Called According to His Purpose: Missionary Letters from China

By Deborah Blumer

Called According To His Purpose
ISBN # 978-0-578-01454-8

All rights reserved. No part of this publication may be reproduced, stored in a retrieval system, or transmitted in any form or by any means: electronic, mechanical, photocopy, recording, or otherwise - except for brief quotations in reviews, without prior permission from the author.

Copyright © 2008 by Deborah Blumer
Published by Deborah Blumer

And we know that in all things God works for the good of those who love him, who have been called according to his purpose.

Romans 8:28

The man with the dagger

"The robbers who attacked Loshan last Saturday night and Kwanshan last Sunday night arrived here early this morning and began their attack on the west gate of the city about 4 a.m. I was awakened at that time by a fusillade of shots which I first thought must be a bunch of firecrackers going off in the city. But when I became a little more awake, I found that it was not firecrackers either, for every once in awhile a bullet went singing overhead. Then I got up and dressed and found my evangelist, teacher, cook, gatekeeper, and carpenter all ready to receive the robbers, if they should be coming. The firing kept up quite sharply for an hour, after which time shots were heard only at intervals; and as it was quiet in the city, I began to think that the robbers had given up the attack. At seven o'clock we then opened the gates, as we heard what we thought to be Kwangchow people walking the street. But as the carpenter opened the outer gate, we were met by two robbers, armed to the teeth, who immediately came in and demanded our rifles and our silver. The carpenter dodged out the door and found some hiding place; the rest of the Chinese with me hid in one of the rooms, and I was left alone to deal with the robbers. They demanded my rifle. I said I had none. Then one of them drew a dagger and commanded me to find the silver. This command he enforced with a stab of his knife in my left arm. I took them into my room and showed them what money I had, but they were not satisfied. They thought I must have money hidden some place, and my explanations to the effect that I had my money in Hankow and used only checks, were either not understood or not believed by them. Neither did it help to tell them that I was a missionary who did not have much money and so had none to give them. There were none of the usual marks of the mission station about my place, of course, as I have not yet had a chapel, etc., set in order. So the man with the dagger stabbed me wickedly several times in both arms, and finally the other honorable robber put his rifle up in my face and said he would shoot if I did not find silver."

CONTENTS

Book One
Through Cloud and Sunshine:
George Oliver Lillegard
1888-1918

1   The Boy----------------------------------5
2   The Young Man---------------------------8
3   The Pastor & Missionary---------------14
4   The Attacked---------------------------30
5   The Worker-----------------------------39
6   The Head of the Family---------------72

Book Two
Neither Death nor Life:
Mr. & Mrs. George O. Lillegard
1918-1927

1   The Courtship-------------------------96
2   The Wedding--------------------------100
3   The Newlyweds------------------------105
4   The Journey to China-----------------126
5   Temporary Homes---------------------149
6   Expecting a Lillegard----------------188
7   "Settled" in Shihnanfu---------------234
8   Back to Shihnan----------------------267
9   Expecting a Lillegard Again--------297
10 An extended visit---------------------326
11 Moving to Wanhsien, Szechwan-------341
12 Wanhsien, New Mission Field--------357
13 A permanent home in China----------397
14 Second Verse, Same as the First------415
15 Number Three-------------------------448

Postscript----------------------------------486

Appendix
    Timeline----------------------------488
    Chinese Names, Old & New------------489
    Sources-----------------------------489

Acknowledgements----------------------------490

Note from Author----------------------------491

Book One

Through Cloud and Sunshine

I need thy presence ev'ry passing hour.
What but thy grace can foil the tempter's pow'r?
Who like thyself my guide and stay can be?
Through cloud and sunshine, oh, abide with me!

Christian Worship, #588, stanza 5

Chapter 1
The Boy

George Oliver Lillegard was born in Calmar, Iowa, on April 23rd, 1888. His parents were Lars Olson Lillegard and Ansoph (maiden name Kaasa) Lillegard. Lars was a Christian day school teacher. George went to public and private schools in Bode, Iowa.

St. Olaf Lutheran Church then and in 1993

Lars Lillegard Family, 1891
Left to right: Sarah, Lars, Lawrence, George, Ansoph, Louise

Lars Lillegard Family, 1895

L to r: Louise, Lars, Lawrence, George, Sarah, Guri (Lars' sister), Anna, and Ansoph holding Olga

Their home in Bode in 1993

Little is known about George's childhood, but one letter written at age 11 has been preserved:

GEORGE WRITES AT AGE 11,"...the biggest hailstorm I ever saw."

Bode, Ia May 24th 1899.

Dear Uncle Lawrence.

"I will try to answer your letter,[1] which I received not a very long while ago. We are well, but I have a cold. Papa is teaching norwegian[2] school in town and has sixty or seventy scholars. Rev. Jorgenson teaches those that are in the Forklaring[3] in the forenoon while papa teaches the smallest, but in the afternoon papa teaches us while the smallest have the afternoons free, but on Wednesday the little ones off all day and we have it free. Papa teaches them then alone. Sarah and I are studying German yet; Christopher Halenger is teaching Joseph Hanson, Otis Monson, two of my school mates, and me Latin. Both of them are about my age. Papa sent for some Latin Norwegian books to Luther Publishing House, but they did not have any so he sent to New York after some Latin English books. We are on the second Declension. There was a hail storm here about four weeks ago. It was the biggest hailstorm I ever saw. Some of the hails were almost as big as a hens egg. They said there were about 300 window panes broken here in town. In our house there was one upstairs window broken to pieces and one of the sitting-room windows was cracked clear across. In the Academy there were thirteen window-panes cracked or broken. In some of the windows there were holes as round as a ball without a crack around it. It was Sunday to just after church. It has been raining every Sunday after that. John went to Minnesota on morning train today. Louisa went over to Josie to keep her company this afternoon. Sarah, Louisa, Lawrence, Anna and I are going to school. At recess we play football most of the time and I have been running so that I have got kind of stiff. I guess this is all I can say this time so I will stop.

Your nephew,
George

P.S. Schreibe bald.[4]
Galba filiis bonae reginae rosas multas dat.[5]"

---

[1] "Uncle Lawrence was only 8 years older than Dad and his mother's youngest brother and I believe he was very fond of him." (George's daughter Laura Lillegard)
[2] (He did not capitalize this...other variations in his writing are left as in original, too.)
[3] Explanation (to the Catechism – Norwegian)
[4] Write soon. (German)
[5] Galba gives many roses to the children of the good Queen. (Latin)

Chapter 2
The Young Man

George attended **Luther College in Decorah, Iowa, at age 15.** He graduated from the Preparatory Department the following spring (1904).

Lars Lillegard Family, 1905
Standing: George, Sarah, Olga, Lawrence, Louise
Seated: Anna, Ansoph, Ella, Lars, Valborg

George participated in many activities with friends at Luther College during the next four years:

Amphie Debating Team, 1907 (George on right)

"A Crazy Picture" (with rare smiles)

Amphie Glee Club (choir), 1908

"The Glenwood Gang," 1908 (George above)

George graduated from the College Department in 1908. The class motto (in Greek) on their graduation photo means: "Neither reckless nor fearful." He spent the following year in Willmar, Minnesota, teaching at Willmar seminary.

GEORGE WRITES A TRAVEL JOURNAL IN 1909.
"MY VACATION TRIP . . .Two Days in the Grand Canyon of Arizona"
"The strange sublime grandeur of it took possession of me,..."

I had been carried swiftly from northern Iowa through Missouri and Kansas to Colorado, where I had visited Pike's Peak, Garden of the Gods, and the other interesting places accessible from Manitou. I had spent a day in Santa Fe, that old, old town, with its plaza, Governor's Palace, and venerable Catholic churches, so suggestive of the rule of Spain. I had noted the scenery, the unique adobe villages, the swarthy, picturesquely-clad Indians, en route westward. I had mingled with all kinds and classes of people, studying and observing - learning from them. And all had been most enjoyable and interesting - a continual revelation of new things to me, Iowa born, Iowa almost all my life hitherto. Then, on a Sunday afternoon, I came to the Grand Canyon of Arizona. It is here I would have you linger longest with me.

On the way to the Canyon, I had made the acquaintance of two young men. We had agreed to make the trip down the Canyon to the Colorado river on foot the next day. As we stood that evening on the rim of the gigantic, fifteen-mile-wide chasm looking out over the mountain peaks below us and down into the dizzy depths, we could see a few white specks out on the gray plateau almost a mile below. These, we heard, were the tents of "Half-way House" - only half-ways! - But we were determined to do as we had planned.

The next morning we were up early and began the zigzag descent down Bright Angel trail, first providing ourselves with a canteen of water and box-lunches. The descent was all such fun as three boyish young men could make it. We would go with a rush down the steep trail, stop, when a turn gave us a new view of the impressive scenery about us, to gaze and wonder and, perhaps, take pictures of the Canyon or each other on the trail. Then on again, racing, laughing, all exhilarated by the fresh, dry, plateau air and the joy of being in such surroundings. Sometimes I would crawl or slide directly down the Canyon-side and land with a clatter of loosened stones - and torn clothing, perhaps - on the trail below, thus gaining on my more staid comrades. Once I came very near going over a precipice, a few hundred feet down. Then I became more staid myself - staid on the trail.

Soon we reached the plateau along which the trail led for a mile. Here we raced with a little brook that ran quietly through shady alleys of its own making - a veritable oasis on the desert plateau. As we looked back from the edge of the plateau up the Canyon, it seemed almost impossible that we should have come down those steep, apparently unbroken walls. But here we were, ready for the final descent to the river, which was by a steep, winding trail. Just for excitement, I followed the smooth rock-bed of a brook, now dry, down a narrow canyon for a while, crawling from ledge to ledge, tobogganing, on my hands, down some smooth slope, and so on again.

Three and a half hours after we set out from the hotel on the rim, we caught sight of the Colorado. With a hurrah! we rushed to the bank of the roaring, turbid stream that seems to have been the creator of this great wonder of nature, the Grand Canyon. Here we clambered along the Canyon-side from rock to rock to gain new views of the tumultuous, raging river in its narrow rocky bed. We watched the seething water; noted how this mighty force had worn and polished the hardest rocks till they shone like glass; torn and broken others; filled in with sand here; washed out whole cliffs there. And we wondered.

At noon, we sat down in the shade of an overhanging wall, and with the rocks as seats and dining table and the roaring river as our orchestra, ate one of the best little meals we have yet tasted. Then freshened and rested, we began the seven-mile ascent up the Canyon, although it was in the heat of the day, and down in between the high walls it was very like an oven. Soon after we started out, we met a party of tourists on horseback. One of them said to us, referring to the steepest, most winding part of the trail, called "Devil's Corkscrew;" "That sure was the Devil's Corkscrew wasn't it?" As we toiled up its blazing turns, we thought it was certainly hot enough to be that. But we kept on, not wishing to stop often to rest, lest we feel fatigue too soon, and reached the rim of the Canyon again in four and a half hours. We rested that night, well satisfied with our day's trip. By making it on foot, we had gained an idea of the immensity of this incomprehensible, mile-and-a-half-deep cut in the face of the earth, such as would have been impossible otherwise, deceptive as distances are to the eye in the clear air of Arizona.

The next morning, we awoke ready for more tramps. We walked then, along the rim out to various "points:" long, narrow promontories, so to speak, jutting far out into the chasm. From these, views could be had of the Colorado, a gray ribbon in between dark walls, and of the Canyon to either side, as far as eye could reach. There was something fascinating in standing out on such a point, where a stone would drop for thousands of feet, gazing dizzily down along the great perpendicular walls, or out over the weird, age-old shapes, rising in columns, or singly here and there, out of the vast gorge. The strange sublime grandeur of it took possession of me, so that I could stand all absorbed in it, oblivious of all else....It was interesting, too, to watch what effect a look over the rim straight down for near a mile had upon different people. Some could not trust themselves near the edge, a sort of insane desire to throw themselves into the abyss seizing them. One little lady timidly approached the edge, looked - then ran back and clung to a tree.

But interesting as the Canyon was, I had to leave it that night, though regretfully, and continue my trip. I travelled then westward to the Pacific Ocean, visiting points of interest all along our sunny west coast and on my return, in the wild and picturesque Canadian Rockies, I found many delightful places, more beautiful though not more grand and impressive than the Canyon - many enchanting places, where a man would gladly while away his time in just idle dreaming and gazing on Lovely Nature - and many interesting places, though perhaps not so very beautiful. Finally I spent two weeks in camping on a pretty little lake in Minnesota, enjoying all the camper's sports.

    All in all, my vacation was most delightful and enjoyable, besides being, as I had expected, a certain education in itself; and it was a real, restful vacation to me, a laborer in the classroom for nine months of the year - all of which applies not least to that part of the trip I spent in the Grand Canyon of Arizona.

Chapter 3
The Pastor & Missionary

In 1909 George entered Luther Seminary at St. Paul, Minn. He graduated in 1912 and was ordained in June at Glenwood, Iowa. He was assistant pastor in Holmen, Wisconsin, from June through September.

Lawrence, George, their father Lars Lillegard, son-in-law Henry Gullixson (married to Sarah), 1912

George (top row, second from right), 1912 (possibly a seminary graduating class picture)

Next he took a call from the Norwegian Evangelical Lutheran Church of America to go to China as a missionary. The Lutheran Herald published this announcement:

"**China Mission**

A few more months, and the Synod new Chinese mission will no longer be in the preliminary stage. Friends of the movement will be interested in the announcement that Rev. George Lillegaard, of Bode, Iowa, the Synod's first missionary to China, passed through Chicago Sept. 16 on his way to New York, whence he sailed for London the latter part of the week.[6] Rev. Lillegaard is taking the Eastern route to China. He will write of his experiences to the Herald, and will later inform our readers at frequent intervals of his observations of heathen life and manners, of the difficulties in his field, and the methods employed in reaching these benighted people with Christ's gospel.

And there is more good news for the friends of Chinese mission – which term, we presume, includes all readers of the Herald - namely this: Within the next six months the field in which our church will now commence work will be visited by Rev. J.R. Birkelund, who has been delegated by the church council of the Synod to make preparations for the inauguration of this new mission in the province of Honan. He will be gone possibly half a year. Rev. Birkelund expects to leave Chicago the first Sunday in October and will travel by the Western route, making Japan on his way. He may have a traveling companion in the person of Rev. M. Sumstad, of Minneapolis, Minn., who has also been called into this work, and whose acceptance of this call is expected."

Luther Anderson

George wrote for the Lutheran Herald on Nov. 27, 1912:

"After spending three days among the mountains and lakes of Switzerland, justly famed for the incomparable beauty and grandeur of its scenery, I came to Genoa, 'The Proud,' the birthplace of our American friend, Columbus. Here I embarked in the good ship 'Luetzow' for my 32 days voyage to Shanghai, China…we have 'taken in' Naples, Italy; Port Said, Egypt; Colombo, Ceylon; Penang and Singapore on the Malay Peninsula; and Hong-Kong, China."

George concluded several articles in the Bode Bugle which described his trip:

"…Monday evening the 2nd of December we arrive at Shanghai. The last week we have had stormy weather. The first three and a half weeks the weather was uniformly fair and calm. A four days trip will bring me from Shanghai to Hankow – whereupon I expect to prepare for my mission work in earnest. What I write thereafter will be printed in 'Lutheran Herald.' As all who would be interested in reading about this mission keep 'Lutheran Herald' – if not, they ought to subscribe for that excellent church paper – I shall not burden the readers of the 'Bode Bugle' with any more of my poor contributions, unless something of more personal interest should happen that would interest Bode friends particularly. So 'thanking you for your attention' and wishing you all a Merry Christmas and Happy New Year, I am

Sincerely yours,
Geo. O. Lillegaard"

George arrived in Shanghai, China, on December 2, 1912. The first news he received upon arrival was the accidental death of his only brother: Lawrence had fallen from a silo. With Lawrence dead and George overseas, Lars felt as if he had lost both of his sons. He pleaded with George to come back right away, but the mission wouldn't allow it.

This was a very unique period in China's history. On January 1, 1912, Sun Yat-Sen had been elected president of the Chinese Republic. On February 12th the last Zing

---

[6] On board the "Oceanic"…The Titanic had sunk on April 14th, 1912.

emperor had abdicated. This was the end of 3,000 years of Chinese monarchy. Mere months later, a late-Zing military strongman succeeded Sun Yat-Sen, dissolved parliament and attempted to restore the monarchy. It was a time of political unrest.

There are few personal letters from this time period in George's files. He mostly kept articles written for "The Lutheran Herald," a magazine published in Decorah, Iowa.

Boat trip in China, ca. 1912

George in rickshaw, ca. 1912

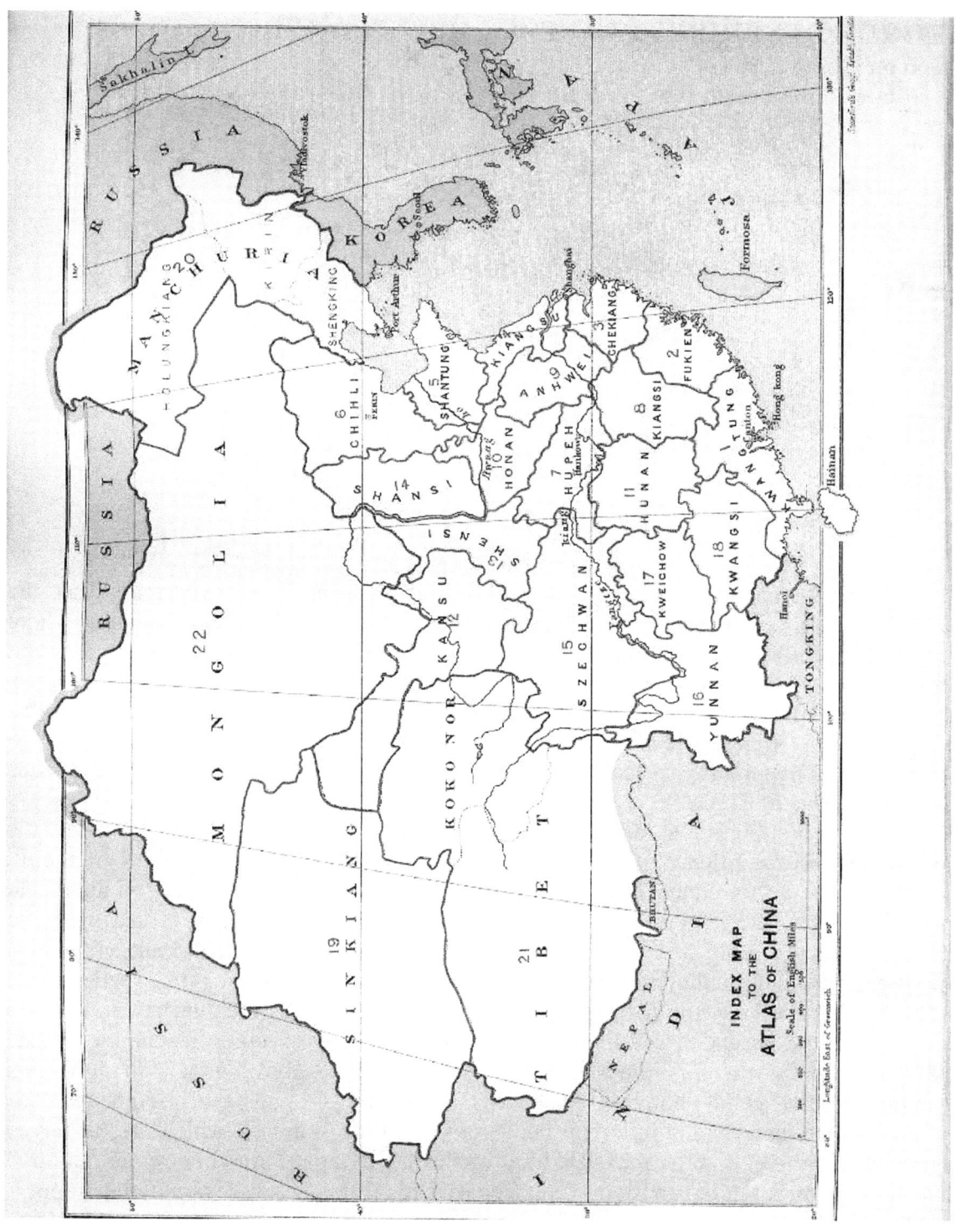

GEORGE DESCRIBES CHINESE LIFE.
"Seen on Chinese Street"
"A chicken balances on top, to eat up the evil spirits flying their way..."

We cannot by any means give a faithful description of everything that the wayfarer sees on a Chinese street. Although one would hardly encounter anything here that would seem strange to a man fresh from the Middle Ages or the time of Luther and even later days in Europe, our modern, perhaps overrefined sensibilities, would receive a distinct shock at the reading of anything like a realistic description of the familiar sights and smells of a Chinese street. We shall not attempt to shock our readers, but merely to relate a few of the sights that have struck our attention or that may serve to give an idea of the conditions in China.

Let us first picture an ordinary Chinese street: from five to fifteen feet wide, the roofs of the houses often almost meeting overhead, laid with stone in the better built cities, with the accumulated filth of the adjoining houses in most cities, winding and crooked so that the evil spirits may not find their way in them, filled with an heterogeneous assembly of people, artisans, tradesmen, dogs, pigs, children and smells. The streets are not public property in China, houseowners claiming the space to the middle of the street in front of their property, and so if it suits their purposes, they do their work in the streets, or sell their goods there. Here is a travelling restaurant planted at a busy street corner, a little stove in a carrying frame above which an unwashed specimen of the genus homo prepares meat dumplings or wheat biscuits, or rice dumplings, or whatever his line may be. Here is a little stand on which are displayed cigarettes of various brands from "Dad knows" to China's patriotic "Love your country" homemade brands. Here is a money changer with his little glass case containing coppers and silver or paper money. There is a frame from which hang various portions of a pig or a cow or a water buffalo or a sheep - or perhaps a dog or mule - all cut in the most unscientific and unorthodox manner. You buy a cut of meat, and the meat vendor chops off a piece in the most convenient place, all portions being sold at the same price from tail to snout. Vegetables, wood, coal - almost anything required for the home - is carried by vendors along the streets or piled at some busy corner.

Some vendors ply their trade into the wee hours of the night. One may hear a musical call: "Hot meatballs for sale," (at home I suppose they would say "Hot dog"), or some harsher voice calling "fried dumplings," while further attention is called to the wares by the beating of some sort or other of instrument: rattle, clapper, bell, gong, or whatnot. It is said that there is an endless variety of such instruments, a whole volume being required to give their names and a description of them.

The shops are open to the street, the whole wall facing the street being made so that it can be removed, except for a counter or stand over which to sell the goods in the shop. From the middle of the street one may look at rolls of the finest satins or silks, at imported foreign goods, or wares of any kind. Here a customer is arguing the price with a very polite shopkeeper. What if an hour or two pass by, if only a copper has been saved! A small shop about twenty feet square may have enough salesmen standing around to run a whole department store at home.

A crowd has gathered about two people engaged in a violent quarrel. To judge from the noise made and the rage shown, murder is sure to be done. The whole excitement started with a customer's attempt to cheat a vendor out of a copper. The disputants are kept from flying at each other's throats by bystanders, and the former are quite content to vent their rage upon the ancestors of their enemy pro tem, there being no greater injury that can be done a man than to curse his ancestors. Finally the storm of words subsides, and the ancestors of the respective quarrellers are again allowed to rest in peace.

At a doorstep we see a woman combing a little pig with a wooden fine comb, and consigning the results of said performance to perdition. Somewhat later, two little girls are performing a similar operation on each other's heads, apparently with the same comb. Within the door a Chinese is subjecting his coat to a kind of "cleaning and pressing" process, not entirely unfamiliar to soldiers in the late war.

We almost stumble over a dog or pig engaged in the usual occupation of scavenging the streets, as we are startled by a series of loud explosions. No, the soldiers have not begun looting. It is only some provident family clearing the air about their home of evil spirits and noxious influences.

According to the Chinese astrological calendar, it is a lucky day. A wedding procession passes: chairs, sedan, occupants, all gaily decorated with red. In front of the procession, several musicians march, blowing their flutes, clarinets or horns, scraping their fiddles and beating their drums and gongs. One snare drum is carried on a boy's back, while a man walks alongside, turning around at an atrocious angle in order to beat the drum with his two sticks. After the musicians come several coolies, carrying baskets or trays containing presents of all descriptions, all done up in red wrappings. Then comes the bride's chair, its gay decorations concealing a frightened young girl, leaving her parental home for the first time, never to return except for short visits perhaps. Then come other chairs with the relatives of the bride and groom, and the procession trails off in a crowd of small boys, "charivari-ing" the wedding, like any crowd of American town boys.

We meet a villainous-looking soldier - an ex-bandit, no doubt, if not still actively employed in that profitable business under the cover of his uniform - carrying a birdcage out to some open court to give his pet bird the air. Another brave warrior is seen flying a dragon kite out among the graves on the hillside.

In a doorway, a little boy is getting a bath. His brown skin glistens in the sun after this unaccustomed treatment. Where the street skirts a pool of water, several women are washing clothes, kneeling beside the pool, paddling the clothes with a wooden paddle, a smooth stone serving as washing board. Another woman is washing her vegetables in the pool, while a coolie is drawing water for somebody's tea.

At a street corner, a priest has erected an altar to the Goddess of Mercy; and men, women and children come to burn incense, prostrate themselves before their favorite idol, and beg for some favor. The stones are worn smooth where the worshippers kneel.

A blind beggar gropes along the street, discoursing sweet music on a homemade, two-stringed fiddle. Other beggars lie by the wayside, some of them hideously deformed, all of them atrociously dirty. Here an old woman sits cross-legged, and in a most athletic manner swings her body forward, pounding her head on the ground, as she wishes a thousand blessings to the passersby who favor her with a copper. She has placed a pad on the ground before her, and her head hits this with a resounding whack, as she bows, that would seem to be enough to break any ordinary head. Hers must be "solid ivory." There is a large worn spot on her forehead.

Another beggar lies moaning and slavering on the ground making an ugly picture of apparently extreme suffering or epileptic weakness. When darkness falls, he picks himself up and proceeds in quite a natural manner to his home "in the suburbs."

It being a day lucky for all and every manner of undertaking, a funeral procession also soon passes by. Eight men carry a heavy coffin, suspended from a carrying frame. A chicken balances on top, to eat up the evil spirits flying their way. Musicians precede the coffin, together with a crowd of priests, coolies and friends, carrying all sorts of paper articles, banners, foodstuffs, paper money, etc, to be burned at the grave. Other men set off long strings of firecrackers as the procession advances, filling the street with smoke. The mourners follow in sedan chairs, all dressed in white, and keeping up a continual moaning and groaning, with some apparent effort, to assure the departed spirit that they truly grieve his loss.

There is no end to the things that thus might be told concerning the sights to be seen on a Chinese street. A full description would involve a book on the whole social life of the Chinese masses. There is little privacy for most people in China, that being a luxury reserved for the rich, so that almost every phase of life could be seen and described from the vantage point of a window overlooking a busy street. This story will at least give an idea of what we see as we go about our mission work in the cities of heathen China.

Geo. O. Lillegard

GEORGE WRITES FROM NANKING[7] UNIVERSITY, DEC. 24, 1912.
"Confucius' Birthday Celebrated at a Modern Mission College"
"For the birthday of Confucius was celebrated in such a wholehearted manner by the (Christian) students of Wesley College in Wuchang that one suspects they have little heart left for Jesus Christ or the true God."

The writer has a vivid recollection of the first Christmas Eve he spent in China. The great Union University at Nanking, supported by several of the strongest American Missionary Societies, was celebrating its Christmas Holidays. The festivities that evening consisted of a Chinese play, given by the University students, which the missionary body attended en masse. After we had witnessed a few murders and other tragic scenes, we left the place alone, sick at heart and as homesick as it ever has been our fate to be in China.

Evidently the usual Reformed indifference to our Church Festivals was at the root of this peculiar "Christmas spirit." But an item in one of the Hankow daily papers a short time ago leads us to think that the indifference may have extended even farther than to the externals of our Church Festivals. For the birthday of Confucius was celebrated in such a wholehearted manner by the students of Wesley College in Wuchang that one suspects they have little heart left for Jesus Christ or the true God. The report, written by a Chinese student, Mr. D.F. Senn, is as follows:

"Wesley College Students Celebrate.
The 27th day of the 8th month (lunar year) was in the past ages as at the present time, and will undoubtedly be in time to come, observed and celebrated on account of the birthday of our great and wide-known sage and philosopher, Confucius, who was born B.C. 551. Usually on this day, the schools, some of the foreign firms and a few government organizations all stop their routine work in order to show their respect to, and do honor to, the Great Man. To go by the regulations of the College and the prevailing custom in our country, the College staff has given to the students this grand and important day as a holiday, on which they are not only hoped to make the best out of it they can, but are also expected to tell the illiterates, with whom they have or have not acquaintance, that over 2,500 years ago there lived in our dear country a great sage, whose virtues and precepts are worth the while to be learned and put into actual practice.

On the evening of the previous day, (Oct. 10th) a celebration meeting was held in the College Assembly Hall; teachers, students, and some outside guests just filling up all the seats and making the gathering very lively. Prof. P.S. Li presided. The meeting was opened by singing the "Hymn to Confucius." Then scripture (note the small "s" in scripture) reading followed, selections from the Book of Great Learning (a Confucian classic) were read by Prof. Hu. After this came the speech by Prof. Tun, who although having a sore throat and being unable to speak, yet harangued to his attentive hearers. The speaker rehearsed about the origin of the Confucian religion, and how and where it and Christianity exactly correspond in their teachings. Exclamations and approbation were continually heard.

After all this, the Wen Ming plays made their appearance. Without any dress rehearsal because of the lack of time, the performances were fairly well done and heartily enjoyed by the audience who could find no leisure to stop laughing and hand-clapping.

The meeting was closed by shouting three cheers in honour of Confucius, and the hurrah of voices broke down the house. Long live the teachings of Confucius!"

The quaint English of the writer does not make this report less tragic, when one considers that it comes from one of the old, well-established Mission Colleges of Central

---

[7] Pronounced/also spelled "Nan-jing'" – west of Shanghai on Yangtze River, in the province of Kiangsu (new Pinyin spelling is "Jiangsu" - see following)

China, to which this country has been looking for the light that is to lead it out of the political, intellectual, and spiritual darkness in which it gropes. And yet all too many of the Mission Colleges in China are of this stamp. If they do not put Confucius above Christ, they at least cater sufficiently to Chinese prejudices to make the students believe that Confucius is fully the equal of Christ and his "religion" fully as good as Christianity. What these Colleges are doing all too many missionaries are also doing or at least neglecting to testify against. Even Lutherans cooperate with such un-Christian "Christians" and seek to correlate their work with that of these deniers of our Lord.

What should <u>we</u> do under these circumstances? It is not enough for us to decry the conditions on the mission fields and perhaps find in them a reason for not supporting foreign missions. It is not enough for us to point out the errors in the conduct of these other missionaries. We should rather work with holy zeal in every way open to us to bring the light of the pure gospel to heathen China. We should rebuke those who hide the Truth of God under the bushel of their "socialized Christianity," not merely by word, but also by deed, showing them that the old Gospel is the only remedy for the evils under which the heathens suffer so much today. We must show our faith in the eternal Word of God by our works with it and for it. As we see other missions losing themselves in the externals of religion - charitable deeds, union organizations, etc. – we should spend our whole energies in bringing those who perish in the darkness of heathenism or Confucian ethics or modern evolutionistic philosophies, the saving gospel of Jesus Christ. What a challenge to our faith and courage are not the mission fields today! Are we going to shrink back from it? Or are we rather, though we be but a Gideon's band, to fight and work in faith in the Almighty God and conquer in His name? There can be only one answer for every true Lutheran.

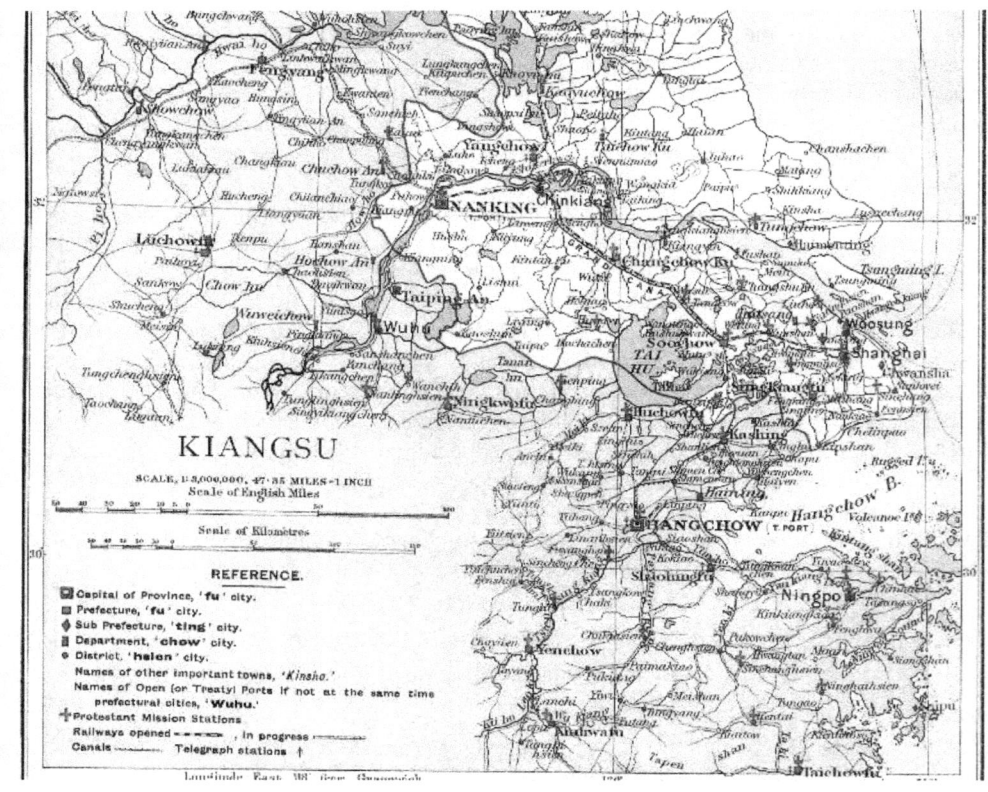

GEORGE WRITES FOR THE LUTHERAN HERALD
"Learning the Chinese Language"
"…I did not understand why you were so earnest about telling the people the way to the *post-office.*"

Nanking,[8] China, Jan. 15, 1913

The revolution in China last year marked the beginning of many new things. It was the beginning, too, of the language school, whose advantages I am now enjoying.

Last winter a large number of missionaries from various parts of central China had taken refuge in Shanghai, where they might be under the protection of foreign guns during the revolutionary disturbances. Many young missionaries, too, on their way to the field, were stranded here for several months. To aid these "newcomers" in the study of the difficult Chinese language and also to give the older missionaries better opportunity to continue their studies profitably, a union language school was started, under the supervision of some of the best Chinese scholars among the foreigners. About 130 were enrolled, and, during the few months of its existence, the language school proved such a decided success that certain missionaries went to work to make the language school permanent. The University of Nanking was induced to give the language school use of part of its buildings, and last fall the school opened here with about 40 young missionaries enrolled. This was all that could be accommodated in the rooms first assigned to the language school. But later twelve more missionaries arrived, clamoring for admission, and arrangements were made to give them quarters in another of the university buildings.

Three of the university professors, among them the President, Prof. Bowen, volunteered to take charge of the class-work, and after some time the required number of fairly good Chinese teachers was secured. The Chinese who really know how to teach a foreigner the language are very few and far between, but the best teachers available were engaged. The language school has been so fortunate as to secure the services of one particularly able Chinese to be the overseer, critic, and general manager of the forty teachers in the school. Thus the teachers, too, are taught, and are spurred on to do their best.

This month our class is enjoying the instruction of one Rev. Cummins, formerly missionary to India, who has made the study of the languages of mission fields his specialty, and who comes prepared to aid beginners by a phonetic method of his own.

In our class, the daily work is carried on about as follows: At 8:45 a.m. the class meets with Prof. Bowen for the study and analysis of the Chinese characters. This is work that the Chinese teachers cannot do, as they cannot give the necessary explanations and most likely do not know how a character is to be analysed themselves. The written characters look at first sight like a wild medley of scratches, but upon closer acquaintance one begins to see a little "method in their madness," too. The Chinese alphabet, if we may call it so, consists of 214 "radicals" (or root characters) and something over 1000 "phonetics" (or sound characters). The radicals are arranged according to the number of strokes required to write them, and in the Chinese dictionaries all characters are grouped under their respective radicals. Thus, to find a character in a dictionary one must know

---

[8] Pronounced/also spelled "Nan-jing':" near Shanghai on eastern coast, Province of Kiangsu (new Pinyin spelling – Jiangsu)

what its radical is, just as we in our dictionaries must know with what letter a word begins. Most radicals and phonetics are complete characters in themselves. They are combined in various ways to make the 50,000 or more additional characters in the written language. Often two or more radicals are combined to form a new character, but generally a radical and phonetic are joined together, the radical giving a clue to the meaning of the character, the phonetic to its sound. E.g., in the character for "table," the radical part means "wood," indicating the material out of which the object is made, and the phonetic part, "djoh," which is itself a character meaning "lofty," gives the sound of the whole character "djoh"=table." This is a rule, however, which has about as many exceptions as examples.

To learn to read and write Chinese characters is a sheer gift of the memory, but it must be done if the great mass of literature in this Chinese script is to be accessible to the missionary, or if he is to reach the educated Chinese by his writings. The movement for the introduction of the Roman alphabet is becoming stronger, both among the Chinese and the missionaries. In time this phonetic method of writing will, no doubt, take the place of the cumbersome old method, even though the great advantage of having one literature for the whole Orient will thus be lost, and the Bible and other works will have to be translated into the multitude of dialects instead of this one written language.

At 9:30 a.m. we meet with Prof. Cummins for drill in the phonetics of the Chinese language. Many of the sounds are hard to get exact, as they are so similar to certain of our sounds, yet not the same – so near, and yet so far. The Chinese b, d, and g, are not b, d, and g, as we say them; neither are they p, t, and k, but something half ways between. Halfway between, yes; but that is a point which it is very hard for the foreign ear and tongue to find. The Chinese "r" is a cross between a "j" or a "zh" and our "r." The p, t, k, ts, and ch sounds are much more strongly aspirated than in English. There are sh, hs, zh, dz, dj, ch and sz sounds in abundance, and they must be clearly distinguished. The spoken language is musical and it is a pleasure to listen to a good Chinese speaker; the only thing that grates on the foreign ear, at first, being the above-mentioned preponderance of sibilant and "buzzing" sounds.

From 10:30 till noon we work with our Chinese teachers. One of the large classrooms on the third floor of the "Girls' School" of the university has been partitioned off into little "cells," into which we retire with our respective teachers, and practice reading, writing, and speaking – and hearing – the language. This is, of course, the principal part of our work. It is from the Chinese themselves that we must get the correct pronunciation, rhythm, accent, etc. In the Chinese language more depends upon correct intonation of the word and the sentence than almost any other language. The meaning of the word changes with the various intonations or inflections given it. In Central China there are five "tones" or inflections that a word can have; a falling tone is at the end of a sentence with us; a rising tone, as when we ask a question; a level, even tone, as when we sing on one note; an explosive and falling tone, which I can best compare, perhaps, to the "tiger" with which American college boys like to close their yells, though, of course, the Chinese are not quite so vociferous about it, except when they are trying to teach foreigners to give it correctly. The fifth tone is a short, quick, high-pitched tone. It is a great advantage, in learning these tones, to have a good ear for music, as it also requires a good ear and a ready tongue to learn to speak the language smoothly and rhythmically. When drilling on these five tones we can, however, console ourselves with the reflection that missionaries in South China are much worse off than we. They have to learn 10-12 tones. The native Chinese do not, of course, have to bother about "tones;" they give words their right inflection naturally. Foreigners must learn the tone of each word, however, much as we in German have to learn the gender of each noun.

The importance of giving the tones correctly may be illustrated by one or two of the many stories told about missionaries who were a little too confident of their ability to speak Chinese correctly. A certain missionary once preached long and earnestly to a large audience about the way to salvation – he thought - , and was quite flattered to note the attention which his sermon commanded. After the service he began angling for compliments from one of his friends who had been present. His friend said: "Yes, you spoke Chinese well, but I did not understand why you were so earnest about telling the people the way to the *post-office*. The word "dju" in the fourth tone means "salvation," but this preacher had given it the second tone, which is plain "post-office."

Again, at a dinner party in a missionary home, the hostess in the course of the dinner asked the Chinese waiter, or "boy" (as the waiters and servants are called throughout the East) to bring in a certain dish. The waiter did not seem to understand the order. She repeated the request, the waiter fidgeted about a little and still delayed. Finally she ordered him to go and bring what she asked for. The "boy" obediently went, and after a lapse of time, returned and, sidling up to the master of the house, presented him in the presence of the astonished company with - a pair of trousers. Anyway, the good mistress got what she had ordered and could hardly blame the servant.

In the afternoon at 2 o'clock we meet with Rev. Cummins for drill in speaking Chinese sentences correctly and fluently; or for the study of Chinese "grammar," if so we may call it. There is really no grammar in the sense we generally use the word. There are no conjugations, declensions, genders, rules, etc., to learn. Chinese words never change in form to denote number, tense, etc. This does not mean that Chinese grammar therefore is easy to learn. For there is a great deal to learn about Chinese *idiom*. Just because of the lack of inflections and forms to denote the various relations of a word in the sentence, so much the more depends upon correct idiom – correct order of words, correct phrasing, correct rhythm. And these are the hardest things to learn in any language, when once the pronunciation of its peculiar sounds has been mastered. In consequence, no foreigner ever gets through studying Chinese "grammar" or idiom. Missionaries who are ambitious to learn the language well, have a Chinese teacher at their beck and call all through their lives, and use every spare hour to study and delve deeper into the wealth of Chinese phrases and idiomatic expressions. Few foreigners there are, indeed, of whom it can be said that they speak Chinese like a Chinaman.

At 3 p.m. we again meet with our Chinese teachers and dig all we can out of them. Yes, "dig it out;" for the Chinese teachers teach you only what you make them teach you. They are so polite that they hardly can be made to correct the mistakes which you notice yourself. Instead they, perhaps, will flatter you on your good "djong-gweh sheng-yin" (Chinese accent), and leave you to correct yourself by what you hear them say when they are off their guard. The great advantage of a language school such as this is that one has the assistance of less polite, but more kind, foreigners, who will not only correct marked defects of pronunciation, etc., but will also see to it that the Chinese teachers are "shook up" once in a while and made to understand what is expected of them. Besides, we change from one teacher to another every week, thus minimizing the chances of teachers becoming so used to his pupil's particular faults and idiosyncrasies that he will not take notice of them.

Besides these advantages, there are the no less real advantages of having other young people to study with, compete with, compare with; and to associate with in the hours of relaxation necessary to keep up physical health and mental vigor in the rather trying climate of these semi-tropical regions. In short, I consider myself fortunate in having secured admission to such a language school, and I hope that the young men and women, whom our synod, I trust, soon will send out to join in the great work, for the uplift of China and the salvation of Christ's redeemed ones in this land, will also be able to enter this school when it opens again next fall. The school closes here in May and thereafter I shall have to study alone with a native teacher. But by that time I should be so far advanced as to be able to teach my teacher how to teach me what I wish to be taught!

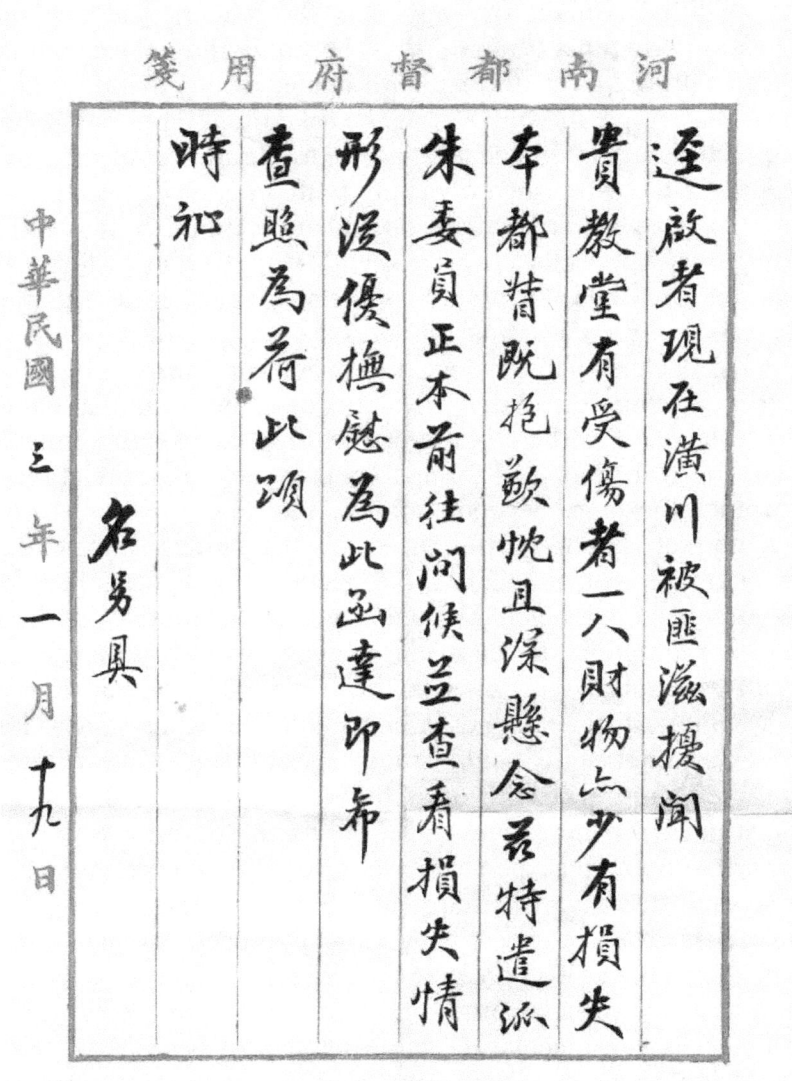

GEORGE WRITES FOR AN AMERICAN MAGAZINE.
"A Chinese Home"
"…many…buy their food ready-cooked at a restaurant or from one of the vendors of 'red-hots,'…"

On the Yangtse River, June 6, 1913

Today I should like to introduce the readers of <u>Lutheran Herald</u> to a Chinese home, as the casual foreign visitor may see it. So stepping out from the high-walled compound of our missionary home, we follow the rough, stone-paved street till we get to what seems to be the average type of a Chinese house. A few feet directly in front of the entrance, we perhaps find a stone wall about 10 feet wide and 8 feet high, which is intended to keep the evil spirits from flying into the house. For the evil spirits (in China, at least) can fly only in a straight line and cannot turn corners, so that such a wall directly in front of the door is effective protection against them. Many houses do not have this wall, but instead have a partition wall inside, directly before the door, so that one has to go through a narrow hallway to the right or the left before gaining entrance to the house proper. Where houses are built on opposite sides of a narrow street facing each other, such a wall can be dispensed with, as they protect each other sufficiently well. To further insure that no evil influences may emanate from the home opposite, the following pious wish is inscribed in prominent characters on the door: "May he who lives opposite prosper, or enjoy all good things." Whatever good these walls may do by way of keeping out the straight-flying spirits of China, they certainly do this much: they keep the cold winds and rain storms from sweeping too strongly into the house. In order further to protect their homes from the evil spirits, the Chinese put over the door an octagonal piece of board with red or blue and white stripes painted on it like the spokes of a wheel. In the center or the hub of this octagonal wheel there is often a small looking-glass. The board is suppose to be a sort of charm which the evil spirits dare not come near, and the idea with the looking-glass is that the spirits upon approaching the door will see their image in the glass and be so frightened at their own ugly appearance that they will flee forthwith, in undignified haste. We find, too, upon the door or above it, even in the most miserable hovel, the character "fuh" or "happiness."

Upon entering, we find ourselves in a paved courtyard, around which the rooms or "giens" (divisions) of a Chinese house are clustered. These are built of stone or brick, with tile roofs; the poorer ones, of mud and straw or cane, with thatched roofs. They are seldom more than one story high. There are generally no windows in the outside walls, but the side which faces the courtyard is almost all window. Only the most modern Chinese homes have glass windows; most of them are simply open lattice-work. In winter when it is cold these windows are sometimes covered with paper to keep out the penetrating north winds, but generally the Chinese house is as open in winter as in summer. The Chinese does not pretend to keep his house warm in the winter. He simply dons a few more garments of wool, or thickly-padded "blue-print" cotton, or fur-lined silk, and thus bids defiance to the biting winter frosts. It is quite amusing to watch the littler toddlers trying to move around under their load of clothes. With a fur cap pulled tight down over their heads and several layers of thick garments around their plump bodies, they, perforce, go with arms sticking straight out and are often literally longer horizontally than perpendicularly, or shorter up and down than sidewise, or thicker east and west than north and south – or whatever way you want to put it. Sometimes the Chinese indicate how cold it is by the number of garments they must wear, e.g.: "Yesterday it was only four garments cold; today it is eight garments cold," etc.

But it is not quite correct to say that the Chinese do not heat their houses at all. For they have ovens for baking, i.e., many of them, not all; for many, too, since fuel is scarce and expensive, buy their food ready-cooked at a restaurant or from one of the vendors of "red-hots," etc., that are continually crying their wares on the streets. And then they have ovens in their beds, - the so-called "kongs." The beds are made of brick, built only a foot or two above the ground, and in one end of these brick beds an oven is fitted up, so that on a cold night the chilled members of the family can go comfortably to sleep on a warm bed. Fuel is not so plentiful that there is much danger of their being roasted.

If we now take a look into the various rooms around the open court, we find the family busy at work, - with spinning and weaving, perhaps. For there are many hundreds of silk looms in Nanking, this city being one of the centers of the silk industry in China, especially fine satins being woven here. The whole family, from the old grandmother (who perhaps is politely showing us around, if we know enough Chinese to be able to explain to her that we wish to see her home) to the grandsons and their young wives, take part in the work. For the women, too, do much work that we would delegate to the men of the household. There is indeed little "housework" for them to do, in the sense that foreigners use the term. We see little furniture; the floor never needs to be washed (for it is simply the bare ground); the meals are not at all the complicated affair that we make them. For each one takes his bowl of rice or cooked vegetables, whenever he gets hungry, and plies his chopsticks busily till he is satisfied and then goes to work again. Family meals, where all sit down to table together, are almost unknown among the Chinese. Even taking care of the numerous children is not much of a problem for the Chinese woman. The little ones are either left to themselves in a little cradle, or carried in "papoose" fashion on the back of an older sister or of the mother herself, while the older ones shift for themselves or help as best they can with the work of the house. And so the women are free to help the men in the fields and gardens and shops and the various industries of China.

If we now have been real polite, the mistress of the home may give us permission to enter the "parlor," too. This is the one room in the average home which is decorated, and where it is evident that pains have been taken to make things look neat and attractive. Here we may see many interesting and valuable old paintings and scrolls and pieces of brassware and a number of books. But we soon learn why this room is thus different from the rest. It is the family "sanctum," where the spirits of the great and good ancestors are reverently remembered and worshiped. We see on one side of the room an altar with a painting, perhaps, of the last patriarch who had left his family, and various scrolls with couplets inscribed on them, setting forth the virtues of the deceased, hanging above it. On the altar are placed little offerings; perhaps incense is burning. And so our pleasure at finding this attractive room in the house vanishes. For here, then, is the greatest bulwark which Chinese heathendom can set up against Christianity: ancestor worship, the Fourth Commandment kept so as to break the First Commandment, that which has been to a certain extent and should only be China's blessing, changed to a curse. For weak, sinful men, though it is right that they be reverently remembered by their own descendants, cannot be made objects of worship by them without degrading the ideals of their worshipers, without pulling these down to an even lower level than their own. And so we who know of a Father of men who was not man and who, though he became man, still is God, the one perfect Being, we keep the Fourth Commandment well to keep the First Commandment better. Then another and greater blessing than this that she "shall live long upon the earth:" will come to China: God will dwell among her people.   Geo. O. Lillegaard

Chinese servants

"the ruins of the yamen in K" (Kwangchow)

Chapter 4
The Attacked

After George finished his first year of schooling at Nanking University in July of 1913, he made a trip to Sinyang, in the province of Honan. From there he went to Kwangchow[9] in the same province, to start the mission.

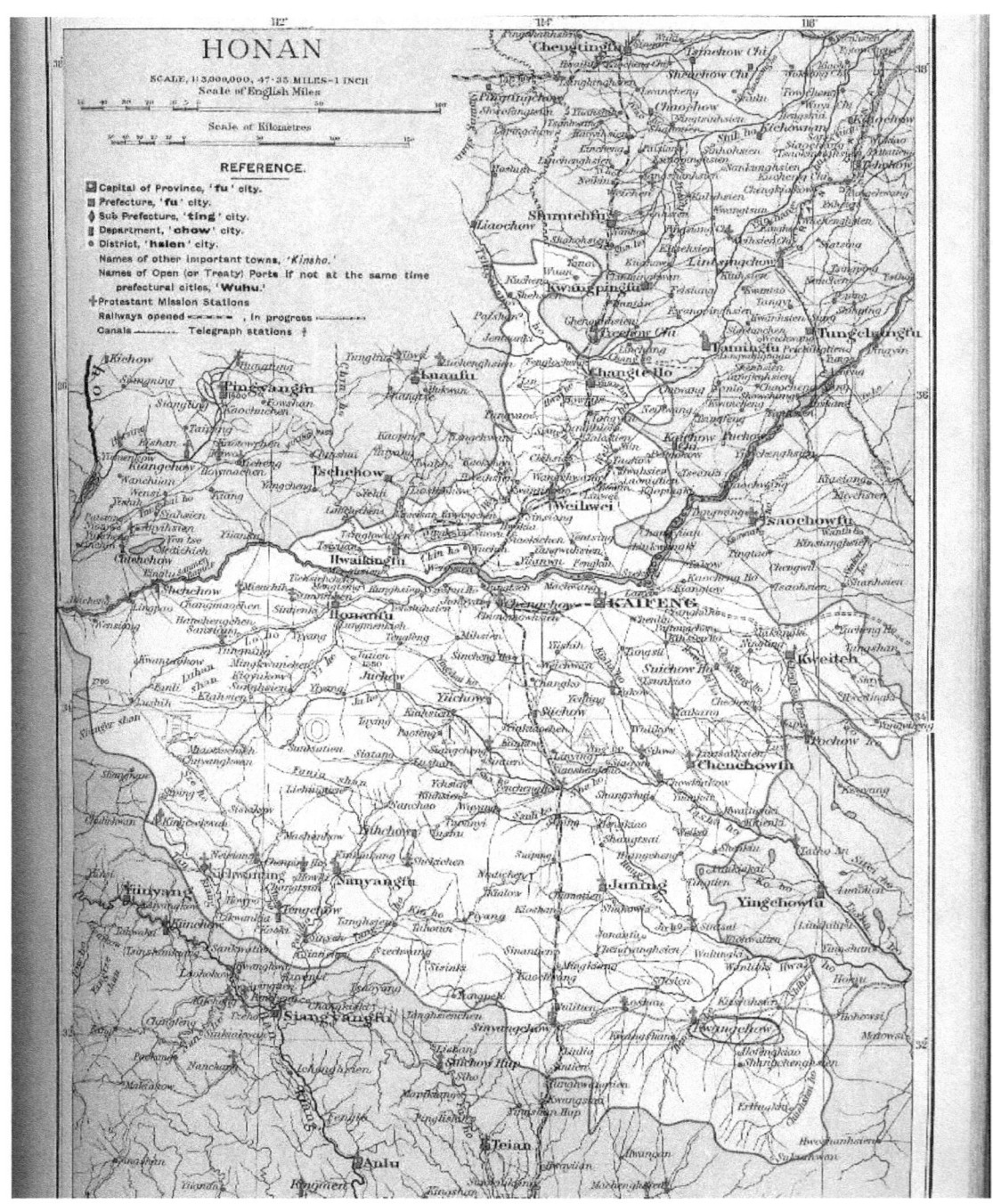

---
[9] Pronounced "Guan-jo;" now called Huangchuan, in Henan (Pinyin spellings)

"The Start" – George's Trip into Inland China

"…river which landed me (George Lillegard, in chair) for the first time in 'Lutheran Synod Mission' territory" (Kikungshan)

Kwangchow had been a city without Lutheran missionaries for years. George was placed in the "North City" on one side of the river. On the other side of the river in "South City" there was an outpost of the China Inland Mission.

THE CHINA INLAND MISSION

Founder—The late Rev. J. HUDSON TAYLOR, M.R.C.S.
General Director—D. E. HOSTE.

HOME OFFICES OF THE MISSION

LONDON	Newington Green, N.
PHILADELPHIA	235 School Lane, Germantown.
TORONTO	507 Church Street.
MELBOURNE	267 Collins Street.

Object.—The China Inland Mission was formed under a deep sense of China's pressing need, and with an earnest desire, constrained by the love of Christ and the hope of His coming, to obey His command to preach the Gospel to every creature.

Character.—It is evangelical and undenominational. It is supported entirely by the free-will offerings of God's people, no personal solicitation and collections being authorised.

Progress.—On January 1, 1908, there were in connection with the Mission, 900 missionaries and associates (including wives), 18 ordained Chinese pastors, 448 assistant Chinese preachers, 208 Chinese school teachers, 227 Colporteurs, 252 Biblewomen, and 546 other unpaid Chinese helpers, 19,054 communicants 27,603 having been baptized from the commencement. There were 547 organised churches, 201 schools, 42 dispensaries, 88 opium refuges, and 8 hospitals.

CHINA'S MILLIONS

The Organ of the China Inland Mission

1d. *Monthly.*   **1s. 6d.** *per Annum.*   **50 cents** *per Annum.*

C.I.M. ANNUAL

CHINA AND THE GOSPEL

An Illustrated Report of the Work of the China Inland Mission

Bound in Green, Red, and Gold (Bronze)

George writes in a letter written on Dec. 15, 1913 (to Rev. Larsen), "I have not been in one place for more than a week at a time for over two months. I will just so barely be settled down here when I will have to go to Kioshan to the wedding and the meeting there." He had no idea of the danger awaiting him in Kwangchow.

"So the man with the dagger stabbed me wickedly several times in both arms,..."

Lutheran Herald.

Entered at the Decorah, Ia., post office as second-class matter.

Stand ye in the ways, and see, and ask for the old paths, where is the good way, and walk therein, and ye shall find rest for your souls. (Jer. 6, 16.)

Vol. IX.　　Decorah, Iowa, February 19, 1914.　　No. 8.

Notes and Comment.

A Day With Robbers in Kwangchow—and the Aftermath.

Lutheran Herald: It was my intention about this time to write the *Lutheran Herald* an account of a journey in a Chinese sedan chair in peaceful southeastern Honan. But I have unfortunately to chronicle first the worst thing that has befallen Kwangchow and this part of Honan for three centuries. It is not certain that this letter will reach America, as the countryside to the west of here, through which the robbers have passed, is now infested by petty thieves and highway robbers, so that the mailmen do not dare to leave. Mr. Mason and I hired two men for ten thousand cash (about four dollars) to run to Sinyang with the principal news from here, and we trust that they will get through safely. The telegraph wires were cut by the robbers before entering Kwangchow, so that we have not been able to make use of the telegraph. Now, however (Jan. 17), about 400 soldiers have come, and as they report everything quiet to the west, it may be that the mail service will soon be established again. The robbers have gone to the southeast, and report has it today that they have attacked Shangcheng but have not yet gained entrance, several of the robbers having been killed. Evidently the soldiers in that city remained true. Without the treachery of the local police here, the robbers certainly would have been a long time about gaining entrance to this city, too.

Mr. and Mrs. Mason and Mrs. Smith[10] returned from their country refuge yesterday. Mr. Smith also returned, a short while before they did. Mr. Mason and I have visited the city official and the captain of the soldiers that just arrived and asked the latter to see to it that his soldiers did not do any mischief in the city. He was very polite to us, and as he seems to be a very decent sort of a man, no doubt the soldiers will prove themselves the friends of the people here. They are supposed to pursue the robbers, but they take their time about it and are careful to let the robbers keep a good distance ahead of them, it seems. How long the robbers will remain in this district, it is not easy to tell. Most likely they will go to the mountains to the south, where in some mountain fastness they could easily defy 3-4 times as many soldiers as now are pursuing them. They have money enough and clothes enough to live royally all the rest of the winter, counting only what they got here in Kwangchow.

The following, then, is a circumstantial account of the experiences I myself have had with the robbers and the results of their visit to the city. It is long, and the writer figures largely in the account. But I trust that the readers of *Lutheran Herald* will understand this as it is meant: simply as a diary of these days' events, and not any elaborately prepared article for the press. I have thought that such a circumstantial

---
[10] Missionaries from the China Inland Mission

account might be of more interest under the circumstances than a more condensed narrative.

Jan. 14, 1914. Well, now I have seen robbers, looked them square in the face, in fact. And I cannot say that I exactly care to see them again, although I must say to their credit that most of them were quite decent robbers. I am no judge, exactly, of what might constitute a decent robber, but there was only one of those who visited me that did me any real harm. But to begin at the beginning: The robbers who attacked Loshan last Saturday night and Kwanshan last Sunday night arrived here early this morning and began their attack on the west gate of the city about 4 a.m. I was awakened at that time by a fusilade of shots which I first thought must be a bunch of firecrackers going off in the city. But when I became a little more awake, I found that it was not firecrackers either, for every once in awhile a bullet went singing overhead. Then I got up and dressed and found my evangelist, teacher, cook, gatekeeper, and carpenter all ready to receive the robbers, if they should be coming. The firing kept up quite sharply for an hour, after which time shots were heard only at intervals; and as it was quiet in the city, I began to think that the robbers had given up the attack. At seven o'clock we then opened the gates, as we heard what we thought to be Kwangchow people walking the street. But as the carpenter opened the outer gate, we were met by two robbers, armed to the teeth, who immediately came in and demanded our rifles and our silver. The carpenter dodged out the door and found some hiding place; the rest of the Chinese with me hid in one of the rooms, and I was left alone to deal with the robbers. They demanded my rifle. I said I had none. Then one of them drew a dagger and commanded me to find the silver. This command he enforced with a stab of his knife in my left arm. I took them into my room and showed them what money I had, but they were not satisfied. They thought I must have money hidden some place, and my explanations to the effect that I had my money in Hankow and used only checks, were either not understood or not believed by them. Neither did it help to tell them that I was a missionary who did not have much money and so had none to give them. There were none of the usual marks of the mission station about my place, of course, as I have not yet had a chapel, etc., set in order. So the man with the dagger stabbed me wickedly several times in both arms, and finally the other honorable robber put his rifle up in my face and said he would shoot if I did not find silver. When I said I had none, he pulled the trigger, but the gun was not loaded, so I did not get even a decent scare over it. Then they went to work to rummage the place for whatever valuables I might have. I opened the boxes that were locked for them and showed them around the place in as hospitable and friendly a way as I could manage under the circumstances. They searched my clothes, too, for valuables, but happily did not find my watch, although they looked through my clothes several times. My L.C. (Luther College) class ring they took. When they had rummaged through everything, they asked me again for silver. The man who had stabbed my arms put his knife to my throat and threatened to kill me if I did not produce a rifle or some silver. As I had a good conscience over it, I could look him in the eye and repeat that I had no silver or any rifles and if he killed me it would not help him or hurt me. I was ready to go to a better country than China. Then he sheathed his knife, saying: "You are not afraid," a compliment which I hardly deserved, however; and the ordeal was over for me. If any of the robbers that entered later began to threaten me, asking for silver, I could tell them that the others had taken all I had, and I had no trouble convincing them of the truth of that.

Then my evangelist, teacher, and cook came out of their hiding places, too, and helped me to explain why it should be so that I had neither rifle nor silver. As I had said, I did not come to China to shoot men, but to save their souls, and as for my money, that was in America or in Hankow. Then some robbers came who were of a little less vicious temper, and we set ourselves to entertaining the robbers for the rest of the time they were in the city. Most of those that came in were quite interested in seeing "the foreign devil" and had a number of questions to ask about where I was from, how old I was, where my wife was, etc. One smiling young fellow wanted to know a number of things about the foreign countries and asked me to take him along to America some time. I said he could go if he would stay here and "study the doctrine" awhile, show himself a good student, etc. Then he wanted me to come along with him and play robber. We should be friends, he said. He and one of the others, too, that came then were quite sympathetic when they saw the way I had been stabbed, and this young friend of mine said he would find the man that had stabbed me and pay him back – something I told him he did not need to trouble to do. This young fellow really felt friendly toward me, I think. He left finally, without taking a single thing with him, and I believe he had half a mind to accept the offer I made him to come back after a while and study the Bible with me, if I saw to that no one took him as a robber and cut his head off. A number of the other robbers, too, were friendly enough. Thus, one gave back the cook's best coat, when I represented to him that my cook was poor and did not have many clothes. And I am very thankful to them for not destroying the things they did not wish to use themselves. I had to answer many questions about my camera, typewriter, violin, skates, music stand, and other articles strange to them; and they not only did not take these things, but left them as whole as when they came. The articles they made use of were my woolen underclothing, towels, suits, and shoes, and the fur rugs that I had lately acquired in China. A saddle that I had just received from M.W. & Co. (as I thought for awhile of buying a horse to use on my travels, instead of using only the Chinese carrying chairs) went on the back of one of their ponies. Most of the men had horses. One man relieved me of my fur cap, another wanted my fur-lined coat (which he left, however, when he went), and another wanted to exchange shoes with me. I went on the principle that "what is mine is thine," so made no objections to complying with their wishes. I have not lost as much as I expected I should, and if it were not for the wounds I have in my arms, and for the memory of a vicious face demanding money from me at the point of a dagger, I should not have such entirely unpleasant remembrances of the visit of "White Wolf's" brigands to Kwangchow. About 2 p.m. the robbers left this part of the city with their booty, and by 4 p.m. the people were out in the streets, and the report was circulated that the robbers had left the city, going to the east, no doubt to attack one of the other "hsien," or district, cities in this region, Gusihsien or Shangcheng.

These robbers were the same band as that which attacked Tsaoyang, where Mr. and Mrs. Fauske, Mr. and Mrs. Holm, and Miss Saether were kept prisoners. They have kept to western Honan hitherto, but they have made a raid to the east. Kioshan, where a number of the U.C. (United Church) missionaries are stationed, was taken last week, a number of smaller places, too, on their way east, and now in quick succession Loshan, Kwanshan, and Kwangchow have been attacked. These robbers are well armed, having good army rifles and plenty of ammunition, evidently. They are becoming very daring, as they have met with no reverses whatever since beginning their brigand career a year or two ago. Most of the robbers are young men between 20 and 30 years of age. Some are older; a number are only boys. It is a disgrace for China that a band of robbers like this should be allowed to terrorize the country. But no serious effort has been made as yet to stop their ravagings. This part of Honan has been very peaceful hitherto, none here being able to remember that robbers have visited the city before. But it was really not to be expected that such a rich district as this should escape such a band of robbers, and now then we have had them. If only they are satisfied with this and do not come back periodically, I shall not complain. I have lost up into the hundred dollars worth of clothes, etc., but I expect to get that back from the Chinese government in the course of time. Meanwhile, I have enough left to get along with. The only article which they took all I had of, was toweling. I have been thinking it is good that they want to use that article anyway. While they were here, some of them washed their faces and made their toilet quite punctiliously. Some day, perhaps, it may turn out so that Jesus Christ, who was crucified between two robbers and who promised one that he should that day be with him in Paradise, will be washing clean the hearts of more than one of these ignorant, misled robbers here in heathen China.

A large number of people in the city have been killed or wounded, it seems. I have not been able to find out yet how it is in other parts of the city, but on this street alone, 20-30 men have been killed. The owner of the house I am occupying was shot through the thigh and was brought into my rooms here, hoping that I should be able to help him. Others, too, have come for medicine or advice as to what to do with this or that wound. I have done the best I could, given them antiseptics, and told them how to bandage the wounds, etc. Never before have I wished so that I was a doctor or that there was a doctor with me. So much could be done to relieve the suffering of these poor people. Cannot some young doctor be found in our large church body who would be willing to come out here to help suffering mankind, instead of eking out a living there at home with a number of neurotics who could do just as well if they never had seen a doctor? Here in all this city of many thousand people, with tonight many hundreds, perhaps, lying with rifle bullets some place in their bodies, or with nasty knife wounds, there is not a single doctor to help. No doubt tomorrow will find a large number added to the list of the dead. As for myself, only 2-3 of the wounds I received went deep enough to matter much. One in the right arm bled freely and is causing me no trouble now. One in the left arm, however, which has not bled much but has turned a little "bad," has been aching most of the day. I had no chance to bandage it till in the afternoon, as the robbers were always with me and I did not care to run the risk of having them run off with the clothes on my back. I had on a thick fur coat at the time I was being told to seek silver and was feeling the point of Mr. Robber's knife, and that, perhaps, saved more of the wounds from being serious.

Jan. 15. Today I have been kept quite busy giving out medicines, cotton bandages, etc., to various people who came to seek help from the foreign "medicine man." I have no large supply, and I shall soon be out of the necessary aseptics and antiseptics. Today we find that up into the hundreds of people have been killed and many more wounded. Next door to me in the group of houses of which I am renting a part, three men were killed. It is indicative of the general change of attitude towards foreigners in China that the robbers should be less fierce with me than with the Chinese. Mr. and Mrs. Mason and Mrs. Smith of the China Inland Mission over in South City made their escape to the country before the robbers entered the South City. The North City was entered about 5 a.m.; the South City not till 8 a.m. So they are in safety at the home of one of their church members in the country and will no doubt remain there till they hear that all is peaceful here in the city. Mr. Smith, who some days ago started out on a trip in the inland, I have not heard anything about. It is to be hoped that he, too, is in some out-of-the-way country place and not in Shangcheng or any larger market-town along the way to that city. For the robber band has in all likelihood gone off to that place.

Soldiers are expected here from the west soon. The people fear that they will be little better than the robbers. But I hope they will at least not kill and torture people like the robbers did. I have said I should speak to the commander of the troops that come, if some man like old Mr. Wen[11] here in South City would come along to add dignity to my appeal for the people. Some hint to the effect that there might be trouble with the foreign governments, if the soldiers should commence to plunder anywheres near the two mission stations, might have some effect, if the soldiers are government soldiers and their captain is a decent sort of a fellow. Anyway, it may be worth trying. In the meantime, my promise to do this has caused some of the leading spirits here in the city, with whom I have spoken, to be a little more at ease with regard to the soldiers who are on their way here. Let us hope that there will be no more killing, plundering, and burning in this city, which surely has seen enough of that kind of treatment for this year anyway.

Jan. 16. Now I have found out how it was that the robbers could enter the city so easily and quickly, in spite of the high, thick walls and the double-doored gates. The city police or guard of 2-300 men have all left the city with the robbers and have turned professional robbers. They opened the gates for the robbers, after pretending for a while to defend them, and then went to rob the money shops and the rich men's places. For, as they were acquainted in the city, they of course sought these places first, whereas the newly-arrived robbers simply went from house to house from the west end of the city to the east end. It had been agreed before then, through "White Wolf's" spies, no doubt, that the city police should help the robbers in this way.

More and more people have come with news of how this man or that man was killed or wounded, and it makes the heart sick to think of all the misery these robbers have left in their wake. Some have been shot through the chest, others through the legs, or arms, etc. And these ignorant Chinese can do nothing to help them but to pray to wooden idols or at best to an unknown God; or if they are church members who are acquainted with the new "muh-si" (pastor) over in North City, they can get a little iodine or some other antiseptic and some cotton and bandages to bind up the wounds of their relatives or friends. I have had to turn away all who did not have real serious wounds, as I have but little medicine left. It will take the people days to recover from the shock, it seems. All business is at a standstill. None has the heart to do anything. Some I imagine have died of fright more than of their wounds. One young man came to me today and wanted some medicine for his heart. It went too fast sometimes, and he could not always keep his balance, he said. I could only give him a little tonic medicine (not "Kuriko," by the way), and some good homeopathic advice about taking things cool and trusting in the Lord in whom he professed belief to help him these days through his troubles. I do not

---

[11] Mr. Wen is one of the most prominent men in the city and the leading spirit in the China Inland Mission congregation over in South City. It is perhaps due most to him that the work there has not stopped these many years that there has been no foreign missionary in Kwangchow.

know that I diagnosed his case correctly, but I judged that it was fright that was bothering his heart more than anything else.

The robbers had little time to waste here, as they knew that soldiers were on the way eastward after them. So they did not destroy many things in mere wantonness, as they did for example in Tsaoyang. The "yamen" (the district governor's residence and office) was burned and some other houses, too. But no attempt was made to set the whole city afire. The governor escaped death, although most of the men with him were killed. He had hidden some place in the rear of his residence where he was not found.

Such are some of the details of a story which now a large number of the cities in Honan could tell. Are the Chinese alone responsible? They are responsible indeed, for they could see to that such a condition of affairs did not exist. But is none else responsible? How about those who sit quietly in the safe shelter of good homes in a civilized community and do nothing to bring "Peace on earth, good will to men" to the ears and into the hearts and lives of China's millions?

G. O. Lillegard

Soldiers going west from Kwangchow

500 soldiers going from Kwangchow to Sinyang

Chapter 5
The Worker

After the bandit incident, *The Bode Bugle* published a story headlined, "Rev. George Lillegaard Shot." Shortly afterwards, Lars received this letter:

ADDRESS OFFICIAL COMMUNICATIONS TO
THE SECRETARY OF STATE, WASHINGTON, D. C.

DEPARTMENT OF STATE
WASHINGTON

January 19, 1914.

Mr. Lars Lillegard,
    Bode, Iowa.

Sir:

    The Department has received from the American Consul General at Hankow, China, Mr. Roger S. Greene, a telegram dated January 18th reporting that your son, George Oliver Lillegard, American Lutheran missionary, has been wounded by robbers who took Kwangchow, Honan, on January 13th. The wounds, the Consul General states, are not serious.

    I am, Sir,

        Your obedient servant,

           For the Secretary of State:

                  Director of the Consular Service.

393.116/54

AMERICAN CONSUL GENERAL WRITES GEORGE
"...troops have been sent to protect you."

AMERICAN CONSULAR SERVICE

Hankow, China, January 23, 1914

Subject: <u>Brigandage in Honan.</u>

Rev. George O. Lillegaard
American Lutheran Mission
Kwangchow, Honan

Sir:

Your letter of the 20th instant arrived last night. I first heard of the attack made on you at Kwangchow, on the evening of the 18th instant by letter from the Rev. Ingvald Daehlen. I immediately reported the matter by telegraph to the Secretary of State at Washington, and to the American Minister at Peking, and at the same time telegraphed to the Governor-General at Kaifeng and to the Minister of War, now acting Governor General of Hupei, demanding that protection be afforded you. Both have replied informing me that troops have been sent to protect you. I have further mailed to both of them an abstract of your report of the affair, calling attention to the treachery of the local soldiers or police who admitted the robbers.

Your complete report sent to Mr. Daehlen was mailed by me to the Legation at Peking by the morning train on the 20th instant.

- 2 -

It now appears that the Government is planning more systematic measures against the robbers than heretofore, and I shall be greatly obliged if you will inform me whether anything effective is actually done. Please continue to keep me informed by direct letters from time to time, that I may act intelligently and promptly in case the promised measures again prove to be ineffective.

I am forwarding to the Legation a copy of your letter under acknowledgment and will inform you of any further action taken.

Please be assured of my deep sympathy with you in the terrible experience through which you have passed. I may add that in my telegram to Washington I mentioned that your injuries were not serious, so I hope your friends will not be unduly alarmed. I trust that your wounds are now healing satisfactorily. I understand that some of them were giving you a little trouble.

Very respectfully yours,

Roger S. Greene
American Consul General

GEORGE REPLIES, STAYS IN CHINA AND CONTINUES WORK.
"...many thanks again for what you have done to help us through this difficulty and to finish "White Wolf..."

The Lutheran Synod Mission,

信義會 光州 河南

Kwangchow,[12] Honan March 4th, 1914

Hon. Roger S. Greene
American Consulate
Hankow, China

Dear sir: I wish to thank you for your telegram received here Monday. Evidently our district magistrate had received orders from Kaifeng Friday the 27th to protect us, and seeing he could do nothing more I suppose he decided to report a future event as already accomplished, in order to set our minds at ease. His moral lapse may be forgiven when one considers the undoubted good effect it had upon the missionaries in this city. As for myself, I take my sleep in spite of rats, brigands, and other nuisances. But the Masons and Smiths over in South City spent sleepless nights until they heard that the robbers had passed Kwangchow and were so far west (the railroad) that they would not be likely to come back. As a result of your representations, a force of soldiers was sent from Sinyang on Sunday the 1st who rather unexpectedly met a band of robbers on the way, fought them, killing a few hundred, and then went on without giving the brigands chase. They did not reach this place, but 100 soldiers arrived from Kwangshan Monday to protect "Fuh Yin Tang." Everything is quiet in this district now. Soldiers are passing through here every day on their way west. All the robbers have scattered to their homes now, those belonging in the district to the east of here, having "melted away" before the soldiers, while those from the west returned practically unhindered to their western homes. There seems little question in the minds of such men as Major Robertson that the soldiers were not in earnest about their pursuit of the robbers. He thinks there is some "hanky-panky" about it, as he says. What that might be, only a Chinese could understand, no doubt. One thing is sure, the troops or whoever is responsible for the troops have not done what he could and should to suppress these brigands. I shall in letters to the daily papers give more details about how the brigands escaped, etc, which will show what was not done by the soldiers. Whether there is anything to be done about it, you shall have to judge. So long as this large band under its present leadership is allowed to ravage the country at will, no one can tell how many foreigners may suffer at their hands. It may be that they will scatter now to their homes, and there will be quiet for a time. But so soon as they begin to suffer a little want again, no doubt they will make another raid. Gen. Wang has ordered this city to receive him as a conqueror. Have

---
[12] Pronounced "Guan-jo"

not the robbers all disappeared? But a foreigner who is not gifted with the Chinese view of what constitutes a victory, cannot but wish that someone would explain at least to the great leaders of this memorable expedition against the robbers, in some practical, tangible manner what a real victory is.

As I expect to be in Hankow before many weeks have passed, I shall not say more about this matter until I can speak to you in person. If there are however any questions with regard to this matter which I could answer, I am at your service. With best greetings to you, and many thanks again for what you have done to help us through this difficulty and to finish "White Wolf," I remain

Respectfully yours,
Geo. O. Lillegard

Rev. Lillegard & Rev. Larsen (Kwangchow?)

GEORGE REPORTS FROM THE CHINESE MISSION FIELD.
"...its real mission in this land: to preach the simple gospel of Jesus Christ ..."

The Lutheran Synod Mission,
信 義 會 光 州 河 南

Jan. 22d, 1914

The Lutheran Synod Mission, representing the Norwegian Evangelical Lutheran Synod of America which is the oldest of the Norwegian church bodies in America, has just begun its work in China and so has nothing to report with regard to work accomplished. The first missionary (George) arrived in December, 1912, and will not be in position to begin active work till towards the end of this year. Eight more workers have come out since the fall of 1913. As soon as these have had their allotted time for language study, the work will be opened in the three cities chosen for our field to begin with. These cities are Kwangchow, Kwangshan, and Sihsien. The president of the Mission Committee of the NELS of A. arrived in December, 1912, to make the necessary arrangements with regard to choice of field for work. After visiting various parts of Central China and conferring with various missionaries and mission officers or boards, it was decided to take up work in Southeastern Honan, with the three cities mentioned as the first stations to be opened. The two "hsien" cities, Kwangshan and Sihsien, which hitherto have been held as outstations by the American Lutheran Mission, were turned over to the Lutheran Synod Mission on the condition that the latter should place foreign workers there within three years. Kwangchow, the largest city in southern Honan, which for a number of years has been without any resident foreign missionary, was considered open territory, and the first pastor of the mission is stationed there now. He is in the "North City," while the China Inland Mission, which now has stationed a foreign missionary in the long-unoccupied city, has its station and the bulk of its work in "South City," across the river.

As to our plans for the future: We expect to station a pastor, woman's worker, and teacher at each of the two "hsien" cities, Kwangshan and Sihsien, within a year. At Kwangchow, two pastors, two teachers, and a nurse will be stationed by the end of this year. A doctor is expected out soon to take up hospital work. It is the plan to build high schools, both for boys and for girls, and a hospital, as well as the necessary chapels, day schools, etc, in Kwangchow as quickly as possible.

The LSM expects to cooperate with other Lutheran Missions in Central China in higher educational work (college and theological seminary), and in literary work. It intends also to adhere to such principles of comity with non-Lutheran missions as the Lutheran Church always has upheld, viz that there shall be no proselytizing, acceptance into membership of men from other churches who are not members in good standing in the churches from which they come, etc.. While the LSM thus will be interested in educational and medical work and in various union projects, it hopes with God's help to remain true through and in it all to its real mission in this land: to preach the simple gospel of Jesus Christ to all whom it will be given these years to reach.

The Lutheran Synod Mission,

信 義 會 光 州 河 南

Kwangchow, Honan_____ 191 .
Jan. 3d, 1914

The Lutheran Synod Mission, representing the Norw. Evangelical Lutheran Synod of America which is the oldest of the Norwegian church bodies in America, has just begun its work in China and so has nothing to report with regard to work accomplished. The first missionary arrived in December, 1912, and will not be in position to begin active work till towards the end of this year. Eight more workers have come out since the fall of 1913. As soon as these have had their allotted time for language study, the work will be opened in the three cities chosen for our field to begin with. These cities are Kwangchow,(   )Kwangshan,(   )and Sihsien(   ). The president of the Mission Committee of the N.E.L.S. of A. arrived in December, 1912, and to make the necessary arrangements with regard to choice of field for work. After visiting various parts of Central China and conferring with various missionaries and mission officers or boards, it was decided to take up work in South-eastern Honan, with the three cities mentioned as the first stations to be opened. The two "hsien" cities, Kwangshan and Sihsien, which hitherto have been held as outstations by the Amer. Luth. Mission, were turned over to the Luth. Syn. Mission on the condition that the latter should place foreign workers there within three years. Kwangchow, the largest city in southern Honan, which for a number of years has been without any resident foreign missionary, was considered open territory, and the first pastor of the mission is stationed there now. He is in the "North City", while the China Inland Mission, which now has stationed a foreign missionary in the long-unoccupied city, has its station and the bulk of its work in "South City", across the river.

As to our plans for the future: We expect to station a pastor, womans worker, and teacher at each of the two "hsien" cities, Kwangshan and Sihsien, within a year. At Kwangchow, two pastors, two teachers, and a nurse will be stationed by the end of this year. A doctor is expected out soon to take up hospital work. It is the plan to build high schools, both, for boys and for girls, and a hospital, as well as the necessary chapels, day schools, etc, in Kwangchow as quickly as possible.

The L.S.M. expects to cooperate with other Lutheran missions in Central China in higher educational work(college and theological seminary), and in literary work. It intends also to adhere to such principles of comity with non-Lutheran missions as the Lutheran Church always has upheld, viz that there shall be no proselytizing, acceptance into membership of men from other churches who are not members in good standing in the churches from which they come, etc..   While the L.S.M. thus will be interested in educational and medical work and in various union projects, it hopes with God's help to remain true through and in it all to its real mission in this land: to preach the simple gospel of Jesus Christ to all whom it will be given these years to reach.

GEORGE ASKS FOR AID TO CHINESE FAMINE VICTIMS.
"...the cry goes up to "Heaven," to the rain-gods, to the dragon of the sea, for rain to refresh the parched earth."

The Lutheran Synod Mission,
信 義 會 光 州 河 南

Chikongshan, Kwangchow, Honan
August 10th, 1914

Lutheran Herald:

A few months ago, I had to chronicle the first real catastrophe that had befallen Kwangchow for something like 300 years, viz., the visit of the White Wolf brigands to SE Honan. Now I have unfortunately to tell about an even worse trouble that has come over this unhappy field of ours: a long-continued drought, in consequence of which lean famine stares a great part of the people in the face. For three months last year, the people suffered under the raids of the brigands and the hardly less terrible oppression of the many thousand soldiers who followed after them. And hardly had the last force of soldiers left for the west on their leisurely pursuit of the brigands, when the possibility of famine came to add its heavy weight to the woes of the people. There had been very little rain throughout the fall and winter and the rice crop (which is harvested in the late fall) was the poorest they had had for many years. The ground was so dry that many fields could not be worked enough to allow of sowing the winter crop of wheat, and the wheat that did grow up was almost totally destroyed by a sandstorm from the north which covered the grain with its dry burning grains so that it was withered away. Thus all the farmers had to rely on for their living the coming year was the rice crop. If they had been able to plant their rice, few would have suffered. For rice is the important crop and this district of Honan is a very wealthy and favoured one, so that it could stand the loss of the wheat crop.

But only little rain fell in the spring, and when the "rainy season," the months of June and July came, there was no rain at all, except for local showers here and there. Rice, you know, must have plenty of water. The rice fields are banked up in such a way that there is always an inch or two of water standing in them. Large pools of water supply the fields when the rains do not come frequently enough to keep them flooded. But now the pools were as dry as the rest of the land. Then the famine began in real earnest. The great part of China's population is agricultural. If the crops fail, millions of people are at starvation's door. There may be tons of grain stored in the cities, but as soon as it is evident that the year's crops will be a failure, prices of all grains go up so quickly as to make it impossible for anyone but the few rich to procure enough to live on any length of time. So it has been in our district. Many have already starved to death. Many have done away with the children whom they found themselves unable to support. Thousands have left their homes and begged their way to other more fortunate parts of China, leaving behind them the old and weak and helpless, the women and children, to starve to death or to end their misery by suicide. Others have turned robbers and eke out a living by surprising some rich farmer and extorting from him what grain he has in store.

All over the land, from rich and poor alike, the cry goes up to "Heaven," to the rain-gods, to the dragon of the sea, for rain to refresh the parched earth. A traveller could almost any day see long processions winding along the country roads or over the mountain paths, carrying banners with an inscription something to this effect: "Great merciful Heaven, have compassion on the parched earth; send us rain from the clouds above." Through the burning heat, heads bared to the lurid sun, chanting weird songs, they march many tens of miles, perhaps, to some favorite temple or sacred spot and beg for rain. But Great Heaven has remained hard as steel, sending down to earth only the most intense heat that has ever been recorded since foreigners came to these parts.

  In a former letter, I noted how it was first when a missionary of our church came to the district that misfortune came upon it. And it is not only I who have noticed that. The heathens are more than ready to blame us foreigners for the disasters that have befallen them. The native Christians are feeling the weight of their hate now. They hear that it is the foreign pastor who has brought these troubles upon them - Heaven is angry because some of China's people have listened to the doctrines of the "foreign devils." Drive out the foreigner, they say, and all will be well. It is hard to say what an ignorant mob might do with a foreigner if they should have him in their power now.

  Just the last few days, however, we have had good rains and the prospects are that a large percentage of the people will be able to live through the winter in some way. They are sowing millet and planting beans and other vegetables and will perhaps manage in that way until the wheat crop is harvested in the spring. If the drought had continued much longer or out into the winter, nine-tenths of the people would have starved to death. As it is now, perhaps seven of these nine will be able to eke out some sort of a living - i.e., if only there is sufficient rain hereafter to keep the crops that now have been planted from drying up. But still there will be two in every ten people who will be starving, if help is not brought them.

  <u>We can help them.</u> We can prove that the foreigner does not bring misfortune with him but blessing, both for time, and for eternity. Jesus fed the hungering multitudes in the wilderness. We can do the same. We <u>should</u> do the same, even though, as in Jesus' time, it is not by giving material aid that we can expect to gain the real converts to Christianity. It will not take such very large sums to relieve the worst of the suffering, now that such a large part of the population will not be affected. It will be <u>possible</u> to help. It will be a good investment for us to help. We can give to those who are sick or helpless. We can make those who are able-bodied work for their food, either with such work as we want done in our station, or such as will benefit the public in general, e.g. work on the roads, which is sorely needed here in China, etc. We <u>can</u> help - and help ourselves while so doing.

  Cannot then our friends at home take of their abundance and give to this poverty-stricken, hunger-wasted people out here to whom we have undertaken to bring the gospel of Jesus Christ, the Bread of Eternal Life? The crumbs from our tables would feed thousands of Lazaruses here. The paltry sum of two dollars would feed a man and wife for a month. How many of our people will be willing to give two dollars that a Chinese family may live?

GEORGE SEEKS AID FROM RELIEF COMMITTEE.
"...there will be millions starving..."

Chikongshan, Honan, China,
August 27th, 1914

Rev. E.C. Lobenstine
Shanghai, China

Dear sir:

As secretary of the committee elected by the missionaries working in the drought-stricken districts of southern Honan, I have been asked to write you to ascertain whether the Permanent Relief Committee in Shanghai had any funds at its disposal which we could make use of, or if we in other ways could get help from you in our relief work. The conditions in South Honan are very serious, an unprecedented drought adding its heavy weight of woes to the sufficiently great distresses the people had suffered at the hands of White Wolf and as the result of a year's poor crops. This year there was neither wheat crop nor anything else and it was impossible to plant rice. The rains that came in the early part of this month made it possible for the farmers to plant vegetables, millet, etc., so that a great many will thus be enabled to keep starvation away from their door. But still there will be millions starving all through this district. All the missions represented in this district are to raise what funds they can in their respective constituencies at home, and we have also cabled through the consul at Hankow for relief from the various benevolent organizations at home. But we cannot expect to get much from home for a month or more yet and many are already going to their station and will no doubt be pressed on all sides for help. If there then are any funds already in China at the disposal of the Relief Committees we should like to get our share. It seems that a great part of China is suffering from some form or other of disaster, and no doubt many claims will be made upon the funds at your disposal; but I doubt that any district needs them more than our district in Southern Honan.

Would you kindly let me know then whether you can help us in any way or not? Thanking you in advance for all favours, I remain

Respectfully yours,

Geo. O. Lillegard

GEORGE GIVES THANKS FOR FAMINE RELIEF.
"What we do, whether in the evangelistic work, or in the medical work, or in such famine relief work seems but as a drop in the ocean."

Feb. 24th, 1915

The Lutheran Herald:

Friends who have so kindly given of their goods to help the famine-stricken people in southern Honan will no doubt be interested in hearing what has been done to relieve the need; so I shall sketch in brief what has been accomplished hitherto and review the present situation.

The first week in December we began to take on men for work on the streets of the city. By the middle of the month we had 400 men engaged. There were thousands of others who wanted work and who no doubt needed it just as bad as those who were given it. We had almost to fight our way at times through the crowds of men begging to be taken on. But with the funds at our disposal, about $1,800, we could not see our way clear to engaging more then. However, later $1,600 more were received and since Christmas we have employed about 800 men. Some have worked for only a few days or weeks, so that by this time perhaps about 1300 men have been in our employ for a longer or shorter time. Besides these who have been thus directly aided, many hundreds of the poor people in the city: men, women and children: have daily earned an extra penny by picking up brickbats and small stones and selling them to us for use in making roads.....

.....There has been much suffering in the country, especially to the south and west; and we have not been able to reach many outside of the city itself. There was an unusually heavy snowfall two weeks ago, during which many people starved and froze to death and many more suffered severely. A few days ago Rev. Larsen and I picked up a beggar boy who was lying in the street, a bundle of rags, skin and bones, almost dead from starvation and cold. We found that both his feet had been frozen so that they now were but one swollen mass of blue, putrid flesh. On these frozen numbed feet he had stumped his way into the city to beg for food. As we could do nothing for him here we sent him to Kioshan to the hospital of the United Church Mission there for treatment. This meant a journey of four days by wheelbarrow overland. Together with him Mr. Mason in South City sent one he had found in like condition. These were cases that just happened to come to our attention. No doubt there are thousands of others in the country round about who would need like medical attendance.

I fear that the doctors in our synod have seen so many appeals for a missionary doctor in the columns of our church papers that they turn over another page when they come to articles on mission topics. But I cannot help but make this another plea for a doctor. It seems so unreasonable that we should have to send such cases these many days journey overland to a doctor already overloaded with work when a church body as large as our synod's now three years ago decided to take up work in China and to send a doctor out as soon as possible. Every day people come to me with ugly wounds or inflamed, half-blind eyes or mysterious aches and pains or still more mysterious descriptions of the aches and pains of a friend or wife or child at home. I can do so little with my limited supply of medicines and my still more limited knowledge of them. But it seems so hard to turn them away, knowing that the Chinese doctor they then must go to will most likely kill them with some vile concoction no animal would ever eat or drink but which deluded men will if they think thereby to prolong a little their miserable, yet beloved lives. It is a good Chinese doctor who has gotten so far that he can prepare a mixture which will do the patient no harm and who so will give nature a chance to do her work. Yes, the need is so great in every way. You at home can never realize what the need is simply by hearing about it. And we out here soon get so used to seeing it all, soon become so blunted that we do not notice it ourselves and so soon fail to tell about it or to describe it aright.

What we do, whether in the evangelistic work, or in the medical work, or in such famine relief work seems but as a drop in the ocean. Still we hope that it is felt more than appears on the surface. Cast a stone into a large pond. It sinks a moment; the ripples play along the surface for a time, and then all is quiet and placid again. But although visible signs of commotion have disappeared, there are many changes in the pool. We make a commotion for a time with our work for the relief of the poor, and it seems but as a ripple on the placid surface of Chinese society. But we hope and believe that our work will have its effect for many years to come, that fruits of the work will show themselves in many little ways, and that the Norwegian Synod will have cause only to bless the time it contributed a few thousand dollars to the poverty-stricken people of Kwangchow and vicinity.

"All who were baptized, except Mr. Yeh, he wasn't present when I took this."

(1st class baptized at Kwangchow)

"my house from the west" (in Kikungshan National park; Jigongshan, Henan Province)

George (in Kikungshan)

GEORGE DESCRIBES HIS CHINESE HOME.
"A Winter in a Chinese House"
"...they (the rats) perhaps were only standing guard over me to defend me from worse specimens of their own kind."

Kwangchow, Honan, October 30th, 1914

The Lutheran Herald:

The words "a Chinese house" generally bring up before one's eyes the dreary picture of a disreputable-looking hut with mud walls, straw roof, or at best unevenly-laid tile roof, small papered windows, poorly-fitting half-broken doors, with the interior of the house damp and dark, the ceiling and walls thickly coated with soot from the chimneyless ovens, mud floors, and dirty furniture and beds with an uncertain number of inhabitants. It was into something like this that I expected to move last winter when I first came to Kwangchow, as so many pioneers in new districts have had to do. But upon arriving here I was made to realize more forcibly than ever that I was not a pioneer, and that pioneer conditions no longer obtained to give spice to the missionary's life. For as good a Chinese house as I have seen was offered me by its wealthy owner. What this is like may be of interest to the readers of "Lutheran Herald," so I shall describe it somewhat in detail in order to make plain if possible under what conditions we live at present.

That the house is a good one does not mean that it comes up in any way to the requirements modern tastes demand. For it was built something like 30 years ago at a time when the Chinese knew even less than now about what was required to make a house liveable. And so, although the buildings with their elaborate carvings and expensive stone and woodwork, no doubt cost far more than a good foreign house would cost, I fear an American housekeeper would hold up her hands in despair at the sight of the accommodations it affords - for dirt.

Like all Chinese houses, the buildings are grouped around a courtyard, which is here all laid with brick, the main building facing the entrance across the courtyard. The entrance is no ordinary gateway. Three separate doors have to be passed through before the courtyard is in sight. These are of heavy timber, and when barred and blocked by the great beam provided for the second door would seem to make access impossible for anyone not armed with modern artillery. To the left of this is a building which we now use as chapel and which seats comfortably enough 100 people. To the right is a smaller room (originally the gatekeeper's quarters but) used at present as a storeroom. Across the courtyard is the main building, higher and wider than the others and more elaborately finished. The large guest room in the center has beautifully carved wooden walls with panels bearing inscriptions in the various styles of writing used at different periods of China's history, and paintings of birds, trees, and flowers which would do credit to many a foreign artist. The floors were originally of brick, but board floors have been put in the whole building and the three rooms have been divided into four larger rooms and two small storerooms. To the right of the courtyard, as one enters, is a smaller building, called "side building," which was last winter used by our evangelist but which has now been turned over to the Chinese woman in Mrs. Gudal's[13] employ. To the left of the courtyard is the kitchen with its brick stove, water "gang" (a large pottery jar), soot-

---

[13] Gudals were fellow missionaries.

blackened walls, and the indispensable Chinese cook. The woodwork in all these houses is painted and the brick walls whitewashed, so that they are comparatively clean. Neither have we noticed that they were inhabited by any of the numerous parasites with which China abounds. For China, as my readers perhaps have heard, is a very densely populated country. There are said to be about 400 million people, and equal number of dogs and pigs (at least these as well as the Chinese are omnipresent), besides numerous other domestic animals, a few billion tame and affectionately disposed insects, and not many fewer rats. We have fortunately been able to shut out all these above-named inhabitants of China as well, with one glaring exception: the rats. For as the houses in this part of the city are built as close together as in any tenement quarter in our big cities at home, "back to back," or "shoulder to shoulder," so to speak, the rats come from one house into the other and simply will not stay away from us. We have tried plastering up their holes. But they soon make new ones or come in some other way hitherto unknown. We have tried to catch them in traps. But they are too smart for that. We have tried to poison them with the "sure-kill poisons" procured at Montgomery Ward & Co., Chicago. But we have seen no signs of the poison being popular in this quarter of the rat world. And so we still have them with us. Evidently these pests have been pests so long that they do not understand how we foreigners feel about them. Last winter, I slept on a low cot bed and used no mosquito net (as now) to keep unwelcome intruders off and out. Often I would wake up in the night to hear (and feel) a rat scamper off the foot of my bed, another leap hastily off the chair at the side of my bed, where he evidently had been investigating the condition of my clothing, another as quickly leave his lookout post on the top of the bureau at the foot of my bed, another dive for the corner back of my bed, another run squeaking along the rafters above me - and I would turn over and try to go to sleep again with the comforting thought that they perhaps were only standing guard over me to defend me from worse specimens of their own kind. And indeed the rats have been kind enough not to destroy anything for me yet, except some rice that I left exposed in the pantry, which evidently was too much of a temptation for them. But they have managed to masticate the major part of a garment belonging to Mr. Gudal; and my cook came to me ruefully one morning and showed me a neat hole which a curious rat had gnawed in his best coat. Evidently rats are an integral part of Chinese houses, so we have resigned ourselves to their company so long as we live in those houses.

Another integral part of even the best of Chinese houses seems to be dirt. It would perhaps be strangest if it were not so. The much carved woodwork, the little nooks and crannies so inaccessible to the hand of the most determined housewife or servant, but so convenient for the germs and the dust; the beams and rafters overhead, way out of reach of the duster or the mop but continually catching dust sifted through the tiles upon them; all make it impossible to keep such a house clean in the way we are wont to at home. Even painted walls are ornamented with dirt that has become so attached to its abiding place that modern soaps and cleansers plus Chinese muscle and industry avail little against it.

In this way then, such houses as these, good and comfortable as they are in many ways, are not such as either missionaries or Chinese can afford to inhabit if more sanitary dwellings are to be found.

GEORGE'S ARTICLES AND HOUSEHOLD GOODS IN CHINA

George, Olive Christensen & Anna Tenwick

"Articles in Kikungshan House, October 1st, 1915"

1 dining room table w. 2 extra boards
6 "   "   chairs
1 sideboard
1 small bookcase
3 cane chairs
1 "   settee
1 "   steamer chair
1 bureau
1 washstand
1 double bed
1 bamboo shavings mattress
1 large mirror
1 cane centre table
1 Chinese table
1 writing desk, with top
1 servants' quarters table
1 "   "   chair
1 kitchen table
2 servants beds (out of commission)
1 large lamp
1 small lamp (Rayo)
1 thermometer
1 portierre[14] and pole
5 roller shades
3 pr. lace curtains

9 glass sauce dishes
1 "   "   bowl
7 water glasses
1 glass water pitcher
1   "   syrup   "
1   "   vinegar cruet
1 pr." salt and pepper shakers
1 crumb pan and brush
6 pint Mason jars
1 quart "   jar
1   "   measure
1 large soup kettle w. cover
1 tin salt shaker
1 strainer, 2 pie tins
1 tin cup, 1 skimmer
1 pancake turner
1 ladle, 1 cake spoon
1 iron kettle with cover
1 granite saucepan
1 large granite pan
1 granite mixing bowl
1   "   teapot
1   "   coffeepot
1 teakettle

---

[14] doorway curtain

2 toilet sets: 2 pitchers, two washbasins, two pails with covers, 2 soapdishes, 1 chamber
1 large Chinese scales
1 small   "   "
1 doormat
1 featherduster
1 tapbell
6 large plates
6 small plates
6 soup   "   , 1 broken
6 butter plates
6 sauce dishes
6 cups and saucers
1 large covered dish
1 butter plate w. cover
1 large platter
1 small platter
1 gravy bowl
1 pickle dish

1 copperbottom boiler
1 rolling pin
1 dipper
1 toaster, 1 collander
1 grater, 1 strainer
1 muffin pan, 3 bread pans
1 dishpan, 2 tin pans
1 large bread pan
2 frying pans
1 flour box, 1 flour sifter
1 iron pail, 2 tubs
1 baking oven
3 water jars (gangs) leaking
1 pr. firetongs
2 Chinese benches
6 veranda curtains
200 ft. rope (extra) for same
1 sugar bowl, w. cover
1 cream pitcher, 1 small bowl

Household Goods on hand (more or less used)

3 white woolen blankets
1 pr. grey woolen army blankets
1 pr. grey cotton blankets
1 heavy quilt
2 bed spreads (single bed)
1 bed spread (double bed)
1 woolen "rickshaw rug"
1 couch cover
4 bed pillows
6 pillowcases
4 sheets (single bed)
3 couch pillows (square)
3 pillow covers
2 portierre curtains
2 linen tablecloths (coarse linen)
6 linen table napkins (coarse linen)
1 green table cover
8 large bath towels
6 hand towels
2 bath rugs
kitchen knives, forks & spoons
3 fur rugs
3 pr. sash curtains
1 table scarf
Furniture enough for a five-room flat here, and the same in China

(Included in a letter from George to Rev. Larsen – another missionary – dated October 14th, 1916, from Chicago, Illinois)

GEORGE DESCRIBES HIS SUNDAY IN KWANGCHOW.[15]
"A Sunday at the Mission Station"
"Time does not hang heavy on a Chinaman's hands."

June 21st, 1915

The Lutheran Herald:

The Chinese have no Sunday. For them it is work, work, day in and day out, except for the New Year's holidays when they take several Sundays free all in one. But those that come regularly to our services, soon learn to count Monday, Tuesday, etc., till Sunday comes around again. And on that day several hundreds could be seen wending their leisurely way to church, whether to the South City or to our chapel in the North City. Many walk 10-20 miles from the country into town. They are up bright and early and long before the hour for services has come, they are seated in the chapel or the guestrooms, waiting for the services to commence. Time does not hang heavy on a Chinaman's hands. It is the one thing of which he has a great and unlimited supply, and he can "kill time" with the greatest ease without any pangs of conscience.

The bell rings; the "muh-si" (pastor) ascends the little platform on which stands the preacher's desk; and when he finally succeeds in composing the rather noisy, restless crowd of men, women, and children, the Chinese evangelist opens with prayer. Then a hymn is announced and read. The organist, a young Chinese catechumen, plays the melody on the organ we have ventured to buy with the synod's money, and the audience sings. It would be hard to do justice to our congregational singing. There is no lack of spirit and vim in it. All who can read - and most of our people, even many of the women, can read - sing with might and main and a fervor that would delight the heart of the average choirmaster at home, who too often finds only the organ and a more or less interested choir making the music, while the congregation dreams on and prepares for the weekly sermon-lulled nap. But there is some lack of harmony in our Chinese singing - in fact there is no trace of it whatever. Any congregation at home that made itself guilty of such singing would be banished by irate neighbours to some desert isle till it repented of its ways. But the organist and the foreigners present struggle on through the hymn, hoping against hope for the day when order shall emerge out of chaos, and China too learns what sacred music is. We hope to train our school boys as a choir to lead the singing and the responses. They have good voices and with proper training could soon learn to sing sweetly enough.

The ritual used in the Norwegian Lutheran Church has been translated into Chinese, and this is followed throughout in our services, except that some of the chants and responses are dropped, since there is no congregation as yet to give the latter. In due order comes the sermon - concerning which perhaps the less said, the better. The Chinese have remarkable control of their facial muscles and let not the shadow of a smile cross their features at the linguistical mistakes or the agonized attempts at finding expression for the thoughts of the foreign preacher. They sit soberly, attentively in many cases, through a long harangue that would send the average churchmember at home laughing or sick with disgust out of the church. There are some, of course, who come simply out of curiosity, and who are inattentive or noisy during the services. It requires

---
[15] Pronounced "Guan-jo".

not a little effort to keep the attention of an audience of Chinese men, women and children, many of whom have never before in all their life been in a place where they could not talk or move about as they pleased. But we cannot complain. It does not take long for them to become better behaved than the average church choir at home.

In the church, the men and women are hidden from each other's view by bamboo screens, as a concession to Chinese views of decency. And as they leave, they go each their way to their homes. Some discuss the "dao-li" on their homeward way. For those who once become interested in the "dao-li," it is not simply a matter of a Sunday's service. It is their daily topic for discussion. It is new to them, this teaching concerning God's love for man. They search the Scriptures, compare them with their own "sacred books," reflect and discuss. Yes, now many have learned to pray for guidance in their study of the word. They <u>wish</u> to know the Way, the Truth and the life. Pray ye for these searchers after truth!

In the afternoon, the men and women meet separately, the women with one of our women's workers, the men with the pastor. The men have this past year been studying the gospel of Luke, somewhat in the way Bible classes are conducted at home. When the pastor has given his exposition of the portion assigned for the day, opportunity is given to the catechumens to ask questions or to give their exposition of the text or discuss any other questions that might arise from what had been read or said. Especially of late, many have availed themselves of this. Thus a knowledge of the Bible is imparted, such as could not readily be given either in the regular services or in the catechetical classes which meet during the week for the study of Luther's Catechism and its explanation. At this meeting roll is called of the 100 odd names that have been entered on our books, i.e. those who have in the presence of the other catechumens expressed their desire to become Christians. If one does not come for three successive Sundays, his name is struck.

In the evening, those of the catechumens who live in the city and who have not too far to walk in the dark to our street chapel, meet there with the Chinese evangelist for a short evening service. Thus a Sunday as different from anything the Chinese before have known as light from darkness has been passed. The monotony of dull lives has been broken. New ideas, new ideals, have sought to open their minds and hearts to the Light. They came at first, perhaps, to scoff, but remained to pray. They cannot be quite the same as before. They have seen men bow their heads in prayer to an unseen God. However little they understood of what they saw and heard, new impressions have been received that cannot but have their effect, if only to lead them to come again and again till they do understand.....

Oh you at home who have been brought up from childhood in Christian homes and schools, under every Christian influence, in the full light of the gospel - pray for these darkened minds and hearts out here; pray with compelling faith, and hearts that long with a little of the Saviour's longing to see them turn to the light and find Him in whom alone is life eternal!

GEORGE REBUTS A LETTER FROM REV. THORSEN
"...the conscious efforts I always had to make not to appear awkward and bashful made me appear the very opposite...It hurt me very much to be considered conceited."

SOUTHERN HONAN FAMINE RELIEF FUND.

COMMITTEE:
Rev. H. J. Mason, *President.*
  Kwangchow, Honan.
Rev. G. O. Lillegaard, *Secretary.*
  Kwangchow, Honan.
Mrs. Prof. E. Sövick, *Treasurer.*
  Shekow, Hupeh.
Rev. C. W. Landahl,
  Sinyehsien, Hupeh.
Rev. J. N. Stotts,
  Kusihsien, Honan.

COMMITTEE:
Rev. L. Kristensen,
  Losban, Honan.
Rev. K. S. Stokke,
  Juning, Honan.
Rev. A. Aandahl,
  Tungpeh, Honan.

Kwangchow, Honan, Nov. 4th, 1914

Dear friend Rev. Thorsen,[16]

    Your letter of Nov. 1st was just received. Thank you. I have not been hurt by it, nor do I think that it shall in any way affect my relations to you, at least for the worse. I believe you wrote it in a Christian spirit, and I shall try to answer it in a like spirit. Before proceeding to discuss the matters I have in mind, however, I should like to remind you that we are as Christians supposed to "tage alting i den bedste mening."[17] The interpretation you have put on some things I have written you was entirely wrong and (though I admit that I am careless in the way I write, especially to friends and those with whom I feel upon confidential terms) I think unnecessary. I trust that you will read this letter patiently, remembering that I wish to write as though I were talking with you.

    I am only sorry that you should have considered it necessary to write as you have done, for it indicates that I have been grating upon you in a way that I had not thought possible. I wish first to beg your pardon for causing you any unpleasantness. I know from my own experience that it is discouraging, especially at first, to find friction where one hoped everything would be good and pleasant.

    As to my being proud: It is no news to me that I should be thought so. There was a time when I was thought modest, though I must say that I believe I was more conceited then than I am now. That was in my days at college when I was a young lad and was always very afraid to offend anybody or to express any opinion that might disagree with that of others or do anything that would lose me the popularity I generally enjoyed. I really was bashful then, though, and very conscious of it. It was first after leaving college when I was pushed out into the world and into society and association with strangers that I began to get the name of being conceited. I think the conscious efforts I always had to make not to appear awkward and bashful made me appear the very opposite, though I did not know it. It was first when I came to the seminary where I expected everybody would be so loving and Christian and kind, that I found out what others thought me to be, when I began, as you put it, "to see myself as others saw me." It hurt me very much to be considered conceited. It was the last thing I wanted to be or at least to be considered. And the more I wanted not to be considered so, and the more I brooded over it and rebelled against it, the more conceited people thought I was. Finally

---

[16] Fellow missionary
[17] Literally "take everything with the best meaning:" "Put the best construction on everything." (Norwegian)

I decided that I was conceited, that this business of not wanting to be considered conceited was itself conceit - and after that life became more liveable again. I know still that certain people before they have learned to know all my corners consider me conceited in ways that I am quite sure I am not. But I do not let that bother me, but try to go my way, to bear patiently contumely[18] as well as praise with all equanimity, and to remember that if others think I have certain faults, that is no more than I think of them, and than they have the right to think of me. I know that I have faults and would indeed be proud not to be ready to admit it. I think pride is the original sin and the last one to be driven out of man's heart. I have generally found others to be conceited in some way or other, too, and have been rather proud sometimes to realize that I knew of my pride better than they evidently knew of theirs. In fact, I have found the most conceited people of all and often the hardest ones to get along with to be those who were proud of their modesty. Seeing that it is the most common form of pride, it is evidently not the most displeasing to the one who first sinned through pride. You will note by this dissertation on pride that I have philosophized some on the subject, and I hope you will so realize that, if I am conceited, it is likely to be in my case an incurable disease, being only too well recognized, and still existing. I do not expect to get rid of all the pride in my heart until I leave this earthly tabernacle. I shall, of course, try to cultivate true Christian humility. I do not think, however, that it is necessary in order to be humble to avoid giving expression to one's opinions, even though they are contrary to those of better men than myself. Neither do I think that it is necessary to attempt to do less for God and man in a false modesty or false fear of what men may think. Nor do I think that a man needs to carry himself as though he were ashamed to show himself. I think true humility is something far different from any of these things. Christ is our model in this as in all things. He who "spoke with authority," even though an unlearned, young man (not so very much older than I), who reproved even in childhood his mother and later in sternest language the leaders of his people, was never even by his own enemies, who considered him but a man, accused of being conceited. (Please do not misunderstand this comparison; I mean simply to show that Jesus as man was no less humble because he did those very things which I above say I do not think are signs of pride.) So much in general with regard to my being proud.....

.....As to my prospects for getting a wife - I have not told you everything about that matter, and so I do not think that you can say that the reason I have not gained anyone's promise is that I am too proud and have offended the girl in question for that reason. Some time when we have a chance to talk together, I may tell you more about it. For the present, I shall just say that what other people think or imagine stands in the way ought not be considered. For they know nothing about the matter. They may guess, but only show their ignorance thereby. I know what stands in the way. My reason for telling you about those matters was not to gain any encouragement or information from you, but simply to let you know enough so that you would not be teasing me to get married, etc. I do not enjoy it, especially when others are around. It may be that I am "repulsive" to certain people. I am not always as much of a gentleman in my speech and actions as I should desire to be. However, I have no cause to complain of not being able to gain the friendship of the fair sex. I have had more cause to complain of becoming a friend of theirs too easily.....

---

[18] rude language or treatment arising from haughtiness or contempt

.....If there is anything you wish to criticize or correct, I shall be glad to have you write me again. Whatever the result of this letter, I hope it will help you to understand me better, and so enable you to help me more. A man must fight his battles alone. But it is good to receive the correction of others......

.....I have argued with you, both on the subject of unionism and of election. Perhaps you have there, too, thought that I showed conceit in so stubbornly defending my position over against yours. If it was only my own, I admit that I might be more modest about presenting it. But since it is the position held by the majority of our church and of the Lutheran church as a whole, I do not feel that I am called upon to keep silent on that subject but that I have a perfect right to argue for the position our church has held as much as I please.....And so I trust that we, even though we may always disagree on certain subjects, can be just as much friends for that, have each other's confidence just as much.....

.....I shall have to ask my friends to be satisfied with seeing me make only slow progress toward the goal set for the one who would follow Christ. It is not easy to be alone with oneself so much as I have been. It either breaks a man or makes him strong and perhaps hard - "a hard customer!" You with your wife and children will never realize what these last two years have been for me, both of good and evil - evil through my weaknesses and faults, which I believe the Lord is trying to purge me of; good through the grace of God and the kindness of his true followers with whom I have met here.

But now it is midnight. I started this after the evening service. When I read this over in the morning, I shall see if there is anything to add. If not, I shall close with this. Thank you again for your letter. I trust my letters will be no worse understood and received than yours have been. My best greetings to your wife. If she shares your views and opinions, perhaps she might read such parts of this letter as you deem right. With best regards to you and the children, I remain as ever

Your sincere friend,
Geo. O. Lillegard

(Excerpts from seven type-written pages)

"Some of the women and girls who were baptized.
Mrs. Giang and her daughter are not here neither is Mrs. Djang."

GEORGE REQUESTED LEAVE FROM THE MISSION because of his father's illness. His request was denied.
"...we felt that we could not grant it under the circumstances."

REV. J. R. BIRKELUND, M. D.,
President
4530 Monticello Ave., Chicago, Ill.
REV. J. A. O. STUB, Stoughton, Wis.
Secretary
REV. G. SMEDAL, Roland, Ia.
REV. S. S. URBERG, Blair, Wis.
REV. R. MALMIN, Thompson, Ia.
REV. S. J. N. YLVISAKER.
Fergus Falls, Minn.

The Board of Foreign Missions
OF
THE SYNOD OF THE NORWEGIAN EVANGELICAL
LUTHERAN CHURCH OF AMERICA

OFFICE OF PRESIDENT
4530 Monticello Ave.
CHICAGO, ILL.
Tel. Irving 1797.
CABLE ADDRESS:
(C.I.M. Code)
BIRKELUND
CHICAGO

May 23, 1915

Dear Rev. Lillegaard!

Yesterday I sent a letter to Rev. Larsen,[19] most of which concerns the whole mission, so I shall write but a few lines to you personally. I hope you have received our cablegram. The enclosed copy of a letter to your father is self-explanatory. A couple of days ago I received the enclosed letter from the post office with an empty torn envelope from you. I hope to get the contents before I leave for Frisco day after tomorrow, and shall then write you again, either before I leave or on the way. I was glad to learn of the progress of the work through Larsen's "Indberetning."[20] There are, however, a number of questions I should like to ask, but presuming that some of them may be answered in your letter I shall wait patiently. In closing let me say that your application for leave of absence was given due and careful consideration, but we felt that we could not grant it under the circumstances. Storaasli's return, even though absolutely necessary, will, I am afraid, throw some cold water on the enthusiasm for the China mission. Let us hope and pray that even this, though we cannot understand it, may be a blessing for our work.

With kindest greetings

Sincerely yours

J.R. Birkelund

---

[19] Fellow missionary
[20] "Report" (Norwegian)

THE CHAIRMAN OF THE BOARD NOTIFIES LARS LILLEGARD.

"Already, therefore, our meager forces have been seriously crippled;..."

George's father Lars Lillegard

May 6, 1915

Mr. L. O. Lillegaard
Bode, Iowa

Dear Mr. Lillegaard:
    Grace and peace in the Lord, Jesus Christ.
    Our hearts go out to you in deepest sympathy. We feel confident that if you could look in upon our thoughts you would rest assured that we entertain only the kindest and most sympathetic regards for yourself, your family and your son, George.
    But as much as we might so desire we cannot advise that George be permitted to return from China already this year.
    Kindly bear with us and consider the reasons which have prevailed with us.

In the first place - this particular mission in China has just been begun. Your son, George, was the first man on the field. No one can have a better understanding of our young mission, its needs and difficulties than your son.

Storaasli has been compelled to return on account of the serious illness of his young wife. We cannot tell you how seriously our young mission forces must feel the loss of every worker.

Already, therefore, our meager forces have been seriously crippled; our thin skirmish line has been weakened almost to the breaking point.

We feel that your son is needed more than ever. If he had but recently arrived, and if he did not have a remarkable capacity for work and a thorough understanding of our field, it would be easier to permit his homecoming.

Your appeals had so touched our sympathies that we were profoundly affected, and were almost moved to act against our better judgment. But it seems to us as though the Lord plainly says "I have need of every one of my workers on the field in China."

In the second place - we know that you with us share the hope common to us Christians.

We know further that also you will cheerfully bear what burdens and tribulations there may be placed upon you.

You cheerfully gave George to this great work. You will not, we feel confident, begrudge the Lord the labor and the efforts of this young soldier of Christ.

In the third place - we are compelled to confess that as much as we would like we cannot make an exception.

Old Dr. Larson surely felt that he parted with his oldest living son for the last time in this life when he bade him God's speed and blessed him as he set out for the distant field. Those of us who were present in Minneapolis in 1913 will surely never forget that parting. We are all the richer for the memory of it. It proves that after all the love of Christ constraineth a parent to make sacrifices which the world cannot understand or appreciate.

Dear Mr. Lillegaard, you will not, we are sure, ask of us that at this time we should jeopardize our whole foreign mission work. An exception such as we would like to make would, however, be fraught with such serious consequences that we cannot with a good conscience make it.

We firmly believe that our missionaries and their dear ones will be willing to abide by the rules and regulations which all missionary societies have found to be useful and necessary.

To make more evident, if it be possible, the sympathy and respect we entertain for you, we are sending Rev. Malmin as the special representative of our committee. We ask that you receive him in the same spirit of kindliness in which he is sent.

So we commend you and yours to him who doth mark the sparrows fall.

Yours in Christ,

J.R. Birkelund, Chairman
J.A.O. Stub, Secretary

GEORGE WRITES STORAASLI, FELLOW MISSIONARY.
"...it looks to me as though there is pretty sure to be a split in our church."

The Lutheran Synod Mission,
信義會光州河南

Kwangchow, Honan, June 28th, 1915

Dear Gynt:

I should have started for the mountain today, but it has rained pitchforks all night and day so that there is little likelihood that I can get started even tomorrow. The rain was needed for the crops, so that I shall not complain because it delayed my trip to the mountain.

But now, since all my books have been packed away and nobody comes around, it being a rainy day, I have nothing particular to do, and so think perhaps this will be as good an opportunity as any to sit me down and write the letter that I have for some time thought to favor you with. You will by this time have had a chance to get acquainted with the present state of affairs within our synod and so you should be prepared to answer what I have to say.

I am becoming more and more certain as the days pass that it would be best for all concerned if I could part company with the rest of our present forces. Though as said in a former letter, there has been a better feeling between us of late than formerly, it is too evidently but a sort of armed truce, which will be broken any time that they find they are strong enough to begin to push their own plans. I am not going to say that it will be wrong for them to do so. It seems that there are more in our church who are more or less secretly of Larsen's[21] opinion than I have thought. I have begun to believe that much of the anti-unionism talk both in the U.C. (United Church[22]) and with the majority of our own synod is meant principally to satisfy the minority in our own church, so that there should be no chance for them to hang their hats on that point. I know that Birkelund[23] is of Larsen's mind pretty much and I fear that his support of us in our position was more official than actuated by his own ideas. Later letters from him have made me feel that he was less conservative on that point than I thought perhaps he was. I believe he is more conservative than Larsen & Co. or at least not so aggressive about his views. But he is not in sympathy with us. I am quite sure that he too was rather pleased that you had to return, and that he would not have sent you if he could have decided the matter. I think they will try still harder hereafter to avoid sending minority men[24] out.

Now, the more I think of giving up the work here in Kwangchow, the less I like it. I should hate very much to have to leave this place. There are a number of comparatively fine Chinese here, who I think are as much attached to me as one could expect a Chinese would be to a foreigner and whom I thus hope to be able to influence for the good also in the future. I have been thinking these days that I have been alone here, how fine it would be if I could continue the evangelistic work here, if you could come out again and take up

---

[21] Fellow missionary
[22] a church body with which there is talk of union (merging), along with the Hauge Synod
[23] chairman of mission board
[24] those who do not approve of the merger if it would mean compromising Scriptural truth

the educational work, and if Lauritz Y. came out to take up the medical work. I think that we three with our wives (if I ever get one) could make as good a combination as any in all China. It means much to have men of somewhat the same mind together in a station. And there are no differences that divide so much as differences in religious convictions. I hope that we would be able to disagree about some things so that life would not become entirely too monotonous for us, but I am quite sure that we would be able to keep mutual respect and esteem. As to your wife - I am also more and more sure that your relations with the other missionaries on the mountain had much more to do with her physical state than you or she perhaps wish to think. These mental troubles are subtle things. They are the real root of physical troubles that we are inclined to ascribe to other causes. Or at least one would be able soon to recover from ailments that are the result of physical defects or injuries if the mental state was what it should be. Dr. Behrents said that he thought she would not be able to stand it here in China because she seemed to be unhappy here. Though she might be more susceptible than most women to the climatic influences that I have before written you about, I am quite sure that she could stand it out here, if she had such company as she liked.

And thus have led up to what I wanted to say: it looks to me as though there is pretty sure to be a split in our church. I believe that the minority will grow with the years, according as some of this unreasoning enthusiasm for union that has possessed so many of the lay people subsides. Now it depends much, of course, upon what turn matters take at home. But I should think it would be possible for the minority to keep at least some of the property belonging to our synod. Luther College and the congregations in that vicinity are quite consistently minority, as I understand it. Our seminary in St. Paul and some of the Twin City congregations likewise. Kwangshan and Sihsien belonged originally to the A.L.M. (American Lutheran Mission), and they are welcome to them. But if there is a split and enough of the synod remains to support a small mission in China, then please fight for Kwangchow, Gynt. That and the country to the north and east, with perhaps Gusihsien when Stotts finally decides to get out, will be all that we shall need. At the present time since the mission fields are beginning to be pretty well occupied, we cannot plan on occupying a large field anyway. Personally I believe it would be much better for our mission work here if the Synod did not join with the U.C. Also I should be glad to see Larsen and Thorsen join the U.C. That is where they both belong. If I had their convictions, I believe I should have joined the U.C. or the Free Church long ago.....

.....Sometimes I hope that the Synod in toto will be able to unite with the more conservative part of the U.C., and that the liberal part of the U.C. will join hands with its natural partner the Free Church. The Hauge's Synod might undergo a similar division. It would be fine if the divisions in our Norwegian Lutheran Church could be reduced to these two and that along natural lines, the more conservative and the more liberal. At least it has for a long time now, 2-3 years, been my prayer that such might be the case. There are a few radicals in our own church who likewise ought to go over to the Free Church, for example our beloved fellow missionaries. I believe that the minority in our synod will not object to union if the new body was cleansed from the liberal elements in the U.C. and the Hauge Synod.

When you answer, kindly give me your opinion as to these matters, as well as the opinions of such men as you have had opportunity to discuss these matters with.

Now I have stated definitely what my plans for the future are. I expect that you will see to it that they are given some chance to be fulfilled, that is, if they agree with your own plans or find acceptance with you. Sometimes I am glad that you are at home to look after mission interests for our minority side. The principal reason I wanted to go home this summer was to feel around a little as to what prospects there were for getting the minority interested in mission work out here in case there should be a split in our synod. But now you can take care of that. I fear that the committee would not have let me go home, even if you had not gone. They were too afraid that I would hurt the union cause. My father at least thinks that is the real reason why they were so against my going. It shows on what a precarious foundation this union rests, does it not, when they have to be so terribly careful to avoid everything that might upset it and when even a small potato like myself is a possible danger or obstacle in the way of union? One almost feels like saying that they condemn themselves and their work for union by such fears and conduct.....

.....Well, I hope to hear from you very soon, Gynt, with regard to these and other matters. Please keep me informed. I hope that your wife is rapidly improving and that you two will be given grace to spend many happy years together, whether at home or here on the mission field. God bless you both and your work for our Lutheran Church.

Sincerely,

Geo. O. Lillegard

Rev. Lillegard & Rev. Larsen

TENSION BETWEEN GEORGE AND OTHER MISSIONARIES

"You see there was a time when it was taken for granted that she (Miss F.) and I were to be married. It was first after it became known or was generally suspected that Miss F. was engaged to Armstrong that their open attitude towards me changed. Then Thorsen wrote me the letter that I have told you about." (Referred to in his letter "George rebuts..." p. 58)

(This letter did not have an addressee. It is believed it was sent to Dr. Birkelund: See p. 83)

June 28, 1915

Anna Tenwick, Sara Xavier & Olive Christensen

I shall review briefly here how it came about that there is this tension between us out here, as I see the matter.

Soon after Larsen came I was made to feel indirectly that he did not agree with me in my standpoint on unionism, etc., although he had said nothing to that effect when we met in Shekow and I spoke to him about it quite a bit. In a letter to him I then asked him his opinion with regard to that matter, saying that I was seeking for light on the subject and that I had not come to any definite decisions in the matter, which was then the case. He then wrote me frankly what his attitude was and defended it. I answered, telling him how I had thought and felt about the matter up to that time, sending him a copy of a letter that I had written to Faye in Africa with regard to that matter. It expressed the standpoint to which I had then tentatively arrived. In order that you may know what that was, I send you a copy of it too. Kindly return it when you write again. In that letter, too, I asked Larsen again for further light on the subject, saying that I wished to learn from my elders. But, evidently because I had ventured not to accept unconditionally what he had to say on the subject, he did not write any more about that subject, did not even refer to my letter with regard to it. This rather surprised me, as I thought I had written in as humble a way as anyone could expect, certainly more humbly by far than I had written to Prof. Brandt with regard to the matter. Later on in the spring he came with a very unnecessary and officious criticism of my letters to the Hankow daily concerning White Wolf, which made me feel that he was even then looking upon me in a way that would mean strained relations. He showed there what both he and Thorsen have shown so many times since, that he considered himself responsible for me and my actions to the general public, as though his own good name would be injured in case mine should in any way be endangered. Now I am not averse to friendly criticism. I think I can take as much of that as anybody. But I do object most strenuously to being fathered by these older men out here. In matters that concern simply my own reputation and good name and in which my actions do not directly affect my fellow missionaries I reserve the right of a fullgrown man to manage my own affairs and to get advice when I want it. As I have written you before, I should be very thankful to you if you would tell them that I will be responsible for my own actions. I have been the president, in the Junior and Senior years at college, of a class in which were men as old as Larsen. I have beaten in an oratorical contest among others a man as old as Thorsen. And I'll be hanged if I think the fact that they are a few years older than I gives them any right to father me out here in this work in which we are supposed to be of equal rank. They will have to show their superiority in other ways than per a birthday book. I have knocked about the world a good deal in my 27 years and have also seen enough of the pastoral work at home to be convinced that ten years or fifteen years work with kvindeforenings,[25] etc., do not conduce to make a Solomon of a man. In this connection, it might also be noted that in the C.I.M.[26] and I think in most other missions, the Senior Missionary is the one that has been longest on the field, no matter how superior attainments a newer arrival may have or may think he has.....

.....Well, when all these people of ours came to the mountain, I was filled with a desire to be of as much service to them in every way as possible. I wanted to help them for the sake of the work which I think I have had as much at heart these years as anybody. For instance, I thought I could help them to "get on to" the changes of pronunciation in the Kwangchow dialect, and to get acquainted with the character and geography of our field. So in two meetings I did thus try to help them. But I must say I never felt more uncomfortable in all my life about anything than I did in those two attempts to be of service to our new arrivals. Can you imagine how the fat woman feels the first time she gets into Barnum's circus and is stared at by the thousands of visitors? I know now. I felt as though I was being tolerated or humoured something like we humour a sick child. In other words, it was considered an unmistakable sign of my conceit and my desire to run things that I should thus presume to try to enlighten them in any respect. I realize now that it might have been better if I had tried to do less for them than I did. My mistakes in that line, however, were due to my interest in the work and nothing else, also perhaps to an undue confidence in that members of my own church would be especially ready to put confidence in me. I certainly shall know better hereafter.....

Now as to our discussions with regard to unionism: Since Larsen did not answer my letter to him with regard to the matter, I had simply to think it out for myself. It was not long before I found out how radical he and Thorsen were. When the Free Church attacked the clause with regard to unionism, both Lutheran Herald and (the Norwegian language church paper) contained editorials with regard to the question. T. & L. expressed dissent with the expressions there used in such a way that I wondered why in the world they did not go and join the Free Church. I said little about the subject, though I did have a few arguments with T. both with regard to that and to election. As I had articles in our own church papers on my own side, it was not hard to get the best of him in such discussions. Once at a meeting of all us missionaries, too, the rest of them agreed that they would not write home about the unionistic practices in which they were indulging lest they should cause remark. I told them, then, that I did not believe in sneaking behind the bushes to do things that I did not dare to do openly, and that I would indulge only in such "unionism" as I could with a good conscience defend before the

---

[25] Ladies' Aide Societies (Norwegian)
[26] China Inland Mission, stationed also in Kwangchow, but across the river from George

whole synodical conference. However the matter ended there then. When I came up to the mountain after New Years, as I have told you before, they wished to have the matter discussed before the whole mission. We discussed it, and though there were no judges of the debate present, I think it was evident enough to all concerned that S. & I felt more that we had proved our case than they did...Perhaps I should not blame T. & L. for getting personal over the matter. Perhaps I would get personal myself under such circumstances. But when they put themselves on the wrong side of the fence as they had done in this matter, they cannot expect but what they will get butted around a little,... I cannot help it that I can show up their arguments and defend my own position. That is what I should do. When we discussed the subject on the mountain, their final argument was that it was so necessary to present a united front against the devil. When I told them that the devil was not so dense that he could be fooled by a simply externally united front they had so little to say that I almost felt sorry for them. So when they cannot disprove my arguments, the only thing they have got left to do is to discredit the source of the arguments, and that they have done enough of both to themselves, me and to others. But so long as our church takes the standpoint it does on this question, I do not see how I can conscientiously do otherwise than I have done. I realize of course when I write to you as I have done about this subject that you yourself are inclined to disagree with the standpoint of our church. I know that from what you said with regard to the matter when we were together here on the mission field. But I have believed that you were not very aggressive or radical about it, and that you would be ready to follow the practice of our church yourself so long as matters stood as they now do in our own church. I have written to you as freely as I have because I knew that you would not make use of what I wrote to in any way hurt Larsen & Thorsen.....

.....Now there is another matter that I mention reluctantly, but of necessity, if you are fully to understand the situation. This letter, whatever purpose it serves otherwise will at least be interesting reading, I trust.

You know that I told you in Hankow that there was a girl I was waiting for, but who was unwilling to go to the mission field. I have hoped that she would get over that feeling as she grew older, and got a little more experience in life. But when I came to Sinyang, it was not long before I found that my wife was already chosen for me. I am not very practical. I have my own ideas about love and marriage. If the ALM[27] people had left Miss F. and me to our own devices, things might have gone differently than they have. Daehlens and Sovicks and Mrs. Dr. B. were not such clumsy matchmakers that they did much harm, but the Kristensens said things in the presence of us both that made things very awkward for us and that practically forced us to try to come to some understanding. Some of the ALM, like Miss Anderson..., and Nelson, who did not want to lose any workers, said things too, though in an unfriendly way that made matters awkward. So towards the end of the summer I told Miss F. about the girl I am waiting for and soon after she told me about the man she is now to marry. As we found some community of interest in criticising a number of the ALM we were pretty much together after that, out into the fall, and as she was not very much in love with the man she had told about, and as I sometimes felt that I had better not wait for the bird in the bush, we might have made a match of it, if we had not quarrelled so much about unionism and the Student Volunteers Movement. We got to quarrelling too often when we should have

---

[27] American Lutheran Mission

been courting, if there was ever to come anything of our friendship. During the summer, I had kept much more company with the Episcopalian ladies whom we met on the boat to Hankow than with Miss F., and some of the ALM were sore at me for doing so. There are many strange things about my relations with Miss F. that I cannot take time to recount in a letter. Suffice it to say that she got a little too fresh to suit me when she found out that Larsen did not agree with me and that our more friendly association ended there. She is too strong-minded to get along with a strong-minded man like me. Every time I get to talking to such a strong-minded woman like that, I feel like administering some of the treatment the shrew in Shakespeare's "The Taming of the Shrew" received. Last spring I was sure again that I wanted to wait for "the one" even if it meant till my furlough came due. Miss F. and I were little together. As an illustration of what kind of talk a missionary community is capable of, I might say that our newcomers had not been on Chikung a month before it was said that Miss Tenwick and I were engaged. At the end of the summer, Miss F. became engaged to Armstrong, the man she had spoken about. It was not easy for her to decide to leave the mission work. She told me about it at the time, with tears in her eyes, and was certainly anything but happy in the way one would expect a newly engaged girl to be. Only Mrs. Hellestad, Miss Hagestande and I knew about it at the time. I do not believe she would ever have become engaged if some of her own mission had not said such unkind things to her. You see there was a time when it was taken for granted that she and I were to be married. At Hellestads' wedding in Kioshan we sat together at the supper table next to the bride and groom. How this came about, I need not tell, except that it was evidently enough according to Miss F.'s, the bride's, and Mrs. B.'s desire. I shall never forget the look on Saeterlie's face during all that supper. It was a mixtum compositum of almost anything you please to think of. I presume it was him who told you that which caused you to ask me in a letter I received last summer how matters were progressing with me and Miss F. In consequence, when summer came, and I kept more company with our own ladies than with Miss F., women like Mrs. K. often said things to Miss F. that stung her much. I think it was principally such things that drove her to accept Armstrong, whom she had refused the winter before, but who with Gudal's encouragement came again to court her in the summer. When I saw how things were with Miss F., I felt that she was making herself unhappy, and I would have saved her from herself if I could. She needed someone to give her some common sense advice. Thus we were together several times again the last part of the summer. She became engaged in August, though the engagement was not announced till November.

Now, there were times when some of the ALM were sore at me because I did not pay as much attention to Miss F. as I might have done. When she became engaged to Mr. Armstrong, there were some of them who knew enough about the real state of affairs to be little affected either over against her or me. But Gudal, who when he knows a little thinks he knows it all, took pains to make it known to our missionaries and others that I had been turned down in spite of having been persistently after her for some time. And so I can explain better than any other way how the things that have taken place between Thorsen, Larsen, and myself have come about. During the summer, though we disagreed about matters, Thorsen & Larsen never showed any open unfriendliness or disrespect for me. When Thorsen was here in September, he was kind as usual, even told me how modest I was, etc, because I wished to wait awhile before taking up the active work. It was first after it became known or was generally suspected that Miss F. was engaged to Armstrong that their open attitude towards me changed. Then Thorsen wrote me the letter that I have told you about. Then (when he was here in November with Miss Zavier) Larsen blurted out with some small personalities that hurt himself more than they did me. Then Gudal and wife took on the half-pitying, half-contemptuous air which Larsen has helped him to continue since. Then Miss T., who had started corresponding with me when I left the mountain, suddenly quit. When I came to the mountain after New Year's, those precious old maids of ours whom I had to beware of lest they propose to me the summer before had become so strangely distant. Do you blame me if the old Adam rose up in me at the sight of such things, knowing why it all was, and if I lit into them all up there in a way that it took them some weeks or months to get over? I am not used to taking that kind of BS from anybody. Of course, I could not very well go around and tell everybody what I am telling you here. If I was anxious enough about my face, I perhaps might. But I do not think it is the part of a gentleman more than of a lady to go and talk about such matters. I do not believe that Miss F. has said much, if anything, to give people the impression that matters were as popularly supposed. It is principally Gudal, and then of course those who had seen that we were somewhat together, who gave people that idea. It has not been easy for me, of course, to know that people think I had made a fool of myself over Miss F.....When I become satisfied that the girl I have been waiting for will not come to the mission field, I know of enough young girls at home whom I can have for the asking, so that I am not worrying about the matter of getting a wife, nor does anyone else need to worry for me.....

.....As I read this letter over, I find it rather unpleasantly personal in several places, in a way that I do not consider right for a generous-minded man's letters or words to be. But sometimes I get sort of tired of being so careful in my expressions when others are not, and willingly let the old Adam in me speak. I have tried in general with God's help to be charitable in my judgements and I believe that I can soon forget all these little personal difficulties and be as friendly with the men I have discussed as I could if there never had been any such unpleasant episodes in our relations.....

.....So now I have passed the great part of a day of waiting. It is still cloudy (today is Tuesday) and if it does not clear up I shall hesitate about starting for the mountain even tomorrow (it is more pleasant down on the plain than up on the mountains during rainy and cloudy weather anyway). But I shall try to get started tomorrow.

So best greetings to you - and when you have finished reading and digesting this letter, please burn it up. Hoping to hear from you soon again and to receive sufficient money to pay our debts, I am as ever,

Very sincerely yours,

Geo. O. Lillegard

Chapter 6
The Head of the Family

In November of 1915, George returned to the U.S. to see his father who was near death. He set sail from Yokohama, Japan, on the 20th.

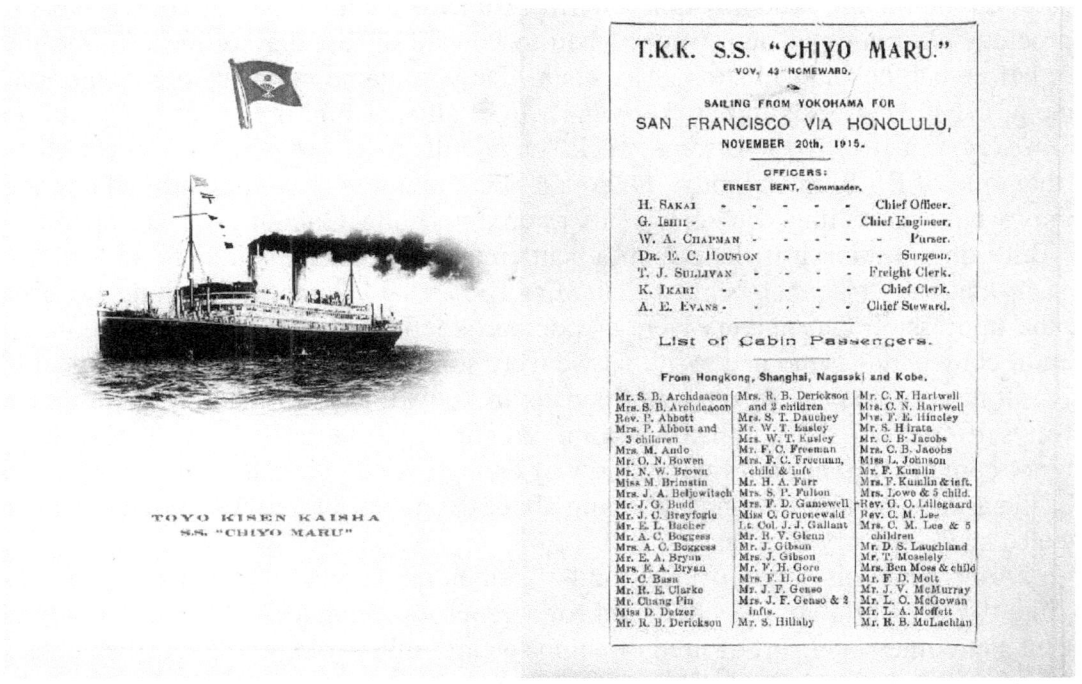

Lars Lillegard

GEORGE WRITES FROM MINNESOTA OF HIS DAD'S DEATH.
"We believe that he is now with the Heavenly Father and so have nothing for which to grieve, except for our own loss."

St. Paul, Minn., Feb. 15th, 1916

Dear friend Miss Christensen:

Thank you very much for your very interesting letter of the 30th of Dec. just received. I shall answer it right away and am going to use the typewriter, by your leave, as I wish to have a copy of this letter. Furthermore, I must take every chance to use this machine as I am just trying it out, and am not sure yet that I want to keep it.

I am glad that you wrote me as soon as you did, as I have been waiting for news from China, and have had considerable more reason for kicking against myself than I thought I might have, on account of my failure to write you from Japan. However, you should have gotten my Christmas mail in time, if it were not for the fact that there is such poor mail service across the Pacific now.

Last time I wrote, it was the night after my father suffered the stroke of paralysis. Contrary to the doctor's belief, he lived through that night and became somewhat better again for a couple days. About a week after he became worse, however, and died on Jan. 19th. I was then in Chicago to attend the meeting of the mission committee, having left home very unwillingly of course under the circumstances.

The funeral was on the 21st. The day after, we received the news that my uncle, Prof. Kaasa, had died that morning. My sister Anna and I went to attend his funeral. He left a wife and six children, the oldest 15 years. You have no doubt seen the account of his funeral as given in Lutheran Herald, so that I shall not say more about that here.

My father suffered greatly the last days, so that it was with some feeling of relief and joy on his account that we saw him released. We believe that he is now with the Heavenly Father and so have nothing for which to grieve, except for our own loss. I am very glad that I could be with him the time I was. It was worth the trouble that it apparently is going to mean for me that I came.

It seems that your forebodings were justified. When Prof. Wold told me that the committee at home might be more ready to believe prejudiced reports from the field rather than my statements, I thought he was mistaken. But it seems that in that respect also I was too sanguine. I did not think that our missionaries would do anything to make my relations with the Committee more difficult. But I must say that Larsen wrote just the kind of letter I asked him not to write. Even those men who had in the main encouraged me to go home - Wold and Mason - were quoted as advising me against it. And so the committee decided without being in the least affected by what I had to say in the matter that I should return to the field immediately. As they demanded an answer right away and I had to leave so hurriedly on account of my father's death, I said there at the committee meeting that I would return to China. The only other thing I could have done there was to resign, and I did not wish to do that then without having considered the matter more fully. But after considering the matter I have decided to ask the committee to let me stay at least till after the Synod Meeting, and have given my very good reasons for making that request. I have not heard yet what they are going to do about that request. Anyway, it is simply impossible for me to return right away. I have gotten so sick of the spirit that has been shown over against me anyway that I would be very doubtful of being willing to stay any length of time, if present conditions in our church were to continue. I want to wait and see how this union question is settled before I try to represent the Synod on the mission field.

It certainly is fierce the way this church war is being waged. And so far as I have been able to judge, the majority party is the one that is making most use of unfair and questionable methods in order to promote its interests. Certainly there is much to be desired in the spirit shown over towards minority people. Just to have talked to Prof. Brandt or to L.S. Swenson seems to be enough to blacklist a man.

I feel that I shall also have to mention a matter that I should like to think of only as a bad dream. I have learned that some of my private letters to B. (Birkelund, the Mission Secretary) have been read in part at least to Dr. Stub and perhaps to other members of the mission committee. In the letters that I thus marked private and confidential, I unburdened myself to B. about the troubles I was having with Larsen and Thorsen and expressed myself with regard to those men very frankly, feeling that I could do so with B. As there was a time when especially Miss T. (Tenwick) showed her disagreement with my views, she also came in for her share of my criticism which is something she will pardon, no doubt, when she remembers how she also at times criticized me to her friends.

I should not mind having B. tell Larsen & Thorsen what I have written him concerning them. But I should not like to have Miss T. think that what I wrote concerning her was said very seriously or that I now would defend my statements at all. I should feel very bad to know that anything should be brought back to her or any of you others, whereas Larsen & Thorsen are welcome to hear all that I have said about them. Neither should I care to have Gudal hear all that I have written concerning him. I believe I might have been more ready to excuse him than I was.

I write you this now, so that you may be forewarned. It seems that it is best to trust no one to be really friendly to one. I cannot understand B.'s action in letting Stub, for example read those letters as anything but a deliberate attempt to harm me in his estimation. And when he did that with Dr. Stub he may do the same with you out there whom he knows to be somewhat friendly to me.

Your account of the people that were baptized was something I had been waiting for. Thank you. I hope those that have been baptized will show themselves true Christians and that you will soon be able to baptize many more. I believe that those who were sore because they were not baptized will get over that in time and perhaps be better churchmembers for having had to wait.

You ask me not to give up Kwangchow. I have not done so yet, and hope that I shall not have to. However, I cannot say definitely yet what I shall be doing. If the committee grants my request, I shall be returning next fall. If not, it will be hard to say how things will go for me.

Thank you very much for the pictures you sent. They are fine. If you get any more - especially such as show the daily life of the Chinese in city and country - I should be very thankful to you if you would send me copies. I may get slides made and use in my lecturing expeditions.

Last Sunday, I was in Holmen, Wis. - preached in Norwegian in the morning, lectured in the afternoon, spoke to the Y.P.S. (Young People Society) in the evening, and to the High School the next day in the morning. Next Sunday I am to go to Decorah, and the 27th to Lake Mills. Several others have also asked me to come, and it seems that all my Sundays will be taken up.

So much, then, for this time. I hope to hear from you soon again in reply to my letters from the boat and to hear that the articles I sent you arrived safely. I enclose a bill which Miss Tenwick will kindly pay for me. How is my boy, Pete, getting along at school? I have not heard anything from Hellestad as to whether my letter to him and the money for Pete's schooling was received or not.

With best greetings to you all, I remain

Very sincerely your friend,

Geo. O. Lillegard

GEORGE QUESTIONS HIS RELEASE FROM MISSION.
"...my last letter to the Committee contained no reference to a resignation..."

St. Paul, Minn., March 19th (1916)

To the Board of Foreign Missions
of the N.E.L. Church of America,

Dear friends:

Your letter of March 8th was received the 14th inst. I thank you. Your letter says: "Our Board feels in conscience constrained to accept your letter as the message that severs our relations," and "Den staaende komite - ser sig nodt til at erklare at - Lillegaard har brudt sin forbindelse med synodens Kinamission."[28] As my last letter to the Committee contained no reference to a resignation or to the possibility of that I might resign, I do not understand how you can refer to it as you do, and should like to ask the Committee to explain why it considers that I have severed my relation with the Mission. I ask this for my own private benefit, and until I hear from the Committee in reply to this question shall make no further answer to its communication of the 8th inst. Hoping to receive an early reply, I remain

Very respectfully yours,

Geo. O. Lillegard

---

[28] "The standing committee sees it to be necessary to declare that Lillegard has broken (severed) his connection (relation) with the synod's China Mission."

GEORGE SENDS LETTER BACK TO CHINA
"...the Committee has fired me,..."

St. Paul, Minn., March 21st (1916)

Dear Miss Christensen:

Your very interesting and newsy letter of Jan...-Feb....th was received here last week, and it has not yet ceased to cause me pleasure and delight to read it. Of course I am most delighted with the nice things that Stotts had to say about me. Talk about the irony of life's happenings! That he above all men should praise me, the rabid anti-unionist, and thus indirectly slam the unionists Larsen and Thorsen, is too good to keep to oneself. I have been wondering if he perhaps has not gotten some inkling of that there has been trouble in our little family circle, and has chosen this way of slamming my venerable fellow missionaries. Or what do you suppose his object with preaching that way was? I do not flatter myself that I have made such an impression upon him that he would preach thus about me without some ulterior object in view. Your letter came very opportunely at the same time as a letter from our Mission Board and as an antidote to it. The letter from the Board stated that I had severed my relations with the Mission. How they can make that out beats me. I simply asked in my letter for leave to stay till after the Synod meeting. But this they say means that I have broken my connections with them. I have asked them to explain what they mean and am now awaiting an answer. In the meantime, you need not take this to mean that I am not coming back to China. I still hope that I shall be able to return to China in due time. Of course much depends upon how things go at the Synod Meeting in May. Now that the Committee has fired me, they will of course be preparing to defend their action, so as not to give the minority a chance to find fault with them. This means, then, that I can expect to be soaked, at least privately and no doubt to a certain extent also publicly in a manner that perhaps few men have had the honor of being soaked at my time of life. Well, I am more or less game to stand the racket. If what they say is true, it will serve me right that people find out about me and so know what kind of a man I am. If it is not true, I believe that they will themselves fall into the pits they dig for me. And so I should worry! Of course there is nothing pleasant about the prospect. But I am in it now and shall have to do the best I can to get out without having lost too much.

I should like to emphasize again what I said in my last letter to you, that I hope you will not let Birkelund or anyone else make you believe that I have it in for any of you ladies or even particularly for Gudal. I have been careless about writing B. But pray, what man is there who would not get into trouble if a confidential friend turned against him and told others everything that his friend had told him, taking care to put everything in the worst light possible, instead of the best light possible! If I could make sure that he would quote things in their connection and would see to that what I wrote was understood in the same way as it was meant by me, I should not worry about the matter. But it is hard to know what to expect nowadays. It seems that affairs in our church are getting to be just as bad as they are in countries that are at war and that there is just as little consideration for opponents as well as just as little regard paid to the Ten Commandments and to "Inter-church Law." I shall keep you informed as to the progress of events here and let you know what the prospects are for that our China Mission will be under better management hereafter. Please keep these communications private, however, that is with you ladies. I am keeping copies of these letters to you, so that I can show people here what I have written, in case I should be accused of making trouble between you ladies and our other missionaries.

The last I heard from Miss Hilleboe, she had decided to wait till next year before going out to China. She has returned the call from the U.C. (United Church) and has given the call from our Church her serious consideration, with the above-mentioned result.

The first Sunday in March I lectured in Red Wing; the second Sunday, I lectured in Anderson's church, and last Sunday I preached and gave a talk to the Sunday School in Aasen's church. Tonight I leave for Chicago, and lecture there in Geo. Gullixon's church tomorrow evening. Sunday I lecture in Lee, Ill., according to present plans. The following Sunday I go to Calmar, Iowa, my birthplace. I have also given talks on China at various Young People Society meetings here in the Twin Cities. The first Monday evening this month, I lectured to the Seminary Mission Society. So you see I am kept busy in that line, and do not get any too much time for study. However, I am putting in considerable time at the University,[29] too, and feel that I am well repaid for taking up work there.

Next year, I plan on going to Chicago. As two of my sisters want to study music there, and a third one plans on taking High School work there, plus some music, a fourth one expects to get a job as nurse there, we figure on setting up housekeeping there next year with our mother as housekeeper.[30] A fifth sister will be teaching school some place or other, and the sixth is married, so that means that we will be "banning gia"[31] for the winter. I hope, at least, that these plans of ours can mature.

I agree with you as to the advisability of getting Miss Saboe to Kwangchow. No doubt Larsen will support you, so that it ought not be so difficult to get arrangement through. Poor Mrs. Thorsen no doubt will feel aggrieved. But I should think she would be getting used to conditions there now soon, and so would feel more satisfied to be alone.

But so much for this time. Please keep me posted on things, and be sure to let me know if you hear anything about me in the lines I have suggested in the "warning" parts of my letter. With best greetings to you all, and best wishes for all success and joy in your work, I remain

Very sincerely yours,

Geo. O. Lillegard

P.S. Kindly excuse my using the typewriter. I believe you understand why I do so.
G.O.L.

---

[29] From Feb. – June of 1916 George studied at the University of Minnesota.
[30] After his father's death, George was the only male left in his family. (See picture following)
[31] (This is most likely a phonetic rendering of a Chinese phrase.)

Ella, Olga, Anna & Valborg Lillegard (George's four youngest sisters), 1913

GEORGE CHASTIZES LARSEN FOR WRITING AGAINST HIM.
"...Prof. Wold...feared that you older men would make trouble for me, and that the Home Board would be unreasonable. I was more optimistic than he in that respect,... although the optimist is the right kind of a man, the pessimist is generally right."

St. Paul, Minn., April 2nd, 1916

Dear Rev. Larsen:

Your letter of Jan. 25th was received about a month ago. Thank you. You have no doubt heard from the ladies how things have been going with me the last months - my father's death, etc. - so I shall not repeat that here. I should just like to add a more personal word.

No doubt you have seen in the church papers by this time what the committee decided in my case. With the evident prejudice Birkelund had against me, the letter you found it necessary to write the committee, and the force-it-through-at-any-cost tactics of the majority party in our church, the decision of the committee is only what one might expect. I did not understand how you could write such things as that Mason and Wold had advised me against going home. For Mason, although he said he was sorry to see me leave, advised me definitely to leave. Prof. Wold advised me to wait awhile, not because he disagreed with me as to the needs on our field or as to the advisability of taking up studies at home again, but because he feared that you older men would make trouble for me, and that the Home Board would be unreasonable. I was more optimistic than he in that respect, and so I have another proof of one of my favorite statements, that although the optimist is the right kind of a man, the pessimist is generally right.

I could of course take your letter only as a proof of that you were not in reality desirous of seeing me return. After the frank talk we had about that matter, it certainly must have been evident to you that I understood the situation, and I do not suppose you will claim that you did not know what action the committee might take in my case under the circumstances. I considered the committee's request to me to return immediately very unreasonable, and their action in announcing that I had "severed my connections with the mission" simply because I asked them once more for leave to stay in this country till after the synod meeting, still more unreasonable. I do not mind for myself. I do not believe that I am limited to the Synod or the proposed new church body for opportunities to serve the Lord. But I am sure that our China Mission will suffer and will continue to suffer unless the committee changes its ways, and there comes also more readiness on the part of missionaries on the field to consider one another. And on that account I am sorry.

There were other statements in your letter to the committee which it might have been best, in the interest of truth, for you to have left out. But I shall not point them out here. It is too late anyway for any correction of yours to do any good. I expect, of course, to be attacked in every way that the committee can attack me now, not excluding even misrepresentations and "kjaerringsladder,"[32] such as I have heard also grown-up men indulge in. But I shall expect to find that they gain little thereby, and so am not worrying about it.

I have thought it in order to send you this frank criticism of your letter, not because it will help me any or even relieve my mind, since I am not much worked up

---

[32] "old woman's gossip" (Norwegian)

over it, but to give you a chance to understand what your letter was and accomplished. It will then depend upon yourself whether this gives you satisfaction or the opposite.

    I trust that the work that has been begun in Kwangchow will prosper in every way, and that the Truth of God will find acceptance in ever increasing measure. With best greetings to your wife and yourself, I remain   Very sincerely yours,

Geo. O. Lillegard

REV. LARSEN ADMITS
"…we frankly criticized you to your face,…"

Kwangchow, Honan, August 4th, 1916

Dear Mr. Lillegard:

It is now not far from a month since I received your note of June 6th. I had thought to acknowledge it before this, but have not gotten around to it. Your note seems to breathe a friendly spirit, and I can assure you I have no desire to be thought of by you as anything but a friend. However, friendship that is real must be genuinely and frankly outspoken, and that is what I wish to be now. You have tried to give the impression that the letters Thorson and I sent home immediately after your departure were not in harmony with the expressions of good will and hopes for your return which we gave utterance to during your last days in Kwangchow, and that consequently Thorson and I have been guilty of double-dealing and hypocrisy. Now I think that in your heart of hearts you know that Thorson and I have not been guilty of double-dealing in your affair. You know that we frankly criticized you to your face, and felt that certain very definite changes in you and your attitude toward us would be necessary as a condition of harmonious work. So far from saying anything to make you think that we considered this change as already having taken place, I do not see how you could leave without feeling that we earnestly hoped that this change might occur before you returned to China. As to writing to the Board, that was our plain duty. And as friends we could have rendered you no worse service than to write only half truths. We are heartily sorry over the turn your affair has taken. And what I said to you in Kwangchow, and wrote to the Board, I repeat now: I for one wish you nothing but that which is good…

With kind greetings,

Sincerely yours,

N. Astrup Larsen

GEORGE WRITES THE MISSION BOARD AFTER HIS RELEASE.
"...I should not have come home when I did, had it not been for my father's condition..."

(Written ca. Dec., 1916)

Friends, Christians:

After reading the twelve-and-a-half-page report or "indberetning" of the Mission Committee, and knowing also what has been said concerning me in private, I suppose I ought to be ashamed to show myself. But here I am. As I have been "unmasked" in a public document, I owe it to my friends, my mother and sisters, and myself, to say something concerning at least parts of the Committee's report...

...I wish first to confess to certain faults and mistakes of mine. For one thing, I talk too much. "And in the multitude of words, there wanteth not sin." In China, where I often had no other pastime than that of writing letters to my friends, I wrote too much, which is still worse. To my friend, Dr. Birkelund, I wrote many and long letters. As he was also the President of our Mission Board, I made the mistake of mixing up mission and private matters in my letters to him, taking for granted that he would know how to separate between the two. Dr. Birkelund made the same mistake himself in writing to Rev. Larsen this last year, so that he had to be asked to write concerning mission matters and concerning the more private matters to Rev. Larsen in separate letters. I have not been asked to do so, and thus have not separated between private and mission matters, leaving it to my friend's judgement to distinguish aright.

This meeting is not the place to discuss my private affairs. If anyone wishes to know full details about them, I shall be glad to speak to him privately at any time. However, I feel that I should make use of this opportunity to thank the Committee publicly for being so kind as to advertise for me, free of charge, that I am looking for a wife. If I am to speak more seriously about this matter, I shall have to call attention to the fact that the letter from which the Mission Committee quotes was written a year and a half ago, and that my circumstances, both financially and otherwise, have now changed so much, that I trust answers to the Committee's advertisement will not come in too soon.

In the next place, I wish to confess to the mistake of having written too freely about our mission's troubles. Concerning this the Committee says: "Der kom lange breve med angreb paa nogle af de andre missionaerer, deriblant et brev, som indeholder saadanne ord og udtalelser, som vi ikke kan gjengive uden at komme I strid ikke blot med de almindelige regler for anstaendighed, men ogsaa med de borgerlige love."[33] In the letter referred to, there is one expression, or perhaps if we stretch a point, a couple more, that might come in under the characterization given by the Committee. At the close of the same letter, I say: "You will, of course, know what in this is supposed to be private and what can be told to others that might be interested. As I read this letter over, I find that it is rather unpleasantly personal in several places, in a way that I do not consider it right for a generous-minded man's letters or words to be. But sometimes I get sort of tired of being so careful in my expressions when others are not, and willingly let the old Adam in

---

[33] "Long letters came with attacks, against some of the other missionaries, including a letter which includes such words and comments which we cannot repeat without getting into controversy not only with the common rules of decency but also with the civil laws." (Norwegian)

me speak…So, when you have finished reading and digesting this letter, please burn it up."[34]

In a letter written on the way home, I write with regard to this and a few other letters: "In previous letters to you, I have written very frankly and sometimes, I recognize, in rather a bad spirit…I suppose that you appreciate that I have written to you at the times when I was rather bitter about some things, and so naturally expressed myself more strongly than I myself in my usual mood would think justifiable. I have also at the time I wrote recognized that some things I (said) wrote were not well put and that others had best, for my own sake perhaps, more than for others' been left out." Since the Synod's attention has been called to the wrong I have done in using questionable expressions and in criticizing my fellow missionaries, I wish to ask forgiveness here. This I would do even though I never have received any rebuke in private, nor refused to better my ways, unless Dr. Stub's suggestion in a conversation with me to the effect that if my letters should be published, they would hurt me in the estimation of a great many people, should be called a rebuke.

Much space is devoted in the Committee's report, to prove that I was needed on the field at the time I left and so should not have left. With regard to this, I can only say here that I should not have come home when I did had it not been for my father's condition. He asked me to tell the Committee that he took all responsibility for calling me home and he told me several times before he died that he had a good conscience about doing so. As to the needs on the field, I shall state that I never have said that I was not needed on the field in this sense that there was nothing for me there to do but that I was needed less at this time than it was to be expected I would be needed later on, as everyone can understand when he remembers that the mission work grows every year. It is also to be noted that when I was in China, my fellow missionaries granted that I might use most of my time this year for study, they insisting only upon that I should stay in China at our station or at some school there. It is since I came home, that they have emphasized that I was needed to help in the pastoral work in Kwangchow. As it would take too much time to go into details, I shall let the matter rest with this…

…I have been blamed for publishing the letter printed in Wiese's Bidrag,[35] both by friends and others. I wish to explain then that I did so, realizing fully that it might bring some such answer as is printed in Synodalberetning.[36] But I considered that the "Erklaering"[37] published in March was put in such a way that it would hurt me in the estimation of our church people more than the whole truth concerning our mission affairs and my private affairs ever could.

To those of my friends who consider that I have acted foolishly in this matter, I would say that I should rather call it foolhardiness. I realized when I left the field that my action in doing so might bring upon me criticism and "kjaerringsladder."[38] After the Committee's Erklaering came out, I knew what was being said about me. But I have refused to be driven from what I considered the right course by fear for my reputation. I have faced dagger and leveled rifle and scorned to fear for my life. And I faced ridicule

---

[34] See the last letter of chapter 5.
[35] Contribution (Norwegian)
[36] Synod report (Norwegian)
[37] "Declaration" (Norwegian)
[38] "Old woman's gossip" (Norwegian)

and dishonour and scorned to fear for that which a man loves better than life – his good name. To quote from a song I like to sing: "I like the fiery heart that dares without a hope of gaining." Therefore, too, I have been a minority man.

I should like to say finally just a word concerning the mission work that I was given the honor of beginning and to which I should gladly have given my life. There is on the mission fields and also in the work for missions at home a marked tendency to emphasize the first part of Christ's last command: "Go ye therefore and make disciples of all nations," and to lay little stress upon the last part, "teaching them to observe all things whatsoever I commanded you."…There we have our orders. Then let obedience to that divine command mean what it will, disobedience is sure as God's eternal word itself to mean – death.

Geo. O. Lillegard

GEORGE WILL FILL IN AS PASTOR IN MINOT, ND. IN SUMMER.

"I...plan to study at least another year here at the University[39]..."

Chicago, Ill., May 25th, 1917

Dear friend Gynt:

Perhaps you are not particularly interested in hearing from me. But I have too many grateful memories from the refreshing oasis in the desert of unionism out in China that you and your wife were to me to be willing to drop you just yet. So here goes.

I had thought for awhile that our gracious Mission Committee was going to unbend enough to give me a call again to go back to China. They were very reasonable about the money side of affairs and I took that to mean that they wanted to be friends again. But since that matter was settled in February, I have had no more evidence of their desire to have me go back, so I am playing the game that has become traditionally good American policy: watchful waiting.

I suppose this war, the poor rate of exchange in China and the consequent increased cost of conducting the work out there, has something to do with the fact that so little attempt is made to get new workers out to the field. And so I for the present plan to study at least another year here at the University, if nothing unexpected turns up to upset my plans. I have been asked to take charge of Gullixson's congregation in Minot this summer, and have accepted that offer...

In another year, things ought to have cleared up sufficiently on the political horizon – as well as the ecclesiastical heavens – to make it possible for me to continue the work I have learned to love. As long as we are in this beastly war, and as high prices and poor exchange prevail in China, I suppose our church will be forced to retrench rather than to increase its work on the foreign fields, and under the circumstances I shall be satisfied to stay at home and continue my studies. That will also give the people a chance to forget the "kjaerringsladder"[40] that has passed current concerning me, and afford me the opportunity to acquire the added "alder og forstand"[41] and pastoral experience in this country that Larsen at least seems to think so necessary to successful foreign mission work. If I am to work alongside of him and his ilk, I suppose it will be necessary to conform somewhat to his ideas of what a missionary should be and to come up to his standards.

All has been well with us this winter. Two of my sisters have been studying music at the American conservatory and the youngest Ella has done very well, we think. I should have liked to have the folks with me next winter too, but they have gotten so homesick that there is no keeping them. So I expect to live in one of the university dormitories next year. Another of my sisters has been practicing as nurse and has been kept busy enough. Just at present she and my mother are visiting relatives in Capron, Ill., about 70 miles west. That is where some of my mother's folks came in early years – in 1842 – and so there is a host of cousins of various degrees there now. We have a number of relatives here in the city too. It is the place where my mother grew up.

---

[39] From October of 1916 through the spring of 1918 George studied at the Divinity School of Chicago University, graduating on April 13th, 1918 with a Master of Arts degree.
[40] "Old woman's gossip" (Norwegian)
[41] "Maturity and understanding" (Norwegian)

I expect to go to the Synod Meeting and trust I shall have a chance to see a little of you there. No doubt there will be such a jam that it will be hard to find anyone, but I trust I can get to shake hands with you anyway. How is everything in your community? Has your trouble been peacefully settled? With best greetings to your wife and yourself, I am as ever,
                                                                                    Geo. O. Lillegard

George at left in bottom row

MISSOURI SYNOD WESTERN DISTRICT AND BOARD OF MISSIONS PRESIDENT ANSWERS GEORGE'S LETTER.
"...we hope that developments in the future may lead to this desirable end."

Board of Foreign Missions

Evangelical Lutheran Synod
of Missouri, Ohio, and Other States

ST. LOUIS, MO., U. S. A.

4/17/18.

Rev. Geo. O. Lillegard
University of Chicago

Dear Brother:

At the last meeting of the Board of Foreign Missions I at last found the opportunity to present your kind letter of February 25th, '18. It was very favorably received and contents noted with special interest.

We indeed would feel very gratified if your good services could be enlisted in behalf of our China Mission and we hope that developments in the future may lead to this desirable end.

Perhaps I may be at Chicago some time to meet you personally and to discuss with you your future plans.

As the Board member who is to visit China also has to go to India, the proposed inspection tour has been postponed until after the war.

Wishing you God's blessing for your studies, I beg to remain,

Very sincerely yours,

R.Kretzschmar

GEORGE WILL ACCEPT CALL TO LAKE VIEW CONGREGATION.
"I shall be through with my examinations today,..."

Chicago, Ill., June 13th, 1918

Mrs. O. E. Brandt
St. Paul, Minn.

Dear friend:

I wrote Dr. Brandt[42] at Fargo last week, inquiring what time he expected to be at home. As I have not heard from him yet, I fear that my letter may not have reached him, and so I shall write you, in the hope that this may find him at home, or at least that you will know what his plans for the next week or two are.

As you perhaps know, I have received a call from Lakeview congregation,[43] and have decided to accept. And so now, before I settle down to congregational work here in the city, I should like to get your husband's advice on a number of matters, as well the practical church work here as the union question, etc.. I shall be through with my examinations today, and expect, then, to leave for home this afternoon. Would you, then, kindly drop me a line at Bode and let me know whether Prof. Brandt expects to be at home next week, between the 16th and 20th, or whether it might be better for me to come later, say between the 23d and the 26th?

I have not been outside of the city of Chicago now since last October and look forward to getting out and meeting some friends in other places again.

With best greetings to you and yours,

Very sincerely yours,

Geo. O. Lillegard

---

[42] Missouri Synod Mission Board member
[43] He served at Lake View Lutheran Church at Roscoe & Osgood Sts. in Chicago, Illinois, from May, 1918 through April, 1921.

GEORGE'S CONGREGATION SEVERS NELCA TIES.
"...no consideration was taken by the Synod of the N.E.L.Church of the congregation's resolution..."

November 25th, 1918

To the Norwegian Lutheran Church of America:

    At its regular monthly meeting on March 5th, 1916, the Norwegian Evangelical Luth. Congregation of Lake View, Chicago, Ill., adopted the following resolution: "Resolved: In the interest of peace, harmony, and the good of the cause, the N.E.L. Congregation of Lake View, Chicago, Ill., respectfully urges the Synod not to take any further action towards amalgamation of the three church bodies or towards dissolution of the Synod, but to attempt first to obtain a clearer agreement in doctrine and church practice than is contained in the 'Opgjør'[44] in its present form."

    At the regular monthly meeting on November 4th, 1918, the N.E.L. Congregation of Lake View, Chicago, Ill., adopted unanimously the following motion: "Moved, that this congregation do not consider itself a member of the Norwegian Evang. Luth. Church of America, since no consideration was taken by the Synod of the N.E.L. Church of the congregation's resolution of March 5th, 1916."

                                                                   Respectfully,

                                                                   Geo. O. Lillegard

---

[44] "Settlement" (Norwegian)
  This was a compromise document attempting to settle the differences between the church bodies (United Lutheran Church, Hauge Synod and Norwegian Synod) that led to a union in 1918 into which all except a minority of the Norwegian Synod (now the ELS) entered.

A CONGREGATIONAL MEMBER PROTESTS WITHDRAWAL.
"...I still wish to remain a member of the Norwegian Lutheran Church of America."

Chicago, April 5, 1919

To the Congregation meeting
Lake View Lutheran Church,

It has <u>accidentally</u> come to my knowledge that the Lake View Lutheran congregation has withdrawn its membership from the Norwegian Lutheran Church of America. I wish to protest against this and also against the manner in which it was done.

No announcement was made at our public services of the intention of withdrawing, neither was there any public mention made of the fact after it had been accomplished. Nor has our parish paper printed a report of it.

An affair of such grave importance should have been officially brought to the knowledge of all adult members of the congregation whether men or women.

To me it is unspeakably sad that this, the oldest Norwegian Lutheran Church in Chicago should have taken this step. A step which throws the undeserved stigma of false doctrine on our beloved church, for I cannot conceive of any other reason which could justify such an action.

I regret that it was done so quietly and that none of the leaders of our church body were asked to explain to you their side as ably and as fully as the minority viewpoint has been expounded to you by the present pastor of the Lake View Congregation.

For my part I still wish to remain a member of the Norwegian Lutheran Church of America.

Respectfully,

Anna C. Reque

"Bessen Luxenburg
Feb. 20th, 1919

Rev. G.O. Lillegard
867 Roscoe SO. Chicago, ILL.

Dear Friend:

I received your letter of Jan. 17th today and I sure was glad to hear from you. I heard about you and your good work from my mother and from my friends in the church. I am very anxious to meet you.

I get the parish paper you send pretty regular but I haven't received the one with Aurthur Hendricksen letter yet. It will come some time.

It doesn't look like we will be home before sometime in July and it sure is hard for us to wait that long. The delay in signing peace makes it hard. I would like nothing better than to hear that we have received our sailing orders.

This town we now are in is very dead. No entertainments of any kind. A fellow can spend his evenings in a cafe but that don't appeal to me.[45] I rather stay in and talk German with the people.

The people that I live with treat me very good. I sleep in a regular bed between white sheets and have hot milk and toast for breakfast and if I come home tired she always give me hot milk. Treat me just like one of their own.

I sure take care of myself as do most of the soldiers, although the life away from home tends to lead the other way. For my part, I have a mother to go back to whose love and respect means a lot to me. Many times this life of waiting to go home, makes a fellow forget for a minute what is right, but I have always done things that I am able to tell my mother and my friends. I am proud of my mother and want her to feel that I have played her square.

I will tell you a little of what we have done in the war but it will be to hard to write a complete story of it so I will give you one of our most exciting experiences and one that we can thank our Lord that we got out of safe.

On the opening of every big drive a wildcat gun is sent out to help the Infantry in their advance and to stay with them and shell out anything that stops them. It is dangerous on account of the exposed position. It was our Halloween Joke on the Kaiser. This happened on the Argenne Muse drive.

On Nov. 1st our gun left our position at Romdin at 3 am and we advanced. The

---

[45] His writing style is left as is, including less-than-perfect grammar.

whole line of Artillery had opened up fire for the big drive. At 3:30 we took a position in the open in front of our first line trenches. We could not fire till daylight so we all layed under our gun for protection. It is impossible to explain how the steady explosion of our barrage looks but it is a sight that makes you wish you were home. My explanation of it now is that it was wonderful. The Huns sent over gas and till 4:50 am we had our masks on. At 5:50 we opened up on a machine gun nest and at 6 am the infantry went over the top. The Hun Artillery had opened fire on us and we had to move. We pushed our gun down a hill and they followed us down with their fire. At 6:15 Hun prisoners came in alone to give themselves up. They sure were a starved looking bunch. At 6:20 we advanced but only got a short distance before they started a machine gun barrage on us and it was 6:30 before we could advance at a mad gallop. We were sitting all around the gun and on the barrel singing, It's home we want to be. You ought to have seen the look on the prisoners face. I guess they thought we were crazy but we were working to make our song come true. As we passed our infantry they sure went wild. Two of our fellows had gone to get some eats and we heard an awful noise in back of us and it was them coming up. One had policed a Hun horse with harness and another a bicycle and they had the traces tied to the bicycle and it sure was a funny sight. I guess the people at home can't imagine the happy go lucky feeling a fellow gets when at or rather in a battle. We took a position but got stuck in the mud and we made prisoners face our gun in the right direction. When the infantry passed us we advance again to a town named Remonville but had to go back as the roads were all shot up. We returned to our battery on Nov. 2nd at 3 am. Not one of us were hurt but we lost 4 horses and our ammunition casson had a direct hit so we left it. It was an experience I am glad I had, but one I am glad is over.

 Well that will have to be all for this time and I hope I will hear from you again or be in Chicago to meet you.

 Please give my best regards to my friends at the Church.

Your Friend,
Alf Nelson
Battery B.
122 U.S.F.A.
American E.F."

GEORGE DEFENDS HIS SISTER ANNA.
"I think...that she has been wounded oftener than she has wounded others."

Anna Lillegard, army nurse, 1916

Chicago, March 1st, 1920

Dear Mr. Skoien:

Your letter of Feb. 25th was received here in due time, and I wish to thank you for your prompt reply. It was quite satisfactory, although I still regret that you should have found it necessary to write as you did in the preceding letter to Anna.

As for Anna's faults: I recognize as well as anyone that she is far from everything she might be, especially in her relations with her male friends. I have often warned her against flirting and all that goes with it. I think, however, that she has been wounded oftener than she has wounded others. And I do not think that you need to think that she has at any time treated you intentionally in any flippant way. If she had been able to believe that you really cared for and would have remained true to her these years while you are at school, she would have done her share to keep up your friendship. However, that is something for you two to settle. I do not know enough about the circumstances to be any judge. She no doubt wrote more, in wounded pride, than she should, and perhaps you for the same reason have likewise written hastily.

I for my part am sorry that Anna did not settle down with a Lutheran and a pastor such as you expect to be. There is nothing better that I could have wished for her. Perhaps it will be much more her loss than yours that the friendship did not ripen into what it might.

May you have success in your studies and make your life a blessing for the church to which you belong! And with this, I hope this regrettable correspondence can be amicably closed,

Sincerely yours,

Geo. O. Lillegard

Book Two

Neither Death nor Life

For I am convinced that neither death nor life, neither angels nor demons, neither the present nor the future, nor any powers, neither height nor depth, nor anything else in all creation, will be able to separate us from the love of God that is in Christ Jesus our Lord.

                                              Romans 8:38-39

Chapter 1
The Courtship

In about 1917, during World War I, George met Bernice Onstad. Their families had known each other for years. Before Bernice or George was born, his father Lars had written in his diary:

"Juleaften, 1881
I have just experienced my happiest Christmas Eve in America at Kittlesby's (Bernice's grandparents). We had a lovely Christmas tree in the parlor. I had to speak a few words and received three gifts, a pair of bedroom slippers, a silk scarf, and a pair of cuff links. Then we read and sang songs and had a very good time."

Lars Lillegard's family lived in the Kittlesby's home town of Calmar, Iowa, from 1881 to 1889 (George was born in 1888). Bernice's parents were married in Calmar in 1896, but were in Manitowoc, Wisconsin on July 17, 1897, when Bernice was born.

Erick J. Onstad Family, 1909

L. to r.: Anna Olava, Elsa, Agnes Bernice, Ragnar, Erick

Bernice went to elementary school in Wittenberg, Wisconsin, where her father was principal of Wittenberg Academy.

Bernice is in second row from left, second person

(Reverse of above photo, written by Bernice)

Bernice went to Bruflat Academy in Portland, ND, while living at Mayville, ND (close by). Her father was principal there, too. Here is her graduation invitation:

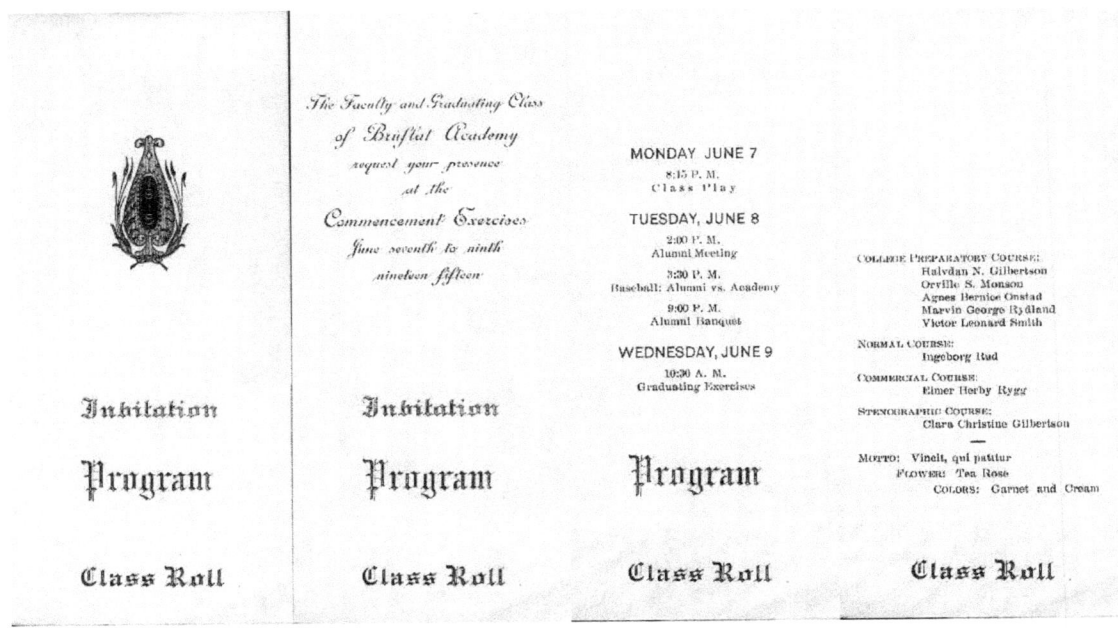

After graduation, she taught in Hampden, North Dakota, for one year. She next taught in the Winnebago Indian mission school in Wittenberg for one year. Then she moved back home to Madison and taught at secretarial school and worked at the French Battery Company plant (now Rayovac).

George and Bernice courted for a couple of years, mostly through letters. Bernice was living at home in Madison, Wisconsin. At first, George addressed her as "Miss Onstad." When he first wrote to her as "Bernice," she wrote back, "Aren't you getting fresh?"[46] (She labeled photo on right, "I got the kinks out of your legs, didn't I?-almost.")

---

[46] Their daughter Laura relates this story.

GEORGE PROPOSED TO BERNICE ON THEIR THIRD DATE, on July 30, 1919. This memorabilia dating to their courtship was found with their letters:

French Revue

given by

French Battery Employees Association

Saturday, April 10, 1920

at the

Lowell School

Program
8:00 O'Clock

A—Overture—Orchestra.
B—Scenes from an Indian Village.
   Indian women have gathered together at sunset
1—They are seen going about their daily tasks:
   INDIAN WOMEN AND CHILDREN
   Gladys Miller, Kate Emerich, Verena Serstad, Katie Stedry, Emma Schnarbusch, Mary Mueller, Charles Ryan, Doris Serstad.
2—Young Indian girls greet the sun with the "Song of the Sunworshipers."
   SUNWORSHIPERS
   Tillie Anderson, Mary Massey, Mrs. B. Peterson, Marie Rindt, Jessie Taylor, Winifred Swenson, Agnes Stedry.
3—Indian Lullaby..Olga Derry
4—Sun Dance..Sunworshipers
5—Weaver's Song..Gertrude O'Keefe
6—"Pipe of Peace" Ceremony—as Indian braves return from the hunt:
   The Indian Chief in order to pacify the Four Winds, which will bring unity from all the Universe, calls on the "North" because the bitter cold comes from there; the "East", to ask for gentle rains for the growing crops; the "West", for the warmth of the sun; the "South", for there lies the Happy Hunting Ground, the place of Departed Spirits. The Peace Pipe is offered to each of the Four Winds in turn, after which the Chief smokes to Mother Earth and then to the upper world of the Great Spirit:
   INDIAN BRAVES
Esther Rolfson ....Chief
Mollie Mueller ....North Wind
Winnabelle Gratiot ....East Wind
Betty Krighaum ....West Wind
Margaret Ripp ....South Wind
   Sadie Grinde, Abbie Ryan, Jennie Friess, Mrs. Sayler

C—Twenty Minutes of Harmony.
D—One Act Play "Heirs at Law."
   (Director, Donald W. Tyrrell)
   Stage Manager, C. J. Bach

In which a rich man, having made a will leaving all his estate to his two heirs, changes his mind and, through his lawyers, executes an amendment to his will, which is to be opened and read one year after his death. The year has now passed and a series of blunders and misrepresentations occur incident to the unsealing and reading of this Codicil, and the interference of the inevitable mother-in-law, played by an all-star cast consisting of:

Richard Doane ....James Hamilton
Leobert Lloyd ....William Balderston
General Lindsay Doane ....Gerald Wiedenbeck
Mrs. Theodosia Rockwood ....Marie Gleason
Gertrude Doane ....Lucille Gruen
Phoebe Rockwood ....Minnie Guerlich
Meta ....Jane Riley
Trixie Fleurette ....Viola Schimming

---

DANCE PROGRAM
9:30 O'Clock

1 One Step_____
2 Waltz_____
3 One Step_____
4 Fox Trot_____
5 Waltz_____
6 One Step_____
7 Fox Trot_____
8 Waltz_____
9 One Step_____
10 Waltz_____

Chapter 2
The Wedding

George and Bernice married on May 26, 1920, in Madison, Wisconsin.

Mr. and Mrs. E. J. Onstad
announce the marriage
of their daughter
Agnes Bernice
to
Rev. George Oliver Lillegard
on Wednesday, May Twenty-sixth
Nineteen hundred and twenty
Madison, Wisconsin

At home
after July 1st
3629 Wilton Avenue
Chicago, Illinois

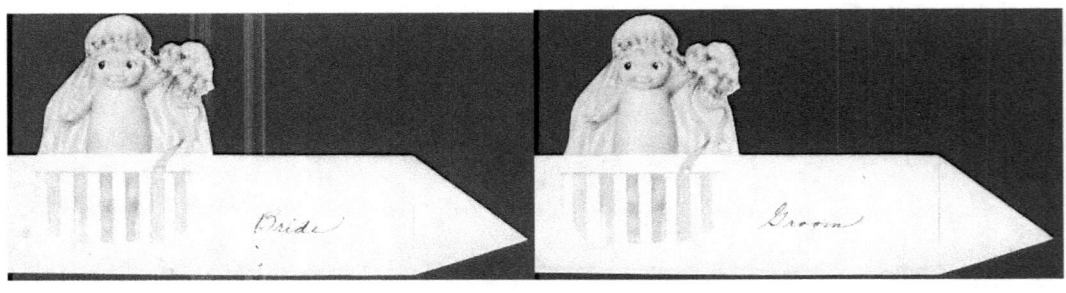

Here is the announcement from the Madison newspaper:

BERNICE ONSTAD WEDS

The marriage of Miss Bernice Onstad, daughter of Mr. and Mrs. E. J. Onstad, 1610 Rutledge street, to the Rev. George O. Lillegard, pastor of Lake View Lutheran church, Chicago, occurred this afternoon in Our Saviour's Lutheran church, the Rev. Holden M. Olsen officiating.

The bride was attended by Miss Alice Jacobson of Galesville as maid of honor, and the Rev. H. A. Preus of Chicago acted as best man. Misses Elsa Onstad, sister of the bride, Valborg Lillegard, Chicago, sister of the groom, acted as bridesmaids, and Ragnar Onstad, brother of the bride, and Andy Norgord of Cambridge acted as groomsmen. Miss Alice Jacobson, music instructor in Gale college, sang "A Song of Joy," by Wheeler.

The bride wore a gown of white crepe de chine, prettily embroidered and beaded, a white tulle veil, and carried a shower bouquet.

After the ceremony, a reception and wedding dinner were served in the church parlors, where covers were laid for 42 guests. The couple will spend a month in Minneapolis and St. Paul, and in Iowa and northern Wisconsin, and will be at home after July 1 at 3629 Wilton avenue, Chicago.

Out of town guests here for the wedding are Mrs. Ansoph Lillegard, Chicago, mother of the groom; Misses Olga and Valborg Lillegard, Chicago; Mrs. M. Tjernagel, Story City, Ia.; and Mrs. H. Gullixson, Bode, Ia., sisters of the groom; Miss Bertha Hegg, Decorah, Ia.; Miss Laura Hegg, Milwaukee Downer college; Otto Onstad, Cambridge; Alice Jacobson, Galesville; and Grace Halvorson, Manitowoc.

Congratulations on their wedding from GA Gullixson, President of ELS

Form 1204

CLASS OF SERVICE	SYMBOL
Telegram	
Day Letter	Blue
Night Message	Nite
Night Letter	N L

If none of these three symbols appears after the check (number of words) this is a telegram. Otherwise its character is indicated by the symbol appearing after the check.

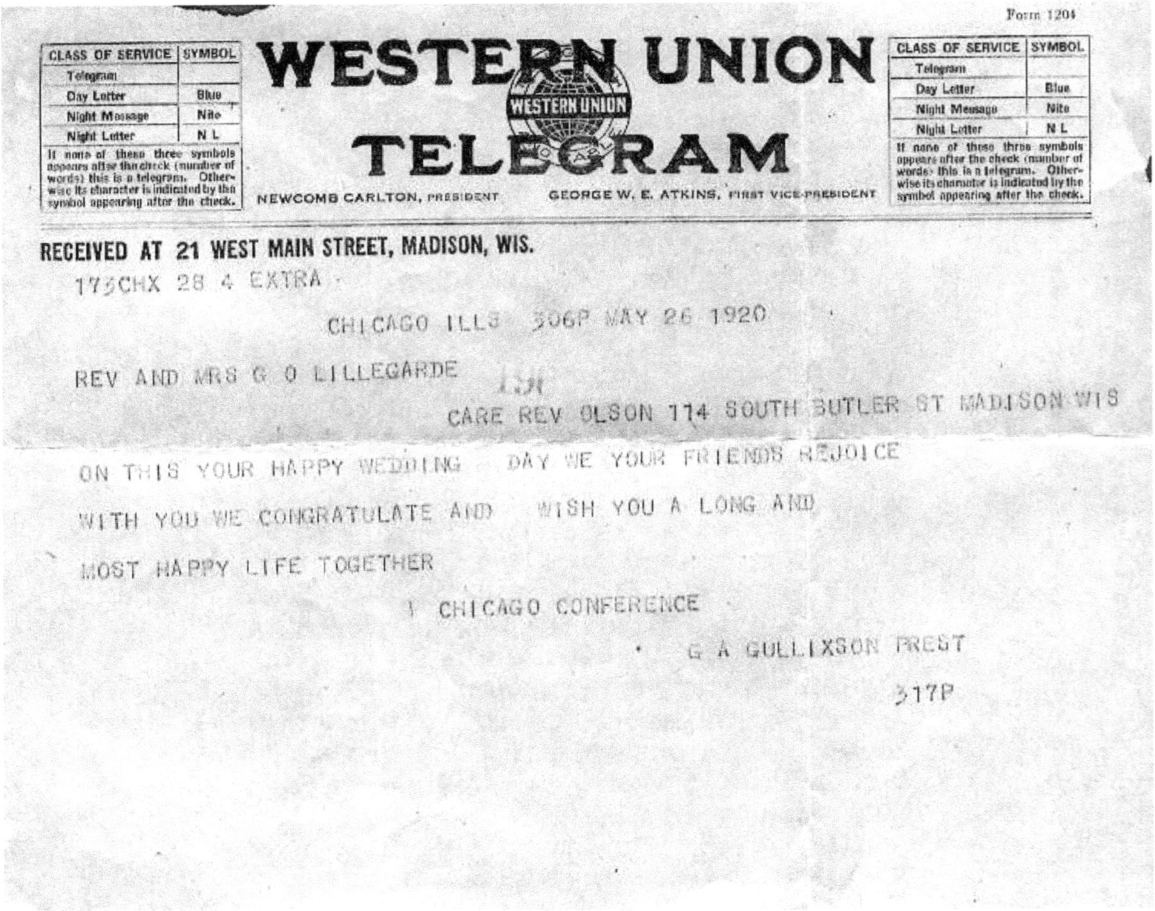

WESTERN UNION TELEGRAM

NEWCOMB CARLTON, PRESIDENT GEORGE W. E. ATKINS, FIRST VICE-PRESIDENT

RECEIVED AT 21 WEST MAIN STREET, MADISON, WIS.

173CHX 28 4 EXTRA

CHICAGO ILLS 306P MAY 26 1920

REV AND MRS G O LILLEGARDE

CARE REV OLSON 114 SOUTH BUTLER ST MADISON WIS

ON THIS YOUR HAPPY WEDDING DAY WE YOUR FRIENDS REJOICE WITH YOU WE CONGRATULATE AND WISH YOU A LONG AND MOST HAPPY LIFE TOGETHER

CHICAGO CONFERENCE

G A GULLIXSON PREST

317P

(Telegram service of Western Union ended in January of 2006.)

The Congregation of the

Lake View Lutheran Church

invites you to a reception given in honor of

Rev. and Mrs. Geo. O. Lillegard

in the church parlors

Monday Evening, June 28th, 1920

at eight o'clock

Bernice and George Lillegard; May 26, 1920

Bernice on wedding trip to the Wisconsin Dells, 1920

Chapter 3
The Newlyweds

MISSOURI SYNOD PRESIDENT WRITES CONCERNING CALL.
"I wish you could have seen how interested all members were in your acceptance."

Board of Foreign Missions

Evangelical Lutheran Synod
of Missouri, Ohio, and Other States

ST. LOUIS, MO., U. S. A.

9/10/'20

My dear Friend Lillegard:

I notice in your paper that the important meeting will be held Sept. 20. We pray to God that He may guide you and your congregation in your deliberations that you may cheerfully accept the call to our foreign mission field in China.

At our last meeting we dwelled on this matter for some time. I wish you could have seen how interested all members were in your acceptance.

We also talked on the salary question which has not been definitely adjusted as yet in our China mission. Do you know what the salary of a missionary in China is on an average in various societies doing mission work in that country? Or could you perhaps on short notice get some data in regard to this matter? The Board suggested that I have a conference with you in regard to this question and we might talk over other matters in regard to our China mission. Since Rev. Brand is elected General Secretary of our foreign missions and he also holds a pass on the C. & A. I suggested that he also go along, which readily was sanctioned by the Board. Would we be welcome to see you on Monday Sept. 20 and in the evening represent our Board at the meeting, or would you prefer to see us come say next Friday or some other day the following week?

With cordial greetings also to Mrs. Lillegard,

Very fraternally yours,

Rich Kretzschmar

KRETZSCHMAR THANKS GEORGE FOR ACCEPTING CALL.
"As soon as you know about the time when you may be ready to sail we ought to try to book passage for you."

9/29/1920

Rev. Geo. Lillegard
Chicago, Ill.

Dear Friend Lillegard:

The Board feels very gratified at the result of your meeting and wishes to thank you and your congregation for your interest in the great cause of our Lord's work among the heathen. May he most bountifully bless you and the congregation for the sacrifices you are willing to make for the missionary cause and may he help you to find a good successor to continue the work which you have been doing very faithfully and successfully.

I do not know whether it would be advisable to write to our missionaries in China so long in advance with regard to a residence. Still the brethren certainly will be glad to hear from you and will be more than willing to render you every assistance. You are personally acquainted with Missionary L. Meyer, 11 Milan Terrace, Hankow, who is the secretary of the missionary conference.

Missionary Arndt is expected to come to America on furlough coming spring. Perhaps arrangements could be made for you to take charge of his work.

I understand the S.S. Lines are all overcrowded and have long waiting lists. As soon as you know about the time when you may be ready to sail we ought to try to book passage for you.

Kindly let me know the date on which your congregation stops to pay your salary and state the amount you have been receiving. You may draw at any time the allowance for outfit ($200) and the amount granted for your reimbursement.

With cordial greetings also to Mrs. Lillegard, I am

Very sincerely yours,

Rich Kretzschmar

GEORGE RESIGNS AS PASTOR OF LAKE VIEW CONGREGATION.

"...I have received a call to the Mission Field of the Missouri and Norwegian Synods..."

Rev. Geo. O. Lillegard
PASTOR OF
Lake View Ev. Lutheran Church
Res. 3629 Wilton Avenue
Telephone Lake View 4420

Chicago, October 4th, 1920.

To Lake View Lutheran Church

Dear Christian Friends:

As I have received a call to the Mission Field of the Missouri and Norwegian Synods in Central China, which I feel it my Christian duty to accept, I hereby resign as pastor of Lake View Lutheran Congregation, with the understanding that I am to serve the congregation as heretofore until a successor has been installed.

May the God of Love and Peace grant to this congregation His blessings in every way, giving it ever faithful pastors who will serve it well, with all zeal for the truth and its propagation.

Respectfully,

Geo. O. Lillegard

GEORGE ACCEPTS CALL TO CHINA.
"...we shall plan on leaving for China about the middle of January."

October 6th, 1920

Rev. R. Kretzschmar
St. Louis, Mo.

Dear friend:

Enclosed you will find my acceptance of the call to your field in China. At the regular congregation meeting last Monday evening, I announced to the congregation that I had decided to accept the call to China. A special meeting will be held in two weeks to call a successor. It may be that we will need the assistance of your Mission Committee (Home Missions), as the congregation seems to be somewhat doubtful of its ability to go ahead alone without any connection with any synod. Our Norwegian Synod[47] will of course be represented at our conferences. But in case the congregation should decide to appeal to the Missouri Synod, whom should I call upon here in Chicago for assistance?

It will be hard to say when I can be free to go. I have promised to stay here until a successor is installed. I hope that may be done by the first of the year at the latest. Then we shall plan on leaving for China about the middle of January.

I would appreciate receiving the $500.00 granted for reimbursement soon. The outfit money, I think had better wait till we know when we will be leaving.

Thanking you very much for your kindness and courtesy in all our dealings, and with hearty greetings to yourself and family from my wife and myself,

Sincerely,

Geo. O. Lillegard

---

[47] The "little Norwegian synod," now known as the Evangelical Lutheran Synod. George was one of the 13 pastors who founded the synod on June 14, 1918.

GEORGE WRITES THE MISSION BOARD OF ACCEPTANCE.
"...with the hope and prayer that my service in this field may be blessed of our Lord to the upbuilding of His kingdom both at home and abroad."

Lake View Ev. Lutheran Church
ROSCOE AND OSGOOD STS.
CHICAGO, ILL.

GEO. O. LILLEGARD, PASTOR
RES. 867 ROSCOE ST
TEL. LAKE VIEW 4428
OFFICE. 1017 ROSCOE ST

G. A. ANDRESEN, SEC.
4251 N. SACRAMENTO AV.
H. C. LAWSON, TREAS.
5067 N. LINCOLN ST.

October 6th, 1920

To
   The Board of Foreign Missions
   of the Ev. Luth. Synod of Missouri, Ohio, and other states,

Dear Christian friends:

    Your letter of May 20th, 1920, calling me to the mission field of the Missouri Synod in Central China, was received in due time. Since my congregation here after due consideration has granted me the release I asked for, I herewith accept your call to the China Mission in the name of the Triune God, with the hope and prayer that my service in this field may be blessed of our Lord to the upbuilding of His kingdom both at home and abroad.

    With cordial greetings,

Respectfully yours,

Geo. O. Lillegard

KRETZSCHMAR ANSWERS GEORGE'S LETTER.
"Your acceptance will gladden the hearts of our missionaries in China..."

Board of Foreign Missions
Evangelical Lutheran Synod
of Missouri, Ohio, and Other States

ST. LOUIS, MO., U. S. A.

(Fall, 1920)

Rev. Geo. Lillegard
Chicago, Ill.

My dear Brother and esteemed Friend:

Your letter of acceptance and other communication of Oct. 6 came to hand. Your acceptance will gladden the hearts of our missionaries in China and all who are interested in that great mission field. May God bless you and make you a blessing.

Would suggest that you get in touch with Rev. Boecler in regard to assistance for your congregation. He undoubtedly will be in a position to advise you. And you know he has a big heart for all church work.

As soon as you are able to fix the date of your sailing approximately we ought to try to make reservations on some Pacific S.S. Line. It is hard to book passage. All lines are overcrowded. Which line would you prefer?

The amount granted for your reimbursement was $425, the amount you mentioned when we spoke about this matter. In your letter you refer to $500 which probably will come nearer to your actual loss than the former sum. But I am not authorized to issue order for payment unless the matter is reconsidered and our former resolution accordingly amended. Do you want me to lay the matter again before the board or should I instruct the treasurer to send you the amount specified in the resolution?

With cordial greetings also to Mrs. L. I am,

Very sincerely with you in Lord's service,

Rich. Kretzschmar

KRETZSCHMAR CORRESPONDS ABOUT MISSION MATTERS.
"We...hope to be successful in supplying our China mission with the sorely needed medical missionary."

Board of Foreign Missions
Evangelical Lutheran Synod
of Missouri, Ohio, and Other States

ST. LOUIS, MO., U. S. A.

(Fall, 1920)

My dear brother Lillegard:

On account of a misunderstanding the mailing of this check has been delayed for several days. The treasurer anticipated you had already proceeded to China.

You may draw at any time also the allowance for equipment for yourself and Mrs. Lillegard @$100. And you will kindly let us know when your salary will cease to be paid by your congregation and we will pay you the same till date of sailing or arrival in China. The board has not yet taken up the salary question of our missionaries in China which we discussed with you some weeks ago. Rev. Brand was not able to attend our last two meetings so we thought it best to postpone action.

Rev. Brand has now accepted our call and will move to St. Louis as soon as he will be able to find a suitable residence.

Prof. Ylvisaker replied to my letter that his brother, the Doctor, could not at present consider a call to the foreign mission field. I made the suggestion to the professor that the board could possibly relieve the Dr. of financial burdens and thus make it possible for him to go.

We are in touch with several other doctors and hope to be successful in supplying our China mission with the sorely needed medical missionary.

If you ever visit Rush Medical College look up Mr. Arnold Nickels of Watertown. He was mentioned to me by his Pastor Rev. H. Eggers.

With cordial greetings also to Mrs. L. I am,

Very sincerely yours,

Rich. Kretzschmar

112

LILLEGARDS ORDER A PIANO.
"...it is destined to go to China,..."

Rev. Geo. O. Lillegard
3629 Wilton Ave.
Chicago, Ill.

Dear Sir:

We are pleased to inform you that we are this day shipping to you the style L Walnut piano ordered by you of Mr. H.A. Oberschulte.

This instrument is sent forward with every confidence that you will be very much pleased with its beautiful tone quality. Some of our own experienced expert tone regulators have volunteered their opinion that this instrument possesses as fine a tone as any piano they have met with, and as it is unusual for piano mechanics to express themselves with regard to any special instrument they produce. This exception marks your piano as an especially desirable acquisition, and so we believe you will find it.

We understand that it is destined to go to China, and we trust that its fine quality will result in a demand for BEHNING instruments in that land.

Wishing you every success in your work, we are

Yours very truly,

BEHNING PIANO CO.

Board of Foreign Missions
Evangelical Lutheran Synod of Missouri, Ohio, and Other States
ST. LOUIS, MO., U. S. A.

14. Dezember 1920.

AN DIE PASTOREN, LEHRER, GEMEINDEN, SCHULEN UND SONNTAGSSCHULEN.

Lieber Kollege im Predigt- oder Schulamt!

Wir moechten Dir und — durch Deine guetige Vermittlung — Deiner Gemeinde, Schule und Sonntagsschule folgendes zur Erwaegung vorlegen. Es ist teils erfreulich, teils betruebend.

Gott hat uns unter den Heiden in Indien ein reiches Erntefeld zugewiesen. Die Tueren stehen nicht nur weit offen, sondern immer wieder werden unsere Missionare sogar aufgefordert, in neuen Gebieten die Arbeit aufzunehmen. Ist das nicht erfreulich? — Aber wie um so betruebender ist es nun, dass unser Feld seiner tuechtigen Arbeitskraefte waehrend des Krieges beraubt worden ist, so dass von vierzehn Missionaren nur noch vier auf ihrem Posten geblieben sind! Und fuer neue Missionare war jahrelang der Zugang versperrt. Alle Notrufe der Missionare, alle Bemuehungen der Kommission schienen vergeblich. Jetzt endlich — welch eine Freude! — werden neue Kraefte nach Indien abreisen. Die Missionare Kuechle und Harms mit ihren Frauen — und ersterer mit zwei Kindern — kehren nach Indien zurueck, wo sie schon unter grossem Segen gearbeitet haben. Mit ihnen gehen hinaus die zwei neuen Missionare P. Heckel und P. Kauffeld und unsere Missionskrankenpflegerin Frl. Ellerman sowie ihre neue Assistentin, Frl. Georgi — also zehn Personen im ganzen. Die Abfahrt erfolgt von New York aus am 30. Dezember. Gott wolle sie beschuetzen auf dieser weiten Reise! Hoffentlich koennen ihnen bald noch mehr Arbeiter nachgeschickt werden.

Auch in China geht das Rettungswerk unserer Heidenmission gut vonstatten. Doch auch dort fehlt es sehr an Arbeitskraeften. Wie erfreulich ist es uns daher, dass ein junger Bruder aus unserer norwegischen Schwestersynode, der schon in China gearbeitet hat, Pastor G. Lillegaard, mit seiner jungen Gattin voraussichtlich bald nach China abreisen und unsern Missionaren zur Seite treten wird. Gott gebe, dass bald noch mehr Friedensboten dorthin ausgesendet werden koennen! Dringend noetig ist fuer unsere Mission in China ein lutherischer Arzt oder Aerztin. Wie viele aerztliche Kraefte haben sich waehrend des Krieges der Regierung zur Verfuegung gestellt, und fuer den heiligen Krieg in der Mission rufen und suchen wir noch immer vergeblich, Gott sei's geklagt! Es fehlt an MAENNERN, es fehlt auch an MITTELN. Grosse Ausgaben stehen uns bevor, und die Kassen sind leer, ja haben Schulden. Wie betruebend! Wir bitten alle Pastoren und Lehrer sowie alle unsere Christen, jung und alt, dieser Not in dieser Weihnachtszeit und besonders am Epiphanienfest ein Ende zu machen und durch ein besonderes Liebesopfer mitzuhelfen, dass auch unter den Heiden Weihnachtsfreude und Epiphanienlicht verbreitet werde. Gott walte es!

Mit herzlichen Segenswuenschen zum Christ- und Epiphanienfest

DIE KOMMISSION FUER HEIDENMISSION.

Rich. Kretzschmar Vorsitzer.

(Translation of preceding German letter announcing George's call to China:)

December 14, 1920

TO THE PASTORS, TEACHERS, CONGREGATIONS, SCHOOLS, AND SUNDAY SCHOOLS:
Dear colleagues in the preaching and teaching ministry,

    We would like to bring to you – and through your good offices your congregation, school, and Sunday School – the following for your consideration. It is partly joyful and partly disturbing.

    God has shown us a rich harvest field among the heathen in India. The doors are not only wide open, but again and again our missionaries are even called upon to begin work in new areas. Is that not wonderful! But how troubling it is that our field has been robbed of its talented manpower during the war, so that only 4 out of 14 missionaries remain at their post. And for new missionaries the way was blocked all year long. All the missionaries' calls for help, all efforts of the commission seemed in vain. Now finally – what a joy! – new manpower will travel to India. Missionaries Kuechle and Harms with their wives – the former with 2 children – are returning to India where they have already worked with great blessing. With them are going two new missionaries, P. Heckel and P. Kauffeld, and our mission's medic, Miss Ellerman as well as her new assistant, Miss Georgi – ten persons in all. Their departure from New York will be on December 30th. May God protect them on this long trip. Hopefully, still more workers can soon be sent after them.

    Also in China the saving work of our mission is well established. But there also there is a severe shortage of manpower. How joyous for us then that a young brother from our Norwegian sister synod, who has already worked in China, Pastor G. Lillegaard, with his young bride, will quite soon travel to China and work side by side with our missionaries. God grant that soon it will be possible to send still more messengers of peace from thence. Urgently needed for our mission in China is a Lutheran doctor. How many medically-trained personnel made themselves available during the war of the government but for the holy war in the mission field we still call and search in vain. God have mercy! It is lacking in MEN, it is also lacking in MEANS. Large expenses loom before us and the coffers are empty, indeed we have debt. How troubling! We pray all our pastors and teachers, as well as all our Christians, young and old, to bring this need to an end this Christmastime and especially at the feast of the Epiphany, and through a special love offering pitch in so that Christmas joy and Epiphany light may be spread also among the heathen. God grant it.

    With hearty wishes for divine blessings at Christmas and Epiphany,

THE COMMISSION FOR WORLD MISSIONS.

Rich Kretzschmar, Chairman

MISSOURI SYNOD VP DESCRIBES GEORGE'S SUCCESSOR.
"...he is unmarried...Danish is his mother-tongue."

Evangelical Lutheran Synod
of
Missouri, Ohio, and Other States.
TREASURER'S OFFICE,
ST. LOUIS, MO.

Springfield, Ill., January 7th, 1921

Rev. Geo. O. Lillegard
Chicago, Ill.

My dear Bro.,

I am very glad to hear that Mrs. Lillegard is mending. May our dear Lord restore her to her former strength and cheerfulness.

The brother I had in mind as your successor is Rev. P. Krey, a graduate of the 1919 class of Springfield Seminary. He is about 26 or 27 years of age, an all around fine man, sincere, gentlemanly in his demeanor and bearing, a good student, acceptable as a speaker, and faithful in his pastoral work. He was my assistant since his graduation from this institution and is at present teaching a class in our day-school besides assisting in preaching. After his graduation he took a course in some normal school in the west and holds a teacher's certificate and diploma of some sort. He is unmarried. He tells me that Danish is his mother tongue. He came to this country with his parents I do not know how long ago and speaks the English language fluently and well. He has no prospects of being called to the pastorate of my present charge, because the Seminary worships in my church and it seems desirable to call an older and more experienced man. You will see this very readily when you consider that the Proffs are members here also. Of course I should not wish to have it made known to my people that I mentioned his name to you. No doubt they would consider that an unfriendly act on my part. But he is too valuable a man to be restricted to the school room, as necessary and blessed the work of teaching our youth is. And I happen to know that he is anxious to get into all the duties of the ministry. I think he would prove himself to be a very active and successful missionary in the service of your church, if your people decide to call him. He was elected to take over the pastoral work during the vacancy and has consented. But I do not see that that would be a bar to his being called to your charge, as you do not intend to leave before some time in Spring. By that time my church may have her own pastor again.

With cordial greetings yours

Frederick Brand

REV. MEYER GIVES PROGRESS OF MISSION IN CHINA.

"I will endeavor to reciprocate your kindness to me some years ago when you gave me the only reliable facts about China that I received before I arrived here...As to our field in Shihnanfu, Hupeh...the political situation has had a bad effect upon the work there."

Hankow, January 12, 1921

Dear Rev. Lillegard:

First of all allow me to bid you and your wife welcome to the China Mission and we hope that before very long we will be given the pleasure of extending this welcome to you personally. We were all very glad to hear that you had accepted a call from our Board and are looking ahead to time when you will be among us as a brother missionary.

One of the things I have learned since I came to China is that it pays to be sparing in dealing out advice to missionaries who are just coming out, but since we can only consider you as returning missionary and not as a novice I will endeavor to reciprocate your kindness to me some years ago when you gave me the only reliable facts about China that I received before I arrived here.

You ask about the progress of our mission. I think that I can truthfully say that our mission is making slow but sure visible progress here in Hankow...During the last year I had twenty-two baptisms and Mrs. Meyer is getting a women's class ready for Easter. We, Mrs. Meyer and I, have three schools running. One is a mixed school for boys and girls, lower and higher primary, the second is a boys school of fifty pupils and the third is a girls school of fifty. These schools are kept up to the mark with a good curriculum...

...As to our field in Shihnanfu, Hupeh - until about two months ago our men out there were very optimistic. Since then the political situation has had a bad effect upon the work there. The fighting there has pretty well disorganized the work for the time being and our people there have not had the easiest of times...To sum up the status of our mission at present I might say this: the men in actual work are making progress and visible results are evident. Our missionary personnel is not very large and need great reinforcements. Our mission as an organization still needs a lot of organizing which we hope will come to pass when the newly elected Rev. Brandt comes out as secretary. We all feel that you will be a great help to us all here and look forward anxiously to your arrival.

Regarding the housing conditions here in Hankow I might say that we all are living in quite nice houses. They could be better of course but we are quite satisfied and very fortunate in getting what we have. You will understand what I mean when I say that we need not be ashamed to invite anyone to come and visit us. It is difficult at times to secure a place that is suitable both to the missionary and to the mission's purse, but we have all found such a place and feel confident that you too will find such a place in a short time.

And now as to your personal effects and as to what you should bring along...Bring all the clothes along that you can...Be sure and bring shoes and let your measure with a good reliable shoestore at home so that you can order by mail. Some people have good luck with the Japanese shoemaker here others do not. It all depends on the shape of your foot...

...As regards furniture: I would advise you not to bring anything along...tables, chairs, stoves - personally I would let them stay at home. Regarding a piano - you must suit yourself. If you stay in Hankow it would be an open question whether you should bring it or not, unless, of course, your wife is a musician and has a pet instrument. But if you go to Shihnanfu I would say not to bring one along. There is one out there and it has cost the mission about 400.00 mex, to get it there from Hankow...The reason I advise bringing along as little as possible is: the present rate of exchange is almost two to one, the freight rates are very high, take the gold that you would use to buy the things with in the States, add the freight rates, and exchange for mexican dollars at the present rate and you have quite a sum of money with which to buy out here. And you eliminate all the shipping trouble and can get your things out here when you want them, and what you want, accomodating yourself to some extent to the place you go to be it Hankow or Shihnanfu...

...When you arrive we hope that you will make your home with us until you have decided where you will take up your work. Personally I hope you will decide to stay with us here in Hankow. The Shihnanfu people want you out there. We both need you. But you will see when you get here what is best.

With kindest regards to you both from the whole missionary personnel and from many other people out here, I remain,

Sincerely yours,

L.Meyer

VP BRAND ARRANGES FOR THE LILLEGARDS' TRIP.
"I am planning to take the Can. Pac.[48] How would that suit you?"

Saint Louis, Mo., February 3rd, 1921

Rev. Geo. O. Lillegard
Chicago, Ill.

My dear Brother,

Brother Kretzschmar handed me your letter of Jan. 31 this forenoon and I hasten to write you such information as I may have. I am not as familiar with the details of this office as brother Kr. is, who has been acting director for the past years, but I trust that I shall soon familiarize myself with my new duties.

It is indeed good news to hear that Mrs. Lillegard is mending so rapidly that you can now make your plans for your trip. I shall answer your questions as they follow in your letter.

1. I shall write our agent at Minneapolis tonight to see whether he can secure a pass for you to the coast. I am under the impression that he cannot get consideration for our ladies, but shall ask him.

2. He will take care of your S.S. ticket also as soon as you have indicated by what line you prefer to travel, whether you wish to touch Honolulu and from which port you are planning to depart.

3. If our agent provides you with a pass or passes you will have an opportunity to stop off wherever you please within the time limit, which will be ample.

4. The Mission treasury pays your freight bill. It will be perfectly all right to ship through Montgomery Ward and Co. (send me the bill).

5. Pastor Kr. tells me that we allow first class on small S.S. and second class on first class S.S. However, I think I should tell you that traffic to the Orient is very heavy at this time and that agents tell me that many Japanese and Chinese travel second class since the war on their return to their respective country. I do not know how that would affect you and your good wife if you had to share a stateroom with them.

6. I have already sent a voucher for $200.00 to our treasurer, which is the allowance for fitting out, one hundred for each one of you, which will mean that Mrs. Lillegard gets the major part of it. The treasurer's check ought to reach you in a few days. Cordially yours,

Frederick Brand

---

[48] Canadian Pacific Railroad

GEORGE ELABORATES ON THE CALL TO LAKE VIEW.
"I have had charge here for the last three years, but have accepted a call to China,..."

Rev. Geo. O. Lillegard
PASTOR OF
Lake View Ev. Lutheran Church
RES. 3629 WILTON AVENUE
TELEPHONE LAKE VIEW 4420

Chicago, February 17th, 1921

Rev. P. Krey
Springfield, Ill.

Dear Rev. Krey:

A call is being sent you today to the pastorate of Lake View Church, and you will no doubt want to know something about the congregation and the work in this section of Chicago. I have had charge here for the last three years, but have accepted a call to China, under the Missouri and Norwegian Synods, and should like to arrange to leave this spring if possible. I have, however, promised to stay here until a successor is installed. The congregation has called two men in the Norwegian Church, but these have after some delay returned the calls. Your name was third on our list, as you were recommended to us as a Scandinavian Lutheran who would be ready to take up the work in a place like this.

The congregation was originally Norwegian Lutheran, the first Norwegian Congregation in Chicago, and belonged to the former Norwegian Synod. Since I took charge, it has been independent, belonging to no synodical organization. I have affiliated with the Norwegian Synod, now a member of the Synodical Conference. There have been no regular Norwegian services held during the past four years, since few of the members desired such services. We have had one Norwegian Communion service during Lent, that is all. The rest of the work is all carried on in English, and the name of the congregation would have been changed ere this to "Lake View Ev. Luth. Church," were it not for certain legal difficulties which would be encountered. This will be done in due time, anyway, without a doubt. The members are practically all Scandinavians, Norwegian still in the majority, Danes almost as numerous, and a few Swedes. The people are scattered over the whole North Side of Chicago, which has made the work in late years somewhat more difficult than before. But there are a number of Missouri Lutherans in the neighborhood, which would make it a good field for a Missourian to work in, if all signs do not fail. The closest Missouri churches are Boecler's, a mile west; Steinhof's (English), a mile and three quarters northwest; Schlerf's (English), three miles north; and Karl Schmidt's, a mile and a half south. Our church is half a mile from the lake. So you will appreciate that there is quite a strip along the lake shore in which no Missouri congregation is found at present. Since there are few Norwegians residing in this section, we have thought that it might be well to have a Missourian working here who could get better in touch with Missouri Synod people living here than a Norwegian Church pastor could.

The congregation is quite small, but has always been self-supporting. It has a property worth $10,000.00 or more, free of debt, including a flat building bringing an income of $600.00 a year besides providing rooms for the janitor, in return for which he does the janitor work. There are only about 100 active communicant members, but a good number of people attend here and count this as their church, without having joined. The total income of the congregation the past year was between three and four thousand dollars...

...The salary now is $130.00 per month, together with offerings at the three great church festivals, and fees for the ministerial acts: baptisms, weddings, and funerals - sometimes sick communions, but not for communion services held in church. The "Extras" have amounted to about $500.00 this past year, and these will increase each year, the longer a man works in a city like Chicago. Thus you would have an income of over $2000.00, which should be enough for a young pastor to live on. This is without parsonage. But there is a flat building back of the church, one floor of which has for many years been used as a parsonage, and which if the new pastor desires it will be put in shape again for such use. There has been talk of putting in electric lights and new hardwood floors. I understand that you are still unmarried. It may be that you could arrange to get a room in the flat, if you so desired, from those who are now renting the flat, or that the congregation could arrange to reserve a room for you. There is an office in the church, fitted with bookcases, desk, and stove, for the use of the pastor, and as long as you are alone, you would not need more than a bedroom besides that.

I mention these things, since you no doubt will be interested in hearing also about such practical matters. There are many things that I should like to say about the prospects in this field, and the conditions in the congregation. But since you are so close to Chicago, perhaps you could arrange to make a short visit to the city, before deciding upon the call, to look over the field at first hand. We shall be glad to take care of you while here, if you will be satisfied with very ordinary entertainment. Rev. Brand is somewhat acquainted with conditions here, and I would refer you to him for such information as he can give. I hope that you will decide to accept this call and that it will not be so very long before you will be in position to take up the work here. I should like to be relieved right after Easter, if possible.

If you cannot come here to talk over the situation with us, I shall be glad to answer any questions that you would like to have answered with regard to the work here.

With best greetings to you and your present charge, and the hope that they and you will both decide that you should accept the call to Lake View, I remain

Very sincerely yours,
Geo. O. Lillegard

REV. KREY RESPONDS ABOUT THE CALL TO LAKE VIEW.
"...though I have been preaching in the English tongue right along, I must confess that I am by no means perfect in that language."

"Springfield, Ill.
Feb. 21, 1921

Dear Rev. Lillegard,

You, undoubtedly, have by this time received the postal by which I notified you of the receipt of the call to Lake View Ev. Luth. Church. You seem to have great confidence in me. This gives me somewhat courage. But nevertheless, I must confess, that I feel quite timid about taking up the work which you leave. And I will tell you why.

1. Being a graduate of the University of Chicago, you undoubtedly are a master of the English language. Lake View therefore is used to hear fine, elegant English sermons. Such I doubt whether I will be able to deliver. For though I have been preaching in the English tongue right along, I must confess that I am by no means perfect in that language. Having acquired the language during the last 12 years, since my migration, you can easily imagine that my speech or pronunciation is not perfect. Now if this cuts no figure with your people, good and well, that's one stone removed. But give me your straight opinion.

2. You must know that your belief of my being a Dane is only half true. I am only half a Dane; my mother being a Dane. I have never yet preached in that language, although I read and understand it perfectly well and also have spoken it in our home.

3. The congregation here, Rev. Brand's, being without a pastor at the present time, makes me doubt whether it would be right and adviseable for me to leave at this present time, unless some other arrangement can be made.

In conclusion I wish to say also that I have written to several brethren for advice. And I should also appreciate, since I do not feel inclined to visit the calling charge, if you would be so kind as to tell me something more about the prospects and the conditions in the calling congregation, and maybe also give me some sound advice, so that I may be better able to decide what to do.

Yours fraternally,

Peter C. Krey
117 East Wash. St.
Springfield, Ill."

GEORGE RESPONDS TO KREY ABOUT CALL.
"After you have preached and spoken only English for a while, I think you will find the language 'opening up' for you."

Chicago, February 25th, 1921

Dear Rev. Krey:

Your letter of the 21st is at hand. I had intended to answer it sooner, but have been busy, so have neglected it.

As to your difficulties over accepting the call to Lake View; I do not think that they are of any great importance. This congregation has had college men of good education from the beginning, and if you lack that, it might make it harder for you in the beginning. But I am sure that any man of ability who tackles the work in a city like Chicago with a will and the determination to make the best use of his opportunities will succeed, whether he have any exceptional educational advantages or not. Most of the people in the congregation are not critical on the fine points of the English language, so that should make little difference, if your work otherwise is acceptable. Not being personally acquainted with you, it is of course hard for me to say whether your limitations in that respect are great enough to be any real handicap in your work. I am sure that the judgment of men like Rev. Brand, who knows what is required in a city like Chicago, is good enough to warrant me in saying that you will be able to handle the situation allright, so far as the language problem is concerned. After you have preached and spoken only English for a while, I think you will find the language "opening up" for you. The Scandinavian language will not be required much hereafter. I think that the one Norwegian Communion service that has been held the past years might just as well also be discontinued. The only prospect of growth in this neighborhood is by work among the people of German descent. And that work you would be able to do better than any full-blooded Scandinavian. At present the congregation is entirely Scandinavian. But in English work, there can be no objections to taking in people of all nationalities. If you get the German Missourians started to coming to this church, the congregation will soon grow and become more of a power in the community.

As to the demands your present call might make upon you: could it not be arranged so that one of the students or professors could take your place until a pastor was installed? I should like to have a man here right after Easter. But I can stay till the latter part of April, if necessary, and still arrange to get away to China this spring. So that you would have till that time to find a man in your place in Springfield.

If you should decide to accept this call - and I hope that action can be taken promptly so that we can make our plans accordingly - I wish you could arrange to visit with us a couple days. There are many things I should like to talk over with you about the work here, the synodical affiliations of the congregation, etc., which I cannot very well discuss satisfactorily in a letter. In the meantime, I think this is all that can well be said or that will need to be said for you to make an intelligent and right decision with regard to the call you have received.

With best greetings to you,

Sincerely yours,
Geo. O. Lillegard

KREY ACCEPTS CALL TO LAKE VIEW CHURCH.
"I have decided, being convinced of the importance of the call, and trusting in the grace of God that He will make me efficient to fill the post to which I have been called by no desire of my own - to ask for my release."

"Springfield, Illinois, March 6, 1921

Dear Rev. Lillegard,

The congregation decided yesterday to consider the call extended to me by Lake View Lutheran Church, in the regular monthly meeting next Sunday afternoon. I have decided, being convinced of the importance of the call, and trusting in the grace of God that He will make me efficient to fill the post to which I have been called by no desire of my own - to ask for my release. Which I think will be granted me without much debating. If you so wish, I can wire you the result next Sunday afternoon.

Yours with fraternal greetings,

Peter C. Krey

Springfield, Illinois, March 13, 1921

Dear Rev. Lillegard,

As you will already know from the fact that you have not received a telegram, I was released this afternoon. But at the same time I was asked to remain in charge of the congregation here as long as possible. How long that is to be, is up to you to decide. However there is no possibility of my leaving here before after Easter. But how soon after Easter would you have me come? Would the 10th suit you? I should like to come and talk this over with you, but there is not the slightest possibility of my getting away, even for a day only, before Tuesday after Easter. Shall I come then?

With fraternal greetings,

yours as ever,
Peter C. Krey"

BRUNN WRITES GEORGE ABOUT KREY.
"...I wrote you a postal card in the german language,..."

PRESIDENT
REV. FR. BRUNN
OAK GLEN, ILL.
PHONE LANSING 63J

1ST VICE-PRESIDENT
REV. J. H. HAAKE
3116 S. RACINE AVE.
CHICAGO, ILL.

2ND VICE-PRESIDENT
REV. P. LUECKE
4943 MONTROSE AVE.
CHICAGO, ILL.

North Illinois District
of the
Synod of Missouri, Ohio, and Other States

SECRETARY
REV. F. P. MERBITZ
4032 MICHIGAN AVE.
CHICAGO, ILL.

SECRETARY OF FINANCE
OTTO C. RENTNER
82 W. WASHINGTON ST.
CHICAGO, ILL.

TREASURER
WM. J. HINZE
BEECHER, ILL.

"Oakglen March 22 '21

Dear Pastor Lillegard!

This morning I wrote you a postal card in the german language, asking you to introduce Rev. Krey as your successor. Tonight the thought stroke my mind, you might not understand our language. Therefore I will repeat it in english. Please fullfill the wish of Rev. Krey and introduce him in your former congregation.

With best regards

yours
Fr. Brunn
President"

KRETZSCHMAR WRITES GEORGE ABOUT INSTALLATION.
"...you are to receive your commission - "Abordnungsfeier"..."

EMMAUS LUTHERAN CHURCH

RICHARD KRETZSCHMAR, Pastor
MARTIN SCHAEFER, Ass't Pastor

2243 SOUTH JEFFERSON AVENUE

Bell Phone: Sidney 856
Kinloch Phone: Victor 815 R

St. Louis, Mo., 3/28/21.

Rev. Geo. Lillegard
Chicago, Ill.

My dear Friend:

Rev. Brand informed me that your successor would be installed on April 17 and that it was your intention to leave Chicago about the same time. He also asked me to make arrangements with you for a solemn service, in which you are to receive your commission - "Abordnungsfeier" as it is our custom whenever a new missionary is sent out in to the foreign field. Have you any wishes in regard to this matter? Which date would suit you best? Which church should be selected for that purpose, perhaps Rev. Boecler's? Who should preach the sermon? (German or English, or in both languages?) The Board would try to send a representative. President Pfotenhauer could also be invited to participate. But before we go any further in this matter, kindly give us your suggestions.

Very cordially yours with greetings to Mrs. L.

Rich. Kretzschmar

Chapter 4
The Journey to China

BERNICE'S FIRST LETTER: ABOUT THEIR SEND-OFF
"The church was filled, so there were at least 1,000 or more there."

Monday, 4/18/21
2127 Leland Ave.

Dear Folks,

    This is my first chance to write since leaving.[49] Have you heard about the speed my train made? We got to Janesville about 3:30 and there we stayed until 8:30. Almost everyone made trips to the lunch room - I bought a couple sandwiches and some fruit. Then we travelled on to Beloit, waited there a few more hours, ditto Caledonia, ditto Crystal Lake - finally arriving in Chicago at 4:30 A.M. Sunday - 5:30 Chicago time. I got to the flat about 6:30. George had been to the depot twice - once around nine o'clock and again at midnight. I came home alone, but it was getting light so I didn't mind at all. I slept a little over an hour and then got up, dressed, had a bite of toast and a cup of coffee at a restaurant, and hurried to church. We had a nice service. Then we went to Olsens' - the Lillegards, Holger Pedersons, Jarga, Bale, and Krey - maybe more. We had a fine, big dinner. Then back to the church. We had a very nice reception - there were so many present both morning and afternoon. The Ladies' Aid served supper. From the reception we went to the German church, where there was a very impressive service. The church was filled, so there were at least 1,000 or more there. We received $50 or more in money from various friends, during the day and evening. $15 were given to me and the rest to George.

    Today we have cleared the flat, sent our trunks down, been down town, and finally "married Anna"[50] - I say "we" Ha! ha! Yes, we had a nice little wedding here, with only the family present. About two hours after we start west tomorrow Jim and Anna leave for New York. Bought a fountain pen today & a black ribbon for it, so I can "hang it on my neck." It doesn't write as well as a pencil yet, since it is rather stiff so I changed off to pencil. Have been scribbling at this since before supper - "af og til."[51] I'm sure the whole letter is more or less disjointed but I'll do better another time. Am sending a schedule of addresses that George made out.

    Please excuse the haste. We leave tomorrow at 10:00 Standard time & land in Des Moines at 7 P.M. Go to Story City Wed. More soon,

In Haste, but with lots of love to all,
Bernice

---

[49] She had been visiting her parents in Madison, Wisconsin.
[50] Anna Lillegard, George's sister (see last letter of Book I, Chap.6 p. 94). She married Jim Reid.
[51] "now and then" (Norwegian)

BERNICE DESCRIBES THE TRIP FROM COLORADO SPRINGS.
"It is so different here from anything I have ever seen."

Erick Onstad Family, 1918
L. to r.: (back row) Bernice, Ragnar, Elsa
(front row) Anna & Erick

Colorado Springs
April 29, 1921
Friday 4:55 PM

Dear Mama,

    Thank you so much for Letter #3 received here yesterday when we arrived. We came in at 3:45 in the afternoon after quite a pleasant trip from Des Moines. We took the sleeper from Des M. and were on a fast train of course, so we felt quite "luxurious" after having been in those dinky local trains. I was not feeling "pitty good" but am glad it was while we were on the train so it did not interfere with our sightseeing.

    The first we did was to find a hotel. We have a nice large room in the "Rex Hotel" at $3 a day. It is not a very modern hotel, but it is nice, clean, and convenient enough. Have hot & cold water in the room - wonderful water from the mountains. It is so soft. We cleaned up, had supper, and then went to a small theater and saw Mary Miles Minter in "The Little Clown." I was feeling somewhat blue & homesick so was glad to see a movie. This morning at nine o'clock we and four others went on a tour. We rode in a fine big Cadillac - such an easy riding car. And we had such a nice trip - went to the Garden of the Gods, Cave of the Winds, and the Seven Falls in the South Cheyenne Canon. I really cannot describe the scenery - I only wish all of you were along with us. It is so different here from anything I have ever seen. Of course The Dells are interesting and wonderful, but the mountains and cliffs are so much <u>bigger</u>. Just think, in going up to the Cave of the Winds we drove <u>up</u> 1400 ft. in two miles. And at the Seven Falls we climbed 297 steps and after that - beyond that - we climbed a mile higher - not a mile in height, but distance. We came up to Helen Hunt's grave then. So now I can say I have really climbed a mountain. We were very anxious to go up Pike's Peak but the road isn't open yet on account of so much snow. So we have to be content with gazing at it from a distance of about 10 to 14 miles. Tomorrow we plan on going to Cripple Creek and then we will leave for Denver around 6 o'clock. Think we will be leaving Denver for Salt Lake City Monday. Am not sure just what George has planned and he isn't here just now. Uf, this pen of mine doesn't feed right. Guess I'll have to look for a Waterman agency here and see if they can fix it for me.

    You should see my face! It is quite sunburned, but have put cream on it and will smear some more on tonight, so I'll be O.K. tomorrow, I'm sure.

    Am sending some pamphlets which describe some of the scenery around here. Believe they are a little better than cards. Suppose you'll be busy moving[52] when this reaches you. Don't work too hard, if you can possibly help it.

With much love to you all,
Bernice & George

Some of the places are owned by private interests so there were some extra charges along the way.

---

[52] They moved out of town to Lake Edge Park, Madison.

BERNICE WRITES OF RAILWAY ADVENTURES.
"We had hit an automobile!"

May 3rd, 1921

Dear Raggie,[53]

Have lots of things to tell about and think you will be quite interested so I shall address this letter to you. The last letter I wrote was on Friday. Well, Saturday was a very exciting day - it was really hard on my nerves...

Sat. morning we got up about 7 o'clock, had our breakfast, and then took our grips to the depot & checked them. Then we took a street car out to where the North and South Cheyenne Canons begin. As I wrote Friday, we went up the So. canon that day and Sat. we tho't we'd walk up the No. canon. It is 2 ½ miles up to the end. Well, we came out there at 9:30 and we had to get back to catch a 10:58 car, as we had another trip planned for the afternoon. So we started out walking and walked as far as we dared - so as to have time to get back in time. It is beautiful up the canon and it is rather a fascinating and fearful experience to find yourself apparently hemmed in completely by unscalable rocky walls. There is a swift, clear rivulet along which the road winds. We walked up about 1 ½ miles or more and then had to hurry back. Altho' we knew there was quite a grade all the way, we didn't appreciate how great it was until we came down again and found it easier to run than walk most of the time. We ran a good deal of the way, both because it seemed easier and because we needed the time. We took a number of pictures and if there are some good ones we'll send samples.

Well the first excitement was in <u>just making</u> the streetcar. Then we went back to town and took the Cripple Creek train. Cripple Creek is a mining town way up in the mountains - elevation is 10,000 feet. Geo. just said Cripple Creek is not quite that high, but the railroad reaches an elevation of 10,600 feet before it gets there. That was an interesting trip! The way that train climbed the mountains was quite marvelous. There was a good deal of snow much of the way. We saw some flourishing little towns here and there and now and then we passed through - or by - what were once thriving, bustling mining towns and are now merely a bunch of deserted buildings. The latter looked so desolate. We saw many, many mines no longer in operation, too. When we were about three-fourths of the way up we came to a wreck. A freight train was wrecked by a rock that had fallen down on the track. The engine and tender were down in the ditch. Fortunately, it was not such a high grade as many places. No one was killed, but the fireman was bruised. We had to get off our train, go around the wreck and board another train (?), called a train, but it was a very rickety affair, with cars somewhat like the elevated cars in Chgo. When we got to Cripple Creek George got off to buy some lunch, since we hadn't had any dinner. I stayed right on the train - luckily, because they

---

[53] Ragnar, Bernice's brother

unloaded and loaded again and started off before George returned. I certainly was all excited. I asked the conductor to stop the train, which he kindly did and George came running, having heard the whistle as we started. Whew! I was relieved when he was safely aboard! The wreck had caused considerable delay, of course, so we were late in returning to Colorado Springs. The Denver train waited, however, so again we made a grand rush and got on that train. Well, I thought that was enough for one day, but about six miles out of Denver we were aroused by a generous dose of gasoline smell and the rather abrupt stopping of our speeding train. We had hit an automobile! A man - the driver, rather - got stalled on the track. I mean the engine was stalled! He tried to push the car - a Cole Eight off, but when he saw he couldn't do it, he ran to a place of safety. The car was carried along for ¼ mile and was the finest mass of wreckage one could wish to see. It took an hour to get it off so we could proceed. Wasn't that considerable excitement for one day? Sunday we took an 80 mile auto ride through the mountains and canons around Denver. We were way on top of Lookout Mountain where we saw Buffalo Bill's grave. It was a wonderful (and extremely dusty) ride.[54] We also saw some of the city of Denver. Yesterday - Monday - we left Denver at 8:30 A.M. and travelled until 11 P.M. We spent the night at Rock Springs, Wyoming instead of taking a sleeper. Left Rock Springs at 9:50 this morning and arrived here at 5:10 P.M. We were 1200 miles from Madison at Denver. We will leave here 7:50 Thursday morning and arrive in Frisco 10 AM Fri. That will be our longest jump. Tomorrow, we are going to Salt Lake City for a few hours. Hope the weather will be as nice as heretofore.

   Now, Raggie, <u>please write</u>! And Elsa owes me a letter. Hope to get mail in San Francisco when we arrive there. Love to all,

<u>Sis</u>

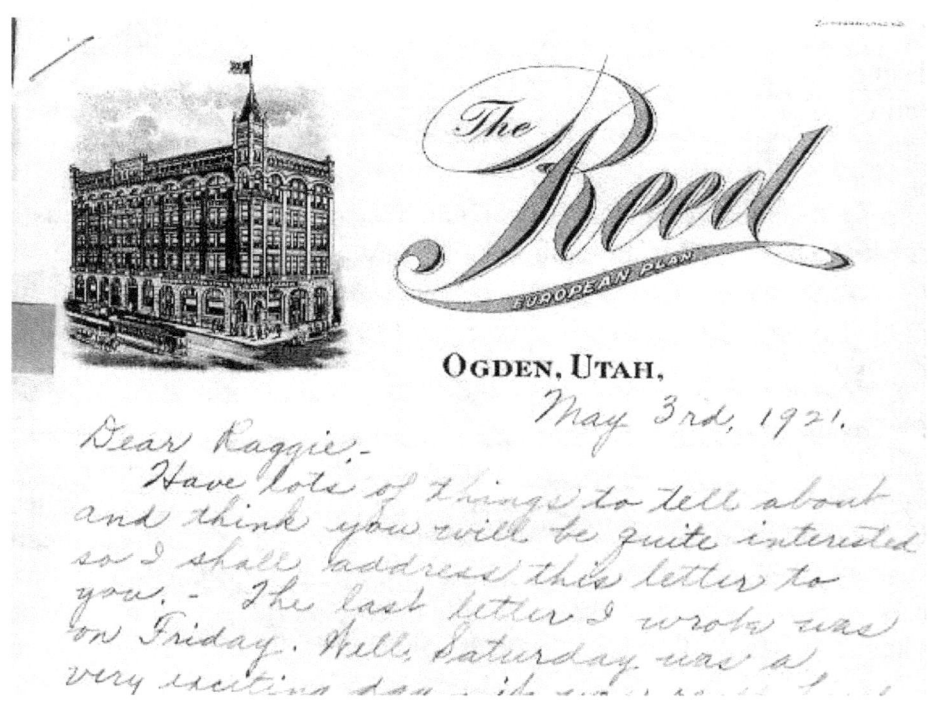

---

[54] Not any more! The road is now all paved. (note from author, who lives in the Denver area)

REV. MEYER ANTICIPATES LILLEGARDS' ARRIVAL IN CHINA.
"...you might telegraph us the name of your boat and we will meet you at the docks."

Hankow, May 30, 1921

Dear Mr. and Mrs. Lillegard;

Welcome to China!

The missionary personnel bid you a hearty and sincere welcome. We are looking forward to your arrival and hope you will soon feel at home among us. May God bless you both and keep you well and happy for the work to which He has called you.

According to the last letter we received from you we are expecting you to arrive in Hankow about the 12th of June. When you leave Shanghai you might telegraph us the name of your boat and we will meet you at the docks. Our cable address is: SYNOD, HANKOW. Arrangements have been made that you stay at Kuling this summer with the Meyers. They are also expecting you to stay with them when you come to Hankow next week.

Rev. Brandt is at present with us in Hankow but will probably be on his way to Shihnanfu when you arrive here. He will be back in about a month. Our conferences will take place in Kuling some time this summer.

May the Lord bless you and keep you, may He make His face to shine upon you and be gracious unto you, may He lift His countenance upon you and give you peace, is the constant prayer of

The China Conference.
Per Meyer

BERNICE WRITES FROM THE SHIP, S.S. TENYO MARU.
"Just a note before we sail...I'm not quite in the pink of condition,.."

May 10th, 1921 11:45 AM

Dear Folks,

Just a note before we sail. As you see by the stationery, we are on board ship now. Mr. Bakkerud, a former schoolmate of George's, is here and will mail this for me. We were at his home for supper last night. Expect Rev. Brohm's and Kirchner's down to see us off. The boat sails at 1 PM. We have gone through the whole boat - around on decks and in the various rooms and find it quite nice. We have a good-sized stateroom and have reserved two steamer chairs. Although I'm not quite in the "pink of condition," I hope to prove myself a pretty good sailor.

Am writing this on a bird's-eye-maple writing desk in a very comfortable room. There are books and magazines to be had also. So our home for the next four weeks will be quite convenient and comfortable, I think. There is a large grand piano - Steinway - also finished in maple and, judging by the few chords George tried on it, it is in good tune.

I had a very nice time playing piano duets with Rev. Kirchner Sunday eve. He is not a bad pianist at all.

From now on I shall try to number my letters and keep records of our correspondence. Hope you have received all I've sent thus far. Will send mail from Honolulu.

Goodbye all for a little while. God bless and keep each one in his tender care!
Yours, with all love,

Bernice

GEORGE WRITES BERNICE'S PARENTS FROM THE SHIP.
"None of us have fed the fishes yet..."

May 12th, 1921

Dear Folks,

The third day out and we have not been seasick yet. That is not so bad is it. Of course we have had perfectly fine weather all along so far, but the ship does move a little even so and if B. and I were not pretty good sailors, I imagine we would have been seasick together with some of the others who are just beginning to put in an appearance.

I shall leave it to Bernice to relate the events of the past few days. I suppose she will be writing you just before we reach Honolulu, so that she can mail her letter there. I am going to impose upon your good nature to ask you to act as our agents in settling the little bills that we still have left to pay in the U.S.A. My father used to do that for me. But now the folks haven't any checking account so that it would mean considerable trouble and expense for them to go and get Money Orders. So I have thought you might be willing to write out checks for the amounts noted in the letters enclosed. I am sending you herewith a Traveler's Check, which you can cash any place, and that will cover these amounts and leave some over for future bills for a similar nature.

We have certainly had an interesting trip so far, and I think that Bernice has enjoyed it as much as I, although she was not at all times in the best of condition. Today she has a dizzy head - as the sea is a little rougher again, I suppose that means that she is on the verge of sea-sickness. None of us have fed the fishes yet, however.

With love to you all, George

GEORGE WRITES SISTER LOUISE AND SPOUSE(TJERNAGELS).
"I certainly have found the Missourians cordial and helpful in every way, and I believe that they will do a good deal in future years for foreign missions."

May 13th, 1921

Dear Folks,

I guess you have not received more than a card or so from us on our way west, but then we have been so busy, when we had time to write, answering the letters we received, that we have had little time for any extra correspondence. And if you want to get letters regularly from us in China, I warn you that you will have to write regularly yourself.

We have had a very pleasant trip so far, although at times rather strenuous. In Bode we visited at Grandma's most of the time. Monday I went up to St. Paul and B. and Grandma went to Lake Mills. I came down to Lake Mills Monday night and we all went back to Bode on Tuesday afternoon. For supper that day we were out at Sarah's. We left for Des Moines Wednesday noon and went right on to Colorado Springs that same evening, arriving at that place Thursday afternoon. Friday and Saturday we took in the sights at that place, the Garden of the Gods, Cave of the Winds, Seven Falls, etc.. We could not get to the top of Pike's Peak as the road was not open yet. Sunday we went to Denver and took a long auto ride through the mountains that day. Monday we went on to Ogden, stopping off over night on the way at Rock Springs. Wednesday we went to Salt Lake City, heard a fine organ concert on the Mormon Tabernacle Organ at noon, and in the evening went on up to the Ogden Canyon. Thursday morning we left for San Francisco where we arrived Friday morning. In Frisco we spent most of our time visiting with friends and a couple Missouri Synod ministers. One day, however, we took a trip up to the top of Mt. Tamalpais, from which we had a fine view out over the bay and the surrounding country. We sailed at 1 o'clock Tuesday and so far have had the finest kind of weather. Neither B. nor I have been sea-sick, although she has not felt very well until today. She was pretty tired out from the trip to Frisco, I guess, and there was something the matter too, so that she had to go and see a doctor. I hope she will be allright after this. It would be pretty bad to start out for China except in the best condition.

There are comparatively few passengers on board ship, and many of them are Japanese. We are the only missionaries, it seems. I shall have to take charge of the services Sunday. Monday morning we are due to arrive at Honolulu, so we will have a chance there to try our land legs again.

The day we sailed we received a large box from Olsons and other members of the Lake View church, containing packages and boxes to be opened one each day until we reach Japan. Hitherto we have found a box of stuffed dates from Lawsons, a towel set from S. Anderson, a house dress for Bernice from Olsons, and a jar of mixed candies from Engquists. It certainly is interesting to have something to look forward to each day. And it is encouraging to have the people in Chicago remember us in this way. In many ways I feel much better about the way our mission work is starting out this trip than I did nine years ago. I certainly have found the Missourians cordial and helpful in every way, and I believe that they will do a good deal in future years for foreign missions. Our Minority[55] is growing too, and no doubt that will be able to give us all the support that we need. I hope that you will help along as best you can in your neighborhood and try to

---

[55] The new Norwegian synod, founded in 1918

make the work in that part of the country succeed.

    I shall mail this at Honolulu when we arrive Monday. If I think of anything more to write then, I shall add a little to this. In the meantime, give our best greetings to all the folks at Follinglo. And much love to you from us both. I enclose the pictures we took.

Your brother,
George

(Here Bernice begins numbering her letters in order to keep track of them.)
BERNICE WRITES HER SISTER FROM THE SHIP.
"If only the menus were written in English so we'd know what we were going to get."
LETTER #1

Friday, May 13, 1921

Dear Elsa,

    Guess you shall have the first letter on board ship - from me, that is. George wrote to papa yesterday.

    We have had such fine weather that I am almost ashamed to admit I have not been feeling well. I think it may be because I was tired out when we started. I have not fed the fishes anything though and I have been to the table every meal except the first breakfast and that doesn't mean anything, as George and I have often gone without breakfasts. But oh! It's my head! My ears feel stuffed and I get so dizzy and, of course, dizziness is inclined to affect the stomach, especially if it is bad. You see, there is a continual motion - a gentle rising and falling - even when the weather is fine and it just seems to "get me" more or less. I am feeling better today and by tomorrow I hope to be back on my legs in A-1 condition. I really have been at a disadvantage - Saturday evening I acquired some bladder trouble. Since it didn't get better I went to a doctor Monday and she (I went to a lady doctor) said it was probably caused by some asparagus I ate. Asparagus irritates the kidneys, so take my advice and never eat much of it. She gave me some pills to take at regular intervals - I take them when I remember to do so, which is at extremely irregular intervals. However, I am almost over that trouble. She also placed me on a temporary diet, which I have tried to observe as well as I could.

    So far I have had a salt-water bath every morning - a whole tub full of water too. We have a small tub of soft water there to rinse off the salt water when we are through. That ought to be quite invigorating and I'm going to try to keep it up the rest of the trip.

    There are five of us at our table in the dining room. Each one has his own place - it is not like in a cafe where you choose your table each meal. Our table is 25A. Across from us are a man and his wife who live in Shanghai. We have not learned their names yet. Evidently they have lived there many years - representing some large business firm, I suppose. At the end of the table is a huge man, Mr. Moses by name. He is trying to reduce and they said he had lost 48# in the U.S. He still weighs 250 lbs.!!! Imagine! And he is some eater, albeit he says he is dieting.

    Am sending you a sample of our dinner menus. We have new menus each meal. Breakfast is served from 8:30 to 9:30, Lunch at 1:00, and Dinner at 7:00 P.M. You see there are no prices on the menus, so we can order anything and as much as we like. The meals are quite good, but my breakfast today did not "sit well." I kept it though. If only the menus were written in English so we'd know what we were going to get.

    Well, I believe this is enough for now. Have some others to write to. Hope you folks are writing right along.

Much love from
Bernice

A TOTAKA   COMMANDER

Luncheon.

Olives   Salami   Pickles

Clam Chowder Boston Style   Beef Bouillon en Tasse

Boiled Halibut Caper Sauce   Pomme Natural

Chicken & Ham Pie Southern Style

Mutton Stew Dublin Style

To Order   Lamb Chops Breaded a la Petit Pois

Boiled Potatoes   Baked Sweet Potatoes

COLD BUFFET

Roast Beef   Boiled Ham   Corned Beef

Ox-Tongue   Mutton   Capon   Bologna Sausage

Salade Combination Mayonnaise

Spring Onions   Lettuce   Tomatoes

Toast Custard

Plum Pie   Cakes Assorted

Lemon Jelly   Pineapple Water Ice

Fresh Fruit

Cheese   American   Swiss   Oregon   Cream

Tea   Coffee   Milk

Friday May 13th, 1941.

LETTER #1 - PART 2

Sunday, May 15, 1921

Dear Mama,

We expect to arrive in Honolulu quite early tomorrow so this will be my last chance to write and get mail off from there. You should receive this letter about May 27th - the day we hope to arrive in Yokohama. That means you will have to wait longer for mail from us after this, since it is hardly likely that any mail will be picked up between Honolulu & Yokohama. But after that time you should receive mail quite regularly.

I am feeling just fine now and have <u>such an appetite</u>! We are also becoming acquainted with more and more of the passengers. We have learned that the other two at our table are Mr. & Mrs. Lipson and we have visited with them a good deal. They are nice people.

George is the only minister on board - in first class, at least - so he was asked to conduct services this morning. He prepared a short sermon and had a very nice little service. We sang some hymns (I played) and he read the Gospel and Epistle lessons and preached. Couldn't use a ritual in such a crowd of course. We tho't the services were very well attended. Today is Pentecost so it was nice that we could have services.

I think I wrote that we received a box by express from Chicago. It came to the boat about the time we did. It was full of packages and letters to be opened on the designated days. There is something for each day from May 10th until May 27th. On the 10th we opened a box of stuffed dates from Lawsons. On the 11th we got a bath towel & wash cloth from Severn Andersons; on the 12th I got a pretty morning dress from Olaf Olsens; on the 13th we got a 2 qt. can of assorted candies from Engquists and on the 14th a letter from Mrs. Engquist. Today we opened a box of fudge from Hazel Andersen. Tomorrow's package is addressed to me - from Alpha Pedersen (Mrs. Holger P.) It is small and I can't imagine what it is. It certainly is very interesting to have parcels for every day.

I didn't tell Elsa that we dress for dinner every night. I have worn my brown outfit - have a new "bib" with collar attached that looks very nice with the sweater - , my silk suit, which I wore as a dress, and have worn my best waists. Tonight I have my light blue dress on. We have fairly good meals, but I really prefer my own cooking!

We walk quite a bit - most of the passengers walk for exercise. Eight times around the deck makes a mile. Have read two books and have started a third. Mama, if you want a thoroughly enjoyable and humorous book, read "Tish" by Mary Roberts Rinehart. It is good! Besides that we have done some writing. Tomorrow we will mail 14 letters (15 if we count the two in this envelope), 3 correspondence cards, and 30 cards. I've sent seven cards to your folks, so you need not worry that we've forgotten them. Have to send Otto's & Leah's cards to your address as we don't know how else to reach them. Sent one to Clara at their Dayton St. address.

Well, I guess there is no more news now and I'm getting sleepy. Oh yes! I can't keep my hair curled here!

Much love to you all
George & Bernice

BERNICE WRITES HER FATHER.
"...many of us who are fond of music have spent several hours listening to Caruso McCormick, Mme. Melba, Galli-Curci, and others."

LETTER #2   Thursday, May 26, 1921

Dear Dad,

      Well, I guess I'm a pretty good sailor after all. For we had some really rough weather last night and early this morning. This boat is not very steady either so we got the full benefit of the weather. About five o'clock this morning our side of the boat got a drenching. Fortunately, we had all but closed our porthole, so not very much water got in, but some rooms got pretty wet, judging by the soaked couch covers, etc. hanging in the halls. There were not many vacant places at breakfast this morning. It is not as rough now either, as we are nearing the coast of Japan. We will arrive in Yokohama tomorrow morning and the boat does not leave again until Monday AM. Then we go to Kobe and spend a day there and on to Nagasaki where we spend another day. That means we will be spending a week in and along the coast of Japan. We intend to sleep on the boat, except perhaps Saturday evening. We plan on going to Tokyo Saturday and remaining there until Sunday. I guess there are street cars between the two cities, so we may not stay in Tokyo after all, George just said. It depends on how long it takes to go from the one city to the other. Tokyo has a population of over two million. The president of the TKKSS (?) has invited all the passengers on the Tenyo to a tea party in his garden tomorrow PM. We did not accept as we did not think we could go to Tokyo tomorrow too. We want to go Saturday because the California team plays its first game of baseball then. I wrote, didn't I, that there are sixteen California boys on board who are going to play the Japan colleges. And can you imagine anything so absurd as to send a bunch of boys off on a tour like this without a coach, or some <u>man</u> to look out for them? They have one or two managers, true but they're no better - they're boys too. And of course this is a Japanese boat and liquor can be had. Result - those who are thus inclined, can and do get what they want to drink. Not all of them do - some are really and truly athletes and some are above such things, but there are some who are weak and become pitifully intoxicated. It is a shame and I feel that the blame should be placed principally on the University for permitting them to go off alone. But one would think that boys between 20-26 (as most of these are, I should judge) would have some college, state & national pride, even if they have no personal pride. If they don't change their mode of living pretty quickly, I fear the tour will result in a triumphant victory for Japan. The Japs are pretty quick. There is a 13-yr.-old Japanese girl on board who won more prizes than anyone else in deck sports. She won in ping pong, quoits, and other sports. It was quite interesting to watch her play against these athletes and beat them. If she is a fair sample of what the Japs can do in sports, our boys will certainly have to cut out drinking & gambling and get down to business. You know, it just makes one sick to see boys, who usually think they know it all - no one can tell them anything - stoop to such folly. Saturday night I saw one boy, who did some spectacular playing in the Honolulu game, with bloodshot eyes and a coat sleeve almost torn out, sitting in the lounge room looking like a fool. One of the other boys was with him to look after him and keep him from making a scene. It made me feel blue all evening. He is such a good-natured fellow when sober, but he has a very weak-looking mouth…It is a pity and am afraid it will cause comment.

We had a nice time in Honolulu. Mr. Moses, Lipsons, and we hired an auto and drove around the city for three hours. It was a very interesting drive. Honolulu has a population of 90,000 and is a pretty city. We saw so many large schools - grade, high schools, and a normal school. And there were children of every color there. This is not the best time of the year to visit there, but we thought there was a profusion of color even so. I think Mama would like Honolulu very much. In the afternoon we went to the baseball games. It was quite exciting, ending with a score of 5-5. There was no time to play off the tie.

Now we have been on board ten days without a sight of land. That is quite a long time, but time has passed by quite quickly. There are quite a few deck sports that one can take part in. And George and I have read quite a bit. Besides, one can develop a great capacity for sleep here. One of the Japanese on board is very wealthy and among other things he has a case of excellent records with him. So, many of us who are fond of music have spent several hours listening to Caruso McCormick, Mme. Melba, Galli-Curci, and others. Although I have not much to complain of, I have had a bad head much of the time. I don't know whether the continual motion of the ship is to blame, or whether the food is. Maybe it is neither. But we are getting tired of ship food. The ravenous appetite I mentioned in my last letter did not last long. I can't say the food is actually bad, but it isn't tasty. Often I study the menu and can find <u>nothing</u> that appeals to me, except olives & fruit. The names on the menu sound very fine, but the food is not so fine. Well, our trip will be at an end in a little over a week. We will arrive in Shanghai Sunday AM June 5th.

Last week we went to bed Thursday evening and arose Saturday morning. We crossed the 180 degree meridian and skipped Friday.

Today is our Paper Wedding.[56] Our last package in the "Chicago Box" contained a box of stationery. Very appropriate, wasn't it? We have not nearly as nice weather as we had a year ago today. Although in some respects this last year has been long, it has gone by very quickly.

If our last mail went through without delay, you should receive our letters about today or tomorrow. The "Shinyo Maru" was due in Frisco May 24th and three or four days more should bring it to the Middle West.

Is the cottage all ready now? I certainly wish I could have seen it when it is all fixed up. Will you be able to get the yard in pretty good shape this year?

What is Ragnar going to do this summer? You can tell him that I wouldn't relish the idea of his driving to the west coast for a number of years to come, after having driven through mountains by auto, and through both mts. and desert by train. There are some mighty desolate stretches through the latter and the mountains are treacherous. He will "Pooh-pooh" at this, of course, but I know of some people living in Denver who won't go up to Lookout Mt. by auto because there are such accidents there. The great things in nature are as terrible as they are wonderful. How is Mama? Hope she is improving. And how is the LPA?

This is all the news for this time. Greet all the relatives & friends around there.

Love to you all,
Bernice

---

[56] Their first anniversary

BERNICE WRITES HER MOTHER
"We arrived in Yokohama yesterday A.M."
Letter No. 3

Saturday, May 28, '21

Dear Mama,

Yesterday we mailed a package to you folks. I hope you will not be too disappointed when I tell you they are not for you. The luncheon set is for <u>Mrs. J.D. Loberg</u> and the kimono for Alice.[57] Both are to serve as wedding presents. We are sending them to you because we thought there might be enough of the $10 George sent to Papa to pay the duty on these things. If there isn't, please let us know and we'll settle with you. You may think these presents are not the most suitable, but I have not felt a bit like shopping for one thing, not having felt pretty good these days, and it is not easy to shop in Japan. They have all sorts of beautiful things in dishes, ivory, silks, etc. etc. but they charge robber prices. Lipsons say we will be able to do better in China, but I wanted to send to Margaret & Alice now. We did pretty well on these things, however, and I thought Alice might appreciate a kimono for her trousseau as much as anything else. I can send her something for her house for Christmas or some such time.

Did you get the package from Honolulu? The fan was not bought there. We got that in Frisco but didn't send it from there because we thought it might as well go with Ragnar's. It is made in China though! We couldn't find anything suitable for Ragnar - it is quite hard to find souvenirs for men and the port city people are wise and charge the tourists too much. Wait until we get way inland!

We arrived in Yokohama yesterday AM. We spent most of the day right on the boat, as it rained & rained & rained. About 3:30 PM we went up and did our shopping - by the time we returned it had stopped raining. After supper 8 of us went to a movie. We came when the programme was half over, but since the performance lasts <u>four hours</u> we saw two different films anyway. We missed <u>three</u>! People in the Orient have more time than in America.

There goes our lunch gong. We did some walking around town today - bought a sun shade for me and looked at Japanese art. Don't know just how we will spend the afternoon.

Must close now. Will write again soon. Have not received any mail here from you as yet. If you have written, it may come before Monday AM.

Much love to you all from George & Bernice

---

[57] Alice Jacobson, a lifelong friend of Bernice (Bernice and Alice pictured)

BERNICE WRITES OF SIGHTSEEING.
"When we go into stores we see rows of these wooden & straw shoes standing outside."

Letter No. 4   Wednesday, June 1, 1921
                                                                                         Kobe, Japan

Dear Mama,
      Your Letter No. 6 of May 8th was received yesterday. You may be sure both George and I were delighted, since this is the first letter we have received since the day we sailed from Frisco. You said you would write again to Yokohama. We have not received any more mail yet, but we may get it in Nagasaki tomorrow or Friday. We left a forwarding address though so we will get it in Hankow, if it doesn't reach us here.

      Even though I was sort of expecting it, the news of Ruth's death was somewhat of a shock. I really cannot realize that she has gone. I know it will be very hard for them all, especially Nona, to get used to her absence. I am going to write to them soon, maybe today. Was her funeral large? I imagine it was.

      By this time I suppose you are pretty well settled. I just know you have the coziest little place. I am wondering what kind of home we will have. Have the men started fixing up the yard? I'll bet your place will look like a million dollars by the time we see it.

      We are almost broke so I think we won't be buying much for a house just yet. Can't say I am really sorry though, as I'm sure we will never have another opportunity to do this much sightseeing. And we have seen some wonderful places. We went to Tokyo last Saturday afternoon - eight of us. We didn't go to the baseball game however, as several didn't want to. We took two autos and spent two hours riding around the city of Tokyo. My, it is interesting to walk along (we got out and walked through some places) a regular Japanese street. There are very few sidewalks, even in the main streets. Why should they have sidewalks when most of the people wear wooden shoes - they are very simple - a flat piece of wood with straps to catch the toes in like this (illustration) and then two pieces in under. Let's see! (illustration) That's the way they look from the side. Sometimes the pieces are so high the wearers seem to be walking on stilts. Some are only an inch or so high. They are supposed to be rain shoes, but they seem to wear them be it rain or shine. And you should hear the clatter, clatter, clatter on a cement floor - like in an electric car station, or some such place. Their stockings, if they may be called that, reach only to the ankle and are divided like a mitten - one place for the big toe and one for the rest. They are not regular <u>stockings</u> as they are heavier and have some kind of padding on sole underneath. Of course they wear these "straw" shoes - you know the slippers we sometimes see in the "States." That would be the "shoe" and the wooden affair the "rain shoe." Quite a few of the men dress in foreign style clothes, but not many women or girls do. We see some wonderful display of color among the latter very often - bright red, pink, etc. The women carry their babies around very much like the Indians do. We see little girls - sisters or nurse girls - carrying babies around like that too. When we go into stores we see rows of these wooden & straw shoes standing outside. They don't go inside with them on.

      We have been into many shops and seen works of Japanese art. They certainly have a great deal of beautiful work in bronze, porcelain, and other ware. We have not bought any dishes though. They are quite expensive and then we have decided to wait a while before buying. We saw some wonderful tea sets - thin as paper and beautifully painted. I'd love to have a set. And if we were rich I'd send a barrelful of stuff home - some real artistic things.

Yesterday AM we arrived in Kobe. We walked up into the hills - or mountains - and saw some beautiful waterfalls. They were many hundred feet high, I am sure. We had no guide, so didn't get details. George wants to go up town to mail this now. Will send mail from Shanghai. Love to you all from us both.

Bernice

BERNICE WRITES UPON ARRIVAL IN CHINA.
"They say traveling up the Yangtsze[58] is the finest method of travel in the world..."
Letter No. 6

Hankow, China
Wed., June 15, 1921

Dear Mother,

Here we are in Hankow at last. We arrived Saturday forenoon and were met at the dock by Mrs. Meyer and several Chinese who helped with the baggage. Revs. Arndt and Bentrup met us on the way to the house. They can never know just when the boats arrive so they didn't get down to the dock in time. Rev. Meyers is not home as he and Rev. Brand have gone to the other station at Shanghai. That is quite a distance inland.

I really do not know just where to begin with news, etc. but think I'll give a diary of events first and then tell about our co-workers.

We had a <u>splendid</u> trip up the Yangtsze River. The river steamers are very comfortable. I really found the "Tuck-wo" much more comfortable in most respects than the "Tenyo." And we had much better food. They say traveling up the Yangtsze is the finest method of travel in the world. There is the ever changing scenery like on a train but without the noise and dirt of a train. And there are the comforts of ocean travel without the motion of the big seas. The only motion there was the throbbing of the boat with the engines. So you see we enjoyed our trip very much. The valley is beautiful too. I really have been quite pleasantly surprised all along the way in China. I imagined it to be a dreary place, etc. and didn't remember that it might be very pretty. And now that I have actually covered the distance, I do not feel nearly as far from home as I imagine you feel I am.

Saturday we stayed right at home all day because it rained. Sunday it was nice and bright, however, and we were out both morning and afternoon. In the morning we went with Mrs. Meyer to one of the chapels and heard a Chinese evangelist preach. He is a very nice man and Mrs. Meyer & George said he preaches well. All I know is that he certainly could talk. All Chinese, young and old alike, are very fluent in their own tongue. One never hears them stumble or hunt for words as we so often do. I noticed, before I was told anything about it, that a young person never seemed embarrassed or at loss when conversing with elder people.

Sunday afternoon at 4:30 we went to Arndts' where Rev. A. conducted services in English. We were there for supper and the evening also. Monday it rained again - during the first half of the day anyway. I did some arranging of our clothes and things and towards evening Magdalene (Mrs. Meyer - we dropped the Mrs. before we started!) and I went shopping. I bought material for a white petticoat and for a white skirt. I find I'm not well equipped with light clothes and must have some made before we go up to Kuling.[59] Yesterday (Tues.) I washed out some clothes - we have sent some to the laundry and Meyer's boy did a little, but I had some waists, etc. etc. that I wanted to do myself. After lunch Mrs. Arndt, Magdalene & I went to one of the schools where Magdalene helps instruct some women. There were some guests here for dinner.

---

[58] This was her spelling.
[59] Pronounced/spelled "Gu'-ling," also known as Kuling-chen - the mountain resort where the missionaries all went in summertime to escape the heat and have conference (<u>National Geographic Atlas of the World</u>, revised Sixth Edition, 1992)

Everything is so late in this country. The usual time for dinner is anytime between seven and nine o'clock. Movies, etc. do not begin until 9:15.

George played tennis yesterday afternoon and he thinks he lost a pound or two. He needs to lose some - he's been gaining right along. I'm glad he can get the exercise as he cannot stand the kind of life we've been living the last two months. He has been badly bothered with hives since we came to China until just these last couple days. We thought at first it was mosquito bites, but he had them in such a variety of places that it didn't seem like that either and when we came here they said change of climate very often affected people that way. Well, George certainly had them. There were big hard lumps all over his body and they itched so that he'd rub the skin off. He's been having a bad cold in his system too. I was rather afraid he would get another attack of tonsillitis, but he took a dose of Sal Hepatica (ha ha!) and it helped some. So I really have stood the trip and the climate better than George so far. They have had an unusually cool spring here - even way in here. It was cool both Sat. & Sun. but yesterday it was quite warm and it is today too. Not so warm, probably, as it is oppressive. But we will be going to Kuling the first of July and they say it is quite cool up there.

Now I'm going to describe Magdalene[60] as well as I can. Some day I'll send a snapshot. She is not as tall as I am - is two, three inches shorter, but is better developed. She has very pretty dark eyes and eyelashes and dark brown hair - almost black. She really is pretty and is also a jolly person. Tetlies and Meyers are very good friends. They came out the same year and were together at the language school in Peking. Magdalene thinks a great deal of both Evelyn and Agnes K. Meyers spent last summer up at Kikungsan (where George used to go) and are therefore well acquainted with all the Norwegian missionaries. Agnes is going home in July and I hope you will have a chance to see her. She would have left earlier, but she is waiting for the arrival of a young Tetlie before leaving. I wish I could see her before she left, but I am afraid I can't. But I expect to see Tetlies this fall when they return to their station.

George and I are going to look at a house this afternoon. We are not sure we will be here, but houses are so scarce here that they advised us to hunt for one now so that we will have a place if we do. It will be easy to secure renters if we don't stay. Meyers have a nice home here - quite convenient, considering they have electric lights and city water. But of course, missionaries cannot afford a real modern flat or home, such as are to be had if one can pay the price. Now I must quit. Maybe George will write a few words too. Received Elsa's letter Monday - was so glad to get it. It had been forwarded from Yokohama to Nagasaki, from there to Shanghai, and then to Hankow. I really think it was on the same boat with us all the way. There is American mail due today, so I hope there will be some from home then. We have also received a letter from Krey here and the "Lake View Lutheran…" How are you feeling now? Do hope you are not all played out by your moving and getting settled. Take care of yourself.

Much love to you all and greetings to all my friends.

Bernice

Elsa is quite a letter writer. Will answer soon.

---

[60] Wife of missionary Lawrence Meyer

Hupeh province (now called Hubei – new Pinyin spelling)

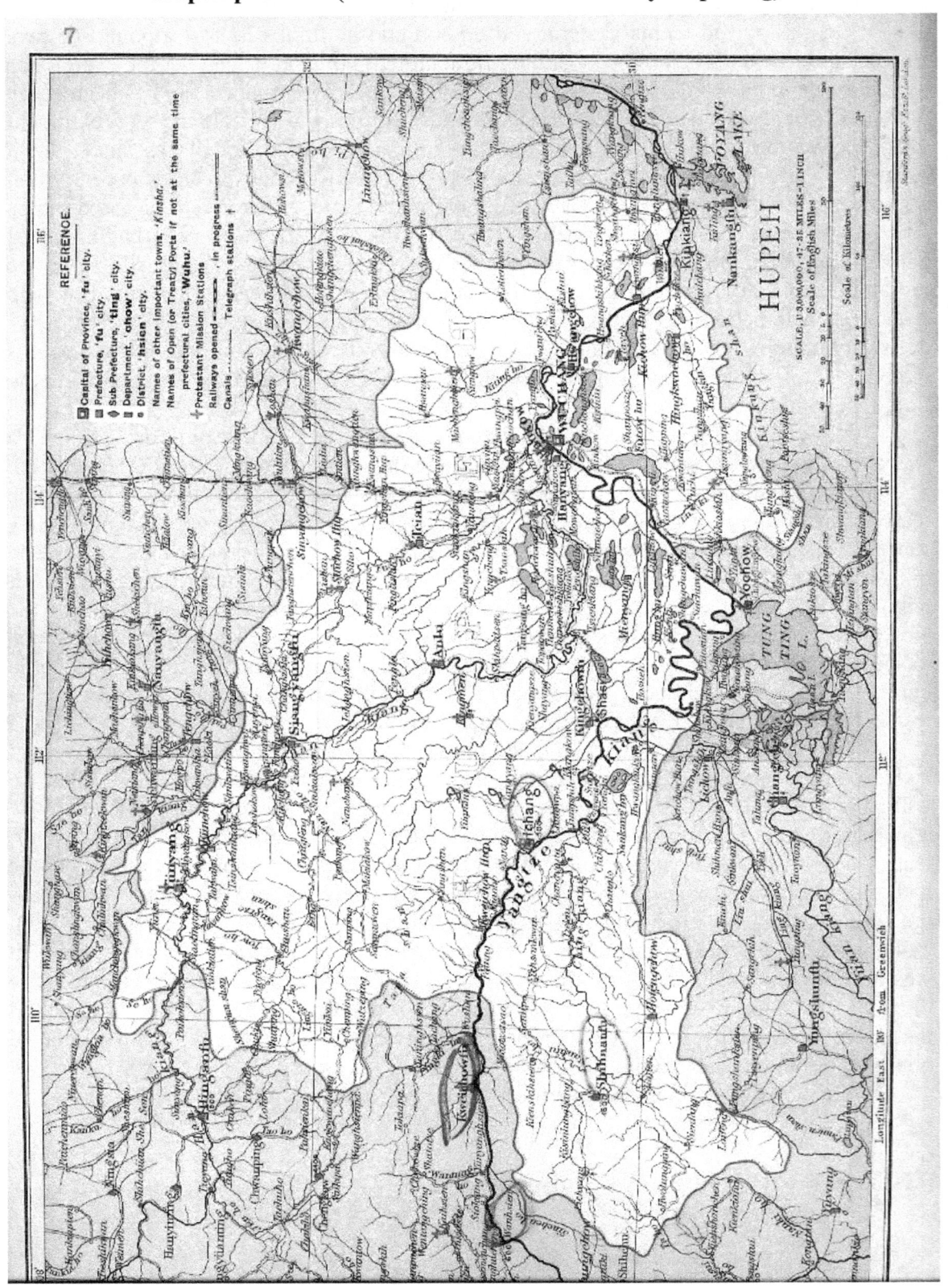

GEORGE WRITES UPON ARRIVAL IN CHINA.
"...it would seem that the work has progressed better than could be expected."

Hankow, China, June 15th, 1921

Rev. R. Kretzschmar
St Louis, Mo.

Dear friend,

We arrived here Saturday morning in good condition, except for a cold which I had contracted on the way up the river. Today, however, I am feeling quite normal again. We found that Rev. Brand had already left for Shinanfu with Meyer, and that Schwartzkopfs, Mrs. Bentrup, and Mrs. Riedel had gone to Kuling. Mrs. Meyer, Arndt, and Bentrup met us at the boat. We are to stay at Meyer's home till they go to Kuling, and also share their summer home with them at the mountain. The missionaries at this place all seemed to be in good health, with the exception of Rev. Arndt, who certainly has been failing. He ought by all means to go home, which I understand he does not plan to do, although his family leaves the latter part of this month. Could he not be persuaded to go home in order to travel about and seek to arouse interest in our China Mission? He should stay for the Conference on Kuling, but could certainly after that. Bentrup and Schwartzkopf would both be ready to take over his work by next fall. A word of advice or exhortation from the Mission Board at home might help to make Arndt realize the desirability of making the trip home.

I have as yet had little opportunity to see what work is being done here. From what has been said, I understand that they have all had their full share of the difficulties that usually surround young missions. But in spite of these, it would seem that the work has progressed better than could be expected. The schools and chapels in Hankow are doing good work and the dispensary just opened will soon be a considerable help to the Mission, although only a Chinese doctor is in attendance.

I enclose a copy of our accounts since leaving Chicago and up to date. I understand that I am to render monthly reports to the Mission treasurer located here after this. I have enquired as to what should be charged up to expense account and trust that this statement will not be found to contain items which should rather have been entered on my private account. We tried to economise as much as possible on our trip, but it seems that it is becoming increasingly difficult to do so.

Just this note now. I hope that I shall be able to write something more about the work here very soon.

With best greetings to you and yours from my wife and myself,

Sincerely yours,

Geo. O. Lillegard

TRAVELLING EXPENSES OF GEO. O. LILLEGARD & WIFE

For Passport	$10.00	
" Japanese and Chinese Visas on passport	4.50	
" Packing Materials, boxes, etc.	12.95	
" carting trunks in Chicago	5.00	
" Mrs. L's RR fare to San Francisco	73.45	
" excess baggage, Chicago to San Francisco	9.15	
" Sleeper fare, for Mr. & Mrs. L. to Frisco	28.15	
" charge for $470 worth of Amer. Express Checks	2.35	
" streetcar fare, Chicago and San Francisco	1.00	
" meals en route to Frisco, one week	23.05	
" transferring trunks at Colorado Springs	1.50	
" " baggage at San Francisco	5.50	
" Hotel at San Francisco	8.00	
" deck chairs on board "Tenyo Maru"	3.00	
" tips to stewards on " "	13.00	
Received from Mission Treasurer for expenses		$300.00
" refund on tickets purchased to Hongkong		55.10
To Balance on hand at time of arrival at Shanghai	154.50	
	355.10	355.10

Balance on hand, 154.50 exchanged for Mexican dollars as follows:

$50.00 gold at 2.07		103.80
$4.50 gold at 2.00		9.00
100.00 " at 2.03		203.00
Received 100.00 taels, paid to Mrs. Netland, Jan., 1921 at 70.9		141.05
For S.S. Fare, Shanghai to Hankow	100.00	
" telegram " " "	1.30	
" Hotel Bill at Shanghai	14.50	
" baggage transfer, Shanghai and Hankow	3.75	
" rickshaws at " "	1.65	
" tips to stewards on River Steamer	1.50	
" Customs charges on freight sent by M.W.&CO.	24.70	
" salary for June	160.41	
Balance on hand, June 15, 1921	148.94 Mex.	
	456.85	436.85

Signed,

Geo. O. Lillegard

Chapter 5
Temporary Homes

BERNICE REQUESTS SEWING PATTERNS.
"...there are many tailors to be had, but they haven't patterns..."
Letter No. 7

> Hankow, China
> June 16th, 1921
> Wednesday Eve.

Dearest Mother,

Your letters - No. 7 & 8 - sent to Shanghai came today. The American mail was due yesterday and we received a pile of magazines and papers, but not much personal mail - only one letter from George's mother. Since the letters from you had to be forwarded they were one day late, but even more appreciated perhaps because we were a little disappointed yesterday. You do write such good letters! And it was nice to get a word from Willard too. It does make me rather homesick to read the letters from home. I think I will learn to be happy here, but I believe most of the missionaries long for home, deep in their hearts, even though they find contentment in their work. I try not to think too much about such things. I know that it takes too much energy to give way to homesickness. And you must not grieve, Mama! You must try to picture China as a pretty country and the part of Hankow in which we will probably live, if we remain here, is quite foreign. The people here - missionary folks, I mean - have comfortable homes. And, except for Arndts, all the people are young. I have met only Rev. Bentrup - his wife and Mrs. Riedel and the children have already gone to Kuling (Gu' ling), Rev. Gihring is up north, and Schwartzkopfs are at Kuling. Mrs. Gihring is in California. I told you about her before we left, I think. And Rev. Gebhardt, the only bachelor, is still at Shinanfu. And if all the girls are as companionable as Magdalene, life will be very bearable here. So you must not worry about me at all. George will take good care of me too, I'm sure.

By the way, I think it would be a good idea for you folks to go to Western Union and register a code address and let us know what it is. Reids (Anna L.) have registered one in Chicago and we have told them to advise you if we ever cable - better send your address to 2127 Leland Ave. Their code address is "Jasreid, Chgo." for James Reid, see? We will get one here and tell you. The conference here is reached by addressing "Synod, Hankow," but we want a personal one also.

Would you send me some patterns? You could use some of the money we sent. You see, there are many tailors to be had, but they haven't patterns and here they make everything, except such people as have money to throw away. Magdalene has had a tailor here all week. He charges $.70 (Mex. or $.35) a day. He is very neat and quite clever, but she cuts the things for him as a rule and then tells him just how to do it. He made a very nice sport shirt yesterday. She cut that by an old shirt which she had carefully ripped up. Today he made a white petticoat and a white duck skirt for me. I used the embroidery you gave me for the skirt - petticoat, I mean and it is so pretty. The skirt is perfectly plain (now I mean the top skirt, ha ha!) but instead of having it gathered, I had it plaited. Yesterday I bought a flowered voile for dress - it is quite dark so will not have to be washed often. I picked out a style in a fashion book - as did Magdalene for a dress of hers - we showed it to the tailor (this is a regular tailor) and told him to make our dresses accordingly. He has no pattern - simply looks at the picture and sews the dress. But to return to patterns for me. I'd like a good shirt pattern for George: size - neck 16" or 16 1/4" and 42" chest. And I'd like a pattern to make petticoats by, and some other simple patterns - so I can cut ordinary clothes, you understand. And if you can find a nice dress pattern to be made up in silk - taffeta or crepe - please send that. I want a nice dress for next fall - one piece, or something suitable, not tight anyway. But you know what is becoming to me better than I do and you needn't worry about picking a pattern when you don't have to make it. The silks here certainly are wonderful. It is so late now I must quit. Much love to all from us both.

Bernice

You should see my legs. Talk about mosquito bites!! I've never had as many in my life. We use a net over our bed, or we'd be bitten to death. House is screened too.

We had a thunderstorm tonight - rained so hard for a while. Has been unspeakably sultry & oppressive today.

GEORGE EXPLAINS WHY SOLDIERS LOOT.
"...when they are disbanded take the law into their own hands and go out to collect their pay."

Hankow, China, June 16th, 1921

Dear father-in-law,

Bernice has written about most of the events these last days, but there is one matter she left me to write about, besides business. That is the disturbances in this neighborhood the last few weeks. I suppose that you will see reports concerning them in the papers at home. Hitherto only a few foreigners have been molested by the brigand soldiers, and in Hankow we are safe enough. Just today a large destroyer or small cruiser came up the river, the U.S.S. Wilmington. And things seem to be quieting down in the Chinese cities also. Wuchang, the capital across the river, was badly looted by the soldiers and much of the city burned down. Ichang, a few hundred miles up the river from Hankow, was also looted and there several foreign firms suffered loss by fire and pillage. But Hankow itself has escaped. It seems that the soldiers do not receive their pay and when they are disbanded take the law into their own hands and go out to collect their pay. There are half a million soldiers scattered throughout China, and it seems that the country is in a quandary to know what to do with them; if they keep them in the government's pay, they will go broke; if they try to disband them, the soldiers will turn robbers and become a danger to the country in more ways than one. Naturally every case of such lawlessness brings the day of foreign intervention closer.

I enclose a check for $20.00 to go on account. Please pay the enclosed bill for $5.99 for Literary Digest, and when you have paid the customs on the package we sent you, let us know what it is, so that we can credit you with that amount also. There will soon be other bills to pay also, but I hope that this check will last for a while.

With love to you all,
George

GEORGE WRITES OF POLITICAL UNREST.

"As a punishment some of the soldiers were taken up the Peking[61] railroad a ways, and when the train reached a town called Siaggan, the cars were riddled with machine gun bullets."

Hankow, June 16th, 1921

Dear mother,

Yesterday American mail came and your letter was the only one of a personal nature. There were a lot of magazines including the package of magazines that you sent. You need not send any more church papers now, as I get them mailed direct to me. But if anything else comes, please forward it.

It was good to hear from you folks again, as we had not gotten anything since leaving San Francisco over a month ago. I got a short letter from Krey when we arrived here last Saturday the 11th, and Bernice got a letter from Elsa. Otherwise the only mail we have had between Frisco and here was a letter at Yokohama from Mrs. O. But now I suppose the mail will begin to come in more regularly.

We came to Shanghai Sunday morning the 5th, and found one of Rev. Arndt's daughters there to meet us. She showed us around a little the two days we were there, and when she was on duty (she is a nurse) we went out shopping and also went out in a carriage to see the sights. We got a carriage for half a day for only 1.00. Tuesday night we left for Hankow, on the river steamer, one of the boats that I had travelled on before, six or nine years ago. We had a nice trip and the weather was very cool for this time of the year all the way. Even now it is not so hot here in Hankow as it usually is. Mrs. Meyer met us at the Hankow docks, and Arndt and Bentrup came a little later. We are staying with Meyers here and will be with them also this summer up at Kuling. We shall have to look for a house now, so that we will have something to move into when fall comes. Our freight was here ahead of us, beating us by about two weeks. So far as I could tell by looking at, it was all in good shape. For the present and until we find a house, it will stay at the storage house of the Shipping Co. Some of the missionaries here have already gone up to Kuling. Meyer has gone with Rev. Brand up the river to the new field in Western Hupeh and is not expected back until July. We may stay here till he comes back, if it does not get all too hot. Two of the other missionaries are in Shinanfu, the field inland that Brand now is visiting. It seems to be decided already that we are to stay in Hankow. In some ways it would be nice to do that, and in other ways I would rather go inland. However, we shall wait till the Conference this summer before making very definite plans.

Mrs. Meyer is a very nice young lady, and in general I have received a good impression of Bentrup also. The other missionaries I have not as yet met. We have a small room here, as none of the missionaries have large quarters. But we shall have to reconcile ourselves to camping until next fall or when we move into our new home. We have spent most of the time since coming here, shopping, unpacking and repacking for Kuling, and in general getting things straightened out, besides visiting with the other missionaries.

---

[61] Pronounced "Bei-jing'," like the modern spelling

Perhaps you have seen in the papers something about the disturbances here in Central China. Shortly before we left Shanghai, we heard that Ichang, a city a few hundred miles up the Yangtse, had been looted by disbanded soldiers, and some foreign property also destroyed. And while we were on the way up the river, Wuchang, the city across the river from Hankow, was also looted by soldiers who were soon to be disbanded. In both cases this was done, it seems, because they did not get all the pay they expected or wanted. Wuchang was badly looted, and big parts of the city burned. Many Chinese were killed but no foreigners were molested. As a punishment some of the soldiers were taken up the Peking railroad a ways, and when the train reached a town called Siaggan, the cars were riddled with machine gun bullets. About 2000 were killed in that way according to reports. So you see China is far from being a quiet and restful place to visit. However, I think that things will be quieting down after this. At any rate, we are safe enough here. There are a number of gunboats here, and just today a large U.S. cruiser came up to Hankow.

I enclose a few pictures taken on the way. If I should send pictures that you have received before, you will have to give them to someone, or send them on to Louise or Anna. We wrote Lunds a card on the S.S. Tenyo, and I also sent a letter enclosing some kodak pictures from here. I mailed to Lunds' old address. You had better enquire if they have received it, forwarded from there.

So much for this time. Please write about the work in Lake View too and let me know how church attendance, etc. is. How does it go with Saturday school? It would be fine if he could get that going.

Lovingly,

George

BERNICE AND GEORGE LEAVE HANKOW FOR KULING.[62]
"...we...are now on our boat. We...arrive tomorrow morning at Kiukiang. From there we travel by auto a distance and then by chair up the mountain."

Letter No. 8

June 26th, 1921

Dear Mother,

  I should have written last week, but it really was so hot and "sticky" that one didn't care to write. Moreover, this letter will catch the same boat anyway. It is pretty sticky today too, but George and I are going to Kuling tonight so I want to get a letter off. I do not know what number this letter should be because my books containing the records is packed. But I am sure the last letter was written on June 17th. Have an idea this is No. 9. Mark the number it should be and I'll put it in my book when I get to Kuling.

  There isn't much news to relate. We have been rather busy getting some things done that had to be attended to before leaving Hankow. Yesterday I made (not quite finished) a bed net. And we had two pads - or mattresses - made. Really neither pad nor mattress, but halfway between. They are for camp cots, for traveling, etc. - single size. Out here they make up what is called a "pu'kai" (pugai) which consists of bedding wrapped in some peculiar oil cloth. When people travel inland they must have them. The oilcloth is placed on the ground and the bed made on that. The oilcloth keeps insects away. Well, these pads are really for a pu'kai, as I understand it. I have had to do some "fixing" on my clothes too, sew buttons & clasps, o.s.v.[63] And I have had a flowered voile dress made. Am sending a sample. You may think it is rather funny, as George did when he saw the material. But now that it is made up he likes it and says it is quite a sober looking dress after all. I doubt that I can describe it well, but I'll try to give you an idea. The sleeves have a puff (drawing) Ha ha! do you get that? There are two ruffles around the waist, much like my white net dress. And there are two panels <u>loose</u> - about four inches wide - in front and in back. On these panels are five ruffles. The panels reach to the hem of the skirt. It is a little different from my others and I hope to be quite satisfied with it. One certainly needs more clothes in such a warm climate, but I believe I am fairly well fitted out for this summer now. I think it is wise to add a dress or two each year, as then it doesn't take so much money at one time and one always has something.

  The summer is here all right now. Wednesday we went to Shelkow (Sā' ko) to attend commencement exercises at the Union Lutheran Seminary (for Chinese). The walk from the station to the school was quite long and <u>very sunny</u>. I really thought it was very hot. But Thursday was worse. I was dizzy with the heat all forenoon. You should have seen the wax candles! They were so soft they bent and twisted. Magdalene and I did some work right along all day to keep our minds off the weather. It is too uncomfortable to lie down. And Friday forenoon it was bad too, but it let up a little towards evening. We ought really have been up on Kuling 'ere this all of us, but circumstances have not been favorable. Only Bentrup and we are going this evening, as the others cannot get away yet. Meyer and Brand just returned from Shinanfu yesterday morning. The trip was very dangerous. They traveled up through the Yangtsze gorges,

---
[62] Pronounced "Gu'-ling;" modern spelling also Guling, in Mount Lushan National Park
[63] o.s.v – and so forth (Norwegian)

where the boats never travel except by daylight. They have told of many interesting incidents!

George and I have had a Chinese teacher the last week; Mr. Chi is his name. I have not done any studying by myself - have only been reading with him. But when we get settled on Kuling I must get to work in real earnest. I think I will find it very interesting, but it is so long since I did any studying that it may take me a while to get into that harness again.

The conference is scheduled to begin July 11th. That means that in a few more weeks we will know where we are to be stationed. It <u>seems</u> that we will be either in Hankow or not very far from here in a new place not yet occupied by the Missourians.

Guess I'll have to cut this short - we have had supper and are now on our boat. We leave 8:30 or 9:00 o'clock and arrive tomorrow morning at Kiukiang. From there we travel by auto a distance and then by chair up the mountain. Will write a letter very soon from there. Don't think I'll give you a Kuling address as this will reach you so late. It takes only a few days more to forward mail to us.

Much love to you all from us both. Hope we get mail this week.

Bernice

Kiangsi province (today Jiangxi)

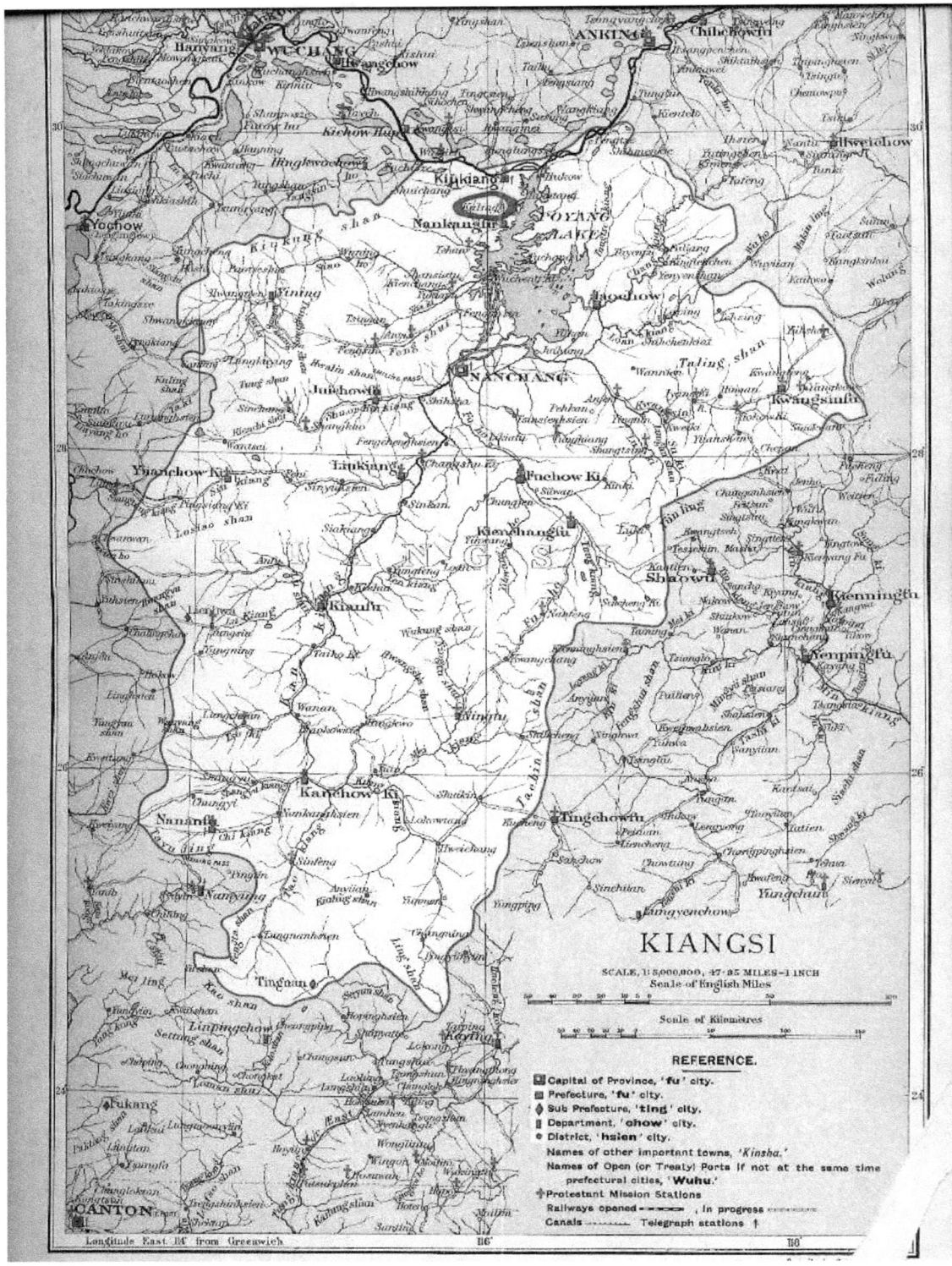

GEORGE ADVISES HIS SUCCESSOR, KREY, ABOUT LOVE.
"It seems that in most cases it takes a girl much longer to make up her mind on the question whom she likes than it does a man."

Kuling, China, June 28th, 1921

Dear friend Krey,

Your letter was the first one to reach us after our arrival in China, so that you may be sure it was appreciated. We were glad to hear that you were satisfied with your work - and with the Royal, and also glad to hear from others that the attendance at the church services bespoke interest on the part of the people in their new minister. May you be given the courage and strength to hew to the line and do a thorough work in Lake View. I was glad to note from the Lake View Lutheran that you were going to start a Saturday school. I shall await eagerly reports as to the attendance, etc. Do not be disappointed, if you have some pretty hard work to keep up the attendance, especially during the summer months.

We were naturally much interested in your confession regarding the state of your heart, since reaching Chicago, and my wife confesses to a burning curiosity as to who the fortunate young lady is that has been honored with your attention. Not knowing who she is, I cannot very well give you any advice; anyway it is an ungrateful task to give advice to anyone in such a position as you say you are. I can give this general advice, however; give the lady time. It seems that in most cases it takes a girl much longer to make up her mind on the question whom she likes than it does a man. And if the man is hasty, he is more than likely to be turned down. Either keep awooing till you are pretty sure of your fair one, or try, try again, till successful or absolutely hopeless. So here's wishing you all success and all happiness. You will need a good helpmate in your work in Chicago. This is written on the assumption that you were thoroughly serious when you wrote your last letter. We were not so sure but that you were writing in a somewhat facetious vein.

We came up to this place, the mountain resort in Central China, yesterday morning. It is certainly a beautiful place, and we are waiting for good weather so that we can enjoy the scenery. Today it is drizzling right along, so we have to stay inside. We are for the present staying in the same house with Bentrups, Schwartzkopfs and Mrs. Riedel and her children. In a few days the house that we are to occupy will be ready. Then we will be with Meyers, Brand, and Gebhardt. The last named are still in Hankow. Bentrup sends best greetings. He is getting along fine here and although he has had quite serious trouble with his eyes is well satisfied to be in China. In two weeks our conference is to commence. Then we will all be together and, I suppose, have some pretty lively discussions. There are a number of things to be discussed, and there is no general agreement amongst the missionaries on any subject, I guess, to judge from what I have heard. That is generally the case.

So much for this time. I enclose a sketch of our activities up to date for the Lake View Lutheran, if you have place for it in one of your next numbers. With best regards to you from Bernice and myself,

Sincerely,
George O. Lillegard

BERNICE DESCRIBES THE CHAIR RIDE TO KULING.
"Often you feel as though your feet are where your head belongs!"

Letter #9   Kuling, July 1st, 1921

Dear Mother,

    Hope Elsa will not feel badly because this letter is not addressed to her. I really intended to write this one to her, but there are several things I wanted to write to you, so I shall try to send her the next one. I am waiting so for mail from you - haven't had any for two weeks, but we expect American mail very soon now as the "Shinyo Maru" was due in Shanghai some days ago. -- I think I shall forget rules of letter writing as regards paragraphing, because it takes too much valuable space. I'll just make a few dashes to indicate paragraphs. --Mrs. Arndt and her daughter Agnes and son Eddie sailed for America the 29th. We sent a little package along for you. We gave them some money for postage, but they took things along for so many that they may forget and ask you for postage money, also for duty expenses, should there be any. I hope you will not mind paying that, however. I looked for some silver for you for your silver wedding, but what was to be had was so expensive, and as you have quite a bit, I thought white brass might please you as well. It may need polishing when it reaches you - I think your silver polish will do the work all right. The tray is for you, the waterpipe for papa, the smell pipe for Ragnar, and the little box for Elsa. The box is really for Chinese ink, but I thought it would make a good stamp box. I do hope you will all like the stuff. Hankow is the home of white brass. You could use the tray for your cream & sugar, probably. People use so much brass here, both white and yellow. The waterpipe is just what they use a great deal here. I wish I could explain how it is used, but I am afraid I cannot. There is a part that contains the tobacco and I guess the smoke passes through the water before it is inhaled. You may be somewhat curious regarding the ink box. They use ink much like paint here. One wets a bar of black ink and writes with a brush which comes to a very fine point. I said "wets a bar" - well, you do it much like with water colors. George brought writing material for me today. There is a little wooden dish or tray that has a groove at one end for water. Dip the bar into that and rub it on the flat surface of the tray so it makes a paint. Do I make myself understood? It is really hard to describe things well on paper.

    We came to Kuling Monday noon. We had a very interesting trip. We left Hankow Sunday evening on the river steamer "Suiyang" - traveled first class Chinese - for two reasons. This boat has no foreign class service and then some of these missionaries have been so economical that they believe in traveling that way. George and I don't, so I hardly think we will travel that way often. We had our "pu'kai" along and slept out on the deck so we were not bothered by any stale air or friendly insects. I slept on the cot and George and Bentrup made their bed right on the deck floor. We had to get up at 5:00 AM though, because they washed the deck. It made me cross almost as I was so tired then. Hadn't slept well the last 2-3 nights in Hankow on account of the heat. Well, we arrived in Kiukiang about 7:30 AM. From there we went by auto for a distance of about seven miles. And the remainder of the trip was made by chair. Except in cases of very heavy people, there are four chairbearers. George persuaded four to carry him too (instead of six) by promising to walk now and then. I can assure you that the trip up the mountain is very interesting and not entirely without danger. There are many places where a misstep on the part of a coolie might send you rolling hundreds of feet down to a narrow gulch or valley. I wasn't really afraid though - I held my breath a couple times, that's all. It is a <u>wonderful climb.</u> Often you feel as though your feet are where your head belongs! No fooling, though, it is so steep some places that Hutte tu!⁶⁴ I think I will dread going down more than climbing up. There were a good many clouds when we came up Monday and I found it very interesting to travel amongst them, for that is really what we did. Much of the time there were such heavy clouds below that we could not see the valleys. Sometimes we would be going along in brightness and suddenly a cloud would come rushing and envelop us. There were two or three so heavy that we could see only a short distance ahead. So we are "living in the clouds" literally speaking. Kuling is a very pretty summer resort. There are several valleys occupied. The largest is called Central Valley - the bottom and sides of the valley are dotted with houses. There are many trees also. I am sure you would like it here as far as scenery goes. There must be many nice people too as there are about 2000 foreigners here during the summer, if I am not mistaken.

    The plans for us this summer are like this. Meyers, Revs. Brand & Gebhardt, Gales (some friends of Meyers - not missionaries) and we are to have a new house for the season - rent it, of course. The house was to be completed by today - July 1st. We heard from the owner before we left Hankow that it was not quite ready, but expected to be able to use a bedroom upstairs and board with the others of our crowd up here. When we arrived Monday we found the house a mess. It was anything but ready! Fortunately they could accommodate us here for the time being and here we have been ever since. George thinks we will be able to move into our bedroom over there tomorrow afternoon, as the upstairs seems to be ready now. But I wonder when the downstairs will be ready. To cap the climax the carpenters have been on a strike since yesterday. Imagine, <u>strikers</u> in China! They seem to think they will come back tomorrow or Monday. I surely hope so. All the rest of the crowd will be coming next week because conference begins the 11th and we can't all live in this cottage. At present we are 7 grownups and five children here. Three of the kiddies are under a year and a half "og du kan tro der er musik her."⁶⁵ Two of them are such crybabies - one is 3 and the other 1 1/2 and they just howl when they get mad. I am tempted to spank them thoroughly at times.

    Since I'll be mentioning the names of our co-workers now and then, I had better introduce you to our mission family. I have not met them all myself, but know the names, anyway. Arndt, of course, you know was the first man out. Next came Riedels, who now have three children. I believe the next man out was Gebhardt, a bachelor. Then came Meyers. They have no children. Next came Schwartzkopfs. They have a cute little boy. And Bentrups came shortly after S's. They also have a baby boy. Besides ourselves, that is all. It is enough to warrant a lively conference this summer, however. Things have been going on pretty much as they would here. And some, especially one, have even become quite unionistic. It seems hard for even a good Missourian to remain conservative here. Do hope things will be straightened out at conference without too much fuss. George and I are not very keen about being in Hankow for several reasons.

---

[64] Literally, Brr, an expression of shivering from cold. Shuddering at the thought of something eerie or unpleasant. (Norwegian)
[65] "and you can believe there is music here." (Norwegian)

For one thing, George would like to be quite independent of the others, because he hopes the Norwegian Synod will be able to support its own mission in time. And if we remain in a place where there are unionistic tendencies on the part of one or two co-workers, there will certainly be more or less friction. The housing problem in Hankow is extremely bad also. I believe it is as bad, or worse than in the States. It seems almost impossible to get a place - there are long waiting lists. One man, who is very friendly toward our missionaries, has offered us a two-room flat and the mission is holding it and paying rent this summer so that whoever is stationed in Hankow will have a place. It was simply circumstance and kindness on Mr. Klein's part that made the place at all available. George would like to go to Peking or else go inland. At any rate, he would prefer to start a new station. I haven't much choice. I would enjoy living where we could have a little garden and could hang our clothes out in the sun. I know I will find it hard to have servants. I am too particular and I hate so to have nice things spoiled or stolen, and pretty things broken. All such things are to be expected, it seems. Well, maybe I'll be lucky enough to get some good "boys." No use crossing bridges yet, I suppose.

If Alice's plans were carried out, I suppose she was married yesterday. I thought of her so often and wished I could be there. Did the kimono get there in time? I hope she will like it. And have the other things come through - the fan & napkin ring? I imagine I'll get mail from you answering some of these questions just after this is mailed. That's usually the way. - Oh, I almost forgot - Tetlies got a little boy Monday June 27th. Had a card from Magdalene today. She says all is well.

Hope you folks are sending about a letter a week. Ragnar & Elsa will have to relieve you when you are too busy. They must write anyway though! Had a letter from Martha Klath this week. Now it is bedtime. Good night all! Please don't be lonesome! You must get well & strong. How are you? Please tell me.

Much love to all from us both,
Bernice

BERNICE WRITES TO HER MOTHER-IN-LAW.
"I should just like to know what you could tell me about Krey this very day. Has he been coming as frequently as ever and does he still gaze at Ella?"
Letter #10

Kuling, China
July 2nd, 1921

Dear Mother and Girls,

It is about time I write a letter to you, I guess. George wrote to the Lake View Lutheran the other day, but he thought I'd better write to you this time, and I'm glad to do it, of course. I feel a little guilty about not having written more than one so far, but we had to divide up on the writing so we have each written to our respective families. We are waiting rather impatiently for American mail every day. So far we have received only one letter from you (Mother's) since we arrived in China. We expect a big bunch of letters now as one of the big boats came to Shanghai this week.

I didn't read what George wrote last time so I don't know just what news you have, but I believe I can write without repeating much.

Sunday, July 3rd...I was interrupted yesterday by the arrival of American mail. Your letter, Val, of May 20-26 was received and one from my mother. Those were all the letters we received, but we have hopes of getting more one of these days. We were mighty glad to get the two, however. I believe that was the reason I dreamt that Val came out here.

And I tho't you brought so many pair of white shoe laces along and I told you, "Why, we can buy _anything_ here!"...I should just like to know what you could tell me about Krey this very day. Has he been coming as frequently as ever and does he still gaze at Ella? It certainly is tough to be so far away that it takes six to eight weeks to exchange news. But you must be sure to keep me posted on all such interesting things. How are Pearl and Columbus getting along? I wonder if they're as thick as ever. And I am anxious to hear how "you all" are spending the summer. If Alice's former plans were carried out, she and Bert were married last Wednesday (6/29). By the time this reaches you she should be in Chicago. If you are not already in touch with each other, please call up J.B. Arneson, D.D.S. on Milwaukee Ave. I'm sure you girls will like Alice very much, as well as vice versa. We're glad to hear the recital was such a success, artistically and financially. We knew you would do well, Ella, but we know getting a crowd in Chicago is not the easiest thing, so we congratulate you muchly. Has it brought any new pupils yet? It doesn't seem fair to me that the proceeds were evenly divided. I can't quite get over the nerve of one in offering her services and then accepting pay! Maybe I am misjudging her? Your dress must be very pretty. Val is quite an artist. No, Val, I am sorry to report that I didn't learn the Hula-hula dance. We had too little time in Honolulu. I imagine they dance best at night and we were off again by that time! And regarding the Gullixson wedding present. I wonder if your eyes weren't bad that day! I certainly cannot understand it, because I myself bought the spoons and ladle and wrote out _both cards_ and I am quite positive I put Mr. & Mrs. G.O. Lillegard on both. At any rate, we intended both to be from us and I cannot explain the incident if the cards were otherwise.

July 4th...Well, it doesn't usually take me three days to write a letter, but it seems I cannot get this written in one "sitting." We got some more American mail yesterday

P.M. but no more from you. There was a letter from Alice tho' saying she was to be married June 18th. It seems as if I've missed so much this spring! Am glad Anna & Jim were married before we left anyway, so we didn't have to lose out on that too.

So you had some hot weather in May: we hear that the spring and early summer has been unusually cool here in China. But the second week we were in Hankow it was terribly hot. I was really dizzy with the heat a couple days. And as you may know, it is not only that the thermometer registers 90° and over in the shade, but the air is <u>so</u> heavy and oppressive. George thought the heat was getting on our nerves and insisted that we go to Kuling and not wait for Meyers, who were not ready to leave. So we left Sunday eve, June 26th. We took a river steamer and since we had to travel first class Chinese, there being no foreign class on this boat and there also being some of our missionaries who believe in extreme economy, we slept on the deck. Rev. Bentrup was with us. We had our cot and bedding along, so George put that up for me and he & Bentrup made their bed on the deck floor. We didn't sleep much during the night and at 5 A.M. just when we <u>were</u> good and sleepy, we were roused and told to get up because the deck was to be washed. Whew! I was peeved. I was so tired from lack of sleep for several nights on account of the heat that I could hardly be anything but peeved!! Believe me, George and I won't travel that way if we can help it. We arrived in Kiukiang, at 7:30 A.M., made arrangements for our baggage and then traveled via auto to the foot of the mountain where we took chairs. Except in cases of very heavy people, there are four chair-bearers per chair. George should have had six, but he promised to walk some so he got away with only four too. I can assure you that the trip up the mountain is very interesting and not without danger. The path is not very wide and a misstep on the part of one of the coolies might send one tumbling down hundreds of feet. And it is so steep that one feels almost as if one's feet are where the head should be. I was not really frightened or nervous – I held my breath a couple times and kept my "tongue in the middle." That sounds better in Norsk – "holdt tungen i midten." The trip is wonderful though. Have you ever been up in the clouds? We are living in them and it is rather fun. The day we came it was rather cloudy and we were in brightness part of the time and part of the time in big clouds. Meyers, Mr. & Mrs. Gale – friends of M's Brand and probably Gebhardt – and we are to live in a new house this summer. We will rent it, of course. This place was to be ready by July 1st. When we came we found it anything but ready and had to live with the missionaries of our crowd already here. We were 7 grownups and 5 children! By Saturday the upstairs was finished enough for us to move in, so here we are living in this place and boarding with the others. It is about a five minute walk over there – over a ridge, so we do some climbing three times a day. We expect the rest up during the week. Hope we can "live" here then and not merely room here. Kuling is a very pretty summer resort and is also large. There are supposed to be about 2000 foreigners here during the summer.

Since I was not very well supplied with summer clothes – I mean light ones – I had to have some made. I had a white skirt made and a flowered voile. The voile is rather dark. I wanted something that won't need to be washed all the time and it is often pretty cool here. Today being the Fourth, it is quite warm! I am not going to have any more made this summer, but next spring I must. One needs more light clothes here because of the heat. You have to change oftener. George had a white duck suit and a pair of white serge (with tiny black stripe) trousers made. With the two old light suits he had, he is fairly well supplied. I certainly felt sorry for him the first week we were in Hankow. He had to have the light suits laundered and most of his other clothes had to be sent to the cleaners. One evening there were guests for supper and all the poor man had to wear were his heavy black trousers and his Prince Albert. I wore my white net dress!!

The sun is so bright here that people with sensitive eyes need dark glasses. George bought an ordinary pair, but I couldn't wear such things over my specs so I had to have a pair ground. We look pretty fierce when we come along with our big brown eyes!

Remember how we spent the Fourth last year? Have it in my diary, but don't know what you did. Bale was over for dinner and after dinner George & I went to the Art Museum. We are going down into the valley today to celebrate. Don't know what they will do but they're going to serve <u>free lunch</u>! We'll be there! Just wish we knew what you are doing! I get homesick when we get letters from Madison[66] & Chicago.

We had a Chinese teacher the second (& last) week we were in Hankow and we expect him up here this week. That means business for me. I read a little with him but did not do any studying by myself. It looks like interesting, and hard work. But believe me I am going to learn it. I get so impatient when all these people talk and I can't understand them. And it is rather hard to give orders to a servant in sign language!

'S nuf for today, I'm thinking. By the way, are there any more "For Love" installments. The last one left off at a most interesting point. We do read them! Got any new snaps for us?

Much Love to you all from George & Bernice

(Written in left margin) Better send our letters to Louise & Sarah too. Please!

BERNICE WRITES HER MOTHER.

"Please let your family have their own way in such matters occasionally – it will do you much good I think."
Letter #11

Kuling, China
July 13th, 1921

Dear Mama,

Thanks so much for all the mail! We have it all now, I am sure, every letter up to No. 13 inclusive and Elsa's letter. I just noticed that letter No. 10 written May 26 was postmarked June 2nd at Madison, while your next letter of the 29th went out May 30th. So the delay, or part of it, was right in Madison. I surely enjoy all the letters and I must say you have written most faithfully, mama. I was quite surprised – <u>very pleasantly</u> so – to receive mail from you directed to Kuling, as I didn't know George had given you our address here. He remembered it after the mail began arriving. I hope you are getting our letters quite regularly now. Elsa's letter amused me very much. Is she changing already? She "sounded" different and appears to have acquired more humor. Oh my! I'd like to come and have a cup of coffee and a good talk with you this afternoon. And I'd give

---
[66] Madison, Wisconsin

<u>anything</u> for a taste of your bread. We haven't tasted really good bread since we left the States. We have good bread, and yet it is so different somehow. We have to use such care with vegetables, fruits, water, etc. that something seems to be lost. But it may be my own cooking would change matters though! Meyers really have a very good cook, though. And the cook and the boy are very artistic. I just wish you could see how they fix things sometimes. The butter – when it has become rather soft – is a marvel of little figures of designs. The pies always have some very fancy figures of pie crust on top. And mashed potatoes are always fixed up some way. The boy – waiter & general house boy – decorates the table with ferns and flowers whenever he can get them. Today the cook made two cakes and you should see the fancy frosting. It looks as though it had come from a bakery.

I have not told you about the location of our house, have I? We are not looking out over the prettiest valley, because this valley is not wooded as the others are, but we do see the most wonderful sunset. I have never seen them quite so beautiful – not that I remember, at least. We are very near the top of one of the highest ridges. There are steps leading from the top to our second story rear entrance. There is a sharp descent from our front porch – we look right down into the valley. And to the west we can look still farther down to another valley. Our view of that valley must be much like that from an airplane. Although we had had dry weather the last two weeks, I cannot remember seeing it <u>perfectly</u> clear in the second valley. There are almost always light clouds or mists hanging over it. Today there were beautiful fluffy white clouds down there. When we have taken some pictures, we will send you views from here. We are able to use most of the house now. The bathroom is not ready, but we can manage very well as it is, if necessary.

Today is Rev. Meyer's birthday and we are going to celebrate. Rev. Gihring & Gebhardt are here and early this morning Gihring went down and bought a big bunch of firecrackers. They were shot off in the bunch and we had some noise. The Chinese are great to celebrate weddings, births, etc. by shooting firecrackers. This afternoon at 4:15 we are going to Russian Pool for picnic supper, and those who desire to will swim. Next Saturday – the 16th – is Mrs. Riedel's birthday and of course mine is Sunday. Don't know if we'll celebrate on the 17th though since Mrs. R. is going to treat the bunch Saturday.

We have nice associates here, I think. I mean our mission crowd. At present we are fourteen grownups – including Rev. Brand – and five children. There are Schwartzkopf, Bentrup, Riedel, Meyer, Lillegard & <u>wives</u>. Brand, Arndt, Gihring, and Gebhardt – <u>bachelors</u>. The first three temporarily, Gebhardt indefinitely!! Mrs. Gihring and Marie Brauer intend to sail from Frisco August 6th. You may be sure Gihring and Lenchen are happy.

Conference began Monday morning. The first day they met over at Arndt's. (The other folks are living in Arndt's house.) Since then, however, they have met here. We ladies are all cordially invited to attend, but we have too many things to tend to and cannot be present all day. Lenchen and I have been present the first hour in the morning, since that hour is devoted to doctrinal discussions. I find that very interesting and instructive. I would like to spend more of the forenoon there, but must devote some time to the study of Chinese. This morning I was able to read quite a few characters, but most of the time I didn't know what I was reading. They express themselves in such a simple way that it is difficult! Ha ha!

Since starting this letter we have been out on our picnic. We went out one way and came back another. It really is very, very pretty around here and I only wish you could take these trips with us. However, I do think you're living in such a beautiful place that you have no cause for envy. I still think Madison is one of the finest places I've seen. But, of course, it is a splendid thing to learn a little about the mountains also. They are so <u>grand</u>, so <u>big</u> – there is so much of nature – insurmountable cliffs, woods, and sparkling rivulets. This evening we saw a most remarkable rock. By water erosion it had become like a big sand pile. It was gray in color, with touches of red.

Today I read over your letter describing the kitchen, etc. and got a fair picture of the place in my mind. Your description was very good, but of course I can't quite <u>see</u> the place as I should like to. Hope Ragnar will take some time exposures of the interior some day. And when the lawn is nice we'll be pleased to have some snaps of the place.

I have actually begun making napkins – to go with my lunch cloth, I mean. I am crocheting around the first napkin – am on the last round so it is almost ready. I think they will be very pretty.

Soon we will be able to tell you where we will be located. The conference will be taking up appointments 'ere long. I'll be glad to know where we are to live, at last. We all like Rev. Brand so much and feel more and more that none better could have been chosen as Secretary of the Foreign Mission Board. And it is certainly splendid for all concerned that he could make this trip.

Did George also tell you when to stop sending mail to Kuling? You had better not send any here after the first week in August. After that time you had better send to Hankow until we give further instructions.

Now I must retire. If I think of more to write, I'll add it tomorrow. I will write to some girls in Madison – the Dorcas Society, I think – sometime, but it seems my time has been very well occupied of late. I'm owing so many letters – received from Edward & Netty the other day too. In the meantime, greet all my friends and tell them I have not forgotten them. If we were wealthy, I would be sending hundreds of Oriental things. Really, I enjoy sending gifts and whenever I see something pretty or odd I wish I could buy it and send it to one of you.

Here I go on writing when I should be undressing. By the way, I hope Dad & Elsa have persuaded you to go to Calmar. Please let your family have their own way in such matters occasionally – it will do you much good I think.

Now, Good night Dear Ones.

Our love to you all –
George and Bernice

BERNICE WRITES HER FATHER.
"He had a pile of nice, soft, "goo-ey" mud and now and then he mixed in some dry grass by treading it in with his bare feet! Hope he enjoyed the feeling."

Letter No. 12

Kuling, China
Monday, July 18, 1921

Dear Dad –

Have I written any letter addressed to you? Have "me doubts"! But of course the letters are all meant to be shared.

Not much happens here at Kuling to write about. We have had unusually dry weather the three weeks we have been here, they say. Have had some rain but have been able to keep our clothes, etc. quite dry. It has certainly been most fortunate for us since the mud plaster in the house has had a chance to dry pretty well. They use a regular mud plaster, these Chinese. I don't suppose they do in an "all-foreign" house, but this house is foreign in style and partly Chinese in construction. I saw one mixing some plaster out here one day. He had a pile of nice, soft, "goo-ey" mud and now and then he mixed in some dry grass by treading it in with his bare feet! Hope he enjoyed the feeling. They do their painting quite differently too. They dip a cloth or wad of rags into the paint and roll that back and forth over the surface to be painted. I doubt that it is the most economical method, as they paint the right hand as far as to the wrist in that way. We surely see many things done in a crude way. From a distance I have seen threshing done both by means of the flail and by treading it out, using water buffaloes for the latter. Water buffaloes are the most common domestic animals in this part of the country. They use them for plowing and all such farm works. Do you know what they are like? All I have seen are equipped with large horns and resemble cows, but are of rather heavier build. I also spied a burro going round and round in a hut, evidently grinding some meal or flour for the housewife.

Saturday was Mrs. Riedel's birthday and we were all invited over for supper. We spent the evening playing games. We had a fine time – it reminded one of YPS (Young People Society) meetings.

Sunday I celebrated my 24th birthday. My, but I'm getting old! Gebhardt and Gihring sneaked up in the morning and hung a book on my door – "The Gateway to China." Inside was written, "To the birthday child in the room above from the occupants of the room below." George gave me a book also – "An Irish Woman in China." Riedel's gave me a unique thing. It is a Chinese dressing table made of mahogany and with quite a bit of inlaid wood of a lighter color. It looks just like a box – 6" X 7" X 9" – but when a piece is withdrawn a mirror, which can be made to stand up, and three small drawers appear. Bentrups gave me a small silver bon-bon dish and Schwartzkopfs gave me three dainty handkerchiefs. I was very pleasantly surprised by all these gifts, you may be sure. All I missed was a letter from home, but I imagine there's mail on the way.

We had communion services yesterday forenoon. Rev. Brand conducted that part of the service, George preached the regular sermon. It was a very nice and solemn service. In the evening Arndt preached.

Rev. Brand has been suffering from an infected toe the last four days. There was no visible bruise so the cause of the infection is rather mysterious. We think it is the result of a bad skin that he got on the trip to Shinanfu last month. Whatever it is, the poor man has certainly suffered much. He is feeling better now and the toe improves daily, we are glad to say.

George says I must "re-tire" now for tomorrow's trip! Good night!

Tuesday AM –

We are sending you some pictures cut out of folders that we got as we did our sightseeing. We have seen the ones I have checked off.

How is the LPA getting along? We have received two copies of La Follette's and I have studied some politics too – in that paper.

Now I must do something else.

Can't say I've learned much Chinese yet. I should like to go to the language school in Peking, but don't suppose that's possible, unless we should <u>happen</u> to be stationed there. Ought to be able to tell where we will be placed by the next time I write, unless Conference draws that out too long.

Much Love to all of you and greetings to all friends who may be interested in receiving them.

Your daughter,
Bernice

BERNICE TELLS OF NEW MISSION LOCATION.
"We are going to Shinanfu[67]...It <u>is</u> hard to access and at present there is no medical aid to be had except from a distant city...But if no doctor volunteers to come this year, we have the promise of the Lord that he will not try us beyond our strength."
Letter No. 13

Kuling, China
July 26, 1921, Tuesday

Dear "Muvver,"

Maybe I wasn't glad when your letter No. 14 and Ragnar's arrived yesterday!! Also one from Margaret H. Loberg. We hadn't received any from you folks for a good two weeks and I was beginning to wonder where our mail had been held up, or whether we had given other addresses, or what. And I was feeling quite blue about noon, the more so because we had received a few letters from Chicago last week, so I knew some American mail had gone through. But I was certainly happy when these three letters came, and I must say Ragnar was quite right when he remarked that his letter was devoid of sense! It was! Evidently he was so excited about the trip before him that he couldn't think. However, I was mighty glad to get it.

Before I forget I might as well tell you that Mrs. Land passed away June 17th or 16th. Am not sure of the exact date. Mother L. was with her the last few hours. She was active until the day before she died and then she slept away, being in a coma the last hours. It seems funny to tell you of something that happened in Chicago, but I doubt that you are communicating with the Chicago folks, so you would not be likely to hear of it. I don't suppose you get the Lake View Lutheran any more, do you? There might be items in there of interest to you and if we can remember, we will tell Krey to send you the paper when we write again.

You say Papa wrote to us in Yokohama. Are you sure he <u>did</u> write, or did he <u>intend</u> to do so? We have received all your letters, two from Elsa, and one from Ragnar, but cannot recall receiving any from Dad, nor have I any record of it. So I have thought he didn't find time to write after all. At least, I hope no letter has been lost. You should have quite a few letters by now and I hope they have contained the kind of news you wanted. Needless to say, your letters are most satisfactory and, although I <u>could</u> thoroughly enjoy a letter a day, I think you have been very faithful in writing. I hope you can continue writing at least once a week.

The tall man on the picture of the clock tower is Rev. Berg of Oakland, Cal. He is a friend of George. There is usually too much to write on the front of the snaps and I thought you copied it below the pictures anyway.

Were certainly surprised to hear of Mrs. Bleken's death. You neglected to state what caused it and if it were sudden or not.

Except for those few very hot days that we experienced in Hankow, I believe you people have suffered more from heat than we have. We read that there has been great heat all over – in France, in the States, and other places. Gales came up last Friday and they report the heat in Hankow has been terrible. It was as high as 101 degrees one day, with a minimum of 83 degrees. With the humidity of that city, that is something awful. One never rests because it is too hot to sleep at night. I'm surely glad we did not have to

---

[67] Pronounced "Sih'-nahn-fu;" see map of Hupeh in Chapter 4, page 146

"sleep there" – excuse me from wandering – I meant live there. There are some mosquitoes distracting my attention here. The sun is hot in Kuling too and it is not pleasant to walk out on the hillside during the middle of the day, but it cools off at night so it is seldom uncomfortably warm.

Well, unless more changes are made, I think I can inform you of our future home – at least for the next year or two. We are going to Shinanfu ('Sin ahn FU). It is inland all right. Since I am not posted on the geography of China yet, I cannot locate the place for you very well. But it is about as far – in miles – from Hankow, as from Chicago to St. Louis. So they tell me. But it is a good week's journey – or more, depending on weather and other circumstances. We have to travel up the Yangtsze River, through the famous Gorges and over mountains and through valleys to Shinan. Rev. Brand says the scenery is wonderful. Gihrings, Riedels and Gebhardt started work in this field. Gebhardt is going back this fall, but not the others. Both Mr. & Mrs. Gihring have had dysentery and they do not deem it advisable to go back for a year or so. Riedels would be willing to go back, it seems, but Mr. R. is not extremely well and they have three children who are not perfectly healthy. I should not put it just that way, because they are pretty well all of them, but one is subject to dysentery and the baby has had some queer spells and Brand thinks they should be under medical care. Now don't think that Shinan is to blame for this unhealthy state of affairs. These people would be just as subject to such ills in Hankow. To a great extent, they themselves are to blame, because they are careless and have neglected certain rules of common sense. We cannot live here as we do at home. There are a number of fundamental principles which must be observed in the tropics and those who are too careless or lazy to do so must suffer the consequences of their neglect. Of course, the most careful may become sick, even as people get sick at home, but much can often be avoided.

Bentrups are supposed to go out there also, but will not be there until after Christmas sometime, if then. Mrs. Bentrup expects to be confined in December, which explains that. So I guess there will be only Gebhardt and we two going at first.

Bentrups have not shown a very good mission spirit in regard to this business. I do not want to judge them and of course Mrs. B. may be excused to a certain degree because of her condition, but it is apparent that they came out with a rather vague idea of what mission work really is. It seems they expected to come out for seven years and that they were to return to the States for good. And Mrs. Bentrup, I have been told, does not believe much in inland work. At any rate, they have been quite disappointed with their being sent to Shinan and am afraid have not been so very nice about it. Be that as it may, here are some of my ideas. Rev. Brand thinks the field is a good one and the work should be continued in spite of difficulties, so someone must go. Why should it not be we as well as someone else? Others have worked with equally difficult problems and survived, why not we? It is hard to access and at present there is no medical aid to be had except from a distant city. The question of medical aid is the most serious, but Brand is working hard to get a doctor and had good hopes of one at the time he left. In that case, we may get a doctor this fall or winter and he will come to Shinan at once. But if no doctor volunteers to come this year, we have the promise of the Lord that he will not try us beyond our strength. Only now have I begun to realize what a wonderful promise that is. And I believe I can truthfully say I am quite ready and willing to go out with Gebhardt and George. There will be sacrifices, I suppose, and difficulties, but all in all I think we will be much more happy and contented inland than we could be in Hankow. I had no particular desire to live in Hankow. The big city is quite likely to spoil the missionaries – in fact, I think Hankow – living there rather – is the reason some of these young fellows seem so afraid to go inland. We had really been placed in Hankow first. George was to be principal of the school for evangelists, but no one seemed willing to go inland except Gebhardt – who offered to go back alone, dear fellow that he is – so George's spirit was somewhat roused and he said he'd go.

Here's something that I hope will please you! Yesterday Rev. Brand said he thought he could guarantee that we would get our first furlough in <u>five years</u>. The recommendation of the conference is that we get the first furlough in five years, the others – the succeeding furloughs, every seven years. I think that's fine! It is not entirely definite yet, as the Board at home has to take it up, but Brand is for it heart and soul and they'll have to do quite a bit of over-ruling to prevent it. So it is <u>possible</u> that we may return in 1926. Please make ready!

This letter had better be your "wedding letter," I believe. Many, many happy returns of September 2nd. May God keep you both healthy, strong, and happy for many years to come! I shall be with you in spirit that day and I hope you'll have a splendid Silver Wedding.

I hear George coming – he has had a committee meeting this eve – and I had better get ready for bed. The mosquitoes are humming around me – they don't bite me but they love to tease. They bite George though!

Will add a few words tomorrow!
Good night.

Wednesday A.M.

Good Morning!

There seems to be no news since last night, but I'll write something anyway. I'll beg, I guess. Please, whenever you find any simple patterns, skirts, waists, or dresses – <u>anything</u> in fact – will you send me some? Everything is made out here as that is the only practical thing to do. I will even have George's BVD's made when he needs new ones. There are no tailors who do foreign sewing in Shinan, but there are two sewing machines out there and I'll have to do what I can and have dresses, etc. made here in Kuling during the summers. And if you should ever send a package and have some little spaces to fill in I might tell you that hairpins – wire <u>invisibles</u> – and bone – toilet soap, Pepsodent, and such things are welcome.

That's all I can think of just now. I can't think anyway today. Am rather tired as we got to bed late – we don't keep as late hours up here as we did in Chicago.

I like the sample of Elsa's blue crepe dress so much. I'm sure it is a beauty.

So much "for denne gang."[68]

Lots of love to you all and greetings to all my friends.

George & Bernice

---

[68] "for this time" (Norwegian)

BERNICE REMEMBERS HER COURTSHIP.
"It is two years ago today since George first came to see me…Have the same dress on too…"
No. 14

Kuling, China
July 29th, 1921

Dear Mother,

    Although I have written once this week, I think I'll write a little again tonight. Letters 15 and 17 came today and the two letters from Ragnar that you forwarded. We were so glad to get them all. No. 16 and the gift are evidently still coming – it may be delivered tomorrow. There are queer irregularities sometimes. Today your letters of June 21st and July 3rd were delivered. And you see we received the other letters written June 19 and 20th several days ago and one from Chicago, written June 19th, over a week ago. So you must not worry if our mail comes to you in bunches too. I can hardly understand how my letter of June 1st could reach you by the 18th – I think four weeks from here is pretty good time. Of course, that one came from Japan, but even so 18 days is mighty speedy service. I wrote to Swerigs on June 4th. And I am sure you have George's note by now dispelling your worries regarding the disturbances around Hankow. There was no trouble right in Hankow – it was in Wuchang across the river. China is so unsettled at present that you will undoubtedly receive reports of uprisings now and then, but please do not be alarmed over them. As long as you don't know positively that we <u>are</u> in danger, don't worry. Time enough to do that when you know there is good reason for it. I believe China is as safe as Chicago anyway.

    Saturday AM 7-30-'21 It was too windy and hot to continue writing last night so I went to bed. Well, letter No. 16 came today. Mange tak[69] for the very pretty collar and vest – I'm sure I'll make good use of it. There was no duty – there should not be duty on first class mail. The picture of Kathryn is so nice – doesn't she resemble Ella? The one of Raggie and Elsa is, as you say, not so good. But it is so good to get them, good or bad. And I am so glad you sent the two letters from Ragnar. He seemed to be enjoying himself and I imagine the experience will do him good. The term is six weeks, is it not?

    Now I want to tell you a few things that may be of value to you. In China there is both import and export duty, because the rate of duty is so small – only 5%. There is no export duty in the States, is there? But the import duties over there are scandalous – not only that, but they put their own valuation on articles. And some customs men work a grand graft, according to reports. Some clever people might get by with stuff, but I guess ordinary mortals cannot make it work well. None of our trunks or packages were opened when we came in to China. I'll bet that wouldn't work coming in to the US. Now I <u>think</u> people coming in are allowed to bring $100 or so worth of stuff with them, but am not sure. However, if Rev. Arndt goes this fall, as he is supposed to, and he has room and is willing, etc. etc. we will send the Christmas presents along with him and risk duty charges. He will hardly have much of his own along since his wife and daughter left so lately and took much with them. We would then send all to you and ask you to distribute the things, or we would send one package to Chicago containing the things for George's

---
[69] "many thanks" (Norwegian)

folks and the rest to you. Would that be OK? But more of this later when things are settled.

Dad said exchange was $.53 on the dollar. We do not know just what he meant, but $1.00 gold exchanges for $2.00+ mex. About $2.06 or so. But George made a suggestion which I am not keen on passing on to you, but since it really is sensible I will anyway. He said that if you ever wanted to send me a little money – like you intended for my birthday – it would be better if you would place that amount to our credit there, as we will have subscriptions to pay, etc. every now and then. And then that amount at the current exchange will be given to me here. In that way neither of us will lose on exchange and it will save us sending a small sum to you and vice versa. But, we don't want you to keep crediting our account so that we always have a balance or anything like that, because of this suggestion. It is offered as an economical method of doing things in case you should feel like squandering some cents.

You asked if George found China different than when he was here. Yes, it is somewhat different. Living expenses are much higher for one thing – the war and famines are responsible for that, I suppose. Living in Hankow is very expensive and even the folks in Shinan found it very expensive way inland. Usually it is considerable cheaper to live inland, but there has been famine out in that region and it was very hard to get things. Canned goods is (sic) out of sight here. Of course, as long as one can get fresh vegetables, it is not so bad, but I for one would relish some canned corn or peas once in a great while. One of those small cans of Campbell's soups cost $.50 mex. Or $.25 Amer. money. Imagine! I have been considering having you send a box of those soups & some such stuff via parcel post. It would have to come to the American PO in Shanghai, however, and be forwarded from there. It wouldn't pay to send freight. But I guess we won't bother. Am afraid it wouldn't pay. Canned pineapple costs $.75 & $.90 a can (Mex.). Our salary is $1000 gold per year minimum exchange two to one. If the exchange gets better, we are to reap the advantage of it. Then we are to have house, traveling expenses, some summer allowance, medical allowance, but not dentist allowance – and dentists rob one here. It is not such a great deal under existing conditions, but we will have to be careful and try to live within our income. –It is two years ago today since George first came to see me. Remember how it rained? And he stayed over & we had our boat ride the next night. They have started movies here in Kuling lately and we may celebrate by going. Have the same dress on too – my tan one.

Much Love to you all.
Your loving daughter Bernice

KREY GIVES AN UPDATE ON HIS LOVE LIFE.
"I can't change the heart of a human being."

Lake View Lutheran Church
ROSCOE AND OSGOOD STS.

Rev. Peter C. Krey, Pastor

Chicago, July 7 1921

"Dear Rev. Lillegard and wife,

I suppose you were somewhat shocked when you had read my last epistle to you. Perhaps it was rather inconsiderate of me to burst out with it that way, but I simple[70] was too full of it and had to have an outlet somewhere for those exuberant feelings; and you were the victims. Since I have received no encouragement from the other side, the affair is off for the present at least, whether there will be a wedding some day or not, God only knows and time only will tell. I am composing myself and setting my mind and things on work. I have seen enough. I can do no more. I can't change the heart of a human being. It is up to the Lord to couple us, if he wants us coupled; and if not, I cannot defy Him. I am going to work harder then ever. I have rented the flat out to Mrs. Tallaxon. She will be as much as my housekeeper, that will give me better headquarters, and a bigger change to save; save for what? for a Ford. With one word I am going to work.

But I have now been talking so much about myself that I feel like making an apology, if it were not for the fact that I know you will overlook; besides the above paragraph is about the only real NEWS that I could give you from Lake View, since I suppose that other writers keep you informed about current events here.

Well I wonder how it feels to be in the land of the Chinese; it is no doubt as hot or may be hotter there as in this wonderful city of ours. We have had a long hot spell now; they say the hottest we ever had. But a fine rain to night has cooled the air off a little. With these remarks I'll close this epistle with the wish that I may soon have a letter from you, and the hope that you are well and in fine spirits,

Yours as ever
P. Krey

P.S. Congregation voted last night to support the mission in which you were engaged. I hope to kill the Santal Mission now since Mrs. Lund is dead, and organize a China Mission Society.

P. K."

---

[70] His mistakes in English are left as is; he is Danish.

KREY DISCLOSES THE OBJECT OF HIS AFFECTIONS.
"God speed the day when I may call her mine;…"

"Chicago, Ill., July 27th, 1921

Dear Friends,

Your letter came a little too late for the July issue of the Lake View Lutheran. (I should have said August issue, for the July issue is out long ago.) So if nothing else comes before Sept. I may use it then. Thank you all the same. As you will notice from the enclosed issue, I've published part of a letter written to your mother, to which I hope you will not object.

As to the work here in Lake View, I must say that I can see no reason whatever why this place shouldn't grow. I know, of course, that I cannot make it grow. I can only do one thing and that is, preach the word, and even that I cannot do of myself. I have done very little "pushing" so far, it has been too fearfully hot. As soon as cool weather sets in, I am going to "push" things a little more, especially my school. At the present time I have only eight pupils, but they are regular. The confirmation class I've dropped; don't know what I will do there yet. The Sunday school is very poorly attended, regular pupils being about 20. The services have been what one may call fairly well attended, I suppose, the regular attendance being between 40 and 50, though it sank to 28 on the third of July.

In general I have found the people here to be a very congenial flock, but I must also confess that I am missing among them the ripe, tried, firm, stouch[71] Lutherans that I am used to be surrounded with. The best man I had was in my estimation Rudolph Jargo, and he has left me now for his home in Wisconsin. Of all the rest I know not a single one in whom I could perfectly confide as in a real "Missourian." But then this does not discourage me. I know there will be more "Missourians" by and by, if God grants me grace to stand firm and to stick long enough in this place. But enough about that.

Let us turn to something in which I am and you also just as intensely interested – but perhaps I am all too outspoken about such a sacred thing as love; I should perhaps not have written anything to you about it. But the crush was too overwhelming to keep my mouth shut. But let it be now. I am now trying to collect the scattered pieces of my heart and may be I will succeed in getting it sewed together before long.* For the present I feel much like the boy who is gathering up the pieces of his little wagon which has been run over and crushed by some unforeseen happening. Your advice is the best that could have been given me for the present time. Thank you. So you will now see that I was deadly in earnest when I wrote my first letter.

Let this suffice for this time. Greetings to Bentrup, Gihring and Riedel, if you see them. With best wishes to you and your courageous wife

From

Peter Krey

---

[71] Perhaps he meant "staunch"?

July 30th

*P.S. This is not true. I never will succeed in doing that. I am "gone." Her name is Ella B. Lillegard; God speed the day when I may call her mine;   Peter"

Ella Lillegard, George's sister

GEORGE CONSOLES AND ADVISES KREY.
"…from what I hear from home,…Ella had become already quite attached before you met her,…"

January 3rd, 1922

Dear friend Krey,

Your interesting letter of October 5th has lain unanswered for some time. Just after it came, I started out on a long and somewhat adventurous trip overland to Shihnan, the inland station that our Mission has occupied the last two years. Gebhardt had been there alone since September, and Schwartzkopf and I, who were to join him, were delayed till the first part of November by the work connected with getting our families settled here in Ichang. I have written to the Church papers about events in Shihnan, so I shall not repeat here. Schw. and I had a fine trip over – beautiful weather all the way. We went up through the Gorges into the province of Szechuan and from there over the mountains a five days' journey to Shihnan. We found that there was little opportunity to do work in Shihnan on account of the fighting that had been going on there, so we all decided to return to Ichang for the present. Gebhardt has gone to Hankow to help out with the work there for the present, and Schw. and I will try to get some work started here in Ichang. We have rented a building near one of the city gates on a busy street, and as soon as that is ready, we shall start work there.

As to matters in Lake View – I am glad that you have determined to try to get matters straightened out in the congregation, and I hope sincerely that you will succeed in your efforts to turn the minds of your people away from liberal and worldly deals for their church work. You have a hard task before you, and it will be no disgrace or discredit to you if you should fail, to get every thing the way it should be in a short time. I did not do all that I should have done in Lake View. The main reason I did not try to clean out the Lodges, etc., was that I felt that I would have to stick it out indefinitely in Lake View, if I was to do anything in that line, and that would mean giving up going to the mission field. So that was left to my successor. One difficulty, of course, is the question of Synodical affiliation. It will be hard for some in the congregation to break entirely with the Norw. Luth. Church. The national bonds are so much stronger with any people than the religious.

As to your private affairs – I am glad that you have "regained your poise," as you put it. There can be nothing more disturbing to a man than some "heart trouble" of the kind you have mentioned. Since I have perhaps encouraged you more than I should have done in my earlier letters to you, I should like to say now that from what I hear from home, it appears that Ella had become already quite attached before you met her, so that she is quite immune to attentions from other quarter. Under the circumstances, I should like to give you this advice: Find some other suitable Christian young lady and cultivate her acquaintance. Often a man is as much in love with love or with an ideal as with a particular, concrete female, so that it is not hard for him to transfer his affection from one individual to the other, and that entirely honesty and wisely, without his ideals or his affections receiving any injuries. It may not seem to be true to the man who thinks himself very much in love with one person. But when the transfer has taken place, it seems the most natural thing in the world. After all, men and women are created so that there are any number of suitable combinations that can be made, and the old romantic idea that there is only one that can suit a certain other one is as dangerous as false. Am I philosophising more than necessary or more than you like? I trust you will put the best construction on everything I write and take it as from a good friend. Rest assured that your confidences in this matter have not been and shall not be abused. I can say the same for Ella and my family. As Ella wrote regarding some other love affairs that she has not told me about: "I believe that if I can spare anybody's feelings by keeping quiet, it is the least I can do." The knowledge that such matters remain a secret between the two or three concerned always helps later on, when conditions perhaps change so that some other woman has the place the first had been expected to occupy.

I have not written to The Lutheran lately, thinking that you might make use of parts of my articles to the church papers, recently sent in. Perhaps extracts from this letter would also be suitable. My wife writes good letters at times, which might also be suitable. You might ask my folks if they have any such letters. You see, I am getting busier right along and find less time for letter-writing than I should like to have. So I have to economize as much as possible.

So much for this time. I hope to hear from you again soon, and that the effect that your campaign in Lake View is bearing good fruit in every way. With best greetings to you and the friends in Lake View,

Sincerely yours,

Geo O. Lillegard

GEORGE DESCRIBES A PICNIC.
(Excerpt from Letter #15, written Monday, August 8th, 1921)

Yesterday afternoon we all went to a little temple about a mile away and enjoyed a picnic supper. Near this temple, which marks the spot where one of the Ming emperors in the 14th or 15th centuries lived for a time as a priest, there is a Grotto in the mountain side, in which is built a temple. We had a fine time, and the real picnicky character of our picnic will be evident to you from the circumstance that we were caught in a shower of rain, after we had stood and watched a storm passing over the valley below. Today it has been raining quite steadily. The rain was very welcome, as it has been quite dry the last five-six weeks. There is little thunder and lightning here and no wind with the rain at all these days.

Temple of Heaven in Peking (Beijing);

you may see a replica in Walt Disney World's Epcot Center at the Chinese village.

THE MISSION WILL NOT SEND THEM TO SHIHNAN.
"...we were scheduled for Ichang[72]...they didn't think it fair that I should go out alone." (as the only woman)

Kuling, Aug. 13, 1921
Saturday

Letter No. 16

Dear Folks,

Last night we received papa's letter of July 11th. And Aug. 9th – Tues. – we received Letter No. 18 of July 14th. So you see how mails come – yours of the 14th arrived three days sooner than the one written three days earlier. You are most likely experiencing the same with our letters. It should not <u>always</u> take four weeks for mail to reach you. What mail comes over on one of the Empress boats should make pretty good time. But, perhaps I had better tell you what little I know regarding boats. The only two boats making a speedy trip across the Pacific are the "Empress of Asia" and the "Empress of Russia." They are CP boats and sail from Vancouver. Boats from Seattle & Frisco make the trip in three or four weeks, as compared with 15 days (approx.), the time required by the two before mentioned. 23 to 28 days is what is required as a rule by average boats – that is between the States & Shanghai. Then you must allow for another three or four days trip on the Yangtsze. Now your letter of July 4th made good time – arriving here August 9th. I imagine you are getting mail from us more regularly now. By the way, when you mention the receipt of letters, will you please mention the number of the letter, or the date it was written? Then we also know which ones you have received, you see.

George is writing a sermon tonight. It was not his turn to preach tomorrow, but Riedel is not feeling well, so they asked George to take his place. That was at supper time tonight, so he was not given much time to prepare. It reminds me a little of our Saturday evenings in Chicago.

Mother, in your letter of 7 – 14 you said you did not go to church the Sunday previous on account of summer complaint. You will be surprised to know that I was sick abed the very same day with much the same trouble. I had such a severe attack of diarrhea that we feared dysentery at first. Fortunately it was not that – we had two microscopic examinations made but no "ameba" (?) – the germ of dysentery – were found. We had had some peaches not as ripe as they should be and also some cucumbers and I am sure they caused the trouble. No one else was sick, though. The attack did not last long, but Rev. Brand watched me with eagle eyes every meal for many days! After that until poor, hungry "me" fairly rebelled. I did not mention this at the time because I was afraid it would cause you <u>useless</u> worry. I have been fine ever since. In fact, I need laxatives every now and then. It seems the climate affects people one way or the other. Some become very "loose" and others the opposite. It seems to have affected me the latter way more or less. You mentioned the ear trouble I had coming over. I have been fine ever since we landed in Shanghai. It was almost strange that the ocean trip should affect my ears and head so much. I really cannot say I felt particularly rested after our three weeks on board ship.

---

[72] Ichang is now called Yichang.

My, I'm glad you have electricity now. Although you folks seemed to think it was rather slow in coming, I must say it was done much sooner than I thought it would be. It seemed to me such things are more likely <u>years</u> in getting through than <u>months</u>. Are you going to have an electric stove? That would certainly be fine!

Papa said in his letter that you folks intended to drive to Iowa. I hope you made the trip, but he said you would stay only a week or so. That is too short a time for you to visit your many sisters and brothers and, if you went, I hope you stayed longer than a week. One week in a place like that is just enough to wear one out completely. Ikke sandt?[73]

By the way, I have written very few letters except to you folks, but you may be relieved to know that I <u>have</u> written one to Grace Halvorsen – quite some time ago.

George told you we were scheduled for Ichang. At least, such are the present plans. We are really more satisfied with that. Had we gone to Shinan we would in all likelihood have been there only a year or two. That meant we would not take all our things out there, because of the difficulties of transportation. Everything has to be carried over the mountains by coolies or on burros. So we would have had to leave the piano with someone, repack books, etc., and take only the most necessary things. Had Gihrings been in Ichang, we would probably have let them use some of our things and we would have used some of their things in Shinan. So in that way, it will be much easier and nicer for us. That is looking at it from a rather selfish point of view, of course. But George is better satisfied with it in other respects, because he feels that it is a more permanent place for him. We may not live right in Ichang so many years, but he is quite sure we will be in the territory about that city. It is not the idea of the Mission to do very extensive work in the city of Ichang – one man is probably all they will want there. But that section of the country looks quite good to most of the men. They think there are great possibilities there.

George didn't tell you how the change came about, as I remember. The day before the Conference closed a little more was said about allocation and Bentrups were placed in Hankow. (I told you they did not want to go out in a previous letter.) That meant only Gebhardt and we two would be going to Shinan, and I'd be the only woman going out. I'll admit it was not so terribly easy to swallow that, but I resolved to do my best and be as cheerful as possible. And I didn't want the other missionaries to know how I felt so I tried to keep a courageous "front." But, that evening a number of the boys had a conference of their own over here and I was rather surprised to learn that they were quite indignant over the fact that the "newcomers" in the mission should go inland practically alone. It wasn't so bad for George as he knows the language and is acquainted with the inland, but they didn't think it fair that I should go out alone. So they talked and talked and decided on what to suggest in the way of changes and carried their plans through the following day. The thing now is, how will Mrs. Gihring take it and how will both Mr. G and she stand it? Both have had dysentery very badly. I think she got over it now while home, but Mr. Gihring went to Hankow Thursday to consult the doctor. He was up near Peking this spring and gained a great deal while there, but he has lost again since he came here. If he is not pretty well by the end of September, he will not dare go inland. Then I don't know just what <u>will</u> be done. It may be that we would have to go out for a few months. I should certainly not like to see Mrs. Schwartzkopf go

---

[73] Don't you agree? (Norwegian)

out alone. She is very game to go inland, however, & I should enjoy being with her. She is about my age, but she is such a sensible and capable person. And she is always so composed. Nothing seems to ruffle her – the right type for a place like Shinan. But I'm not worrying about these things. It won't help matters any and then I don't care much where we live temporarily, even tho' I'd love to get settled down for a change.

I wrote a letter to Evelyn Tetlie the other day. The poor girl has had quite a time this summer. She got along nicely after the boy came and was up several days – during which time Agnes left for the States. Then she had to go back to bed and has been there ever since suffering from sprue. Sprue is a diseased condition of the entire alimentary canal.[74] Poor Evelyn has had such a sore mouth that she couldn't talk at all some days. And it takes a long time to become entirely cured – often the only cure is change of climate. I hope she will get over it without having to go home. That would be very hard on the mission just now, having lost Dr. Distad and Rev. Stokke in June and also a Mrs. Nelson. The baby is well, fortunately.

Conditions are worse and worse, politically speaking, aren't they? Have been reading some in La Follette's and it is really appalling to see what Harding is doing and what the "representatives of the people" will do. It will be a terrible thing if a panic is going to be necessary to straighten things out. I imagine a panic would affect us quite a bit too. Let us hope and pray it can be avoided.

I have bought a few dishes this summer. Kiukiang – down at the foot of the mountain – is the city for dishes and there are many peddlers here in Kuling. Some weeks ago Mrs. Meyer and I bargained for 18 cups & saucers & 2 plates. We got them very reasonably. So we have half each – a good tea set. Today I bought one rather small and one large China bowls. I didn't have anything for mixing salads, etc, and for sauce. The two cost me $1.60 – 80 cents gold. You'd have to pay over $2.00 gold & then some for the same quality over there. Nei, nu maa jeg virkelig slutte. Dette blir for langt. Hils alle.[75]

Much love to you all,
Bernice

---

[74] Celiac sprue is gluten intolerance.
[75] No (well), now I must really close (this letter). This is getting too long. Greetings to all. (Norwegian)

BERNICE DESCRIBES THE HUMIDITY.
"The salt is almost always more or less wet."

(Letter #17 is missing)
Letter No. 18

Kuling, China
August 25th, 1921

Dear Dad, Mother, and Elsa,

  Ragnar must not feel slighted because this is not addressed to him, since I have just answered the letter he wrote on my birthday. His came through in a little less time than yours. You will note that your letter of July 14th came here just two weeks earlier than that of the 17th. But oh, I was so glad to get this letter and the one from the Buerger-Lee-Eighmy bunch. Thank you so much for remembering me that way. George said last night that if I was going to get silly when I got letters from home, he thought he'd have to tell you not to write!! We get our mail late in the evening as a rule up here. That is because the boats from Shanghai come in to Kuikiang about 4:00 P.M., then the mail has to be carried up the mountain, and then distributed, so occasionally the mailman comes after we have gone to bed at night. I must write to Netty now too, as we are owing them two letters. But I really have had very few letters from my friends so far – I haven't written many, either! I imagine I'll hear from Alice soon, altho' she has probably been quite busy getting settled.

  I wonder if you have had any rain this month! July was dry up here too, but we have had quite a bit of rain this month. And after the rain and fogs, we watch for a real bright day, hang out all our clothes, take out our bedding, and put out our dresser drawers. We have been very fortunate thus far in not having things get moldy. There has been a little on our shoes and a couple pieces of clothing have had a few spots, but they were brushed out quite easily. I used to think it would be just terrible to have to watch the clothes, sun them, etc. etc. but have not found it half bad. One does not feel the dampness ordinarily, but you can tell it on the salt and sugar. The salt is almost <u>always</u> more or less wet. Haven't seen any salt shakers out here. I'll tell you what is worst – to have straight hair like mine. When I first came to China I simply couldn't do <u>anything</u> with my hair. It felt much as if I had just washed it and it was not dry. I use a curling iron now and that helps a little bit – dries it out in front anyway.

  My, I haven't done any studying for over a week and I'll be so helpless when we get to housekeeping. I know some words, all right, but when it comes to <u>talking</u>, I never know all the words. I know one or two that I need and that's all. I can write a few characters – it is really fun to do that with a Chinese brush. But you have to train your memory – the strokes of the character must be made in their certain order and it is quite an art to write well. I'll send you a sample of my writing some day.

  Mama, you asked if we had "eftermiddags kaffe"[76] out here. Well, we have had coffee two, three times, but we have tea generally. Here in the Orient customs are quite European – British, strictly speaking. Since the British & Americans mingle and the former predominate in numbers, their customs also predominate. I don't like it very well, I must say, but then we can do things our own way when we get settled in our own home. The trouble is, if you mix at all with other people who have their dinner at 7:30 or

---

[76] "Afternoon coffee" (Norwegian)

8:00 PM, for instance, and make their calls between 4:00 and 7:00 P.M. and you have your dinner at 6:00, why someone might come and call while you were eating. Etc. etc. So one has to conform to general customs to a certain extent, unless you are isolated. There is one advantage in serving tea – it is much less work and cheaper! But I prefer coffee!!

Mrs. Gihring and Marie Brauer came yesterday. You can imagine how happy Mr. G. and Magdalene are. Gihring met them in Shanghai. The girls came out on the maiden trip of the Empire State, the boat which was to sail May 14th and the one George and I wanted to sail on. We won't go on a Japanese boat again, if we can help it.

You mention receiving the money we sent from Hankow, but you have never said anything about the first Amer. Exp. (American Express) check for $10 that we sent. Am sure we sent that from Honolulu – maybe from Frisco, but I think from H. I hope it wasn't lost, as $10 "er ikke at forsmaa"[77] – not for missionaries getting $165 Mex. Your letter sent to Yokohama has not been received even yet, Dad. Am so sorry!

Elsa, you said you'd send me something when you saw what I might like. I'm going to mention a few more things that are welcome out here. It is hardest to get the little things out here – needles, buttons of every kind and description, clasps, black & white, hooks & eyes – ditto, embroidery or beading transfer patterns, "og saadanne ting."[78] They could be put in letters now and then. There are some things we would like to have you buy for us especially if you should find bargains. One thing is stockings. We are not in need of any just now and I believe we are pretty well fixed for the winter, except that I could probably use some good mercerized (?) black ones. I wear 9 or 9 ½ and George wears size 11 or 11 ½. Now when you buy things that we ask you to buy, please keep record of it and if we have any money there, good & well, draw on that. If not, let us know so we can send some. I'll not worry about little things like needles, etc. because I can send you trimmings, or such things that you may use or like to have. Many pretty things – bags for instance – can be made out of the Chinese embroideries taken from Mandarin coats. These peddlers come around with strips from old coats and the older they are the more valuable they are and the finer the embroidery. Some of them need to be cleaned in gasoline, which we will leave to whoever gets such pieces, as gasoline is quite a luxury here.

Friday 8-26-21

Mrs. Gale, who has been with us most of the summer (I think I told you about Gales – they are business people), thought I ought to make over my old blue serge suit skirt. I have been wearing it as a "rainy-day-skirt." She is a very ingenious person naturally and I guess people develop some ingenuity in this country too. But she does know how to sew – can make suits and all kinds of garments. So I have ripped up my skirt and washed it. Her plan is to turn the skirt, cut off some from the bottom – I mean make less flare, it is gored quite a bit – and put that at the top, raise the whole skirt and make plaits on the sides. If it is made right, I think it will be quite nice.

I am so sorry, Elsa, that I didn't write you a special birthday letter some time ago. I didn't think of it soon enough and this will be quite late. But I'll think of you. I should like to have sent you a birthday present, but I guess the fan and little box will have to be

---

[77] "is not to be belittled/despised" or "is not to be sneezed at" (colloquial) (Norwegian)
[78] "and things like this" (Norwegian)

your birthday presents. Hope the things I sent with Agnes Arndt have reached you by this time.

We have a cook and a Boy now. The cook is experienced and said to be very good. George wants a <u>good</u> cook at least until I can speak Chinese fairly well. If I want to train in a new cook after that, good and well. The boy looks like a nice fellow. He has been Boy for a year, but doesn't know how to wash clothes, although he is willing to learn. I am really glad of that as he will learn to do it my way then. I can't tell you how glad I am that I have washboard, wringer, and boiler with me. It is true, one <u>can</u> buy all such things out here, but <u>they cost so much</u>.

Is there a pretty good beach in Monona Lake over your way? Wouldn't mind joining your swimming party some night. Now this is a pretty long letter – I spend so much time writing letters to our folks that my friends are neglected! It is most fun to write to one's own folks.

Much Love to each one of you – Mother, Dad, Raggie & Elsa. Haven't you some snaps for us?

George & Bernice.

Greet my friends.

(Written in margin: Cannot give another address yet. Send to Hankow.)

BERNICE FINDS OUT ABOUT THEIR NEW ICHANG[79] HOME.
"It is a foreign-style house, owned by Chinese Chamber of Commerce,…"

Hankow, China
September 6th, 1921

Dear Sarah,

Congratulations on the arrival of "Sonny"! We were so glad to hear of it and of course are happy it is a boy this time, as I am sure all of you are. Mother only told us he had arrived, however, and we are waiting to hear how big he is, what his name is, and such details. Also how you yourself are feeling.

When I wrote to Mother "L" a week ago I didn't know how soon we would be coming down to Hankow. George left Kuling a week ago yesterday (Mon.) and Meyers and I left two days later. When we came to Hankow I found that George had already left for Ichang. He is up there trying to find a place for us to live in. I hear houses are very scarce and hard to get so I'm anxious to hear what luck he has. Expect him back in a few days, if the disturbances up that way do not keep him longer. There seems to be some looting going on up there and it may be he won't be able to get away while that lasts. I do not think he is in any physical danger though. The Chinese have certainly been having a fine time by themselves this summer. I don't know what all the fighting is about – doubt that they themselves are quite clear on that point! Everyone seems to think they'll cool off now and be quiet until next summer perhaps. Great life! Sometimes the foreigners are in danger and then it is not so pleasant, but, understand, these attacks are not directed at foreigners. Now I hope this is not worrying you. <u>We</u> are not worried! In fact, we feel quite as safe as you people in the States do.

This week I must try to get a few things sewed. I haven't made a good start by any means because it has been rather warm – quite a bit warmer than up in the mountain. And heat always makes me sort of pepless. Today it is beautiful and as soon as there is some hot water I'm going to wash out a few pieces that I didn't want to send to the laundry. This afternoon I may try to sew some on a serge skirt I am making over. The trouble is, I'm such a poor stick at sewing. I really don't know anything about it, but maybe I'll learn a little by and by…

(The remainder of the letter is missing.)

The following excerpt is from a page of notes made by Bernice, dated September 7th, 1921. It is a quote by George:

"It's an ill wind that blows nobody good. The excitement in Ichang helped me to secure a house at a good figure. It is a foreign-style house, owned by Chinese Chamber of Commerce, and they were glad to get me in there so that soldiers would not be appropriating it and paying them no rent. The rent is 25.00 gold – 7 rooms, 6 smaller rooms in the servant and kitchen quarters. Nice yard – walled (8 ft.) – palms and other trees – Foreigners –"

---

[79] Ichang is now called Yichang; it is on the Yangtze River.

GEORGE TRAVELS AND BERNICE WAITS TO GET SETTLED.
"I was glad when George came back, even though he assures me he was in no particular danger."

Letter No. 22
(Written in left margin: I've caught up with you now, only your numbers started in April, mine in May.)

Hankow, China, September 15, 1921

Dear Mumsie,

    Here comes my "weekly," although there isn't much news. I can always find something to write home though. Am glad George wrote to papa on his return from Ichang, as he could write intelligibly on the conditions up there and I can't. I was glad when George came back, even though he assures me he was in no particular danger. Hope they quit squabbling up there soon, because I can hardly wait to get settled down. The house he has rented is large, but I guess that is about the best that can be said for it. The walls, woodwork, & floors are not nice, George says, but we may be able to fix it quite nice with a few quarts of paint. And we are going to get along with just as little furniture as possible until we can add good pieces gradually. I am so sorry we didn't bring our dandy brass bed with us. Beds are sky-high out here. I tell George we had better use a Chinese bed for the present. We slept on one all summer and that's what I have now. They are just a frame with cane, straw or wicker – no not wicker – I don't know what you call it – reinforced with ropes in under (drawing). This stands on "horses." I think I could sleep on most anything after this summer, because we certainly haven't been pampered with soft beds. Once in awhile we have enjoyed that luxury. If we did start out with a Chinese bed, we could put our mattress on top of it. We brought our own along, you maybe know.

    Well, George came back Saturday A.M. and left again Tuesday forenoon – for Kwangchow this time. He left here at 11:00 A.M. by train and arrived in Sinyang at 7:00 P.M. where he spent the night. Then he had a long trip overland. He had hoped to make it in two days, but a card from him today reported that the roads were bad on account of rain and he expected to spend three days on the road.

    Previously we had planned that I should meet him in Sinyang when he came back…We were to visit at Blys and then go on together to Kikungsan, where we would visit Tetlies. I had decided to give up the trip, because I felt we couldn't afford even a small extra expense now, but today I received a letter from Evelyn and she says she is so anxious to have me come up that I wrote & told her I would come next Monday. I won't go to Sinyang, however. Evelyn says she has been feeling much better the last few days and feels much encouraged. She has certainly had a hard summer though, has been up only a few hours a day and for weeks she wasn't up at all. Have I told you what sprue[80] is? If not, it is a diseased condition of the entire alimentary canal. Evelyn's mouth was so sore some days that she couldn't talk. I hope she is really improving now. I have heard so much good about her that I am anxious to meet her, as well as Mr. Tetlie and Bunnie & Baby Norman. And then it will be so nice to know someone who really belongs to the family here in this foreign country. (Written in margin: Evelyn is my

---
[80] Celiac sprue is intolerance to gluten found in wheat and other grains.

cousin's daughter. Lava [Anna Olava, Bernice's mother]) O saa skal det blive rigtig godt at komme iblandt Norske folk igjen. Vi trives nok med Tyskerne, men vi er nok ikke et folk alligevel.[81]

Are you pretty well fixed in your new home now? You've not mentioned the bathroom and I've been wondering if it can be used. I don't suppose you have water. Will you have a pressure pump put in this fall? I am <u>so glad</u> for all you that you have the place. I think it would look quite like a palace to me now. The homes I've been in so far out here certainly are not convenient. Gales have a fine flat, for instance, but it is a place where one has to run a lot of steps. It is called a <u>flat</u>, but they have rooms on three floors. Imagine! And that is one of the quite expensive places too.

In many ways I dread starting in housekeeping. I know that all my wonderful kitchen utensils and most everything won't be very "lovely" for long. The servants are awfully hard on everything – and yet servants are a necessity here, since we do not have the public servants that you have. And, of course, men cannot understand why we women feel that way about things. George asks, "What's the use of having things if they're so nice you can't use them?" But now I'm crossing the bridge too soon again. Have already discharged the Boy we had hired. He wanted higher wages and did not want to do washing & ironing, and was, all in all, quite independent, so I'm glad to be rid of him. Like as not there will be plenty of boys in Ichang who will be glad of a place to work now after all this trouble up there.

Monday evening Arndt left for Shanghai on his way to the States. We sent our Christmas presents with him and everything will be coming to you for distribution. I take advantage of you, don't I, Mine Mother? You see, you've always done so much for me and now I make more and more demands. Well, I couldn't put any tags on the things because of the custom inspection, but I have a list and description of the articles and I'll send that to you together with instructions and think you'll have no trouble. Maybe you will feel somewhat repaid for your trouble since you'll see a lot of Chinese things. Please do not open the packages so anyone else sees you. The kids & Dad can see the things to be sent away when you've sorted them out, if they want to, but please keep their presents until Christmas Eve. The only perplexing thing is – how are you going to open & sort things without seeing your own? Maybe you will recognize them without having to look at them carefully, so they can be inspected anyway Christmas time. Your birthday present is there too – one for Christmas, one for Jan. 20th, but I guess you'll have to open them both at one time. Will write regarding postage, etc. later on. There ought not be much duty, if Arndt knows his business, but he's so forgetful that I worry a little about the stuff. I'll make out the list one of these days and send in a later letter. I imagine it will reach you before the packages by a good deal anyway, but I wanted to give you fair warning now.

Much Love to Youse all,
Bernice

…As far as I know, I haven't used a telephone since we left Chicago! Believe such a thing would scare me now.

---

[81] And so shall it be very good to come among Norwegian people again. Of course we get along with the Germans, but to be sure we are still not one people. (Norwegian)

Chapter 6
Expecting a Lillegard

BERNICE IS EXPECTING, FOR THE SECOND TIME.
"I have been feeling ever and ever so much better all along than I did a year ago…I have great hopes that everything is all right this time."[82]
<u>Letter No. 23</u>

8 Milan Terrace
Hankow, China
September 26, 1921

Dear Mother,

    My letter is late this time, but I see there were five letters written between Sept. 2-15, so you must have received quite a bunch at about the same time. Your letters No. 23 and 24 came last Saturday – the 17th, I mean. I was glad to hear that you did finally go to Calmar and I'm sure you enjoyed your visit, not to mention the pleasure it must have given all your relatives and friends. Did you know that Agnes Kittilsby arrived in Northfield the 19th of August – the day you went to Calmar?

    You asked a couple questions that give me quite a bit to write about. I tho't I had told you about the water, etc., altho' I knew about that before we came out here, so I probably neglected saying anything. Our great care in use of water and vegetables is due to the farming methods and general unsanitary living habits of the Chinese. (What I'm going to write now doesn't sound refined or nice, but you might as well know the truth about such things out here!) As you may have heard, China is a man's country. Women are disregarded – if they see things they shouldn't, it is their own fault, according to the men. They should keep out of the way – "if you don't like it, keep your distance" is the idea. In both Japan & China the ideas of modesty are quite perverted. The dress is modest, but the habits!! Especially those of the men. It doesn't bother them if there is no toilet near at hand – they wouldn't take the trouble of hunting for such a place. The middle of the street or any public place will do just as well. The fact that there are women and others around is of no concern. So we are often forced to witness men standing around tending to their private business in public. We do not see women doing such things, but they nurse their children any place & every place. And they nurse them until they are two and three years old, so they say they often see them nursing two and preparing for the arrival of a third. Easy to get wet-nurses here, I should judge! It is really funny to see them sit down on a box and have a little fellow <u>standing</u> and getting a meal from his mother. But I'm getting away from the subject. I must tell about the fertilizer the Chinese use. In most homes in the cities – I refer to the average home such as a missionary has, not the elegant, modern flats – the bathroom is equipped with a "box." In this box is a pail or jar and this is the kind of toilet we have. Every morning one of the city scavengers comes and empties this & cleans the pail. Now the farmers come in and get this refuse and use it on their gardens as fertilizer. They have wonderful looking gardens, but they do not smell so wonderfully good! You can tell when you are nearing a Chinese garden some time before you can see it.

---

[82] I didn't find any letters of Bernice before 1921 to fill in the details of her premature delivery during their first year of marriage.

You can understand, therefore, that the water is never quite safe in this country and we prefer to boil even the spring water in the mountains than run any risks. And for the same reasons, we eat almost no raw vegetables – they must be thoroughly cleaned and boiled. We do eat tomatoes, because the boiling water poured over them to peel them sterilizes them pretty well. We eat raw fruits, but they should first be washed, preferably in a disinfectant solution, and they must always be peeled, if one wants to be perfectly safe. Do you realize what freedom you have in the States now? You can eat raw onions without inquiring whether they're from your own or someone else's garden, you can go into the orchard and relish an apple right from the tree, or eat fruit on the way home from the fruit store. Still, I do think the American people would profit by a little more precaution and I understand perfectly well now why George would ask so often – "Has this been washed?" "Is this clean?" etc., etc. One gets that way after living here awhile. You ask what we eat. We have a lot of vegetables here and if one learns to use the Chinese vegetables, there is a great variety that can be served. The other day we had some bamboo sprouts and they were fine. And we have had a lot of eggplant this summer, prepared in half a dozen different ways. I am a good Chinaman, George says. We had a Chinese dinner a couple weeks ago and it was delicious. I managed the chop sticks just fine too. A Chinese banquet is probably the most elaborate affair thinkable – at a big affair they have 30-60 courses, or more, George says. That's not fooling either! They have innumerable fish and meat dishes. I've tasted four new fruits and am fond of them all. There are the loquats, a small fruit resembling peaches somewhat. They were in season when we came in June. They are very good. And now there are pomelo, "Yang-tao," and persimmons. The pomelos are a trifle like grapefruit, but sweeter, and the skin is different. Each section has a tough white skin around it. "Yang-tao" is a Chinese fruit and is delicious. Have had only one each of the raw fruit and it has a banana and gooseberry flavor combined. The canned fruit is so much like gooseberries, that I cannot detect the difference. I think the raw fruit has more banana taste tho.' Persimmons are a large (& small!) yellow or red fruit that look very much like tomatoes, but they are so luscious. So fruits can be had here, but they are quite expensive. It is a good thing we are able to eat a few raw things. All this boiled stuff can hardly be the very best for one's stomach. We can get fresh milk here in Hankow and at Kuling, but of course, the milk has to be sterilized too. So if we have a mania for sterilizing and washing things when we come home, don't feel insulted, but recall that we have to use extreme measures here. There are people who are rather careless – Riedels for instance – but you may be sure they suffer for it. In the spring, summer, and fall it is never safe to save meat and vegetables until the next day – prepare what we need for one day and eat it. Some people follow that rule the year round. We eat mostly beef – at least during the summer. I have had pork chops once, I think. But we have had bacon and ham. Beef is the stand-by, however, and we prepare it in every possible way. The pigs are such scavengers here that the pork isn't very good. I hope we can have some this winter. And I guess mutton & veal are available – we had veal here the other night.

  As to what housework I do, I can tell better when I get into my own home how much I will do. The cook is supposed to do all the cooking and the "Boy" is to set the table, serve the meals, clean & dust daily, make beds, etc. etc. There are so many things to do here because of the lack of the most ordinary conveniences at home and because of all the precautions, etc. that one could hardly do one's own housework alone. Besides the language study and mission work we women should do and the rearing of families, there are countless little things one does not want the servants to do and I guess one could keep busy the whole day just supervising the servants. One has to keep an eagle eye on everything.

Now then, for some news. Last Monday I went to Kikungsan to visit Tetlies. I was as far as I know, the only foreigner on the train, but the Chinese in the compartment with me were very nice and friendly. They even offered me dinner – it smelt good and believe I could have eaten it and enjoyed it had I not carried my own lunch. I was the only one going up the mountain too, but I managed very nicely. I had a fine visit and enjoyed it so very much. Both Evelyn and Joe are most likeable people and Sister Bergitta, who is taking care of Evelyn, is also a pleasant and good hearted girl. Bunny is three years old and a fine little girl. She is a bright youngster too. Little Richard Norman is positively the best baby I've ever known, a blessing for his sick mother, you can be sure. I was there from Monday evening until Friday morning and in all that time he never really cried. As Joe said, he would expostulate and complain and try to explain that he needed attention at times. He is a healthy looking fellow too, even tho' he must of necessity be raised on a bottle. Evelyn is not well by any means. She is up a few hours every day, but there is no steady improvement. Some days she feels quite well and other days she feels quite badly. Last week it was decided they should go to Shanghai where a Dr. Blumenstock practices and seems to have had excellent results with sprue patients. That was the plan Friday and yesterday I received a note from her saying Dr. Skinsness, who doctored her all summer, had telegraphed and said they should go on home and not stop in Shanghai. So it is quite possible they will sail for the States this fall. I am anxious to hear definitely what they will do.

George came to Kikung Thursday noon. He had a bad trip to Kwangchow because of the wet roads. It took him 3 ½ days to travel from Sinyang to Kwangchow, a distance of about 80 miles. So he spent three nights on the road, two of them in Chinese inns. He made the same distance in two days coming back. Poor boy! He was certainly all tuckered out and badly bitten up. He looked quite worn and thin – he walked a good deal on the trip over – and he's not felt rested until today.

By the way, did George write that you should send letters to Ichang? Please send them to Hankow as before. We may be here indefinitely and it will be an easy matter and little delay to have mail forwarded to Ichang, should we be able to go up quite soon. They are still fighting up there and it is useless to go up until it becomes more quiet. I don't want George to go up until he can take me with him. I get too lonesome when he leaves me here.

Received the patterns last night. Mange tak![83] I like the dress pattern – it is Elsa's, isn't it? But, I do not expect to get a new dress this fall, so I'll have a summer dress made that way next spring.

Would you like to do some shopping for me? I am asking favors in every letter, but I really think you'll enjoy this one. I know I should like to do it myself, but cannot very well. First I must tell you a "big secret"…we are expecting a Lillegard in March, if all goes well. I haven't told you before because I did not want to worry you, especially since our place of abode was so indefinite. I have been feeling ever and ever so much better all along than I did a year ago. Have had more sleep and regular hours and have

---

[83] Many thanks! (Norwegian)

had practically nothing I had to do, so I could take it easy when I didn't feel well. Haven't had any of those real weak spells and suffered less from nausea, altho' I have, of course, sacrificed not so few meals. Seem to be over that now, however, as I've had an enormous appetite and kept all meals the last three weeks. I have great hopes that everything is all right this time. Have developed quite a bit and believe it is not so much fat as proper development. At least, I certainly hope so. We are expecting Dr. Doederlein here in a week or two and then I will have him give me a thorough examination. Dr. D. is a specialist in women's diseases and a surgeon of repute in Chicago, so I can trust him fully. (You have, I take for granted, read that he is going out to India for two years to start the medical work. Do you keep the "Lutheran Witness"? I wish very much that you would, as you will find more news of our work as well as articles by "us missionaries" in that paper. So I would urge you to subscribe. Moreover, it is one of the best church papers to be had.) I have had a little discomfort "down stairs" right along, but have not been alarmed over it. Have had pains now and then, but I think I know the reason. Do you remember that I went to a doctor in Oakland the day before we sailed? I had such painful urination at that time and she tho't it might be caused by asparagus – it is such a kidney irritant. She also found that my uterus was way down and somewhat back. Of course she couldn't do much for me, but she put a tampon in that day and showed me the correct knee-chest position. I do not know when the trouble was brought on – it may have been more or less gradual, but I am quite sure I hurt myself climbing mountains in Colorado Springs. I haven't been worried about it, but I imagine that is what has caused the pains I've had and I have been most awfully bothered with constipation all summer. I have discovered that taking the knee-chest position at night often helps to relieve that, and I've used mild cathartics[84] pretty much.

    Now for the shopping favor. Will you buy little things for me – the things that have to be bought? They can be bought here, but everyone tells me they are so expensive that it pays to have them sent from home, and frequently there is not duty here on parcel post packages. Mrs. S. says value to $12.00 goes through duty free. Papa will probably know about the postal regulations. Now, as George wrote, his "preste kjole"[85] has been sold by Ylvisaker for $35.00 and we have asked him to send that money to you folks. As soon as you get that, there should be enough money to take care of this shopping and then some. I'd like to have shirts, stockings and other little things that I should have. I believe it would be wise to have you send the soap and talcum powder, etc. too, as soap, for instance, is sky high here. I'll get flannel here. Emma ordered a bolt yesterday – 46 yds, and we will divide that. But I would like some yards of birdseye for the first "ones," some nice nainsook – or whatever you say – for the little dresses, a little challie or batiste (?) for a couple nightingales and the sweet nightingale patterns you have. And I might add – some good safety pins. As I have written before, many such little things, pins, toilet articles, thread, etc. etc. are so expensive here, while silks, embroideries, and other fancy work are cheap. The latter are made here and the former imported, which accounts for such a state of affairs. And then I wonder if you could secure the book, "The Healthy Baby" by Dennett for me. The Macmillan Co. publish it. Mrs. Klein, a good doctor here, suggested that I get it. She says it is a helpful book. I have asked Alice to send me a set of patterns. She was the only one I wrote to about this during the summer and I turned to

---

[84] Laxatives
[85] "Pastor's gown" (Norwegian)

her because I didn't want to tell any of our folks until I was far enough along to see if things weren't better. And then I didn't know but what we might have to go out to Shinan where there is no doctor, so I kept it quiet as far as the U.S. was concerned. Had we gone to Shinan, we would of course have returned to Ichang or Hankow in January or February. There is a foreign doctor and hospital in Ichang. I would rather like to have you send these things as soon as you can, if you will please. Later there is the Christmas rush and after Christmas would be rather late. Oh yes! I've been thinking I'd like some eiderdown – either for a square blanket or for one of these hood & blanket combination things. I may not need the latter very much, as it would be April anyway before the little one can go out "visiting" and then it will be quite warm here. By a year from now one could hardly use that, so maybe a blanket will do as well – bound with blue ribbon. I always like the other things, but they would take more material and I must economize. When you buy things for us, will you please keep an itemized account and send that to us so we can know how we stand with you? Because we want to keep our own accounts straight here and we want to be sure there is enough money there to pay for things. How much commission do you charge? I'll send you some handmade laces when I can pick up something nice…

Well, this is quite lengthy & George and I are going out to an auction inspection now. Haven't the list of presents ready to send yet, but it will be coming soon. Hope you will enjoy your "duties" as prospective grandmother & not find it too much trouble. I'd love to do that shopping myself!

Much Love to you all from
George and Bernice

Chinese banquet

GEORGE PREPARES THE HOUSE IN ICHANG.[86]
"...we make this our family headquarters. I shall have to be away most of the time, in Shinan[87]...for a month or more at a time."

Ichang, Hupeh,
Oct. 12th, '21

My dear mother,

Your letter of Sept. 9th reached me yesterday, forwarded in a letter from Bernice at Hankow. So your mail has been coming even more irregularly than ours. Five weeks is pretty bad though. I am sure two weeks is the longest time that we have waited with writing you, so the other three weeks are due to poor mail service across the Pacific.

I have been in Ichang since last Wednesday. I came alone, partly because I wanted to make sure that it would be safe to bring Bernice along, partly because I needed to get some work done on the house here before trying to move all our goods over; and the fewer there are under such "roughing it" conditions, the better. I have had several carpenters and masons, repairing the house and whitewashing the walls. Tomorrow the painters are coming. And by the end of the week it ought to be possible to use most of the house.

It will be a pretty respectable place, I think, when it once gets fixed up. I shall send you some pictures, as soon as I get the ones I have taken printed. Ichang is a port city, that is, a city that has been open to foreign businessmen for 50 years, and that is a commercial center, about 400 miles northwest of Hankow, on the Yangtse river, in the same province as Hankow. I am about 400 miles due west of Kwangchow. This is a beautiful city, I think, that is the surrounding country is very picturesque. Sunday afternoon I went out to some temples in the hills back of the city, and got some really wonderful views of the river and the mountains beyond them.

I have told you about my trip to Kwangchow. I did not see any of the former Synod people as they are all home on furlough. But of course I saw a number of other people that I knew in earlier years. I met the Masons on their way back from England.

Our goods has been standing in storage all this time in Hankow. It should be coming this week, though, about the time the house is ready for it. We haven't had a look at the inside of the boxes, but so far as we can tell from the outside everything is allright. A couple of the dishes we had with us in our trunks were broken, however, and some others chipped...

I hope you have succeeded in renting the house in Bode by this time. Valborg wrote that several people were inquiring about it. I think it would be a good thing for Olga to stay in the country this year. It is too bad she is not in position to help you people a little with your expenses. How is Anna getting along in her home? Everybody happy? We have not heard from her for awhile now.

Has Bernice written you yet, I wonder, that we are preparing for a little Chinaman around the first of March? Bernice has been much better this year than last year, and has also been quite contented and happy, so that we hope everything will be allright this time. There is a Scotch doctor here, and a room in their hospital for the use of foreigners, so

---

[86] Pronounced "Ee'-chang;" today is spelled Yichang
[87] Pronounced "Sih'-nahn," spelled correctly, Shihnan or Shihnanfu; today is Enshih.

she will be taken care of allright. One reason we decided to stay here in Ichang was that she might have medical attention.

Rev. Gihring, one of the men who was to go to Shinan, is so sick now of dysentery that he will be unable to go. Since they need more help there, we shall not open any work here in Ichang yet for awhile, even though we make this our family headquarters. I shall have to be away most of the time in Shinan and the country between Shinan and here, for a month or more at a time. Of course, we don't like that, but we have to make some sacrifices for the sake of the work. We have good servants, that can manage the housework pretty well, so Bernice will be allright alone here. Mrs. Schwartzkopf will live here too, in the west half of the house, so she will have company. Then we are going to try to arrange so that Schwartzkopf and I will not both be away at the same time.

The Szechuanese soldiers have now retreated about 20-30 miles, so that everything is quiet in the city. But the Northern soldiers make themselves a general nuisance about the place. Everything is so expensive here now too, on account of them. The latest report is that the Northerners were defeated in their last battle, so that we may have the Szechuanese coming down this way again. However there are a number of foreign gunboats here, so that foreigners should be pretty safe. The steamers have been unable to go up the river beyond Ichang these last weeks, because the Szechuanese fire on them. As long as that state of affairs continues, I shall be unable to go to Shinan. But perhaps by the time I get ready to go, things will be quiet again also up river.

These days that the men are working on the house I am living most of the time in a little room (the storeroom) that the servants will use later. I shall make a plan of our place on the opposite page. Apart from the fact that the woodwork is poor, and in general the interior is very rough, the house is good. This plan is exact, except that the partition downstairs has been taken down, making one large parlor and sitting room. Upstairs we will have four bedrooms, two for the use of guests and our missionaries on the way to Shinan. At present I shall have my study upstairs, and our parlor will have to be in what I have marked "study."

Schwartzkopfs will occupy the west half of the house this year, and make use of one of the rooms in the rear for kitchen. It is going to be rather crowded for two families, but we can get along, I am sure. The hall is much bigger than it needs to be. Perhaps we can make use of that some way, by building closets in it upstairs. There are downstairs.

Now it is getting to be bedtime, although it is only 9 P.M. Can you believe it? I have been waking up so early these mornings, and so have gone to bed early. For one thing there are soldiers right next door, and they begin tooting their horns about 4:30 A.M. I have been up most of the time since leaving Kuling between 5:30 and 6:30 A.M.

So much for this time. Please write often, mother. It is good to get your letters, and now I suppose that the girls are so busy with their "fellows" that they don't find time to think of us very often, and so you must write.

With much love to you and the girls,

Your Son,
George

Map of House in Ichang at 37, Wen Gi Lu (by George)

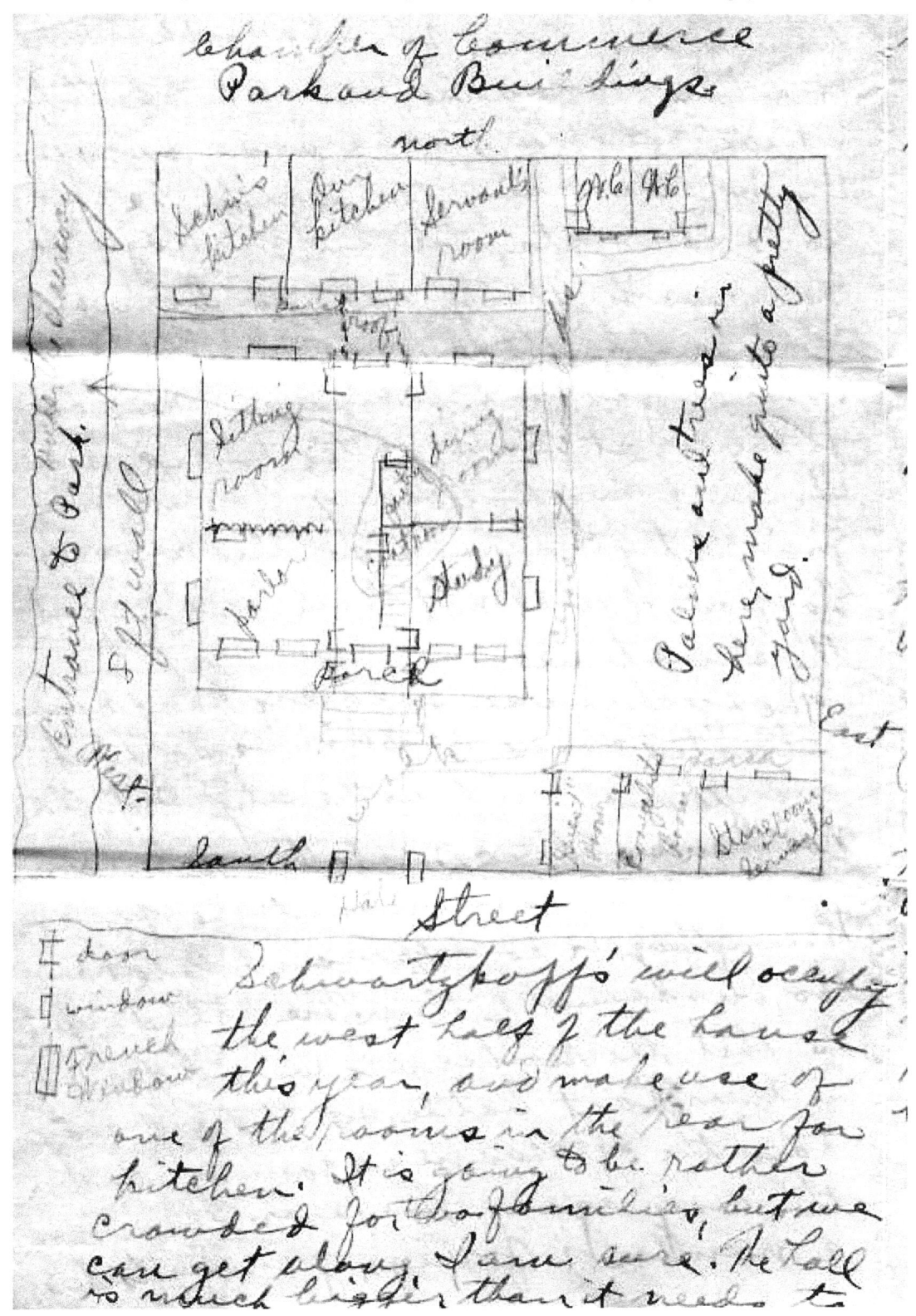

BERNICE'S MOVE TO ICHANG
"I would as soon make the trip alone…I had been so lonesome that I couldn't wait to get off."

Letter No. 25

S.S. "Tung Wo"
Thurs. Oct. 13th 1921.

Dear Dad,

Am sorry that this letter will not reach you quite in time to wish you a very happy birthday and many happy returns of November 7th. I wonder if you will have an oyster supper! I'd like to join you!

As you see by the stationery I am using, I am on the river steamer "Tung Wo" bound for Ichang. Am making the trip alone too, if you please! Received a wire from George a week ago saying "Bring family," which indicated that it was safe for Schwartzkopf and us ladies to come up. And a couple days later I had a letter in which he suggested, more or less directly, that I come up on the first steamer <u>if I wanted to.</u> There were a certain number of things that I had to attend to before I could get away, but I found out that the first British steamer going up was Tuesday eve. Well, Schwartzkopf was to have auction on his household furniture Wednesday and he tho't he could manage to get away Wednesday evening if his stuff went fairly high. So they tho't I might as well wait one more day and come with them. I let it go at that, but Monday evening I just made up my mind I'd go Tuesday anyway. I would as soon make the trip alone and it didn't make any difference to S—s whether I went with them or not. Besides, if they couldn't get away Wednesday, I'd be one day to the good. One day meant 24 long hours to me, because in spite of keeping busy all day long, I had been so lonesome that I couldn't wait to get off. I packed until late Monday evening and all Tuesday I "flrög rundt som en forvilda veggelus"[88] securing passage, ordering a few groceries, hunting for half a dozen dining room chairs, and doing a number of other things. For the first time since I was married I had to tend to a certain number of business affairs myself. I have depended on George so entirely that I didn't have a great deal of confidence in myself when I started. To my surprise I discovered I wasn't so helpless after all. Of course, I had to have someone get coolies to take my baggage down and take care of things at the boat. A woman cannot bargain with coolies very successfully – they take advantage of her. Mr. Bentrup took care of that for me.

George wrote that furniture was very expensive in Ichang and that most foreigners brought theirs along from Hankow. Fortunately, George and I had ordered quite a bit of wicker – we have a little rocker and small table for our bedroom, a table – also quite small – 25" dia. – settee, and four chairs for our parlor, besides a steamer chair and clothes hamper. All those pieces cost us a little more than $35 Mex. And Tuesday I went out for dining room chairs. Must have gone to about eight furniture stores before I finally found something I tho't would do both as to style and price. Got half a dozen oak (Japanese oak, I believe – not as fine as oak at home) with good cane seats for $20. That

---
[88] "flew around like a bewildered bedbug" (Norwegian)

is enough, but it could be worse. It <u>sure do</u> take lots of money to fit a house even very meagerly!

George reports that all groceries can be secured in Ichang, but they are a little higher so I ordered a few. I am allowed a ton of baggage on the boat, so it doesn't cost us anything to get all this stuff along. Pretty nice, isn't it?

Mama inquired about our freight. It has been in a godown all summer. "Godown" is the word used out here for warehouse or storehouse. Our freight is on this boat too, so we will have all our "belongings" with us in Ichang except the freight that is enroute from Kwangchow. I think that will be coming in a week or so.

I hope to arrive in Ichang sometime during the day tomorrow – Friday. If we do not arrive until towards evening, we may sleep on the boat, because otherwise I will have to get out my bedding and sleep on a cot. We have not bought any bed yet – they're <u>terribly</u> expensive out here. There is a steel cot and a single bed coming from Kwangchow and we plan on using them this winter. We had also planned on using a Chinese kitchen stove, which is a brick affair with holes in which to burn charcoal, but there is a Swedish missionary on board, a Mr. Nelton, who told me last night that he had a couple kitchen stoves he wished to dispose of. I gathered that he would sell them quite reasonably, so George may buy one.

Am having a splendid trip. It was quite cold yesterday, but today it has been quite comfortable. I have a cabin to myself, but have let Mrs. Nelton sleep in the extra bed because they have a baby and really need three beds to be comfortable. We have good meals and good service. I have cabin No. 1 – it is next to the "dining-lounge room." On these small boats the dining room also serves the purpose of living room or lounge, as it is called. I have been spending my time eating, sleeping, writing letters, and knitting. Expect to finish George's sweater before I get to Ichang. (This paper will not take ink on this side.)

Here is something of more especial interest to Mother. I have finally made over my old blue serge suit skirt. Put it on a waist. It looks fine, in spite of the fact that it has been darned several places and I'm immensely proud of myself. I hemmed it by hand and surprised myself by doing a good job.

Am wearing it today with the middy made from my cape lining and enjoy a secret satisfaction in my "made-over outfit." It looks nice, if I do say so myself!

By the way, there is something I have been thinking of telling you people. The majority of us out here are <u>still wearing our summer hats!</u> And I have also been using my sunshade! I guess we will be shifting to more wintry clothes now, although it was positively <u>hot</u> in Hankow last Monday.

We have been going past great flooded areas today. I was told that about 3/5 of the land on the one side of the river (this P.M's traveling) has been under water. One can see water miles back now. It is certainly hard on the poor Chinese farmers.

Five minutes left until dinner. Please have Raggie give you 54 pats for me!

Much Love to you all from
Bernice

Greet all the friends who kindly inquire about me.
Now you may send our mail to us at
    Ichang, Hupeh
    Evan. Luth. Mission, China

BERNICE DREADS GEORGE'S DEPARTURE.
"George and Lou plan on going out to Shinan sometime next week…they seem to plan on staying until shortly before the Christmas holidays."

26   Ichang, Hupeh China
                                                                                           October 24, 1921

Dear Mama,

    This is 10:40 A.M. Monday. Great time to be writing letters, but there is nothing especially urgent to do this morning, although I must say I wouldn't have to look far for work. I consider it more important, in fact, that I get this letter written, since I failed to write last week. There was too much muss and work then to be able to sit down to write.

    My last letter – No. 25 to Dad – was written Thursday the 13th. The following evening at about 6:30 the boat anchored at Ichang. There are no docks here, because the water rises and falls so much that they would have to put them out too far. George came down to get me in a little while and we made our way to the house through the rain. First I guess I shall draw a diagram of our place…

    George had had carpenters and painters here and things were getting into shape slowly. Our two rooms upstairs had been painted & whitewashed and our downstairs rooms were almost dry. The paint is anything but beautiful, but it covers a multitude of faults even so. It is a peculiar red – quite a barn paint, in fact. The Chinese use some stuff made – or rather, colored with or blood as a sort of filler. Then they put on a red paint. But you know one can get used to many things and I find I do not mind the color & the woodwork, etc. so much when I get my things about the room. It is really so nice to get into one's own home again.

    Schwartzkopfs arrived early Sunday morning. They got all their baggage and freight up with them that day, but we couldn't get our freight up until Tuesday because we had to wait for the bill of lading. So Schw's got as settled as they could until they get more furniture, before we did. We had more to unpack too, I believe. Well, I don't know just what to say about our freight. All my nice dishes & cut glass ware came through fine. Only a few saucers, a cup, and a couple oatmeal dishes were broken of my every day dishes. So I consider it fortunate that the frail things came through so well. But oh my, how they must have handled our bigger pieces!! George believes the boxes must have had the roughest handling between Hankow and here. It is hard to say, of course. Well, my heart almost lost a beat when they opened the piano. The front piece (on which the music stands) had been shaken loose. The lock was sprung and the piano open. We were pretty frightened at first, but <u>most fortunately</u>, we could find no damage to the inside (the works, etc.) and what scratches there were are on the inside. And it is in as good tune as when we left – which was a <u>little out of tune</u>! Not very badly out of tune tho'! And what a <u>joy</u> it is to have it!! The mirror in my dresser is broken, worse luck. It seems as though a rod was jammed right through the crate, as there is a little hole to show where it went in. Again it is fortunate that the whole thing was not splintered. Almost 2/3 of the mirror is usable and when we can afford a whole mirror for the dresser, we will use what there is left for something else. At present we have the broken mirror up – the piece that is unbroken, I should say! My nice glass washboard is broken too. That also is broken in such a way that I can have a small washboard made for washing out handkerchiefs, baby things, etc. And then my dresser fared badly. It was well crated, but it was "sprung." Two of the drawers are cracked a little and George had to put a board across the bottom to hold it firmly as the legs were inclined to spread.

Tuesday Morning. How do you do! Didn't finish this yesterday after all, so I'll do it now. At least, I'll make an attempt to do so. Have a woman washing for me today, but she is inexperienced so I have to show her how and help her now and then. She is our Boy's wife – both are very young. He is 20 – looks like 15 – and she is 21. He too is inexperienced so I have to train them both. That is really preferable, however, as then they learn to do things my way. I hope to train this woman to wash, iron, and mend. If she proves to be O.K. I want to use her as amah when the baby comes.

I suppose it does sound quite luxurious to have a cook, Boy, and amah. Well, it is nice to have someone do the dirty work, and I think I have a pretty good cook. But, I am quite positive you would not exchange with me. I am young and can learn to get over some of my "finicky habits" I guess, but you couldn't endure the carelessness. I have been here only a little over a week and today almost all my dishtowels are in the wash and all of them were by far filthier than I ever got them – could have used two and had less dirt. And that in spite of the fact that George has told them how they're to be used, that I have watched them and taken them away every day or so, and have even washed dishes with them to show them how to be clean. Now that is only one of the many things to be watched continually. But of course some servants can be trained to do quite well and can be trusted quite far. But we can never tempt them. My cupboard, or little cubbyhole, is locked and I give out the eggs, milk, potatoes, etc. Some time when I am not so busy I shall try to tell you about the "squeeze system" out here and also about "losing face." They are two of China's curses, as we see it. I cannot dwell on those subjects now.

I was telling about our freight yesterday at the time I quit writing. The bookcase came through in good shape and my kitchen utensils also. My cedar chest has warped a little, but was unhurt by the trip, for which I'm thankful. And all my nice linens and things in it looked so nice. It was a pleasure to unpack that box. Yesterday George's freight came from Kwangchow. I was quite surprised to see the dishes he had. There are almost enough for our every day use. They are blue willow pattern dishes and there are three each of the large plates, supper plates, cups & saucers, soup plates, besides sugar bowl & creamer, pitcher, vegetable dish, platter, & butter dish. He also had several odd pieces and a few kitchen utensils. It is lots of fun to see his old bachelor things. He must have had quite a nice home. He also has a ¾ size bed & a cot bed. We have put the bed up and George built out on one side so we could put our big mattress on. Some furniture in our room, I tell you! That contraption for a bed, part of a mirror, and a very original wash-stand made by George out of one of our boxes. Then we have a chest of drawers – red in color. Tomorrow a white wardrobe is coming. We should care! Some day we'll paint the chest of drawers white and have a new bed, and new mirror. In the study we have one wall lined with bookcases (?) made of packing boxes and more are to be made today or tomorrow. We have to economize where we can as our salary is already way overdrawn. One must have some things in order to start housekeeping.

By the way, I want to tell you I have three tiny shirts – smallest size – and two of those bands – 1 yr. old size. Maybe it would be better to send a few shirts a little larger. Have no stockings. But don't buy more than you think I really need, because George's life insurance premium has to be paid the first of next year and we will need $40.00 some then. Expect that our heater stove in Chicago will be sold before then and hope the $35.00 for his gown will be paid soon. Then we'll be able to cover nicely, I believe. I have 23 yds. of flannel – Emma & I bought a bolt together because we saved about 20¢ a yard by doing so.

Wednesday. This is great – three days on a letter! However no boat has gone down the river in that time so it will reach you just as soon, unless the overland mail route between here and Hankow has been re-established. It was discontinued this fall during the trouble around here.

In a few days I hope we will be quite settled. Our wardrobe, a desk for George, and a cupboard for dining room should be here today. The latter is out in the hall, as a matter of fact, but they have to put another shelf in. Will keep my dishes, silverware, and dishtowels in that. There are wooden doors only – inclosing shelves above & below. In the middle are two drawers. It is by no means a wonderful piece of furniture, but it will serve the purpose. It has been oiled to look about same as our dining room chairs. They – the chairs – are the most decent pieces we have bought, I believe. Hope our wardrobe will be nice. George ordered all these things before I came, so I don't know just what they're like until they are brought here.

Yesterday P.M. I had two callers – both are ladies in the Scotch Mission. One is the wife of the doctor. Another doctor in that mission will return to Ichang the first of the year, I have heard.

My woman is learning to iron this morning. As she is still on the first pieces, I cannot tell how apt she will be. She did my washing very nicely, tho.' The clothes got so white. But I take some of the credit for it, because I spent an hour Monday evening soaking the things. I rubbed soap on each piece and gave it a couple rubs on the board. It certainly is worth one's time – the clothes are much easier to wash and get nicer. Then yesterday I took care of the boiler entirely and helped her – saw to that she had enough water, o.s.v. – o.s.v.[89] And now I'm sitting around here taking a hand in the ironing every so often. The Chinese are terribly slow. You are undoubtedly surprised that there is anything left for me to do with so many servants. So far I have surely not lacked for work but of course we are just getting settled. However, I am not anticipating a great deal of leisure. There will be enough household cares, and there are so many other things I want to and should do, that I expect to be quite busy all the time.

I have a rather bad cold. It rained all last week and was miserably cold around here and Saturday I had sore throat. I doctored up that night with quinine, a woolen sock, hot water bottle, hot lemonade, & gargling. It helped a good deal, but now it is in my nose & head and I cannot seem to reach it as effectively. George too has a little cold, but it didn't get such a good hold on him evidently. We have had beautiful weather this week, regular October weather like you have at home.

George and Lou plan on going out to Shinan sometime next week. They don't know just how long they will be gone, but they seem to plan on staying until shortly before the Christmas holidays. I certainly do not look forward to the coming two months! It is nice that Emma is here but I get so lonesome anyway. Maybe I can overcome it by keeping myself occupied all the time. That doesn't always help tho'. Oh well, such is life and many are much worse off than I. And next year we hope we can live a more settled life.

---

[89] Og så videre – etcetera (Norwegian)

This will never do! I cannot write in peace, so I'm going to quit right here. Have to wash all my nice dishes, some pictures, etc. George is still unpacking books. My, he has a big library!

Am finishing this with a steel pen. First time I've used one in months!

Will try to write again very soon. Am feeling just fine. Except for the cold in my head.

<u>Much Love</u> to all of you,
From George & Bernice

It will take mail a little longer to come from here, especially if the overland route is not re-opened.

Just tho't of a couple things. The little building in front is a "gate house." Mr. Li is a general helper – in business matters that is. We will use him as teacher as soon as we can settle down and study. He is a mission employee you understand. The "guest room" is for Chinese who may come for this or that. It won't be used much, I imagine, until we get work established here.

CHINESE ROOMS ARE HARD TO HEAT.
"Our rooms here are about twelve ft. high."

Letter No. 27

37 Wen Chi Lu
Ichang, Hupeh, China
November 1st, 1921

Dear Sis,

Letter No. 26 was written to Mother October 17-19 and I forgot to put the number on, I believe. Ikke sandt?[90]

It is rather late to start a letter and I'm quite sleepy too, but when I get a letter started, I usually get it finished sooner or later.

This evening I made a batch of fudge in my chafing dish – up here in the study. It didn't turn out to be as good as it should because the milk curdled as soon as the stuff got hot. It was not sour when I put it in, but was evidently too old. Am getting fresh milk now – get seven bottles, which is less than that many quarts, for $1.00 (Mex.) It is cheaper than canned milk however. I imagine I will use my chafing dish quite often here, since it is not so convenient to be in the kitchen, and of course it heats quicker than a stove fire. And our study is quite cozy so we are upstairs most of the time. The only times we have been downstairs are meal time and the time we spend at the piano, or entertaining. Haven't done much "entertaining," but have had several callers. People are more punctilious about many things out here and I have had more callers within my first two weeks here than in six months in Chicago.

Today has been such a beautiful day, so at noon Emma, Louis, George and I decided to drop our work and go out in the country on a hike and picnic. We put up a little lunch hurriedly and were off at 2:30. We walked for an hour, at the end of which time we had arrived at a temple near the Yangtsze. We had a fine view of the country and we are in beautiful country too, I want to tell you! All about us we see mountains and in between them a fertile valley. Across the river from Ichang there is a ridge of mountains that resemble pyramids. One is especially large and fine and that is called The Pyramid. Back of the mountains along the river are other ridges considerably higher and of a great variety of shapes. It was such a treat to get out in the quiet, restful country! And you can imagine how I enjoyed the changing leaves. They reminded me so much of Wittenberg. We saw several unusually beautiful trees with leaves of all colors. Picked some leaves to bring home. At one place the boys, who were a little ahead of us, walked right into a bunch of pheasants. They flew up right under them and they deplored the fact that they didn't have shotguns. There is pretty good hunting around here, I think, but guns cost fearfully much! After we had eaten our lunch we went down to the river – not the river proper but an arm of it separating a rather long island from the mainland – and hired a "wadse" to take us back to the city. A "wadse" is a sort of boat – it looks something like what we call a scow in the U.S. Had a nice ride home and we felt we had had a regular picnic and enjoyable afternoon.

George is in bed, so I must hurry. He has been calling me right along. Good night!

---

[90] Literally - Not so? (Didn't I?) (Norwegian)

Wed. P.M.

We are fairly well settled now. I have no curtains up on the windows nor on our "bookcases," but am in no particular rush about that. I do not miss curtains very much here. The windows are all these doors that open in and in both the parlor and study there are doors opening out upon the veranda- half of the door is glass, half is wood, so they are not really French doors. I have been wondering how I can use my parlor curtains. There are three windows – I count the doors as windows of course – in both parlor and study. And then, they are not suitable anyway. Since all the doors and windows "open in," the best thing is to have curtains on the window, fastened at both top and bottom with rods. And then one can have some drapes way to the side. These are the only kind of windows I have seen in China. In many ways I like them better than the kind we are used to. They're easier to wash, for one thing. But they surely are not very tight and I would not want them in a cold climate.

We have our stoves now too. People have been telling me how terribly they mind the cold out here during the winter, especially after they have been here two, three years. They seem to think their blood gets thinner. That may be very true and one does feel cold more where there is dampness. However, I believe there are other good reasons which explain the cold here. First, the houses are not built to withstand cold. They are built for warm climates – windows & doors are loose and the rooms are dreadfully high. Our rooms here are about twelve ft. high. Imagine heating such rooms! And then what they use for heating would be considered a joke by you folks. I suppose they are little better in the southern U.S.A. For downstairs we have a heater (??) about the size of the little stove we had in our bedroom in Portland. Remember? That is to heat both dining room and parlor. We have it in the dining room. At first we thought we would try to get along with that this winter, since I will be alone more or less probably, but we decided to get another to put up here in the study, so George bought another one yesterday – <u>smaller</u> than the one we have downstairs! There is no chimney in this house so we have to run the pipes out through the windows. The top of the four panes in one "door" is replaced by a piece of tin or galvanized iron and the pipe is run through that. It works fine, especially on second floor where the pipe can be extended up outside and the smoke carried away better. We cannot have a pipe come up to the top of the house from the first floor because it is too expensive and consequently some smoke comes up along the side of the house. But I guess it won't bother much. Can keep the window on that side closed as well as not.

We like our new home very much. There is nothing elaborate and I must admit our houses have always been much finer, as well as furniture, o.s.v.[91] but I am quite satisfied and some day we will probably have some nicer things to put in our house. Our bedroom could take a prize for variety of pieces and colors, but really I think it looks quite nice when it is all fixed up. I have some curtains on the washstand and it doesn't look half bad. And we have such dandy verandas, both upstairs and down. We appreciate the upper one especially. There is no grass in our yard, but there are some palms and a few other trees and we have good place to hang out our clothes. Will send some snaps – they're not very good, but may give a faint idea of our present home.

By the way, mama evidently forgot to put those snaps in her letter No. 27. She said she would send some, but I didn't find them. That letter came Sunday. We surely

---

[91] Og så videre – etcetera (Norwegian)

haven't had much American mail the last three & a half weeks. There cannot have been any big boats coming in lately – to Shanghai, that is.

Have had a woman here over a week and have gotten quite a number of things done. She has washed clothes twice and I have both bednets, George's bathrobe – summer one – and a number of other smaller pieces clean and ready to put away for the winter. Have also washed our big grey sweaters and the steamer rug. Still have a few extra pieces, but will take them gradually. She mends well too and I have had her mend George's fall w. suits. Some of them are mostly patches, but he can wear them very well. They look quite artistic! His B.V.D.'s are all nicely mended and put away too. Today she has been putting patches on his coat linings. One coat is next to relined!!!!

George is in bed again – have been writing at this off and on, you see. He is not feeling well. We both had colds last week, but at that time I was much worse off than he. The other night I doctored him up and he felt better again yesterday, but this afternoon he felt so punk again that he took a hot footbath tonight and I gave him a cup of hot milk with butter and pepper. Then I wrapped him in a wool blanket. I don't believe it is only a cold. I think we must have eaten something that wasn't quite good for us, as our "tummies" seem to be a little off. I haven't felt quite right the last days either. Guess we shall each take a good dose of Epsom Salts tomorrow morning and see if that doesn't help. We have decided not to have breakfast also, because it is good to eat less.

The bags may leave for Shinan Sunday. There is a boat going up river then and if George gets over this spell they plan on leaving at that time. I don't like to have him go, naturally, but the sooner they go the sooner they will return, I suppose.

I wonder if I'll be able to manage things alone here satisfactorily. I really have picked up a lot of Chinese since we came to Ichang and our cook is quite clever, so he and I get along quite well. I can show the boy & the woman how to do things. Mr. Li had to go home Sunday because his wife is ill, otherwise I should have begun studying this week. I will be so glad when I can really talk a little instead of using some words and more signs to make myself understood.

Now I am going to bed too and I am also going to have a cup of hot milk. I am so tired this evening. Write often, Elsa, and tell about your school work, etc. etc. etc. Ragnar too. You kids cannot expect mama to tell everything, you know. It is so long since I had a letter from Raggie. Oh, I really had intended to answer Willard's letter before this. I still have it, you can tell him, and will answer some day. Give my best regards to all who inquire about me – and other friends.

My love to you all
Bernice

BERNICE EXPLAINS THE WAR IN HUPEH PROVINCE.

"…China is in the hands of two governments…The Northern government has been the recognized one and is located at Peking. I don't know anything about the Southern government.[92] But the province of Hupeh is between the North and South and makes a fine thing to fight about."

Letter No. 29

Ichang, Hupeh
Nov. 18, 1921

Dear Mother,

    I am rather pepless today, so I will not promise a long, or perhaps very cheerful letter. But if I do sound a little blue, or "down in the dumps," please don't be at all alarmed. Take it for what it is worth – now that George is gone and I cannot spill all my imaginary troubles into his ear, I may unload. However, I shall try to be considerate and then I'm not feeling as badly as this introduction might indicate! The fact is, I am troubled with a spell of diarrhea today and so do not feel quite right. I don't know what caused it, but the early part of the week I was troubled the other way so took some pills and Epsom Salts and since then I've been eating a good deal of fruit and yesterday the cook prepared spinach. It may have been the crowning touch. I do not think my bowels have been <u>normal</u> for almost seven months. Have used more laxatives in that time than since my castor oil days, I'm sure, and have had several spells of diarrhea. Don't know whether to attribute it to the climate or to my condition.

    Friday, a week ago today, I received your letter No. 31 and the one you sent on for Netty. Today the package of patterns, and the La Follette's inclosed, came. Thank you so very much for everything – clasps, needles, patterns, all your trouble, o.s.v.[93] You are really too good to me, Mama!

    I am going to send you a package one of these days – not today, because I dare not go down to the P.O. but maybe tomorrow or Monday. It contains 6 yds. of torsion (?) insertion and 6 yds. of lace edging to match. It is <u>hand made lace</u>, if you please. That is all we buy out here. It was just by chance that I saw this and I thought it was so beautiful that I bought it for Elsa's graduation dress! Though it is very fine, I am sure it is strong and will wear well. The reason I'm sending it now is because Christmas mail is often exempt from duty and so I hope to save you that. I do hope you can use it for her dress – it ought to make up beautifully with a fine lawn or organdie. And if you and Elsa would like me to, I'd enjoy scouring the fashion books and my own brains for the style of dress – I could make suggestions, that is. Now I don't know as I shall make this a present exactly. I should like nothing better, as far as desire goes, but George says we have spent a good deal on presents this year. So I have been thinking this could help pay for some of the things you are buying for us. It won't go very far, but it will help some. The lace – all of it – is worth about $2.50 gold. Do you think it is expensive – less than 21¢ gold per

---

[92] The Southerners were led by Sun Yat-sen, who had been the first president of the government following the Qing or Manchu dynasty. He was later exiled to the far south in Canton (by Hong Kong). His faction was known by many names: Nationalist Party, Kuomintang (Guomindang), or KMT. This conflict was his failed attempt to take over China. Sun Yat-sen was the first one to welcome the Communists from Russia as members and financiers.

[93] Og så videre – etc. (Norwegian)

yard for handmade lace! I hope you will like it as well as I do! You may not need it all for a dress, but of course you can find use for what is left for either yourself or Elsa.

Well, George and Lou left here Nov. 10th, a week ago yesterday. It was pretty hard to have them go, but we are living in hopes that they will return in two, three weeks or so. They did not have an easy time of it when starting out. They intended to leave the boat at Patung (Ba dung') and travel overland from there, but learned – while the boat stopped there – that they could not secure any coolies. You see, they need coolies to carry their baggage (clothes, bed, bedding, supplies, etc.) and should have chair bearers to carry them. They remained on the boat and went up to Kweifu. There they could get five coolies, but no chair bearers, so they started off on foot with these coolies. Today we received letters written last Sunday. They had traveled about 60 li then, or approx. 20 miles – maybe not quite that many miles, as they were climbing mountains all that distance and there are more "li" up hill than down. That's the Chinese for you! On the level, a Chinese "li" averages about 1/3 mile. The boys expected to get a couple chairbearers at the place they stopped Sunday and so have one chair between them. George, dear man, does not complain, but I'm sure he was quite tired out. It's not so easy to climb and walk all day when you're not used to it. He said the scenery was wonderful and they had splendid weather. Until the last couple days – we had over a week of weather more like summer than fall. The last two days have been cooler and quite autumn like.

Well, I was going to say, the reason it is so difficult to get men is because the armies have taken almost all the coolies available.

You have asked what they're fighting about and I do not know whether your question has ever been satisfactorily answered, or whether I can do so now. I'll try. As I understand it, China is in the hands of two governments, so to speak. The Northern government has been the recognized one and is located at Peking. I don't know anything about the Southern government. But the province of Hupeh is between the North and South and makes a fine thing to fight about. South and western Hupeh has been the play ground for the two armies for several months now. Shinan has been in the midst of it. For instance: Oct. 27th the city was captured by the Southerners, on Oct. 28th by the Northerners, and on November 1st the Southerners were there again. Mr. Gebhardt has written that he is quite safe and George says they are in no particular danger. But if conditions do not improve, he says they may leave Shinan for the present and try to bring Gebhardt back with them. You may be sure I hope that is what they'll do.

I surely am glad Emma is here. We visit together a good deal – usually for only a few minutes at the time, but you know it is nice to have someone to talk to. But, of course, no one can take George's place and I surely do miss him. It isn't that I haven't enough to do, because there are ever and ever so many things I do not seem to find time to do. I've had quite a bit of correspondence to do this last week and now I must get Christmas mail out. All that takes a good deal of time. And I have been trying to put in two and three hours a day at language study. So my time seems more than taken up.

It is a year tomorrow (today by the day) since you came to Chicago. How I wish you could pay me a visit now! And do you remember our Thanksgiving? Emma and I tho't of having some of the marines over next Thursday, but we've lost the pep for it. We plan on saving now and having more of a "splurge" at Christmas time when the boys can be with us.

You ask if we have to pay our house rent. No, that is mission expense. You ask about vegetables out here. Well, I guess the only one I've missed is lettuce. We have carrots, cabbage, spinach, a Chinese celery, bamboo roots, and other Chinese vegetables. We have one or two kinds for dinner and supper. But today I'm not eating vegetables!

Now since George left I've been out with the servants every evening for devotion. Our cook is baptized and he reads and explains to the others. They all seem quite interested. Two of them cannot read – our boy and Emma's cook. But our boy has learned the Lord's Prayer. I was so pleased when he repeated it last night. The cook taught it to him.

This is quite a long letter after all, but now I must write a little to George. Have written to him every day. By the way, you hadn't told why Raggie was short of money, so I was curious until this last letter came.

Much Love to each one of you four.
Bernice

Another note from George. Vi er rent overrrasket[94] - two letters in one day. We didn't expect mail to come through so quickly. They traveled 97 li Monday – had one chair between them so they could change off. George says the scenery is most wonderful and he seems to be enjoying the trip. Am so glad of that! And he says their grub is holding out fine – have plenty to eat.

---

[94] We are completely surprised. (Norwegian)

BERNICE GIVES THE TELEGRAM CODE FOR BIRTH.
"...<u>Below</u> is the regular code word for 'Everything & everybody all well,'..."
Letter #33

Ichang, Hupeh
December 17, 1921
Saturday Eve.

Dear Mother,

Guess I'd better hurry or this letter won't be written this week and I believe I have been getting my "weeklies" off quite regularly of late.

Just think! One week from this evening is Christmas Eve. I am quite excited about it! It will be quite different from what I am used to though. In the first place, it looks more like October than December here. Gardens are still green and leaves are still falling. The willows in back of us are quite green and full of leaves and the palms in our yard are rather "summery" even now. So it isn't likely we'll have a white Christmas. The last few days have been so mild too. We have had fire down here in the dining room right along, but only enough to keep it going, and yesterday and today I was upstairs a good deal and was entirely comfortable with my sweater on. Tonight it is colder again though. And then we won't have "ludefisk,"[95] which always seemed so essential to the Christmas meals. Worst of all, however, we are not going to have a tree. We could get some sort of evergreen here, but we have no trimmings and cannot even get popcorn, so we will let it go entirely. Next summer we are going to order trimmings from the States – Monkey-Ward's,[96] I s'pose. Anyway, I am determined that we shall have a tree whenever possible to get one and not be hampered by lack of trimmings. Lou and Emma will have a tree this year and will let us look at it! And we are to have Christmas dinner with them – we'll eat one goose then. New Year's Day I'll entertain and then goodbye to the other goose! I have "me doots,"[97] as to the increased bulk of our geese, but at least we know what they've been eating for a month. You see, these Chinese geese are so particular they refuse to eat foreign leftovers. Gave them some biscuits soaked in warm water once and they positively preferred starvation to them, even when I put oats on top. They ate the oats and left the bread. So you see "hvor fin de er paa det."[98] But I say I'm glad I know they've not been feeding on Chinese rubbish the last month.

I am going to make it as Christmassy as possible though. Expect to have curtains in the parlor, dining room and our bedroom. Don't know just what to do in the study as curtains will make it rather dark, I fear. But we have just put up dark curtains in front of all the bookcases, as it looks fairly respectable in there now.

The other day I made a batch of ginger cookies – my first attempt. My cooky cutter is smaller than yours and I got close to 200 cookies. They are not like yours, of course, but they will do – they have to! I suppose I needed a little more flour than you do in order to roll them, and I believe I should have put in a little more ginger. They are quite thin and crisp, though, and remind me of yours anyway!! This week I must try the white ones and perhaps Berliner Krandser and fried cakes too. Lard is quite expensive,

---

[95] Lutefisk is cod soaked in lye which gives it a rubbery texture. It's eaten with melted butter.
[96] Montgomery Ward's
[97] "My doubts"
[98] "how particular they are." (Norwegian)

but one feels like forgetting that once in a while. I've never made fried cakes in my life, either.

It seems holly grows around here and, believe me, we're going to try to get lots and lots of it and make this house look so festive that - - ! And then when one <u>feels</u> festive, why everything appears festive. I'm so glad that the men are not going to spend Christmas in Shihnan that ludefisk, etc. are immaterial.

An American mail(boat) arrived in Shanghai last Tuesday, so we ought to be getting some Christmas mail soon. If it missed that boat we will have to wait another couple weeks.

George and I take walks almost every afternoon. He has been studying all forenoon lately and I am busy about the house, so when four o'clock comes we feel we need exercise and fresh air. It is so interesting to go out together. Some days we do not walk so very far, but loiter along and watch the activities of the barbers, fortune tellers, cooks, etc. etc. and peek into the various shops. Yesterday we walked into the city (the walled city) and saw so much of interest. One sees something new each day. After we had walked in some distance we went up on the city wall and continued our walk, going around the whole city. Ichang has expanded a great deal and in many places there seems to be as much outside the wall as inside. We were out for two hours yesterday.

Sunday

I felt so sort of restless last night I had to quit writing – it seemed I couldn't sit still and think.

Gebhardt went down to Hankow last Wednesday. They wired for him saying they needed his help as they are rushed with work. He is not to stay very long – we told him we would expect him here for New Year's Dinner. Everybody likes Gyps – too bad he hasn't a good wife!

Yesterday forenoon Emma and I packed some little Christmas boxes full of candy and cookies and sent them to our new missionaries, who are at the language school in Peking. There are eight there – three married couples, one single lady and a single man.

It is so nice today and George and I just took a few snaps. We are also going to take a couple of our Da si fu (cook) and Tsao si fu, our boy. Si fu means <u>help</u> or <u>helper</u>. "Da" means big, great, large, and the head servant is usually called the Da si fu. Tsao is our boy's name and the "si fu" is added, partly because it doesn't sound well to call him only Tsao and also to indicate that he is a servant.

Since Gyps left we have been having only two meals a day. We were eating breakfast anytime between eight and nine o'clock, dinner at one, and supper at seven. George has been reading about the great benefits of fasting, etc. and thought we were eating too much so I was game to have two meals. We did it for some time in Chicago and it worked fine. We eat some fruit when we come down and that is enough until between ten and eleven, when we have breakfast. About three or four o'clock we usually have a little tea or coffee and a few cookies, but not any more than we'd have for coffee any other time. We have our dinner between six and half past. I really do think the plan a good one. Three hearty meals a day are too much for people not leading an active outdoor life and one doesn't have much zest for eating so often. And in this way we surely have longer days.

Upton Sinclair is a staunch advocate of the fast cure. He claims it cured him of both nervous and organic troubles when everything else had failed to give relief.

We have rented a place for chapel here. It is on a very busy street and is only about two and a half blocks from our house. It is being remodeled just now but hope it will be ready in a couple weeks.

Well, the vaccination did not work on me and I doubt that it really worked on George. He got sores on his arm, but not bad ones and he didn't feel sick. We'll have to see whether they leave any scars. Instead of scratching the arm one place, they make three or four scratches. Guess that is the British way. Dr. Borthwick is Scotch.

There are not very many soldiers here now – at least, not in this section of the city. They have been sent south and west of here, it is said. And Ichang certainly is coming to life again. When I came here in October we saw rickshaws only now and then, streets were quiet and some places almost deserted. But now, the place is a busy, bustling city. The streets are crowded with small shops, food stalls, candy booths, fortune tellers, shoppers, barbers, and all the other things one finds in a Chinese street. New houses and shops are being built in places where the looters ruined property. And still they say it will be a long time before Ichang again reaches the economic prosperity it had attained before the lootings and the recent fighting.

I am inclosing a letter to the "Dorcas" girls. I thought you might like to read it and then will you please see that it reaches the president or secretary of "Dorcas"? I believe it would be easiest to give it to Rev. Olsen.

We plan on sending a cablegram to Chicago as soon as we have news for you. Jim has registered there at Western Union so we can send a four word cable, unless there should be no code word to cover the message. In the first place, you had better get in touch with Anna at once and give her your address. Her name and address is Mrs. Jas. D. Reid, 4503 No. Winchester Ave., Ch'go. They will then wire you as soon as they receive a message from us. And here is the code:

Widow – Baby girl, dead
Woman –   "   " , well & fine
Worry – Baby boy, dead
Youth -   "   " , well & fine

These words are from the extra code words in the Western Union Code book. My condition will be a word added or prefixed to one of these words, taken from the code book under Business & Health. For instance, <u>Below</u> is the regular code word for "Everything & everybody all well," so we might send the code "Belowyouth" or "Belowwoman." If you want to secure a code book and want the message as it comes, you can tell Anna so. Anyway, you people can make your own arrangements about that. As to when to expect a message – of course, that is rather indefinite. March 3rd is the middle of the fortnight we can expect a "party" here and then we would probably want to wait a couple days or more before sending a cable. Now I know you will be impatient and probably anxious those weeks, but do not worry, please. I have been in fine condition all the time and am sure we'll all be happy in a few months. I cannot realize that I am really to be a mother – it seems too good to be true. A year ago today (by day, tomorrow by date) I stayed home in bed – it was the beginning of my trouble. Am glad I have been spared that so far this time.

I'm going to play for George now.

Much Love to all, Bernice

GEORGE DETAILS THE WAR IN SHIHNAN & ICHANG, HUPEH.
"...we decided to leave that station for the present, and wait till conditions grew more settled before taking up the work more aggressively there."

Dec. 20, 1921

It is now some time since the missionary's life was in general taken to be one of constant danger and hardship, spent among savage peoples of fickle passions and special fondness for "roasted or stewed missionaries," so long, in fact, that the missionary-cannibal joke is about worn out. But the conditions in war-ridden China today are rapidly becoming such that the missionary in almost any part of the country can begin to appreciate what Paul meant when he wrote to the Corinthians: "In journeyings often, in perils of waters, in perils of robbers, in perils by my own countrymen, in perils by the heathen, in perils in the city, in perils in the wilderness, in perils in the sea, in perils among false brethren." The undersigned came to Ichang together with Mr. Gebhardt the first of September to find it the center of the conflict between the Szechuanese revolutionists and the Northerners. Mr. Gebhardt proceeded to Shihnan, getting through the enemy lines by taking passage on the foreign river-steamer to Szechuan and going south from there into western Hupeh. It was not long before Shihnan became the center of operations, as the victorious Northerners advanced, driving the Szechuanese for a time even out of this westernmost city near the Szechuan border. When the Szechuanese first left Shihnan in the middle of October, the task of guarding the city was taken over by a force of local guard organized by a certain Mr. Yang. In a few days, the Szechuanese returned, demanding the unconditional surrender of these local troops together with their leader. To save the city from the horrors of a siege and capture by a superior force, Mr. Gebhardt, the only foreigner in the city, was asked to negotiate with the Szechuan general on behalf of the city and the local guards. An attempt to reach the enemy quarters by flying…flag failed, since these flags were fired upon, and those flying them had to take refuge from the shots. So Mr. Gebhardt together with a Chinese gentleman were let down over the city wall in an unobserved place, and proceeded by a round-about way through the hills to the rear of the Szechuanese, from where they were brought to the general's headquarters. This trip was made twice in the course of one night and once again the next day, but the Szechuanese seemed bent up on attacking the city, apparently in order to get revenge on Yang and his soldiers, who had made the business of the brigand chiefs in that neighborhood rather too unsafe for some time in the past. This branch of the Szechuanese army was evidently made up largely of the brigands who roam the wild mountains on the border between the provinces of Hupeh, Szechuan, Kweichow, and Hunan. So in spite of the understanding that Mr. Gebhardt finally succeeded in arranging with the General, the Szechuanese stormed the city walls the morning of the third day and wreaked their revenge on the local guards. In their search for the leader, Mr. Yang, they ransacked the premises of the Catholic and Episcopalian Missions, quite unceremoniously and became also quite offensive at our Mission Premises. A few days later the Northerners appeared and began firing on the city from the hills around it. The Szechuanese fled, killing and maiming all their prisoners most barbarously. Many of the wounded were brought to our Mission premises for treatment, and with the help of one of the army doctors, were cared for as best we could with our inadequate facilities and untrained assistants. The Northerners entered the city quietly but only to leave it again in two days, narrowly escaping being trapped there by the reinforced Szechuanese. When the Szechuanese entered the city this time, they looted and carried on in the barbarous fashion that has become the style throughout the country of late years. Generally in such cases the premises of foreigners, or at least the mission stations, have been unmolested. But here, these were all attacked. Without any warning several shots were fired through the closed door of our mission premises, killing one Chinese who was about to open the door. Mr. Gebhardt was also about to proceed to the door at this time, so that it is only through a kind Providence that we can still have him with us. At the Episcopalian Mission, thirty or forty shots were fired through the doors into the chapel, and the Catholic Mission was even looted. The people in Shihnan and vicinity fled from the city in streams, leaving the place almost depopulated. After a month of peace and quiet a good half of them were still in hiding. Through the fighting and the panic, Mr. Gebhardt stayed on alone, no word of the situation in Shihnan reaching the rest of the country till all was quiet again. The undersigned together with Mr. Schwartzkopf managed to reach the place by November 16th, after a week's journey, made strenuous by the difficulty we found securing coolies to carry our baggage over the mountains and buying food for use on the way. On the way we met many wounded soldiers being brought back to Szechuanese Army Hospitals from the fighting front, and found many other evidences of the state of war in which this whole section was at the time. The soldiers stationed in the towns along the road were quite pleasant, being proud of their recent victories over the Northerners, but it seemed that there was an anti-foreign sentiment spreading among the Szechuanese which at any time might break out in ugly fashion. Partly for this reason, and partly because war conditions made it impossible to do much in Shihnan, we decided to leave that station for the present, and wait till conditions grew more settled before taking up the work more aggressively there.

 Mr. Gebhardt has gone to Hankow to help out for the present with the work crowding upon the brethren in that busy port city, while Mr. Schwartzkopf and the undersigned open up the work in Ichang.

 This city is finally showing some signs of its normal life. Twice it has been looted by the Northern soldiers; for two months this fall it was in a state of siege. And it has taken another two months for the people to return to their normal activities, and for those who had fled to safer places to return in some degree to their homes. But now is the opportune time for us to begin work. We have therefore rented a part of a new building, on a busy street near one of the city gates, for temporary chapel quarters. Here we hope in a short time to be able to propagate the gospel by the spoken and written Word, and point out to this much-visited people, the way of salvation from every ill, both temporal and eternal. We entreat the prayers of our home church for that measure of quiet and peace which will enable us to do this work unhindered and without interruption.

Geo. O. Lillegard

BERNICE RECEIVED A CHIT BOOK FOR CHRISTMAS.
"…when we want to get messages to our friends or neighbors we write notes and send them via servant."
Letter No. 36

Ichang, Hupeh, China
December 31st, 1921
<u>New Year's Eve</u>

Dear All-o'-Youse!

    'Tis as fitting to end the Old Year right as to begin the New Year properly, sez I, so I shall at least start a letter to you folks. If I have to finish tomorrow, I will consider the New Year properly begun! However, I do not expect to have much time for writing tomorrow, so I will do my best now.

    It is now almost six o' clock here – doesn't that mean it is New Year's Day there now? If o meridian is at Greenwich, then we are west and the sun gets here considerably later than at Madison. We had a discussion on that subject at Mr. Hawkins' on Thanksgiving Day, but I couldn't get head or tail out of it. But it got clearer when I thought it over by myself. Now I'll venture you people will have a discussion and if you get to arguing as to whether you lose or gain a day coming from San Francisco to China, I'll just tell you a day is lost. We went to bed on Thursday evening, May 19, and arose Saturday morning, May 21st.

    This week has been quite a vacation for me – the first regular vacation for several years, as I didn't have any when with the French Battery and I don't consider lying in bed, like last year, a vacation exactly. A year ago this evening I sat in the morris chair and had supper. I entered in my diary for that meal – "Had ludefisk and apple sauce!" We will not have a very orthodox supper tonight, but I did tell the cook to make some "kjöd kager."[99] Besides we are to have peas, mashed potatoes, and prune whip and fresh buns. If the buns taste as good as they look, I'll be mighty happy. The bread has been getting on my nerves lately and still I felt sort of helpless, because the cook uses some kind of perpetual yeast and I don't know how to use it. But I finally got desperate and tho't I'd risk a batch with the yeast I bought in Hankow. I did all the sponging, etc. myself but the next morning I was preparing part of the sponge for biscuits and told the cook to knead the bread. Well, he made a mess of it because he had too much flour and even though I added the biscuit sponge and more milk, the batch looked anything but promising. I fear the yeast was no good either. Anyway he fed that bread to the geese. But the cook grasped my idea of breadbaking anyway and what he made today looks better than any he baked before.

    But before I dwell on the news, I must tell you that the Christmas package arrived Thursday, Dec. 29th. It really made very good time, as it often takes a couple months – occasionally even more – for packages to get through. Well, the one you sent first, containing all the material and so forth, has not come yet. Tusind tak[100] for the presents! "Det var nok morsomt at faa en pakke ifra Dere."[101] It <u>did</u> make me a little homesick! The package came through in fine shape – the soap might have fared better, if the wrappers had been on, but none of the bars were broken, they were just chipped a little.

---

[99] "meat cakes" (Norwegian)
[100] Thousand thanks (Norwegian)
[101] "It was certainly nice to receive a package from you." (Norwegian)

That Creme Oil soap surely reminds me of home! And I am especially grateful for the Pepsodent since I am rather more particular about toothpaste than George. The doily is very pretty, of course, and you know I am ever so pleased to be the possessor of it, always having wanted one. And I'm quite "crazy" about George's belt buckle and you may be sure he is not a little pleased. It is a beauty! I was very glad to get some cotton stockings as I do not need to wear silk here all the time and still I didn't have any others. Now I can be more saving on my silk ones. Ja, tak for alt![102]

We are now very well supplied with toilet articles and almost all small things that we prefer to get from the U.S. My sewing box is well supplied too.

Mama, in your little private letter to me you said, "I don't like this way of giving presents." I couldn't understand what you meant then, but think I do now. We were very glad to get all these things, but I suppose you would have enjoyed sending something else than the toilet articles, for instance. Was that what you meant? Well, we plan on sending orders to Monkey-Ward's now and then from now on and hope to relieve you of much of this sort of shopping. I feel that we have given you too much trouble altogether this fall. Of course, when it came to baby things I felt you would do that shopping the best of anyone and I did not want to order such things from a mail order house. But we can easily get many of the other smaller things from them. So I shall try not to abuse your kindness. Don't imagine, though, that we were not pleased with the Christmas package.

We have not received any Christmas mail – greetings or anything else – from our Chicago folks. There should be a couple big American mails in next week, however, and we look for a bunch of letters then. We received a package from Louise the same day as yours came. There were a pair of embroidered pillow cases, a pair of stockings for George, and a couple bars of candy. A couple weeks ago we received a picture of Louise and the baby. She is quite a girl all right. I believe the dress I sent for her will soon fit her. Didn't you think the dress was pretty?

---

[102] Yes, thanks for everything! (Norwegian)

January First 1922

Happy New Year! May 1922 be a better year for each in every way!

Papa and Mama, do you remember when I came home (in No. Dak.) after several New Year "Wakes" and very stealthily climbed the stairs, only to be met with the chorus "Hap'py New Year!!" shouted as with one voice? You counted 1-2-3 first. And you seemed to think it a pretty good joke on me, as I suppose it was.

We spent the evening with Schwartzkopfs. We didn't go up until about nine o'clock (they live upstairs in the study, while we live in our dining room. That's so we can get along with one stove.) About eleven o'clock we started to play "Rook" and kept on until after twelve. At twelve the gunboats certainly did their share to announce the birth of the New Year. I imagine you had that sort of noise in Manitowoc. The "Elcano" siren has a most unearthly and weird sound.

Today I have the dinner party. We will have our big meal at noon this time. Besides Emma and Lou, we have invited Mr. Hawkins, Mr. Hawley, and Mr. Ross. The first two are temporary bachelors, both having wives living in the U.S. Mr. Ross is a regular bachelor – he is postmaster here. You see, I still have more gentlemen guests than ladies! We are to have goose, stuffing, mashed potatoes, carrots (prepared a la cook), baked water chestnuts, apple pickles (from the only precious can I put up last year), cranberries, buns, butterscotch pie, cookies, coffee. Oh yes! We start out with soup.

What do you think of my hubby! He puts presents away so that he forgets all about them. Marie Brauer wants my typewriting manual, so the other night George had to dig around in the storeroom for it and what did he find but another present for me! It is a chit book. Maybe you people are wiser than I was when I came to China and know what a chit book is. I didn't, so I'll explain it. You know we haven't many telephones here – none in Ichang that I know of – so when we want to get messages to our friends or neighbors we write notes and send them via servant. A chit book is a book with the owner's name on it in which the name of the person the note is addressed to, is written. There is a space on the side for the signature of the addressee, to indicate receipt. Understand?

We had quite a busy week last week – that is, there were quite a number of parties. I told you in my last letter that we were at Nilsen's for coffee Monday afternoon and the "Elcano" boys gave an entertainment that evening. The boys displayed more or less talent, but it was rather misused, we thought. It was a vaudeville performance. Tuesday noon we had a fine dinner, or tiffin, on Capt. Evenson's boat. Wednesday afternoon the Ichang Bachelors entertained for young and old. They had a Christmas tree and Santa Claus, plus a present for each foreign child. Sonnie received a fine teddy bear. And Thursday afternoon Emma had a little tea party. Then I read "Richard Carvel" during the week, enjoying it very much. This evening George and I are invited over to Mr. Franzen's for 6:30 supper. Mr. F. is one of the Swedish missionaries.

Now we must buckle down to work. We have had a splendid teacher during December and George has done a lot of studying, putting in three, four hours a day. Now I am going to put in a little time each day. Then the chapel will be ready soon and then George will have considerable work there and I must get some sewing done. My woman sews nicely when I show her what to do, so she can relieve me of a good deal. And I believe she is as anxious to help prepare for a little one as I am. She wants me to be very careful and is quite interested in everything. I was very pleased with her ironing the other day. She has learned quite quickly.

So you had a good laugh at my Norsk. I meant to write "flrög"[103] – I was making an attempt to express "den tykke 'l'."[104] So now!

My oh my! After eleven and oodles to do before 12:30.

Much Love to all,
Bernice

---

[103] "flew" (Norwegian)
[104] "the thick l" (Norwegian)

GEORGE ANSWERS HIS SISTER'S QUESTIONS.
"…there are about 100 foreigners in all,…we are kept almost too busy attending social functions,…"

Evangelical Lutheran Mission,
ICHANG, HUPEH, CHINA.

GEO. O. LILLEGARD,

Ichang, January 3d, 1922

Dear sister Louise:—

Your letter of Nov.2d together with the photograph of you and the baby came about the middle of December, and your Christmas package came a few days ago. Thank you ever so much for it all. We appreciated it very much. We used the new pillowcases New Year's Day by way of celebrating, and I have also made use of the stockings.

We have received no package from the homefolks, but did get a package from the Onstads at the same time as yours. They sent mostly certain supplies that we had asked them to buy for us, but I received also a fine silver belt buckle and Bernice got a doily. Some of our Christmas mail was delayed, by the wrecking of a boat on the river, and several bags of mail were lost. We hope that none of our packages were among the lost and damaged articles. We should get them in a few days now.

We have not answered all your letters directly, I notice. But we have taken for granted that you get the letters we send to Chicago. However, we appreciate very much the letters you send, and I hope you will keep up writing to us, even if we do not answer so regularly.

We have been sort of wondering why Nehemias did not write to us. He used to be a pretty regular correspondent. You might tell him we are beginning to think he is down on us or something!

We were certainly glad to hear that Olga was improving so much. I hope that she continues to improve and suffers no relapses. Tell her I shall answer her letter soon, and that we would appreciate very much hearing from her regularly.

You have asked a number of questions in your letters, which I shall answer as best I can this time. Yes, our piano is here and is in very good tune. It had been handled pretty roughly some place, but in spite of that it kept in good shape as far as the strings and tone quality are concerned. We enjoy it very much. Bernice gets more time to play here than she did in Chicago. There are not so many other things to do, in the social way.

By the way, it just occurred to me that I have not yet sent that $5.00 to Miss Nelson that Mr. Lovik gave me for her. It has simply slipped my mind most of the time, and when I have thought of it, I have not been in a position to look up her address. But I shall get to work right away and send it to her, and you may tell Mr. Lovik from me that the money has been sent at last. He did not know her address himself, so I did not have a note of it. It is Siangyang, Hupeh.

I like Ichang pretty well, in many ways better than Kwangchow. Of course the life in port cities like Ichang and Hankow, where there are so many other foreigners, is not like it is in inland cities where you perhaps are the only foreigner. Here there are about 100 foreigners in all, outside of the sailors on the British, American, and Japanese gunboats in port. So we are quite a community. Every once in awhile there is a garden party or some program to which everyone is invited, so that we are kept almost too busy attending social functions, at times. We shall have to cut out some of it. In a place like Ichang, there are not so many foreigners but what all are invited to most everything. Thus in the last week, we have been to two programs given by the American and British sailors, to a boat race between the two gunboats, to a Christmas Tree Party given by the Bachelors, besides to tea at a couple homes and to dinner on board one of the river steamers, the captain of which is a Norwegian. We have English services every Sunday for the benefit of the Lutherans in town - a Norwegian family by the name of Nilsen, and some of the sailor boys being Lutherans. Shihnan, the city is inland it is a beautiful place, and if I should eventually go there, I think that I should like that place also considerably better than Kwangchow. It is in a picturesque valley, and one can see the high mountains from almost any point of vantage in the city, such as the city wall or a second story building.

Yes, we can get anything in Hankow, and even in Ichang, as foreign goods of all kinds are imported, but of course many of them are too expensive by the time they get here for the missionaries' purse. We have coffee right along, but here most people have tea in the afternoon, English style. Candy can be bought, but we do not like to eat the Chinese candies, tempting as they are, because it is not clean or safe, and the foreign candy is pretty expensive. However, Bernice can make better candy than any we buy. Sugar is cheaper here than at home, and peanuts, walnuts, etc., are very plentiful and cheap. We have had pears, oranges, mandarin oranges, pomelos, persimmons, and lemons all fall, and in this part of the country there is generally some fruit to be had at all times of the year. Apples are scarce here, but we got some imported apples for Christmas from the Hankow brethren, so that we are getting even them. Peaches, plums, etc., are plentiful in season.

I have lost in weight, because I went to work to get rid of some fat. 200 lbs. is too fat for me. Tennis and mountain climbing are pretty good fat reducers. I have been feeling better if anything since coming to China than before. Bernice has been getting fatter, I think, since coming here, and in general looks better than before.

I have quite a few letters that I must try to get off my hands soon, so I shall close with this. Best greetings to Sande and the Tjernagels.

And love to you and family from Bernice and myself,

Your brother,

George

REPORT FOR TERM ENDING DECEMBER 31ST, 1921
Geo. O. Lillegard

Together with Rev. Gebhardt I left Kuling August 29th. After a couple days spent in Hankow, we started out for Ichang, at which place I had been stationed. When we arrived, we found the city in a state of siege, as the Szechuanese had attacked the Northern troops on both sides of the river. The day we landed, the Northerners were cleared out of the hills on the right bank of the river across from Ichang, and the sounds of battle ceased for a couple days, while the opposing armies reorganized and cleared the battle fields of dead and wounded. In this latter work, we assisted one day together with some other foreigners in Ichang, having been asked to look after the Northern wounded left back of the Szechuan lines.

In spite of the excitement, we were fortunately able to rent a house at a reasonable rental not far from the new South Gate of the Chinese city. The house with the necessary repairs could be made suitable for two families, and as Rev. Schwartzkopf could not proceed to Shihnan under the existing conditions, arrangements were made to house his family there also for the time being. Rev. Gebhardt, however, proceeded to Shihnan, succeeding in getting through the Szechuan lines by traveling via the foreign river steamer, although the boat was heavily fired upon.

Since it was impossible to do anything more at the time, I returned within a week to Hankow, from which place I made a hurried trip to Kwangchow, Honan, to gather up the belongings I had left there since 1915. The first part of October I returned to Ichang, to find the city just beginning to recover from the attack that had finally been beaten off. That month was required, however, to get the house repaired and put in order, our goods unpacked, and the household put in "running order," so that I could leave my wife, inexperienced as she was in things Chinese, to the tender mercies of our servants and neighbors.

November 10th Rev. Schwartzkopf and I started out for Shihnan to help Rev. Gebhardt in the work which he had taken upon himself or to save him from the danger that he was in, whichever the circumstances might require. We had just heard that Shihnan had been the scene of severe fighting between Szechuanese, Northerners, and local troops, that the city had been looted, the Missions raided, one man killed on our Mission place, and that the situation was still uncertain. But we could not ask Rev. Gebhardt to leave his station without knowing something at firsthand with regard to the conditions and seeing what work there was at Shihnan to detain him there through such dangerous times as this. We arrived at Shihnan, traveling via Kwei-fu and Tai-Chi on November 17th. We found our Mission station full of orphan boys and wounded soldiers. But since the people had fled from the city in large number, and those left were afraid to venture out on the streets any more than necessary on account of the presence of the very soldiers who had twice attacked and looted the city, there was little opportunity to do active mission work. We had also been given good reason to believe that the Szechuanese were preparing another attack on the Northern troops, and that the Northerners were also preparing for an aggressive campaign to drive the Szechuanese out of the province of Hupeh. Thus it appeared that Shihnan would be the center of military operations for some (time) to come, and might become an exceptionally dangerous place for a foreigner to stay, since the Szechuan soldiers had shown an increasingly anti-foreign spirit. In view of all the circumstances, we decided after talking the matter thoroughly over to leave Shihnan for the time being, and to put in our time getting the work in Ichang started and investigating the field with a view to determining which centers should next be occupied by our expanding Mission. After arrangements had been made with a group of reliable Chinese catechumens to look after the orphans and wounded soldiers on our premises, we left Shihnan, traveling again via Tai-Chi and Kwei-fu, and arriving at Ichang on Nov. 27th. Since that time, I have put in the greater part of my time studying the Chinese language in the effort to recover the command of the language which I lost during my six years' absence in the States. We have also arranged to open work here. A very suitable location was found, near the new South Gate, on a very busy street. Here we have rented two sections of a foreign-style building, just built, where we will have room for a chapel to seat 150 people, a reading-room where guests or visitors will have an opportunity to read the Scriptures and Christian literature, which is also to be on sale there, a school-room or street-chapel, and room enough for a gatekeeper and evangelist to make themselves at home in.

Since we have no evangelist or teacher that we can put in charge of this place, we have had to content ourselves with engaging a somewhat stupid and therefore fairly reliable man as janitor and gatekeeper, and a Chinese gentleman of good family and some leisure to receive visitors and seek to interest them in our Christian literature. Since the chapel is only a short distance from our residence, it will be possible for us to spend considerable time in the reading-room each day to interview men who seem interested in our work as well as to conduct catechumen classes, as soon as we have some catechumens definitely enrolled.

May the New Year, 1922, find the work of the Lord prospering in this city as well as in the other sections of the province which has been chosen as our field for sowing the precious seed of God's eternal Word.

BERNICE'S SECOND PREMATURE DELIVERY
"We shall pray that the good Lord will bless us with healthy children in his own good time."

Ichang, January 21st, 1922

Dear folks,

This time I shall have to do the writing for the family, as Bernice is in bed in the hospital. Last night at 7:30 she gave birth to a still-born girl, who arrived about two months too early, apparently, or at least something over a month. Bernice is doing very well, and so far as we can tell now will be on her feet again quite in proper season.

But to begin at the beginning: Sunday morning, just as she was about to leave the house to attend the services in our new chapel, she noticed that she was "flowing" a little. I had already gone to the chapel. But she lay down, while Mrs. Schwartzkopf went for the doctor. He gave her a morphine injection, and by 2 P.M. she was in a private room in the hospital. Since examination showed that she was in the preparatory stages of delivery, the Dr. advised keeping her here, although she did not flow any more after the first attack, and seemed to grow better for a couple days. She stayed on her back in bed all the time. I slept here nights, and the Chinese woman that we have been training waited on her when I wasn't here during the day. And of course the nurse and Dr. looked in every once in awhile. The end came rather suddenly last night. The "waters" had been coming quite freely in the afternoon, and then about 7 P.M. came an abnormal amount of more "waters." The birth followed very soon after. The Dr. and nurse were in attendance and she was given chloroform during the worst of the pains, which were not as severe as usual, it seems. The afterbirth came away with the child, so that everything was over by 7:30. By 9 P.M. she was dressed and ready to see me again.

Miscarriages are common occurrences here in China. The climate seems to affect the nervous system of foreign women, so that they have often severe menstruations, and are much more subject to abortions and miscarriages than at home. The immediate cause of this miscarriage <u>may</u> have been a rather long rickshaw ride which Bernice had the evening before. We had been invited then to the Swedish Mission to meet one of their missionaries from the Belgian Congo. We did not know that rickshaws were dangerous. Afterwards the Dr. said that he should have warned us against using them on these rough streets here. We shall certainly be more careful another time.

The Dr. says that he will be able to say in a couple days more definitely whether or no Bernice will suffer any complications. So far she has been fine. She has no fever – her appetite is good – and her cheeks are as pink as ever! It is, of course, a terrible disappointment to us both that things should go this way, now that we have been planning and preparing so long. But we must not complain. We shall pray that the good Lord will bless us with healthy children in his own good time.

Mother's letter was received yesterday. B. wanted to write you, Mutter,[105] but did not feel well enough, since she was rather expecting to give you the title of "grandmother" as her birthday present to you. We would have rejoiced very much if we

---

[105] German for mother

could have sent you a cable to that effect, on your 50th birthday. Our best wishes anyway for a blessed and happy 50th year.

I have little other news to relate than this that our new chapel was formally opened last Sunday. The weather was bad, so we had no other auditors than our servants and teacher. The hour was also bad – 10 A.M., when the Chinese eat their first meal. Hereafter we shall meet at 2 P.M. Sunday Schwartzkopf & Gebhardt preached, and I read the service. Tomorrow I shall ask Schw. to take charge of the services.

Gebhardt left yesterday morning for Shihnan. Just last night, we heard that a Catholic priest had been killed by bandits at Lichwan, 50 miles west of Shihnan. We have sent a messenger after Gebhardt asking him to return, as we do not think he ought to go out there so long as conditions are as unsettled as they are.

I shall write again in a couple days and let you know how Bernice is faring. In the meantime, I hope you people will not worry about her. She suffered no lacerations whatever and she is in good hands here. We have a large comfortable room in the hospital. It has been cold these days, but with a little nursing, the tiny stove we have, manages to keep the room warm enough. It snowed and rained last Saturday, Sunday, Monday, and was really quite bitterly cold until yesterday P.M. Then it let up a little. So much for this time.

Love and greetings from us two – still us two – to you all,
George

(Over)

(Written by Bernice)

Dear Mama,

Am flat on my back so my penmanship is kind of funny! Am sorry you couldn't have been grandma on your 50th birthday, but we are not so fortunate. But I am feeling pretty fine and you must not worry one bit. By the time you get this I'll be up and managing my household as usual.

Will write a regular letter as soon as I can move a bit. Am well taken care of by everyone.

Much Love,
<u>Bernice</u>

BERNICE EXPRESSES DISAPPOINTMENT OVER LOSS.
"…God in His Wisdom has seen fit not to grant us a child yet."

Hospital, Ichang, Hupeh
January 23rd, 1922

Dear Mumsie,

You don't care how this letter looks, as long as you can decipher it, do you? I feel so crippled today that I'm writing under great difficulties. Had tho't to write a long letter, but fear it won't be that this time. Have really been doing splendidly – beyond everyone's expectations, I think. My temperature and pulse were quite normal until last night, and the nurse says I'm normal "downstairs." But I must confess I'm not comfortable today, and that is because milk is being secreted, in spite of attempts to prevent that. And so I have a little higher temperature – it has been less than 100° so far, however, so it isn't alarming! Nurse Jeffrey bound my breasts Saturday morning, but either she didn't get the bandage high enough, or else it simply would not be stopped. She did her best for me, I know. I surely have been, and am, bound up with all this bandage and padding around my breasts and a binder around much of the rest of me! And while my size has decreased in the one region, I now have quite a mountain farther up. I told Dr. Borthwick this forenoon that I tho't I had enough for twins and he did laugh so.

I know you wonder why it happened. Would we knew, Mother! All we know is that God in His Wisdom has seen fit not to grant us a child yet. Maybe we are quite unworthy of such happiness and we both feel we received a lesson and must try to better ourselves – by His Grace. I need not tell you we feel keenly disappointed, but maybe another time all will go well.

George mentioned a rickshaw ride as a possible cause, but I must tell you that now all is over – well before that too, in fact – the doctor does not think so. Just at first he tho't so, because the roads were bad that day. But had that been the cause, it would not have taken five days to bring on the birth. During the month or so preceding this I experienced a great deal of discomfort and various pains. Especially did I suffer with backaches. At night I was anxious to get to bed and in the morning I was glad to get up. I went to the doctor and he came & examined me also and everything appeared OK. My urine was all right – it was tested at regular intervals – and my bowels were loose. But what I noticed particularly was the sudden and quick change in my sizes. I became so large in just about three weeks that it didn't seem quite right. But there was no satisfaction to be had. Well, then on the 15th there was the sudden and rather slight hemorrhage. The following morning, and every other day thereafter, the doctor examined me and found the birth canal gradually opening. He says he never saw it open so easily. Well, it's all right for them to say that, but they probably don't know what my back felt like those days, even tho' I said it felt like a sore tooth and a boil. Then I had pains – or pain, as it was a steady pain almost – in the uterus too. I could feel it expand often, but not contract. But from Thurs. at midnight I evidently began to be in labor, tho' no one recognized it as such since it was not the usual thing. I had a most awful back and sore uterus – that's the only way I can describe the abdominal pains – all the time with spells of violent pain. But they were not the bearing down pains. But at noon the waters began to come and kept on coming faster gradually until at 7 o' clock P.M., when I had been <u>really</u> sick for awhile, and then in one "shot" there came an <u>excessive</u> amount of water. Why, I pretty near drowned myself! In spite of all efforts to keep it somewhat "centrally located," some of it ran over and almost to my neck. And after that things happened so fast that I kept the doctor & nurses running. Doctor kept telling me I was having a mighty easy time of it, and I guess I really must have, Mama, compared with many. But they gave me a little chloroform towards the last to keep me more quiet and to relieve me. It was not enough to put me entirely "under" tho.'

So my large size is explained. The nurse had also examined me – she has had special obstetrical training – and tho't I must have a large baby, so we were all in great hopes the little life would be saved, even tho' it came prematurely. It did kick a little only a couple hours before the birth, but the poor little thing could not outlive that ordeal. Well, so much for this. I have repeated not a little of what George wrote, but I had to in order to be coherent. So, "blease eggscuse"!

Disappointed as I am, I try not to dwell on it too much. I think I shall continue making small garments at odd times right along. And I'm going to delve into Chinese and athletics for some months. So I'll keep my mind as busy as I can. And Emma says I may be foster-mother to her baby when it comes. I think I will feel my loss keenest when hers arrives. Aa ja![106] Please, will you send me a "Bunting" pattern? I don't know how to go about it and I'd like a pattern now so I can make a real pretty one- take my time at it. You sent 1 1/3 yds. you know. By the way, I had just finished four nighties the week before this happened. Had no shirts tho'! Next time I'm going to be ready early – probably before I know whether there's need or not!!

Nurse says she is going to put a Belladonna plaster on me tonight, which should give me relief. So I guess I'll be O.K. tomorrow. Expect to get home in a couple days if my breasts give no more trouble. Travel via stretcher! When I can sit up more, I'll attempt to answer some of your questions in recent letters.

In the meantime – So long!

Much Love to you all from
Your same old daughter

Bernice

---

[106] Literally Oh, yes; Oh, well

"Chicago March 7th 1922. Tuesday

Dear George & Bernice,

Last Sat. March 3rd we received Bernice's letter written the 28th of Jan. telling about that she was just out of the hostital[107] & home again. We were so shocked as we had not heard any thing before that. But today we received two letters one from each of you telling all about your troubles. They were written the 20th & 24th of Jan. You both have the sympety from us all. We do feel so sorry for you. But still there are many things to be thankful for. If you only get well & strong again Bernice we will all be happy & it is a blessing that the child dyed when it was not just right, and it may not happen again so let us not worry about that. God willing evry thing may be perfectly alright & lovely another time…& wise men don't know any more than other's why such things happen.

George you ask about your father's family. I don't think there were any miscariages. They were five in the family. Guri the eldest then Lein that died just after they came to this country the same time that there mother died, and then Astri & papa & a brother younger that died when a few days old. Heis name was Mikkel. And there was three years between them all.

Your grandpa had a bad leg for years & was a cripple & died from that disease. It must have been tuberculosis.

Here we are all well & getting along as usual. But Grandma has been quite sick with pneumonia again. Lawrence has been to see her several times. She was getting over it allright they thot, but today we had a letter from Olga saying she was worse. Olga is there she had just came when she wrote us & they would like to have me came & I don't know what to do. Its such an inconvenient time for me to leave. We are trying to rent our flat furnished & thot we had succeeded they the party said they wanted it, but I guess they could not give the reffrences that Mr. Wolf our Landlord demanded. He is doing the buissness for us. We are asking $80 per month. I think we could have rented it to another party if this one had not fooled us. Now we will have to put an add in the paper again.

Yes we received your letter explaining the rode,[108] But man proposes. God disposes.

We were beginning to wonder why we did not get a cable. In your last letters Geo you said Bernice was troubled with backache. I told the girls that was a bad synton and besides you said you took long walks evry day. Now that was the worst thing to do. She should have been very quiet then. Bernice I think you are a very brave little woman to write as cheerfully as you do and that is the way to be. Let not your hearts be troubled. Ye believe in God, believe also in me, the bible says.

Mr. & Mrs. Rennen lost their little girl a few weeks ago. Geo you babtized her just before you left for China. Rev. Krey performed the funeral services.

Oscar Sörlien from Bode called on us one evening he say things are picking up a little in Bode again. You know J.T. Temple is postmaster now. Adelaide assistant. They are in my building but I have not heard a word from Temple. Oscar said he would speak to him. Of course, they will want the building. I have soon got 3 months rent coming. Well I must quit now hoping to hear from you soon that all is well.

With love from
Mother. (Ansoph Lillegard)"

---

[107] It's curious to note that her spelling of some simpler words is wrong, but she spelled other more difficult ones correctly; maybe she was using a dictionary?
[108] This possibly refers to the bumpy ride Bernice had before the premature delivery.

Missouri Synod Western Dist. Pres. offers sympathies on their still-born baby.

OFFICE OF PRESIDENT
Ev. Lutheran Synod of Missouri, Ohio, and other States
WESTERN DISTRICT
CONCORDIA SEMINARY (ST. LOUIS) BOARD OF CONTROL
BOARD OF FOREIGN MISSIONS

Emmaus Lutheran Church
JEFFERSON AVE. AND ARMAND PL.

Bell Phone: Sidney 1526 J
Kinloch Phone: Victor 816 R

RICH. KRETZSCHMAR, PASTOR
2243 S. JEFFERSON AVE.

ST. LOUIS, MO. 4/13 1922

Rev. & Mrs. Geo. Lillegard,
Ichang, China.

My dear Friends:

When I received your letter of Febr. 10 it moved me to sincere sympathy. How sad, that your fond hopes were turned to sorrowful disappointment. May the Lord cheer your hearts with the comforting assurance that even though His thoughts are unfathomable they certainly are thoughts of peace and not of evil and that under His kind providence all things must work together for good to them that love God.

Thank you for the report on your activities since conference at Kuling, also Mrs. L. for the article which was published in the Kirke Tidende.

The account given by Rev. Schwartzkopf on your trip to Shinanfu made me send up to God expressions of gratitude, for His gracious deliverence and protection He gave you in great dangers. We hope the days of warfare and bloodshed may be over and that the work of messengers of peace may now go on unobstructed.

Rev. Brand is now on his trip to Europe. We hope to see him in St. Louis in June. I am very anxious to see him back. I cannot give the foreign missions the time necessary, and the other members of the board are not yet sufficiently posted to give me the urgent relief.

Yesterday Mr. Pettus the manager of the Peking Union Language School was here to see me. We had a long conference and I was very favorably impressed. He understands our doctrinal position much better than most people belonging to sectarian churches and I think we can make satisfactoy arrangements with him in regard to our misionaries who wish to study at his school.

With cordial Easter greetings,

Faithfully yours,

Rich. Kretzschmar

Vice-President Brand sends sympathies also.

BOARD OF FOREIGN MISSIONS.
SUBCOMMITTEE AT ST. LOUIS.
REV. RICH. KRETZSCHMAR, PRESIDENT,
　2213 S. JEFFERSON AVE.
REV. O. CHR. BARTH, SECRETARY,
　4528 ALASKA AVE.
MR. WM. LEHR, TREASURER
　3603 OHIO AVE.
PROF. L. FUERBRINGER,
　CONCORDIA SEMINARY.
PROF. E. PARDIECK, CONCORDIA SEMINARY.
MR. O. SCHMIDT, 3712 NEBRASKA AVE.

MEMBERS AT LARGE
REV. J. F. BOERGER.
REV. P. ROESENER.
PROF. S. YLVISAKER, PH. D.
REV. H. M. ZORN.
PROF. F. ZUCKER.

Evangelical Lutheran Synod
of
Missouri, Ohio, and Other States.

BOARD OF FOREIGN MISSIONS.
REV. FREDERICK BRAND,
Director and General Secretary,
St. Louis, Mo. U. S. A.

OFFICERS OF SYNOD.
REV. F. PFOTENHAUER, D. D. PRESIDENT,
　415 W. 62D ST., CHICAGO, ILL.
REV. F. BRAND, 1ST VICE-PRESIDENT,
　3316 S. JEFFERSON AVE.
　　ST. LOUIS, MO.
REV. J. W. MILLER, 2ND VICE-PRESIDENT,
　1126 BARR ST., FORT WAYNE, IND.
REV. O. A. BERNTHAL, 3RD VICE-PRESIDENT,
　969 EDDY ST., SAN FRANCISCO, CAL.
REV. H. P. ECKHARDT, 4TH VICE-PRES.,
　318 MOREWOOD AVE.,
　　PITTSBURGH, PA.
REV. M. KRETZMANN, SECRETARY,
　309 S. OAK ST., KENDALLVILLE, IND.
MR. E. SEUEL, TREASURER,
　3558 S. JEFFERSON AVE.,
　　ST. LOUIS, MO.

Chemnitz i/S, Germany,
April 23, 1922.

Rev. Geo. O. Lillegard,
Ichang, China.

My dear Brother,

　　Your quaterly report and letter dated February 10th were sent me from India to Chemnitz, and I was deeply interested in all you wrote. Allow me to express both my wife's and my own sympathy in your second disappointment. The Lord knows just what He is doing. May he grant you and your good wife firm trust in his leading. Mrs Brand and I passed through a similar disappointment and surely feel with you.

　　We left India a few weks earlier than we had intended, first, because I was through with my work, and then, because it was impossible to get passage to Europe during April, May and the first half of June. As my synodical work begins in June, I had to be at home at that time, if it was at all possible. Our voyage from India to Europe was uneventful. Here I find things less favorable than I had expected. The brethren are urging me to remain over for their synod which is to be held in June, but I have not yet decided to remain.

　　I thank God that you are now firmly located in Ichang. I have no doubt that this city had to be occupied in the interest of our Shinan work. We can only plant. Success must come from the Lord. May he look favorably upon your labors.

　　I know that you will look to consistent Lutheran practice. We might as well fold our tents and 'hie ourselves away' if we are not faithful and true to our convictions which are based upon the Word. Do not be afraid to testify in love whenever it becomes necessary. That we can not please the Reformed church with our firm stand for the truth, is plain. Neither do we intend to please. Nor are we called to do this. Let us be satisfied to please the Lord who commissioned us to do his work.

　　You and the brethren in Ichang have experienced the gracious protection of our Lord. In future disturbances he will be no less able to keep you. If we missionaries wish to wait until all war clouds blow over, the Lord's work will never be done.

　　It is my earnest intention to keep looking for a doctor or at least a trained nurse for Shinan. But the Lord is the giver. Therfore let us keep asking him to provide.

　　As soon as I dig through the mountain of mail I found here in Chemnitz and which all claims my immediate attention I shall write you again.

　　Please remember me to brother Gebhard and the Schwartzkopfs. I trust the latter have had an increase in their family by this time.

　　With cordial regards to Mrs. Lillegard and yourself
　　　I am truly yours in Christ

　　　　　　　　　　Frederick Brand

GEORGE RESPONDS WITH THANKS FOR SYMPATHIES.
"…we hope that someday 'everything will be allright.'"

Kuling, China, July 11th, 1922

The Rev. Fr. Brand
St. Louis, MO

Dear friend,

Your letter of April 23rd – which happens to have been my birthday, by the way – was received at Ichang, upon our return from Shihnan. Thank you very much for your cheering words. My wife has been gaining in health and strength right along, and we hope that some day "everything will be allright."

I enclose my report for the year past, to be presented to the Conference this summer. It is largely a repetition of the reports already sent in, but you will no doubt be interested also in a copy of this. I certainly hope that my wife and I can lead a more settled life next year. Our life has not lacked in interest and in valuable experience, but I do not feel that I have gotten as much studying or mission work done as I should. Politically things seem to be clearing up a little in China, so that it may be that we will have no further disturbances on our field to break up our work. But nobody can tell. Gebhardt reports exciting times in Shihnan the last weeks, as the troops that were there all spring packed up and left for Szechuan shortly after my wife and I departed, taking ten or fifteen thousand dollars of the people's money with them. Thereafter, one band of the soldiers after the other came, demanded money, and left. Now, according to his last letter, the Northern soldiers should have arrived, which means that the road from Shihnan will be open and that peace should prevail throughout that district, until the Szechuanese start another "Save Hupeh" expedition.

We find the new missionaries a very attractive set of young people, physically handsome, mentally alert, and apparently as earnest and sincere about mission work and their Lutheranism as one could wish. May the Missouri Synod be given grace to continue sending of its best to the foreign fields so that it may be possible to build up a truly Evangelical Lutheran Church also in the heart of this heathen stronghold. We look forward to a profitable Conference, with considerable emphasis laid upon the doctrinal papers to be read by Schwartzkopf on "The Means of Grace" and by Zschiegner on "The Congregation." I have a paper on "Chinese Superstitious Customs." We have also arranged for Chinese services on Sunday afternoons, and for special meetings for the benefit of the ladies of our mission, to be held during the week, to study some book of the Bible, or this year, Introduction to the New Testament Books. Klein has been asked to take charge of these meetings this summer. For Sunday evenings, we have arranged to have a series of doctrinal sermons. In this way, we hope that the theological study, which we so sadly neglect during the year under the stress of our mission work and language study, will be stimulated and encouraged.

We are waiting rather anxiously to hear what the Board decides with regard to the recommendations we made last summer. So much will depend on that. One difficult question for us is going to be the school question. If Meyer is to go home on furlough next year, we really ought to have his successor appointed this year, so that he could get somewhat into the work this year. The question of securing workers for Shihnan may also cause some trouble, unless it is solved this way that Gebhardt and we stay there, together with one of the new couples.

Nagel sailed from Australia in June and is expected some time this week. He is to stay with us in Arndt's house. Miss Arndt and Mrs. Wampner from Shanghai may also be staying with us for a few weeks this summer. The last two-three weeks we have been alone – for the first time since we came to China – and we have enjoyed the novelty.

Have you heard anything more with regard to Rev. Backerud, the man in San Francisco whom I spoke to you about last summer? There are no calls available in the Norw. Syn. and so he still is inactive. If someone would speak to the proper authorities in the Mis. Synod about his case, make a frank investigation in case there is any doubt about his fitness for the ministry, and then act accordingly, I feel that a good man would be gained for the work of the Church. He is not the kind who will do anything himself in order to gain a call, so that he may be forgotten if someone else does not take his case up. His pastor, Rev. Brohm, has promised him that he will do something about the matter, but seems to be very slow in acting. I take it upon myself to mention this matter to you, since I spoke to you last summer about him, and you know something about the spiritual trials through which he has passed these last years.

My wife sends best greetings to you and your family. We hope to hear soon that you have arrived safe and sound in the States and are hard at work for the great mission cause. With best wishes to you,

Sincerely yours,

Geo. O. Lillegard

BERNICE WRITES 2 ½ WEEKS AFTER DAUGHTER STILLBORN.

"Ichang is also at the entrance of the famous Yangtze Gorges, which for grandeur rival Niagara Falls, if indeed they do not surpass them."

A LETTER FROM CHINA Ichang, February 7th, 1922

The many questions asked by friends in the States have given me a clue to the thoughts which may arise also in the minds of readers of this paper upon being reminded of our China Mission. Therefore, I hope the following may be of interest to some of you.

Those of you who have read other articles from the mission field will know that we are living in the city of Ichang this year. Have you located Ichang? It is approximately 30 degrees north latitude, 111 degrees east longitude, in the province of Hupeh, and on the Yangtze River. Via that river we are about 1000 miles from the Pacific coast and of course the river forms the route of travel, there being no railroads completed in this section. Ichang is also at the entrance of the famous Yangtze Gorges, which for grandeur rival Niagara Falls, if indeed they do not surpass them. The city itself lies in a little valley encircled by high hills and mountains. The mountains directly across the river are very interesting, there being a series which are pyramidical in shape. The largest of these is a landmark, one may say, and has won the name "Old Pyramid." The name "Old Sentinel" would appeal to me, as it seems to me to be a big guardian. Ichang has an estimated population of 80,000, and some think it may be larger. It is a port city, but there are no foreign concessions and the foreign community is comparatively small. I should say 100 foreigners is a fair estimate, excluding, however, the sailors on the several foreign gunboats stationed here.

I wish you could take a walk with me in "Chinese City," as we usually call the section within the city wall. The city has been growing and there is quite a large area occupied without the walled city. We live in this latter section. Unless you had made a study of Chinese habits and customs or had been warned by friends, you would undoubtedly be shocked, as well as interested. The Chinese have many filthy habits, but I prefer not to dwell on them. But in spite of bad smells and offensive sights, I have thoroughly enjoyed the many long walks my husband and I have taken through the Chinese streets. Not only are the streets very narrow in the first place, but several feet on each side are taken up by a variety of stalls and booths, selling food, vegetables, tobacco, fish, meat, and all such things. Or one sees trays filled with stockings, towels, brass ware, and crockery. And then a barber may come along and, finding someone who desires a shave, be it on his face or head, forthwith deposits his portable barber shop, consisting of a stool, wash basin, warm water, towel, soap, and "tools," and gets to work. So you understand a street is not a public thoroughfare only, but is utilized fully as much by individuals for individual purposes.

Upon our arrival in the Orient last summer I discovered that my ideas regarding the dress of the Japanese and the Chinese respectively had been very vague. And not long ago I read a statement by an American author, which indicated that also habits and customs of the one people are confused with those of the other. In Japan both men and women wear kimonos, in China neither wear them. Here the Mandarin coats are worn. Formerly these coats were full and had very wide, loose sleeves. The present style is more conservative, the sleeves being made to fit quite tightly and the coat having no fullness. Chinese men wear trousers which are held in tightly at the ankle by a ribbon. Over these and some short "coats," which take the place of Occidental underwear, are worn the Mandarin coats reaching to the ankles. Outside of these again are frequently worn short, rather tight coats reaching to the waist. The women wear trousers reaching about to the ankle and coats which vary in length, but I believe the really modest wear them knee-length. Some wear both shorter trousers and coats. Such is the characteristic dress, but occasionally one sees men dressed in foreign style and women wearing skirts. However, the Chinese cling to their native dress more tenaciously than do the Japanese, especially than the men of the latter country.

There is one thing that has bothered me more or less ever since we came to China and that is the sight of bound feet. It is most pitiful to see Chinese women hobbling along on their tiny feet. If there were anything dainty or attractive about a bound foot, one might understand their submission to such torture, but we from the Occident, at least, fail to find anything about it which appeals to our sense of beauty. On the other hand, those women who have been spared that pain have the daintiest feet and shapely ankles. There are, however, comparatively few in the latter class. I have not seen a naked bound foot yet but it has been described to me as follows: All the toes are brought under the foot toward the arch and they walk on the heel and the toes thus turned. Naturally the instep is forced up and there is a large, round bunch of flesh and bones where the ankle ought to be. It is a terrible practice! Many women suffer a great deal much of the time, not only during the growing period.

One of the questions most frequently asked is, "What do you eat?" We have practically the same foods here that we were accustomed to having in the States, with the exception of some of the luxuries – at least, they seem luxuries to me now! We can buy many of the foreign vegetables and we use native vegetables, which are very good. Fruits are available in season, especially here in Ichang, this country being quite rich in fruits. In a city like Hankow all sorts of foreign goods may be had for the money. Ichang has two stores that carry quite a complete line of canned goods, but prices are almost prohibitive so we indulge in such things only rarely. So far I have been fortunate enough to get some fresh milk, but at present I get less than a pint a day. Pork, mutton, beef, chicken, and fish are to be had, but we eat beef as a rule, or sometimes chicken, as we consider them the safest and most desirable from several standpoints. When one has seen how the pigs live and what they have to eat, one's appetite for pork is not particularly stimulated. The meat vendors do not distinguish between various cuts of meat so we simply order a quantity of beef, or whatever it is – not a sirloin steak, a roast, or a soup bone. Although generally quite satisfactory, it must be admitted that choice meats are not to be had. The Chinese have no scruples about putting an animal on the market that has died of old age or disease!

When I tell you that we have three servants you will undoubtedly be astonished and also consider us extravagant. In the first place I must tell you that for the three we pay the equivalent of $10.00 – American money – per month and they furnish their own food and bedding. However, if we didn't actually need them, the fact that wages are small would surely not induce us to keep them. When you consider how many public servants you have, you may appreciate that we who lack all those must either have private servants or spend all our time in merely existing. We have no telephone, no water works or wells, no electricity, no gas, no furnaces or base burners, and many other things. If I wish to get word to a friend, I must send the "Boy" with a note. The cook must make daily trips to the markets to do the purchasing. Our water must be carried from the Yangtze and filtered before it can be used at all, also boiled before it can be used for drinking or cooking. Much time has to be spent in sterilizing foods and fruits, the filthy habits of the Chinese making them unsafe.

In spite of having several servants, a missionary's wife finds more than enough work to keep her occupied each day. Not a little time is required to superintend the work of the servants – Chinese servants require constant supervision and the exercises of various moral virtues, such as patience and self-control. She is also expected to devote as much time as can be spared from the household duties to the study of the language and to mission work. As long as one is attempting to acquire Chinese there will be no lack of work, and it is a life-long task!

Mrs. Geo. O. Lillegard

Chinese restaurant on the river front, Ichang, February, 1922

GEORGE COMPLAINS TO THE TELEGRAPH OFFICE.
"...the telegram...was delivered only after we had come, seen, and conquered our destination..."

February 22nd, 1922

To the Chinese Telegraph Administration:

The undersigned have been under the impression that a telegram was supposed to be able to make better time to a certain destination than anything or anybody else. The telegraph service in Ichang, however, seems to be planned on such leisurely lines that, like the hare in the old fable, it can be beaten by almost any Chinese coolie with a wheelbarrow. The undersigned had two telegrams sent them in December, neither of which was delivered at all, although the telegraph office had been notified of our arrival in the city and our address noted. February 10th, we paid $12.00, perfectly good Mexican dollars, to have our address registered, hoping fondly that this would ensure the prompt delivery of our telegrams. But on February 17th, we sent a telegram from Itu to Ichang, announcing our arrival on the Shasi-Ichang launch that evening. The telegram was sent "15:35," and arrived at Ichang "18:36." But for all that it was not delivered till about 14 hours later. Our residence is a five minutes' walk from the telegraph office, in a perfectly accessible place, that one does not need the light of the sun or even a lantern to find. But still the telegram which read: "Coming tonight," was delivered only after we had come, seen, and conquered our destination and had enjoyed a good breakfast on top of it.

We should like to be given some assurance that our telegrams will be delivered with reasonable promptness hereafter, or get our $12.00 perfectly good Mexican dollars back. Will someone in the proper office please register our little complaint and do us the honor of paying us a <u>little</u> attention?

Most respectfully yours,

Geo. O. Lillegard

Chapter 7
"Settled" in Shihnanfu

BERNICE WRITES OF MOVE TO SHIHNAN.
"…we're not afraid,…"
No. 45
Friday Eve.

Ev. Luth. Mission
Ichang, Hupeh, China
March 3rd, 1922

Dear Mama,

Night before last your letter No. 48 arrived. I was glad to hear the lace had arrived. You must allow extra time for all packages, it seems. I hope the two letters – 33 and 34 – came through O.K. They probably went on a slower boat. Too bad you should have had such a cold. And isn't it funny it should happen just when I was sick too? That is the second time you have been feeling badly at the same time as I have, but I guess I had the worst of it both times. Soon I will be getting superstitious and imagine you're not well every time I am not! Yes, and when I read of all the goodies you had on the 20th – it makes me almost homesick, although I was not very hungry just at that time. It is just six weeks ago tonight since that unfortunate evening and today is about the time we expected things to happen. It makes me feel a bit blue, but on the whole I've been quite happy lately. I study almost every forenoon and usually have enough to keep me busy afternoon and evening, so I do not have too much time to sit and brood over things. I'm feeling so well now and George and I are taking our almost daily walks again. But I do not particularly enjoy going into my cedar chest. There are so many dear little things there. By the time I have a little one I think I will have quite a respectable collection of things. There are many articles lacking however, and I will have plenty of preparation to enjoy. You'll send me a Bunting pattern, won't you? And some day I'd like to have you get a good maternity corset for me. I didn't have one – couldn't get a satisfactory one here and it was too late to send for one. The doctors and nurses strongly advise the use of them. I do not expect to need one for some time, but you could send one at any time, because in order to get any good of it I should have one on hand for the time I do need it. I like both Warner's and La Camille. Burdick's handle the latter. I also like front lace, low bust, and soft boning. At present I am not sure what my normal waist line measures, but I'll send that some other time. But I tho't I'd give the other description now while I thought of it and maybe you could keep this letter until you decide to buy one for me. Can do?

I am making a silk shirt for Emma's little one…I am waiting rather impatiently for the little jackets you have sent. They should come one of these days. Here you, who have so much to do, have been making so many things for me – oh well – I believe you rather enjoyed it and I shall be so glad to have them. It is fun to make such tiny things…

You say you've had nice weather. Received a letter from Netty at the same time as yours and she complained of the cold and snow. We have had a mild winter here. They say it has been milder than ordinary, at least. Now the trees are getting green again and here and there one sees new patches of grass. Have also seen a number of fields with some sort of grain coming up. The vegetable gardens have been in evidence all the time. I don't know how they took care of them during the cold weather.

Saturday Eve. – George was so tired last night that he wanted to go to bed early so I didn't finish this. Can you guess what big job we have been doing this week? We spent three evenings pasting in Kodak pictures. And we pasted in 384. Besides that we spent one evening pasting shortly after Christmas. So we have put in between 400-500. We have only a couple dozen or so left now and we will leave them until we can get some art corners. We are using them in my new album. In that album we have our wedding trip pictures, our trip last year, and some China pictures. I have written under some of them but still have quite a bit left of that to do…

…Now I have done all the calling I had left to do, but I ought to entertain a little. I am anxious to have the nurses and Mrs. Borthwick to tea. They have been so kind to me. But I may not be able to have them now – guess I'll have to make a special effort. You see I plan on going to Shihnan with George pretty soon. The doctor said I could go the latter part of this month, but I am feeling so well I hope he will let me go in a couple weeks. Gyps[109] is pretty rushed and we really must go soon. I am quite anxious to go. I think the experience will be quite worth while and I am eager to see the Gorges. Tho' the trip may not be so pleasant now, it will most likely be wonderful when we come back. Besides, if it gets to be a case of our having to go out there next year, I will know what it is like, and if we don't go, I may be able to encourage whoever does go. Because of a series of unfortunate circumstances Shihnan has been criticized and badly spoken of with the result that most of these young fellows are afraid to go out. Lou certainly seems to fear the place and is undoubtedly glad that we are going out and leaving Ichang to him for the present. Of course, George and I are not very anxious to be stationed there, but we have other reasons – we're not afraid, as I expect to prove to them now. Oh, I bet there'll be some fun at the Conference this summer! George is chairman and we hope he'll be able to keep calm and help things to run as smoothly as possible…

Hutte tu![110] I'm getting cold, so I guess I'll "beat it" to bed. Had a letter from Mrs. Flott the other night. I wrote to her in December – first time since we were married. Good Night, Everybody!

Much Love to all from George and Bernice

Please, Papa, will you send us a statement of our accounts?

Yichang (Ichang) in 1999 (photo by David Furholmen)

---

[109] Nickname for fellow missionary Arnold Gebhardt
[110] Brr! (Norwegian)

TO MOTHER – PRIVATE! (Written on outside of letter)
"Elsa is always wanting a ring…"

No. 46-B

Thursday A.M. (March 8, 1922)

Dear Mama,

    This is to be a sort of private note to you, unless you choose to let the children read it. Since we plan on leaving for Shihnan so soon we will have to do some things now that we might otherwise postpone for awhile. The other day George and I went into a big jewelry store here more out of curiosity than anything else. We asked to see a few things and found a very pretty ring which we finally purchased. Elsa is always wanting a ring and since she will graduate this spring a ring would not be inappropriate and this is as pretty and cheaper than you could get there. I wonder if Ragnar would like to go in on it with us. If he wants to put in $2.00 or so gold we will be glad to pay the rest. I am "crazy" about the ring myself. It is entirely Chinese – Chinese gold and workmanship. The set is black – about the size of my signet ring – and has a flower inlaid in colored stone. It fits my little finger and makes a nice little-finger-ring, but it could be sized if it is too small or if she wants it for the third finger. Maybe you think I am encouraging jewelry, etc. for Elsa, but I know she likes a little and what I can get here is better quality for less money, besides having the novelty of coming from China attached to them. Besides I think jewelry is more welcome at graduation time. However, I do not think it will get there in time for that event. I'm sorry, but the fact is we are afraid the duty would be high and so are going to ask Riedel to take a little package along for us when he goes home this spring. We do not know just when that will be. We don't know just what else we will send, but can let you know that later. I do intend to send you a silk scarf, a mate to the one George gave me for Christmas. It is not to be a special present but is to help pay for the many things you have sent and not charged us for – patterns, needles, etc. etc.

    Tuesday Dr. Borthwick gave me an examination again. He found that my uterus is retroverted. At present it is <u>not down</u>, for which I am thankful. And I feel much encouraged because the indications of a "fallen wall" in the vagina seem to have disappeared. When I tell you that a few weeks ago he was almost convinced that I would need an operation by a specialist at some future time, you will know I was glad to hear that he now said he would want to see my condition much worse before advising an operation. But of course it is bad enough for a young person to have any such trouble "downstairs." I have great hopes of overcoming it tho.' Tomorrow afternoon I am going to the hospital to have the womb put back where it belongs. An instrument is to be placed inside the uterus and then turned on its axis, thus bring the organ back into position. Dr. said I'd need no anesthetic and he tho't it would not hurt at all. If conditions are not bad, he thinks it will stay in place after that.[111]

    Yesterday afternoon I received two American packages – one of them from you, containing the jackets. There are just as dear and pretty as can be. I surely am glad to

---

[111] Bernice's next letter (March 12, 1922): "The doctor couldn't do anything for me last Friday. The uterus fell right back again."

have them and it was awfully good of you to make them. I showed them to my woman and she was delighted with them. Especially did she admire the ribbon bows.

The Chinese do not dress their babies at all like we do, but she tho't "foreign fashion" was very fine. The other package was from Chicago and contained a fine white knitted (or crocheted) hood with pretty blue ribbon bows – from Valborg, a pair of hose and rubber "pants" from Ella, a pair of white kid shoes and long white petticoat from Anna.[112] Beside there was a box of face powder for me. Everything is so dainty and pretty. The little shoes <u>are cute</u>! I'll be able to devote my time to making dresses, petticoats, and bedding next time.

Well, I must study now. I'm getting a mania for radicals – I like to analyze the characters, but whew! It taxes one's memory!

Much love to you all from
George and Bernice

Continue sending our letters to Ichang.

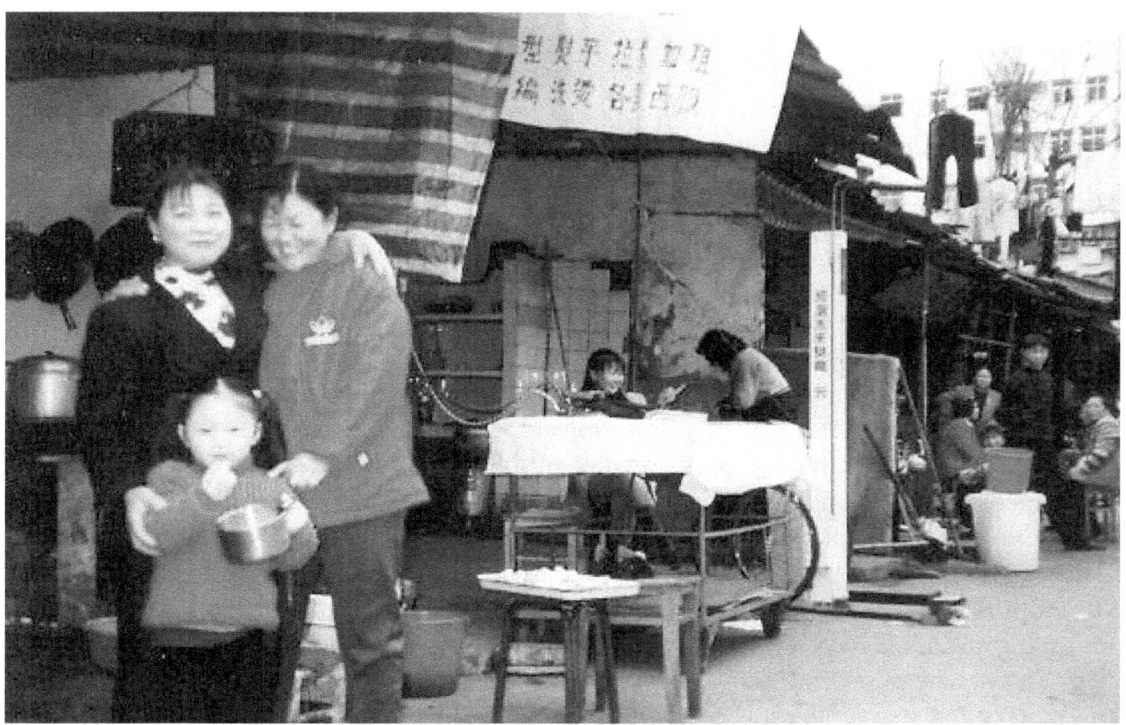

Yichang in 1999 (photo by David Furholmen)

---

[112] All three: George's sisters

BERNICE ENJOYS THE MAILBOAT TRIP ALONG THE GORGES.
"We have even seen 'cave dwellers' – "

Letter No. 48　　　　　　　　　　　　　　　　　　　　In a mail boat "cabin"
Sunday　　　　　　　　　　　　　　　　　　　　　　On the Yangtze Kiang
　　　　　　　　　　　　　　　　　　　　　　　　　　March 19th, 1922

Dear Folks,

　　　　Here we are on our way to Shihnan. I wish you were all along, altho' we would need a larger boat. We were mighty busy the last couple days in Ichang. We had so many things to attend to – doing spring housecleaning (sort of), packing for the summer, for Kuling, and for Shihnan, taking down the stoves, o.s.v. And our kitchen utensils – the "rustable" ones- had to be washed and greased. Lots of excitement. Fortunately, only one day was cloudy and rainy, so we got our things dried. We had all our stuff packed by Friday evening, except our bedding and a few toilet articles. Do you wonder what we use for such traveling? Well for our clothes and such things we have, for this trip, two large baskets or corries about 36" x 20" x 8" at a rough guess. The 8" can be made about 14" though when packed full. In one of these we carry the bedding we use on the way. Then we have three suit cases and a bag. For our "grub" we have baskets without covers. They have no covers but there is a rope net to pull over the top so as to keep things in. The baskets are made for such traveling purposes and are reinforced. Our camp cots are tied together and carried separately. We will try to get a picture of our party when we get on the road so you can get an idea of how our baggage is carried. We will also try to get a good picture of our boat. But even if our pictures are good, you will have to wait a long time for them because we have to send them to Hankow to be developed and printed and then they have to be sent back to Shihnan.

　　　　We left Ichang yesterday – Saturday – about 10:45 – 11:00 A.M. on one of the mail boats. These don't take passengers as a rule but if the postmaster chooses to favor anyone with the use of them at times, he may do so. This boat is 40-50 feet long and probably ten feet at the widest part. In the middle is a little cabin which we occupy. There is also a layer of mail bags on the floor and our stuff is piled on top of these. By the way, the reason we take a boat like this is that the foreign steamers are not running up here yet. The water gets so low for several months that no large steamers can go up. Next month the water will most likely be high enough for them to resume traffic. But we are enjoying the ideal way of seeing the Gorges. The large steamers go so fast that the scenery can not be appreciated to fullest extent. Yesterday we made only 75 li, or about 25 miles. We have several ways of "getting ahead." The boat is manned by twelve men. Sometimes ten of them row while the "lao ban" or boss and another man take turns guiding the "steering gear" or rudder. Part of the time six, seven men "track." That is, they pull the boat along. And when the wind is favorable we sail.

　　　　The Chinese do not row like we do. They have two methods. One – the method used on this boat – is where they use the principle we do but go at it differently. They stand at the front of the boat and face in the direction they are going. They have long oars and the rower stands on the side of the boat opposite that on which the oar dips. Do I make myself clear?

Monday, 20th – The other method is one that seems awkward to us. The oars work on the same principle as a fish's tail. The oar just "wiggles back and forth" without being taken out of the water to speak of.

Tuesday – My pen went dry after these few lines yesterday and I didn't fill it, but sat outside and watched the scenery. It is really so interesting that I haven't done any reading or writing. – I was going to try to tell a little about tracking. The main rope – the one which they pull – is fastened to the boat proper. Another rope, however, comes from the top of the mast. (Drawing) That's not a very good picture, but our boat looks a little like that, only longer in front of the cabin. With the rope from the mast they can raise or lower the other rope so that it can go over other masts or boats that we pass. The ropes used for pulling are made of bamboo. It may be the rope coming from the mast is there for other purposes than the one I mentioned, but I don't claim to know about all such things.

Wed. Such a letter! I really cannot seem to keep at it more than a few minutes at a time. We have had good weather all the time and so I like to sit out here on the back of the boat and look at the scenery. I have now brought my stuff out here and can both write and keep an eye on everything.

We haven't had a favorable wind more than one day, however, and that was Monday. We made good time that day – must have made about 70 miles. Sunday we had a strong wind against us and there was so much sand blowing in the faces of the men that we rested about three hours one place. Right after that we went up a bad rapids, so we understood why they didn't want to go in the face of all the sand. George and I got out and walked twice that day for the fun and the exercise. Once we came to quite a stream and were not able to find footing all the way across (and keep dry, that is) so a Chinese carried us across on his back. Great sport! Early Monday morning we came to the worst rapids, called the Shin Tan. There was a rushing and roaring that reminded me of the flood at Wittenberg. And there surely was quite a drop. We got out and walked around that, since it is only a couple weeks since a mail boat was smashed there. They said it took about 100 men to pull this boat up. Four ropes were used; two for pulling the boat up, two for holding the boat near shore. This going up the rapids is great sport! Hard work for the men though. And one night we had quite a thrill. About 6:00 P.M. a favorable wind came up and everybody wanted to make use of it because there was some hard going ahead. So those who had already stopped and were making ready for the night put up their sails and started off again. And then there was a river full of boats, big and little! Some of these river boats are immense things and look terribly unmanageable. Besides having a rudder, there is a huge, long pole sticking out in front of the boat for steering. Well one time it looked rather as though we were going to be crushed in between a rock and one of these river "elephants." We weren't panic stricken or even much frightened, but it was sort of exciting. One day two of these big boats bumped into each other and the front of one was smashed off. Believe it was able to go down river tho'. Today the going is not so easy. The current is swift so much of the time and there have been rapids every little while. Besides that, there is quite a strong wind against us.

I wish you could see the immense cliffs and precipices along this river. Some are about as straight up and down as they can be. And it is interesting to see all the different rock formations, the caves, temples in seemingly unapproachable places – on the tops of high mountains – huts on the cliff sides, goats climbing around, and many such things.

We have even seen "cave dwellers" – in truth, we saw several caves used for houses, just yesterday. Life is very primitive in these little mountain villages. I have noticed that most of the women are fairer and have pink cheeks too.

Today we expect to get to Tai Chi. If we get there early and the coolies from Shihnan have arrived, we will probably start out over the mountains today.

We are going to have chicken for dinner today. We have a little charcoal stove along for use on the boat and cook our meals on that. On the road we will find stoves at the inns. For utensils we have a little tea kettle, frying pan, and an iron kettle (handle on) and we get along fine. By the time we have a furlough I think good meat and plenty variety will be <u>some luxury</u>. Even chicken gets too common to be enjoyed much. The chickens here are nothing to brag of anyway. But I'm hungry today!

Lots of Love to all of
You from
George and Bernice

Enroute from Yuyangkwan to Itu, Feb., 1922

"Mail boats (like the one we travelled in last March, 1922)

sailing up through the Gorges of the Yangtse."

Letter No. 49 (written by Bernice)

Shihnanfu, Hupeh, China
March 28, 1922

Dear All-of-you,

Am owing you all letters, so this letter is especially for each one of you!! We arrived here in Shihnan about 9:00 P.M. Saturday and found letters 49, 50, & 51 – which included Ragnar's and the one from Mrs. Hanson – besides one from Bertha Wangsness and one from Peggy Shoulders, awaiting us. Of course we were more than pleased. And then who wouldn't be rather pleasantly surprised and happy to suddenly discover one was not forgotten entirely by one's brother! It was nice to get a letter that could make me laugh after our strenuous trip. Sorry you flunked in Mechanics (or whatever it was), Raggy, but imagine you will make it up some way. It's a pretty stiff course, isn't it? And it is good to hear Elsa is getting along well. And at last I know where Andy is! Did he receive my Christmas card? Haven't seen him since the day after our wedding. Tell him I'd enjoy a letter from him. Before I tell about our trip, etc., I'm going over these letters and will answer questions as I find them.

Lenchen and Magdalene are one and the same. All the women in our Mission are supposed to learn the language. Meyers & Gyps are the only ones who have been at the language school so far, but now all the new missionaries are at Peking studying. There are three couples, one each unmarried man and woman up there. Mrs. Riedel, who has been here about five years, handles Chinese quite well, but the other women have not done much, as they all have babies. But they can all manage to get along with servants, etc. pretty well. They cannot do work among the women tho'.

Now, mama, I'll accept your correction on the spelling of "scarfs" but not on "Yangtsze." It doesn't <u>have</u> to be spelled that way but tsze is one Romanization of the Chinese character which is really pronounced "dz." As a matter of fact, I think "tzu" would be a better way and that is used very much for expressing that sound.

There was a nice piece of nainsook in the Christmas package. Thanks! Yes, we paid a little duty on the packages – were glad to, tho.' Packages of $5.00 or less value are duty free. It's in the U.S. that the duty is such a big item.

Well, on the question of time George says we're both partly right and partly wrong. I have no geography, but someone said the day started at the prime meridian or Greenwich. If that were true, why what I wrote was correct, because the sun moves westward and the day would "move westward" too, so to speak. Am I not correct? But since the day begins at the 180 meridian, of course we are ahead of you. But now let me ask a question or two. If we went to bed on Thurs. eve. and arose Sat. A.M. did we gain or lose a day? When we return, if we go to bed on Thurs. eve. and arise on Thurs. morning again, do we gain or lose a day? I should say that I had lost a day when I had only six days in a week, while eight days in one week seems like gaining a day. So, your laugh at me was not entirely justified. Of course, I should have known that the day did not start at Greenwich, but since I had heard that and believed it (having forgotten my geography), why, my reasoning was logical. So there! (All laugh – Ha Ha!)
I think of Cora so much. It hardly seems possible – it is distressing – and one's heart goes out to her. Raggie, please be patient with me! These months have not been the best and I haven't done any shopping for you yet. (The rest of the letter is missing.)

BERNICE DESCRIBES THEIR NEW HOME, ABOVE SCHOOL.
"There are about 100 day pupils and they are here from morning until night."

Letter No. 50

Shihnanfu, Hupeh
April 4th, 1922

Dear Folks,

  This time I am going to economize on time and type a letter for the whole Onstad-Lillegard "slegt"[113] – rather, those of the said "slegt" nearest to us, who are most interested, I suppose.

  The main subject of this letter will naturally be Shihnan. We have been here almost a week and a half now and I am still alive and happy, which may surprise some of our own missionaries out here after all the slander this place has suffered!! In order to save some rather futile descriptions I have made a rough sketch of a part of the house in which we are now living.[114] The plan is that of the second floor. This is an immense Chinese house – the largest in this city of about 50,000 inhabitants. Here I am starting off wrong – I should of course tell about the city of Shihnan first and then tell about our house. Well, I am glad this is not a composition which is to be submitted to some very critical University professor. I have made a bad beginning, but I shall start over again in another paragraph and tell things in better order, <u>if possible</u>. First, however, I wish to apologize for what evidently will not be a very neat letter. You may put the bulk of the blame on this wonderful "Corona," which is nothing to boast of when in good condition and certainly quite hopeless when it is afflicted with a variety of "unfixable" faults. But I have to use it in order to secure carbon copies. All right, then. All set!!

  When we descended into what is known as the Shihnan valley, we were confronted with such a mass of hill-tops as I have never before seen. Well, Wittenberg is indeed in a hilly region, but I never had a view of that from a mountain top. It was an interesting sight. Most of these "hills" are young mountains, if you please, but when one is so high above them, they are not unlike so many cocks of hay. In this country the mountains are also fairly well wooded, which adds much to its beauty. I might say here that as a general rule the mountains are quite bare, because the Chinese use every scrap of wood and grass for fuel. One does not have to fight his way through a lot of underbrush, and such things, in China. The people even crawl up tree trunks and cut off all but a few of the topmost branches for fuel. It is too bad, as there must be vast supplies of coal in these mountains. On one mountain top we even saw coal right on the outside. It was this terrible bareness that made me just a bit nervous sometimes when we made a big climb and we could look down thousands of feet into a narrow gorge. I always felt that there was hardly a blade of grass to stop one's fall, should one have such an accident. Well, as I said, in this section there is more wood and there are many rice fields. It is truly beautiful! And in this valley lies the city of Shihnan, the largest and most important for many miles around. All around are hills and mountains; far in the distance we can see on clear days, the very high ranges with ranges of varying heights intervening. Our house is in the eastern part of the city, but a short distance from the East Gate and with the city

---

[113] "family" (Norwegian)
[114] They had living quarters in the Hu property, according to p.43, <u>Biographical Sketches of LC-MS Mainland China Missionaries</u>.

wall right in back of this property. Right beyond the wall back here the land slopes abruptly to the river, which has the clearest water at all times except after heavy rains when so much sediment is carried along that it looks almost like the Yangtze. Across the river from us is a range of five mountains with nicely rounded tops. On one top a little farther on stands a pagoda, guarding the city. Oh, really it is beautiful around here!

Now then, I can tell about our present home. The only foreign thing about this house is that it has two stories, which is not the usual Chinese style. The downstairs is used for several purposes. And there is much more space in the building than is indicated on the sketch – there is more building in back and there is also a little square, or piece, or ground in back of the house. The "windows" in this house are Chinese in style. Well, there are a few panes of glass here and there, but they hardly count. I am rather at loss just how to describe them to you, but I will have to try. In our rooms – sitting room, bedroom, etc. – there are windows on two walls. About two thirds of the wall (all except three, four feet at the bottom) is sort of lattice work. Over this lattice work thin paper is pasted and that makes the window. I thought I wouldn't like them at all, but they are not half bad. This house was built by a wealthy Chinese and is quite artistic in some respects. The lattice works are rather pretty. The way it is now, you notice we have dining room and kitchen together. It is all right temporarily, but if we should come here to live for a longer time, I think we would put a partition in. On the whole I like this place. Since Gihring's furniture and much other stuff is for sale, we are renting that just now. We are quite comfortable and fairly cosy, but I know I could make this place look pretty nice if we had our own things here. In some respects I think this house is more desirable than the one in Ichang.

Now I have told mostly about the pleasant things. I must confess, however, it is not ideal in every way. The last couple years Shihnan has suffered greatly at the hands of soldiers and there has been much famine and relief work to do. In fact, the work of the mission has been more along that line than regular mission or evangelistic work. Many orphans and poor, starving, or helpless people have been taken in and cared for. So even now we are running a sort of orphanage here. At present there are some over forty boys here. They live in various rooms downstairs. The older ones are learning trades, some the bamboo trade, making baskets, etc., others are learning weaving. You can imagine all these little fellows are not the most quiet. Chinese are not quiet anyway, as far as I know. To me they seem to be a very, very noisy race!! Besides, the schools are under us too! You can never know what that means until you have heard one. Descriptions do not do a Chinese school justice, that's all!! There are about 100 day pupils and they are here from morning until night. In China it is the custom for children to come to school at dawn and stay until dusk. They go home twice during the day for meals. And when the day pupils are through, the orphans begin! That is not all. The house is right on a Chinese street, no lawn or even a couple feet of sidewalk or anything else between house and street, if you please. And from that quarter there is always noise, venders calling their wares, people gossiping or fighting, children yelling and playing or hollering at the tops of their big voices because someone refuses to let them have their own way, and so on. When I say fighting I do not mean fist fights. The Chinese do not resort to that method very quickly, but they have a grand "curse fest" and <u>threaten</u> to become very violent. Besides all the noises mentioned, every door in the house has a remarkable, resounding squeak!! There are no hinges such as we are used to – there are some wooden hinges and – well, I doubt a burglar could come in through a door without giving a very satisfactory alarm! So you see there are a multitude of sounds assailing our ears.

It seems George and I must have become somewhat susceptible to the wiles of a body of cold germs after our rather long trip. A day or two after we arrived we fortified ourselves by taking a dose each of Castor Oil. But evidently there was a rebel body of germs awaiting our arrival and on Thursday they descended upon us both. We had a grand and glorious fight, but for awhile George and I were losing ground to the enemy. Re-enforcements came to our aid in the form of Epsom Salts, hot foot baths, Nyal's Analgesic, etc, and George began to get the upper hand. I, however, had more of a struggle. My head ached and my ears were stuffed. Saturday I stayed in bed until the middle of the afternoon. Sunday I felt better, but yesterday (Mon.) I had such a stiff neck and shoulders and neuralgia in the outer part of my right ear. I really was quite a sorry specimen and felt rather miserable. Today I feel pretty well though and have had to get rid of some superfluous gaiety by pestering that noble person, my husband. Oh, yes, I forgot to say that the orphans are to be moved into another building in a couple days, so that will help just a little, anyway.

(The remainder is in script.)

So much typing for this time. My neck is still a little stiff and I feel a bit tired. Seems to me I'm always tired! I believe one's capacity for sleep increases very much in China. And I never accomplish anything in the evenings here, mostly on account of the poor light, I think. These lamps are a nuisance! When they are turned up so one gets a fairly decent light they smoke and have to be turned down. George has sometimes said it was hard to have such lamps and remain a good missionary!! When we can afford it I guess we will have to invest in a gas lamp – gasoline lamp, maybe it is called. Like the lantern they used to have at Onstad's.

My, I am waiting so for mail! I haven't been particularly lonesome here so far, but these days when I felt so punk I was rather homesick. It seems <u>so</u> <u>long</u> since I saw you all. And it is soon a year too, while the longest I was ever away in one stretch before was five months – at the Indian Mission.

We three have taken several walks around in Shihnan. Have had about four days of rain tho' so we couldn't go out those days. Most streets are bad in wet weather, but Chinese streets are worse! Some day we expect to make a trip on the river – it will be great sport because there's a good current and lots of rapids.

Bushels of love to you all,
George and Bernice

The second floor of their mission compound in Shihnanfu (by Bernice)

```
┌──────────┬──────────────────────┬─────────────────┐
│ Go       │ Small, dark          │                 │
│ kitchen  │ Courtyard            │                 │
│          ├──────────────────────┼─────────────────┤
│          │ ← Veranda →          │ Stairway        │
├──────────┴──────────────────────┴─────────────────┤
│                                                    │
│  These three rooms are used for                    │
│  storing Riedel's and Gehring's things             │
│  and hospital supplies just now.                   │
│  When Gehring's were here, they lived              │
│  in these rooms.                                   │
├──────────────┬──────────────────┬─────────────────┤
│ Have supplies│ ← Veranda →      │ Our water jugs  │
│ stored in    │                  │ and wood are    │
│ here.        │                  │ here            │
├──────────────┤                  ├─────────────────┤
│              │ ↑                │ Kitchen         │
│ This is      │                  │ part            │
│ reserved by  │   Courtyard      │                 │
│ landlord     │   (Cement floor) │                 │
│ for storing  │   Stone          │                 │
│ some of      │                  │ Dining          │
│ his goods.   │ ← Veranda →      │ room            │
│              │ ↓                │                 │
├──────────────┼──────────────────┼─────────────────┤
│ Stairway     │ ← Veranda →      │ Stairway        │
├────────┬─────┬──────┬──────────┬─────────────────┤
│Gebhardt│Geb- │ not  │  Our     │  Our            │
│'s      │hardt│ used │  bedroom │  sitting-       │
│Study   │'s   │ now  │          │  room           │
│        │bed- │      │          │                 │
│        │room │      │          │                 │
├────────┴─────┴──────┴──────────┴─────────────────┤
│              ← Veranda →                          │
└───────────────────────────────────────────────────┘
                 Chinese Street
```

Have indicated doors. There are windows facing inner veranda and Chinese street. Hang our clothes on the inner veranda.

Plan of Second Floor.

GEORGE PROPOSES CHANGYANG AS A NEW MISSION FIELD.
"**It is only 15 miles from the Yangtze, and can be reached by launch down the Yangtze twenty miles, then by chair the rest of the way over a fairly easy road, in a little over half a day.**"

Shihnanfu, Hupeh, May 5th, 1922

The Rev. Fr. Brand,
St. Louis, Mo.,

Dear friend:

It is now some time since we received your letter of Feb. 28th, but I suppose this will reach the States about as early as you will anyway, so you would not notice the delay. As you perhaps have heard already, my wife and I left Ichang as soon as she was strong enough to make the journey over the two mountains after her sickness. Schwartzkopf's family was increased by the advent of another baby boy a few days after we left, which explains why they did not come out here as originally intended. He is in charge of the work in Ichang which is growing as rapidly as it could in reason be expected to do. The chapel services have been very well attended right along, and thirty or more have signified their desire to study the gospel teachings more fully. I think the results of the work done there already prove that we were justified in opening work in that center. And it certainly does mean a good deal to us at this place to have a man at Ichang to look after the freight, mail, etc., that is transhipped at that point, besides its being a haven of refuge in time of trouble and sickness much closer to our field than Hankow would be. I suppose Schwartzkopf has already written you more in full concerning the work there, so I shall not expatiate on it here. If I remember aright, I also wrote you, in the letter sent to India, about our change of plans.

An outline of events since I wrote that letter, Feb. 10th, will no doubt be of some interest to you, dry enumeration of places and dates though it may be.

Feb. 13th Schwartzkopf and I took a week off and made a trip to Changyang, Yuyangkwan, and the country southwest of Ichang. We found it a most interesting section of this great republic, and not at all so sparsely populated and poor as we had been led to believe from the statements of some others that had traversed the country. It was our opinion that Changyang should be occupied as soon as possible, since it would be a convenient center from which to reach a dozen or more large market towns in a section entirely untouched by mission effort of any kind, not even Catholics. The town itself is small, but a well-built, clean, and evidently enlightened place. I could wish nothing better myself than to work in such a place, although it would mean considerable travelling to evangelize the surrounding territory. Distances are somewhat more formidable there due to the rough character of the country than they would be in a more level country. I believe that our mission should attempt to occupy this place very soon, working out from Ichang to begin with. It is only 15 miles from the Yangtze, and can be reached by launch down the Yangtze twenty miles, then by chair the rest of the way over a fairly easy road, in a little over half a day.

March 18th my wife and I started out for Shihnan. She decided that she would rather brave the unknown with me than be left alone in Ichang. We secured a mailboat through the kind offices of Postmaster Rose at Ichang, to take us up to Taichi, as the foreign steamers were not yet running. We had only a small cabin, which was lined with mail sacks, but managed to make ourselves fairly comfortable for the five days that it took us to reach our destination. We had no trouble on the way, though there had been robberies and disturbances along the river for some time before, and still are for that matter. The Szechuanese soldiers were somewhat unpleasant in one place, and we passed close to some boats of robbers, who according to our boatmen would have robbed the boat if they had not seen us foreigners sitting at the stern. But we enjoyed the trip very much, the scenery of the gorges naturally being more impressive in a little sailboat that in the large, swift steamers. The rapids also gave us a few thrills. They were at their worst at that season. The trip from Taichi we also enjoyed very much, although we did not enjoy the inns. We had good weather and with four good chairbearers for Bernice and a sturdy mule for me, we managed to make the trip in three days, so that we had only three nights of hotels a la Chinoise, which was not so bad. Bernice stood the trip fine. We both had bad colds after we came here, but we do not know whether to blame that to the trip or to Gebhardt, since the latter had had similar attacks of Grippe shortly before we arrived.

  We found Gebhardt too busy to be lonesome. The school, which he opened the last part of February, had over 100 pupils. The Chinese gentry in the city were quite profuse in their words of praise for our missionary, although their admiration unfortunately did not extend to the doctrine which we preach. Shortly after we came, Gebhardt was presented with three large "signs," two long "tablets," and a score of scrolls, all praising him for his work in saving the city and surrounding from famine, war, and other troubles – even ascribing to him the ability to make the stones "sit up and take notice," when he preached! Gebhardt had done his best to avoid this display, but someone had collected money from the businessmen, which amounted to over 100 strings of cash, so that they were able to make quite a splurge. There must have been one or two hundred people here paying him their respects. Lately Mr. Gebhardt has been asked to serve as chairman of the local famine relief committee. All this shows that there is no prejudice against the foreigner as such in this country, and it should be possible for us to build up a good work here. The city gentry are loath to study the doctrinal books that we have, however, so that it may be some time before we will be able to baptize any one. Personally I would rather wait awhile and make sure that the men we do baptize are well grounded in our Lutheran faith. We have some good material here, men who are capable and cultured, and who would make fine workers in the church, if they are given grace to experience a thorough repentance and a living faith.

  My wife and I have enjoyed our stay here so far very much. We like the house, the surrounding country is a treat to sore eyes, and we enjoy the work, and our association with Gebhardt. The weather remained quite cold until a couple weeks ago, when it turned real warm. This week it rained three four days, but yesterday and today have been ideal. Services on Sunday have been well attended, many people coming in from the country. We have special meetings with these country people on Sunday afternoons, teaching them the Catechism and Explanation. We have services and catechetical instruction every evening of the week, which meetings have not been so well attended. Besides that, my wife and I have had two meetings each week with a group of women and girls, who are reading an easy Gospel Reader. Gebhardt and I take turns at the services, and weekday meetings. He has general supervision of the whole plant, and teaches religion in the lower classes of the school, while I teach English and Religion in the upper classes, and music to the whole school. In all I have 21 hours of meetings and classes per week. So with the other work that I have tried to do here – straightening out Gihring's affairs, helping with the management, etc. – I have had little time for study. So I am glad that I had the leisure I did in Ichang this winter to brush up on Chinese and make some further inroads into the "wild and troubled domains" of Chinese language and literature.

I shall try to write an article for one of the church papers about the city and work here, so shall not expatiate further on that now. We hope to hear soon that you have returned safely from India and that you will be able to do great things for the cause of missions in China as well as India. The more I read and hear about conditions on the mission field, the more I feel that it is up to the conservative Lutheran Church now more than ever before to hold the banner of the cross up before the eyes of the heathen world, that at least a few of also these Gentile nations may be brought to see and love the Light of the world.

My wife joins me in hearty greetings to yourself and family,

Sincerely yours,
George Lillegard

"The house we are in, and Bernice"

Kuling

BERNICE DESCRIBES CHINESE FUNERAL CUSTOMS.
"…the priest moved his hands…in the most fantastic manner…"
No. 57

>Shinanfu, Hupeh, China
>May 15th, 1922

Dear Folks,

Here comes another typed letter to "youse." Guess most of the news is of general interest anyway, so why write it twice?

There isn't much in the line of news, to tell the truth. Life in Shihnan has not been very exciting in the "foreign circles." Not exciting, did I say? Probably not, but there has been plenty of noise and excitement of a kind in the street directly in front of the house and in the house opposite. Permit me to relate! I only regret that I am not versed in Chinese superstitions, as that would make the following doubly interesting, I am quite sure. However, I shall do the best I can…Friday, at about noon time, an old man across the way died. Although we were not sure there was a death there just at first, we were suspicious because we heard the cymbals, drum, and flute. Unlike our custom of preserving a dignified silence as much as possible, the Chinese make a great deal of noise to keep the evil spirits away so that they will not molest the spirit of the deceased. So, I suppose musicians (?) were summoned at the earliest possible moment and they immediately proceeded to frighten or entertain the evil spirits. During the day the noise was more or less intermittent, but at night, especially at about the time we went to bed, there was lots of noise. Let's see, though – I guess the musicians did not have the floor that first evening. There was a fellow with a violin who sang, played, and cracked coarse jokes out in the street. Whether he had been requested to come or not, I will not dare to say definitely. But since that and the following night are the only times we have heard him during the several weeks we have been here, it is not very unreasonable to assume that he was not out here purely by accident, is it? Saturday morning we were awakened at dawn by the wailing of two, three women. They were rapidly repeating words mingled with a kind of sob and wail the likes of which I have heard only in China. George says he has read that they mourn that way to assure the departed one's spirit that they mourn their loss so that it – the spirit – will not come back and torment them. I can at least say that this morning at dawn by some of the women is the only indication of mourning there has been in this instance. During the day, Saturday, there was again the intermittent noise of the cymbals and drums. The family were hurriedly being supplied by hastily-made white caps and garments, white being the color of mourning in this land. A couple pictures representing heaven and hell, respectively, (I suppose) were hung outside and incense sticks kept burning. And towards evening they rigged up a contraption out in the middle of the street. There were benches arranged thusly: On the "steps" were placed incense sticks and candles. At one end was a table adorned in like manner. Lights were also placed on the street at the opposite end. Oh yes, a white strip of cloth was first placed over the benches. As I understand it, that evening the priest, assisted by the musicians, performed the task of bringing the departed spirit safely across the "Styx." Paper money was also burned. I am enclosing a sample of this paper money. The Chinese have much the same idea as the Indians had with regard to the need of this world's goods in the next world. So they burn things with the idea, according to a book I have just read, that the smoke is "supposed to waft them through ether to the waiting spirit." Money would naturally be needed, but the Chinese could never afford to burn real money so they have found this way out of it. They cut up this ordinary Chinese paper and stamp it to resemble coins. This paper can be bought for a few coppers a package. I do not know how much money is represented though, I am sorry to say. I must ask Mr. Rao some day.

Sunday morning at dawn we were again awakened by the wailing of the women and during the day there was again the music. But the big "show" was in the evening!! A sort of platform had been rigged up and table placed on top of it. About eight o'clock a dish of something (food?) was started burning, as well as candles and incense sticks. The priest, decked in a brown silk robe, a crimson satin surplice (I think you call it a surplice) and a crown, took his place at the head of the table and the musicians lined up on the sides. Then followed a truly Oriental and weird scene, albeit it impressed us as very superficial. It <u>is</u> superficial, of course, but not all such scenes would give one the impression of a lack of sincerity. The chanting of the musicians, accompanied by a "violin," drum, and cymbals was <u>very Oriental</u> and not unpleasing. If I only were a composer! I would surely make use of that chant in an Oriental composition. During this chanting the priest moved his hand – hands only – in a most fantastic manner (it was rather clever and graceful, too) and handled various objects in peculiar ways. While this was going on money – paper, I should say – was being burned by the package. The excitement kept on until after we had been in bed for some time.

Tuesday, the 16th. Yesterday morning there was some noise also, but it was more quiet during the day and evening. However, when out for our walk, we saw them piling up hundreds of packages of paper "money" and when we came back there was a veritable furnace. This was on the stones along the river. This morning we were graciously permitted to sleep a little longer. If there was any extra noise we didn't hear it. But it was not long before another set of musicians started up and they have been at it intermittently all day. Today the friends of the departed are coming to pay their respects – I think they "kou tou" – kneel on the floor and bow their heads – before the coffin. And our "Boy" said the burying would take place tomorrow.

What I have related above is an account of a funeral in a family where money is not too scarce. A funeral is a very expensive thing in China. Poor people cannot afford such affairs and it is more of a burden than many can carry merely to have a coffin and have it taken out to its burying place. Very often women and children have no coffin at all, but are merely buried in the ground. Isn't it terrible? The coffins are carried by coolies, usually eight in number. The casket is fastened to a long, stout pole, which in turn is suspended by ropes from the coolies' carrying poles. As they move along with steps peculiar to burden carriers, they sing lustily. Often a chicken is fastened to the top of the coffin. This is supposed to clear the road of demons. If one may judge a man's wealth by the size of his funeral procession, as seems to be the case, we saw the funeral of a very wealthy person in Ichang just before we left for this place. The procession was very long and there were tables of food to be left at the grave and many paper images, which I imagine were to be burned there.

What would we think if a son or friend should present us with a coffin for a gift? That, however, is a very appropriate and most acceptable gift in China. It may be many years before it is put to its intended use, but in the meantime it serves many useful purposes. It is handy to keep clothes in and makes a good bench to sit or lie on also. Oh, there are many things upside down here!! Some day I may sit down and tell about some of the things that are just opposite to our customs.

Right here I cannot refrain from telling about one thing which certainly tickled my funny bone. In Ichang we used to hear one of the night watchmen making his rounds. About every minute he pounded his big brass disc twice. It used to make me think he was sounding a warning – "Here I come! Run for your lives, all ye doers of the deeds of darkness, before I arrive!!"

LETTER NO. 57

5/16/22

Dear Mom,

Since I am perched here on top of Giles' giant Chinese dictionary, I may as well continue typing. I am beginning to be able to manage this instrument honored with the name typewriter. Today we received a nice bunch of American mail, to our great delight and joy. Your letters 57 and 58, together with one from papa including a statement of our account were among some from George's folks and some other mail. Thanks very much for letters and also the money enclosed. It is great fun to see some regular American money again, but I would suggest, if I may, that you do not make a practice of sending money to us. You see, we really lose on the exchange, especially so when the quantities are not real large. You understand it is not that we do not appreciate it, of course, and it is all right to slip in a dollar bill once in a while, if you like to do so. I only mention it so that you will not do it often.

On May 2nd one of the steamers plying between Ichang and Hankow burned on the down river trip and quite a bit of mail – all the mail it carried, I think – from Western China burned. It is barely possible that one or two letters from us were in that mail. I wrote Letter 51 to Ragnar on April 12th and 52 to Papa April 18th-20th. If either of these were in the bunch destroyed, it would most likely be the latter. I hope not, however. But there was nothing specially important in that letter, as I remember. I told Papa I was exercising every day, for one thing![115]

Now I want to answer some of your questions. You mentioned Elsa and her plans, rather that she had no definite plans. Well, I agree with you entirely that it is not a thing to worry about and it would be very nice for her to stay at home with you for a year or two. A girl needs all the housekeeping experience she can get. Let her take the housekeeping responsibilities off your shoulders for a couple weeks at a time, for instance. It would do both of you good. Please, Mama, give her the full responsibility sometimes. It is much more interesting than to know that you are sort of under orders. You know what I mean. It is all right to give orders, but I know that I did much better work and took 100% more interest when I knew it depended on me. And then she will never regret it if she learns to sew, at least enough to make her underclothes and simple dresses. In sewing it is not so easy to be left entirely to one's self. Then too, I am sure Elsa will never regret having had the opportunity to stay at home with her mother for awhile and really becoming acquainted with her. I am so glad for you that you have the "Daylight." You have not said whether it is a one tub affair, whether the tub is wooden or copper, etc. I can imagine the wringer pleases you.[116]

The pictures we took of the cook and the boy were not very good and we haven't taken any of "lajla," as you call her. Their winter clothes are not very becoming because they are so padded. Will try to remember to take some more. But now, don't forget that we, too, like to receive pictures! You ask how I converse with the servants. Why, I talk Chinese to them! They do not understand any English. The cook understands a few terms, such as scrambled - "chi (gee) dan," pudding, custard, omelet, and a number of

---

[115] The letters were not burned; they are in the collection with all the rest.
[116] This must be an old-fashioned washing machine which consisted of a tub with agitator and hand-fed wringer to squeeze out the water from the clothes.

other words. When I was unable to express myself so they could grasp my idea, I appealed to George. Now, however, I get along pretty well. Mr. Rao told me yesterday that I spoke much better now than when we came to Shihnan. I never called the boy's wife anything as a rule. But "amah" is the usual term. Lajla is a good suggestion though…

Nei,[117] I think I have written about enough for one letter. What do you do with all my letters? If some of the things I write about China can be made use of to stimulate mission interest, I shall indeed be very happy. We never hear anything about or from Rev. Olsen. Will you tell him that we would appreciate even a short letter from him? George has received almost no letters from his Norw. Synod friends in the ministry and he is not at all pleased about it. Do they think that because we are in China we have lost our interest in the church at home? That is what the dignified silence Gullixson and Moldstad have maintained would lead us to suspect. We have heard from Preus once. Krey has written several times but his letters contain mostly Lake View news, which we are, of course, glad to get.

Oh yes, do you still have the dog that you wrote about?

With oceans of love to the whole E.J. Onstad family,

George and Bernice.

仁 仁 This character is pronounced "ren" in a lower even tone. It means Benevolence.

Would you mind sending some of my letters to Netty to read, some with "things" Chinese in them? She has been writing to me almost every month and I simply cannot write all this stuff to all my correspondents.

---

[117] No (Norwegian)

GEORGE DETAILS THE BRIGANDAGE IN SZECHUAN.
"**The soldiers are the real power in all districts.**"

Shihnanfu, Hupeh, May 12th, 1922

Central China Post:

Since Tang Tsu Mou and Yang Chun Fang with their robber bands were driven out of Shihnan and Lichwan districts, peace and prosperity have again made a nodding acquaintance with western Hupeh. The soldiers of General Pan Chen Tao, who are under the command of Li Yueh Sen, have behaved as well as soldiers in China are expected to behave and have maintained order throughout the districts under their command. In accordance with the treaty drawn up by Wu Pei Fu's representatives and the Szechuanese, the Fu of Shihnan is to constitute an independent district with its own representative government. Representatives from the various hsiens have met at Shihnan and organized some sort of an Assembly. Its powers are so vague, however, that its members seem hitherto to have even refrained from exercising their powers of speech. At any rate it is very little in evidence. Similar organizations have been effected in the six hsiens to function in the local government. The soldiers are the real power in all districts.

Due to the heavy burden which these soldiers, even the best of them, are, prices are still very high. Although conditions are better than they were last spring, there promises to be a small-sized famine in certain parts of the district. A Famine Relief Association was organized lately by representatives from several districts residing in Shihnan, and an attempt is to be made to raise funds and organize relief work through the worst months, June and July. The greater part of the 500,000 strings sent by the government for relief in this district last year did not find its way out of the pockets of the agent sent out to superintend the distribution of the funds. It remains to be seen whether the Committee now organized to recover some of these funds and collect others can do better by the poor people. One of the missionaries in Shihnan has been asked to take care of the funds. Apparently he is the only man to be trusted in the neighborhood.

One is curious to know, at times, when the Chinese will take the business of getting rid of the numerous robber bands in the country seriously. Several months ago, it was decreed in Szechuan headquarters that Yang Chun Fang and Tang Tsu Mou must be punished for their misdeeds, including the murder of Father Adons[118] in Lichwan. Instead of seeking to capture and disband them, with suitable punishments for the responsible parties, they have simply been shooed from one corner to the other. First they were asked to withdraw from Shihnan. They did so with ill grace, only to make Lichwan the scene of their depredations. Then General Li Yueh Seng was ordered to attack him there. Instead of fighting him, he sent word ahead, warning him that he must retire to a safer place. Then Yang and another band of his men were asked to leave Chungchow and the Yangtze, where they had been making merry with all river traffic for a season, including the Chinese mails. The result was that Yang Chun Fang and Tang Tsu Mou, birds of a feather, have gathered their forces in the four hsiens in the southeast "tongue" of Szechuan, Yuyang, Hsiushan, Chiengiang, and Penshui. Here they are carrying on a systematic brigandage under the guise of apprehending and punishing

---

[118] This part of the carbon copy has run off the bottom edge of the paper and is indecipherable.

thieves and robbers, who fortunately for their purses seem in all cases to be men of wealth. It is also feared that they will soon cross over into Hupeh, a prospect which does not please the inhabitants of these districts at all. They are making overtures to Li Yueh Sen to have him take them under their wing, and he is said to be considering the matter favorably. Under whatever pretext they enter the province, the people do not trust them to show themselves as anything but robbers. These are not the ordinary enlisted "rough-necks," turned loose for an occasional looting bee. They are professional robbers, who have made it their mission in life to relieve the rich of their superfluous wealth, not always taking the trouble to investigate carefully the size of their victim's budget so as to make sure that he belonged in the local "Four Hundred." So if they enter the province, there will no doubt be a considerable emigration on the part of the local gentry to some healthier climate. We hear also that the Szechuanese are waiting only to get their domestic tangles straightened out, whereupon they will make another descent upon Ichang. We wonder if someone could persuade Liu Hsiang that it would be more to his interest to clear the province of brigands, in some effective manner, than to try his luck again at downing the redoubtable Wu Pei Fu. And also if he and our other Tuchans would try some other method of dealing with them than that of shooing them off into their neighbors' preserves. Some other way could hardly be any more expensive and troublesome than the one hitherto so popular.

GEORGE WRITES KRETZSCHMAR OF NEW STATION

Rev. R. Kretzschmar   Shihnanfu, Hupeh, May 22nd, 1922
St. Louis, Mo.
Dear friend,

    Thank you for your kind letter of April 13th received today, as well as for your post card of Jan. 31st received some time ago. I was glad to hear that Missionary Faye was coming to St. Louis soon, and I hope to hear that some of the other missionaries will also join in with the Missouri Synod. Too bad that Rev. Brand could not have arranged to visit Africa too on his trip around the world. It might have made considerable difference to the workers there as well as to the Mission Board at home.

    As you perhaps have noticed from the date line above, we are now in Shihnan – have been here for two months. Bernice decided that she would rather go with me than be left alone in Ichang, although it was not so very long since she had been in the hospital. I have already written to Rev. Brand about the trip to this place, so shall not repeat here, as you may have had an opportunity to read his letters from the Mission field. We have enjoyed our stay here very much, and like Shihnan and surrounding country better than any Chinese city we have yet seen. There has been much work to do here, so that we have kept busy. Although my wife is the only white woman in a radius of over a hundred miles, she has not been lonesome. The language study keeps her busy, and she has also enjoyed meeting the Chinese women and entertaining them as best she could. We have meetings twice a week with the women, at which I instruct while my wife acts as chaperone. Even so the "better class" women find it improper to come. We need a lady worker who can go out to the homes and instruct the women there. In the larger families or clans, one could easily work up large classes of catechumens in this way.

    We have over a hundred pupils in our school here, with three teachers devoting full time, and two more teaching certain classes. Mr. Gebhardt teaches religion in the lower grades, while I have religion in the upper grades, as well as English and Music. Then we take turns at the meetings with the catechumens every evening and the Sunday services. Gebhardt has general supervision of the work, as well as accounts, and the care of the orphan boys. So we are both kept real busy and find little time for study. We have secured a mortgage on the house which we have been renting. We are to pay $3000.00 Mex., and this sum is to be repaid at the end of the mortgage term, five years hence, or any time later that the owner wishes to within twenty years. If it is not paid then the property reverts to us. As the owner would not sell the place for less than $15,000.00, and it is worth even more than that to us, I consider that we got a bargain on the terms of this mortgage. Even if we do not manage to buy land right away and build houses, we will be provided with the necessary quarters for as many missionaries as would be expected to live here.

    The work in Ichang, according to Mr. Schwartzkopf, is progressing as rapidly as could be expected. The results already justify the opening of a station in that place. It has also been a great convenience to us to have a man at Ichang. Without him, we would have had to trouble some other mission to forward boxes and packages for us and act as our agent. It seems to me that an effort ought to be made to open work throughout the whole field west of Hupeh as soon as possible.

We are waiting rather eagerly to hear what the Board decides with regard to the numerous matters discussed at our last summer's Conference. It will be rather hard for us to accomplish what we should at this next Conference, if we do not know what action the Board takes re those recommendations. I hope Rev. Brand will be home early enough so that the Board can send us the necessary instructions before our Conference. We plan to meet on Kuling from August 9th on. We have a number of papers, a large number of Committee reports, and not a few other matters to be discussed. I suppose the question that will cause most trouble is that of stationing. However, we hope to settle the difficult matter of stationing men at Shihnan by calling for volunteers, among whom we expect to be. And I trust Meyer will not make too strenuous objections to continuing with the school work in Hankow, so that there will be no difficulty over that question. Is there no prospect of our getting a doctor for the Shihnan field? It is really no easy matter for women with little children or expecting such gifts to be so far away from doctor as we are here. There are two graves about a mile south of the city, marking the end of the Pittsburgh Bible Society's work in this district. Both the women laid to rest there could no doubt have been working yet, if adequate medical aid had been at hand. And a man and boy would very likely also have joined them if a doctor had not arrived from Ichang in the nick of time, after a very strenuous trip of ten days over the mountains. Sickness of the missionaries in this field has cost our mission also enough by this time to go pretty far towards paying the salary and expenses of a doctor, or at least a well-trained nurse. Of course sickness comes to those who have doctors next door also. But then they at least have the chance to do what is humanly possible to cure the sickness, whereas here the lack of a doctor is enough in itself to kill a certain class of patients through the destructive effects of fear and worry.

There are many other things that could be written up. But I shall give the main points in the report for the last four months, which I enclose herewith. My wife and I will also be writing articles on various phases of the life and the work. Gebhardt and I were appointed a "Prompting Committee," to suggest articles to the various members of our mission. We have written to all the men on the field, giving them a list of subjects on which to write articles to the church papers at home. But so far as we know none have been written, or been published. I hope we can give our mission work more publicity hereafter.

Politically things have been quiet the last few months. There have been rumors to the effect that the band of robbers or disbanded soldiers that terrorized this region last fall and winter were about to return from Szechuan. But so far the rumors have not materialized. Today we hear that a band of a few hundred robbers is operating on the main road to Ichang, and that soldiers have been sent to fight them. But as long as we are in the city and the soldiers remain loyal, there should be no danger on their account. Wu Pei Fu's victory may mean peace – and it may mean still more war. Nobody knows, except perhaps a few Chinese and they do not talk. The Szechuanese in this section are not at all pleased over the situation, and it is as yet hard to say what the effect will be on them. We hope that they will decide not to make any more attacks on Ichang so as to make this district the battleground again.

With best greetings to you and your family from Bernice and myself,

Sincerely yours, Geo. O. Lillegard

Summary of Accounts from June 30th, 1921 to June 30th, 1922.

MONTHLY REPORT.

Name Geo.O.Lillegard,   Place.,Kuling,Ichang,Shihnan, July 1st,1921 to June 30th,1922.

IN ACCOUNT WITH

BOARD OF FOREIGN MISSIONS OF EV. LUTH. SYNOD OF MO, OHIO & OTHER STATES.

		Dr.	Cr.
1.	Salaries of teachers & evangelists,& gatekeepers,Ichang,		45.00
2.	Rents of schools & chapels & residences ,Ichang,		310.00
3.	Missionary's salary		1924.92
4.	Allowance for children		
5.	Travel,including Schwartzkopf's trip to Shihnan,Nov.1921,		832.91
6.	Personal teacher		59.00
7.	Medical		56.00
8.	Missionary's rent for residence ,Ichang,Sept.-March,Kuling,1921&1922,		667.00
9.	Books & tracts		137.64
10.	Sundries ,Telegrams,Stationery supplies,registering cable address at Ichang,		26.85
11.	Freight on household goods from Kwangchow to Ichang,and storage and freight		
12.	at Hankow and from Hankow to Ichang,		116.74
13.	Repairs on residence in Ichang,		139.60
14.	Furniture and supplies for chapel and guestrooms in Ichang,		261.50
15.	Upkeep of chapel in Ichang,Jan.-March,1922,		15.15
16.	For registering mortgage deed on property at Shihnan,at Amer.Consulate,		15.00
17.			
18.			
19.			
20.			
21.	Received from Treasurer Received interest on deposits,1921,	4565.00 3.27	
22.	Balance of , June 30th,1921,	427.59	
	TOTAL	4995.86 4607.31	4607.31

TOTAL BALANCE ,June 30th,'22 388.55

KREY WRITES OF LAKE VIEW JOINING MERGER.
"I printed my resignation…"

Chicago, Illinois
June 7th, 1922

Dear brother Lillegard,

You will be anxious to hear, I suppose, how things stand in Lake View. Probably you have heard already what has happened. On Monday the first of May the congregation held a special meeting to determine synodical affiliation. This meeting had been decided upon in the regular meeting on the first Monday in April. The special meeting was duly announced. I also preached two sermons on the two preceding Sundays, April 23, and 30, bearing on the joining of a synod. But it was all of no avail. When the time came, there were 17 voting members present, (the greatest number that I ever had) but their minds were all set. They wouldn't listen to God's Word, nor to common sense, though I talked back and forth with them for nearly three hours. Rev. Karl Schmidt, my visitor, was present, but they would not let him have the floor. When the final vote was cast, it was found that 16 were for and only one against going in to the merger. That one vote was P. Widding. The majority, of course rules in Lake View, and therefore they considered themselves from that moment on, members of the "Norwegian Lutheran Church in America." A delegate for the extra convention in June was immediately elected, and I was told that it "was up to me to act now," meaning of course that they expected me to take the same step. I had told them in a previous meeting that I could not go with them, and that I would have to resign, so I just stated, what they all knew, that they would have my decision within the next few days. I printed my resignation in the "Lake View Lutheran" and read it on the following Sunday May seventh. My somewhat quick action caused a great stir. They had not expected that I would "lay down on the job" like that. But just that was one reason why I did it. I wanted to stir them up, in the hope that they might come to their senses. But that hope has been vain so far. Several of our faithful over there are now attending Boecler's church, and one family Hemmeter's. Church attendance is very poor over in Lake View, I hear. The plot-makers don't show up anymore I hear, still they are the ones that want to run things, and are still running things. The congregation is now calling Rev. Darwig from somewhere here in Chicago. I feel very sorry for Lake View, for I really had gotten to like the place. But I could not go with them in what they so deliberately and determinedly set out to do and accomplished. Rev. Schmidt said too, after the meeting "it was all cut and dried."

It will interest you, no doubt, to hear, that Rev. Arndt from China is in Chicago these days, and that he got a hold of me yesterday, and, of course, as soon as he heard that I was out of office began to talk China mission to me and stuck to it too, like a postage stamp to an envelope. I am to see him tonight again. But I hardly think it any use. I have two calls in hand already, and I doubt very much whether I am a fit man for China. Notwithstanding I am between fires. If only Rev. Brand were here. He knows me quite well, and I place a lot in his judgment. But as it is, the matter must be decided before he comes, for the calls that I have are both urgent, and it would be unjust to keep the congregations waiting.

With fraternal greetings,
P.C. Krey

THEY ARE BACK IN KULING FOR THE SUMMER.
"…I've lived many places and have put up with inconveniences, but we felt like turning back when we saw this place."
Letter No. 62[119]

Kuling, China
June 28th, 1922

Dear Mom,

Had intended to write sooner, but I guess it is a good thing I didn't – I'm in somewhat better humor today than I have been for a number of days.

Your letters 62 and 63 came last Saturday, the 24th. They came back from Ichang, or we'd have had them earlier. But of course we did not intend to come up here so soon. It was "awfully" nice to get your letters! Maybe you don't think I'd like to visit you and see your lovely home!! I guess I was more homesick these last days than I've been for a long time. I won't go into details about house arrangement. Suffice to say we left it to Meyers, since we were so far away. Well, we received a letter in Ichang saying we would live in last year's house and I needn't bring anything along except for our own room. When we arrived in Hankow there was a misunderstanding or two and it was finally decided we were to occupy Arndt's house. Well, people furnish their own cutlery as a rule, but here was I without any along. Walter Arndt helped me out though, so I was satisfied. Aber![120] Instructions had been given to repair the house and we thought it would be <u>quite</u> livable, at least until we could fix it up a little. But, oh my! What did we find? Well, I've lived many places and have put up with inconveniences, but we felt like turning back when we saw this place. Dirt – uf, how some people can leave things when they go away "gaar ud af min forstand og helt ind i prestens."[121] The repairs were really not noticeable. There is one missionary who has been up here a month or over and he certainly could have had the place cleaned up for us when he had nothing else special to do and we surely do not feel very grateful for the way he managed things. However, we had the cook clean up the best room and we put up a bed and slept there the first night. The next morning we found a horde of bed bugs in the bed net. That was almost the last straw! We simply packed up our suitcases, made the rooms as airtight as possible and then fumigated three rooms. The new couples invited us to spend the night with them. Sunday we had the bed washed with both kerosene and disinfectant and we have found only one half dead one since. These days carpenters, masons, grass cutters, etc. have been busy and very gradually things are being repaired and the house made livable.

Thursday (written over Mon.) Guess I'm dreaming, since I'm writing Monday for Thursday! Oh well, I'm hardly responsible these days. Not only has this place been terribly upset, but we have had so much rain that we cannot do much work and everything is getting so damp. Sometimes I just feel like taking the next boat home and occasionally a wave of disgust or dislike of Chinese passes over me. Aa ja![122] It's only temporary. On the whole I'm very contented and I guess I'll be happy enough when the sun comes out.

---

[119] This is the last letter to her family, which I have, until January of 1923.
[120] But! (German)
[121] "goes beyond my understanding and completely into the pastor's (understanding.)" (Norwegian)
[122] Literally, Oh yes! Oh well! (Norwegian)

Uf, George is trying out a Chinese teacher and the latter is an "<u>unmusical comedy</u>"! Some of these teachers – would-be teachers – are a huge joke.

Well, let me introduce you to our new missionaries. As George wrote, they are quite a fine looking set of young people. Mr. and Mrs. Klein, Mr. and Mrs. Theiss, Mr. and Mrs. Scholtz, and Mr. Zschiegner (pronounce Chēgner – the German ch on the "g"). These girls are between 22 and 24 years of age and the boys between 24 and 26. As I have said, Zschiegner is to be married this fall. Then there is Miss Olive Gruen, our lady worker, who is not young in years, but very much so in spirit. She is 39, if we are not misinformed. She is a game girl and it appears she has the true mission spirit.

Last night we went up to Bentrup's, where Theiss's are living, to help Mr. Theiss celebrate his birthday. We had firecrackers along and also a number of tiny presents done up in countless wrappings. There was a lot of paper wasted!

The board at home has not reported on the 5-year furlough question – or anything else – as yet. Brand went to India and Europe and did not return to the States until May or June.

I cannot collect my thoughts so you'll have to wait for a decent letter, which I hope to be able to write when we get settled.

Much love to you all
From Bernice & George

Greetings to all.

Our house no. is 1140.

Mrs. Klein, Miss Gruen & Bernice, 1923

GEORGE INFORMS HIS FAMILY THAT…
"…we got away from Shihnan just in time…"

Kuling, China, July 4th, 1922

Dear folks,

Today being the Glorious Fourth, I shall celebrate our independence by writing a letter to all you home folks at once. I am sending copies of this to Anna and Valborg at Chicago, Louise at Story City, and the rest of you at Bode. For once I have letters from all those places to answer. Guess I am the one that will have to plead guilty to negligence in writing letters now. We really have been so unsettled the last weeks, however, that it has been hard to get anything done. Now we are finally getting somewhat composed in our cottage on Kuling and hope to get down to some good, hard studying the rest of the summer.

Louise's letter of May 9th is the first one to be answered. That was received in Ichang upon our arrival there June 10th. It seems that we got away from Shihnan just in time to escape considerable excitement. Although this part of the country was not directly involved in the fighting in May, it was affected by it to a large extent. And a few days after we left, things began to move in Shihnan. There seems to have been considerable danger at times that the city would be looted by the soldiers who had been there all winter. But they finally left the city for Szechuan, satisfied with the $20,000 that they demanded from the city. That was only another and more respectable way of robbing the people, of course. Since they left, about the middle of June, one band of soldiers after the other has come to the city and rumors of all kinds have kept the people in a state of fear and suspense. According to the last letters received from Gebhardt, a thousand northern soldiers, who had been wandering about the country, have now arrived. They demanded several thousand dollars right away but otherwise have caused no trouble. They may behave themselves allright. But this goes to show that Shihnan is still in a dangerous zone. There are robber bands terrorizing the country all over. In southwestern Honan, a company of ex-soldiers looted a town in which some Norw. missionaries lived, burned the mission station, took the missionaries prisoners, and kept one single lady for several days in a place outside the city. It seems that none of them were harmed, however. There are so many soldiers in China that the country cannot support them out of its lawful taxes, so the soldiers just take the law into their own hands and help themselves to what they can find, whenever they get hard enough up.

The province in which Kuling is situated is at present the storm center. But the fighting is some distance to the south of us, and there should be little danger of any of the soldiers coming up here. The only difficulty is that we might be cut off from our source of supplies, if the fighting should get as far north as this. There is a possibility, however, that the opposing parties will make peace.

Louise's and Ella's letter of May 23rd reached us a few days ago. We were sorry to hear of Aunt Astrid's[123] sickness. Hope she will improve again. I should think that it would be best for her to remain quietly at home when she is so weak. Visiting is generally hard work. How is Guri[124] managing all alone out there anyway? If Astrid is

---

[123] Lars Lillegard's sister
[124] Another sister of Lars Lillegard

not there when you receive this, you had better send it on to her. I will suggest that the Chicago copy be sent on to her, as there will not be so many there to share it.

Yes, I have heard from Krey as well as Anna with regard to events in Lake View. It is of course too bad that Krey should have made himself personally unpopular. But I fear he would have had a hard time with that bunch anyway, as soon as he tried to get them to cut out lodges, etc. I could not do anything with them myself, as you know. I had sort of expected that some of the old lodge members would drop out and that Krey would be able to pick up some new members from among the Missourians in the neighborhood and that in this way they could keep the congregation going. I hope you Chicago people will go to Gullixson's or some Mis. Synod church after this. Please do not let our family get divided along church lines anyway. You will feel more at home among the Minority people, anyway, I am sure than with Hauge or U.C. crowd. I certainly am glad that I am with the Missourians out here. We have a fine bunch of young people here now. You should see the handsome men and ladies we have. I think we are the handsomest crowd in Kuling – myself and wife helping along to earn that distinction, of course! And they all seem to be good loyal Missourians, too.

I cannot say that I approve of your playing in the Union churches, Valborg and Ella. It will draw you into their company more than might be good for you. Furthermore, you need not fool yourself into thinking that they are going to be particularly grateful to you for your work. You may meet more criticisms than praise. As long as you folks are in Bode, of course you have to go to our church there. Madson is allright and it may not be long before he decides to join us.[125] Perhaps the congregation will get its eyes open, too. The $500,000 debt they are in ought to help some of these lay people to see what kind of a crowd has been running the affairs of the church of late.

Mother's letter of May 21st reached us at the same time as Anna's of the same date. If you stay in Bode this next year, I think you had better store the furniture in Chicago, or continue to rent it out as you have been doing the past months. It would be a good investment financially anyway. Jim,[126] I suppose, could help you to manage it. Are not things beginning to pick up a little in the country now? How has Henry[127] been managing during these hard times?

We are renting Rev. Arndt's house this summer. It is a very old house and has not been taken care of either, so that we have had a rather hard time getting things fixed up decent. When we came one of the missionaries had gotten some repair work done but with the result that the place looked worse than ever. Mud was plastered all over everything, this being what they used to repair the broken places in the ceiling and walls. I got workmen busy right away, and now after ten days it is beginning to look somewhat civilized. There were no kitchen utensils either. So we could not keep house til last Wednesday. Then we bought some utensils and borrowed others. Up to that time we had boarded at Schwartzkopf's. One night we slept at the house we occupied last year, which the new missionaries share now. We were driven out of this place by a well-organized attack on the part of an army of bed-bugs. We counter-attacked that afternoon and the next night by a scientific gas-attack, sulphur fumigators, which routed the enemy

---

[125] Norman A. Madson did later join the ELS.
[126] Reid, Anna's husband
[127] Gullixson, Sarah's husband

completely, so that we have seen no signs of them since. Pretty soon we will think that this house is a little better than a Chinese inn. It rained a little every day too last week, in fact ever since we came up, so that it has been pretty muddy and disagreeable. The result has been that both my honorable helpmate and myself have broken our records for grouchiness and general ill-nature. Hope the weather will be better hereafter, so that we can get out and exercise a little.

    I enclose some pictures taken on our trip to and from Shihnan. I am sending some to each of you. If you wish to exchange and see what they all are like, send them around. If you have received any of these before, I suppose you can divide the duplicates among you. We expect to see a baseball game this afternoon, and perhaps we will also celebrate by having a picnic meal some place, if the weather is good. It has rained a little this morning, but promises to clear up now. Bernice just finished playing a couple sets of tennis. She plays pretty well, having learned the game in her school days at Bruflat.

    So much for this time. Please write again soon, and we shall try to answer more promptly too. With best greetings to all friends in Bode, Story City, and Chicago, and our love to you all,

George

Bernice's parents hosted Rev. Brand in Madison, WI.

BOARD OF FOREIGN MISSIONS.
Subcommittee at St. Louis.
REV. RICH. KRETZSCHMAR, *President*,
  2243 S. Jefferson Ave.
PROF. W. ARNDT, *Secretary*,
  Concordia Seminary.
MR. WM. LEHR, *Treasurer*,
  3693 Ohio Ave.
PROF. M. S. SOMMER,
  Concordia Seminary.
REV. H. HOHENSTEIN, 3506 Caroline St.
MR. G. SCHMIDT, 3712 Nebraska Ave.

MEMBERS AT LARGE.
REV. J. F. BOERGER.
REV. P. ROESENER.
PROF. S. YLVISAKER, PH. D.
REV. H. M. ZORN.
PROF. F. ZUCKER.

Evangelical Lutheran Synod
of
Missouri, Ohio, and Other States.

BOARD OF FOREIGN MISSIONS.
REV. FREDERICK BRAND,
Director and General Secretary,
St. Louis, Mo., U. S. A.

OFFICERS OF SYNOD.
REV. F. PFOTENHAUER, D. D., *President*,
  415 W. 62d St., CHICAGO, ILL.
REV. F. BRAND, *1st Vice-President*,
  3316 S. Jefferson Ave.,
    ST. LOUIS, MO.
REV. J. W. MILLER, *2d Vice-President*,
  1126 Barr St., FORT WAYNE, IND.
REV. G. A. BERNTHAL, *3d Vice-President*,
  969 Eddy St., SAN FRANCISCO, CAL.
REV. H. P. ECKHARDT, *4th Vice-Pres.*,
  318 Morewood Ave.,
    PITTSBURGH, PA.
REV. M. F. KRETZMANN, *Secretary*,
  309 S. Oak St., KENDALLVILLE, IND.
MR. E. SEUEL, *Treasurer*,
  3558 S. Jefferson Ave.,
    ST. LOUIS, MO.

Saint Louis, Mo.
August 7th, 1922.

The Rev. Geo. O. Lillegard,
Kuling,
China.

My dear Brother,

    Your report for the year ending June 30th, 1922, just now came to hand. It affords very interesting reading, rehearsing as it does the chief events of the past year.

    Your success in planting Ichang station counts for a great deal, seeing that the odds were against you.

    Let us hope that it may please the Lord to make Ichang a great center for our work in that section of China.

    A week or so ago I had the great pleasure of reporting on my trip around the world in the interest of our missions to the Norwegian sister-synod. The brethren were exceedingly kind, giving me all the rope in the way of time I could possibly expect. I trust the effect of the report was to impart new impetus for our work in China. Some of the Norwegian brethren promised me to urge a special offering for the building fund in China. Unfortunately I have not heard how successful they were.

    While at Madison I had the good fortune to enjoy an evening with the good parents of Mrs. Lillegard. My own relatives could not have been friendlier. Mrs. Lillegards parents are the embodiment of old time Christian hospitality. Some day when I must rest up, I shall write to them to allow me to slip up to them, and I know they will have that famous bed I used in order for me.

    Please see to it that the minutes of the Conference get into my hands as soon after the Conference as possible. We cannot give the addresses of our missionaries in China in the 1923 Annual unless the report gets into my hands before the first week in September.

    With cordial regards to all the missionary body, especially to Mrs. Lillegard and yourself,

    I am

        Sincerely yours

        Frederick Brand

The views are very fine. Thanks. I was not nearly so successful.

Chapter 8
Back to Shihnan

GEORGE ELABORATES ON THE CONFERENCE REPORT.
"Mr. Gebhardt, my wife, and I are now on the way up to Ichang…we hope to be ready to proceed up river in a week or two. Then the Kleins and Miss Gruen will join us."

The Rev. Fr. Brand September 7th, 1922
St. Louis, Mo.

Dear friend Rev. Brand,
    Enclosed you will find a statement which Klein and I were supposed to work out on the question of Higher Education and send in to the Board. It is not exactly a part of the Conference Minutes and so comes this way.

    This year Meyer and Arndt will have charge of the school (in Hankow). It was the understanding, however, that it might be necessary to call one of the older men from the other stations to help out later on in the year, if the work got too heavy for these two. Since it is rather expected that Meyer will be going home on furlough next spring, the man who goes to Hankow to help out this season ought to be the one who will be appointed to take Meyer's place next year, in case he goes home. It was manifestly difficult for the Conference to take definite action regarding this now. I would therefore suggest that the Board appoint Meyer's successor at the same time as it reports on the matter of his furlough. This would relieve us here of a rather difficult situation. The situation is this: If Riedel should take Meyer's place next year, almost anyone of us might help out in Hankow this year, and we could appoint the one for whom it would be most convenient to take up this new or extra work to this temporary job. If Riedel, however, is not to take Meyer's place, that one of the men out here who should take Meyer's place ought also to be given the work of assisting in Hankow this year, in order to save unnecessary moving about and give him a chance to get acquainted with the work. The Conference left the matter of supplying a vacancy in the hands of the Executive Committee. It would be an easy matter to do this if we knew by, say the New Year, who was to take charge of the school next year…

    You ask for a full report on the Shihnan Yamen deal. There is nothing more to say beyond what is contained in the report sent in last year, except that the Chinese government has paid back the 8,000 strings of cash. We lost on the exchange… The amount of money spent on repairs was not all lost, as some material was recovered. There was nothing more to do about the case, as the government was obstinate. After my conversation with the consul last summer, I cannot but feel that the Government acted arbitrarily in the matter, and that we should have had the property. But it is hard for the foreigners to do anything in China now, so that we simply have to take our loss and grin and bear it.

    As for the property we mortgaged. You understand that our plan was to keep that for the Chinese work, if possible – schools, church, evangelists' residence, etc. It would be the cheapest and best possible place we could get in Shihnan for that purpose. Our mortgage of it should not affect our plans for land-buying and building made last summer. We will still need our residences, and land for future hospital and perhaps boarding school. So we hope to hear soon that the appropriations passed upon last summer have been made by the Board. We need to get busy at the landbuying question when we arrive at Shihnan, if our building program and our work in general is not to be held up for lack of adequate accommodations. Since there are to be so many of us in Shihnan this year, we shall have to find some other place for the schools, and it may not be so easy to do that. Next year, if nurses and a doctor come out, I do not know what we shall do for house room for them all. The downstairs rooms would not be healthful places to live in, I fear. At least it would take considerable repairs to put them in habitable shape. I think that we shall be able to get land and put up residences for much less than the amounts recommended last year. Shihnan is going to be a far cheaper place to carry on mission work than Hankow or even Ichang...

Mr. Gebhardt, my wife, and I are now on the way up to Ichang. Gebhardt will proceed to Shihnan while we pack our belongings. We hope to be ready to proceed up river in a week or two. Then the Kleins and Miss Gruen will join us. I am glad that it was decided to send Miss Gruen along, as she is a brave girl who is not afraid of the real or supposed dangers of the Shihnan field, and is a good friend of the Kleins, who could do more than anyone else to keep up their courage. Mrs. Klein is a rather nervous person. She underwent a minor operation in Hankow last Sunday, and has been very worried about having to go to Shihnan where there is no doctor. But we hope she will like it better when she gets out there than she thinks she will. I think, too, that we in many ways need a woman worker more in Shihnan than we do in Hankow, since the men can carry on the work among the women better in Hankow than they can in a place like Shihnan. We hope that we can keep her in Shihnan and that others will be sent out to take care of the work in Hankow.

We are hoping that the Board will decide to send a nurse out even this year. The Shihnan Conference was elected as a Committee to present the need of a doctor to the Board, and you will no doubt hear from us as soon as we are all gathered in Shihnan.

After we had decided to appoint Miss Gruen to Shihnan, we learned that her call read: "to the school work in Hankow." Does that mean that she was expected to do only schoolwork and that we went against the spirit of her call when we appointed her to Shihnan? If so, there will fortunately be no particular harm done this year, since her main duty as yet is to study the language and she might as well do that in Shihnan as in Hankow. If the Board wants her in Hankow, it will be time enough for her to take up her work there next year. In the meantime she will gain some valuable experience in the inland.

Gebhardt was elected Chairman and I Secretary for next year. As all official communications from the Board are to be circulated in the Mission, I was to appoint someone in Hankow as Assistant Secretary, to whom the communications of the Board should be addressed. Mr. Zschiegner, who is to be the General Treasurer, will also be Assistant Secretary, so I shall ask you to address all official communications to him. He will send them on the Ichang and Shihnan, where they will be retained in the Secretary's files and answered.

Mr. Gebhardt has had some interesting conversations with a Catholic priest who speaks German. He says that the Catholics are going to move their Theol. Sem. from Hankow to Kinchow, near Shasi. Their reason is stated to be that they have more land and room in Kinchow, and perhaps also that they look upon it as a better place for theologians, since it lacks some of the temptations of the big city. We are wondering whether Hankow is the place for our Theol. Seminary too – that is, as permanent location. Before we build a Seminary building, the whole question of where to locate our Higher Schools ought to be one (looked) into thoroughly. This priest tells us also that the Catholics are uniting and correlating their Higher School work. They are to make this Seminary in Kinchow the Seminary for the two provinces of Hupeh and Hunan. This year they will have over thirty pupils. The other Seminaries that they have had in the four bishoprics of Hankow, Ichang, Laohokow, and Hunan, will become sort of pre-seminary schools only. Their course covers a period of 15 years from the beginning of the primary work to the end of the Seminary work. Then the graduates are fullfledged priests. Our course as at present outlined covers a period of 14 years – seven Primary, four Middle School, and three Seminary. Ought we not as soon as possible add at least two years Junior College work? That would give our men at least as good a training as the Catholic priests, if not as good as some of the college-bred pastors of the Reformed Missions. I retail this information to you, as Gebhardt thought you would be interested in hearing about the Catholic work.

Our Conference passed off pleasantly enough, although there was some tension connected with the stationing of our forces. Shihnan is going to be a difficult station to man properly, it seems, if we do not get a doctor out soon. It might be well for the Board to make clear to those who are to go out to China that their call implies going to a place such as Shihnan, so that they will not have any excuse, when they come out, to the effect that they were not called to Shihnan, etc. The question was solved this year by Klein's willingness to try it for a year. But we must try to get a different attitude towards the stationing of men in an inland station. The fact that a man has children, e.g., should not be considered a valid reason for refusing to go to Shihnan or taking one's family along. The fact that we have a station like Hankow where one can live very much the same as at home is rather demoralizing to our missionaries. Naturally all would like to stay there and invidious comparisons are likely to be made between their position and that of those who have to go to Shihnan.

There are still a number of loose ends in our organization that need to be gathered up. I hope that we can get them finally straightened out next year, after the Board has passed on all our recommendations and made such other changes and regulations as it finds fit. Then we shall be able to push ahead with our work and not be in quite such great danger of forging rapidly ahead on the wrong path.

This got to be quite a long, gossipy letter. But it relieves my mind of a number of matters that needed to be mentioned in explanation of the actions and resolutions of the Conference. If there are any other matters in the Secretary's Minutes which are in need of fuller elaborations, I shall be glad to write you about them as soon as I hear from you again.

My best greetings to you and the other members of the Board. Mr. Gebhardt also sends greetings. He has also been busy on our voyage writing letters. Soon we shall all be busy climbing mountains and clinging to the backs of our little mules!

Sincerely yours,
Geo. O. Lillegard

George plans the move back to Shihnan.

Evangelical Lutheran Mission.

GEO. O. LILLEGARD,
37. Wen Gi Lu.

ICHANG, HUPEH, CHINA.

宜昌信義會

Ichang, September 22d, 1922

The Rev. Fr. Brand,
St. Louis, Mo.,

Dear friend:- Your letter of August 7th was received here yesterday. Thank you! We had already heard from Madison with regard to your visit there, and were very glad that the Norw. Synod had an opportunity to hear your report on our missions and that the Onstads had a chance to see and meet you. Bernice's parents express their great appreciation of your visit.

I enclose the report on Medical Missions which the Shihnan Conference was to send in to the Board. Gebhardt and Klein have both reviewed it, so it expresses their ideas on the subject also, as, I take it, of the whole Conference. We hope to hear soon that your return to the States has meant greater success for the efforts of the Board to secure medical men for our foreign missions.

We are still in Ichang, as we had to wait till we got word from Gebhardt that coolies and mules had been sent to meet us at Patung. Gebhardt went up two weeks ago, having come to Ichang with us at that time. On the way, he learned that some of the defeated Sechuanese soldiers in the role of bandits were coming to attack Miaoyutsao. So he went another road from there and arrived safely at Shihnan. He advised us to travel the Patung road as the Taichi road was still reported unsafe. Fortunately the telegraph is now in operation to Shihnan, so that we could make arrangements for the change of plans by telegraph. Otherwise we would have been delayed here another week. However, we did not get through with our packing until Wednesday this week, so that there has been little time lost as yet. We expect to leave Ichang Monday, and should arrive at Shihnan by the end of next week, if we are favored with good weather and our coolies prove good travelers. Miss Gruen, Mrs. Klein, and my wife will travel by chair, and Klein and I on muleback. Gebhardt is sending a reliable Chinese to meet us at Patung, who will take our baggage along up to Taichi and see to that it is brought overland from there. It is too expensive to transport all our goods by coolie from Patung. At Taichi, there are packmules to be had. The Patung road is not the easiest to travel, since there are thirty or forty thousand Northern soldiers along that road, no inns are open, and there are few villages the first two or three days' journey. However, we hope that we will manage allright. It makes it bad that we have to go the Patung road now when we have so much baggage, but there is no help for it. It seems that there may yet be another Hupeh-Szechuan war, though perhaps not this year. Wu-Pei-fu would be the attacker in this case.

My wife and I are both well. We look forward to getting settled in Shihnan as we have been on the move so much the last year that we are tired of it. The Kleins and Miss Gruen are also in good health and spirits. They arrived here last Monday. We were so crowded in this house that Kleins and Miss Gruen accepted Rev. Cooper's invitation to pass the nights at his house. We will be able to repay his hospitality when Cooper makes his annual visit to Shihnan this fall.

With best greetings to yourself and family from us both,

Faithfully yours,

GEORGE DESCRIBES THE TRIP TO SHIHNAN.
"...the ladies spent one cold night out in a farmyard."

Shihnanfu, Hupeh, October 15th, 1922

Dear friend Zschiegner,

We have not received any very definite news from Hankow as to the date of the arrival of our new missionaries. But we presume that they will all be in Hankow by the time this reaches you, if they are not already there. I hear from home that Mrs. Ziegler is a Norwegian-American, which, of course, interests my wife and myself especially. We are glad to welcome another Norwegian into our mission. May there be many more of them before many years have passed! We have also heard that you are taking a peculiar interest in the arrival of the new missionaries. We hope that you by this time are in good position to debate the old question: Resolved, that the pleasure of anticipation is greater than the pleasure of realization. No doubt you will be able to defend the negative successfully.

I have not written more than one postal card to Schwartzkopf since our arrival. I was taken sick on the way from Patung and I seem to have lost my pep for a considerable time in consequence. However, I am feeling pretty good again now, and we are getting into the work here a little deeper each day. Gyps[128] has charge of the school and the advanced catechetical class, Klein of the sanitation, etc,. at this plant where we live, and of the station accounts, and I have charge of the Orphanage, the new catechetical class, and the services. This does not mean that we divide the work in this way, but only the responsibility. I teach a religion class in the school, Klein teaches English, and Gyps and I take turns at the services and street chapel meetings. Miss Gruen has charge of the women's work, and I help out with the preaching and teaching of the women temporarily, until Miss Gruen and the other ladies can do that work themselves.

We had a pleasant enough trip over the mountains, although my sickness made it strenuous for me. We had fine weather all the way. Klein's mule developed a sore back from carrying him, and Klein did not fare much better. I had a horse this time, who managed his heavy burden pretty well. The ladies stood the trip better than we men did. We had considerable difficulty finding food for the coolies on the road, and securing a roof for over our heads in the evenings. Klein and I slept outside on the "verandahs" two nights and the ladies spent one cold night out in a farmyard. They preferred that to the hovel that was at our disposal. Our baggage, which was sent on via Kweifu in care of a Chinese who met us at Patung, has not arrived yet. It should be here any day now. Brigands infest the road from Taichi to Shihnan, so no baggage can be transported that way. Our groceries and some of Gyps' baggage, which he took along, is still in Taichi, awaiting more peaceful times. If the baggage and groceries sent via Kweifu does not arrive pretty soon we will be minus butter, milk, sugar, salt, and a number of other necessaries. We took a minimum of our baggage along with us via Patung too, so that we have been rather short of clothing these last two, rather chilly, weeks. However, all things have an end, and no doubt this situation will also some day cease to be. I am

---

[128] Arnold Gebhardt, fellow missionary

rather expecting to see the coolies come trotting in with our baggage about the time our last ounce of butter butters our bread – which means tomorrow or thereabouts.

Prospects for the work here are very good this year. The attendance at our meetings is as large as one could wish, and there are many whom we expect will be preparing definitely for baptism. The school and orphans home are running smoothly enough.

We are wondering when "the great event of the year" is to take place. Let us know the date in time, if possible, so that we can celebrate with you Hankow-ites in spirit. We are also waiting to hear with regard to Arndt's arrival and the kind of arrangements made for the work in Hankow. Is the "language school" in existence yet? Have you heard from the Board?

I have asked Rev. Brand to mail all letters for the Conference to you first. You are thereby appointed as assistant secretary. Kindly forward all official communications promptly to Ichang, as soon as you in Hankow have read them, and ask Theiss or Schw. to forward them with equal promptness to me here. How do you like your treasurer job? As you in the capacity of treasurer will be communicating regularly with the Board anyway, Meyer and I thought you might as well receive the Secretary's mail first also. There will not be so very much of it.

Some of our goods has arrived since I started writing this letter. Only 17 pieces out of about 75 so far, however. The rest is presumably on the way. Now we will be busy unpacking and getting these things put in place. We rest the greater part of our goods and books in Ichang, but even so there is enough to make it a problem just how to dispose of things and where to put them all.

Best greetings to Nagel's and the rest of the missionaries in Hankow from my wife and myself. Please remember us especially to Mrs. Ziegler and Mrs. Zschiegner, when they arrive. Bernice will be writing ere long to them, I think.

Sincerely yours,
Geo. O. Lillegard

George writes his sister about the work in Shihnan; Bernice adds a postscript.
(Her letters from 63 to 84 to her family are curiously all missing.)

Shihnanfu, Hupeh, October 26th, 1922.

Dear Louise:-

Your letter of Aug. 20th came shortly after we arrived at this place and helped to keep us from worrying about the home folks. We did not get any other letters than yours between Aug. 25th and Oct 16th, when we got a letter from Anna. Today we received a short letter from Mother. I must say that my sisters are not very good correspondents. I am beginning to feel that I do not know much about what they are doing any more. Anna's last letter stated that she was in bed, but mother says nothing more about her, so I suppose she got over her sick spell. Hope so anyway'. Mother's letter contained a few shocks,--Astrid's and Gerhard Berrum's death , I feel rather relieved in a way about Astrid, as it must have been a blessing for her to get to go "home", sick and frail and alone as she was. But I certainly feel sorry for the Berrums. Gerhard was a rather wild boy. I hope he had a chance to consider seriously what might come after death for him and that his parents will have the comfort that he died a Christian.

We have been very busy since coming to Shihnan There are so many meetings to attend and so many things to look after that it keeps us all humping right along. I have done more language study since I came here too, as we have a good teacher now. But I have done less letter-writing than ever before. The result is that I am getting quite unused to the art of letterwriting and that it is increasingly hard for me to do any writing. If you people do not write oftener, I will soon be getting to be as poor a correspondent as the rest of you. Bernice writes every week to her folks, and gets letters every week or oftener too. Mr. Onstad did good work in the Political Campaign in Wisconsin and will very likely get a good office in the course of the year. La Follette and the others of his party won out at the Primary elections by a larger majority than ever before, and they give Onstad a good deal of the credit. LaFollette may be the next President yet, and then I suppose my honorable Father-in law will have a chance at something big too!

I guess nobody has written you any details about our work here yet. Well, I start the day's work by teaching religion in our boys' school from 8 tp 9 in the morning. Then I read with my teacher for an hour. Am studying the Chinese Classics now, which are pretty hard stuff. After that I generally study by myself for an hour or two. There are so many things to talk over and arrange now with regard to the work with the school, the catechumens, and the orphan boys, that most of the afternoon goes in looking after various business details. Then we are having repairs made on the place by several carpenters, who have to be looked after more or less. I have also been trying to look after the furniture and other goods that Gihring and Riedel left behind here in this house. We have bought some of Gihring's goods, and are renting some of Riedels, but still there is a good deal left. I have finally got it put away in a storeroom now, out of our way. Then we have meetings almost every evening. Tuesdays and Fridays I also have a class of women in the catechism. On Wednesdays, Thursdays, undays and Mondays, I also have meetings with the men. So you see we do not get very much lesiure. We have no Chinese Christians here yet to whom we can entrust things, so that all the work and responsibility devolves upon us. It is Mr. Gebhardt and I that have to do everything. Mr. Klein has been in China less than a year and cannot do much yet.

Today we invited our Chinese teachers to a meal. They invited us one of the first days we were here so this was return party. We had,--what do you guess?--a regular coon meal. The meat tastes very good, I think,--very much like pork. Did you ever eat it? The Chinese raccoon seems to be very much the same as the kind we have at home. Tomorrow we are going to have wild duck. This mountain country is a good place to get game, if one only knows where to go for it.

Friday A.M. -- George did not finish this letter last night, so he suggested that I do so. We certainly have been a busy family since we came to Shihnan. We used to go out for walks very often last spring, but so far we have hardly been out these weeks. I need the exercise, too. We three girls went out for an hour last night.

BERNICE AND COMPANY GO TO A CHINESE WEDDING FEAST.
"The bedroom holds quite an honorable place amongst the Chinese, it seems, as there is where we were entertained."

Sunday Evening, October 29th, 1922

We have just returned from a Chinese wedding feast and I feel like writing it up while it is fresh in my memory. I know I cannot do justice to it in words but I want to tell you about it as best I can, at least.

Several days ago each one of us – we are six here – received individual invitations on red paper about 4-1/2" x 9" enclosed in a red envelope a little larger. The invitation stated that the feast was to be at about two o'clock, which means that they would probably feast at about five o'clock or later. Therefore, we went over between three and four o'clock. Arriving at the house, we women were immediately escorted to one of the bedrooms, and the men were taken to some other room – we did not see them for some time, so the following account does not include them. The bedroom holds quite an honorable place amongst the Chinese, it seems, as there is where we were entertained. The room into which we were ushered was well furnished, this family being quite wealthy. It was not large, and having only one window, opening into the courtyard, it was also rather dark. There were two beds, one of them about the size of our double beds, I should judge, and the other somewhat smaller. I wish I could describe the bed so you could really get a picture of it in your mind! In some ways it makes one think of the old fashioned four-posters. It is, however, more closed in than they were, if I am not quite mistaken. This bed was almost like a little room. The bed stood lengthwise along the wall and had a carved frame work from which hung white muslin curtains, entirely closing it off on one side and both ends. The curtains in front were embroidered and were draped like we sometimes drape our window curtains.

On the open side was a little entrance, if you please – a platform at each end of which was a little railing enclosing a small cupboard, which also made an excellent seat. Underneath the platform were some drawers. The wood was all a dark mahogany finish, except for the platform floor, which was almost black. On the bed itself were a muslin spread embroidered in black, a number of quilts nicely folded, and a pillow very similar to our bolsters. On these were very pretty embroidered pieces and there were also two embroidered ornaments hanging down, one on each side, next to the draped curtain. They had some pretty vases, the inevitable clock, several mirrors, some embroidered pieces all on or over a table across from the bed. The bed is the seat of honor and so we were asked to sit down on it. This we did and we must have spent about an hour in the room trying to get an idea of Chinese homes impressed on our minds, struggling to converse with the many women sitting or standing around, and eating or drinking the things brought to us. We had not met any of these ladies before and so, like the majority of Chinese, they were quite sure they would not understand any Chinese a foreigner might attempt to speak. Therefore almost at once they said to me, "We do not understand you." Well, I know I cannot speak much Chinese, but I have been told that what I do say is entirely intelligible. However, when some of these Chinese get a notion they cannot understand a foreigner, they simply do not try to understand. Consequently, the conversation lagged for awhile. It was not as embarrassing as it might have been, though, because they first brought us sweet tea with nuts in, then a bowl of some sort of syrup or sweet soup with puffed rice in and finally a cup of tea. Sipping that helped to pass the time pleasantly enough.

And then! We were taken to another bedroom, namely the bride's room. And there we saw the bride sitting in state! The bed was similar to the one just described and the bride was sitting on it. The tables were filled with wedding gifts, such as tea pots and cups, a clock, etc. and over in the corner we saw nicely varnished little tubs, such as they use for washing dishes and clothes, also a pair of water buckets.

The bride was an eighteen year old girl and very sweet faced. She had her hair combed back very neatly in the approved fashion and in back were several very pretty hair ornaments. Her face was rouged, and although it was not just according to our American style, it was not unbecoming. Her tiny feet were clothed with pink stockings and embroidered red satin shoes. She wore a long black skirt and a coat – they do not wear waists – of grey brocaded satin. About her neck was a sort of black crocheted collar and on her bosom a large red flower made of some kind of material, I think. She also wore two chains, on one of which was a silver watch. She had three pair of bracelets – one pair of solid jade; one of amber beads; and the third of gold. She also had two pair of rings, one pair of solid jade, which were worn on the third or ring finger and one pair of gold rings with a jade stone set in each, which were worn on the second or middle finger. Of course her garb is not what we Americans would care to appear in, but nevertheless it was pretty and it was a sight pleasing to one's eye. The bride was very shy and modest, as is becoming to a bride in China. She is not supposed to look up, but must cast her eyes down all the time. Neither is she supposed to speak, but men and women alike may say what they please to her. It is customary to tease and say embarrassing things, and among the poorer classes it is generally the case that very filthy and horrid things are said to the poor frightened bride. It seems, however, that among the more respectable classes they limit themselves to tricks and jokes.

In the bride's room we were served noodles and other dainties. Then when it appeared that we were to leave that room, we asked if they would not like to have us take some snapshots of them. They seemed quite pleased with the idea, and we even persuaded the bride to come out, although it took a great deal of urging and gentle pulling on the part of half a dozen of us. We took a number of pictures in the courtyard but it was rather dark in there, and we fear the snaps will prove failures.

After taking the pictures we were again taken to the room in which we had first been entertained. By that time I was beginning to think that we must have been mistaken about the feast part of it, and that we had actually been invited to "tea." I was almost on the verge of suggesting that we should return home when we were summoned to the feast. Because we are foreigners, the Chinese allow us almost any privileges, even though it is quite contrary to their customs, so now they arranged a table for the six of us and three Chinese gentlemen, two of whom are in our employ and the third had been in our employ at one time. We were told that the ladies were afraid they could not entertain us, so they wanted us to eat with the men.

Our "equipment" at the table was a pair of chopsticks, a brass spoon and small brass saucer for it to rest on, and two small china saucers. When we were seated, the first course was brought in. The first course of a Chinese feast corresponds with our last course. Eleven dishes were brought in – Mandarin oranges, peanuts, melon seeds, sweet meats (literally), cold meats, pickled eggs, etc. Our wine cups, which are very small and do not hold as much as the average wine glass at home, were filled with wine and some sweet or sugared fruit. These things were left standing on the table until near the end of the meal. When we had eaten what we wished of the first course, a dish of "sea slugs" and something else was brought in. This having been tasted, it was taken off and replaced by another dish. Each dish is a course and we had about eight or more varieties brought in dish by dish. There were chicken and chestnuts (delicious!), Mongolian mushrooms and meat, fish, meat balls, tripe, pear soup, etc. Everything was very well prepared and it surely tasted good. The gravies in which all these things were served were most delicious. Finally everything was cleared off the table, we were each given a bowl of rice; and two, three dishes of pork, vegetables, and other meat were placed on the table. Having done justice to this, tea and smokes were brought. We ladies did not smoke even though it is quite the proper thing for ladies as well as men to smoke pipes and cigarettes.

Do you not envy us our privilege of being permitted to go into these Chinese homes, partaking of their food, and so on? It is most interesting. The Chinese consider it very polite to help each other to food and it is fun to have this one and that one giving you some food, even though you may not care to eat any of that particular dish, or want as much. Then they drink to each other's health and that is quite a formality. They look into each other's cup to see how much wine each has, drink, and then look again to see how much the other drank to his health. If one does not wish to drink much, he may do as one of the gentlemen did this evening, "You drink a cupful, I will drink half a cup!" (Please remember that these <u>cups</u> are very small!) The wine they use is very strong, but as a rule not much is consumed during a meal and it is taken in sips between courses, so it does not often affect them. It is rarely that one sees an intoxicated Chinese.

Do you wonder if we get enough to eat when we use chopsticks? You know, I think, that all the food is cut very small and a knife is not needed. We really enjoy using the chopsticks very much and we always get plenty. Usually the complaint is that we have eaten too much when we have had Chinese meals, especially when our own cook prepares them for us.

When the last course has been served it is polite to get up and leave. In fact, they almost hurry you, it seems!!!! Anyway, I did not have a chance to drink all my tea! One does not need to excuse himself for being "like a tramp, who eats and runs."

Bernice, 1922

GEORGE GIVES CORRECTIONS TO HIS PUBLISHINGS.
"One whole line had been left out, with the result that I was made to say just exactly the opposite of what I meant to say,…"

Shihnanfu, Hupeh, November 24th, 1922

Dear friend Ylvisaker:

Your letter of Aug. 31st, which reached me about the middle of last month has been unanswered much longer than it should have been. But we have been so rushed with our work here that it seems increasingly hard for me to catch up with it. Furthermore, I have begun to rely so much upon my wife to take care of our correspondence that I am getting pretty much out of the habit of writing letters. Therefore, it becomes increasingly hard to get at it.

Your letter brought much information regarding church affairs which I was very glad to get. I do not find our church papers as newsy or as illuminative of conditions in the Norwegian Church as it seems to me it might be. Could the Synod not do something about getting a little more "live" paper – and one with a smaller percentage of mistakes per line. Your article, which was, of course, an important one, was all too full of misprints. It weakens the force of a statement to have it murdered by the printer's devil that one has to puzzle to get at the meaning. When I read my article on "The World and the Church," printed last summer, I felt like throwing a fit. One whole line had been left out, with the result that I was made to say just exactly the opposite of what I meant to say – and unfortunately it read as smooth as could be wished so that none could suspect that there was a mistake there. And a large number of other foolish and entirely unnecessary misprints had also been made. I think it would be worth the while of the Synod to engage a professional proof reader…Could not you do something about this?

Since we have been in Shihnan since the 1st of October, we have not as yet seen the new arrivals. Our news from Hankow has also been rather meager. But I understand that the new arrivals are considered a good addition to our missionary force and I hope they will prove to be so. We will no doubt have our share of conflicts and difficulties out here on the mission field. There are those in our midst too whose heart is not exactly in the right place on all questions of principle. But we have some very fine men too. Gebhardt and Klein, who are with us in Shihnan, are both entirely reliable and conscientious men. Gebhardt is an especially fine fellow, very tactful and considerate besides being thorough and capable. Miss Gruen is a very sensible woman, who in time will make a good missionary, I am sure. All of us out here are busy with our routine work, language study, teaching and preaching, and seem never to find time for all that could and should be done. My wife is doing considerable mission work also, besides putting in more time with the language than ever before.

Everything has been peaceful in this region this fall, although robbers and ex-soldiers hold sway in the neighboring districts. When we came out in September, the best route to Shihnan was blocked by defeated Szechuanese soldiers. We took another route and made the trip without incident, but our freight, which had to be sent the other way took a month in getting to us. Fortunately it came through allright, for which we were duly thankful. No doubt you have read in the home papers about the disturbances in Honan, in the former Synod field, as well as other parts of the province. According to last reports, Kwangchow has been taken again. The paper said nothing about Larsens or

Miss Christensen, although it stated that some of the other missionaries there had arrived at a place of safety.

These are troubled times, and it is hard to say what effect these robber outrages will have on the country and our mission work. It may lead eventually to intervention by the foreign powers, which in my opinion will not be a good thing.

Hitherto we have all been quite well, except for the usual colds and attacks of stomach trouble, which we expect to have out here every so often. The new missionaries were very much worried about having to go out to a place like Shihnan, so far away from a doctor and all that. But now that the Kleins are here, they do not seem to mind it, although Klein had been ordered by the doctors who examined him at home to be in a place where he could be under medical supervision. His lungs are not the best, they say. Brand says they are trying to get a doctor and a couple nurses, but hitherto without success. I wonder if it would not be easier to find qualified nurses in our Norwegian circles than in the Missouri Synod. They seem to have few young women with a higher education in their church than we have. We need single women to take up the work among the women in our various stations too. I wonder if some of our parochial school teachers might be made interested in that. Harstad wrote to me once about his two daughters coming out as nurses, but I have heard nothing more from him for a long time. Do you know if there is any chance to get them? It would be a great help to have a well-trained nurse, of course.

We have been discussing the question of opening new stations next fall at some length in our local conferences. In case it is decided to open a new station next fall, very likely I will be the one to do the opening. It would be my wish to get into a new field where I could start on the lines that I think best. Too many things have been started wrong in the older stations to make it easy to develop the work on the right lines. I have been wondering if there is any prospect that the Norw. Synod will grow so much as to be able to support a station in China, besides contributing something to the other missions in which we are interested. It would mean something like $3000.00 per year to run a whole station, including the missionary's salary – and more after awhile as the work develops. Has any particular effort been made to raise funds for foreign missions, or has it been the general feeling that all the Synod's efforts should be concentrated on Home Mission work – which I notice Lee calls proselytizing. Will someone give a few facts in answer to show how the Union Church has been proselytizing among those who wished to join us and would have done so if they had been left alone? Perhaps it would be as well under the circumstances to avoid every appearance of seeking after their pastors and church members. The people are beginning to get their eyes open, and the reaction may bring a great many into our Synod. An interesting reaction is taking place in the political world now – LaFollette a few years ago almost ousted from the Senate, now a Presidential possibility – and similar reactions may take place in the church.

I hope this reaches you in time to bring you our heartiest wishes for a very Blessed Christmas season and a Happy and Prosperous New Year, full of every good thing for all of your family. Kindly give my greetings also to your brothers and mother, as well as the Overns, Faye, and such other acquaintances as there may be in your circles at this time. Fraternally yours,

Geo. O. Lillegard

HANKOW MISSIONARY MEYER'S FURLOUGH DENIED
"It will,…be better for the work to have you here another year,…"

Shihnanfu, Hupeh, December 2nd, 1922

Dear friend Meyer:

Your letter of Nov. 12th was received something like a week ago, and we were all glad to get some news with regard to the work in Hankow – something we had been entirely in the dark with regard to before. Hope Arndt is back by this time and helping out with his share of the work.

Did the letter from the Board lay you out? Hope you were in your secret heart half expecting to be disappointed so that you are not too much disappointed now. It will, of course, be better for the work to have you here another year, till our new arrivals are better able to help out with our growing work. Perhaps this will be a consoling feature of it to you also…

Gyps has already forwarded our official view on the question of a Conference this winter. If necessary the Executive Committee could meet and discuss our problems, but personally I doubt the advisability of calling a "representative Conference," or a General Conference. Travelling to and from Shihnan is likely to be rather difficult at Chinese New Year's time, as snow and ice make the roads in places almost impassable. The expense is also an item to be taken into consideration. At our last Conference the question of supplying help at the Hankow schools was definitely left to the Executive Committee. I doubt that it would be proper to change that decision now. It may take time to decide some of these questions by correspondence, but there would even so be less loss of energy and valuable time than a Conference would entail. For us at Shihnan, e.g., it would mean the loss of a month's time to go to a Conference at Ichang during midwinter.

We are all kept busy here, and seem to find it harder every day to keep up with the work resting upon us. The fact that we have no evangelists or trained teachers naturally makes it so much harder for us, as all detail rests upon us and we have to take so much time for little things that could as well be managed by Chinese if we had them. This is a phase of mission work in the beginning stages which can hardly be avoided without sacrificing more important things than the time and energy of a new missionary. In a year or so, our work ought to be so far on that one man could manage what two are required to do now. But then the work of opening up out-stations in the country towns round about should be taken up in good earnest. Nothing has been done in that respect so far, or can be done under the circumstances…

…we are all satisfied with our rooms. Too bad that this place did not have some lawn or garden space around it. If it did not open right out on the street as it does, it would make a pretty good residence. As it is we lack privacy, especially here in the front where we live. If we can secure the place next door for our schools and Orphanage that we are trying to get now, we may put our chapel and guestrooms there too. That will give us more privacy than now. As it is now, the whole congregation is treated regularly every week to a panoramic view of our wardrobe, at least the part of it that passes through the washerwoman's hands.

The work here is promising enough, although we of course meet with many disappointments. I think it is the usual experience of all missions in heathen lands that very much cannot be expected of the first converts to our faith. It takes the second generation, trained up in Christian homes and schools, to show more of the fruits of the Christian faith. There are exceptions enough only to prove the rule. With your school work as old as it is in Hankow, you ought to find more encouraging material to work with in the near future. Let us but work in faith and hope.

Greetings to you from us all. Everybody is well at present, and we are almost through with the process of getting settled – not quite.

Sincerely yours,
Geo. O. Lillegard

Fellow missionary Louis J. Schwartzkopf promises a Christmas package!

Ichang, December 18, 1922.

Dear Friends: GREETINGS!

Cheer up, ladies and gentlemen, Santa Claus is beginning to get busy. Until now five parcels have arrived and I am trying my best to persuade the coolie to have these in your hands by a week from today, Christmas Day.

One parcel for Klein,

One " " Gyps (a young barrel),

One " " Lillegard,

Two parcels for Miss Gruen,

Four bundles of newspapers & magazines,

Four bottles of U.B. ------Theiss & I hope this will do you some good

The coolie has received five ($5.00) dollars. It is understood that IN CASE you have something to send back with him, he is to receive from you four ($4.00) dollars, making a total of nine ($9.00). Should he, however, find a "load" somewhere else, then he is to receive from you only three ($3.00), making a total of 8.00. Get that? And yet I promised to pay him nine dollars if he would be able to hand you the stuff, by at the latest, on the 25th in the evening. I'm still half asleep, so I'll have to "repeat what I really mean":
Due him for the whole trip 9.00
          paid......5.00

$4.00 which you will give him, or less 1.00 if he finds a job elsewhere.

Another big mail due to-morrow.
No sign of Gihring's freight as yet.
All's well here.
The house next doors has finally been turned over to us; badly in need of repairs; T. will probably "move over" about the first of January.

A MERRY C H R I S T M A S   A N D   A   H A P P Y   N E W   Y E A R.

Regards,

J.S.

rope, basket & oil paper ours — or yours, as you like.
J.S.

BERNICE DESCRIBES THEIR LIFE FOR GEORGE'S SISTER.
"I did not see a white woman for twelve weeks."

Shihnanfu, Hupeh, China

December 2nd, 1922

Dear Louise,

Your letter was all sealed and ready to be mailed the day your last letter was received. We certainly appreciate that you write so regularly. You are the only one on the Lillegard side that does write regularly, too. We are still waiting for some mail from Chicago, the last letter being received October 16th. Well, we did receive a letter from Mother the 26th of October, but it was written from Bode.

There are a number of questions in your letter that would have been answered for you last spring, if the letters we wrote had been forwarded to you, as we thought most of them were. You ask first if there are many other foreigners here. Didn't you know that we were only three foreigners last spring, with the exception of a Belgian priest, and we have nothing to do with him and very, very seldom see him, so he hardly counts as far as foreign community is concerned. All that I have seen of him was a glimpse of his back as he walked down the street. I did not see a white woman for twelve weeks. Didn't you read anything about Shihnan, that is, didn't you see any of our letters? The nearest hospital and doctors are at Ichang, about three hundred miles from here. There are, of course, no foreign stores, but I think we could manage to live all right, if necessary, even if we did not bring so many supplies with us. We were pretty short here for awhile because our freight was delayed so long, and at that time we were able to buy sweetened condensed milk to keep us going, but it did cost frightfully much. We cannot buy cornstarch, baking powder, butter, spices, refined salt or sugar, and such things, so we bring our supply of canned goods and groceries along from Hankow. What we use in that line right along is milk, butter, flour, baking powder and spices, sugar, salt and such necessities, but we buy vegetables – we always have plenty – and meat on the street. Clothing is something that we usually provide ourselves with during the summer. So far, George and I have not invested in any winter clothing to speak of. There are cloth shops, naturally, but I do not know how much they have or just what they carry, because I have not had occasion to do any shopping as yet. I expect to look for something for curtains for some of our small windows pretty soon. I will be looking for something heavy though, not regular curtain material.

You also ask if we are permanently stationed here. Well, we don't know that yet. Since George is one of the older men, it may be that he will have to open a new station next year. We will have to wait until after next summer's Conference before we know. We did not take more than the most necessary things along with us this winter just because we want to be sure we are definitely settled before we move everything again. We sold all the furniture we had made last year to Theiss's and put our nice dishes, cut glass, best silver, and many other things including most of George's books into storage. I hope that if we are ever to move again it will be next year, so that we may finally get settled. We both like Shihnan very much and would be perfectly happy to stay here, unless certain others should also be stationed here. It is not as easy to get along with some people as others. We six that are here now are a congenial bunch and have been getting along beautifully so far. Here is hoping we do so the whole year!!

Shihnan has been very quiet and peaceful this fall, for which we are duly thankful. Just at present Honan, the province in which George lived before, has been terrorized by a number of bandits again. You may have read about it in the papers. We are all glad that we have been spared such troubles. Here the soldiers and their officers have been very friendly to us and also the other people.

Did you have a big Thanksgiving dinner? We entertained the family here Thursday evening and I shall give you the menu: 1- Soup (beef stock flavored with half a dozen or more different vegetables and cream). 2- Fish and potato chips. 3- Roast pheasant and chicken, dressing, mashed potatoes, gravy, cranberry jelly (made of dehydrated cranberries), creamed peas, carrots (shredded and fried in a way that brings out the finest flavor), cucumber pickles, and baking powder biscuit. 4- Pumpkin pie – delicious. 5- Peanuts, walnuts, and candied ginger – and lastly coffee. It really was a delicious meal, one of the best my cook has served, I believe. After chickens had been butchered he accidentally found a pheasant, but we did not think it was enough for six people, so also roasted a chicken. Our pumpkin pies are about as cheap as anything. Yesterday we bought three good sized pumpkins for seventeen cents Mexican or about eight cents American money. The candied ginger is some we put up ourselves this fall. We like it better than the stuff we buy and it is <u>ever so much cheaper.</u> I s'pose if the church people heard that we had such fine meals they would cut down their contributions to the mission "kasse"[129] You had better not publish the menu! It is getting more expensive to live in China too, though. Eggs used to be very cheap, but now we have been paying two cents a piece. And we burn wood in both stoves, and I tell you, that costs, but what are we to do? We cannot get decent coal here, so there is nothing else to burn. We plan on trying charcoal a little just to compare and see if it comes higher or cheaper.

My, it was cold here for a few days! A week ago we had rain and also a little snow. What fell here melted as soon as it touched anything, but the highest mountain right across the river had a nice cap of snow for a few hours. It made us so excited! The boys thought we ought to go up and get some to make some ice cream! It really is no fun when it is so cold here because our houses are such cold, draughty places. The walls, except the outside one, are of thin boards and full of cracks and the floors are so cold. Here the other day I was sitting quite close to the stove and my back was cold, while my face was hot. That is the way, what is next to the stove is warm and what isn't is cold. At that I certainly mind the cold less than the heat. We were just looking at the map the other day and we find we are as far south as Galveston, Texas.

Come and have some peanuts and Mandarin oranges with me? We have bought quite a supply of peanuts, chestnuts, walnuts, and such things. You see, we live more like they did in olden times here – in many ways. The best thing to do is to buy things when they are in season, because afterwards they are scarce and, of course, expensive…Please greet all the Tjernagels from us and tell Nehemias his letter was received the other day. George intends to answer it soon. A happy New Year to all of you.

Love from us both,
Bernice

---

[129] Literally "cash box" – fund (Norwegian)

DECEMBER NEWS
"We have the schools in another building now, so that the place is fairly quiet most of the time."

School in Shihnan

Shihnanfu, Hupeh, Dec. 8th, 1922

Dear friend Riedel:

We have heard indirectly that another member has been added to your family since last summer. Congratulations! We hope everything is well with the new arrival and your wife.

How does it feel to be back in the States again? Have you forgotten China since you came back, or are you beginning to get homesick for some of its sights, sounds and smells? We hope you and your family are all looking forward to the return trip to China, and that you will come back in due time, with renewed strength and health for the great tasks that await us in the harvest fields in the heathen world…

We are all getting along very well here. We have had the rooms fixed up a little so as to provide more comfortable quarters for us six. Thus Kleins have a partition in the large north-room, making a dining-room and study out of that room, and we have a partition in the kitchen, separating that from the dining-room. We have also put in a pantry between the kitchen and Miss Gruen's room – the south room in the main building – and another store room for wood, water-gangs, etc., at this end between the dining room and our study-parlor. We occupy the rooms you used to have, you see, and Kleins and Miss Gruen have the main-building rooms. We have also put a partition in the middle room between our bedroom and Gyps's, making two closets and a bathroom out of that place. We have the schools in another building now, so that the place is fairly quiet most of the time. We still have services here, however.

There might be much to write about the work here that would interest you, but we are kept too busy to do much writing about our "business."

Let us hear regarding your activities in the States and your plans. Hoping to receive some good news regarding the packages in due season, I remain, with best wishes for a Blessed and Happy New Year to you and yours, Sincerely yours,

Geo. O. Lillegard

CHRISTMAS IN SHIHNAN
"...they made elaborate paper decorations, including some whose ornateness and beauty we failed to discover,..."

December 28th, 1922

Dear friend Meyer:

Your letter of Dec. 12th and the note enclosed in your wife's letter to Bernice are at hand – the latter just arrived. Thank you for them both. I shall not accept your apologies, as I consider no apologies necessary. Let us call it a misunderstanding and forget about it! I hope neither of us will have occasion in the future to feel anything but confidence in the other, however violently we might disagree on certain questions, whether it be the amount of pepper to use with one's eggs, or anything else. Enough for that.

We have had quite an enjoyable Christmas week so far, although not everything was done just as we would like. The Chinese got the idea that they wanted to have it more "reh nao"[130] here than the Episcopalian or Catholic Missions could have it, so they made elaborate paper decorations, including some whose ornateness and beauty we failed to discover, and prepared feasts for everyone connected with our mission. There were about 100 people from the country who had their meal on Christmas day noon, about as many school children in the afternoon, after the school program, and about 60 men and women from the city on second Christmas day. We had services on Christmas day morning, school program in the P.M., and again on Second Christmas Day in the evening. The school program was well rendered. We had the crowd sitting in the courtyard, using the middle room in the main building as "stage." The Chinese collected about 160,000 cash for the Christmas festivities - at that they are in debt. We shall have to try to keep them from celebrating in that manner hereafter. They have not gotten the idea of our Christmas celebration as yet, which is only to be expected, I suppose, under the circumstances.

We are waiting for American mail – have not had any now for over two weeks. No Christmas mail has arrived either, except a few packages forwarded from Ichang by Schwartzkopf...(the last line of the letter runs off the page and is missing)

Geo. O. Lillegard

---

[130] (Chinese)

Our First Christians in Shihnanfu (Jan. 1923)

On the First Sunday in Epiphany, the Rev. A. Gebhardt baptized five adults and twelve children – the first-fruits of our mission work in this part of China. Three children and one man were, indeed, baptized in earlier years. But these were in all cases such as had been under our care in the hospital or during the famine relief work and they died soon after their baptism. The baptisms which marked the beginning of the New Year are of a different character, since they imply the establishment of a congregation in this center – a congregation which we hope will grow in grace and strength as the years advance. It may seem that we have had to wait a long time for these first visible fruits, since we have been working in Shihnan for almost three years. But the work has been interrupted so often by political disturbances, by the sickness of the missionaries in charge, and by protracted absences of the missionary force from the station, that we cannot be considered to have put more than a year or two of real missionary effort into this field.

"For første gang, det giver mangen smaating rang,"[131] says a Norwegian poet. And since these are the first Lutheran Christians in Shihnan, a somewhat more complete account concerning them may be of interest to our church people. The five adults who were baptized are: Mr. Jao Hsi-ju, Mr. Liu Yueh-ting, Mr. Hsü Tzu-chien, Mrs. Hsü, baptized "Ya-na," and the son of the two latter, baptized "Yo-han." The twelve children were: Mr. Jao's boy, Szu-shi (meaning "Judge"), and girl, Ngan-wei, (Comfort); Mr. Liu's two boys, Ya-peh and Ya-lwen (the reader may discover that these two names are the Chinese equivalent of Abel and Aaron respectively); Mr. & Mrs. Hsü's two boys, Yo-Peh and Yo-seh, and two girls, His-ngan and Ping-ngan, (Compassion and Peace); and four orphan boys, Chen Yo-er, Wu Hsi-men, Wu Pao-lo, a blind boy, and Wu Ya-koh, a deaf and dumb boy, popularly called "Jimmy."

Mr. Jao has been assisting us the last year with our orphan and famine relief work as well as with other business details. He is a member of the most prominent and influential family in the city, whose members in years past have held even the highest offices, such as that of provincial governor, and now also hold important political offices in various parts of China. Our Mr. Jao is a man of independent means, a capable and clever man, who could become a most valuable worker in the Chinese Lutheran Church, if only Christian zeal and love were given him in adequate measure to fill out his other talents. Mr. Liu has been teacher in our schools the last two years, has proven a reliable man in his work, and an interested student of the Bible. He has a good education and has some means of his own. Mr. & Mrs. Hsü came to us about two years ago, down and out financially, and were given employment in connection with the Famine Relief work to help them over their difficulties. They come of good stock and are intelligent and interesting people. Mr. Hsü seems to be that rather rare specimen, a Chinese that does not care for money. His own money he spent and gave away so freely that he was finally left stranded when the hard years came. At the same time, he wants us to be very saving with our money. He is unusually straightforward and frank about expressing his opinions, so that we have in him that very useful element in a mission – an agent through whom to find out the real facts of a case. We foreigners live so much in a world apart, due to the difficulties of the language and customs of the people, that it is extremely difficult for us to know what to think about men and affairs unless we have some Chinese

---

[131] "At first, many trivial things (matters) are given importance." (Norwegian)

about, whom we can rely upon to give us an unvarnished account of things. Mrs. Hsü is a capable woman, whom we hope to make good use of in the future in connection with the work among the women. She has hitherto been a "mother" to the orphan boys, giving especial attention to those who were too young to take care of themselves. For a time, she cared for a little baby girl, left at our door by some poverty-stricken mother. The foundling, whom we named "Ma-ta," never recovered from the effects of the starvation she had suffered under apparently from her birth, but died last summer, not long after she had been baptized.

Mr. & Mrs. Hsü's oldest son, Yo-han, is a good, bright boy, whom Mr. Gebhardt is helping through school in return for such services as he can render during free hours. Nine of the twelve children baptized have been receiving some instruction in the Scripture truths. The blind boy can read a little according to the Braille system and the deaf and dumb boy has also been taught a few characters. These two unfortunates are bright and happy in spite of their physical defects. Miss Gruen has undertaken the care of little Pao-lo, while "Jimmy" is the especial protégé of Mrs. Klein.

On the Third Sunday in Epiphany, a new-born son of Mrs. Liu's was baptized, being given the name "Shou-Ling," which means, "Receiving the Spirit." On Second Sunday in Epiphany, the five adults, together with the missionaries in Shihnan, received their first Communion. They have also shown their sense of the responsibilities of their church membership by subscribing several dollars a month for mission work in this district – which means up to six percent of their total income. May these young Christians be given grace to remain steadfast in the true faith and grow in wisdom, zeal, and holiness throughout their life. To this end we ask the prayers of our friends in the Homeland.

Geo. O. Lillegard

GEORGE REPORTS ON POLITICS AND OPIUM.

The Central China Post   Shihnanfu, Hupeh, China, January 22nd, 1923
Hankow, China

    This corner of the world has been so quiet and peaceful since last summer that one is inclined to believe that it may be reverting to its original character as an out of the way place which saw other parts of the country torn by wars and brigand outrages and famines and what not while its own life flowed on in its even tenor. If it were not for the presence of one or two thousand northern soldiers whose discordant trumpets wake us long before dawn every morning, we might imagine ourselves back to "the good, old days," when the word of an emperor was better than a hundred thousand modern republican soldiers. But the hard work and incessant drilling to which these soldiers are put lends considerable color to the rumor that the Northerners are preparing to attack Szechuan, with the help of the remnants of Yan Sen's army and the disaffected elements in Szechuan itself.

    Yang Sen's troops are at present quartered in Lichwanhsien on the border of Szechuan, from where it's only a short march to Wanhsien or Chungchow on the Yangtse over fairly good roads…There has been little brigandage near Shihnan or on the highways leading to it. In the southwestern corner of the province and in Lichwanhsien, conditions have been worse. Occasionally one hears reports of Shen Ping activities. The soldiers in Lichwan have not been so careful to observe the letter of the law as the Northern soldiers here have been, with the result that the people are ready to break out against them at any favorable opportunity and drive them out, as they did two years ago, when the Southerners occupied this section of Hupeh.

    The soldiers in Shihnan seem to be pretty well-behaved. They are well officered and many of them seem to be a little better than the brigand class that too often makes up a large part of China's armies.

    A great deal of opium is being raised in this part of the country, and opium smoking is indulged in openly everywhere from the magistrate's yamen to the wayside hovel. It is said that the soldiers offer to guarantee safe delivery of the black stuff past the Customs barrier for so much per ounce. Last spring a prominent gentleman in this city moved to Wuchang, and transported together with his household Penates, slave-girls, and other valuables a considerable quantity of opium. On the way to Ichang he was held up by some of General Djao's soldiers, who immediately relieved him of his opium. He complained to General Djao of the robbery committed upon him by his soldiers, with the result that these two honorable gentlemen indulged in an exchange of compliments of a character not provided for in the "Li Chi," and our Shihnanite departed better off only to the extent to which he had relieved his surcharged mind. The opium business apparently brings poor profit to all except the soldiers and such others as may be "on the inside" with them. No attempt is being made here either by the civil or military officials to suppress the growing or selling or using of opium. The soldiers derive a considerable part of their support from the taxes imposed upon opium, and the civil officials also find it a generous source of profit, no doubt. Between the soldiers and corrupt officials, the Chinese people seem to be in a fair way to reach the bottom of national corruption a few jumps ahead of any of the rest of the nations. Is this what the Great Powers wish to see – or why do they not try to do something about it?

SCHWARTZKOPF WRITES FROM ICHANG.
"People living in glass houses should not throw bricks!
Take that in your pipe and smoke it."

Louis J. Schwartzkopf
No. 37 Yuin Kee Luh.

Evangelical Lutheran Mission
Synod of Missouri, Ohio, and Other States
會 義 信 教 督 基

湖北省宜昌　許慈叩牧師

Ichang February 4, 1923.

Dear Lillegard:

Your well-meant reminder under date of Feb. 1, slipped into my hands about ten minutes ago. Do you want me to send you a calendar for 1923? I noticed that your letter was dated "February 1," while the stamp of "Shihnanfu" was dated "Ih reh san si ih." You want to be careful with your dates…getting ma hu tih,[132] I presume. At any rate, let me assure you, we were very glad to hear from you people for a change; hadn't heard from you for practically one month. Too deeply sunk in your love for…who knows what, eh? Or is it possible that you are still clinging to your beds, hugging the sickness, which, according to a report from Gyps, was trying to entangle you in its friendship? We sincerely hope that you are well or, at least, recovering by the time this note reaches you. I was under the weather about a week or so ago, but I managed to laugh the malady away quite promptly. It is very evident that the long and drawnout spell of dry weather had considerable to do with my health during the past season. But as soon as the rainy season set in, about two weeks ago (altho of short duration), I began to feel somewhat better. With the rain, however, also came cold weather, and that is something which I dread for a two-fold reason: first, a wee bit of wind is sufficient to make me sneeze nights, br-r-r! It rained all day today, getting still colder in consequence thereof.

The enclosed report was written, as you will notice, on the day of the first anniversary of our mission work here in Ichang. And my reason for not letting you people – honorable critics – have a copy of it before this, was because I don't believe in advertising. No, it is not false modesty on my part at all. Just read it, and I am sure you will give me credit for not "showing the thing to outsiders." I received a letter from Rev. Brand on the day we returned from our last trip to Changyang, and because he urged me to send him an article on our work at Ichang "immediately," I lost no time, but sat down and hammered off something, well, it is "something" alright. Brand may consider the paper valuable for its fire-kindling quality. But, I have sent a report in anyway. Next. "Phonetic System." I have been discussing this matter at great length with a member of the Scotch Mission, and have decided to write to Shanghai for information and books in connection with the Phonetic system. It is evident that we should make use of this new system; certainly we should try it with our illiterate catechumens. Next. Chinese

---

[132] (Chinese)

Literature. You may take for granted that I hesitated about ordering tracts and books when I was obliged to ship such a large quantity of parcels of books and tracts to you during the past year. I will confess, however, that I took the liberty to open some of the more or less damaged packages, and that I kept a small number of them as samples. You don't blame me for swiping also two copies of the "Chi tuh t'u iao shioh," do you. Came in very handy. Shall order some for this place. Found a number of other booklets in the lot, which I should like to order, but I forget the names of them; my teacher is making use of some of them at present. Yes, I wish you would give me a list of tracts and books and that as soon as possible, because later on I may be tied down to other work. I am preparing an article for the Kinder-und Jugenblatt now, during February there will be "this and that," besides preparing to open our school after the Chinese New Year, and thereafter I'll undoubtedly be swimming in work.

People living in glass houses should not throw bricks! Take that in your pipe and smoke it. You poor fish…don't get so gay. It is a good thing that you added, "at least, we have heard nothing about any such productions to date"…that saved your hide. Application of the soft pedal is worth a great deal under certain circumstances, eh? As for such "productions," however, you will remember that I sent a long-winded report to the Board last spring; one of the members wrote and thanked me for the "very fine and <u>fascinating</u> article"…wonder why he didn't say "decorative"…for it more than likely enhanced the beauty of one of the spacious wastepaper-baskets! Oi, oi! It is due to this fact (that my article hasn't appeared in print to date) that I have decided to keep my home town "Bugle" supplied with news reports from China. There is always somebody around who appreciates a good thing when he sees it. What is a man going to do? I write a long report, then they say it's windy, and if I make it short, they are apt to jump on my neck and say I am lazy. Furthermore, I wasn't born to become a great writer. I wonder, would it help matters along if I would send some cumshaw[133] along with my next report. I have a good notion to try that once.

Say, James, will it suit you alright if I turn the remainder of my debt over to Gyps? I mean, what I owe you. If you prefer, however, I shall send you a money order for the amount. Say the word. Talk about being hard up for cash, man, you may be floating, but yours truly has already sunk and is still sinking deeper and deeper. They say, "go while going is good," and I sure am going. I still have hopes of discovering a goldmine in the Changyang district.

I suppose Gyps is preparing to leave Shihnan tomorrow. Too bad he can't make as good time as your last letter did coming over. Rev. Karl Nelton of the Swedish Mission left last Wednesday. The doctors of Hankow and Wuchang advised him to take his wife, who has been ill for some time, to Sweden. He sold all of his furniture before leaving. We grabbed a number of wicker chairs and tables, a rocker, (real American), and his organ. A good bargain we made there.

Say, will you help me save a three-center, by asking Miss Gruen whether or not she still has two of my books, "Through the Yangtze Gorges," by Capt. Plant, and "Handbook for China" by Carl Crow. Thanks.

Best Regards to the whole Crew.
Fraternally yours, Louis J. S.

---

[133] From the Chinese "kam sia" for "grateful thanks" – meaning a present or gratuity

GEORGE GIVES IT RIGHT BACK TO SCHWARTZKOPF.
"Don't get so fresh about my dates!"

Feb. 20th, 1923

Dear friend Schwartzkopf:

Thank you for your letter of the 4th, with all its news and philosophy of life and missions, etc. – not to mention the hot air. We were quite excited when we read about the fire that came so close to your place. We wondered how our piano fared during the excitement. Was it moved or did it just stand there through all the excitement? Do you realize that I had had the insurance transferred to the house next door, and that if the house had gone up in smoke, with the piano in it, my insurance would have done me no good? I think I would have had a fit if it had gone. However, since it did not happen, it did not, and there is no use worrying about it. Has Theiss moved the piano over to his place yet?

I sent your report on to Hankow a day or two after I received it. It was interesting. Enclosed you will find Personal and Station Reports for Shihnan. Please send them on to Hankow, when you Ichangites are through reading them, with directions to return to Gyps, the Historian, when they are through with it there.

As for our accounts, if you have not already sent the balance due me along with Gyps, a check will be quite acceptable, thank you. Please send me a statement showing what you have paid for the various articles procured for us. Debts!?! Let us all strike for higher wages. "Hao buh hao."[134]

Miss Gruen says that she still has the two books you mentioned and that she is taking good care of them. Furthermore, she even promises to return them some time. What more do you want?

As for tracts – would you kindly read and report on the following at your earliest opportunity: Life of Luther, by Fritz; The Nestorian Tablet; The Fact of Christ, by MacGillivray: and if you have time, I should like to have you look through Faber's "Civilization." I have looked through a number of tracts and have a few others waiting to be operated upon. I have found a number of really good and useful booklets.

Will you kindly take our beds out of the storeroom in the chapel and put them in your empty room upstairs, now that you have room? I feel they would be better off in the house, and then they might come in handy for your visitors. How about that chest of drawers? Is that in the house? I would be thankful for some information with regard to these articles.

By the way, next time you send coolies to Shihnan, kindly give them bigger loads. They can easily carry 80-90 gin each, if the packages are compact. They carry 60 gin when they go along with us, but when there is no need to hurry, they can just as well carry more. Our freight bills are so big that we will have to be as saving as possible.

Don't get so fresh about my dates! I dated those letters ahead, thinking I would wait with sending them. Then, since I got them all ready on the 31st, I decided to send them on anyway. I did not think anyone would be so critical as to examine the Chinese date on the envelope! Are you satisfied?

---

[134] Literally, "good, not good;" OK? (Chinese)

I am entirely over my cold at last, but Bernice has been sick for three weeks and is not improving. She had a bad attack of bronchitis, which later turned into pleurisy. She has such a sore side that she can hardly move at times. Her cold is still bad, too, although it now affects her head more than her lungs. She is trying to take good care of herself, which is about the only thing to do for such ailments. No medicine is of much help. The weather has been so dark and gloomy most of the time this winter, and we have all been kept so busy that we have perhaps neglected outdoor exercise all too much. If only it would warm up pretty soon, I think Bernice would recover sooner. This cloudy weather is rather dispiriting when one does not feel very good to begin with. Klein has been a little under the weather lately, too – stomach trouble mostly. We are going to get this place fixed up so that we can have it a little more private hereafter. I suppose the fact that our courtyard serves as a depository for the spit and filth of the Chinese who come to our meetings and hang around our guestrooms has something to do with our colds and illnesses. Almost every Chinese we know has had or is having some form or other of cold or "grippe." Have you had mostly dark, cloudy weather in Ichang, too, this winter? Or is it only in these mountains that we have so much cloudy weather?

Everything has been very quiet around our place the last couple weeks. Nobody comes out for evening services. Sunday services have been pretty well attended, however. Last Sunday there was not a soul in from the country – they are scared stiff of being taken by the soldiers. Most of the soldiers in this city have "gone west," to Lichwan preparatory to going still farther west to Szechuan, and then going west some more, undoubtedly, after the fighting has begun. I do not think that this little war in Szechuan is going to affect us adversely. It may help to bring prices down a little that so many of them have moved away from this district. There are still about 500 soldiers here, but that's nothing compared to what we have had before. I lost two good catechumens, however, when the soldiers left – one captain and one "twan fu," the second in command of the troops in this section. One young soldier boy had also been a faithful catechumen.

Guess I will go to bed now. If I think of anything more that I might write to enlighten the darkness of Ichang with, I shall write it in the morning.

Wednesday morning: Last night about two o'clock we were aroused from sleep by a messenger from the yamen with a circular letter, stating that the dollar now was to exchange for 2,200 cash. Exciting news to wake us up in the middle of the night for, was it not? What is the exchange in Ichang now?

How is my tennis racquet? Hope you did not forget to send it along with Gyps. I am quite anxious to see my biggest Christmas present. Hope it came through in good condition to Ichang.

So much for this time. With best greetings to your neighbors and your whole family from Bernice and myself,

Sincerely yours,
Geo. O. Lillegard

Shihnanfu Station Report for Period closing Feb. 15th, 1923
(Excerpts from eight type-written pages)

I. Evangelistic Work:

The western portion of Hupeh with its twelve counties and population of about three million has only one mission center, that of Shihnan, where the Episcopalians have a small congregation with a native pastor in charge and where our work has been carried on intermittently for the past three years…All classes of people have been represented among our catechumens. For a time many of the soldiers quartered in Shihnan also attended our services…Now, however, most of these soldiers and their officers have left for Szechuan, where it appears that China's next civil war is likely to be staged…

…The result of this work was the baptism on Jan. 7th of this year of Mr. Jao Hei-ju, Mr. Liu Huey-ting, Mr. & Mrs. Had Tzu-chien, and Mr.& Mrs. Had Tung-hwa. Together with them were baptized their children and four orphan boys, seventeen in all…

…the approximate attendance for the week commencing Nov. 5th was as follows: Sunday morning, 200; Sunday evening, 165; Monday evening, 55; Wednesday evening, 65; Thursday evening, 210; Saturday evening, 75…

Special meetings have been held with the women and girls each Tuesday and Friday afternoon. A few of these are able to read more or less, and the rest are quite anxious to learn. Miss Gruen, Mrs. Klein, and Mrs. Lillegard have taken charge of these classes, spending an hour helping them to read the Bible History and Catechism…

Since we have no native evangelists here as yet, all the work of preaching and teaching has devolved upon Mr. Gebhardt and Mr. Lillegard, who have divided the work between them as evenly as possible…

For our Evangelistic work, the rooms on first floor of our Chinese mansion have hitherto been used. These make fine quarters for the purpose, but it makes our home on second floor rather too public a place, so that we hope to find other suitable quarters for chapel and guestrooms soon, if this building has to be used much longer as residence for several missionary families.

II. Educational Work:

The Lower Primary and Higher Primary Schools begun last winter were continued this fall, work being taken up again after the summer vacation about Sept. 1st…Attendance before Christmas averaged about 60 in the Lower Primary and 12 in the Higher Primary, out of a total enrollment for the year of 91 in the Lower Primary and 22 in the Higher Primary…

This last autumn the school was moved out of the first floor rooms in our residence and over to some rented buildings near by…

III. Literary Work. IV. Medical Work.

…Mr. Gebhardt, and especially Miss Gruen, have done this work…Miss Gruen's fame as a dispenser of healing medicines and "First Aid" has spread abroad, with the result that she is forced to spend more time binding up filthy sores and wounds and burns than she perhaps can afford…No foreign-trained doctor in a radius of 240 miles, 10 days' journey!...Will not doctors and nurses soon come over and help us?

V. Institutional Work. VI. Charity and Relief Work.

This autumn a number of the boys in the orphanage were returned to their homes, all those who had relatives capable of supporting them being dismissed with a few dollars to start them out with in the world, or to help their people support them. Thus we have had only 19 boys under our care since October…Some of the boys have made fair progress in their studies and a few have been diligent in their work, cloth or bamboo weaving…

A few weeks ago, a little girl was brought to our place for medical treatment by some of the little girls who attend our meetings. She had been found on the streets, shivering in the cold. Her head was one great sore, and her body was covered with bruises and sores, presumably the results of the beatings she had received from her cruel mistress. Upon inquiry, it was learned that she was a "slave girl," bought from her parents for the sum of $6.00 Mex., and lately driven out from her master's home, as she was ailing and presumably not good for anything any more. Miss Gruen bound up her wounds and sores as best she could and Mrs. Had has consented to take care of her in her own home. This makes an addition to our company of orphans, which we could not refuse to burden ourselves with, as the little unfortunate would surely have been left to die out on the cold streets, if we had not taken her in. Of all the pitiful, miserable specimens of humanity that one sees in China, she is one of the most wretched it has been my lot to see in all my five years here. She is perhaps about ten years of age, but acts like an infant, so stunted and warped has her nature become, no doubt as a result of the treatment she has endured the last year or two…

VII. Buying, Building, Improvements, General Upkeep of Mission Plant.

Since we have a mortgage on the Chinese mansion we reside in, we have felt free to make such repairs and alterations in the place as are necessary in order to make it a suitable residence for six people, besides providing for chapel and Chinese guestrooms. Last fall the floors were painted, some partitions were put in to make the immense rooms somewhat less barn-like, and storerooms for the Hospital supplies and Mr. Riedel's goods, etc., built down stairs. This month, the two large rooms on the street are being partitioned off to serve as guestrooms, reading room, and chapel. Hitherto rooms in the main building have been used for this purpose, which necessitated opening the whole building to the public. Under the new arrangement, we will be able to keep the courtyard closed and thus secure greater privacy for ourselves, as well as, incidentally, more sanitary quarters. As it has been, our courtyard has always been but little better than the filthy streets outside…

VIII. Relation to Other Denominations and to the Community and the State.

The Catholic Mission here, which is in the charge of a Belgian Franciscan priest, has hitherto been very little in evidence, so far as our work is concerned. The same must be said of the Episcopalian Mission, with its native pastor. There seems to be little of the spirit of unionism in this latter Mission, but rather a spirit of competition, which can do no harm so long as it is limited to a rivalry in doing good and in educating and evangelizing the people…

IX. The Territory. X. Prospects.

The fact that there is another Protestant Mission in this city does not mean that we have entered a territory already sufficiently occupied. In all the country west of Ichang, there are only two Episcopalian workers, the pastor at Shihnan, and an evangelist at Taweichia-pa, both Chinese. There are twelve "hsien" (county) cities, at least half of which ought to be occupied by foreign missionaries and made the center of aggressive work throughout the surrounding country as soon as possible. Besides this, we are really a unit geographically with the eastern part of Szechuan – six prosperous counties with about three million inhabitants, and with two large centers, Kweifu and Wanhsien, on the Yangtse river, now easily reached from Ichang by foreign steamboats. This territory has only three small mission stations of the China Inland Mission, and has the smallest proportion of Christians of any part of China. Truly the fields are white to the harvest, and our Lutheran Church here has an opportunity before it which it cannot afford to ignore or let pass by. A population of six million, practically untouched by the work of Protestant Missions, with the smallest percentage of Christians of any part of the world, perhaps, except for such sparsely settled countries as Tibet and Mongolia – what a field is there not here for zealous missionaries, who like Paul would prefer "to preach the gospel, not where Christ was already named, lest they should build upon another man's foundation"! The doors are open before us, the great artery of China's commerce, the Yangtse river, bisects the territory named and renders every part of it easily accessible, the people are as friendly as anywhere in China – far more so, in fact, than they are in old port cities like Hankow and Shanghai. With consecrated men to carry the gospel to these people, it will be possible for our Church to do the most blessed work offered it in this world, that of planting the true Church of Christ where it has virgin soil in which to grow and thrive. May God grant that our Lutheran Church will be given the grace to grasp the opportunities before it, and "be a blessing," according as it is blessed by Jehovah, our Savior and Lord. For the Shihnan Conference, Geo. O. Lillegard

Bernice and girls who attended our chapel

Chapter 9
Expecting a Lillegard again

BERNICE ANNOUNCES HER THIRD PREGNANCY.
"Should He see fit not to answer our prayers this time either, He will give us strength to bear it."

<u>Letter 94</u>

China
Shihnanfu, Hupeh
March 8th, 1923

Dear Mother,

    The mails have been rather slow of late. A week ago I received your letter of January 14th, but we surely ought to have all the January mail soon. Yesterday the three copies of "Woman's Home Companion," addressed by Papa, but with Ella's name as sender, were received. If they're from Ella, then, will you please thank her very much from me? They are very welcome, especially since I have received no magazines this year. George wrote to the publishers of the "Designer" and asked them to send subscription bill to you folks. Have you received it? No copies have come as yet. I really liked "The Designer" very much as I found a great deal of useful material in it.

    Guess what I've spent considerable time doing this last week! You know I had that club subscription and received two magazines for one year and two for two years. Well, it seemed too bad to pay out so much money for subscriptions, read the stories mostly – and then eventually throw the papers away. So when I was still in bed a year ago I looked through all my old magazines and tore out all the pages on which there were recipes, household hints, and whatever else I thought I'd like to keep. Sometimes there are good knitting patterns, suggestions for entertaining, and also "beauty hints"! I left the "Modern Priscillas," as they are <u>full</u> of good stuff. Well, I got quite a pile of loose sheets, but of course it was nothing compared with the pile of magazines. In Hankow I secured two big scrap books and these days I've been working at them. It was great fun to do the work and I can tell you I'm getting together a lot of serviceable information. I have one book for recipes, menus, and such things only. The other is for household hints, miscellaneous articles, "Your Baby and You," and house plans – "Against the Time we Build." I don't know just how useful the latter will prove, but if we ever do get into a new house, I may find useful suggestions for making attractive rooms. On the whole, don't you think it's a good plan? I have another bunch of Designers that I must go over soon. When I catch up it will be easy to keep my books up to date, as it doesn't take more than a few minutes to paste in a good many clippings.

    Since I wrote the above I've had dinner, practiced half an hour, and rested a little. Also – received your letter No. 97, which means 96 is missing. It will probably come tomorrow. It is a shame that I so often forget to number my letters. George's are not to be numbered, so mine of Dec. 26th was no. 84. #85, 86, 87, 88, and 89 were written January 4, 12, 16, 20, and 24 respectively…

    Have you my article written in the Lutheran Sentinel a year ago? If you'd read that again, I believe you'd be clearer as to the Chinese dress. A Chinese <u>gentleman</u> wears his coat about <u>ankle</u> length. Coolies wear their coats short (when they wear any) about to the waist – or like Tsao si fu's. Women wear their coats about to the <u>knees</u>. So you think

I ought to ask my amah to wear dresses! Well, I'm sure the Chinese women think we foreigners are very immodest and ought to adopt their styles. I wouldn't want a Chinese woman to wear dresses – only those who either live right amongst foreigners in this country or live abroad and who learn how to dress in foreign style throughout would appear well in our style of clothes. Some Chinese women wear skirts over their trousers and that looks all right, but that seems to be true only in port cities and in foreign institutions. No, they don't always wear white – by no means. Blue is the favorite shade used for ordinary clothes. Grey is very popular – especially do the men like long grey silk coats. Black, purple, and of course, red. But it doesn't seem the grown people use red so much for garments anymore, unless it should be in official circles. Red is used a good deal for children, also blue & white "prints." But old clothes, the kind brought to us for sale, are usually red. That is the color for all joyous and festive occasions. White is the color for mourning. In summer a good deal of white is worn, especially in the port cities, it seems to me.

    I got the wire stand for my Pyrex casserole myself – the dish was a gift. How we do use that casserole! We are fond of escalloped and baked dishes. How often I wish I were doing my own cooking.

    And now my scrap book makes me wish I were in the States where I could get many of the little things which often add so much to the tastiness of dishes. I think I should like cooking very much – now, at least. I've been so discouraged with the servants these days I've felt like firing the bunch of them. And as for sympathy on that score from George – he gets after me for being too particular! Saa gaar det![135]

    You want a hint as to what to send me for the "17th"!! Well, you ought not send me anything – but I could give lots of hints. (Ha ha!) Valborg asked me the same question. Here's a don't – Don't ever send me any gorgette[136] waists! Can't wear them here. Have worn my brown one only a couple times and you may be sure I also had my sweater on. First, let me tell you something – Raise the flag of HOPE again! Yes, I'm very happy to tell you my hopes are soaring again. George and I look forward to the end of September or early October (really, Oct. 4th is when I should expect to be confined) very much and hope the months will pass quickly. I didn't like to say anything before, since I was feeling so punk, but I am much better now as far as my cold and side are concerned. I cough only a very little. But there is still a great deal of discharge from my head and I wonder if that doesn't explain the headaches. I suppose my condition has been somewhat to blame for my inability to throw off this long attack. Otherwise I have been remarkably well, considering. You will appreciate that when I tell you I am almost half through the third month and to date I have retained all my meals – some of them with difficulty, I'll admit, but even so – I think I have learned what I can eat and what I cannot. For instance, some bad days I ate almost only soup and "kavringer."[137] But I'm sure you never had as easy a time. My only trouble is constipation. I am constantly on the warpath and nothing seems to help. I sometimes improve for a few days, but usually have to resort to an enema or other desperate means. I've eaten almost five pounds of prunes and drunk gallons of water! I expect to write to Dr. Borthwick soon.

---

[135] So it goes! (Norwegian)
[136] I think she misspelled "georgette" on purpose to drop a hint.
[137] "crackers" (Norwegian)

Now then, Mumsie, I've told you pretty early this time, but you must not worry. If you do, it is almost sure to be conveyed to me by mental telepathy or other means! You are not to worry about anything – travelling, etc. etc. It won't help a mite. But what will help a lot will be for all you dear ones to remember me in your prayers. I shall take the best care of myself that I know how and that is all I or anyone can do. Surely, I need not fear to trust myself and my little one to the Great Physician. "Beder og det skal eder gives" – "En retfardigs bön formaar meget naar den er alvorlig."[138] Should He see fit not to answer our prayers this time either, He will give us strength to bear it. So we must all be happy and look forward to the great Day.

Now, tell me, how do you like Elizabeth Ann for a girl's name? I should want to call her "Bettie Ann," I think. (We sort of expect a daughter!) Sometimes I am quite undecided as to whether or not I really do like that name. George says he does. And for a boy, George is quite anxious to have the name Lawrence – for his brother. What would go with that? I want the name Onstad, but Lawrence Onstad doesn't appeal strongly to me because that would be the same as Uncle Henry's boy. I also like the name Norman. Any suggestions?

I haven't written to anybody about this – you're first to know it in the States – rather, first outside of Shihnan. At the time I asked about wool quilt I didn't know I'd need it so soon. I haven't any bedding, except pillow. I have just had the amah pick out all the quilts so I have an all-down baby pillow. George thinks I should try to get blankets in Hankow – wool ones. If you'd please price them at home and write at once, I'd be in position to compare prices when I'm in Hankow. As to wool quilt – I don't know whether raw wool can be bought or not in Hankow. I'd like quilt big enough to use for several years. If you can buy wool to advantage at this time of the year and should have a good opportunity, why just go ahead, if you will, please. I plan on making some dresses and petticoats soon. Have nothing in that line yet. But I have shirts, stockings, shoes, caps, nightingales, etc. One wouldn't have much use for wraps in Shihnan! Not the first year, at least.

Nok for denne gang.[139] Have just read this over and my letter isn't any too coherent. Regarding the "news," please use your judgment as to whom you wish to tell and whom not – and instruct Ragnar & Elsa accordingly. It really makes no difference to me. I am not informing our missionaries – we girls are going to surprise them! Miss Gruen is still in bed. She has improved some, but she isn't making any progress now, it seems. Oh, for some sunshine!! It is considerably milder than it was.
(Written in left margin:)
Still next to impossible to buy things on the street. Cook manages to get some eggs & vegetables, tho,' so we get along.

Much love to you all from Bernice

---

[138] "Pray and it will be given to you" (Luke 11:9) – "The prayer of a righteous person avails much when it is earnest." (James 5:16) (Norwegian)
[139] Enough for this time. (Norwegian)

BERNICE LAMENTS THE STATE OF AMERICAN SOCIETY.
"Present conditions in the United States ought to be a warning to all Christians that a renewal of zeal for the Lord's work is absolutely necessary."

Letter No. 96

Shihnanfu, Hupeh, China
March 21st, 1923

Dear Dad, Mother, Ragnar, and Elsa,

  That is the way I must address this letter, because yesterday I received one letter from each of you. I think it is the first time I have received a letter from each individual at the same time <u>in separate envelopes</u>. I have had birthday letters from you all at one time, I believe. Well, it was extremely interesting and I do not object to such very pleasant surprises in the least. The letters received were the ones written by you between February 4th and 10th.

  First, then, Papa's letter – we were ever so glad that you wrote about your work and so on. You need not be afraid of boring us with details. I feel that I ought to know something about my father's work! It is good to hear that you like your work and with a congenial office force, one's work can be made very pleasant. And I know that one can get the service he wants from those under him, if he treats them right. So I have no fear that you will have any trouble in that line, because I believe you could get along with anybody. You told of counting money all night. I can understand such nights perfectly well. I am sometimes forced to realize that I have a constitution more nervous than is entirely desirable. Yesterday we girls were out in our garden trying to plant a few vegetables. We have no rakes, hoes, etc. and the Chinese implements were no good for making the earth fine, so we were helping along as best we could, with the result that we became quite tired from our efforts. And I planted garden all night!

  George and I were rather relieved to hear that Madison had finally secured a pastor, and of course any congregation should be congratulated on securing such a fine man as Dr. Ylvisaker. I met his wife when we were in Minneapolis three years ago and thought she was a very nice woman. We were all entertained at Ylvisaker's one evening during Synod meeting. I am sure you will all like her. Now I only hope the young people can be roused and induced to take an interest in the work of the Church. Present conditions in the United States ought to be a warning to all Christians that a renewal of zeal for the Lord's work is absolutely necessary. Is it any wonder that a nation falls from grace when everything is sacrificed at the altars of the "ungodly Mammon"? When one thinks seriously about it, are not the majority of the people in a country like our own beloved States worse than heathens, in spite of their boasted civilization? Here we can at least preach to those who have never heard the name of God, to a people who have not had Him, instead of to those who have already rejected Him. I, too, feel that Our Saviour's Church ought to do something more directly for Missions. When you get something started, it is possible that you might like something special in the way of information. If I can help, I shall be glad to do so.

  Mother, you say you think of so many things to write about during the week and when you sit down to write you have forgotten them. Permit me to make a suggestion. If you would have a little pad and pencil handy, you could take about one minute to jot down a note when you thought of something and by the end of the week you would have so much to write about that writing a letter would be almost no task at all. It does not take long to write, you know, when one knows just what to tell about. Please tell me, who are Prescotts? You say you were over there for dinner one Sunday. Where will Ylvisakers live? They had such a nice home in St. Paul that I hope they will get something fairly nice in Madison. The parsonage is not much to brag of. How long now until you will need to take the Ladies' Aide again? Couple years?

    Next, Ragnar – in answer to your first question, "How are you, where are you, when are you, and why?" I am <u>fine</u>; I am in <u>Shihnan</u>; I <u>AM </u>all the time; and <u>because</u> I am married! Also, I must inform you that receiving these several letters from my one and only brother has given me one of the pleasantest sensations I have enjoyed for a long time. If there is anything I can do to encourage you to keep it up, just "holler." George and I are not quite prepared to buy out a whole hardware store, but I can very easily answer the questions you asked me. First, can we make use of a vacuum bottle? Well, I had just about decided to purchase one for His Highness, my husband, as a birthday gift, but the kind I could afford to get in Hankow are breakable and I had decided to postpone my shopping until I got there. We certainly could make excellent use of one. Can you not imagine the advantages of having something hot to drink all ready for one when one (takes) these long overland trips. At such times, one feels that a vacuum bottle serves a real practical use and I have often wished for one. It could save us the bother of waiting to boil water at noon, for instance, when we are in a hurry to be moving. And then when it is so hot and we have to drink often during the day, I think hot drinks are more satisfying than lukewarm water. Next you ask about a flashlight. Well, picture yourself living in a house with only kerosene lamps for light and when wanting to get something from another room either having to light a lamp, or candle to find some little thing. Or, imagine yourself out on Kuling some evening and finding it necessary to carry a lantern to go the distance of a block or so. There are probably more uses for a flashlight here than many places. My own, which was a small one, is spoiled. George uses an Auto-strop razor and that is quite all right, as yet, but last summer he had to pay $2.25 Mex. for one dozen razor blades. He thought that was very high as compared with what he had to pay in the States. As for cork-screw, thank you, we are as supplied as necessary! And as for eye-openers! I believe you, too, would find China quite an eye-opener. We learn, to our despair, that we are not quite as smart as we thought when we get at these Chinese characters. Also, we see that the Chinese are not accustomed to applying rules of sanitation to the extent that we "furriners"[140] are. We might be able to make use of a "nose-closer" when we are compelled to walk the Chinese streets or pass a freshly fertilized field! However, you write as though you would like to send us some of this as gifts. George will be glad to put in an order for the razor blades. As for the other two, I have not the least idea in the world what they would cost and I am afraid that if I should order them I might find that I was indulging beyond the means of our pocket book. I tell you, if you find it in your generous heart to send us something like that and feel that you can afford it, I shall make a very special effort to find something Chinese that would please you.

    I will be interested in hearing about your school work, Elsa. Now that you have had such a long vacation from school work, you ought to have a good deal of zest for study. You say you have new frames for your glasses and that they do not go back of the

---

[140] "foreigners"

ear. Are they regular pinchers, or is there something new in the way of spectacle rims too? Do you wear your glasses all the time?

Now for a little news. First and foremost – indications are that spring is here and our extremely long, sunshineless period has come to an end. Yesterday and this morning the sun was shining when I got up, and I tell you that was the first time in many months that we had a day starting out with sunshine. It certainly gives one renewed energy and pep. Although it was quite cold the other day, the thermometer has risen to a little over 70 degrees now (2:00 P.M.) and I feel that it is about time to get out of my red middy.

Another item, which is of interest, but which ought not have to be told again, is that George has again had a little spell. I have told him that hereafter I shall have to insist on his taking "P.C." regularly during such times as he cannot take long walks or play tennis. I am sure that it is only the lack of exercise which brings on these attacks. At that he is out more than either Gyps or Klein and now and then he exercises with his steel dumb bells. But, it seems he is the sort of man who needs a great deal of exercise to keep in good condition. He felt very punk Monday so he went to bed about eight o'clock. I wrapped him in a woolen blanket, rubbed his chest with eucalyptus, and gave him hot milk with butter and pepper. He must have had quite a fever, but at midnight he began to perspire and he just steamed! Although he was better, I did not think it wise for him to get up, so he stayed in bed all yesterday and as he kept right on sweating, his temperature kept going down. He perspired last night also, but not so freely, and this morning he got up. He feels pretty good, but is not eating very much. He says this is the last time he is going to get sick!

Our cook, too, is on the sick list… So I will prepare supper today, breakfast and dinner tomorrow, which will give him a good day and half to rest. Tomorrow evening we are invited to Klein's. They are going to entertain our Chinese Christians, the adults, that is.

The boys are at a tennis court in real earnest now. Just now they are having Conference, then I guess they will spend some time in the garden, and after that they intend to play some tennis. The court is not entirely level yet, but they are not going to wait for that. It will give them good practice to try for crooked bounces! I suppose I will have to go easy on tennis this year!!

Have you heard that Louise has another girl? We do not know the exact date – it was early in February – as Valborg only mentioned it assuming that Martin would have written us all about it. Perhaps their letter got on a slow boat…

Now that we again have sunshine there are so many things to look after that have had to wait, such as washing blankets, sweaters, and the like. And I must also hurry to get some spring clothes in order. As soon as the sun does come, it gets plenty warm enough. The less fuel we have to burn, the better I like it, both because of the money and the dirt. We have been burning some charcoal the last ten days and it is much cleaner. I doubt that it would pay to burn that in real cold weather, though, as it is quite expensive. For mild weather when one just wants to take the chill out of the room, I think it is better than wood. Our stove is anything but suited to wood anyway. We have to keep a big fire all the time, or else it goes out on us. If we have to burn wood again next year, we plan on having a stove made out of galvanized iron, like the one Olive[141] had made here. It makes a very satisfactory stove.

---

[141] Miss Gruen

It is time for me to curl my hair and fix up a little. I will have to get a hustle on if I am to get all done that I feel I ought to before we leave for Kuling.[142] Which reminds me, from May 1st until the 15th or so, it might be best to address our mail in care of Max Zschiegner, No. 6 Milan Terrace, Hankow. After that send it to Kuling. Since we have no house or room as yet, just send it to Kuling, unless I can send you a number before that time. It is quite likely I will be up on Kuling by the time mail begins to arrive and will be able to leave directions with the Post master. Our things, which I have ordered, had better be sent to Kuling also, unless they are sent rather early. It is possible that I will try to arrange to leave Shihnan about the middle of May. If I do not leave then, it will be in early June most likely. We will all have to be on Kuling fairly early this year, since Conference is to open about the 4th or 5th of July. Please give our regards to Dr. and Mrs. Ylvisaker, Hansons, Swerigs, Bensons, Pritchards, and so on, and so on. I cannot write all the names. Lots of love to each one of you from us two.

Yours,
Bernice

P.S. Have just had some Chinese cards printed for myself and am enclosing one for each.

Da Me Guek} American
Li
Ben Hsin I Hwei} Chinese name of our church
Shih? Ngan
Nan?
Ding
Men
Fu
Yin
Tang.

Li – Our name
Ben – formerly
Ngan – Onstad

Shihnan East Gate "Glad Tidings Hall" or} Chapel

Fu Yin is literally Glad Sound or tidings. It is used for Gospel.

---

[142] Every summer they had a mission conference in Kuling and spent the summer there where it was cooler.

BERNICE SENDS A PLAN OF THEIR FIRST FLOOR.
"…our place is becoming more and more pleasant and by and by we missionaries will have a really private place."
Letter No. 97

China
Shihnanfu, Hupeh
March 29th, 1923
2:00 P.M. Good Friday

Dear Mother,

Summer has come! You see the time of day above and it is 86° in the shade. Two hours ago it was 82°. I feel as though we have entirely skipped Spring this year. Two weeks ago it was quite chilly and we needed a fairly good fire when we bathed. A week ago I was glad to change to summer underwear. I certainly am a poor one in warm weather and this weather would seem to indicate a long and hot summer. I am sitting out on the veranda, where I have a wicker chair and table, and am dressed in my ancient blue Norfolk, and white slippers and stockings. But, I guess I must have made a mistake in coming out here at noon, even though the sun never gets at this side, as I noticed our front room is cooler. However, I believe that will soon be warm too, since the sun shines in during the afternoons.

Perhaps you notice this is the first time I ever talked of living out on the veranda. Well, our place is becoming more and more pleasant and by and by we missionaries will have a really private place. Our reading room and guest rooms were all "inside" before – off the inner side of the court. Now we have just had that changed.

1. Room used for girls' school and women's meetings.
2. Our big entrance hall.
3. Reading room (doors opening in to hall and also directly on street).
4. Women's guest room.
5. Book room (not open to public – a supply room, rather).
6. Men's guest room entered from reading room.
7. Large double doors – opened for Sunday services and public services during week, and when very distinguished guests arrive.

These rooms are under our and Gyps' rooms. Now, then, really only our servants and language teachers are supposed to come into the courtyard. Of course, some sneak in, especially since the rulings are still quite new, but it is nothing as compared with before. We have had the place whitewashed, posts scrubbed and today the windows down there have been washed till they shine. We have a few glass windows in chapel, etc. And when our flowers come up and bloom, it will certainly be nice. Our flowers are peeping up now, in fact, and both radishes and lettuce are up. We will have them on our tables within a few weeks. My! It will be nice to eat something raw.

Today I should like to have you see our front room. I believe even you would approve of its appearance this one day. I told the boy to tear the paper off yesterday morning and put on fresh "windows." We had double paper on during the winter and it was very dirty by now. I hadn't planned to do housecleaning, as I wanted to pack away winter clothes, etc., but I did that and cleaned too. I took all the pictures down and washed them, swept the walls a little, washed the windows (they are almost impossible to wash without taking them out so they've only been washed on the inside all year), and saw to it that Hsiao-deh pasted the paper on nice. His job was slow and took almost all day, but by night we had all done except dusting and a few little things. The big rug had been pounded, too. This morning the Boy dusted real well and then I put some fresh doilies around and hung some new white curtains. I have only short ones – curtains. There are three panes of glass on the outer wall and the sun shines in half the day, so I need curtains to protect my rug. And for once the room <u>felt</u> and looked quite clean. It was a pleasant sensation, because even washing the floor, using the sweeper, and dusting once or twice a day, didn't seem to make any impression on the looks. And just a little while ago one of the women across the street came with a lovely bouquet of red blossoms. They call them tea blossoms in Chinese, but the tree is neither the cultivated nor the wild tea tree. And both Edna's and my boys are out for flowers now. We are to have decorations for Easter. The other day Hsiao-deh brought me a <u>beautiful</u> bouquet of peach blossoms. They are almost wilted now.

My! It is almost stifling up here. I feel much tempted to move down in the courtyard, furniture and all. If this weather keeps on, I shall make such a move some day soon. Up to 90°.

I've lengthened the dress you sent. You know I faced it last summer, but even so it shrunk and was all too short finally. Now I put a big false hem on, turned it up on the right side and piped with organdie. I made it plenty long and will have to baste in a tuck until it has been washed a few times. And since the belt isn't big enough to allow for much growth, I intend to make an organdie sash. I happened to buy ½ yard of organdie last summer. Perhaps I will trim the sash ends with the dress material. Now there's the clothes question again. I plan on fixing up most of my old things and then I won't wear them again. I have just received material from Korea for one dress – a very small blue & white check. Then I must have a new white middy. I don't know whether I can put one of my white skirts on a waist or not. They're not full at all. But I do intend to fix my blue silk (accordion plaited) dress. I certainly haven't worn it much and I've decided I'll wear it. When the plaits come out, I'll just have to wash the skirt and make it up some other way. Don't you think that best, too? The dress will be <u>ancient</u> before I've worn it twenty times.

The boys just came back with flowers. They have some pretty branches with tiny pink blossoms, but they say there were some soldiers who swiped most of what they'd gathered.

Tuesday evening we six had a Chinese meal at our place. I had been wanting one for about two months and it tasted good. Everyone seemed to enjoy it so much. I plan on entertaining them all Easter Sunday too. We've been at Klein's so often lately.

It has taken me all too long to write this letter, considering that I didn't have to think what to write next. I suppose sitting out here is not conducive to speed. George & I are going to take a walk now. I meant to tell you we six and our Chinese Christians had Communion services last night. We also have regular services this evening instead of meetings.

     Much love to all of you from us both.   Ever, Bernice

GEORGE ANNOUNCES THE PREGNANCY TO HIS FAMILY.
"The Chinese think it is a great show to see us play (tennis) and they crowd around us by the hundred some time."

Shihnanfu, April 11th, 1923

Dear Martin and Louise:

    Congratulations on the new member of the Tjernagel family! May the tribe continue to increase! We were glad to hear that you were all well. It is going to be very interesting to get back home and see all the new relatives. If we are not badly mistaken, our Mission will be introducing the plan of giving the first furlough after five years, so now we have only three years left. However, we do not know for certain yet. If everything goes allright there will be one more Lillegard about the first of October. That is the name that could stand to have a few more representatives. And as I am the only one that is in a position to perpetuate the name, I hope we shall not suffer any more disappointments. Bernice has not been as sick this time as the other times and looks real well. It was too bad that she should have had that attack of bronchitis and pleurisy in February. But she seems to have regained all her strength now. She is getting real plump. Now that we see the sun a little oftener, the climate here seems to agree with her pretty well. Mrs. Klein, too, is prospering in Shihnan. It really is a good country to live in, I think, as we are up to 1500 feet above sea level, and the mountains and hills round about help to make it attractive and healthful. All of us have enjoyed our year in Shihnan very much so far. We have been kept very busy, which is perhaps the main reason why we enjoyed it. But the fact that we have all lived together harmoniously may have had a good deal to do with it too. We are to begin our Annual Conference this summer on July 4th, so that we shall have to leave quite early in June, which means we have only two months left. The year seems to have passed very rapidly. It is over 90 degrees in the shade today – much hotter for the season than it was last year – so it seems that we are to have an early summer. If that is to be the case, it may be a good thing that we have our Conference so early. The reason we put it at that date, however, was that Meyer wants to attend the Conference before leaving for the States on his furlough.

    I have not been feeling as "peppy" as I might wish the last weeks, as I still have a cold in the head, which I cannot get rid of. I have been exercising regularly, too, lately, besides eating very little, so that I cannot understand why I do not get better. We have fixed up a tennis court not far from our house and play every day for an hour or so when the weather permits. Today Gebhardt and Klein are out in the country on an evangelistic trip, so I do not suppose we will play any tennis. Miss Gruen and Mrs. Klein play too. Bernice has sworn off for the time being. The Chinese think it is a great show to see us play and they crowd around us by the hundred some times.

    I have four meetings a week now with a group of catechumens, whom we hope to baptize on Pentecost Sunday. Most of them are of the scholar class, so that it is easy and interesting to instruct them…

Just got a letter from Ella today, so shall write to her also…

With loving greetings to you and yours from Bernice and myself,

Sincerely, George

GEORGE DESCRIBES MORE POLITICAL UNREST.
"Homes were entered at all times of the day and night in search for men…"

Hupeh, May 11th, 1923

Dear friend Ylvisaker:

Your Christmas greetings were received in due time. Thank you! I had intended to write you long ago, of course, but time has been speeding so fast that I could not begin to arrest it long enough to make it produce the letters that it should. In consequence I have quite a formidable pile of letters in my desk awaiting answers.

First let me wish you God's richest blessing upon you and your work in Madison. We are naturally especially interested in your accepting the call to that place, since we look upon it as our "home town" too. I see by the Prestekalender that you were born there, so I suppose you feel as though you were getting back to your old home too. I am sure you will enjoy living in beautiful Madison and that the congregation will appreciate the work you will be able to do for them under God's guidance. I know Onstad is very glad that the congregation secured your services. He says that the difficulties they have had securing a pastor, etc., seem to have bound the members closer together. They have lost no members during this transition and I hope to see the congregation growing in grace and strength yearly hereafter. My wife thinks that the young people have been too much neglected in Madison and that they especially need to have something done for them…

Is Faye going to take your place at Concordia or is someone else expected to take over your work next fall? I just received a letter from Rev. Brand, saying that he had met Faye. According to that letter, I gather that the Missouri Synod will be ready to start a mission in Africa if Faye wants to go back. I have heard that Miss Anena Christensen is also going to leave the Norw. Church and affiliate with us or the Mis. Synod. Is it not about time that Astrup also "gets on the bandwagon"? It is a source of increasing wonder to me how the conservatives in the Union Church can tolerate the things they do. The discussion regarding Student Volunteer's Movement, Smedal's and Stub's answers to Berrum's article, Smedal's repeated statements in a "Post-chiliastic" direction, etc., it seems to me, ought to open the eyes of these conservatives to the fact that they are out of place in the Union Church. Or are they losing all their conscientiousness as a result of hardening themselves so long?

My wife and I have been quite well the past winter except for some bad attacks of "cold." I still have a cold or at least very bad catarrh, which has staid with me ever since the New Year. Hope that I will be able to throw it off very soon. It is far from pleasant. We shall be leaving for Kuling within a month, as our Conference is to commence about the first of July, and I have some things to attend to in Ichang and Hankow. I expect that we will have some arguments at this Conference, as we are going to take up a number of questions of Mission policy and method, on which there seems to be little agreement as yet among our missionaries. I hope we will be able to improve matters somewhat anyway.

We have enjoyed a quiet year in this part of China, the most undisturbed of any for several years past. Several thousand Northern soldiers have been quartered in this section of Hupeh, and as they were all kept under strict discipline, the country has been spared the brigandage and looting by ex-soldiers and robbers that the province of Honan especially has suffered under. These Northern soldiers are under the command of Wu Pei-fu, who seems to have better understanding than most of China's generals of what is required of an army. During Chinese New Year's, most of these Northern soldiers went to Szechuan, where they now have gained control of the eastern part of that rich province. When they left, there was some excitement among the people here, as several thousand coolies were required to help transport the army baggage and ammunition. People of all classes were pressed into service, there being no system about their "conscription system" at all, except that of getting their hands on every able-bodied man they could find. Houses were entered at all times of the day and night in search for men, with the result that many men staid away from home, hiding in the hills and caves, until the soldiers were gone. Our Mission station also became a refuge for all that could find an excuse for coming to our place. We found several refugees sleeping in the sheds in the rear of our premises and heard that a good many more had been there during the night, in spite of the fact that we had given orders to keep such coolies out. We could, of course, not make our mission a refuge for all the men that might desire to escape military service, and so make it a point to protect only those who were in our immediate employ. The Chinese military still have enough respect for the foreigners that they will grant those in the employ of the Mission immunity from the burdens imposed upon other Chinese.

  Our Mission work has been carried on along the same lines as last year, except for the school which has undergone a considerable reorganization. Last year we had some teachers who were not Christians. This year we decided to engage only Christian teachers and to limit our attendance, if necessary, to the number that the two Christians we had could take care of. As the government opened its Middle School this year – it had been closed for six-seven years – a number of our pupils went to that school. Still our attendance now is over 60, as compared with about 100 last year. Considering the fact that the teachers we dismissed were some of the well-known teachers in the city who naturally drew some pupils away from our school when they left, this shows that our school is now on a solid footing and can expect to grow as rapidly as we will be able to manage it hereafter.

  Mr. Gebhardt and I take turns about conducting the Sunday and midweek services. Besides this I have had four meetings a week with a catechumen class, most of whom we expect to baptize on Pentecost Sunday. We have been kept so busy with the work in the city that we have not done much in the country districts. But lately Mr. Gebhardt and Mr. Klein have made trips out to neighboring villages, preaching and teaching. The woman's work has progressed rapidly under the care of Miss Gruen. We need many more single ladies to take up the work among the women in our stations. Miss Gruen will be going to Hankow next fall, and a new lady will be coming out to Shihnan. But it will be two years before she will have sufficient command of the language to do much work among the women, so that I suppose the work will be neglected here again next year. The Missouri Synod has been all too slow about sending out lady workers. Miss Gruen also started a girls' school this spring, which will have to close next fall, I suppose. In time we will presumably get the workers required to take proper care of this whole field.

Geo. O. Lillegard

Dear sister Louise: Shihnanfu, Hupeh, May 28th, 1923

    Your letter of March 18th reached us some time ago – a whole month in fact, and it is about time that I was answering it… We have all been busy, especially the last weeks. I baptized eight adults and six children on Pentecost Sunday, and had been meeting with them five times a week for a couple months before that. Then there are so many things that need to be looked after towards the end of the season. We decided that I should take the ladies down to Kuling, as Klein did not care to take the responsibility of looking after the coolies, freight, etc. Besides he is rather afraid to have the responsibility of taking care of Bernice. You know, I suppose, that we are expecting a new Lillegard about Oct. 1st. We hope everything will go allright this time. Bernice has been feeling better than the other times anyway and neither of us has been worrying about matters. We thought it best to get away early, however, as it is a pretty strenuous proposition to travel overland so far. Mrs. Klein is also expecting "her first One" about the middle of December. So you see I have quite a family to take care of on the way down. Miss Gruen will be going along, too, and as she is to be in Hankow next year, she is taking all her goods along with her. So there will be a good deal of baggage to look after also. I got twelve coolies sent off today with six big loads, and we will have to take another six or seven coolies along to look after our hand baggage, food baskets, bedding, etc. There will be three chairs with four bearers for each. I will ride a mule, and the cook and boy will share another mule. Would you not like to see our "train" on the road? We expect to make the trip in four days. If only we have good weather, we will make it in that time easy enough… I really do not like to leave the station so early, but under the circumstances there was no help for it. Our Conference is to commence early this year, and I intend to spend a week exploring some new fields that we plan to occupy in the future, before proceeding down river. I shall see the ladies safely on board the steamship at Kweifu, and they will wait for me at Ichang, while I go up the Yangtse to Wanhsien, which is the main place I want to visit. There are a number of matters that I have to attend to at Ichang and Hankow, too, so that I do not expect to get up to Kuling till after the middle of June. Then I will have two weeks to write out my reports and prepare for the Conference. Tomorrow we shall have to do the rest of our packing, attend to various odds and ends, and then early Wednesday morning we hope to start out. If it rains, of course we shall have to wait.

    I am still bothered with a very bad catarrh. I think I must have gotten some sort of infection in the nose other than the ordinary cold…Last week I was quite sick for a while – had fever up to 103 one day – and stayed in bed a couple days. Now I feel pretty good, but still have that abominable discharge from the nose. My nose is sore, too, so that it is hard work to blow my nose the way it needs to be done! Don't you feel sorry for me? I have been trying to take care of myself – have been dieting, fasting, trying various medicines, and all. I shall be glad to get a chance to see a doctor now. Hope I will get my nose cleaned out for once.

    It is getting late and I am sleepy, so I shall cut this letter short. We hope to hear from you again soon that everything is well with you and your two babies. Best greetings to all the Tjernagels, and love to you and yours from Bernice and myself,

                                                        Your brother,   George

GEORGE REPORTS BAPTISMS AT SHIHNAN.
"…we baptized only 30 people, including 14 adults."

Kuling, China, June 22nd, 1923

Dear friend Riedel:

Your letter of Jan. 26th was received a long time ago, and it has been my honest intention for a very long time to answer it. But I seem to be getting very loathe to do any letter-writing and yours is not the only letter that has been lying this long in my desk unanswered. However, here goes.

We were glad to hear that your family were all so well at the time of your writing. We have lately heard some rumours to the effect that some of them were sick again. I hope that is not true. We have not heard yet from any source as to when you may be expected back, but we hope to hear soon that you will be here next September. We need you. I understand that you are slated for the Seminary and Middle School. Meyer will be going home on his furlough after the Conference, and we will need an older man to look after the school work in Hankow. The Board authorizes the opening of two new stations, one in the Shihnan territory and another in the Han River Territory, or wherever the Conference decides. If we are to do that, we will need all the men we have on our list. We cannot afford any more losses such as Gihring's. I understand that they are both well again. Do you think there is any chance that they will consider going out to China again, when they have fully recovered their health?

Our work in Shihnan went about as well as we could expect. There was no startling movement towards the church, and we baptized only 30 people, including 14 adults. But I for my part prefer to see things going a little slow to begin with. It is important to get the foundations laid properly. I think that you will be glad to see the changes that have been made in our mission methods. We have eliminated all heathen teachers in our schools,[143] and are trying to get the Hankow people to eliminate all of their non-Lutherans too. Guess perhaps we will succeed this summer, as the Board backs us up in our view of the matter. There are still some ragged ends that need to be gathered up, of course, but if everyone has the will, it can always be done in time.

We expect to get our Mission Homes started this summer also. We have the lots and the money for the buildings. There has been some delay in getting the buildings started due to disagreement with regard to the kind of houses that should be built. But we hope to settle that soon. Bentrup has built a fine, little house, just below Cederlof's, No.2281, where we live again this year. Kleins, Zschiegners, and Miss Gruen are with us. Schmidt, Ziegler, and Gyps have Bullock's house, Theiss and Scholz have a house on the ridge above us, and the rest are in Arndt's and Schwartzkopf's houses. So we are all close together. Schwartzkopf's tennis court was put in good shape last summer, was the gathering place then, and no doubt will be also this summer. By next year, we should have our own tennis courts on our mission lots.

It is fine and cool up here on Kuling now, almost cold today, in spite of the bright sunshine. It rained yesterday, you see. Of course this is fairly early in the season, but then we have our Conference so early this year. We are to begin July 4th. I came down

---

[143] "The school was moved out already last fall to a group of buildings immediately across the street from our dwelling." (From a letter written the same day to the Rev. R. Kretzschmar, Missouri Synod Western District President…Frederick Pfotenhauer was president of the entire Missouri Synod.)

this early as someone had to go along with Mrs. Klein and my wife. We look for an addition to our number the latter part of September, and the Kleins ditto about the middle of December. We thought it best to avoid the dangerous third and seventh months for our ladies, so made the trip overland from Shihnan in May for that reason. You know it is a pretty strenuous trip to make under such circumstances. They all got along very well, however, except for little spells of sickness on the way. Mrs. Klein was worst off. She felt pretty punk all the last three days.[144]

    I enclose a copy of another letter, giving other news that may interest you, and so shall close with this. Let us hear from you!

Sincerely yours,
Geo. O. Lillegard

Bernice & George, June 12, 1923

---

[144] "Our trip overland from Shihnan to Kweifu was a rather strenuous one, as the roads were slippery the first day or two, and the chair-bearers gave the ladies many a bump as they slipped or fell. Then we had some excitement in the Kweifu Gorge, as some bandits there fired several shots at us and ordered us to 'come across.' But when they learned that we were foreigners, they let us pass. We were naturally very glad that the Szechuanese are still so far behind the times that they had not learned the modern trick of taking foreigners and holding them for ransom." (From a letter written the same day to Rev. Kretzschmar)

BERNICE DESCRIBES HER SURPRISE BIRTHDAY PARTY.
"…before I even got up I was presented with a pretty ivory brooch, two hundred engraved cards and the plate, and a dainty embroidered dress for 'Sunbeam,' by His Honor, My Husband."

July 18th, 1923

Yesterday I had an exciting birthday – the most interesting and full of surprises that I have experienced for many years. I shall have to tell all about it in detail. I hope it won't bore you.

Miss Gruen's birthday was in June, but since it was just two days after we had come up the mountain, we were busy and did not celebrate by having guests. We planned at that time to have the girls (when I say "girls," I mean the ladies of our Mission. We are all girls yet) over some time later. So when Miss Gruen suggested we have a tea on my birthday, I said we might celebrate both hers and mine at the same time. Later on I suggested that we do not have a tea, since this is the last week the Meyers will be here and I thought they would be "swamped" with invitations, so I thought we could just as well postpone our party until later. My suggestion did not meet with Miss Gruen's approval, however, although she did not say a great deal. So it was decided that we invite all the girls. Besides we four in this house, there are nine others. Well, there are really only eight that are missionaries' wives – the ninth one is a sister of Mrs. Meyer. Of course we consider her one of us. We sent out our little note on Monday, asking the girls to come at 3:30 P.M.

It seemed as though we were going to have a perfect day, as it dawned bright and sunny. We have had so much rain since we came up to Kuling, that it means something to have a nice day, you see. I spent the forenoon sunning dresser drawers and the things in my trunk. Of course, I had just got everything nicely arranged when the clouds began coming up from the valley and hovering around us! That has been my luck all summer. Here I am running ahead – I should have told you that before I even got up I was presented with a pretty ivory brooch, two hundred engraved cards and the plate, and a dainty embroidered dress for "Sunbeam," by His Honor, My Husband. Miss Gruen had also given him a little parcel to hand to me and it contained a chain of beautiful blue beads with two silk tassels. I call them blue, but at times one wonders whether they are closer to green than blue. At any rate, they are very suited to me. As soon as I came out the bedroom I was greeted by Eddie, Mrs. Klein, and she gave me some pretty insertion, which she had crocheted, for a sheet for the "small bed" we are hoping to use next winter.

Immediately after dinner Helen (Mrs. Zschiegner) stirred up a light cake, after which we sent her upstairs to rest. We three were busy making sandwiches, dusting and putting fresh doilies around, etc., etc. The servants we have here are no good at going ahead and preparing things, so rather than run the risk of having things half done, we "dug" in and did most of the work ourselves. As a result, none of us were ready at 3:30, but since none of the girls came promptly, we were ready to receive them when they did arrive. Most of them knew it was my birthday, so they were giving me good wishes. When all had come, we served sardine sandwiches, egg sandwiches, dill pickles, chocolate cake, and light cake with delicious fresh cocoanut filling and icing, and fudge. They had their choice of tea and coffee.

When most of them were through – I was still eating, since I had helped serve – one of the servants came in with a big basket heaped full of bundles and I was called to come to see what the mailman had brought. When I heard that, it dawned on me that they were giving a shower. That was a surprise on me, of course, but the real fun was that it was also a shower on both Helen and Eddie, who are expecting "birthday parties" too. Both the girls had been planning with the rest for the shower on me, so when they had to sit down and open their share of the parcels, it was a lot of fun. And such a lot of pretties as we did receive – and all such beautiful things. Olive gave me the prettiest little embroidered silk dress and another gave me a dress made of dainty lawn. Besides, "Sunbeam" received these things: one flannelette and three white Gertrude petticoats, an embroidered cap, a pair of booties, a pair of stockings, a nightingale, Swiss lace for some dresses, and a bottle (for emergency only, I hope). Isn't that a lot of fine and useful gifts? They are all such pretty things that I only wish you could see them…
(The rest of the page is cut off.)

The China Mission Conference

The third annual Conference of the Evangelical Lutheran China Mission met on Kuling from July 4th to 17th (**1923**) and proved perhaps the most profitable conference that our China Mission as yet has held. A number of important measures were decided upon, affecting the whole spirit and method of our mission work among the heathen China. We venture to say that if our resolutions are consistently carried out, our Mission will be found doing a unique work as compared with other Missions working in China today, and certainly a truly Lutheran brand of Mission work.

For one thing, the Conference decided to adopt as its Chinese name a direct translation of "Evangelical Lutheran," since we agreed with Dr. Walther that the retention of the name "Lutheran" was in itself a confession, which we could not neglect to make in this liberal age. Practically all Lutheran societies working in China have taken the name "Hsin-I-Hwei," which means "The Faith-Righteousness Society." Our own Mission has used this name during most of its ten years in China, since this name was used by others as the equivalent of Lutheran, and sufficient thought had not been given the matter for our members to appreciate that this involved a departure from the historical name of "Lutheran." Now that our attention was directed to the question, we could not but change our name to "Lutheran," inconvenient though it might be in some cases to discontinue the use of the name by which we have been known hitherto.

The question of Christian education took up much of our time. Our lower schools have been a great expense to our Mission and have not in all cases had good, Christian teachers. Now we have decided to employ only qualified Christian teachers in our schools, to establish a Normal School for the training of Christian teachers in connection with the Middle School already in operation in Hankow, and to make our schools self-supporting as soon and as far as possible. The local congregations will be expected to conduct and support the school, the Mission only subsidizing these congregational schools when necessary. Where no congregation as yet exists, the Mission may still conduct schools as a mission agency, but perhaps not to the extent that has been done in the past.

It was also decided to make our Training-School for Evangelists a full-fledged Practical Theological Seminary, giving a course corresponding to the Springfield Seminary Course, so that the men graduated from it may be ordained as native pastors. Most missions make large use of so-called "evangelists" – laymen who have been given a little training as preachers and teachers of the Word. The results of the work of such evangelists have not been such as to justify anyone in waging their use except as an aid in emergencies. We plan, therefore, to give the evangelists at present in our employ such a training as will make them fitted for the ordained ministry and in the future use, if possible, only men with a thorough theological training for the office of preacher and teacher of the Word.

Many missions have expended large sums of money in chapels and schools for the native Christians. The result has been that they have taught the natives to rely upon the foreigners' purse, not only for all church expenses, but perhaps also for their own sustenance. The folly of this practice has been forced upon the attention of all missions during these last years of financial depression and rise in the cost of living in China. We have now put it down as our policy and purpose to make the native Christians responsible from the very beginning for the erection and maintenance of their churches and schools. This does not mean that we expect the handful of Christians that we now have to build adequate churches right away. Until our congregations grow larger, they will need help. But this help we plan to give either in the form of loans, on the plan of our Church Extension Funds at home, or as subsidies to the congregations, the property thus becoming the property of the local congregation and not of the Mission. To this end we have asked for an appropriation of $10,000.00 to serve as a Church Extension Fund. Another advantage with this plan is that it will give the native churches a greater measure of responsibility for and control over the church property than is customary in most Missions, even now after the propaganda that has been carried on so many years for self-support and independence of the Chinese congregations, from foreign control.

Our China Mission has hitherto been working in only three centres: Hankow, Ichang, and Shihnan. This year it was decided to open three new stations, one at some point between Hankow and Ichang, a second at Kweifu, Szechuan,[145] the port on the Yangtse for the western part of Hupeh and Shihnan which we already have occupied; and a third at Wanhsien, in Szechuan, the third largest city in that province, and the port for the westernmost part of Hupeh and the eastern part of Szechuan, which we hope to occupy in due time. Messrs. Scholz and Theiss were appointed to the new station between Hankow and Ichang, Messrs. Klein and Nagel, our brother from Australia, to Kweifu, and the undersigned to Wanhsien. Messrs. Arndt and Riedel will have charge of our Middle School and Training School for Evangelists in Hankow; Messrs. Bentrup, Zschiegner, and Schmidt have charge of the evangelistic and school work, and Miss Gruen of the women's and girls' schools' work in Hankow; Mr. Schwartzkopf continues his work at Ichang; and Messrs. Gebhardt and Ziegler will work at Shihnan. The Misses Oehlschlaeger, one a nurse, the other a teacher, will also proceed to Shihnan this autumn as soon as they arrive from the States. Thus our Mission is growing in numbers and is reaching out to the great unevangelized sections of western China, at the same time as it is strengthening its foundations and seeking in all things to "teach them to observe all things that our Lord has commanded."

Work on the mission bungalows at Kuling is proceeding apace, and three, perhaps four, buildings will be ready by next summer, accommodating most of our missionaries for the hot season. But we have as yet not property whatever in any of our stations. We hope to secure sufficient funds soon to enable us to buy land in each of our stations immediately and then proceed with the building of the most necessary houses as soon as possible. Our bill for houserent has been a great drain on our mission funds, and the sooner this "leak" is stopped, the better off will our Mission be financially. Our Conference asked for a total of $42,200.00 Mex. for the purchase of land, and of $58,000.00 for buildings – or a total of about $50,000.00 gold. The Walther League is providing funds for the erection of summer homes. Our total budget for this was set at Mex. $15,000.00 for this year, most of which has already been collected by the Walther Leaguers.

There is now a great deal of Christian literature published by the various Reformed Societies for the Christian Church, but only a small part of it is suitable for our use, since so much is vitiated by modern or distinctively Reformed tendencies. A Committee elected two years ago had reviewed much of this literature and now published

---

[145] See preceding map of Szechwan, also Szechuan or Sichuan (modern Pinyin spelling)

a list of recommended books and tracts. There still remains much work for us to do in the line of translating Lutheran books and publishing other sound Lutheran literature. This year we took a step in advance by deciding to publish a church paper for our Christians, to be issued monthly, besides publishing tracts for the heathen at regular intervals. We have also arranged to publish the following translations as soon as the work is completed: Schwan's Explanation, A Liturgy and Agenda, a Prayer Book, Walther's "Die Rechte Gestalt," The whole Book of Concord, besides some briefer pamphlets. The creation of a Chinese Lutheran Literature is one of the most important tasks that lies before us, and we need the prayers and support of our home churches if this work is to be done properly and well.

The following officers were elected for the coming year: Chairman, Gebhardt; Secretary, Lillegard; Treasurer, Zschiegner; Executive Committee members: Bentrup, Schwartzkopf, Gebhardt, Scholz, Klein, and Lillegard.

Our third Annual Conference closed with a communion service conducted by the Rev. L. Meyer, who now has left for the States on his furlough. May the Lord grant our missionaries faithfulness in their work and our Lutheran congregations in the homeland open hearts and willing hands for the cause of missions to the heathen Chinese that so long have lived without the light of the gospel of the Savior of the world!

Geo. O. Lillegard

Course of Study in the Chinese Language, pursued by Geo. O. Lillegard, Ichang, Hupeh, Evangelical Lutheran Mission

First Year.

The equivalent of the present required course, as given at the Nanking Language School, 1912-1913. Private study continued along the same lines for the rest of the year. Examination by Prof. Wilson, Nanking. Standing: About 98%

Second Year.

(Baller, 30 Lessons) – Mateer Lessons I to CXX – Life of Pastor Hsi, Baller; Bible – Acts. Gospels; the Lutheran Catechism and Explanation; The Lutheran Church Ritual; Pilgrim's Progress, Part I; Bible Histories, Old & New Testaments.
Character Writing – about 1000 characters.
English Reading – several dozen books on China, Mission Methods, etc.
Examination for this work was given by Prof. Edwins, Shekow, Hupeh, Luth. Theol. Seminary. The examiner attended a service conducted by the undersigned at Kikungshan, Honan, before the regular congregation and seemed to think that no further examination was required. No standing reported. Date of Examination, Dec. 1914

Third Year.

Department A. Pilgrim's Progress, Part II. Half Credit.
    Martin's Evidences of Christianity, Half Credit.
    The Sacred Edict. One Credit.
Department B. Mandarin Lessons, Mateer, Lessons 121 to 158. Two Credits.
Department C. Romans, One Credit,
    Genesis, One Credit.
Department D. Baller's Wenli Lessons and Hirth's Notes on Documentary Style, Two credits,
    Total: Eight Credits.

Fourth Year.

Department B. Mandarin Lessons, Mateer, Lessons 159-200. Two Credits.
Department C. Ephesians, Half Credit.
    The Psalms, One Credit.
Department D. The Great Learning, Half Credit.
    Total: Four credits.

Fifth Year.

Department D. The Analects, Three Credits.

Besides the above, a large number of tracts and booklets have been read, and all the Four Books studied in a cursory manner. (I left China November, 1915, returned June, 1921, and have had to spend much of my time the last two years reviewing the first two years' work.)

Geo. O. Lillegard,
House No. 2281, Kuling, China

George's 3rd and 4th year grades in Mandarin Chinese, 1923

THE UNIVERSITY OF NANKING
NANKING, CHINA
DEPT. OF MISSIONARY TRAINING

#73 Kuling.
August 8, 1923.

Mr. Geo O. Lillegard,
House No. 2281,
Kuling.

My dear Mr. Lillegard,

Mr. Wang has handed to me the grades on the examinations taken last Monday morning, covering twelve credits of work - viz, third and fourth year's of language study. Below are the grades allowed -

<u>Third Year</u>

Pilgrim's Progress Part II	90%
The Sacred Edict	86.5
Mateer's Lessons 121-158	91%
Romans	96%
Hebrews	94%
Genesis	94%
Baller - Hirth	89.5

<u>Fourth Year</u>

Mateer's Lessons 159 - 200	90%
Ephesians	95%
Psalms	94%
The Great Learning	86%

In many of the subjects Mr. Wang gave a grade each on reading, and use or explanation, and the grade I have given above is an average of the two. Allowing for the fact that some subjects are "half-credit", others "one" or "two" credits, your general average for the third year figures 91.2%, and for the fourth year 91.1%. Certificates for the work of these two years will be mailed to you on my return to Nanking.

I have not forgotten about the bulletins, but will send you several copies on receipt of the new supply now ordered from Nanking.

With kind regards, I am,

Sincerely yours,

Maude L. Leyda

3rd Year Certificate of Chinese Study

The University of Nanking

Department of Missionary Training

Certificate

This is to certify that _____George O. Hillyard_____ has Satisfactorily Completed the Third Year of the Course of Study of the Department of Missionary Training, thus securing Thirty-eight of the Forty-five Credits Required for Graduation, and is Thereby Entitled to Pursue his Studies in the Fourth Year Course.

In witness whereof _____ President

_____Maude L. Zeysta_____ Acting Dean

Nanking, Kiangsu, _____May 26_____ 19__44__

GEORGE WRITES HIS FATHER-IN-LAW AT WIFE'S REQUEST.
"So long as we do the work for which we have been called, I feel that our lives are in God's hands, and that we are, even humanly speaking, as safe here as any other place."

Kuling, China, August 8th, 1923

Dear Father:

Bernice wants me to write you a little about the political situation in China. Although that is a pretty large order, I shall try to give you an idea of what the situation is. You may find it worth while to have a little first-hand information with regard to China, now that the public eye is turned so much to China and its troubles.

From one point of view, conditions in China are about as chaotic and bad as it would seem they could ever become. We have no President, no Cabinet, no Parliament, no recognized government at all in fact. Such powers-that-be as there are have apparently little control of affairs even in their best-controlled sections. Banditry flourishes at the gates of the cities where the armies are gathered, and no serious attempt seems to be made to check the bandit outrages. No doubt the soldiers are in cahoots with the bandits. The various provinces are controlled nominally by a half-dozen different military leaders, the strongest of whom as yet is Wu-Pei-fu. He is having a hard time holding his own at present, as he has wars on his hands in Szechuan, in Fukien, in Kwangtung, and war is threatening his control also of Hunan, Hupeh, and Shantung provinces, not to mention the continual threat of trouble again with Chang Tso-lin in Manchuria. Of all the eighteen provinces of China, only three can be said to be free from wars or banditry. The province of Shansi has a "good governor" who for many years has been able to keep his province at peace and do constructive work for his people, while wars and revolutions and banditry raged all about him. Chekiang and Kiangsu, on the coast, have also been quite peaceful the last few years. Trouble is threatening there, too, now, however. So you see conditions in the country cannot very well be painted any too black.

As a result of these conditions, trade has almost come to a standstill, the cost of living is rising in all sections of the country, and the people are reduced to starvation or banditry. Foreigners are in greater danger than at any time since the Boxer War. In fact, many seem to think that we are heading for another Boxer uprising against all foreigners. The foreign powers would be largely to blame, if that happens. They have their gunboats at every port, soldiers, too, in many places. They are continually interfering with Chinese affairs, demanding this and demanding that in the most irritating manner. But the worst part of it is that they do not interfere <u>effectively</u>, with the result that they succeed in exasperating the Chinese without accomplishing anything for the benefit of the foreign powers or impressing the Chinese with the necessity of their behaving themselves over towards the foreigners. The settlement of the Lincheng affair has put a premium upon kidnapping foreigners, and made it doubly hard for foreigners to live or travel in the interior. In short, I think that the foreign powers are acting like foolish parents, who threaten their children a great deal, but never punish them properly so as to teach them respect for authority. The Powers ought either to back up their threats and demands with real force and make the Chinese bandits and rough-necks, who are running the country at present, come to time – or else clear out entirely. It would be a lot better for us foreigners here if the Powers would withdraw the gunboats entirely, leave China strictly alone, and treat with China as they would with any other sovereign power, than to have things go on as they are doing at present. The present policy serves only to irritate and cause anti-foreign feeling without doing any good at all. Conditions in China might become such that the foreigners would have to leave the country entirely if China were thus left to work out its own salvation. But in the end, it might be better for us after all than to have things go on as they have been going lately. The only other alternative is for the Powers to step in and take effective control of the situation in China. This view of the situation is held very generally, I believe, among foreigners who are conversant with the situation in China. Most of them would prefer to see the foreign powers take control of China – a few would rather have the foreigners withdraw entirely, believing that the Chinese would be able to manage very well, if foreigners did not interfere and "ball things up for them." As a matter of fact, there is evidence enough that the foreign powers are largely to blame for the present situation.

A great deal more might be said. But I cannot very well write a book about the affairs of China. So far as our own personal safety is concerned, I do not think there is any need to worry. So long as we do the work for which we have been called, I feel that our lives are in God's hands, and that we are, even humanly speaking, as safe here as any other place. If conditions become too bad, we have been directed by the Board to go to Hankow or some port city, where we should be safe, unless the Chinese take up war against the whole world. They are hardly stupid enough to try that now. If we travel in the inland, there is, of course, a chance that we may run into bandits, but we need not worry about that bridge till we get to it. We shall take all precautions and try to keep out of districts in which bandits are operating. So far as we know, the Shihnan territory is still quite peaceful…

…Are there any more States falling in line and coming over to the Progressive side? Just what is the Progressive platform with regard to foreign policies? Would they apply the principle of keeping clear of other powers to China also? Would LaFollette, for example, favor asserting the rights of Americans in China, or would he tell them that it was up to them to look after themselves if they wanted to be in a country like China, as Wilson told the Americans in Mexico in 1915? One difficulty in a country like China is that America almost has to work together with other powers. If Americans, for example, should say that they did not want their government to protect them, while other powers still protected their subjects or citizens, Americans in China would still be in the same position as other foreigners. The U.S. have no concessions in China, like other powers have. They did not wish to accept them when offered to them. But Americans live in the foreign concessions granted to England, France, etc., and would not be able to do any work in China at present unless they had these concessions to live in. This applies only to business people, of course. We hold property only in the concessions or treaty ports. And so, if America took an entirely different line of policy over towards China, it would not help the situation much, unless the other foreign powers agreed to that policy also.

I plan to leave for Kweifu next week some time. Shall spend a day or two at Hankow and Ichang, both, on the way, shopping. I shall stay in Kweifu, looking after affairs there, until it is time to go down to Ichang and take care of Bernice. In October, I shall go to Shihnan for awhile. We hope that it will be possible for me to leave Shihnan in November, so that we can get settled in Wanhsien before Christmas. What is the news from the Synod Meeting? Who were your representatives to Princeton? Have you read my articles this year on "Grantism in the Lutheran Churches," the "Lutheran World Convention," and others earlier? Mother has said nothing about them, so that I have been wondering if you failed to notice that G.O.L., meant me and that your honorable son-in-law was still taking part in the polemics of our Synod at home. I see that Mommsen had quite a time in his congregations and that the Norw. Luth. Church was quite exercised over the matter and took action to save the congregations in his call for the Union. How are things really going in that Union? Is it true that the denominational lines are disappearing, as the editor of Luther. Church Herald says?

So much for this time. With the young books that my wife writes regularly home I am sure there is no news for me to relate. With love to you all,

George

GEORGE ADVISES ZIEGLER ABOUT MOVING TO SHIHNAN.
"Gyps (Gebhardt) reports that the Shihnan territory is enjoying greater peace and prosperity than for a long time before."

Ichang, October 1st, 1923

Dear friend Ziegler:

    I should have written you long ago. But all last week I was so much under the weather that I had to spend most of the time in bed and the rest of the time trying to get my freight and baggage packed for the trip up river. It aggravated my headache to read or write, so correspondence went by the board. Today I feel somewhat more normal again. At least my fever has left me.

    I enclose my steamship ticket together with a letter addressed to the Jardine Mathisen Co. If you have not already procured tickets for yourself, you might have this ticket transferred to your name. If you already have tickets, then to one of the Oehlschlaeger ladies. I could get only $22.50 back in cash on this ticket, and as a ticket to Ichang costs $45.00, it would save the Mission a good bit to get this ticket transferred so that it could be used. Mr. Ross, the agent here, thought that the Hankow Office would surely be willing to transfer the ticket under the conditions mentioned in my letter to the Co. So I hope you will succeed in getting this ticket endorsed for passage of one of your people on the way to Ichang.

    Perhaps the new arrivals will be in Hankow by the time this reaches you. If so, I shall herewith wish them a hearty welcome to China and all happiness and success in their linguistic pursuits this coming year.

    Bernice is still at home. But we certainly cannot wait very much longer. I plan on being ready to leave Ichang about the middle of the month. If the new ladies arrive by Wednesday or Thursday, they would then have a week in which to get ready. I think you can plan on leaving the 12th or 13th, which would bring you here about the 16th. I shall write to Gyps soon and ask him to have coolies at Kweifu for us the 19th or 20th. That would allow us a day here and a day at Kweifu to look after baggage and freight.

    Klein is leaving for Kweifu from Shihnan today, according to his last letter, together with one of our Chinese teachers from Shihnan. There should be no difficulty about his getting the house they were bargaining for, as the owner had written them that the soldiers were on the move and that they now could have the house for $750.00, which means he will come down still more, I suppose. Anyway we ought to have a place to camp in when we get to Kweifu.

    Perhaps I had better remind you again of how you should prepare for your trip across country. Everything that you expect to use on the road should be in small parcels or boxes, weighing preferably not more than about 30 gin each. Do not pack your corries too full – that is those you want to use on the road. Get as much clothing, etc., as you will need for a month or thereabouts into corries or trunks – in such case the corries may be packed full – which two men may carry. That is, they should not weigh more than about 110 gin each. This applies also to the ladies. All the rest of your freight we will arrange to have sent through a freight "hang" at Dai-chi. Although the goods may come through in a week, it may be delayed indefinitely, if there are bandits along the road or conditions are unsettled in that region. You remember, of course, that there are plenty of household goods of all kinds to get along with in Shihnan, with Riedel's and our things, so that you need not take anything in that line along, except your silverware. That had better be packed in your trunks. Besides the provisions that you buy for use in Shihnan, get a few canned goods for the trip overland. Ask your wife to plan picnic meals for five people for a week in the mountains and then buy accordingly! Have this packed separately. I have baskets in which we can pack our food. Bread, cakes, etc., we will get here. I also have milk here. The rest you will have to get. Keep account of this separately also, so that we can figure up our board expenses without too much trouble.

As for other information regarding the trip, I shall refer you to Miss Gruen. Don't worry about the journey. I think we will have fine weather now for a time, and as long as the sun is shining, it is not cold, except at night. You will have to take plenty of covers along, of course. If you will see to that the pieces of baggage you need on the road are not too heavy, I think I can promise that we will make fast time while on the road, that we will not have to travel such very long hours, and that we will make Shihnan in four easy stages, with fairly decent inns at each stop. Much depends, of course, on the weather we strike.

The political situation is rather uncertain. The last reports are that there is heavy fighting in Chungking and some seem to think that the Northerners will not be able to hold out in Szechuan. I hope that this is not the case. If only the Northerners can hold the ground they already have gained, the territory in which we expect to work will be peaceful enough, so far as we can foresee now. Gyps reports that the Shihnan territory is enjoying greater peace and prosperity than for a long time before. Here in Ichang there was a little excitement last Wednesday night. Some soldiers tried to start a looting bee, but were opposed by the local police and some loyal soldiers, with the result that the thing fizzled out within half an hour. There was some firing, though, for a half hour around midnight. Most of our people slept through it all. I was awake and heard it all, but it did not sound serious, so I stayed in bed.

I hope you have been able to help the Hankowites get their troubles with the Sem. settled peaceably. I am sure you will find enough to do these days, helping with those matters, and also helping Miss Gruen to prepare for the new arrivals. Then when they come, you will have something to do again, helping them to get settled.

Everyone here is well, except for my wife, who has a cold. She was quite well last week while I was sick, but has been getting a rather bad cold in the head the last couple days. I hope she will be allright again soon.

We shall telegraph you when "the event"[146] comes off, and at the same time I shall mention the date on which I think you people should leave Hankow for Ichang. With best greetings to you and the rest of the Hankowites,

Sincerely yours,
Geo. O. Lillegard

---

[146] Bernice is due to deliver Oct. 4th.

Chapter 10
An extended visit

ELIZABETH ANN LILLEGARD ARRIVES.
"…she must be going to become a great singer some day."

Ichang, Hupeh, October 8th, 1923

Dear folks:

Just a note today to inform you that a little Miss Lillegard, more specifically Elizabeth Ann Lillegard, arrived for an extended visit last night at 1 A.M. Bernice is doing well and the baby is fine. Believe me, she has good lungs. She kept them going for a couple hours – until Bernice nursed her. Then she finally kept still and went to sleep. I cannot expatiate on her good points as she was sleeping when I came in this morning and I could see only a round face, fat as need be, with a little nose which I presume will some day be like mine, and a mouth which may be like Bernice's. Bernice said she had lots of hair. As for her voice, I think she must be going to become a great singer some day. She could hang on to high Z about as long as Galli-Curci and if she does not crack her voice practicing, I think she will beat her some day!

Bernice is very weak this morning, having lost a great deal of blood, but the doctor and nurse say everything is allright, and that she had really an easy time of it. The pains started yesterday morning, but were not severe. In the afternoon, there were very few pains again. About ten o'clock in the evening, they began again more severely, and by 11 P.M. she was in real labor. But everything was over with by 1 A.M. The afterbirth came immediately after the child. The afterpains seemed to trouble her most. She did not get very much sleep last night either, as the baby was so noisy. So the nurse says she shall remain entirely quiet for a couple days – no visitors allowed, etc.

You may be sure that we are thankful to our gracious God for granting us the little girl we have been waiting for so long. We hope that we will be able to bring her up in the fear and nurture of the Lord and that she will some day become a blessing to all who know her.

I shall send a cablegram this morning to this effect: Onstad, Madison, Wis., "Girl All O.K." – or if they will not accept that as one word, then "Girl well." If that does not go either, I shall sign the telegram "Bothwell," instead of Lillegard and hope that you will realize that this means that both Bernice and the baby are well.

I shall write more later. Now I want to go to the telegraph office and get the cable and some telegrams off.

With loving greetings to you all,

Affectionately,
Geo.O.L.

GEBHARDT SUGGESTS A NAME FOR BABY.
"...a beautiful name for a futuristic lady with bobbed hair."

Shihnan, Hupeh, October 9, 1923

Dear Lillegard:

Your telegram of the 8th arrived about half past eight o'clock last night.

Permit me to congratulate you upon the arrival of your daughter. May she grow up to be a true "Lily" of physical perfection, mental gifts and accomplishments, and Christian soul beauty. I can understand how great your joy is, and I want to assure you that I rejoice with you.

Please do not forget that "Gyps"[147] is a beautiful name for a futuristic lady with bobbed hair. You will understand that you owe me an explanation if you fail to choose this name; so weigh your decision carefully.

I am having two chairs fixed up ready to meet you at Taichi. Klein has two chairs at Kweifu.[148] The mule also is there. The extra chair, I suppose, can easily be gotten at Kweifu. I shall send the local chairs early enough to be in Taichi on the 19th. You should bear in mind that the local military authorities advise coming via Patung[149] (to get to Shihnanfu). Klein writes that the road was safe;[150] at least he said nothing about bandits. I take it that there are no large bands of bandits anywhere near this road, but that there are occasional robberies, as is usual all over the country. The military has not a well established line between Kienshih and Kweifu; so for this reason, I surmise, they would feel safer in having us go via Patung. The merchants are still shipping all kinds of freight on this Taichi road, although they must also take the risk if anything gets lost. If you so desire you can, no doubt, get soldiers to escort you; but this might take some time too, for all I know. The local soldiers were ready to give Klein an escort. I hope that you will have a safe trip.

Yours fraternally,
A.H. Gebhardt

P.S. Give my kindest regards to Mrs. Lillegard and the new pilgrim in your family, please.

---

[147] Gyps is his (Gebhardt's) nickname.
[148] Also called Kweichowfu, (now Fengjie), on the Yangtze River
[149] Patung (now Badong) is on the Yangtze between Ichang (where Ziegler & new arrivals meet up with George to travel) and Kweifu farther west on the river.
[150] Klein had taken the other route, from Shihnanfu to Kweifu.

Gebhardt assures George & company that the road from Kweifu to Shihnanfu is safe.

The coolies returning from Kweifu report that the road is quiet, and that many people are traveling this route now. They claim there are now no bandits along this road. I think that this statement is quite reliable. The road was the same way when I came over in August. There are no soldiers in that neighborhood, and, consequently, the authorities, I take it, would feel more at ease to have you take a road which is guarded all along by soldiers. It seems to me you need not worry about this; but decide for yourself.

       Yours truly,

                  A. H. Gebhardt

Shihnan, Oct. 11, 1923.

Gebhardt second-guesses himself.

Shihnan, Hupeh, October 14, 1923.

Dear Lillegard:-

The enclosed letter was at first intended for all of the party, but on reading it over, I thought it might be well to send it to you alone. I have also sent a letter for the whole party containing no reference to the present situation. As this may be better for the morale of your party, I leave it to your discretion to withhold the enclosed letter from the other members of your party. I should like to urge upon you, however, that you try to take all precautions. To my knowledge, the road is open and fairly safe. If the situation in Szechwan is not quite normal adjust your plans accordingly. I do not want to be held responsible for the safety of any one else.

I hope you will be here in ten days. Your letter of the 8th reached me all right. I shall be glad to see you and to discuss any number of questions.

May God be with you and lead you safely across the mountains to Shihnan.

Fraternally yours,

A. G. Gebhardt

Shihnan, Hupeh, October 14, 1923.

To The Party of Missionaries Bound for Shihnan.

Dear Friends:-

Two chairs are being sent to meet you at Taichi. One of these could well be made more water-proof by placing an oil cloth over the roof. Klein has one, if I am not mistaken. I found only one brass foot-warmer, which I am sending through Hsü Tung-hua, my boy, who can help you in any way you see fit to use him. The coolies coming from Shihnan, eight in number have been paid seventy tiao, so they will not need any money on the way back. You may help them out to the extent of thirty tiao, if they need money. That is all that is due them.

Whether the political situation is or is not favorable you can tell better in Kweifu than I can here. Shihnan is quiet, and so is Kienshih; so once you get so far, you may feel quite at ease. The road between here and Taichi is being used right along now. Whether the Kweifu end of the route is or is not safe, you will have to find out in Kweifu, as I cannot tell that from here.

In general, this part of the country has been peaceful, and there have been no robberies like those of Honan, Shantung, and recently also North Hupeh. There are no large bands of robbers in this territory; so unless bands of scattered or deserting soldiers come down from the province of Szechwan, there should not be any danger. It will be well for you to make inquiries before leaving Kweifu, so that you will not take unnecessary chances. If the situation looks doubtful, it would not be out of the question for you to delay your departure a few days or to return to Patung and come that way. I hope that you will not find it necessary to alter the route of travel once you have arrived in Kweifu. I want to ask you to take all precautions, but I do not want you to feel worried over the situation. I would not worry about making the trip myself, but I should like to have you decide for yourself, as I cannot take the responsibility for any one else.

May the Lord be with you and protect you.

Fraternally yours,

GEORGE GIVES SPECS OF BIRTH AND HIS OWN MALADY.
"Baby weighed 7 lbs. 4 oz…21 inches in length - - - the doctor examined my blood and found that I had malaria."

Ichang, Hupeh, Oct. 11th, '23

Dear Louise:

Your letter of Aug. 27th was received a week ago. Thank you! I suppose you have heard from the Chicago folks by this time that our little Elizabeth Ann arrived last Monday morning at 1 A.M. We sent a cablegram to Onstads on Monday, and I hope they passed the news on to the Chicago people and you. Bernice is doing quite well now, though she was very weak until yesterday. And the baby is showing herself a perfectly healthy little rascal, with a fine pair of lungs, considerable vocal ambitions, an artistic temperament, or at least temper, and an insatiable appetite. She has been crying a great deal hitherto, as Bernice has not had anything for her till today, and that does not seem to be enough. Anyway I fed her some milk the nurse had prepared this P.M., using a spoon, just after Bernice had nursed her, as she was not satisfied and began crying again. She is a smart girl! She did not have to be taught either to nurse or to eat out of a spoon. She just took to both like a duck to water. Takes after me, you see!

Baby weighed 7 lbs. 4 oz. the first day and measured about 21 inches in length. She has tiny little ears set close to the head, pretty hands and feet, good chest and shoulders, and a well-shaped head. Right now, only four days old, she is a pretty good-looking baby, if I do have to say it myself. She has such fat cheeks. She has lots of hair, too.

I have been pretty much under the weather myself the last two-three weeks. Yesterday the doctor examined my blood and found that I had malaria. So now I shall have to feed on quinine until the germ has been driven out of my system. I think I must have had this malaria in my system ever since last fall. For I had so many attacks of fever and cold which I could not account for. I am glad I know what is the matter with me anyway. Then I can take measures accordingly. Quinine is a specific against malaria, so I ought to be able to keep it from getting the best of me again.

We have not heard from the Board, yet, as to whether they agree to opening up Wanhsien as a mission station, but I hope we will hear soon. Wanhsien has only a few foreigners, as I believe I have mentioned already – a few British missionaries, a few business men of various nationalities, and a few foreigners in the Chinese Customs and Post Office services. The nearest hospital would be at Chungchow, half a day's journey by steamer up river. I think it is the Canadian Methodists who are working there. I have been trying to persuade Olga to come out to China to help with the work in our station. If she would only finish her Nurses' Training Course at the Presb. Hospital and then take some special Maternity work, she would be a great help to us out here. She thinks she is not strong enough to come to China, and I suppose it would not be worth while for her to try it, as long as she is not sure of herself. I do wish she would finish her Nurses' Training Course, though. It would make her so much more independent and useful. The Board is trying to get a doctor from Germany now. One nurse is coming out, or rather has come out – this fall.

I shall have to be going out to Shihnan next week with Zieglers and the two new ladies, who are expected to arrive here next Wednesday. Bernice will have good care here in the hospital until she is able to take care of herself. Then she will be living with the Theiss's until she is ready to join me. She has a good Amah and our old cook will be staying here, too, so that she will manage allright. Of course I do not like to leave her at this time, but we cannot do anything else under the circumstances.

Now baby has woke up and is crying again. She is hungry and angry because she does not get what she wants when she wants it. Just like a girl!

Best greetings to all the folks at Follinglo.

With love to you from Bernice, Elizabeth Ann and myself,
George

Bernice & Betty, Oct. 25, 1923,
Rankine Memorial Hospital, Ichang

Dzang amah & Betty, Oct. 25, 1923

MAX ZIEGLER CONGRATULATES LILLEGARDS.

Hankow, Oct. 14, 1923

Dear George,

Heartiest congratulation to you and your wife on the arrival of your long looked for sunbeam, your precious daughter, Betty Ann. May this tender blessing from God be a source of happiness and comfort to you both all the days of your life and an honor to our gracious Father in Heaven. This is the wish and prayer of myself and family, which now consists in four members, my wife, baby and brother "Bud" Fischer.

I too will not make many words now, but I can't tell you how we rejoice with you. We wish the best of health to Bernice and Betty and to yourself too. Let's hope that malaria that is bothering you will soon remove itself to the uttermost parts of Tibet. Not the best thing to take with you on your trip to Shihnan. But I suppose you will have a plentiful supply of quinine along. Many thanks for the cigars on Betty (nice name). Smoked the second one after dinner to-day. Good ones. Tak fer smoken.[151] Tak tak from "Bud" too. He says it will be some time before you will smoke one on him for the same reason. Well, you never can tell.

But to come to some business. Your letter today requests some kale, altogether $800, I take it. So I will deposit $800 in the International Bank…

The paper says that no boat is leaving for Ichang until Tues. But I have hopes that this will go by the overland route tomorrow and still reach you at Ichang. In that case will you please send us a copy of the 1921 minutes of the General Conference. Perhaps Iny has spoken to you about it. We would like to have them as soon as possible. If you have them packed of course it is mei yu fa-tze.[152] But as soon as you can please send us a copy. If you want it back I will copy it and return it.

Everything is pretty fine here, all of us well, including the babies. Our little son is making himself heard right steadily too. Great how they sleep and eat – and yell. Now don't spoil her George by trying to stop her every time she cries. We asked Buswell one time if there was any danger of baby hurting himself by crying too long and he said no, there was more danger of us spoiling him by picking him up every time he cries. So Max Jr. has had some lessons lately. Glad to hear Betty has a good appetite. Guess she takes after her dad.

To-day Ben dedicated his new church. It is really a fine building, very roomy, but neat and simple. Let us hope that this is the beginning of a healthy congregation. We were all there except Helen and Louise. Ben conducted the services. Good attendance.

Hope everything will continue peaceful up the river especially in the neighborhood of Kweifu, Shihnan and also Wanhsien.

Nagels are coming to Hankow Tuesday on the Kung-wo.

Wanted to write you long ago, George, but just did not get down to it. Here's wishing you and the new Shihnanites a safe journey to Shihnan, and hoping that you will find your dear wife and baby well when you return for them.

Greetings to all at Ichang, and to Klein and Gyps.

Yours as always, Max Z.

---

[151] Thanks for the smoke. (Norwegian – but butchered!)
[152] (Chinese)

BERNICE HAS BEEN AT HOME FOR A WEEK.
"George left me two days after I came home (from the hospital)...and I have had rather hard work keeping cheerful."
Letter 126   Ichang, Hupeh, China
                                                                                     Nov. 7th, 1923

Dear Father,
      On this, your fifty-sixth birthday, I must address you with more respect – "Father" – not "Dad"! Sunbeam and I – and George, too, I'm sure – send you our very heartiest congratulations and best wishes. May you continue in good health and enjoy many years of service to your fellowmen and to Our Lord. I am very ashamed, Papa, to think I didn't write a letter to reach you on your birthday, but you will forgive me, I'm sure. I wasn't quite responsible during September, I'm afraid. I wonder if you are having oyster stew for supper. Wouldn't it be wonderful if we could have a family gathering tonight? I'd like very much to introduce you to our daughter, even though she is a little displeased with me just now because I won't pick her up. I held her too long after her supper and she seems to think she prefers being held to her snug little bed.
      Yesterday afternoon the little wool quilt and the flag arrived. They made very good time. The quilt is surely all one could desire for a baby bed and I am so grateful to you and mama for getting the wool, and so on and so forth. But please charge me up what I owe you and then "mange tusind tak"[153] for all the trouble. I like the material ever so much, anything lighter in color would not be serviceable, and this is delicate, too, but not too delicate for a sweet little girl. The flag is a dandy and we certainly are most thankful for it. Mama, please convey our sincere thanks and appreciation to the "Vikings." I will surely try to write them a letter as soon as I am able to and I believe they will be patient if you tell them I have been quite sick and my strength is slow in coming back. You see, I am even late with my "weekly" – it is about ten days since I wrote – and I am afraid I'll be taking liberties if I stay up to finish this tonight. Will have to see how fast I can write.
      It is a week ago today (Oct. 31) since I came home from the hospital. Have we written that George moved all my things over to Theisses and I am now living with Erna (Mrs. T.)? When we came in the door we saw a big bunch of Amer. mail awaiting us on the table. That was a splendid homecoming gift! From Madison there were Nos. 130 and 131 and Elsa's of Sept. 29th. Many thanks! And I also received a homecoming gift from George, namely a dark green wool scarf. My! How I appreciate it! I have sweaters, but they are not always the thing to wear and I've been wanting something I could throw over my shoulders. I have already made so much use of this scarf. At night when I feed Sunbeam it is just the thing.
      The day I left the hospital Dr. B. gave me quite a lecture on what I could and could not do the next month. In fact, he allowed me so few privileges that I felt rather discouraged. The amah I engaged when I came in Sept. had proved to be a person of doubtful character so had to be discharged, although she did her work well. We had two others in mind, but both were inexperienced. After Dr. had given me such a "talking to" George decided to ask the amah who had been helping in the hospital all during my

---
[153] "Many thousand thanks" (Norwegian)

confinement to come and help me for a month at least. She is a very capable Chinese woman and has helped various ones in the Scotch Mission off and on for the last 15-20 years. She bathed the baby after the eighth day and was with me every night after the first. She also assisted the nurse & Dr. when necessary. She can get pretty high wages, but she wants to go home nights, so she agreed to come with me for three dollars or so less than she could have elsewhere. My, I am glad I have her, as she can wash, iron, etc. without my having to bother at all. She can help with the baby also when I want her to.

I guess I'm making as good progress as can be expected. I have bathed Sunbeam myself every day since I came home save one and have also given her all the other attention necessary, but that is practically all I have done. I do not _feel_ so weak, but my milk is rather low, my nerves are "punk," and I perspire terribly every night. My color is getting better, I believe, but I'm sure all of you can hardly picture how pale I was, especially my lips. The doctor ordered me to rest the greater part of the time for the next month – and since it is past nine now I'll have to finish tomorrow. I _must_ hurry to bed for my baby's sake.

Almost noon. Well, something has happened to me, what it is, I don't know, but I feel so much better today. I guess I'm subject to good & bad spells. George left me two days after I came home (Fri. night) and I have had rather hard work keeping cheerful. George calls me _his_ baby and I guess I deserve the name, because I certainly don't like to have him leave me. But I have Betty Ann to think of and as I get stronger I think I will get more used to the idea of being separated awhile. Heinie (Mr. T.) is gone so both Erna and I are grass widows. Erna is a splendid girl and I am so happy I can stay here. You perhaps do not remember, but Erna is Mrs. Holst's niece. I mentioned the fact over a year ago. Both she and Heinie are quiet people, very congenial, and their little Ruth, one year old today, is as sweet a girl as can be – pretty, too. But Theisses will be going to a new station this winter and I'm wondering if they will move before I can leave Ichang. I surely hope not, as that would mean I'd have to move back to Schwartzkopf's. We expect Mr. Theiss home any day and are anxious to hear what he has to say.

Schwartzkopfs have moved to another house about two blocks up from here (this house is next door to where we used to live). I haven't seen their new home, as they moved while I was in the hospital, but they say it is very nice. Last Friday morning, Nov. 2nd, Schwartzkopfs were made happy by the arrival of a big baby girl. They have two boys and Emma was pretty sure this would be a boy, too, much as she wanted a girl. Of course she was delighted when she heard she had a daughter. Six of the seven babies have arrived – three girls and three boys. It will be interesting to learn which will be in the majority when Edna's baby arrives.

I have had no word from George yet, but I expect some from Kweifu any time now and I ought to receive a telegram from Shihnan today or tomorrow. I hope George had a pleasant trip.

This year I fear my Christmas gifts will arrive late. I had thought I'd surely be able to get them off in Oct. but here it is already Nov. 8th. I will try to get them off very soon, but I must ask your pardon for tardiness…

Betty Ann is one month old today and I weighed her again. She weighed 9# 2 oz. I have a hunch the hospital scale was not as accurate as the one I used today and I think perhaps Baby has weighed more. She looked more than 7# 4 oz. when she arrived. Anyway, she has gained steadily and is doing fine. She has blue eyes and brown hair –

what hair she has. Almost everyone says she resembles George, but I think there's a good deal of Kittilsby about her. She probably looks like George below the eyes, but beginning with her eyes and up, I think she looks like me and like Mama. She is pretty young yet to show any marked resemblance. I'm sure I don't care whom she looks like as long as she is a healthy baby and not homely. She is very sweet now and she gets sweeter and dearer day by day. Sometimes I think she looks a little like Elsa did when a baby. You would just love our baby, Papa. And it seems almost too good to be true that at last we have a child. George is just as happy and you should have seen him love her up. Guess it is no fun for him to have to go away now, but then Baby will be much more interested in her parents and the world in general after a month or two and I hope George and I can settle down some place then.

George was rather displeased with me to hear I had written letters which upset & bothered you folks. I told him he had read all my letters, but I guess they must have sounded worse to you folks than to him. Anyway, don't worry about us. I'm sure we'll get settled down some place some time and in the meantime we must try to realize our sacrifices for the work are very insignificant as compared with what others have made. I should be ashamed to complain and I'll try to think more of His Service & less of myself.

Much, much love to all you dear people from Sunbeam & Bernice

Betty & Bernice, Nov. 23, Ichang

BERNICE WAS IN HOSPITAL THREE WEEKS AFTER BIRTH.
"For some time she was in considerable danger."

Shihnanfu, Hupeh, November 24th, 1923

Dear friend Mueller:

Your interesting letter of Sept. 21st reached me the last of October, just before I left Ichang for Shihnan. I envy you your trip through the southern states. That is one part of our country which I have never visited, and which I am curious to know something about at first hand. My sister Valborg was out on a Chautauqua tour last summer, travelling in a Ford. Among other states, they also travelled through Texas, Arkansas, Missouri, and Oklahoma. She writes that she found in the Ozarks a class of ignorant farmers who seemed to belong to an earlier century. She did not realize before how backward things were in some sections of our country. The way she described the people and conditions in that country, they were somewhat worse off than the Chinese in this section of China: Perhaps you travelled through a more enlightened section of the South, however. You did not state how you came to be making such a trip as that. It wasn't your wedding trip, was it?!?

The chief bit of news that I can report to you now is this: On October 8th Elizabeth Ann Lillegard made her debut into the world, by giving a concert that lasted over two hours. Nothing wrong with her lungs anyway! Bernice did not fare very well and had to be in the hospital for over three weeks. For some time she was in considerable danger. But now she is picking up strength gradually, and we hope she will be her old self again soon. Our little "Sunbeam," as Bernice likes to call her, is a fat, healthy little thing, whose only complaint in life seems to be that she does not always get what she wants just when she wants it – something like other women! They all say that she looks just like me, and that she is "the sweetest thing" – bows and blushes from Daddy's quarter – and, of course, we always agree with such sentiments. I comfort my wife by telling her that Betty Ann has enough of her mother's features mixed in with mine to make her good-looking!! Hence we still have peace in the family.

I left my wife in Ichang and came to Shihnan as soon as I could leave her after her sickness. She has to be under the doctor's care for a time yet, so that we could not consider having her make this strenuous trip over the mountains. It gets pretty cold up in the mountains at this time of the year. In December, January, and February, there is often snow and ice, so that the roads in places become impassable for longer or shorter periods of time. I expect to stay here till some time next month, when I hope to be able to leave this place and prepare to start work in Wanhsien, a city on the Yangtse in Szechwan, to which I have been appointed. If we get started there, my wife and child can join me again, as foreign steamers ply the river to Wanhsien also during the winter months now. The political situation is rather uncertain in that quarter, as the city is full of soldiers, about 40,000 of them being quartered in the city and its immediate environs. Fighting is going on above Wanhsien, and although the prospects are that it will not reach Wanhsien itself, one can never know what will turn up next in China. However, I plan on going ahead with opening the work there as soon as this station here can get along without my help. Often a missionary can get the best start just during such disturbed times as Wanhsien is enjoying at present – fishing in disturbed waters, so to speak. Thus we in Kweifu succeeded in renting a part of a palace, because the soldiers had been using the buildings so long and of course destroying them so that the owner was glad to get a foreigner on the place to keep the soldiers away. The foreigners are the only ones who are not subject to the oppression of soldier-bandits and bandit-soldiers that rule China today.

    This should reach you about Christmas time. So I would wish you herewith a very joyous Christmas tide and a very happy and prosperous New Year, marked by the fulfillment of your most cherished ambitions and hopes. My wife and our little Betty Ann join in the greeting. Hoping to hear from you again soon, and with best greetings to other acquaintances at the U. of C., I am

Your friend,
Geo. O. Lillegard

Betty's birth needs to be reported to the Hankow district.

AMERICAN CONSULAR SERVICE

Chungking, China, May 26th, 1924.

Geo. O. Lillegard, Esquire,
　　Evangelical Lutheran Mission,
　　　　Wanhsien, Szechuan.

Sir:

In response to your letter of May 20th, your Department of State passport No. 3339C, issued July 24, 1923, has been duly extended for a final period of one year ending July 24th, 1925. The passport is enclosed herewith.

In reference to the birth of Elizabeth Ann Lillegard, you are advised that births of American children abroad should be promptly reported to the American consular officer for the district in which the child is born. If you have not already reported the birth of your child to the Hankow Consulate General, it should be done at once, on the forms enclosed herewith. In case you have made report, please return the blank forms to this Consulate.

The registration of your child on the blank submitted by you under date of March 5th, 1924, is quite in order, and has been submitted to the Department of State for approval.

Very respectfully yours,

C. J. Spiker,
American Consul.

Enclosures:
　Passport, as described above.
　Report of birth forms & form of physician's certificate.

June 2, 1924

The American Consulate
Hankow, China

Gentlemen:

It has just lately come to my attention that American law requires that the birth of a child to American parents in China shall be registered separately. Upon application to the Consulate at Chungking, I was informed that the birth should be registered in the consular district to which the place of birth belongs. I am sending you accordingly the registration forms, which I trust have been correctly filled out, together with the doctor's certificate. Kindly return the doctor's certificate when you are through with it, if you do not require that it be filed in your office.

Thanking you for your services, I remain

Very respectfully yours,

Geo. O. Lillegard

Chapter 11
Moving to Wanhsien

GEORGE DISPUTES NEWSPAPER REPORTS.
"We passed through Kweifu at the very time these reports were printed and found it in the hands of some 10,000 Northern and 'Second Army' soldiers who did not seem to be worrying about their position at all."

Shihnanfu, Hupeh, November 22nd, 1923

The Central China Post
Hankow, China

If the reports which the copies of the C.C. Post to hand contain concerning the situation in Szechwan were correct, we should hardly be enjoying the peace and quiet that we are in this western part of Hupeh on the Szechwan border. The Szechwanese must have some good propagandists in Hankow to get the kind of reports about the military situation in their province printed in Wu Pei-Fu's own territory. According to these reports, Wanhsien[154] has on several occasions been captured by the Szechwanese in the course of the year, no explanation being offered as to why it should need to be captured by the same armies so often. The latest printed report to reach us states that the Northerners have suffered a "debacle," that one army has retreated to Chienshih and Lichwanhsien, another to Patung and vicinity, and that Yang Sen himself is holding a precarious position at Kweifu. We passed through Kweifu at the very time these reports were printed and found it in the hands of some 10,000 Northern and "Second Army" soldiers who did not seem to be worrying about their position at all. In fact we were told by one of the highest officers in the army there that Yang Sen considered himself in a far stronger position than last year, that he expected to continue his fight for the control of Szechwan, and that at this very time, fighting was being begun again above Wanhsien. The border counties of Hupeh are practically free of soldiers of any kind and are enjoying greater peace and prosperity than for many years past. Wanhsien is occupied by some 40,000 Northern troops who apparently have not the slightest idea of retreating any farther down river. And shipping on the river has been less afflicted by sniping from soldiers than for most of the summer and fall. In the face of these facts, one can but admire the temerity of the Szechwan reporters who fight their battle in the newspaper news columns. Or perhaps the Szechwan time-table has only been a little delayed by the laziness of the Northern soldiers, who have been too leisurely in their retreat to follow the schedule prepared for them by their opponents!

The territory controlled by the Northerners has been quite free of bandits these last months. It is rather strange that this part of the country which for so long has been in the war zone should be free of this pest, while Honan and other parts of the country in the very heart of the territory controlled by the cohorts of Wu Pei-fu are overrun by bandits.

---

[154] Pronounced "Wahn-shen';" now it is called Wanxian and at the time of this writing is being gradually abandoned as the city is rebuilt on higher ground in anticipation of the flooding that will drown the city once the Three Gorges Dam is completed.

But such is the case, whatever the explanation. In this connection, we shall have to contradict another report which appeared in the C.C. Post not long ago, to the effect that Lichwanhsien on the western border of Hupeh had been looted by local bandits. Though we are only 60 miles distant from that place, we have not been able to get any confirmation of this supposedly "official report." We should like to warn the C.C. Post that if it prints any reports to the effect that our city of Shihnan has been captured by Szechwanese or bandits, before we who reside here know anything about it, we shall be strongly tempted to deny also that report!

Although the burden of supporting large sections of Wu Pei-fu's and Yang Sen's armies has been removed from the shoulders of the people in this district, prices of all commodities are still very high. This is due now mainly to the fact that a good two-thirds of the fields are growing the poppy instead of more useful plants. The military derive an immense revenue from the growth of the weed, several million dollars in taxes being collected from the "hsien" alone, not to mention the profit derived from the trade in the stuff. And so nobody dares to raise his voice against the cultivation of poppy in such great quantities. The result will eventually be a shortage of food products in this section, since the lack of waterways and the mountainous character of the country forbid the importation of grains to any extent. One can only hope that the wars in China may soon cease, so that at least one excuse for growing opium will be removed. Just at present, although prices are high, there seems to be no suffering among the people, everyone apparently having enough to do and enough to eat. But people cannot live on opium, and if the cultivation of rice and other grains is neglected for any length of time, the food scarcity is likely to lead to such another near-famine as we had three years ago.

A LETTER SENT TO THE AMERICAN CONSULAR SERVICE
"…if there are any reasons why the American Government would prefer to keep American citizens out of the province of Szechwan,…I would like to learn of them,"

Shihnanfu, Hupeh, Nov. 24th, 1923

The American Consul
Chungking,[155] Szechwan

Dear sir:

I have been informed that the American Government has advised Missionary Societies not to send any missionaries into the province of Szechwan at present on account of the civil wars and banditry that have prevailed there for so long. Our Mission had planned to open stations in Kweifu and Wanhsien since last summer and Kweifu has now been opened, that having been done before we received this notice from our Mission Board. Now I should like to learn direct from you whether the recommendations of our State Department apply to Wanhsien. We shall to begin with not be doing any work in the country surrounding Wanhsien, and it would seem that a near-port city like Wanhsien, where foreign gun-boats are generally stationed should be a safe enough place for any foreigner. However, if there are any reasons why the American Government would prefer to keep American citizens out of the province of Szechwan, even the eastern portions, where the Northerners have control, I should like to learn of them in order that we may be guided correctly in our work in this district. We do not wish to go against the recommendations of our Government.

I have hitherto been registered in the Hankow Consulate. If nothing hinders I shall be coming to Wanhsien about the first of the new year, and should, I suppose, register in the Chungking Consulate at that time. Registration blanks I should like to have sent to Ichang, Hupeh, in the meantime.

Hoping to hear in due time that the American Government no longer places any restriction on residence in at least Eastern Szechwan – Wanhsien and Kweifu – I remain

Very respectfully yours,

Geo. O. Lillegard

---

[155] Chungking is now called Chonqing and has a new province.

BERNICE UNLEASHES HER FRUSTRATIONS.
"Edna[156] and I surely should have gone to the U.S.A. We're grass-widows anyway…"

Ichang, December 3, 1923

Dear George,

Nine o'clock and I am only starting this letter. Erna[157] is in bed with a very bad throat, tonsillitis in the <u>one tonsil</u>, she has, I believe. Her throat was sore yesterday morning & I gave her some Listerine to gargle with then, but she felt so much better during the day that she neglected taking care of herself and last night she felt pretty punk. She has been hanging around all today and finally she sent for Dr. B. He said she <u>must</u> stay in bed. Edna came down after supper and helped Erna doctor herself. But Ruth is naughty tonight of all nights and won't go to sleep as usual. Betty Ann has fussed a little, too. She seems to have settled down now, though.

Your letter of the 29th and card of the 28th came today. Am glad the box of sweets arrived so promptly. But, Georgie, if you were so very thankful and appreciative, how could you write all that "stuff" and_____ Oh dear! I don't know what to do or say! I can't get your idea, for one thing. You say, "_ _ _ _ _, it would not be so far for me to come back to get you after I have found a house in Wanhsien, - - -" I never expected you to come back to get me. I tho't you could come to Ichang now, make all arrangements here as regards freight, etc., proceed to Wanhsien and remain there. Then I would bring my baby and baggage when you said the word. If I am to take care of everything here in Ichang, I don't see any use in your coming back to Kweifu to get <u>me</u>. I can manage myself & baby, but I certainly <u>don't see</u> how I am going to handle the other business here with boxes in the godown half-packed, a bookcase here, and – oh, a million other things to look after. I don't know what we have here or where it is. Now, if you want to save travelling expense, and also, if you had planned on coming down to K. to get me, why I say, come to Ichang now and I'll come alone later.

Here are a few questions. If you must await definite word from the Board, how can you go ahead to Wanhsien? How long would you expect to stay in K. with your family? I am only now beginning to feel fit, and how am I to get the various things done which must be done here and besides move to K.? Moreover, there may be something wrong with me "downstairs." Both yesterday and today I experienced that feeling of fullness in the vagina and I am pretty <u>sure</u> it is not my uterus, so it may be there is something else. I told Dr. B. about it tonight and he said I should wait a couple days – believe he wants to see if I'll menstruate first. What I fear is that the wall of the vagina has fallen. Certainly, something is not as it should be.

I enquired about steamers today and Mr. Windham told me there are six, seven, or more up-river boats, so there will be at least several each week. But there is a period when <u>no</u> steamers go up, usually in Jan. or Feb. Now then, to be sure you would get to Wanhsien, you'd have to leave about New Year time, I imagine. And shall I move to K. and sit around there for who-knows-how-long? All for a few days that will be only "teasers." Believe it would be almost easier to stay here than to have you for only a few days and then be left again. I don't want to be unkind or unloving, but, Honey, it does

---

[156] Wife of missionary Herman Klein, was stationed with Lillegards in Shihnanfu, to be beginning a new mission in Kweichowfu

[157] Wife of missionary Henry Theiss, stationed in Ichang

seem as if you are asking a good deal. Outside of Gyps and Herman, I feel pretty confident none of the other men would think so much of the mission funds that they'd ask their wives to move alone. Why, they can't even come from Kuling alone. Edna & I surely should have gone to the U.S.A. We're grass-widows anyway & we'd certainly have been happier with our own folks than sitting around in other people's homes. Georgie dear, you <u>can't</u> possibly know how we girls feel about this moving & boarding, it seems, or I think you would rather have <u>walked</u> to Ichang! I feel so blue and so puzzled about what to do, and my back is aching, and the tears are all ready to come full force. It isn't fair, that's all!

Here's what I shall do for the present, if possible. With Erna sick and my own menstruation a possibility, I can't make promises as to what I'll do. Have had Christmas parcels lying here a <u>week</u> waiting for notes or letters to be enclosed. However, I'll get the tailor busy and try to get my dress and other things done and I'll have to do some sewing myself, besides other jobs. Then, when you get this letter, please consider the question and <u>wire</u> me whether to pack up and (move) to Kweifu or whether you'll come here, or whatever you decide. We should worry about a couple dollars for telegram, so I'll surely expect some sort of wire from you upon receipt of this.

"It's a great life if you don't weaken," but I'm weakening. Don't come with tales of business men, etc. – I didn't marry one. You're probably disappointed in me and think I'm a poor sport. All right, then, I <u>am</u> a poor sport – and you can tell the world.

Now I'm going to feed Precious and then I'm going to bed to cry a little. Don't care if I am a Baby.   Your Naughty Girl,

Tues. A.M. Didn't cry anyway, as I had several things to attend to and the tears went back where they belong. Hope this letter doesn't make you feel bad – but it's a cinch. I don't know what to do. How can I get ready in such a short time. <u>Can't</u> do these things I want done in Kweifu.

Baby weighed 11 lbs. yesterday. Another ten ounce gain.

Lovingly,
"B." XX

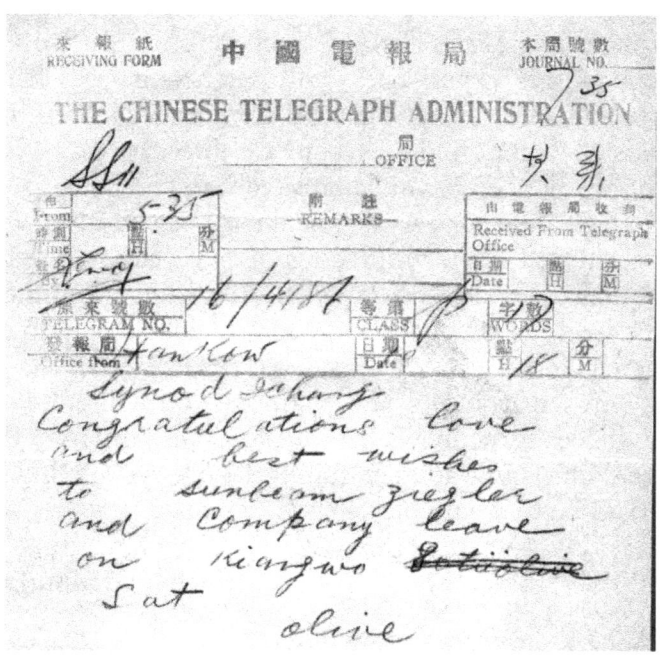

BERNICE HOPES TO AVOID MOVING TO KWEIFU AT XMAS.
"George may change his mind & come here for the holidays anyway when he receives my letters."

Ichang, Hupeh, China
December 5, 1923

Dear Louise,

About a week ago I started a letter to you, but the paper didn't take the ink and I didn't finish, so now the time has passed without my getting it written. It seems so hard for me to get my correspondence taken care of now that George is gone, because he likes to have me write to him every day. A letter a day is pretty near all I can manage now and how my Christmas mail has suffered! You will excuse me for my tardiness this year, won't you? I think I would have got my Christmas parcels ready before I went to the hospital if I had known how long I would have to stay. And it has taken me quite a while to get back into condition again, so I have done practically nothing save take care of Betty Ann and myself. That seems to have consumed a great deal of time. How do you manage with your two? I enjoyed the pictures you sent very much. Since you say Sarah looks like George and everybody here says Betty Ann is the picture of her Daddy, why it would seem that our babies must look somewhat alike. What do you think? I never saw any snaps of Baby Sarah when she was real small.

I'm feeling pretty well now, but I did think I was pretty slow. It is hardly strange though, since I was sick quite a while and then it took so much of my strength to feed my big Baby. She has been so very healthy all the time, but I think my condition made her rather fussy. The nurse always used to tell me not to worry. "She'll settle down pretty soon," she would say. Baby has been a long time in learning how to feed properly. She used to nurse so fast that she sucked in air and then she suffered so with flatulence. Now she nurses more slowly as a rule and when she does get air I always help her get it up by patting her back. She is a pretty good baby and gets more interesting every day. She has such large blue eyes and she certainly uses them. And she is such a fatty, Louise. She has gained steadily and last Mon., Dec. 3, at eight weeks she weighed eleven pounds. She gained ten ounces last week and also the week before. But, you with your two girls know all the things a mother experiences with her babies, so I'll not rave too much. Suffice to say, George and I are so very thankful to have a healthy little child.

I wish I could tell you definitely where we three are going to spend Christmas. George wrote that he may not be able to come to Ichang and he suggested that Betty Ann and I meet him in Kweifu and spend Christmas there. I could live with Nagels, but you perhaps can appreciate how I hate to move again. We certainly have wandered about these years and I do hope we can settle down before spring – and then we must pack up & go to Kuling! Such is life in China! George may change his mind & come here for the holidays anyway when he receives my letters.

Am sorry my gift will come so late, but hope you will enjoy it anyway. Sarah's children are the only nieces & nephews that are receiving gifts – I tho't they needed it. Will try to remember your girls another time. I hope you will have had a pleasant Christmas and may 1924 be rich with blessings for you & yours.

Much love from Betty Ann & Bernice

BERNICE DETAILS THE CHRISTMAS SEASON.
"This is the first time it has taken almost a week to write a letter home."
Letter No. 132   Ichang, Hupeh, China
December 28, 1923

Dear Folks,

      Here is hoping each one of you has had a very merry and happy Christmas. How I wish George, Betty Ann and I could have gathered around the tree, gone to church, and in general celebrated with you. I miss the regular Christmas "routine" that we enjoyed so much. Our Christmases these four years have been rather funny. In 1920 I was in the hospital; 1921 we had no tree, I was feeling rather sick, and we spent part of the evening with Schwartzkopfs and part in our own rooms; 1922 we had supper and spent the evening in Kleins' rooms; 1923, this year, here in Ichang with Theisses. Of them all, I think last year was in many ways the pleasantest. But this year we have our precious Betty Ann, of course.

      Well, let me tell you what news there is. On Wednesday, the 19th, a telegram from George arrived asking me to send the cook (he'd been cooking for us here) to Wanhsien. The telegram came from Kweifu. When that came I had to hurry and tend to things – George wanted some boxes from the godown and I had to get some groceries. Herman helped in enquiring about boat, arranging for the freight, etc. And then I wanted to make Christmas as pleasant as possible for George, so I opened the big package from you and took out the knife, and also the parcel from Chicago. Then I fixed up a box of sweets for him – some of our fruit cake, cookies, some of the cookies from you, and a pound of candy. Then I sent the last bunch of American mail, church papers, etc. The idea of not being together Christmas was anything but pleasant, but I guess both George and I felt we'd make that sacrifice quite willingly if it meant we could settle in a home of our own sooner by doing so. I got the cook and everything off O.K. and then Erna and I were very busy the rest of the week trying to get things ready for the holidays. I wanted to get Betty Ann's bunting ready, there were cookies to make (Erna made several batches), candy – well, you know what one likes to get done, but you <u>don't</u> know what it means to have only one warm room in the house and having to use it for living room, dining room, bathroom – everything save bedroom and kitchen, I guess.

<u>Sunday, the 30<u>th</u></u>. Didn't get this finished as soon as I had expected to. I'll continue right on with the news and events in their order. On Thursday before Christmas my amah was offended because I spoke to her several times about doing her work more quickly and left me – unironed clothes in the tub and others on the line. Well, I guess I didn't lose much of a servant, altho' she had been doing what she did quite satisfactorily. I ironed some diapers and did a few things myself that afternoon and the next day Erna's amah helped me. And Friday afternoon (21st) I managed to get another amah who had had many years experience. I have to pay her more than I care to, but I'll have her only these few weeks I am in Ichang and I can't afford to spend all my time training in "green" women. I felt real punk that Friday and didn't do much. I had a cold and felt miserable in general. I went to bed early that evening for a change. Saturday and Sunday we were busy doing this and that, Sunday evening all of us were at Schwartzkopf's, where we were entertained by Herman and Edna. First we had a service during which little Robert Ernst was baptized. I held him and Schw. and Erna also witnessed. After that we had a big chicken supper.

Monday (Dec. 24th) was a big day. The tree had to be trimmed and we elected Heinie for that job. This room had to be cleaned up, etc. etc. And in the afternoon there was a Community Christmas Party for all the foreign kiddies in Ichang. After dinner I remembered we hadn't washed the cut glass fruit dish, some vases, etc. and so I hurried to shine them. As I was standing here scrubbing one of the articles Erna told me someone was coming to the door and asked me to open it. I thought her request slightly strange but went to the door and saw - - <u>my hubby</u>! I had entirely given up seeing him in Ichang.

Mon. "Saa gaar det!"[158] Will I ever get this finished? I have so much to tell. Well, <u>of course</u>, I was as pleased and happy as anything to have George here for Christmas. It was mere luck that he could come, too. The boat he went up on got stuck on the rocks a little ways above Wanhsien and had to come right back. George had done about all that could be done for a few days, so he took the boat back again and <u>just</u> made Ichang in time for the festivities. After he came I had to hurry to get Betty Ann and myself dressed for the Community Party. The amah had done the last sewing on the bunting so it was ready. And I put on the blue cap from Elsa – it is so becoming to blue-eyed Betty. When we returned from the party I had to wrap a few gifts, as there was something left to the last minute as usual. We went up to the chapel right after supper to a short program given by some Chinese children and then we came home to our own tree. That morning we had received American mail, among them your Christmas letter, Mama. And that afternoon our package from you arrived, so this year I think all our Christmas mail, except a parcel from Netty, arrived on time. At least, I don't know of any more parcels on the way. There were a good many presents and I guess Ruth and Betty received most. Both babies were too tired and sleepy to look at the tree, though, so we let them sleep in their beds. Betty Ann will have to tell about her own gifts – they were all so pretty and we are as thankful for them as she!!

But I received many gifts also, which I must tell about. First I want to say many, many thanks for the lovely wool quilt, the silk bloomers, the knife and socks for George, cookies, etc. The latter were broken up a little, but it didn't affect the taste at all. It was mighty nice to have some of your Berliner krandser and ginger snaps again. And I feel very fortunate to receive such splendid wool comforters. I don't believe any of the girls in the mission have as warm and light bedding for their babies. Here in Ichang the girls all envy me the comforters. Betty Ann certainly is snug and warm in her bed. I have already worn the bloomers and they are fine. George is very glad to have such good socks and he will appreciate the knife (he missed the cook, so didn't receive the gifts I sent up). He will get that now when he arrives in Wanhsien. Now I must tell about my other gifts. George didn't have much time to think of presents this year. He gave me a beautiful dresser scarf and then he says I may buy whatever I need and consider it a gift from him. Well, when he left he gave me $30.<u>00</u> received for piano rent and said I could have that. From George's folks in Chicago I received some very nice talcum powder, a box of complexion cream and three cakes of complexion soap "to match," a linen towel with an embroidered "L," and a rubber lined travelling bag or case, which can be worn like an apron while dressing. Louise sent me a muslin apron with such a pretty appliqué design. Netty sent a nightie; Alice a handkerchief and camisole tape; Olive a beautiful dresser scarf; Edna gave me a pretty tray cloth or center piece; Erna a h'd'k'f; and Emma

---

[158] "So it goes!" (Norwegian)

a box of candy. And Mrs. Nilsen (do you remember my telling of her two years ago?) gave me a <u>beautiful</u> padded handkerchief case (blue silk with <u>pretty</u> embroidered cover) and three handkerchiefs. Cousins Marie and Bertha also sent a h'd'k'f. Believe I have mentioned all my gifts now. I'm not sure I remember all George's, but I guess I know most of them. I am giving him Kreitzman's "Old Testament Commentary, Vol. I" (it hasn't come yet) and I also gave him a white brass desk set consisting of corners (for large desk blotter), pencil holder, ruler, letter opener, blotter (one of these curved things) and stamp – or Chinese ink-box. I also gave him a tie, so did Betty Ann. His folks in Chicago sent him a tie, shirt, two tennis balls; and Louise sent a pair of silk stockings. Netty & Edw. sent him a pretty tie. That's all I can recall. I wanted to tell you that Christmas Eve was beautiful and very mild.

    Christmas Day there were Chinese services in the forenoon – really about noon – and we had our English services at 5:00 P.M. In the evening we entertained the crowd here serving a goose dinner. Wednesday George got busy and packed the cedar chest and several sections of the bookcase. And Tsao sifu was sick, so Erna and I had to help with the work. I was Boy! You should have seen the lamps when <u>I</u> got through with them. They were cleaner and brighter than before or since.

    Thursday was a rainy, unpleasant day and that forenoon Scholzes arrived from Hankow…Friday George enquired about steamers, arranged for freight, etc. etc. I spent a little time packing some in my trunk. I want to have things as ready as possible so that I can leave in a hurry, should it be necessary.

    Saturday forenoon, at eleven o'clock, Betty Ann and I were at Dr. Borthwick's for vaccination. I had it done on my left arm again, but he vaccinated Betty Ann on the sole of her left foot. Have you ever heard of having it done there. I think it is a convenient place, as I can still give her tub baths and just have the amah hold that foot out of the water. Betty Ann usually needs her bath quite badly! The vaccination seems to be working on me this time. My arm itches so and it has begun blistering. Then I seem to be unusually sleepy and "dopey." I really cannot tell much about Baby. Two of the four scratches seemed to be blistering today and seems to me she, too, has been very sleepy. Hope she won't be too uncomfortable. That afternoon Baby and I went to Mrs. Nilsen's for "eftermiddags kaffe."[159] Betty Ann looked so sweet in her blue cap and the bunting. The cap and bunting lining match <u>very</u> well. There were a Swedish lady and a Danish lady at Mrs. Nilsen's also, so our conversation was carried on in three languages. I do not know much Norwegian, tho' – have forgotten a good deal and also get it mixed with Chinese now.

    Saturday evening George and I were out to dinner. Mr. Wilse is postmaster here now and he also is Norwegian, so he had invited Nilsens and us for dinner.

<u>**1924**</u>. Happy New Year! Just think! I started this letter in 1923 and it is still unfinished. Will write more later – <u>today</u>. Good Morning! - - - - - - **9:15 P.M**. The foregoing greetings were written at 12:12 A.M. and now is the first chance I've had to sit down to write. It is almost impossible to do any letter writing here – we are always so many people in this one room and you know what that means.

    Saturday George was busy getting the piano into its box and down to the boat. My! I am so glad we are to have it with us. Now that George has got rid of most of the malaria (we hope so, at least) his voice is better and I anticipate some pleasant hours

---

[159] "afternoon coffee" (Norwegian)

singing and playing. Am so anxious to play for Betty Ann, too. I rather think she will like music. She smiles such wide big smiles sometimes when I sing for her. I suppose my imagination is working overtime, but it pleased me to think she smiled especially much when I sang "Hark the Herald Angels Sing"!

George left Saturday evening after we returned from Mr. Wilse's, that is, he boarded the steamer. I wish I could have gone along, but Betty Ann and I will be going up soon. We must get over the vaccination first and then we will go as soon as there is a decent steamer going up. It won't take me long to pack, as I have only Betty Ann's and my things left. I can go up any time as far as house is concerned, as George says he will have some sort of room ready. Besides there is a Mr. Hawley in Wanhsien, whom we learned to know here two years ago, and he said we could live with him temporarily, if we couldn't find a place right away. Well, I told George he should simply think of Betty Ann. I can put up with anything for awhile, just so I have a room where I can bathe and take care of Baby. I hope we can find and fix up a place before I have to leave again for Kuling so that we will have a home to come back to next fall…

I miss the old way of spending the holidays. Yesterday – New Year's Eve – this room was as mussy as usual, if not worse. It seems we girls spend all forenoon with our babies. That is the way when there are so many in one house. After supper we had to hurry to Schw's where we had a Sylvester and Confessional service. I was so sleepy I could hardly hold my head. I believe I was "dopey" and then the room was too warm and close. The rest of the folks stayed awhile, but I came home to look after my Baby and to finish this letter! (The latter is a joke! This is the first time it has taken almost a week to write a letter home.)

Wish you could see our Betty Ann! She is so sweet and mornings she is so happy she doesn't know how to act. She kicks, smiles, and squeals and has a fine time. She has been more fussy than usual lately, but I fear it is due to my late hours. She has gained, though, and yesterday at twelve weeks she weighed 13# 2oz. She is some fatty! And I have put dresses on every day the last week. She is getting too big to be in nighties all the time. Betty Ann is "meget alvorlig,"[160] I think. She smiles, etc. when lying down, but when she sits up or is carried with her head up, she looks around so seriously and no one can produce a smile. Baby is <u>such a joy</u> to me and I must say that 1923 was a year to be thankful for. What wonderful things babies are!

Now I <u>must</u> close. Oh, by the way! #140 came the other day ahead of #139 and I gather that Mama has been to the hospital, but I haven't any idea what for. Hope I get some more information soon. It is rather disconcerting to receive letters out of their order.

May 1924 bring you all spiritual and material blessings.

'Scuse abruptness! I'm so tired I'm getting silly.

Much love to you all from
Betty Ann and Bernice

---

[160] "very serious" (Norwegian)

Lillegards sell household goods in preparation for move.

SALE! Wonderful Bargains in all kinds of Household Goods! Sale!

Don't miss this Opportunity of a Lifetime!!

Removal Sale!

Since the undersigned are removing to new quarters in the city of Wanhsien, our non-transportable (MUST be sold) goods are offered at a GREAT SACRIFICE! SALE!

```
 1. Large Lamp with two extra chimneys and extra wick,---    6.00
 2. Small lamp shade and one chimney,                        1.30
 3. Sleeve Ironing Board,---                                  .20
 4. Two Walnut Bookcases,--                                 20.00
 5. Walnut Library Table,                                   10.00
 6. Kitchen knife box,                                        .20
 7. Iron Bed and Spring,                                    32.00
 8. China Cabinet,                                           5.00
 9. Kitchen Cabinet,                                        14.00
10. American Washtub,                                        2.00
11. Bathtub,                                                 1.00
12. Cane Cabinet,                                            2.00
13.  "   Flower Vase,                                        1.00
14. Brass Flower Jardiniere,                                 1.00
15. Three crockery Flower bowls,                              .50
16. Small Wall Mirror,                                       1.00
17. Cane Center Table,                                       3.00
18.  "   Sewing Table,                                       3.00
19. Two Cane Chairs,                                         7.00
20. One Cane Rocker,                                         2.50
21. Cane Clothes Hamper,                                     3.00
22. Iron Flour Barrel,                                       1.75
23.  "   Sugar  "                                             .85
24. Two Iron Pails,                                          1.50
25. One large Water Container,                               1.25
26. One Small  "    "                                         .75
27. One Broom and one mopstick,                               .50
28. Set of tools,                                            2.00
29. Reed Mats,                                               1.00
30. Kitchen Lamp,                                             .75
31. One Granite Water Pitcher,                               2.00
32. One Stove with pipes, and stove board,                  11.00
33. Borax and Lux, etc.,                                      .60
34. Set for filling lamps,                                    .30
35. Chinese scales,                                          3.00
36. Electric Bell supplies,                                   .70
37. Washboard
```

51.00
1.30
10.00
62.30

Geo. F. Lillegard

$143.85
  .70
144.55

Ziegler — $70.00
Gebhardt — 6.00
Ladies — 38.00
Unsold — 91.55 — 47.55 = 30.00
144.55

FRIENDS SEND MONEY FOR CHRISTMAS
"...the amount is to you personally."

San Francisco, Calif.,
Nov. 12, 1923

Rev. & Mrs. Geo. O. Lillegard
Shihnanfu, Hupeh
China

Dear Friends:

Through the U.S. Postal Dept., we have just now sent you a little token of our love and esteem. Together with it, we desire to express our best wishes for a blessed Christmas season and a bright and happy new year.

It may seem a little early to venture upon such a matter now, but since affairs seem somewhat uncertain in China, we wish to do what we reasonably can to make for certainty. If our greetings reach you somewhat too soon, we feel that it will be better than to have them reach you too late. So we are taking time by the forelock.

To avoid misunderstanding let me state that the amount (which was referred to above, and which should reach you about the same time as this note) is to you personally. If it may serve in some way to make life a little more tolerable, to secure for you some little bodily comfort, or to fill some little want in your labor of love, we are certain that the mission will be benefitted as well.

We are all enjoying good health, and we trust that your health and strength have not suffered any in yon strange and turbulent country. May God's blessing abide with you.

Your friends,

M.B. Backerud & Family

2 ½ MONTHS OF SEPARATION END; BERNICE RECOVERS.
"Bernice had a rather bad time of it, as she sustained internal injuries which the doctor did not suspect the existence of, with the result that some infection started."

Wanhsien, Szechwan, January 21st, 1924

Dear friend Backerud:

Your letter of Nov. 12th reached me on Christmas Eve, though my wife had seen it some days earlier. And your very generous Christmas present reached us a couple weeks later. That you should remember us in this way as well as the value of the gift itself made our Christmas a more happy occasion even than we had hoped for, since nothing warms the heart quite so much as to find remembrances awaiting one at Christmas Eve from unexpected sources. We are not so rich on our missionary salary either that we cannot make very good use of the money sent us. So we thank you heartily all of us, Bernice, Betty Ann, and myself.

But that is right, you do not know who Betty Ann is. Since I last wrote you, the Lord has granted us that greatest of good gifts on this earth, a healthy little baby, who came to us on October 8th. Bernice had a rather bad time of it, as she sustained internal injuries which the doctor did not suspect the existence of, with the result that some infection started. But she recovered in time. Elizabeth Ann has been most healthy from the start. Today, her 15th week, she weighed almost 15 lbs. She is so fat her cheeks look as though they were ready to pop. She is very active too, and possesses a good pair of lungs which she exercises on occasion and a voice which she is training for the high notes of Grand Opera. However, she sleeps nights and has given us very little trouble so far.

I have seen very little of our baby till now, since I have been separated from my family for most of the last three months. I left Bernice and the baby in Ichang, where they could be under doctor's care, and went to Shihnan, the first week in November, staying there looking after my share of the mission work in that place till the 15th of December. Then I left for this city, which we hope to make our home and the center of our mission labors hereafter. I managed to get enough done here, so that I could leave for Ichang in time to spend Christmas with my "family." I stayed there five days, spending all but Christmas Day in the pleasant job of packing up our belongings in that place. I have been here since the first of the year. Bernice and baby arrived a week ago. We are settled temporarily in a few rooms on the second floor of a large Chinese building in the heart of the business section of this city. Our rooms are light and airy, and with the cleaning and repairing that I put on them make fairly good quarters. We expect to stay here a few months, while finding and repairing some place that we can keep permanently, or until we can buy land and build. You may be sure that we are happy to be living together again anyway and to have the prospect of staying in this one place for some time. We have been moving about so much the last three years that we have hardly felt that we had a home. We brought a piano with us from the States but have had little chance to use it, as it has been in Ichang all the time, while we have been in Hankow, Kuling, and Shihnan. We were settled in Ichang for only half a year.

Wanhsien is a large city on the Yangtse in the eastern part of China's largest and wealthiest province, Szechwan. It is the third largest city in this province and has a population of about 300,000. There has been only one Mission working here so far, the English Episcopalian, and that has at present only two workers. So you will appreciate that there has been comparatively little mission work done in this section of the country. As a matter of fact, this section of China is reported to have a smaller proportion of Christians, and less Christian work than any other part of China proper, which means that it is about as needy a field as one could find in all the world. It has been my ambition to do work in some new field like this, and I hope that I will be able to put in some good solid years at the preaching of the gospel to these people who need it so badly. I have also hoped that the Norwegian Synod would in time grow strong enough to support all the work in this place and that it even now would take especial interest in our field.

We are just having a little fun with Betty Ann. She recently discovered her fingers and of course had to try sucking them. We do not want her to do that, so have her hands bandaged up. She resents that very much and yells in a most unladylike manner at times, when she finds that she cannot get her beloved fingers in her mouth. Just now Bernice pinned a little rattle – a toy – to her bandaged hand, and Betty seems to be quite pleased with the results she gets from swinging her hands around with this new appendage. It is great fun, I think, to watch a little child grow and develop. You see, I am not so young any more – 35 years old before I became a father – and I perhaps am more interested in my new duties than a younger man would be. At any rate, I find it hard not to spend more time with the little one than I perhaps ought to. I suppose you have been a father so long by this time that you get no particular thrill out of it at all!

We are getting a doctor out in our Mission at last. He is from Germany – Ph.D. as well as an M.D. – and presumably a good and capable man. He will be proceeding to Shihnan, where we should have a hospital, schools, and every branch of mission work, since it is the center of a large district entirely untouched by Protestant Mission work. Two young ladies came out this fall, one a nurse, the other a teacher. We need many more such workers too.

I have been quite well the last two-three months, but I had a bad attack of malaria in October, which kept me on the unfit list for some weeks. I ate quinine at the rate of 30 grains a day for awhile and have taken it in smaller quantities since, so that I hope I have gotten the poison out of my system by this time. Still I may have to take more quinine when the spring comes, the malaria season, to be on the safe side. As long as I can continue with my work I shall be satisfied.

I should have written you long ago, acknowledging the receipt of your letter and present, but I have been so busy with getting settled in our new quarters, and so unsettled and "messed up," since Christmas that I have not written even to my folks before. I hope this reaches you promptly, however, so that you will know that your remittance reached me safely, before too long a time has elapsed. Hereafter I hope to get some studying done again. My Personal Report which should have been sent in at Christmas time is also waiting to be written.

With best greetings to you and your family from Bernice, Betty Ann, and myself, and "tusind tak"[161] again for your kind remembrance, Sincerely yours,

Geo. O. Lillegard

---

[161] "thousand thanks" (Norwegian)

FELLOW MISSIONARY SENDS A BRIEF NOTE.
"I wanted to let you know that I am still here;..."

Shihnan, Hupeh, December 30, 1923

Dear Lillegard:

Your letter written at Patung arrived yesterday. I intend to send this letter to Ichang, but am not certain whether it will reach you there or not.

Our Christmas celebrations are now past. The children's program was fairly satisfactory. The singing out in the open court on Monday evening was fine, for the boys kept the right tone almost throughout. The second time the program was rendered, on Christmas Day, the rendition was very poor. The Chinese must have their feast again this year, and it was quite a nuisance. Ziegler, by the way, preached a twenty minute sermon on Christmas Eve.

The books ordered from the Tract Society arrived a few days ago. We are sending out some books for New Year's. Only ten Bibles arrived. If there are more, I suppose they will get here in the course of time.

A letter from the Mission in South America (Brazil) arrived today. I opened it, as it was addressed to the secretary of the Mission.

Everything is normal here. It was very warm during the holidays, but snow fell in the mountains about two days ago. We can see it from here. Today it is colder again.

I hope that you will get settled safely in Wanhsien, and that you do not have any trouble getting there. Let me know how you fare. I imagine you will have a great amount of work the first month or two.

I wanted to let you know that I am still here; hence this brief note. I wish you a very happy year on the threshold of 1924, the wish to apply to Mrs. Lillegard and the baby too.

Fraternally yours,

A.H. Gebhardt

GEORGE WANTS GEBHARDT'S OPINION.
"What do you think of old Chang as a guestroom attendant?"

Wanhsien, Szechwan, Jan. 24th, 1924

Dear friend Gebhardt:

Your letter of Dec. 30th reached me a week or two ago, and just the last few days I received your communication regarding the Chinese Conference. Thank you for both. I am enclosing my Personal Report for the last quarter herewith. I found it hard to settle down to anything like reading or writing these days that I was camping here, so got rather late with my report. I have not seen anything of anybody else's either, so that they perhaps are not so very much speedier than I.

Bernice and Betty Ann arrived a week ago and we are fairly comfortably settled now in the temporary quarters I have rented in the building of the Robert Dollar Co. Agents. I could get this whole building, but the rent is higher than I wish to pay - $800.00 per year. I believe that is what the present renters are paying as rents really are high in this section of the city – the big business section. Although it would be a fine location for our chapel work, it is not a good place for residence, so I plan on renting some place in the outskirts of the city for residence and a smaller place for chapel in the business section…I have another place in view now. It has rather poor buildings – only mud walls- but there is a fine garden, the location is good, and the buildings could be made livable without any great expense. In the meantime, we will have to stay here until that place is put in repair. This house is not so bad, as the rooms are light and airy, we have a "shai lou"[162] on top of the roof which commands fine views of the surrounding city and country besides providing a good place for drying clothes, and it was not hard to put the rooms in shape so that they would serve as a temporary residence. Some scrubbing and a coat of whitewash is all that was needed. The worst trouble with living here is that we get about smoked out sometimes. Everybody burns coal here, and the air reminds us of Chicago in consequence.

I have no place here that I can use for chapel or guestroom, so have been able to do no mission work as yet. After Chinese New Years I hope to be able to start in some kind of a place, however. I am looking for a site for chapel now. What do you think of old Chang as a guestroom attendant? If my residence is to be in some other place than the chapel I will have to engage somebody to act as guestroom attendant and gatekeeper. The only men I have in view yet are Chang and old Feng in Hankow, who I understand is out of a job at present. I do not know whether Chang cares to come or not… However, I shall await word from you before definitely asking for Feng to come up.

We are all well and happy – glad to be together again for a change, even if we do have to rough it a little. Betty Ann is a source of considerable amusement as well as a welcome companion. She has been a good girl – sleeps nights and cries no more during the day than she has a right to. She weighed almost fifteen lbs. at the 15th week, which means she is keeping pretty close to young Ziegler's record. Her cheeks are so fat she can hardly smile. With best greetings to all you Shihnanites from Bernice, Betty Ann, and myself,

Sincerely yours,

Geo. O. Lillegard

---

[162] (Chinese)

Chapter 12
Our New Mission Field in Wanhsien, Szechwan

At our 1923 Mission Conference on Kuling, it was decided to open three new stations, subject to the consent of the Mission Board. One of these has now been opened in Shasi, Hupeh, on the Yangtse River between Hankow and Ichang, the second in Kweifu, Szechwan, 110 miles above Ichang on the same river, and the third in Wanhsien, Szechwan, 65 miles farther west, well into the largest of China's eighteen provinces. A brief description of this new mission field in Wanhsien will, no doubt, interest all those who are active in supporting our Foreign Mission cause.

When Shihnanfu, Hupeh, was opened as a mission station four years ago, our missionaries were the only foreign messengers of the Gospel of Peace in all western Hupeh, a territory with a population of over two million inhabitants. One reason why this section of the province had been left so long without permanent Christian work was to be found in the mountainous character of the country which made it comparatively inaccessible. While there are several smaller towns in this district which our Mission hopes to occupy with foreign missionaries in the course of time, we found it necessary first to link up our work in Shihnan with the older work in Hankow as much as possible. For that reason, Ichang, Kweifu, and Shasi, three large cities on the Yangtse River, have been made mission stations. In all these places, other missions have carried on work for some time, although to an entirely inadequate extent, so that our Mission finds in them needier fields than our first field, Hankow, at the same time as our young congregations are thus brought geographically somewhat closer together. Wanhsien is out of the direct line between these stations, being west of Shihnan. But it is the river port for the westernmost county in Hupeh, Lichwanhsien, which is one of the places which our Mission hopes to occupy when our missionary force has increased sufficiently to enable us to place men at the smaller places in our mission field.

The main reason, however, for occupying Wanhsien was that it is the neediest field, while at the same time accessible and easily worked, of any that perhaps is to be found in all the heathen world. With a population of over 200,000, it has only two Protestant missionaries and a Christian congregation of about 200 souls. While Chungking, the largest city in Szechwan, with a population of about 600,000, has almost 100 missionaries, and Chengtu, the provincial capital, has over two hundred representatives of several Mission Societies, Wanhsien, the third largest city in the province, has a missionary force of only five foreigners, no more than many a town of a few thousand inhabitants has in other parts of the country. To the east, it is 65 miles to the nearest mission station, to the north and south 50 miles, to the west 100 miles. That is, in a territory as large as the State of West Virginia, there is only one mission station manned by two pastors, and three women workers. And this is not a thinly populated part of the world, like Tibet or Mongolia, where the number of missionaries is even comparatively still smaller, due to the inaccessibility of the country, but a rich country, supporting a large population, and easily accessible via the Yangtse River, China's great artery of trade. In proportion to population, there is presumably no part of our field that has had less Christian work done in it than this in and about Wanhsien, so that we have here as near to virgin territory as could be found in this late stage of Protestant mission endeavor.

Wanhsien – which means "The City of Ten Thousands" – is situated on the Yangtse River, 180 miles above Ichang, or about 1300 miles from Shanghai. Foreign steamboats now run regularly from Ichang to Wanhsien and beyond, going in high water season as far as to Kiatingfu, Szechwan, almost 2000 miles from the coast. It was opened to foreign trade in 1917, although it is not "an open port," so that foreigners outside of missionaries may not buy and own property here, but can carry on business only "in transit," while establishing residence in some "port city" like Chungking or Ichang. In spite of these restrictions, there are a few foreigners engaged in business, besides the foreigners in the employ of the Chinese Customs and Post Office. They are either bachelors or "married" to Japanese or Chinese women, or have left their families in the homelands, so that the only foreign ladies in the place are those in the missionary families. The chief business in which foreigners are interested here is the export of wood-oil, which is used throughout the world in the manufacture of varnishes. The wood-oil, expressed from the nuts of a certain tree which grows in the mountainous country in western Hupeh and eastern Szechwan, is brought to Wanhsien by thousands of farmers and wood-oil tree growers. Here it is tested, packed in wood caskets and shipped down river and to all parts of the world. Perhaps more of the varnishes in the homes of our readers than one might suspect come from Wanhsien originally. So when you look at the bright polish on your floor or furniture, please think of Wanhsien and the thousands of heathen Chinese who are vitally interested in selling you such products and whom we are seeking to interest in something greater: the Light of the World.

As Chinese cities go, Wanhsien is a beautiful place. It is situated at a turn of the Great River, where a little mountain stream joins it and the river valley widens out considerably, affording good building sites on the banks of both water courses. The original walled city has been outgrown many times over. The city now extends for several miles along the north bank of the Yangtse and on both sides of the little stream for two or three miles inland. In one section the city extends for a mile or more up the hillside to the base of an immense "bluff" that overlooks the city, called "The Precipice of Peace." Perhaps the first feature of the scenery that would attract the attention of the traveller is the steep mountain peaks back of the city, crowned with fortresses. One of these is a town in itself, as it has a wide, flat top, affording room for many buildings. This particular hilltop is a natural fortress, requiring no walls to make it impregnable, since the sides for a few hundred feet from the top are as perpendicular as they could be made, so that the only way to get to the top is via steps cut zigzag in the face of the precipice. In these disturbed times, this place has become the refuge for most of the wealthy people in the city and surrounding country, who have brought their portable wealth with them and left their mansions to the tender mercies of the bandit-soldiers who have been occupying the city in smaller or larger numbers from the time of the Revolution, 13 years ago. With a few armed men to guard the approach to this hill fortress, they are safe here – until the soldiers bring their new aeroplanes into use!

Protestant mission work has been carried on in Wanhsien since 1888 by members of the China Inland Mission. In this part of the country, this mission is represented by English Episcopalians and a few German Lutherans. The C.I.M. Station is located a mile or more from the Yangtse, near the little stream. There are good school buildings, a church, and a large foreign-style residence. The Catholics have been in this part of China for over 100 years. Foreign priests have not at all times been able to come here on account of the anti-foreign prejudices of the people, but the Church has had its representatives here ever since their work was begun in this province. There are now several hundred Catholics in the city under the care of a French priest, representing "The Foreign Mission of Paris," a Society founded in the 17th century. An imposing church, in cathedral style, dominates the most important section of the city, the "new" city where most of the shipping and "big business" interests are located.

Our temporary quarters are located near the Catholic Church and about two miles distant from the C.I.M. Station. We hope to secure buildings suitable for street chapel work in this same part of the city, while residing in some less congested section, until we can buy land and erect the required buildings. It is our hope and prayer that our Lutheran Church will awake to the great opportunities and responsibilities it has in this vast unevangelized territory and do what it can to bring many also of this part of "the land of Sinim" to the true faith in the Savior of the World.

Geo. O. Lillegard

Baby Max Zschiegner "writes" to baby Betty.

Hankow China, Jan. 7th, 1924.

Dear Betty Ann,

i hope You will xcuse the typewriter and all the misstakes i make becaws this Is my very first lettre.

O what a nice lettre, and what a pretty bib You sent me for Christmas! i thank You so much. wat till we get to that mountain called cooling that mamma is talking about an i will pick You a big big bunch of flowers bigger than any uf tha other boys can. All i can say now is, tak, tak, tak, wich i suppose You will unnerstand.

My, how far You are going away up in China. i made a short trip aready but not so far. Are you afraid of coolies and water? Hope You enjoy Your morning tub as much as me. But don't be afraid. You and I went thru a harder xperience than the trip You are going to make, when the Great Loving FATHER sent us to make our papas and mammas happy and He will will be with You and Your dear Parents. Just keep happy and keep on growing, but don't beat me by too much. Pa and mamma are raving about me all the time, how big i am getting, but shucks, at this rate i don't think i will be able to lick Keith by nex summer. I have lots of fun. It tickles my daddy and mamma so much wen i laff all day long (after i have had plenty to eat), but wen nite comes i just let loose and holler with all my mite and main and make a terrific racket, enuff to wake up the whole naborhood an specialy Mr. Fischer. Well, you see, they are trying to break me of the habit of feeding in the nite an the nurse always even woke me up to get my feeds during the nite. Don't You just love Your mamma tho. i love mine.

Well, i haf to go to bed now. Betty, would You be mad if i asked You for a pictchur of You. Pa has failed to get a good one of me so he is going to take me over to some Chinee by tha name uf Tsung Yen or som thing an hav my pictchur took.

Good nite, sleep tite,

Max Zschiegner Junior.

Dear Mrs. Lillegard,

Now that my son is thru with the typewriter, will you excuse me if I answer your letter of December 6th in great haste? I am awful at answering letters, but this has also been an unusually busy time for us.

I am enclosing the budget that you so kindly sent me and thank you for your trouble. It was the 1923 budget that I wanted tho. But perhaps that is not to be had.

We were very glad to get George's card from which we first learned that he was with you at Ichang over Christmas. I do not need to ask if you had a happy Christmas. Ours was very happy too. It would take more time and space than I have left to tell you about it. The last couple days American mail has been pouring into Hankow. So I guess you folks will be getting yours too when this reaches you. Hope you all fare as well as we did. How is everyone in Ichang? No one has heard from Scholzs here since they arrived. Are they all well? How is Heinie getting along? And Betty and Bobby, and their mammas? And how is Mrs. Louie and Buddy's sister? All quite well in Hankow.

Very sincerely yours,

Max Zschiegner.

P.S. Helen will write soon.

MAX SR. WRITES ABOUT LACK OF FUNDS FOR FURNITURE.
"Let's all take our beds and chairs and tables to Kuling next summer."

Hankow, China, January 7th, 1924

Dear George,

It's a trick to keep track of where you people "are at," but I guess I am going right by addressing this to Wanhsien. Hope your lone journey has brought you there safely and that you have found comfortable temporary quarters, at least, if you have not found something that you can hope to call <u>home</u> some day. Good luck to you, George, and God's blessings upon all your efforts. May the end of this new year of grace find great progress in the broadcasting of the Gospel Message at Wanhsien.

I have your letter of December 9th, written in Shihnan, and your card of Dec. 28th, written in Ichang to answer. We also received a very dear letter, or rather, our little Max did, from Betty Ann in Ichang and he wants to thank her papa also for that pretty bib.

The rush of the X'mas season has left me uncertain as to where I stand with my correspondence. I may not have written you that on Dec. 19th I deposited $2000 to your account in the International Bank and credited it to the Wanhsien Station as you requested in your letter of the 9th. But, as your card indicated, you took that for granted, which was correct. Your card was welcome. It contained the first news we received of Scholz's arrival in Ichang. Was glad to hear that you were able to spend Christmas with your family after so long a separation.

Fischer is making four copies of a letter that was received by Schmidt today from Brand addressed to the General Conference in your name but in his care. The original will go off to you tonight.

All well in Hankow. Had a fine Christmas, but busy "teh hen."[163] Lutheran Witness will be off the press by the 12th. Please let me know how many copies you want in Wanhsien. Did you get your calendars from somewhere? I sent 600 to Shihnan. But no doubt Iny gave you some when he arrived.

Ben is up at Kuling just now but will be back tomorrow probably. Yang Lao Pan claims he needs at least a thousand more than he bid on the job and has come to us with his plea. Says he did not want to run away on the job, but hopes that we will come across, otherwise he cannot complete the houses. There was nothing to do but for Ben to go up and make a thorough investigation. As it stands Yang has received $9400 and still has $1200 coming. Wants an additional $1000. As a matter of fact, the Mountain Retreat Fund has only a little over $300 left. The complete contributions to the fund have not yet been received by me from the States. AND Brand's letter says only Walther League money should be used for the furnishing of the houses, or rather that the Board sanctions the furnishing of the houses if there is enough money in the Mountain Retreat treasury. So there. Let's all take our beds and chairs and tables to Kuling next summer.

Let us know how things are going with you. Will try to write more news next time.

Fraternally yours,
Max Zschiegner

---

[163] (Chinese)

FELLOW MISSIONARY PRAYS FOR LILLEGARDS.
"You must have been travelling very near the time that Captain Brandt was murdered."

Hankow, Jan. 15, 1924

Dear Friend George,

Just a line to accompany the enclosed paper. Please read it and answer immediately.

Received your letter of Jan. 5th, written at Wanhsien. Glad to hear that you arrived O.K., especially since we are reading so much about the activities of bandits near Wanhsien lately. You must have been traveling very near the time that Captain Brandt was murdered. Have you any news concerning that case? Hope nothing will turn up any nearer to you than that. I suppose Bernice and Betty Ann are on their way to you now. God be with them and protect them from all harm. We certainly were pleased to hear that you succeeded in renting part of the Robert Dollar building as a temporary residence at least. That is more than the Shasi folk have been able to do so far. I hear Scholz and Theiss are living in a Chinese hotel, still looking for a place to rent. Hope you will all succeed in securing permanent living quarters before long, as it certainly is not agreeable to have no place that you can call home.

We are all well and baby is doing fine. Hope the same is true of your family. No special news from Hankow. No action has been taken on the recommendation from Shihnan to cut the Seminary down to a half a day. Just now we are waiting for a report from the instructors on the ground covered and still to be covered in the Sem. and the length of time it will take. Of the other resolutions as much will be put into effect as possibly can be this year. Bentrup continues his class with the teachers and Riedel will also take a class with them. Some are doing good work at memorizing Bible passages and the Catechism.

Riedel has received the Liturgy but there were no corrections made by the revision committee. Was this an oversight? Gebhardt stated that corrections would have to be made. The Liturgy and Agenda is something that we need, and ought to be pushed, in my opinion. We have instructed Riedel to go thru it again. Of course it cannot be printed for some time yet, as the Conference has decided, but it would have helped had there been corrections sent along by the revision com., since we are making use of it in the chapels. But I trust it was an oversight.

With sincere greetings to you and yours,

Fraternally,
Max Zschiegner

P.S. Was about to mail this when yours of the 9th came to hand. Thanks for the extra personal report. I think that is required, altho' your personal account can be figured out from the report you sent, which I have forwarded to Brand.

On Dec. 19th (no harm in mentioning it again) I deposited $2000 to your account in International. That was the last to date.

Will deposit $1000 to your account in International tomorrow Jan. 17th, & credit to Wanhsien Station, as you request. I realize it takes a long time for mail to reach you during this season. Perhaps the bank's notification on that last $2000 will have reached you before this arrives in Wanhsien. I think, in general, you are quite safe in writing out checks before having received *notification from me of a deposit, as long as you are <u>sure</u> you wrote me to make a deposit. At any rate I make it a point to deposit immediately upon receipt of requests from our station treasurers.*

It appears you have succeeded in getting something more than a temporary residence, and I congratulate you. I am sure with Bernice and Betty Ann arriving soon the place will be real "homey" before long, even if you are way up across the border of Hupeh at our farthest station at "the front."

Helen & baby send special greetings & love to Bernice and Betty Ann.

God be with you all in your difficult work and grant you a contented home.

Yours,
Max

GEORGE RESPONDS ABOUT THE CAPTAIN'S MURDER.
"I was on board the Tzesui and saw the captain the night before…"

Wanhsien, Szechwan, January 30th, 1924

Dear friend Max:

Your letters of Jan. 7th and 15th have just been received, both coming at the same time, which is a fair sample of the kind of mail service we are having here at this time. As for the Bank question – the Wanhsien "Conference" (!) votes in favor of transferring the accounts to the International Bank as soon as convenient.

I wonder if the American Business interests are getting scared away from China since this distinctively Oriental bank is closing down.

I should like to have fifty or a hundred copies of the Lutheran Witness sent me, if you have that many to spare. I have received no copies of the Calendar, but I shall not worry about it, as I have little opportunity to sell many of them at this stage of the game and later on, it would be too late. However, if you have more in Hankow than you can make good use of would you kindly send me a hundred or two? They would make good advertising posters at least.

As for the Liturgy – the lone copy of that work was in Gyps' hands all last year and he reviewed it all. His idea was that the original translator ought to revise it or work it over more thoroughly before submitting it to the Reviewing Committee for suggestions. Too much of the work handed to us so far has been of such a nature that it could not be "reviewed," but required a new translation. I have thus made an entirely new translation of the Tract on Lutheran Doctrine (Pieper's) turned in by Meyer, as the other was so inaccurate and loose a translation that it was quite unusable. Gyps considered that the Translation Committee ought to be required to do more careful work before turning their work over to the reviewers. Otherwise the Reviewing Committee becomes a translation Committee too, and might as well do the whole work from the beginning. This explains why no suggestions were made to Riedel regarding the Liturgy. Gebhardt asked him to work it over again first. I agree with him that this is the right procedure. In our literary work also, it will not pay to sacrifice quality to quantity. Gebhardt writes that some of the material turned in by Arndt for the Chinese paper was so unclear that his Chinese secretary could get no sense out of it – which means that it cannot be used or will have to be returned to Arndt for correction. Too much of our literary work has suffered from Arndt's passion for speed and quantity production, with the result that it is quite useless.

Thank you for your interesting letter to Betty Ann, or rather Max Jr.'s letter! Betty Ann is doing fine. She has kept on gaining this month in spite of vaccination and moving and everything. She weighed 15 lbs. last Monday, her 16th week. Can Max beat that? We are fairly well settled in our quarters here now, except for that we lack some necessary articles of furniture. It is hard to get things made at this time. The landlord has loaned us several of the most necessary pieces however, so that we are getting along allright. I have not succeeded in securing a chapel yet, but hope to get one soon. In the meantime, I shall have to (do) what I can by conversation and "guestroom work."

Everything is quiet and peaceful in this country now so far as I know. I hear little about the progress of the fighting in Szechwan and nothing whatever about brigandage in this section, although I understand conditions are far from normal. The murder of Capt.

Brand was a peculiar business. I have heard nothing more about it than what has been printed in the papers. It seems that he had gained his enemies in this province and that they had warned him several times to stay away. It may be these who were responsible for his murder. I was on board the Tzesui and saw the captain the night before his murder, while the boat was anchored here at Wanhsien. You may imagine what a shock it was to me to hear about his death, having just conversed with him and had a glass of wine with him in his cabin the day before. It reminded me again of how dependent we are on the protection of the Almighty God at all times and how necessary it is to be prepared at all times to meet Him face to face as friend or enemy.

I shall be sending you my fiscal report for the month in a couple days. Or perhaps I will get it ready tomorrow and mail it with this letter.

With best greetings to you all from myself and "family,"

Fraternally yours,
Geo. O. Lillegard

THE AMERICAN CONSULAR SERVICE RESPONDS.
"**Wanhsien has experienced some very critical moments during the recent hostilities and two incidents which transpired marked the place as one of grave danger to foreigners under certain conditions.**"

Chungking, China, December 4th, 1923

Geo. O. Lillegard, Esquire
Evangelical Lutheran Mission
Shihnanfu, Hupei

Sir:

    In response to your letter of November 24th relative to the recent action of the American Government in advising the several church missionary boards to refrain from sending further missionaries to the province of Szechuan at this time, you are advised that the action taken applies to all places within the province of Szechuan. Because of its strategic importance, Wanhsien has experienced some very critical moments during the recent hostilities, and two incidents which transpired marked the place as one of grave danger to foreigners under certain conditions.

    It may be that with a change in the military situation, conditions will improve and will warrant the removal of the existing restrictions on the coming of further missionaries into the Szechuan field, but at the present juncture, this Consulate is not in a position to approve of the removal of such restrictions. It is regretted that a more favorable reply cannot be given, but you are undoubtedly in a position to appreciate the situation.

Very respectfully yours,
C.J. Spiker
C.J. Spiker,
American Consul.

300.
CJS/Y.

GEORGE REPLIES TO THE CONSULATE.
"Your letter of December 4th reached me…only after my departure…"

Wanhsien, Szechwan, February 4th, 1924

Mr. C. J. Spiker
Chungking, Szechwan

Dear sir:

Your letter of December 4th reached me at Wanhsien the first part of last month, having been forwarded from Shihnan which place it reached only after my departure on December 14th. Since we learned that the Northerners had left Wanhsien for the west, I decided that Wanhsien must be as accessible a place as any to go to in China and took for granted that you or the American Government would make no objections to having American citizens residing in this place. I interviewed the Captain of the Monocacy upon my arrival here and he stated that there were no objections at the present time to Americans coming here, so far as he knew. No doubt the military situation has now changed sufficiently to enable the American Government to remove the restrictions which it had placed upon travel in Szechwan.

I would appreciate information as to whether or no I should now register at the Consulate in Chungking, or whether my registration in the Hankow Consulate is sufficient for the time being.

Thanking you for your letter, I remain

Respectfully yours,
Geo. O. Lillegard
Lutheran Mission,
Wanhsien Szechwan

GEORGE WRITES TO THE CENTRAL CHINA POST.
"I feel that all the circumstances of his death point to a deliberate plot to put him (Capt. Brand) out of the way,..."

The Editor of the C.C. Post   Wanhsien, Szechwan, February 4th, 1924
Hankow, China

Dear Mr. Archibald:

       I should have asked you before this perhaps with regard to whether or no you want me to send important news by telegram or, in how far you will undertake to pay for telegrams that I may send you regarding events in this corner of the country. This question was forced upon my attention at the time of the murder of Captain Brand. I was probably the first foreigner to learn of his death, as a telegram was received here at the office of the Robert Dollar Co. Agents, in whose buildings I have rented temporary quarters, soon after the attack on the Tzesui. I hesitated to telegraph you with regard to the matter at the time, since I had no authority to do so, and I did not write about it, as I was certain your correspondents in Ichang or Chungking would telegraph you with regard to the matter before my letter could reach you.

       With regard to this attack on Captain Brand, I might make some remarks to you, leaving it to you to publish what you please, if any of it.

       I note that your Ichang correspondent calls the matter a plain case of piracy and nothing more. The Customs men here are working on the theory that the junkmen were back of the attack on Brand. The C.I.M. Missionary, the Rev. Darlington, at Wanhsien has another theory which appeals to me as more in harmony with the facts of the case. What I write here is in part his statements, in part my own, and you may take them for what they are worth.

       It has been an open secret that the Tzesui has been engaged in carrying arms and ammunition, especially for the Yang Sen faction in Szechwan. His boat has never been fired upon and has been able to make trips at times when other boats were prohibited practically from going. The only time, he was not able to go was when the Yang Sen faction was ousted from Chungking. Of late, however, Yang Sen has not needed his services, since he can make use of the boats bought by Wu Pei-fu for the purpose. The Tzesui has therefore been suspected of carrying arms and ammunition for the anti-Yang Sen faction. The attack on the Tzesui would seem to be something else than plain piracy, although brigands were of course engaged in the task of "bumping of" Captain Brand. For no attempt was made to take anything but the ready cash on board, her cargo being left untouched. Furthermore, pirates have not ordinarily shot officers in cold blood. Captain Brand was pulled out of his bed without having any opportunity to make any defense, was hauled outside on the deck, stood up against the smokestack and shot in cold blood, and then thrown overboard. He was not the kind of man to rouse their ire by unavailing attempts at escape or self-defense, since he was known for his diplomatic treatment of the Chinese in general. I feel that all the circumstances of his death point to a deliberate plot to put him out of the way, the robbing of passengers, etc., being the reward granted those engaged to carry out the cowardly plot. Captain Brand had made his enemies in Szechwan. He may have been wanted out of the way by Yang Sen who feared he would carry arms for the Szechuanese, now that Yang himself no longer required his services. He may have been attacked by those who knew of his relations with Yang Sen and who now found no other means of getting revenge, since Yang Sen apparently has conquered the province. At any rate, all those "in the know" are inclined to look upon this affair as something directly connected with Captain Brand's activities as an agent in the arms business rather than as an act of piracy pure and simple. For this reason also, it cannot be taken as indicating anything in particular with regard to the status of foreigners in this province. In this connection, might it not be apropos to say that "the falling prestige" of foreigners in China is due mainly, if not entirely, to the illicit activities of foreigners, in the opium-running business, and arms-smuggling ventures, and to the fact that men like Widler are held prisoners by the Chinese officials or military for acts which no foreign power could defend? I am quite convinced that the prestige of the foreign powers would be raised more quickly and effectively by the wholesale deportation of all such questionable characters by their respective governments than by all the gunboats and diplomatic requests that could be produced. So long as foreign criminals are allowed to run wild in China, with only an occasional "vacation" in a comfortable prison in the port cities, we can hardly blame anybody or anything else if foreign prestige sinks according as the activities of such criminals become more and more generally known. In this city, for example, the fact that a foreigner was held prisoner by the military made all too many people look upon all foreigners with an appreciably greater contempt than before. It would seem that our foreign-language press could wage a campaign as profitably along this line as any other.

It would be difficult to make any choice between the two theories suggested above as to the authors of the plot against Captain Brand. Rev. Darlington believes that Yang Sen was back of it. The fact that Yang Sen's soldiers examined the Tzesui the night before it was attacked, that armed brigands could hardly have boarded the boat here at Wanhsien without the knowledge of these soldiers, and that the attack was made at a place entirely under the control of Yang Sen's forces, and that no attempt has been made by them to discover or find the culprits, would point to the correctness of this theory. However, the well-known hostility of the Szechwanese to the Northerners and hence to Yang Sen who now is entirely in the power of the Northerners, would point rather to the possibility that Yang Sen's enemies were back of this attack on one who had assisted Yang Sen with arms and ammunition at crucial periods in his campaigns. Since the real facts are not likely to come to light, one may have his choice of these two theories. There is little doubt but what one of them is correct…

Everything is quiet in this section of the province now. The Northerners are nearing Chengtu, and Hsiung Keh wu is reported as having fled to the country north of Chengtu. The Northerners are closing in on the provincial capital from the south and east. Just at present there is no fighting, the campaign having reached the stage of negotiation, or rather of shooting with bullets of silver, various "neutrals" and "independent" generals being in the market to the highest bidder. Hsiung Keh wu's prospects seem to be about annihilated. Now we shall see what Yang Sen will be able to do with this turbulent brigand country, Szechwan.

With best greetings to you, I remain, Respectfully yours,

Geo. O. Lillegard

ANSWER TO A STATESIDE LETTER FROM A FELLOW REV.
"I have always liked children, but did not realize till I got one of my own how much a child could be loved."

Wanhsien, Szechwan, February 6th, 1924

Dear friend Preus:[164]

Thank you for your letter of Nov. 27th received just a month ago.[165] It was forwarded to me here from Ichang. I have been here since the first of the year, and Bernice and Betty Ann have been here since the middle of January. I have rented some rooms on the second floor of a building occupied by the Agents (Chinese) of the Robert Dollar S.S. Co. which make serviceable temporary quarters, although they are not what I want for permanent residence and chapel. I have not been able to secure any building for chapel purposes yet, but hope to get one soon. In the meantime I have been busy getting our goods unpacked, putting our temporary quarters into inhabitable shape, and attending to Committee duties: translation work, correspondence, language study, etc. I have finally gotten a guestroom fixed up where I can meet Chinese and do a little mission work by talking to people. I have also distributed some Bibles and Christian literature. One does not feel quite right, however, about not having any preaching services when Sundays come around. But I am not the kind that can go out on the street corners and do my preaching, so that I shall have to wait until I can get a chapel fixed up.

Everything is quiet here now politically, although fighting is still going on further west in the province. The Northerners seem to have gained practical control of the province. If they do so and are able to prevent new revolutions from breaking out, we should enjoy peace for a time. Conditions have been as bad as they could be in most parts of the country and I am optimistic enough to believe that they will take a turn for the better now. I think that Wu Pei-fu, the Northern General, is going to succeed in his aim of uniting the provinces by military force. If only his own lieutenants and allies do not turn against him and start some more civil wars within his ranks again.

This city has suffered a great deal from the presence of nearly 100,000 soldiers for a few weeks last fall and of a minimum of perhaps 10,000 men the rest of the past year. As a result prices have gone way up, labor is scarce, and living conditions in general are very difficult. Every home had its quota of soldiers quartered upon it for awhile this fall. The Northerners were forced to retreat from Chungking for a couple months then and their forces were concentrated at this place with the result than even this great city of three or four hundred thousand inhabitants could not take care of them. Farmers and sellers of all kinds of produce did not dare to enter the city with their produce for fear that the soldiers would grab them as coolies. The worst of it at such times is that cesspools and "privies" do not get cleaned out either, as in this country it is the farmers who do that work, making use of the muck for fertilizing their fields. The filth on the streets accumulates also. However, by the time I arrived the worst was over, and we hope that prices will be coming down and things in general returning to normal soon.

---

[164] H.A. Preus

[165] Preus writes: "Sometimes I wonder if we in Chicago are much more advanced than the heathen Chinese – here with our gunmen and murderers of which, not to forget, the reckless auto drivers – over 600 auto deaths here so far this year – and hundreds dead from moonshine!"

Our little Elizabeth Ann is a healthy, happy little girl and is great company for us. I have always liked children, but did not realize till I got one of my own how much a child could be loved. It's great to watch her grow and develop! She has more than doubled her birth weight in less than four months, which is doing pretty well as Mrs. Moldstad might tell you – we will not expect you to appreciate it yourself![166] Come on in, man, the water's fine. If you are going to wait till you get rich before you get married, it will not be any fun any more. Any girl worth her salt will be glad to share your poverty and your hardships with you. And your congregation would without a doubt get busy and raise your salary if you get married. So just go ahead and take pity on some lonely girl waiting for a lover and make her happy and yourself the same in the bargain, "Nichts für Ungut."[167]

If my subscription to the Luth. Sentinel has not been paid yet, kindly send the bill to Mr. E.J. Onstad, State Capitol, Treas. Dept. Madison, who will pay for me.

With best greetings to you from Bernice, Betty Ann, and myself,

Fraternally yours,

Geo. O. Lillegard

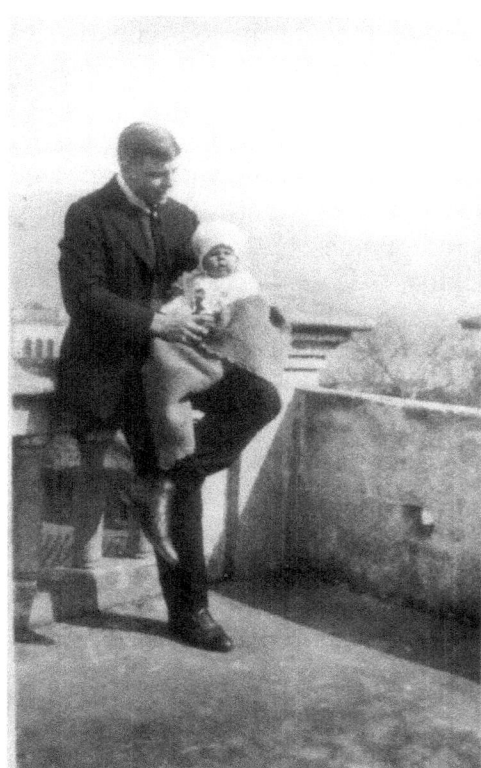

George & Betty on roof of Robert Dollar Steamship Company, Feb. 1924

---

[166] Preus writes: "When that (church building program) is done and I perhaps get a raise in salary from $100 – which I had since pre-war days – then I might get married. It would be folly now."
[167] "Nothing to lose" (German)

BERNICE LAMENTS THE COAL DUST.
"If you ever write to me that your house is dirty, I think I shall scream,..."

Wanhsien, Szechuan, China
February 14th, 1924

Letter No. 136
Dear Mother,

  We have received two of the three American mails received this year since I last wrote. On February 2nd your nos. 142 and 143 came and last Monday, the 11th we received a big bunch. We were at the supper table when the mailman came and I went out on the veranda to get the mail. The mailman is rather important and he very deliberately handed out the mail piece by piece. There were six letters from you folks – 144,-5,-6, two from Papa, and one from Elsa – and one from Olga. Well, I have not been so excited for a long time and I could hardly finish my supper. I just felt like dancing around and yelling! I enjoyed them all so much. I said I, but I am sure George enjoys them just as much as I, or at least almost, and he is always impatient to read them. He thought Papa's letters were just fine and ever so newsy and I think he will answer before long. He just wrote last week, though, so he may wait a while.

  Were you surprised when you read in George's letter that our cook is sick? I do not remember telling you, as I thought it best not to worry you. He contracted a cold in Shihnan about a year ago and has been coughing ever since. When the warm weather came and he still kept on coughing, I though it looked bad and said so to George. I hoped, however, that he would get over it this summer when he was home. But he was still coughing when he returned in the fall and I was glad when we came to Ichang and could send him to the hospital. George was present when he was examined and the Dr. said he had malaria and perhaps some bronchitis. He said that Da sifu did <u>not</u> have <u>consumption</u>,[168] so I thought he probably had chronic bronchitis and was in hopes that he would improve in time. He was in the hospital a week and claimed he felt better after that. But, either he did have consumption and climbing the many steps in the city here has brought it to light, or else his trouble has lately developed into that disease. The day after he arrived in Wanhsien (George was on his way down to Ichang) he spit blood for the first time. He seemed better then for a few days, but the day I arrived here he had spit blood again and George said it was just awful. If we had not been in such a predicament, we would have sent him off at once, but I had left a good amah in Ichang, thinking I could get along with Da sifu and Hsiao-deh's help until such a time as I could find someone here that I could train in. We wrote to Ichang and asked Theiss to find out if the amah could come and then I figured I could manage the cooking with Hsiao-deh's help until I could train him in as cook. But, the other morning we received a telegram from Heinie reading "Amah not available." Klein had written that they and Nagels did not need two cooks there and would send one up here, if we wanted them to. He said Nagels had rather planned on dismissing their cook later on anyway. We wrote them to send him here, if that was the case, and this evening, to our great surprise, he arrived. We do not need to feel particularly indebted to Nagels, however, as he had dismissed the cook before our letter arrived and it was only our good fortune that this fellow had not already

---
[168] tuberculosis

gone down river. Our cook is very weak and is anxious to go, so he will most likely be going down on a mailboat in a day or two. George will enquire tomorrow. This boy looks quite husky, so I hope he will be able to help considerably and leave Hsiao-deh free to help me more. Oh yes! I must not forget to tell you that our coolie, whom the soldiers had taken, has returned. We are so glad, because we could not get decent water while he was gone and we were really afraid to drink the stuff even after it had been boiled a long time. And there (are) so many things for him to do – carry away the dirty water and the ashes, sweep and wash verandas, floors, etc.

My! I certainly hope things will ease up a little now. I have <u>so many</u> things that ought to be done at once, but I have had to let everything go in order to keep ourselves and Betty Ann somewhat supplied with clean clothes. George's and my clothes are in terrible condition, especially George's, which need mending, cleaning, and pressing. Betty Ann is outgrowing all hers and I do not seem to be getting things made for her in a hurry. I have made one flannel gertrude and am at a nainsook one. I have cut out two dresses for her, but she will need three, four more. It is so terribly dirty around here that I just know you cannot even imagine how it is. We have a good sized stove in here and the coal is not so bad, as far as coal goes, but the place for ashes is so small that it fills up in just a little while and then we have to <u>shovel</u> the ashes out. There is no ash pan and we cannot have one made, because there is a rod right through the center of the space, and it would be impossible to put a pan in. Well, those ashes have to be taken out four to six times a day, if we have to keep a fair fire going, and you know what it means to shovel ashes out. Why, the room needs to be dusted after each time – but we think we are very smart if we manage to dust twice a day and most of the time we have to be content with once. Of course putting the coal on is dirty business too. Dirt! Dirt!! Dirt!!! If you ever write to me that your house is dirty, I think I shall scream, because I feel as though you don't know what dirt is!!! Your tales of housecleaning are enough to make me – laugh – or weep. Why, I suppose your house is cleaner just when you start housecleaning than mine is at any time. You need not think I am raving and exaggerating a lot, because I <u>ain't</u>! I have to change pillow slips twice a week here and <u>then</u> they are never clean, it seems. And George and I wash good with warm water every night and I usually brush my hair well. I have to change the cloth on the ironing board at least once a week, but there is so much smoke and soot flying around in the kitchen that it stays white only about one day. But, I have other things than dirt to write about, so shall desist.

I have been wanting to tell you how much I have appreciated the things you have sent for Betty Ann. I have told you how I like the wool comforter, but there are so many things that she has been using right along. The "Bya," of course, is just the thing and is in constant use. I am so thankful for that. The little golf cape has been worn so much and washed so often that it looks quite old already. The small pair of bootees have been worn a lot, but are too small now and are to be carefully put away for "Brother." The long bootees you sent are being worn every day and before very long they, too, will be getting small. I have some larger ones that I can use later on. The nightingale you sent has not been worn so much, as I had to save that for best – it was too pretty for every day – and now it is not safe to put it on her, because I am afraid it will split across the back! I can not think of closing it in front. She looked so sweet in that and you know she wore that the day she was baptized. The cap Elsa sent has been made good use of too. It is the only cap she has that is really becoming to Baby. And blue is so nice on her. I am so glad to have those Baby pins also. They will be coming in very handy now.

Did I tell you about the parcel that came about two weeks ago, containing gifts for Betty Ann from Olive's Mother? There were a white silk cap somewhat similar in style to the one from Elsa, a dress, and a pair of wool stockings. The cap is altogether too small, unfortunately. And the dress, which that dear old lady (She is over eighty, if I remember correctly) has evidently made herself, is small too, although Baby wore it one day. I did not button the top button. I think the stockings are large enough, but I have two pair in use and that seems to be all I need. I sent off a letter to Mrs. Gruen today – Olive will have to forward it for me, as I do not know the address.

Two weeks ago this coming Saturday the weather was so beautiful that George thought we ought to go out, so we went down to the Standard Oil place to call on Mr. Swift of that Co. and Mr. Jenkins, of Gillespie's, who lives with Mr. Swift. We went down river in a small boat and since the water is so low now, we had a long climb before we finally came to the house – it took us about twenty minutes to go up the many steps. When we stepped into that house we could have imagined we were back in the U.S. It is nicely built and furnished with lots of comfortable furniture, and they also have electric lights. We had a pleasant visit and also had tea with them. Mr. Jenkins is a rather young man and is the one who is to be married this fall. I met his fiancée at Cooper's last June. Mr. Swift lent me his sedan chair and carriers to come home and I enjoyed that ride ever so much. I should have said that the house is beautifully located and commands a very fine view of the river and the country across.

Last Sunday we were at Mr. Hawley's for tiffin[169] and tea. Mr. Hawley was in Ichang the first year we were there and we became acquainted with him then. He was at our place for New Year's tiffin, 1922. His wife and two children are in Florida, but it may be that his wife will come out next year. It would be nice if there were a few more women here.

I am so tired and sleepy now and George has announced that he is ready to retire, so I shall have to finish this tomorrow. That is getting to be the usual story with me, isn't it? Perhaps it is because I have been writing such long letters lately to make up for lack in number. Good Night!

Friday Afternoon, 4.00 o'clock – Have just been doing some featherstitching on Betty Ann's gertrude, but I will leave that till later and try to finish this letter now. I am working with yellow thread. What do you think of that for a little girl? I know that you like yellow. This might have been a lighter shade, but I had no choice, since I have only the one skein you sent me. I am afraid the blue is rather dark for Baby dresses, but I intend to try it out. Will you please be on the lookout for good dress patterns for me after this? I believe I will learn to sew enough to make all Baby's clothes, but I must have patterns, because I do not know enough about what patterns should look like to work without. I will be wanting to put her in rompers when she is eight, nine months, I think, and I have no pattern for that either. And I have not thought about coat for next winter, but I shouldn't wonder if I could make her something out of some old clothes here. I will have to go through all our trunks and boxes as soon as I can and then I will find out what we have.

---

[169] Luncheon (British)

We are still looking around for place for permanent residence. The other day we went way up the hill almost to the foot of the mountain and looked at a place. It appealed very much to me, because it is not such a huge place and it seems to be in pretty good condition. And there are ceilings in most of the rooms, which would save us some trouble when it comes to fixing up the place. This afternoon we looked at another place. I guess it "can do" when fixed up, if we should bargain for that. The Chinese are becoming aware of the fact that we are in no special hurry to close a deal, so there seem to be more places offered for rent. If they get the idea that we want a certain place and want it badly, they surely screw up the prices and are most unreasonable.

George has been telling me that I ought to write more often and less at the time. He just said I should put down a "punktum" and sign my name, send this and then keep on writing.

What do you think of the card cases I ordered for the "Vikings"? I wanted the pagoda on one side instead of the tree, but they must have misunderstood, but it does not make much difference. Will you please launder them and then fold them when you iron them? It hardly pays for me to launder them here when they have to travel so far through the mail. The extra case is for Mrs. Ylvisaker – I thought she might like one also. I have one and think it is so handy. I had to carry my cards in a part of an envelope, which was not so very nice. I have been wondering, though, if these are rather useless gifts for you folks? Do the "Vikings" all have visiting cards and do they go calling enough to make use of them? I have found that I needed cards out here. One day just before I left Ichang, Erna and I made six calls. But I really could not afford to send any bigger gifts, so I hope they will like these.

I wish you could see the bathtub a tinner made for us. It is something new in style!! The man seemed so confident that he knew what was wanted when George tried to explain that George thought he would be getting the right thing, but we had to laugh when it was delivered. The length is all right, but it is the same width all the way to the top and is high, so when we want to use our arms we are sure to knock our elbows into the sides. Here is the way it looks (drawing). We are having it fixed up so that we will have room enough to get a decent bath in it.

My, how I would enjoy spending a "regular" Christmas again. We have had such funny Christmases since we were married. Of course, we must not depend on the outward things for our happiness, but it would be nice to follow the old customs that I have been brought up in. I enjoy thinking back to the days when we children were little – My! It was hard to wait until the dishes were washed on Christmas Eve, and how we did wait for the signal to come up to the study. It never took us long to get up the steps after Papa had called…

You say Johannes weighed twenty-two pounds at five months. That certainly is an awful weight – he doubled his birth weight in five months then. Well, Betty Ann doubled her birth weight in four months, but of course Johannes had three more pounds to double. Well, our Baby is plenty heavy enough. She did not like to lie in her bed alone in the other room just now and was crying so hard that I finally took her in here and now she is sitting in a chair and looking at me. I do not like to have her sit too much, but she really sits very nicely when she is propped up with pillows and I do not think it will hurt her back. She seems to have a strong back. My, she is so lively when I bathe her that I often have all I can do to keep her on my lap. She is never so happy as when she is entirely naked and can kick away to her heart's content. Next best to being entirely undressed is having her diapers off. How she does wave her arms, kick, and jump. She certainly exercises. She is beginning to play with me now and is so cute. She puts her little hand up to my mouth and I pretend to eat it and then she pulls it away.

Last Sunday she was sleeping up on Mr. Hawley's bed while we were eating. We heard her about the time we were through, but then all was quiet. When I came up there she was sucking her fingers, had one eye closed and the other partly open. She must have thought it was a good joke on me, as she was so happy and she laughed the hardest she has ever done. The hair on top of her head is getting quite long now, but she hasn't much of any in back. Did you say I had lots of hair when I was born?

I washed my head yesterday morning and it is almost occasion for tears. So much comes out when I wash and I'll say enough comes out every day without having an excessive amount now and then. My hair is so thin I do not know how to put it up becomingly. I think I shall get my old switch out and see if the color is the same now. If I was not afraid that I might look pretty awful with bobbed hair, believe me, I would have George cut it off in a hurry. He is going to trim it for me right along now to see if that will help any.

I shall enjoy a good Wisconsin winter when we come home on furlough. I always enjoyed the winters. We have had very mild weather all this winter. They say that Wanhsien has a milder climate than Ichang, but it was mild in Ichang too this year. Still, it was colder there than it has been here. It is fairly cold in the mornings – around 40 degrees – but it warms up towards noon. Yesterday was about as cold as any day we have had since I came. As I have said before, I am glad we do not have colder weather in this country, because of our poor heating systems…

The lady that was taken by bandits in Honan was Mrs. Kilen. Mr. Hoff died from the wounds received and Mrs. Kilen spent three weeks with the bandits, enduring some horrible experiences. Do you keep any of the "Big Church" papers? There will probably be an account in one of them.

Well, I hate to see our old cook leave, in spite of his failings. He was a pretty faithful old fellow and I fear we won't like the new cook so well. We have already had a clash with him about a little money matter and George and I were all ready to send him off. We do not either of us care about having any fuss with servants – I would rather dig in and do all the work myself with Hsiao-deh's help. But, he finally "came across" and I hope that he understands that George is boss and not he. If he knows that, we ought not have any trouble.

I had intended to do some sewing tonight, but this business with the new Da sifu has taken up time and now it is time to feed Precious. (You see this has been written at intervals since 4.00 P.M.) Lots and lots of love to you all from the three of us,

Bernice

BERNICE DISCOVERS SOMETHING ABOUT BABIES.
"...she seldom cries for temper. She usually has cause to cry."

Letter No. 138

Wanhsien, Szechuan
February 27, 1924

Dear Mama,

Since George is writing to Papa, I'll write a little to you. I'm way behind on my letters to you, I guess. I counted up for 1923, though, and I find I wrote 48 letters and George 8, making 56 from us. You alone wrote 53 to us. Well, I hope I will be able to do better, if we ever get properly settled. You know it is much easier to write if one writes often. At least, I find it so, because then you can follow the daily events more closely.

First I will answer some questions in your last letters. You ask about a birthday gift for Esther. We cannot buy any embroidery here and since it will be too late after we come to Kuling, I have decided to ask Olive to help. I am sure she will be glad to and she has good taste…

Then, you ask about distances.

Hankow – 595 miles (via Yangtze River) from Shanghai
      About four days steamer trip   "   "   (up stream – less going down)
Ichang – 1000 miles from Shanghai – 3 or 4 days trip from Hankow   "

Kweifu[170] – 1110 " " "   - 1 day from Ichang (high water)
                            - 2 " " "   (low ")
Wanhsien – 1175 "   "   "   - 2 " " "   high "
                            - 3 " " "   low "

Shihnan – Approx. 300 mi. from Ichang – It is an 8-10 day trip overland; or, 1 day steamer + 4 days overland.

Kuling, rather Kiukiang, the port, is a twelve hour steamer trip – going down – from Hankow. From the river to the mountain is a half day's trip. I don't know the distance in miles and the "Survey" doesn't give it. No, Wanhsien isn't far from Kweifu. To be exact, we are just 67 miles from there, making these two stations closer than any of the others.

A day or two ago we received a letter from Nagel (Kweifu) with rather disturbing news. Herman has been very sick. He has always had a weak stomach and often suffered from more or less severe attacks of indigestion. About two weeks ago he had an attack, but it didn't pass over as usual. He had very severe pains and they feared appendicitis. It happens there is a Dr. Masoni in Kweifu – a Norwegian subject, but a Finn by birth. He came out under some Mission Soc'y years ago, but has been independent for a long time now. He received his medical education at Hamline, Minn., but he has given up allopathy in favor of hydrotherapy. He is a <u>very peculiar</u> old man and is regarded quite a crank by most people who know him. However, he has been with our missionaries in Kweifu more or less and he cured Nagel's "boy" of pneumonia with his water cure. So, when Herman was so sick they called Dr. Masoni. He couldn't diagnose the case at once, but began applying hot fomentations, which finally gave relief. And after a day or so the Dr. said Herman had suffered with a severe attack of peritonitis.

---

[170] Also called "Kweichowfu;" now has a completely different name- Fengjie

And Nagel thinks Masoni and his water cure are just all right…I am so glad Nagels and Masoni were there. Edna is no good in the sick room and I guess she has been quite upset – and no wonder. But, Edna is "growing up" quickly and she has learned more than I'd have believed possible in the last year…

How I wish you could enjoy Betty Ann with us! George and I certainly have many good laughs over her. She is so funny – and so cute and dear. Sometimes when we come to pick her up after she has been crying, she grunts in such a funny, satisfied way, just as if to say, "Now then! I got what I wanted anyway!" And when she kicks and plays on my lap, she often goes at it in such a business-like way. The <u>funniest</u> thing is when she gets a lively streak while sitting on the chamber (pot). Imagine her kicking and having a good time then! It makes me laugh just to think of it. She is learning to take hold of things now and once in a while she tries to grab my watch. She often holds on to my arm when I'm fussing with her. Yesterday morning & the day before she was so lively in the bathtub that she fairly showered us with water. She is a tough little youngster and has had her bath when the thermometer registered below 60°. I suppose it was warmer by the stove, although our small stove doesn't throw so much heat. I don't like such a cold room, but it couldn't be helped and if I waited with her bath, I'd have to change on her in the morning anyway and that is almost as bad as giving her a bath. Well, Betty Ann didn't seem to mind at all. I had hard work trying to keep her covered a little more than usual. Her only trouble seems to be gas, air, or whatever you call it, on her tummy. So often she cries and we have to pick her up and pat her back until she belches – then she is perfectly happy again. I used to think it was a temper cry, but have discovered that she seldom cries for temper. She usually has cause to cry. Oh, she gets tired and crabby, of course, but that is different. If only she would get over her desire to suck her fingers! I still wrap them.

2/28 – Had intended to write more but George wants to mail his letter, so I'll just enclose this, and try to continue tonight if possible. Lots of Love to you all from us three,

Bernice

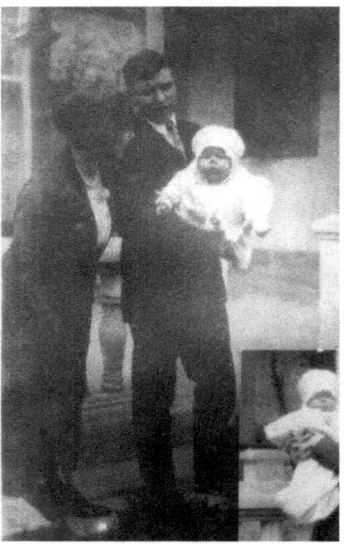

(photo taken at Mr.Hawley's)

GEORGE DESCRIBES THEIR NEW HOME IN WANHSIEN.
"…is located upon the hill above the city, at the foot of the Precipice of Peace,…"

Wanshien, Szechwan, February 27th, 1924

Dear Dad:

I will have to start addressing you by that term, since it is what I usually hear Bernice call you, - or perhaps it should be "grandpa" now?!

Thank you so much for your Christmas and New Year's letters received some time ago. Both the political and the church news were of the highest interest to me. I had heard nothing about developments in the South Africa field, so that what you wrote about the situation there was news to me, although it was only what I had expected. Too bad that Astrup was not smart enough to see how things were when he was in America, so that he could have made definite arrangements in person with the Missouri Synod at that time. But then Faye is in the States now, which will help somewhat. I should think that it would be a good idea to ask the Synodical Conference to undertake the support of the South Africa mission, or perhaps even only the Wisconsin Synod. The Wisconsin Synod has no mission work whatever in foreign countries, and it would be a good thing for it if some work were forced upon it. Faye could do something to stimulate interest in the work by lecturing on South Africa and the Missions. It is too bad that the Norwegian Synod is not strong enough to support the Schreuder Mission. Is it not strange that so many of our good Synod people can stand for the things that they do stand for in that new Church Body? Are there no indications whatever that they are going to protest effectively against the looseness in that church, and withdraw if their protests pass unheeded? Ten years ago, nobody could ever have made me believe that men like Brandt, Hove, and hundreds of others in the former Synod could stand to work in a church body that was so liberal as this Union is. It seems to me that the United Body is going farther along the path of Unionism and Liberalism than even the former U.C. ever did. And our Minority people were going to be a salt in the Union! Verily the salt has lost its savor!

I was glad to hear that our Synod Mission Committee was getting busy and that it would come with definite recommendations to the next Synod Meeting with regard to Foreign Mission work. It has always been my hope that the Norw. Synod would support my work, in part to begin with, and eventually, entirely. $3000.00 gold would be enough to cover all expenses at this station per year, including my salary, although not the purchase of land and building. Is it too much to expect that the Norwegian Synod should be able to raise that much for the China Mission? Although our membership is small, $3000.00 would not mean any large amount per capita. If the will were there, it could surely be done. I fear that some of our pastors are not very much interested in heathen Missions. It seems to be the case that those who are zealous for the preservation of the true doctrine are likely to be less zealous for its propagation throughout the world and to confine themselves to the work in their immediate neighborhood with those who already are Christians. I suppose that is because it is hard for mortal men to be zealous for the carrying out of every part of such an all-inclusive command as: Go ye forth into <u>all</u> the world, teaching them to observe <u>all</u> things. If one part is carried out, the other is likely to be neglected. The Reformed Churches emphasize the first part, the Missouri Synod and other conservative Lutherans have emphasized the latter part. Only in exceptional cases do men seem to have a real interest in the work of carrying out both parts of the command. But I wish that the Norwegian Synod as a whole could show itself such an exception!

I have been thinking of addressing a statement with regard to my new field of work to the next Synod Meeting. Do you think that would be in order and that it would be welcomed by our people? Now that I am in a station that I can look upon as my particular field of work, and that I can ask the Norw. Synod to look upon as its particular Foreign Mission field, I should like to get the Synod started at really doing something towards my support. I fear there is a tendency in our circles to rely upon the "big, strong Missouri Synod" to support us more than really necessary. I do not know what the statistics of our Church are at present, but I should judge that we have a membership large enough to do not so little work if only our people would give as generously as they ought to our various activities. Sometimes, I wonder if some of our lay-people have not joined us to get away from the effective financial organization of the Union Church, which seems to be able to squeeze the money out of the people whether they want to give or not! I may be doing them an injustice, but, "det er cheapare"[171] to belong to the Norwegian Synod, may have helped more than one to stay with us.

As for the Missouri Synod, it seems that they are just beginning to expect their people to give liberally to church purposes. Hitherto contributions especially to outside purposes have been very small on the average in that Synod. Whether because the Germans are "tight," or because the pastors have not emphasized the duty of giving, I do not know. The Norwegians have shown themselves more liberal anyway.

As for Politics, it would be interesting now to have some Journal that would give me a digest of the events of interest in American politics. My daily paper is a British concern and does not give much American news. I have been reading some telegrams about the Oil-land-lease scandal – which seems to be a "first-class scandal" – and I am wondering how it will affect the political situation. Coolidge is bucking the Senate in a way that, I should think, would prove dangerous to his chances for re-election next fall. I hope they get the mess properly straightened out anyway.

As for news here – Bernice has written about everything except the house we finally have secured. This is not the place Bernice mentioned in one of her last letters, but a larger place, which I have had "on the string" ever since I came. The owner finally came down to my figure - $200.00 rent per year – besides a deposit of $500.00, which is to be repaid when I vacate the house. I have drawn a rough sketch of the place on this sheet. It may seem like quite a palace to you, but Bernice suggests calling it "The Barns," which describes it more accurately than palace would.[172] The grounds are fine, however, or rather have fine possibilities, as we have plenty of room within the walls of the "compound" or yard, for gardens. There are also a number of trees, fruit trees, flowering trees, bamboo groves, some big rocks, etc., so that after a while we expect to have a pretty nice place. The buildings are very old and poor – mud walls, tiled roofs, mud floors, dark and dirty. Some of them are really only sheds. But there are some rooms, which I have indicated on the plan, that can be fixed up so as to make comfortable living quarters. At any rate we will be away from the dirt and smells of the city, as this place is located upon the hill above the city, at the foot of the Precipice of Peace, and

---

[171] "it is cheaper" (Norwegian)
[172] George writes in his station report: "There are almost forty rooms, grouped about five courtyards,…"

almost in the country. There are few buildings farther out than this place, but we have not far to go to get to the street. We have a number of orange trees on the place too, so that now I hope Bernice will be getting all the oranges she can eat without bankrupting me as she has tried to do this season! I intend to get this place all fixed up before we move. Right now there are soldiers in the place, and we will have to get them out before I can get workmen started. They came in, too, after I had rented the place, and I have had to go to some trouble to get word to the commanding officer and ask them to order these soldiers out again. In the meantime they are mussing up the place something fierce. A house that the soldiers have occupied for some time is lucky if it has at least the shell left standing when the soldiers go. Sometimes they leave nothing but the mud walls! They burn everything that can be used for fuel, as they are too lazy to go out and cut fuel in the mountains.

I have not succeeded in finding a place for chapel yet, but I hope to secure a place soon. In the meantime I have a chance to do a little work in this place here. The owner asked me to preach to his office force – ten or fifteen men – making use of his guesthall for that purpose. I started this evening. Two of the young men are members of the China Inland Mission in the city – the rest are heathens. It will be a start anyway. Perhaps some of these men will become interested enough to continue coming for regular instruction when we start meetings in our own chapel.

I enclose a copy of our Mission Rules and Regulations, collected and collated from our Conference minutes and the Board's Letters. Your Committee might find this handy. It will give you a clearer idea of what our organization is like than all the scattered minutes and letters would do. I made 31 copies with my Hektograph outfit, one for each missionary, several for the Board, and a few are on hand for future use.

How do our accounts stand now? I imagine we will need to send you some money again soon. As soon as we hear from you, we shall remit. Kindly send me copies of all bills that you pay, if the original bill is not available. This applies particularly to the Book bills at the Synod Book Co.

Bernice is writing to mother this evening, and she no doubt is telling all about our Betty Ann, so that I have no excuse for raving about her. Suffice it to say that she is getting brighter every day – understands me when I talk to her, and answers in Chinese, German, English, Norwegian, Greek, Latin, Hebrew, French, Swedish, Danish, Pigeon English, or Old English, as the case may be. Bernice does not understand her as well as I do because she does not know as many languages as Betty and I do.

Shucks! George doesn't understand any Winnebago!

With love to you all from us three,
George

Unnamed city gate

HOUSE HUNTING TAKES A DRAMATIC TURN.
"It was rather an interesting little affair – just like a scene from some movie, or a chapter from a dime novel."

China
Wanhsien, Szechuan
February 29, 1924

Letter No. 39

Dear Mama,

    I was too tired to write last night and I am pretty tired this evening also, but I will at least start a letter. The reason I'm sort of tuckered out now is that our precious baby has had a little spell of stomach trouble. We cannot imagine what caused it. Wednesday evening she was restless and seemed to have a good deal of "ch'i" (chee) – the Chinese for air, gas, etc. – on her tummy. I gave her a little peppermint water finally and she settled down until eleven o'clock, when I fed her. After we got to bed we noticed she seemed to be spitting every now and then and we both looked at her. Her pillow, or rather the cloth over it, was all wet. What she got up seemed to be watery. I changed the cloth and we went back to bed. But she was so restless – I could hear her turn her head from side to side and she kept making noises with her mouth and spitting. Several times I jumped out of bed so fast that – well, at eleven o'clock I heard her vomit and I jumped up so quickly that I felt fairly sick. That time she vomited milk all over so I had to change both her nightie and her shirt. Altho' it was four hours after her feed, the milk seemed practically unchanged. It certainly was neither curdled nor sour. She settled down some after four o'clock – she had not cried a bit all this time, just seemed glad to be put back in her bed after each time I had picked her up. She seemed hungry at six in the morning and I tho't I could feed her a little. And after getting a feed both she and I slept soundly until eight o'clock. Then when I got up and went to her bed, she had just awakened. I can't remember why I was going to pick her up – guess she must have been restless and I was going to pat her back. Anyway, I just turned the covers back and – oh! how she vomited. It came out in a regular stream, without any apparent effort on her part. She didn't cry, only protested a little when her stomach seemed to be churning a bit and there was nothing left to come up. I went and ate a bite and George took care of her and then he ate his breakfast, while I prepared to give her a bath. She didn't have any fever, so we decided we should have her bath, and altho' more quiet than usual, she brightened up and enjoyed it. I gave her only water after that and then put her in her bed, nice & fresh with clean sheets. She slept good for a couple hours then. I didn't feed her anything but water until 1:30 P.M. and at that time I gave her a little. After that she had a stool of almost undigested milk and the odor was so peculiar. We had given her "Castoria" in the morning. She was better in the afternoon and she retained all she had eaten, but I didn't feed her again until six o'clock. Since I made her wait so long, I didn't think it quite fair to make her lie in her bed all the time and I walked with her, entertained her, etc. from a little after 4:00 until six. She woke up about 10:30 P.M. and I fed her a little, but she vomited some watery stuff then. I think perhaps she stretched too much for her sensitive stomach – she was stretching so while I changed on her.

    Mon. March 3rd – It is taking me much longer to get this letter finished than I thought it would. But last night, when I had intended to write, George felt like "bumming" so we spent an hour playing games with the "Rook" cards and then we went to bed early for a change. Betty Ann has been pretty well these days, but she had tummy ache Friday night and I think she has been rather cross. She hasn't been quite so active either, but she was quite lively this noon and her stools are getting more normal…Well, I cannot imagine why she should get sick. I hadn't eaten anything that I haven't eaten before and I was feeling as usual. And I cannot understand why she always has so much "ch'i" on her tummy and why it should bother her so. She nurses quite nicely now. George is inclined to think she is a little over-fed and I've been considering a longer interval between feeds. Trouble is, she always gets so impatient, especially in the afternoons. In the mornings she doesn't mind. Yesterday morning she was fed between 3:00 – 4:00 A.M. She didn't wake up until 7:00 A.M. and then I was too sleepy to realize she should be fed. She didn't fuss much, so we slept until almost eight o'clock. Then it dawned on me she should have been fed. So I dressed quickly and gave her a bath before we had our breakfast. Now Betty is sitting propped up with pillows in a chair beside me. I have fastened her Bunny rattle to her "gloves" and she is trying to stick the whole thing in her mouth. She is feeling all right again and is happy as usual. I just changed on her (naughty girl! she wet her diaper while I was unpinning it. I'll be glad when she can wear bloomers that can be slipped down in a hurry.) and I said to her, "You're a little 'mitchuf'!" Either the sound of the words pleased her or something else tickled her, because she laughed so heartily. We weighed her this morning, but for the first time she has failed to gain anything. But so much for Betty Ann this time.

Must tell you we are very well pleased with our new cook. Either the talk George gave him when he came did him good, or else he was out of humor because of being dismissed by Nagel and showed his worst side. Anyway he has prepared very satisfactory meals for us and has been very pleasant so far. In some respects I think he is a better cook than our old Da sifu – he bakes better, it seems. He has made some good sunshine cakes…The cook made ginger snaps the other day and they taste very much like yours, although I didn't give him your recipe. And he made some good white cookies too. The old cook never made rolled cookies, only the soft drop cookies. This cook has made fairly good bread but he hasn't made buns yet. George and I eat very little bread – guess it must be because it isn't as light as it might be and also because we have no jam or jelly whatsoever. I'm starved for some of your good jam, Mama!...You know it is a nuisance to go to Kuling and I surely would not care much about going if it weren't so terribly damp and hot. I don't look forward to going to Kuling at all this summer, but they tell us Wanshien is unbearable…

Saturday Mr. Swift and Mr. Jenkins were here for "tiffin." We had invited them for last Sunday noon (week ago yesterday) but they themselves were entertaining that day, so George said they should come when it suited them best and they chose Saturday.

Must tell you a little incident in connection with our house hunting and renting. You remember I spoke of a place which appealed quite a bit to me – the small place. It is owned by a Mr. Tsen. The place we have rented is the "T'an Chia" (gia) or the T'an Home. T'an is the family name – pronounce it like the Norwegian for tooth. Some weeks ago the Tan people asked such an outrageous price that we simply didn't care to negotiate at all and George made enquiries about Mr. Tsen's place. Evidently he was anxious to rent and Mr. Dzang, who has been acting as teacher for Geo. and was middleman in this case, was also anxious to see the deal closed. I suppose the latter expected a generous commission. So, although George had not said he definitely wanted the place, Mr. Dzang drew up a lease and was trying to hurry the deal through. When George finally rented the other place, Mr. Tsen was very disappointed and I suppose, put out. The same afternoon that George decided in favor of the "Tan Chia," Mr. Dzang came two, three times – Mr. Tsen would be willing to consider a lower price, Mr. Tsen would repair this and that, and so on. When they realized George really had made up his mind, Mr. Dzang came in quite late in the evening and said he'd heard a member of the Tan family, who would have some say in the matter, was not in the city, that he was a "black sheep" and would cause trouble. And the following morning George found a letter on his desk <u>purporting</u> to come from the Tan clan and saying that if this deal went through there would be murder done. We enquired how the letter came and found that a little boy had brought it to the gatekeeper downstairs and he in turn gave it to our coolie's son, who put it on George's desk. Of course, we felt sure at once it was from Mr. Tsen and were not alarmed. It was rather laughable instead. George showed it to Mr. Dzang, who seemed to suspect Mr. Tsen, also, and tho't it was going pretty far. George dealt with two of the Tan gentlemen and they claim there is no one else who would have a say, nor is there any "black sheep" wandering about, as George understands. It was rather an interesting little affair – just like a scene from some movie, or a chapter from a dime novel!

One day last week George and I went up to our future home and on the way we saw a woman combing a little pig with a fine comb! We saw that she captured one "udyr"[173] while we were passing.

Speaking of combs – I wouldn't have needed a comb & brush set so badly – for Baby, that is – but, you see, I haven't even a fine comb. When she was only a few weeks old she had so much crust on her head and I had to borrow a fine comb from Edna to get that off. I put vaseline on in the evening and then it came off so nicely. The ivory comb is much better for getting a little dandruff out, tho', than a fine comb. And brushing is good for their scalps. Betty Ann's hair is getting so nice in front, but she is still pretty bald on the back of her head. Her hair is about the color of mine, which probably means it will be quite dark later on.

I'm wondering how our account is…I need a new corset and I don't know what size to order. I always wore a #21, but that doesn't fit me now and I'm wondering if I will ever be as small around the waist as I was. I had to wear my maternity corset until a few weeks ago - Betty Ann was four months – and my old one isn't comfortable yet. So I guess I'll ask for at least a #22…

Your #149 and a letter from Ella E. came Saturday…Today is Tante Emma's birthday. Some ten-odd years ago you'd call up #34 in the A.M. and I s'pose it sounded like this. "Hello, Hans? This is Ole. Gratulerer.[174] O.S.V.[175] "Them" were the days! Time to close.

Lots of love to you all from
George, Betty Ann, & Bernice

---

[173] "beast" (Norwegian)
[174] Congratulations. (Norwegian)
[175] Etc. (Norwegian)

BERNICE & BETTY RIDE IN A SEDAN CHAIR.
"There are no rickshaws in Wanhsien, since there are so many steps,…"

Wanhsien, Szechuan, China
March 28th, 1924

Letter 142
Dear Mama,

  Am rather late with my weekly again, but I have been sort of waiting for American mail. Last night we finally received some, among the letters being yours to Betty Ann and #153. No. 152 has not come yet. I thought it might arrive today, but it must have been put in another mail sack and I suppose it will most likely come with the next boat. I hope so. I have been waiting for mail rather impatiently this time. It seemed so long, somehow.

  We have been having such warm weather lately. It has been quite a bit like it was last March, only it has not been hot as it was then. It has been getting ready for rain and today it did rain. It rained last Saturday and Sunday also. That is the first real rain we have had since I came and it was badly needed. They say it has been so dry that the bean crop is not much good and that is a very important crop in this country. So many varieties of beans are raised in China and they are used in so many ways. I like rain – when there is not too much of it – but it is rather bad if it rains just when I am out of clothes for Betty Ann and things will not get dry. I thought I was going to be out of luck last Monday, since it was raining in the morning, but it cleared up before dinner and we had fine drying weather.

  George and I are anxiously awaiting the day when we can move up to "The Barns." I think I will have to find a new name for the place in spite of the big, empty, barnlike buildings there will be. Our section of the house looks rather promising and I am quite sure our compound is not going to look like a barnyard at any rate. And how nice it will be to get up there where we will have pure, fresh air. Now the fields are full of yellow flowers that look very much like wild mustard, except that the plants are much taller. And when we get up near our place the air is just sweet with the perfume from these flowers. When we get settled up there we will undoubtedly find that there are disadvantages and things are not quite as ideal as we are inclined to picture them now, but I hope we won't have too great disappointments…

Sunday P.M. – Got at this letter rather late Friday evening and last night I was so sleepy that I did not think I would be able to write a decent letter. And here it is Sunday already. The time goes by so quickly.

  Betty Ann and I just had a ride in our new "giao dze," or sedan chair. There are no rickshaws in Wanhsien, since there are so many steps, and people use sedan chairs. I do not think we will have to pay for the chair ourselves. George says the Mission has to pay that. In Hankow the Mission pays for the missionaries' rickshaws and half the rickshaw coolie's wages, so it is reasonable to expect them to pay for our chair. A rickshaw costs about $150.00, while our chair cost only $15.00. Our Hsü sifu (Shy – if you pronounce the 'y' as you do when saying the Norwegian alphabet), who has been our water carrier and man-of-all-work and will be our gardener, is also a good chair bearer. The gatekeeper can carry, too, so that takes care of two bearers. We intend to try to make arrangements with a couple men in the neighborhood so that we can call them whenever we want to use four bearers. Today two of the coolies, who are working up at the house, carried. We just made a trip up to the house and back. Betty Ann enjoyed the ride very much. On the way up she was all attention and looked around at everything, but on the way home she was too tired and fell asleep. She is still sleeping…

She is such a mischief! She reaches out for everything now – I can hardly powder her in the morning after her bath – she wants the powder can! She plays with her toes sometimes when I dress her and she liked the rose colored Chinese slippers she wore today so much. Everything goes to her mouth, of course. Seems to me she is awfully bad in that respect for such a young baby. Is it an indication that she is beginning to teethe?

George bought a cute little wicker chair for her the other day. It is Chinese style – has a little "table" in front, also two little posts with a little rod between on which are a few rings of bamboo that can easily be twirled around. The chair is very small and is just right for her now. I am so glad we have it, because Betty Ann refuses to lie in her bed when awake during the day and it is unsatisfactory to prop her up with pillows in a big chair. In this little chair her feet hang down and she cannot slide around. I fasten her little bunny rattle, her rubber dolly from you, and a jade (glass, in reality) bracelet, to the posts so they will not drop to the floor. She likes them pretty well, but she prefers her fingers. This last week I have not kept her hands wrapped during the day, except sometimes when I put her to bed for a nap, because I want her to learn to use her hands. I wrap them at night, however. But the way she goes for her fingers is a fright and I do not know what to do about it. I have tried slapping her hands and if she is tired or feeling out of sorts, she cries hard, but if she is feeling good, she just smiles and thinks it is fun. Have I told you that I broke her of night feeding at five months? It is over four weeks now since she had a night feed. It was not very hard to break her. She woke up for a number of nights and a few times when she fussed too much I let her get at her fingers. I figured that it couldn't do much harm, since she already had the habit so bad, and I knew it would not be long before her stomach got used to being without that feed and she would not wake up. Frequently she wakes up in the morning about six o'clock and does not even call me. Several times she has wakened me with her kicking and making some little noise and I have found her with all the bed clothes off. It is only lately that she has been doing that and I guess it has been too warm for her. She is such a warm little thing – I am afraid the hot weather will be hard on her. I hope the gift from Grandpa comes through quickly. I am sure Betty Ann will be delighted with the "La-la-by swing," as Monkey-Ward calls them. I imagine she will swing some when she gets used to it, as she is so active.

I am sure you are wondering if Betty Ann has shown a liking for music. She is not interested in piano music as yet, but she loves to have us sing – has liked it ever (since) she was a tiny baby. Usually she opens her mouth wide in a big smile when we sing to her…Betty Ann also enjoys whistling. I suppose she will like piano music better when she grows older.

Seems to me there were some other things I wanted to write about, but I neglected to jot them down. I do not think there was anything of importance. Anyway, I must close this now, because I want to write one or two other letters this evening. Oh, yes! I was going to tell you that my hair is not falling now – not worth mentioning. I certainly am glad that I did not get entirely bald! I have the least I have ever had, though. Betty Ann's hair is growing so nicely and it is about the color of mine.

I will try my best to write again in a few days. I hope your 152 will come and one from Elsa, as it seems she must have written, also. At least, I have had no letter from her telling about her salary, etc. to date.

Give my regards to the Borges, Ylvisakers, Grandma Rasmussen, the Anderson girls, etc. etc. Mrs. Swerig, etc. You had better pin a sign to you – "Greetings from Bernice"!!!

Lots of love to all you folks from George, Betty Ann, and Bernice

Bernice and Betty Ann in chair on way to T'an Chia – new place

Bernice & Betty at main entrance to T'an place

POTTY TRAINING IS WAY AHEAD OF ITS TIME.
"She will be six months old…I just tie her in this little chair, go about my duties, and pick her up when she has 'performed'."

Wanhsien, Szechuan, China
April 6th, 1924

Letter No. 143
Dear Mama,

    In my last letter I said I would try hard to write within a few days and that was written a week ago. Time flies so that it seems I am writing my weekly oftener than every week rather than less. I felt so terribly pepless for a few weeks that I could not seem to accomplish anything, but I have been feeling better the last days. I have been waiting so for a boat, because I expect your #152, but the water has been so low again that no boats have come up and several steamers that got to Chungking have had to remain there up to the present time. We have had some good rains the last week, however, and the water is rising, so there should be boats any time now. But we did receive the package containing the little iron, the rubber ball and valentine and Betty Ann says "Mange tak"[176] for everything except the candy, which George and I ate and appreciated very much. And the little iron will be very handy. Just now the few dresses Betty Ann has have butterfly sleeves, but I want some with set-in sleeves and yokes as soon as I get some sort of pattern, and then a small iron is so useful. Her long dresses had set-in sleeves, but they are put away now…

    We have had some very mild weather the last weeks, except for those days that it rained. Last week we had quite a bit of rain. It is so nice not to have to keep the stove going all day. Hsiao-deh builds fire in the morning so it will be comfortable for Betty Ann's bath, but after that we let it go out. We have packed away much of our winter clothing, etc. and I have changed underwear, but have not been wearing my light dresses or shoes yet. I enjoy wearing summer clothes but it means a lot of washing and ironing and I am wondering if Hsiao-deh will be able to iron my dresses. He has been doing the ordinary ironing <u>fairly</u> well, although I often think of you when the ironing comes in and wonder what you would say, if you saw it. Perhaps it will be easier to help out with that part of the work when we have moved up to the other place. I expect the kitchen to be cleaner and then our rooms are connected, so I will not have to take a walk every time I want to go to the kitchen. And now I can have Betty Ann sitting near me in her little chair, which is a great advantage.

    Yesterday afternoon we went up to "The Barns," Betty Ann and I riding in the "giao tze" and this afternoon we walked up, carrying Baby with us. It is so pleasant up there, even if the workmen are busy and things are still just in the process of getting fixed up. There is a bush of bridal wreath blossoming just outside our bedroom – wish we were living there already. By the time we have moved, I fear it will be through blossoming.

    We took some pictures of Betty Ann yesterday, some of them in the room. If the negatives are good, we should have some of her smiles, as she had a very fine expression on several. I hope the weather will be nice Tuesday. She will be six months old – just

---
[176] "Many thanks" (Norwegian)

think of it! – and we are anxious to get some snaps of her in her birthday dress. She has such a beautiful body – hardly any flabby fat, except on the "hams," perhaps, and not a large tummy.

George had invited Mr. Fuller of the Customs over for supper Thursday evening, also a Mr. Neuman, a German who is going to bring our groceries from Ichang, if they have not already been forwarded. Mr. Neuman came in about six o'clock and asked to be excused since the junk, on which he was going down to Ichang, would be leaving that night and he had to make preparations. He went down with a load of wood oil. We waited until half past seven for Mr. Fuller, but he did not appear, neither did he send an excuse, so we asked Mr. Chang, one of George's teachers, if he would like to eat with us. We had intended to have him for a meal sometime and it was nice to be able to invite him when everything was prepared. He lives here while working for George, so that is how we could invite him at the last minute. I was pretty much put out to think Mr. Fuller should play a trick like that – he sent an excuse late the next afternoon. Fine time to excuse himself!! George thinks some of these bachelors are afraid of coming here, since it is so long since they have seen women, but I say that is no excuse for forgetting his manners and it will be a <u>long</u> time before he gets another invitation. We invited him once before, but that time we sent the invitation the same day and he had made other arrangements, so we were too late.

I meant to tell you something funny in my last letter, but forgot to do so. First I must tell you that the Chinese have a great variety of haircuts, that is, the children. Some shave off all except the scalp lock, while others shave off only the scalp lock; some shave all except a little strip in front, and others have little patches of hair here and there. Well, one day Wen-tien, our coolie's son who does odd jobs, etc. for us, had had a haircut, but I saw a little hair sticking out over the ears and so I told George to have him take his cap off. The lower half of his head was shaved and he explained to us that the barber wanted 200 cash (about seven, eight cents Mex.) to shave his whole head and Wen-tien did not have more than 100 cash. He tried to persuade the barber to do it for that, but the latter was very hard-hearted (!) and refused, so Wen-tien said he should shave half his head and he would give him 100 cash, half price. Although the haircut in itself was nothing particularly strange to our eyes, we had to laugh when he told us about it.

Betty Ann had grass-green stools all last week, too, and Friday I decided to try castor oil again. I gave her a good dose and it seems to have helped some. She had only two stools yesterday and they looked much better, though still rather dark. She must have teeth coming, because she acts that way and we think her lower gums look as though there were a couple coming. Although she seemed well all the time, she did take a lot of my time those days. I could never catch her stools in the chamber and so I had to wash her several times a day. One morning I had not even finished making my bed when I had to take her and undress her entirely, as her vest, or band, was soiled. So the whole morning was gone without my having accomplished anything. I have kept a wool stomach band on her the last week in the hopes that it would help and also to prevent any chance of her catching cold. We have another chair for her now – not one for her to sit and play in, though. I had to sit and hold her over – rather, help her keep her balance on – the chamber so long sometimes and so many times during the day that it took a great deal of my time. Now I just tie her in this little chair, go about my duties, and pick her up when she has "performed." It certainly is a time saver and I hope it will help to make her more regular in her habits. She looks so cute when sitting in either of her chairs, Mama! Well, she is a little darling and grows cuter and dearer day by day. She grabs for everything – George used to think she was not of a very acquisitive nature, but he has changed his mind since he sees how she grabs his book when she sits on his lap. This morning she was trying to help him play the piano. While George was playing, she also put her whole hand on the keys and she seemed to think it great fun.

You say you did not use powder on me. Didn't you have it for any of your babies? How did you keep them from getting chafed? I have used more powder than would probably have been necessary, but even so I have a hard time keeping her from getting chafed where she has fat wrinkles, like around the wrist, and under her arms, etc…

Yesterday I – or Betty Ann – received a crib cover and pillow slip from Alice. It is pink and has bunnies worked on them. I am glad to have something to protect her quilts and blankets, but I think I will save it for awhile. I am sure Betty Ann will enjoy the bunnies when she gets a little older. She likes the yellow flower on my apron (from Louise) so well. I think the cover will be plenty large for the bed we intend having made for her. (Some day we are going to have a bed made for ourselves. When we put a regular bed in our bedroom, I think I shall celebrate!)

You ask if there are pretty curtains in China. I really don't know, Mom. I suppose they can be had, if one pays the price. All the windows I have seen in this country are the kind that open in like doors, so most of our girls have some net, scrim, or something like that, fastened to the windows by rods at top and bottom and then they have some sort of drapes. I have seen some drapes of silk…I did not have any except in the dining room and some short ones in the living room in Shihnan. We will not have much glass here either…

The servants told us that two boats came up today, so I look forward to receiving some mail tomorrow. I shall be very disappointed if there is not some.

Greetings to all and lots of love to all of you from us three.

Your daughter, Bernice

Bernice & Betty in front of dining room, T'an home

THEIR COMPOUND IS UNDER CONSTRUCTION.
"We are putting in floors,…"

Wanhsien, Szechwan, April 9th, 1924

Dear sister Louise:

Your letter of March 2nd was received a couple days ago. Thank you! We always wait and look so for home mail. We were glad to hear that you and your little ones were well, and that the Tjernagels all apparently are prospering. We received an interesting letter from Nehemias too the other day. I shall answer it soon, you may tell him…

Most of my time lately has been taken up with translation work. I have revised or re-translated Luther's Catechism, a Doctrinal Tract by Pieper, a short "Forklaring"[177] by Rev. Hanser, besides written some articles for our Chinese monthly "Lutheran Witness." Then I have had meetings three or four times a week for the Chinese in the neighborhood of our temporary residence. The owner of this place offered us the use of a guestroom for meetings. It is not the most suitable place, but will do as a temporary place. I have not been able to find a place for chapel yet, as it is hard to get suitable buildings at this time of the year without paying a higher rent than I care to pay. I shall fix up a place for chapel in the group of buildings we have rented for residence too, so that we can get along for the time being without a street chapel. I do not expect that many people will come to these temporary chapels, but it is better than doing nothing anyway.

We hope to be able to move into our new residence in a couple weeks. At least I should like to celebrate my birthday there. We think we are going to like the place real well. The buildings are old and poor, but a coat of whitewash and a coat of paint will make them look quite respectable. We are putting in floors, of course. But what pleases us about this place is the garden, the trees, and fresh air, that we will be able to enjoy. There are lots of bamboos, a number of fruit trees, some big pines and other large trees, and some big rocks, so that it will be very easy to make it look like a regular park. When we get settled, we shall take some pictures of the place, so that you can judge for yourself. The scenery in this country is very fine, too. Mountains, the Yangtze, and the city, the fields all look fine from our place, and right back of us there is a steep bluff. We are really fortunate to be able to live in such surroundings and still be close enough to our work.

Betty Ann is doing fine. She was six months yesterday and weighed almost 18 lbs. She gives us so much joy. It is fun to watch her play. Right now she is sitting in a little cane chair that I found for her in a cane-maker's shop, playing with her toys, and jumping, and swinging her arms, as though she thought she were playing some modern music on the piano a la the bang-em-hard impressionistic school, or whatever you call it. The chair has a little table in front, something like a high chair, and she just fits in it now. She is such an active little one. She does not like to lie in her bed, but wants to sit up all the time when she is awake, which is most of the day now. We are having a time keeping her bedding on, as she kicks it off so often. But the weather is getting quite mild now, so that there is no particular danger of her catching a cold. We are waiting for more pictures of Betty Ann to come any day. They were ordered a long time ago. There is no good photographer here, so we have to send to Ichang or even still farther down river. I could do my own developing and printing, but it is hard to find the time, and the work can be

---

[177] Explanation (to the catechism - Norwegian)

done about as cheap here at Chinese Photographer shops as one could do it himself. Perhaps when we get settled in our new home, I will fix up a dark room and begin to do my own developing again.

Bernice has not been so very well the last month, but there does not seem to be anything serious the matter. I guess she will feel better when she gets settled in her new home and can be outside in the fresh air more. Here we are in the heart of the Chinese city, the streets in our neighborhood are most filthy and smelly, and she does not get outside at all except on the verandah. Betty Ann ought to get outside more too. I walk up to our future residence once or twice a day to look after the workmen, but it is too far for Bernice to walk. We have taken Betty along with us up there a few times, sometimes in a chair, sometimes walking. Betty Ann is a pretty good burden to carry any distance, however. You talk about carrying your heavy girls around. Do you not have a baby carriage? We could not use a baby carriage here as the streets are too hilly – all steps. But grandpa Onstad is sending Betty Ann one of these La-la-by Swings. When that comes, we expect that Betty Ann will be sitting in it most of the day. We shall try to get a little cart made to take her around in, too. We have room enough within our own "compound," up at the new place, for tennis courts, for little walks, and all, so that there will be plenty of chance there to get exercise.

Bernice has not seen any foreign ladies since she left Ichang. The wife of the British missionary has not been over to call yet. They are kept pretty busy over there, and live a couple miles away, so I suppose we cannot blame them for not coming over. There are some more American missionaries here now – the representatives of a Bible School in Pittsburgh. They are staying temporarily over at the China Inland Mission. They are having quite a time finding a house, as the soldiers have occupied practically every desirable house in the part of the city where they intend to work. They have been here over a month now. At present there is only a married couple here, but there are half a dozen single ladies of the same Mission staying for the time being in Ichang, who will be coming up as soon as quarters can be found here. I have been more fortunate than they anyway about getting house. This Mission will locate over in the old Chinese city, across the "little river" from where I will be, and over a mile away. You see there is plenty of room for several missions in this city. These Pittsburgh people are rather a peculiar set. They believe in praying over everything, down to the question of accepting an invitation to tea, and are very strict about some things. At the same time, they do not believe in a Hell or in the existence of a devil, nor in eternal punishment, so that I am rather inclined to hope that they will not last long in this place. Some representatives of the same Society were in Shihnanfu for two or three years, before our Mission started there.

This will have to be enough for this time. Greet the Tjernagels and other friends there from us. Tell Gus I will be writing him soon. I have just received $2.00 for Elizabeth Ann, which is reported as having been sent by him to the Norw. Synod Treasurer.

With love to you all from us three, Your brother,

George

An answer to George's offer as correspondent

March 19th, 1924.

Mr. G. Lillegard,
American Lutheran Mission,
Wanhsien, Szechwan.

Dear Sir,

We are in receipt of your letter of February 29th, and thank you for your offer of services. Before entering into any arrangements with you we should like to be able to form some opinion regarding your ability as a correspondent; will you therefore be good enough to send us a specimen article as soon as possible. Unless there is any particularly sensational news we should not require you to send anything by wire.

Awaiting your further news,

Yours faithfully,

THE CHINA PRESS, INC.,
Harold C. Norman

George's specimen article:

Wanhsien, Szechwan, April 15th, 1924

The China Press
Shanghai, China

At present, we are enjoying that peaceful state of affairs which makers of history and purveyors of news consider dull and uninteresting, in this section of Szechwan. If there is any warfare being waged in any part of the province, we hear little about it. We do, indeed, hear that brigands and robbers are carrying on in their usual manner in country districts and along the Yangtse. But this is the normal state of affairs in turbulent Szechwan. Brigands, like the poor, we have always with us, and we would feel lonesome without them. The numerous mountain fortresses in this part of China bear eloquent witness to the fact that brigands have been an ever-present danger in times past as well as now. Several of these fortresses loom up in the neighborhood of Wanhsien itself, and are occupied at present by the wealthiest people of the city, who can from their well-nigh inaccessible heights bid defiance even to the armies that still occupy Wanhsien.

The river has been open to traffic to Chungking all winter. Since the attack on Captain Brandt in January, no foreign boats have been molested. Junks are still in danger of attack, however, and travel as a rule only with military escort. We suspect that the military see to that there are brigands at points along the river so as to ensure that the junks will be willing to pay the escort tax levied upon them. A few weeks ago, a representative of the Carlowitz Co., travelling down river with a fleet of junks, loaded with wood-oil, was attacked by brigands near Kweifu. The military escort drove the brigands away, and though a great number of shots were exchanged, no casualties were reported. There are tens of thousands of soldiers stationed along the river, who have nothing particular to do, but no attempt is made to suppress brigandage or to keep the river clear. It is to the interest of the military, apparently, to keep all trade dependent upon them for protection, even if it results in killing the goose that lays the golden eggs for them.

There are still over 20,000 soldiers stationed in Wanhsien, which is a considerable improvement over the situation last autumn, when there were up to 100,000. The military occupation has resulted in unusually high prices on all kinds of produce and on labor. Although the fighting is presumably over with for the time being, all Divisions are busy recruiting new soldiers. The "awkward squad" can be seen performing in almost any part of the city. These military preparations are ostensibly being made for an attack on Kweichow and Yunnan. But there is much talk about dissensions within the ranks of the victorious troops, especially between the Northerners and Yang Sen's Szechwanese. We are inclined to think, however, that Wu Pei-fu's position is too strong to be challenged by any party in Szechwan at present. If Hsiung Keh-wu succeeds in procuring the required arms and ammunition from Yunnan's foreign neighbors, some of the factions that hitherto have aided Wu Pei-fu may go over to him in an attempt to drive the Northerners out and to reserve the spoils of the province again for Szechwan grafters alone. But until that time, we predict peace for this section of China – that is, such qualified peace as brigands and unruly soldiers are willing to grant us.

A number of changes are just being made in the foreign population of Wanhsien, the offices of Commissioner of Customs, Postmaster, and Standard Oil Agent, receiving new occupants to replace those who have "held down" Wanhsien during the last year or two of wars and disturbance. The female population, which hitherto has been conspicuous for its small proportions, is being increased by the advent of the Pittsburgh Bible Society with a missionary couple and five or six lady workers. The Evangelical Lutheran Mission of America has also opened work in this city, being represented at present by one missionary couple. Since this city has a population of about 300,000, ranking as the third city of Szechwan, it provides ample room for these new Mission Societies, besides the China Inland Mission which has been working here for over 30 years. If conditions would only improve politically, the foreign business community would no doubt also be materially increased in a comparatively short time, since this place affords a good centre for trade of all kinds.

Big tree and shrine on crest of hill overlooking the Yangtze,

Wanhsien, China, 1924

Chapter 13
A Permanent Home in China

BERNICE DETAILS PROS AND CONS OF NEW RESIDENCE.
"...tomorrow our bedroom & closet are to be fumigated..."

[Letterhead: EVANGELICAL LUTHERAN MISSION, WANHSIEN, SZECHWAN. GEO. O. LILLEGARD. 師牧德立黎 會德路道音福縣萬川四]

Letter No. 146. Wanhsien, Szechwan, April 29th, 1921

Dear Mama,

At last we received American mail. Have not had any since the 10th and those were delayed letters. We have been waiting so – I have been quite impatient – but I guess we were lucky to receive this batch at all. You should see how the letters look! They have been <u>soaked</u>. The S.S. "Pakiang" (Bajang) struck the rocks down in the Gorges and we hear the ship is a total loss. This mail was on that boat, so you see it is fortunate it was saved. They could have saved the boat if it hadn't been for a rise of 15-20 feet in the river before a pump came up from Ichang. Your 155 and 156 and Papa's letter of March 16th came and although they had been soaked, they were all legible. But alas! a fine, <u>long</u> letter from Alice (I've been waiting for it for months) is illegible. The letter is four stationery sheets (16 pages) long. I can make out the first page "saa vidt"[178] – but of the rest of the letter I can glean only a few words here and there. Isn't it too bad? But then, I'm glad it wasn't yours and I must say that we have been fortunate in receiving mail so far. The swing has not come yet, but we hear that a lot of mail-boats are at Kweifu, have been for some time, and are afraid to proceed because of robbers. Perhaps they will come when they think they are a large enough fleet, or it may be they will be able to secure a military escort. Just so the swing gets here sometime, I don't mind, although I know Betty Ann would enjoy it ever so much now.

You know it is a long time since I wrote – besides being busy (thinking I was, at any rate) I have been sort of putting it off in the hopes that "tomorrow" would bring mail. Big and little steamers have been coming up the last ten days and I tho't it pretty awful when ten or twelve steamers came in <u>two</u> days and not a letter from home!

Have my diary here and will have to look at that to see what has been going on since I wrote last. Did I mention in Elsa's letter that Parkers (Mr. & Mrs.) called on us Good Friday? So I have seen one foreign woman since I came. Mrs. Parker looks like a very sweet little woman. She wanted to hold Betty Ann. For a while she sat on her lap with a questioning, sober face, but soon she puckered up her face and cried a little in such a coaxing way.

Mr. Jenkins sent us such beautiful roses for Easter. Flowers certainly trim and brighten a room. Easter Sunday was warm and also somewhat close. Got Betty Ann and

---
[178] "barely" (Norwegian)

myself all dressed up before dinner and George and I had our devotion also. After dinner, about 2:30, we went up to "The Barns" for awhile.

A week ago tomorrow we three went down to the Standard Oil bungalow for tea. Since the river is quite a bit higher, Betty Ann and I went over and back in the "giao dze." George took a boat most of the way down and walked back. It was really hot along the Chinese streets, but there was a good breeze up at the S.O. and it was very comfortable. Mr. Swift will leave soon and his successor, Mr. Finch, is here. Besides, Mr. Hawley was there, so with Mr. Jenkins and George, there were five men – only Betty Ann and I to represent the ladies. Betty Ann did not like the gentlemen very well. She does not struggle to get away, but cries in a rather quiet way and the tears roll down her cheeks. Mr. Hawley has carried her around before, so he wanted to take care of her while we had tea, but George finally went to get her. She really didn't want to be with anyone except me the rest of the afternoon. She is very quick to notice strange surroundings. It isn't at all strange that she is afraid of other people, since none save we two ever handle her. She likes Chinese quite well, but she doesn't care to have them come too close either.

We didn't do much celebrating on George's birthday. The tie I had intended as a birthday gift became an additional Christmas gift! But I made an angel's food cake and a batch of fudge and we had chicken supper. Mr. Neumann, one of the Germans, came over for coffee (not tea) and we invited him to stay for supper also…

It just struck ten, so it will be almost eleven before I can get to sleep. Therefore, "finis" for tonight. "Godnat."[179]

Wed. Eve Have not been feeling very well today and feel especially punk this evening. My "digestive tract" seems to be off, for some reason or other. Ate breakfast and dinner and even a little at tea time, but had no appetite for supper. For Betty Ann's sake I ate a boiled egg and small piece of toast. I'd like to know what ails me anyhow! I've certainly had all too many complaints ever since Betty Ann arrived, it seems. Have been so troubled with pimples in my scalp, forehead, ears, and more or less all over. My blood must be in poor condition. Then I have no pep, get so little done and don't seem to care! Well, it's nothing to worry about. Shouldn't wonder but what all I need is plenty of outdoor exercise and maybe I can get that now...

We have finally moved into "The Barns"! Things were not all ready, but George became more impatient each day when he came up here, saw the trees, breathed the fragrant air, etc. so he thought we had better move up anyway. Accordingly, we did some packing Friday and Saturday we had eight coolies carrying our stuff up. All the necessary things, save the stove, were brought and by evening I had most of the dresser and chiffonier drawers filled again. And we have a wash-stand at last. We feel terribly "luxurious" with a regular wash-stand of our own. It has three deep drawers, one a long one, the other two short. How much easier to move when one has place to put things.

We are so well pleased with our new home. It is much more convenient than any place we've had so far. The floors need another coat of oil, but we may wait awhile with that. How wonderful it is to step out of our doors to the earth, not a veranda only or a filthy street! And it has been so fragrant around here. There have been several flowering trees, including several orange trees, and now the pomelo trees will soon be through. There are six of the latter and they have been loaded with blossoms, which have such a

---

[179] "Good night" (Norwegian)

perfume that it fills the house. At times it is really almost too heavy a perfume. Do you remember that the pomelo is a fruit somewhat similar to the grapefruit? A good, sweet pomelo is most delicious, but some varieties are sour and bitter. Hope these trees bear sweet ones. There are so many large trees, fruit trees, bamboos, and young trees in this compound and we certainly do enjoy them. Only wait until we get our grass and garden seeds and get our lawn and garden into proper shape!

Perfect joy is not to be expected in this world, though, and so we have to confess there are a few things we cannot appreciate. Especially is that true of the welcome we have received from a <u>great</u> variety of bugs and insects. So happy are they to have us here that they force their company upon us in spite of screens, whitewash, paint, and persistent use of several swatters. Among the host are moths (by the hundred), mosquitoes, flies (big & little), red ants, white ants (in some of the woodwork), flying ants (big black things), cockroaches, fleas, bedbugs, and the like. Why, I hadn't been here half an hour before some tiny gnats had left their cards on my arm. Of them all, the cockroaches and bedbugs – well, fleas, too – bother us most – mentally, at least. We think the former may be making their home in a huge cupboard, which we are using. The owners of this place have offered us the use of considerable furniture so as to protect it from the soldiers, who are very ruthless. But, where do the bedbugs come from? We have found several in the bednet, but a thorough search of all bedding failed to reveal a single trace. However, tomorrow our bedroom & closet are to be fumigated with several pounds of sulphur, if I don't feel too punk to put up with the inconvenience of closing off those rooms. We will certainly do it in a day or two, anyway. I am going to close this letter now so as to get it mailed. Will tell all about house in next letter. Betty Ann is as cute as can be. She loves to pull herself to her feet in her little chair. But she hasn't gained the last weeks and we don't know why. Since Mon. I have given her one bottle feed a day. Tho't it might be that my milk was getting a little low, and I had to feed from both breasts twice last week. Usually she gets all she wants from one. She is happy and active, though, and quite a chatterbox, though probably not as bad as her mother was. She says "mama" just as plainly and sometimes I think she means to call me.

Better address mail to Kuling after receiving this. Just Ev. Luth. Mission.

Best regards to relative & friends and lots of love to all of you from

George, Betty Ann, & Bernice

Don't know the house no. as yet.

GEORGE DISCUSSES DETAILS OF TRANSLATION WORK.
"Our (Chinese) writers...are not accustomed to writing Mandarin and that shows in the Chinese they produce."

May 6th, 1924

Dear friend Gyps:

Your letter of April 14th and card of the 16th were received some time ago. I had intended to answer your questions sooner. But during the last week of April we moved up to our new place, and since the first of the month, both Bernice and I have been under the weather. We took sick at the same time with a rather bad case of diarrhea. Bernice was pretty sick the first night and scared me enough to make me send for Mrs. Darlington, who is a trained nurse. We are both better now although not entirely out of the woods. I think perhaps the water up here does not just agree with us. Betty Ann thrived through it all. We started giving her a couple bottle feeds each day, when Bernice took sick, and last week she gained 14 oz., whether because of the additional feeds, or because of the change of residence or both. We enjoy our new home very much, although it has its disadvantages. Insects of all kinds have been so numerous that we have been quite distracted at times. Today we are fumigating our bed and bathrooms, and hope that will rid us of the most obnoxious ones anyway. It is strange that there should be so many bugs in a house after it has been all freshly painted and whitewashed. But here they are.

As to our literary work – I agree with you that mimeographed work should be limited to that required by the teachers at the Seminary. Since mimeographing is twice as expensive as printing, this would seem entirely reasonable, even to Arndt perhaps. I hope you have received the revised copies of the Questions and Answers and of Luther's Catechism which I sent you. I sent them by registered mail some time ago. I worked them over quite carefully, making much use of a concordance in order to get the exact biblical phrase used. I note, by the way, that there are a number of phrases which you have changed in Pieper's Tract, which I do not think it would have been necessary to change, as what I had was the phrase or language used in the Bible in many corresponding passages. I suppose the phrase you substituted was correct also, although it seems to me the sense is changed somewhat – perhaps your German copy is slightly different in construction from my English translation – so there is no need to discuss the question in detail here. It would take too long. There is just one phrase which I would refer to for your reconsideration: "For the sake of," as in, "For Christ's sake." I have not tabulated all the Bible passages, where this phrase is used, but in many "wei Chi-tuh" is used, in others "wei Chi-tuh-ty yuen-ku." No doubt there is a slight difference in the meaning of the two, although I have not studied the passages closely enough yet to discover where one should be used and where the other. However, I would suggest that you decide this matter before making changes in the places where I have "wei Chi-tuh," in Pieper's Tract, as well as in the Catechism and Questions and Answers. It is not easy to discuss such points by correspondence. How about making a list of such phrases, and then we can study them together some time this summer?...

Pardon me for innocently enough slamming your and Djang's Chinese, in my reference to the sermon in the Feb. number! Why did you not tell me that I don't know what good Chinese is? Perhaps the fact that it was not a translation, but an original work, accounted for a certain difference in style which I felt, without examining it closely to see whether it was good or not. Anyway I have looked it over again, and shall ask permission to revise my judgment of its Chinese. I found nothing that was not clear in meaning, nor apparently good Chinese. Our writers, however, are not accustomed to writing Mandarin and that shows in the Chinese they produce. They will have to be encouraged to read the Bible and other pure Mandarin literature, so that they do not get too much newspaper Wenli into their style. I note that the Bulletin of the Christian Council is written in simple Mandarin, much more like that of the Bible, than most of the papers one sees. Many tracts, too, of course, are written in good Mandarin. Could not Djang be encouraged to read all the Mandarin literature you can get ahold of, so that he can soak himself in the Mandarin style? He is not too old to learn. Lai Pei-Kweh, I consider, would not be able to adapt himself to any new style of writing.

You ask about the question of English in Primary Schools. The Education Committee has been requested by the last three Conferences to look into that matter and report to the next Conference. I have not done anything more about it than to study the schedules put out by the Government and the Christian Educational Association. The C.O.C.E.A. recommends that English be taught first in the Middle School. The Government schedule allows it at an earlier stage, but I doubt that many Government schools are able to give any real instruction in English in Primary Grades. Personally I consider it a nuisance to spend time and money teaching all kinds of heathen children English. I believe we ought to shut down on it immediately, and I am sure that the Board would approve, or rather that it disapproves strongly of having the missionaries spending so much time as they have been doing in Hankow in teaching English. As for Chinese Government School Laws – I do not believe we need to pay much attention to them, as they are continually being changed and never being enforced. It would be better to follow the recommendations of the Educational Associations. Cf.[180] for example the Ed. Com. Report. That urges strongly that many schools be closed and that quality rather than numbers be emphasized hereafter. Did you read the article in the Dec. Recorder on Educational Work, by a Nanking Prof.? Look it up and read it. It is worth while – and it is not long.

Congratulations on the new members of Shihnan congregation.[181] May they prove to be sincere and faithful Christians that will help you to build up a true Lutheran congregation. My report, of which I enclose a copy for Shihnan Station, will show what progress or lack of progress I have been making here. There have been so many other things to attend to that I really have not had much "pep" left to do aggressive mission work. I hope to get started with that in good earnest next fall.

So much for this time. Let us hear from you again soon. With best greetings to you all from Bernice, Betty Ann, and myself,

Sincerely yours,
Geo. O. Lillegard

---

[180] Confer (compare)
[181] See following page.

"List of People Baptized at Shihnan, April 13, 1924"

徐世端 (God parents)	張幹俪	明喜	德	陳復
咸師母	饒廉儒	明春	泰	陳復
劉利未	張幹俪	世賓	光	王復
劉月亭	咸極樂	保學	善	張復

劉月亭	高合德	尭	德	舒路
劉月亭	咸極樂	昌學	拿	陳約 (Brother of Chen Yo-ceh)
徐世端	高合德		西	陳約
歐福鹿	徐亞拿	順英	音	龍福
歐美鹿	徐亞拿	王堂喜 (Daughter of Tsang Elias Tseng)	天	林
	劉月亭		哈拿	段

李	張	黃	賴	段	李	李	陳	伍
復懷再守信	新天生信真 (Father of Pi Tai-chen)	偉 (Father of Chang Kan-cheng)	理曉佩名代	堂霞國棠	真氏	氏	氏	氏
	永體道謙 (Mother of Pi Tai-chen)	壽仁慰光	程譚張簡 (Embroidery Worker)					
程龍劉舒林陳劉	見 (Ling Tai-sao)	由東 (wife of Liu Hsieh-ling)	鄒屈張龍傅 (Annah) (Mother of Chien Yo-seh) (Wife of Tailor)	亞安保珍祈利亞				

List of People baptized at Shihnan, April 13, 1924.
16 Adults + 10 Children.

GEORGE WOULD BE HAPPY TO SEE HIS BOOK COME TO LIFE.
"…I shall be glad to make an attempt at writing such a book on our Mission work in China…I have been thinking it over somewhat these days…"

May 19th, 1924

Prof. L. Fuerbringer
St. Louis, Mo.

Dear Professor Fuerbringer:

Thank you for your letter of March 18th received some days ago. I was glad to note that efforts were being made to bring the cause of Foreign Missions more adequately to the attention of our church people. Though I feel that you are doing me an honor and giving me[182] responsibility that some other person might rather bear, I shall be glad to make an attempt at writing such a book on our Mission work in China as you suggest. I have been thinking it over somewhat these days, and have wondered if a description of our western field and the conditions under which a missionary works in the inland, written in story form, that is, telling it all in the form of the experiences of a missionary couple, this to be sort of a "composite missionary" rather than any individual at present on our field, or the "ideal missionary." I shall have to find out from Missionary Meyer what he is writing, so that I do not cover the same ground.

It will be impossible for me, I fear, to get this book written before the end of the year. In the meantime I would appreciate such suggestions as you wish to make regarding the contents, literary form, etc., of the proposed book.

With best greetings to you, I am

Respectfully yours,

Geo. O. Lillegard

---

[182] These last four words are covered in illegible strike-overs.

BERNICE SCOLDS HER BROTHER FOR NOT WRITING MORE.
"Are you two kids engaged or not?...You might just recall that you wanted plenty information when I was being courted…"

Letter No. 148	Wanhsien, Szechuan, China
May 20th, 1924

Dear Ragnar,

You don't really deserve a letter, do you, considering all the mail you've sent in this direction. Since Aug. 31, 1923 you have written only one letter and I must say news about you and your affairs has been extremely scarce. Mother said you took a trip last fall and that you would write about it – to date, I've been left to wonder what sort of trip that was. Do you know, it gives me a terribly "brotherless" and lonesome feeling to be so – sort of on the outside. Do you read the letters from China, or have you simply forgotten that you have a sister? Well, "vi skal tage alle ting i den bedste mening,"[183] so I shall just have to think that you have been attending school all year (I heard you registered last fall, anyway), have been working hard, making good grades, and are preparing to graduate. And if this letter goes through promptly, it should reach you about commencement time, I judge. I won't indulge in a lot of stereotyped phrases, but will just say that George and I wish you the very best of everything and send our hearty congratulations. How I wish we could be with you instead of having to send our wishes from so far away. I'm sending you a small gift. Wish it were more, but hope you will make good use of both tie and pin. The character is "Ngan" (say 'sing' then start with that 'ng' sound and add än) and is what the Chinese suggested as the Chinese of Onstad. "Ngan" means peace. So, you may tell those who ask, that the pin has your Chinese name.

I am so anxious to hear what your plans are. Hope you will be able to find a desirable position in Madison, as that city surely is hard to beat. And I don't imagine you'll go very far from there as long as Esther graces the city with her presence. How about it? Are you two kids engaged or not? Don't be so stingy with your information. You might just recall that you wanted plenty information when I was being courted and you were pretty peeved when you came from Cambridge and learned how far things had gone without your knowledge & consent!

Don't make plans for any wedding until we hear whether or not we will get a five-year furlough. If we get that, then hold on until I get there! By the way! Where is that letter from Esther? What kind of person does she think I am, if she's so afraid to write to me? I won't hurt her!

There isn't much to report from here since I last wrote. Have had rain most of the time. Last Thursday it was beautiful, tho,' and every bit of bedding and all the clothes in the wardrobe were thoroughly sunned. It certainly needed it – it has been awfully damp. Although we had part of a wash left to dry, I had Hsiao deh wash again that day and had the cook help with ironing. Sunday it was nice, and yesterday also. Had rain early this morning, but cleared up in the course of the A.M. and it was fine this afternoon…I am so glad it has been cool, because I want to stay here as long as possible. Have lots I want to do, and then we are enjoying our new home so much.

---

[183] "we shall put the best construction on everything" (Norwegian)

You should see Betty Ann! She gets two "Lactogen" feeds regularly each day now and she is getting fatter than ever. She weighed 19 lbs. 6 oz. yesterday. Believe me, she's something to carry around. And she's so lively that I can hardly handle her at times. Sometimes she gets so excited and wild that she doesn't know how to act. She jumps so in her swing, too, that it's funny she doesn't get dizzy.

Sunday afternoon we took Betty Ann along and climbed up to the temple on the side of the "Precipice of Peace." It was quite a climb, but there are steps all the way and we took it easy, so it was not half bad. Including rests, it took us an hour to go up. It was a worthwhile trip, as we found when we got there. The temple is most interesting and very well preserved. Evidently "business is good." We could see that considerable repairing has been done lately and there were several either new or re-guilded gods. We hear the bells & drums every day and often most of the night so there must be many worshippers that climb up to offer their prayers and burn incense. Will write to Mama soon. Now, please, Raggie, write to me now and then.

Lots of love to you all from us three.

Bernice

Buddhist temple moon door

Wanhsien, Szechuan, China

(This is a selection from a thirteen-page document, "Our China Mission" – Wanhsien)

The Temple at Tai-beh Ngai

Above Wanhsien towers a high cliff that runs the length of "the new city," over which access can be had to the city from the inland only by one or two passes which are walled and guarded, in peace or war. In the middle of this cliff, high up under the rim, hangs a temple, one of the historic spots in this province. It is named after a famous poet, Li Tai-beh, who once lived in the cave now turned into a temple. This poet was the Omar Khayam of China, being noted as much for the dissoluteness of his life as for the charm and beauty of his verse. So thoroughly did he enjoy the delights of the cup whose praises he sang that he met his death while boating on the Yangtse, in a drunken attempt at seizing the moon whose lovely image he saw floating in the waters. In the beautiful spot where he once dwelt, his image now stands, the object of worship for thousands of people who especially at New Year's time come to pay homage to the greatest of China's "Immortals."

Above his image, in the highest tier of temples, stands an image of "Shang-Di," the Pearly Emperor, the supreme god of the Taoist Pantheon, once a famous wizard and exorcist. Beneath him in the main temple building, stand the images of Lao-Tze, Confucius, and Buddha, the founders of China's three religions. Atheistic philosophers, lying exorcists and magicians, and drunken poets – such are the gods and saints of heathen China!

At the foot of this temple lies the chapel of the Evangelical Lutheran Mission. Is the Gospel of God's grace and love, through our efforts, to be the means of turning the hearts of these people away from their shameful idols, or are these to stand in their filth and glitter till Judgment Day rends the cliff from which they reign over this teeming city and destroys them and their deluded servants eternally?

Geo. O. Lillegard

AMERICAN HYGIENE HAS CHANGED FOR THE BETTER!
"..a woman ought to wash her hair every two weeks and a man twice a week."

Letter No. 149   Wanhsien, Szechwan, May 27th, 1924
Dear Mother,

About your turn to get a letter, I should say. Although there have been as many letters as usual sent this month, you have not received more than two, unless you count the one from Betty Ann.

There are a number of questions in your last letters and I think I shall begin by trying to answer them. It is a nuisance to answer, excuse me, to <u>ask</u> questions and then not have them answered, so I like to go over the letters and take them first. You ask if young girls do not go out as baby tenders, etc. Chinese customs are so very different from ours in that respect. In the first place, girls are almost always married at an early age, so that the unmarried girls are often little more than children. I do not think it is customary for girls to work for other people even among the poor classes – they do washing for soldiers or others, that is women in general, and may have some work for others, but they do not go to the homes of other people like hired girls at home. Women servants are usually married or widows. People of means often have slave girls – the Raos in Shihnan, for instance, had some slave girls. If people are at all in the position to do so, they keep their girls very much secluded until marriage. It is improper for young girls to be seen on the streets. I guess I will not try to tell any more about Chinese customs in this respect – I might get into deep water. I surely need to read more about China. --- I do not know whether to have my hair bobbed or not. If I had been any place within reach of a hairdresser last winter, it would not have taken me long to decide, and I had the fever when I received your letter and heard that Elsa had hers bobbed. But, I really do not know whether or not I have the nerve now. No hair is coming out now – I hardly ever have a hair on the brush or comb that I can wind around the end of my braid at night – and there is a good deal of new hair. <u>If I knew what I would look like!!</u> It must be nice to be able to wash the hair often and not have to worry so about getting it dry, etc. We just received Mac Fadden's book on Hair Culture, which gives a lot of practical advice. One theory is blown up and that is that (it) is bad for the hair to be washed often. He says that a woman ought to wash her hair every two weeks and a man twice a week. I was pleased to read that, as I like to wash my hair quite often. If it gets too dry, it will have to be rubbed with Vaseline. I would certainly advise Elsa to shampoo her hair oftener now, if she is still troubled as much with dandruff as she used to be. If she is not careful to get rid of dandruff, she will be losing her hair, too, later on, and it is rather late to get busy after one's hair has fallen and is thin.

Well, as you know by this time, we are well pleased with our home, so I am not even envious of the Standard Oil bachelors. Just wait till we get all our furniture! In Wanhsien there is no city electric plant. I think they have a Delco plant at the S.O. place. Delco plants are quite popular in China. Many of the larger cities have electric plants, but the one in Ichang is closed down and I hear the one at Shasi has closed lately. Not enough business to make it pay, I think.

You ask if the Chinese do not build common size houses. In the country one sees many small farm houses, but in the city it is different. You see, the Chinese live so differently. Every young couple does not try to get a home of their own, as is so common at home. It is much more on the "apartment style" idea here. One man builds a big place and then rents out to ever so many families. And in a big family it takes lots of room for just the family, because you probably know it is the custom for all the sons to bring their wives to the paternal home. You can understand, then, that if there are several sons, there will soon be several families – oh, there are relatives and relatives, it seems, who sort of sponge on each other. Really, I think you would enjoy getting a good book on China and becoming a little acquainted with Chinese customs. I cannot do justice to such things in my letters, chiefly because I am not well enough posted myself. What I know is mostly what I have learned from observation, and that has been quite limited, of course. --- I believe some of the questions you have asked must have been answered in previous letters, however, I will repeat just to be on the safe side. We do not have dirt floors in the rooms we use, as we had board floors put in. They are not very nice looking floors – the boards are of various widths and are not grooved, so soon there will be cracks here and there, and the planing is very imperfect, being done with some little hand planes. And as for level floors – they may have them in the big port cities, where there are foreign contractors and where Chinese do things more or less according to foreign ways, but "there ain't been any sich animil" in the houses we have occupied. It is because the carpenters do not have spirit levels and so the leveling is all guess work. Result: furniture of any sort and description has to be moved around until it will stand firmly, or, as is more usual, a little piece of wood or some paper is tucked under one leg. I do not know what to answer about lathing – George says they must have used some kind of laths or bamboo or something as foundation for the inside plastered wall at the Dollar Co. building. So, the Chinese must know something about it. What is more common is to have the outside walls of mud or brick and plaster them, while the inside "walls" are merely thin board partitions. Do you remember that I told about the plaster they were making for #2281 on Kuling the first summer we were in China? That was mud plaster mixed with grass by means of bare feet – wallowing around in it barefooted! They also make plaster by mixing lime and some coarse paper that has been soaked in something. They either have not learned to use sand, or there is some other reason for not using that material. Bricks? You bet they have bricks in this country and you would think so if you could see the city walls built of bricks – <u>huge</u> things. They make very pretty arched bridges of bricks, also. Our stove works so much better now that we have a chimney up through the roof, and how much cleaner than running a pipe out the window! We cannot get hard coal here, so we could not use a heater. In Ichang and Hankow where people can afford to get the stoves and the hard coal, they have a better type of stove. The small Swedish hard coal heaters are excellent for this climate and we have been told they are now obtainable at Shanghai, but under the circumstances it will do us no good to invest. I would certainly like an oil stove for cooking, but as you say, it would hardly be practical, especially in the winter, as we do need the heat then. Since the Standard Oil have an installation here, we can easily obtain the oil and I wonder if it would not be just as cheap, since fuel has been such a big item. Since I expect to be doing my baking and some of the cooking next year, I could also run it more economically than a cook would, I believe. But, I suppose we will have to give up that idea. I think we will enquire about prices this summer, however, as it might pay to run one during the fall and spring. There really are not many months of the year that we need heat…The Standard Oil Co. ought to handle such things here and I imagine they send things in their own ships, which ought to make it cheaper…

Not long ago you wrote that you thought you would do things differently if you could start your married life over again – that you would not work quite so hard, I think you meant. I wonder though. You said you had learned a number of things, but I felt like scolding you hard when I received your last two letters. Why in the world should you get so excited about cleaning, washing curtains, etc. etc. etc. just because Marie Brauer was coming, and why worry about the looks of the place when Meyers come? I know you well enough to know that your house always looks nice and I should judge that your new home is even more immaculate than anything you have had before, so it almost gives me a "fit" (excuse!) to hear about your flying around, cleaning and so on. I would not say anything to your changing your schedule so as to have things more convenient – regarding washing and the like – but why do so much extra work? Why not do just the every day or weekly cleaning, as it may be, and let it go at that? You should enjoy your company, but how can you enjoy <u>anything</u> when you wear yourself out to a frazzle beforehand? I am loath to believe that you have reformed very much and I doubt not that you will be shocked at your eldest daughter when you find out how easy-going she has become as compared with her mother. I am so glad to hear that you have slept better and I hope it is a permanent change for the better…

…a great part of the day, it is necessary to put Betty Ann on her little chair every fifteen minutes, if I want to keep her dry. If she is very much interested in something, she holds out a little longer, but on the other hand, if she has nothing to absorb her attention, she is good for only about ten minutes. I am not exaggerating, as I usually look at my watch when I am interested in saving diapers. But, she has been pretty good otherwise this month – have had very few soiled ones all the month of May. Occasionally there is an accident, but that is to be expected, until she is able to express herself in some way or other to let me know. Betty Ann has been so fussy the last two days – here she is soon eight months old and no teeth are through yet…

We have been living on apricots these days. For breakfast we have them plain and for supper we have had them with sugar and cream. Have eight pints of jam, but one is a salt jar and the cover is not tight, so it may be we will have to eat that this spring. Still, I may try sealing it with paraffin…

…I plan on training in Hsiao deh as cook. He will be able to prepare vegetables, do all the dishwashing, and so on, so it means that I will have only the baking and desserts as a general rule. I think I will enjoy it, since the kitchen is so convenient. And it will be nice to work in the kitchen with the servant for awhile and teach him to keep things in the order I like and to do the work in the way I want it done. I sometimes wonder if Hsiao deh will do; he is quite forgetful and rather careless, but he is such a young boy that he should be able to learn and he has a good temper. And then, although I become quite provoked with him at times and discouraged at others, I like the youngster and feel more as if he belonged to the family than as if he were a servant only. He does not like to wash and iron very well, although he has not said so himself to me, but he seems to be well pleased with the idea of helping me cook. I hope to be able to locate a suitable woman this fall to do washing, ironing, and the like. My! I hope I have lots of pep this fall – there are so many things I want to do, one of which is language study. Just think! I have not studied for over a year. It is really terrible and I am sure I have forgotten much of what I had learned.

Monday George and I celebrated our fourth wedding anniversary. We did not do much <u>celebrating,</u> though. It was cloudy and rather close – and I was crabby and blue! However, I dressed up in my white dress and we had coffee – not tea – and a delicious sunshine cake in the afternoon and we had a chicken supper. In the evening we passed the time by looking through Monkey Ward's catalogue and ordering – or writing down on an order blank – some toys for Betty Ann. One of these days George will write a letter to M-W and send the whole business on to you for forwarding, if you will.

Yesterday afternoon we called on Darlingtons. I thought I ought to go over, since she was kind enough to come when we were sick. I like Mrs. D. and she was very nice – said that if there was <u>anything</u> she could do for me, she would like to do so. Considering that they are short two lady workers and she has her hands full with girls' and women's work, not to mention a great deal of dispensary work, I thought it was offering a great deal. Betty Ann upset George's teacup which resulted in quite a deluge. She is so quick and she grabs for everything, so it is a nuisance to hold her if there is anything within reach. Sunday George took her along to the dinner table. I warned him he had better not, but he seemed to think he could manage. It was not long before she had jerked the tablecloth and we just saved everything from going on the floor. The mischief put her hand into George's salmon as soon as she had pulled the cloth enough to get the plate within reach! I guess we will have a lively time training her. She has a will of her own, all right, but I hope we will be given wisdom and strength to help her to be a good child.

If I do not quit about this time, I will soon hear something like this from my honorable hubby, "Now, don't write a whole book!"

Don't know when we will be leaving for Kuling – Betty Ann and I, that is. So far we have had very cool and pleasant weather and I surely will not leave as long as that holds out. It was quite warm until four o'clock this afternoon – up to eighty-two or four degrees – but then there was a cool breeze and it is just as comfortable now as one could wish.

"Ja, det faar vare nok med denne lange skrivningen"[184] – who knows where I got that? !!!?? By the way, it just entered my head that it will be thirty years the fourteenth of June since you and Papa were engaged. Haven't I a "long" memory, though?

Nu maa jeg endelig sige "Godnat." Hils alle.[185] The gas lamp is going out!

Lots of love to you all from us three.

Din,[186]
Bernice

---

[184] "Well, this lengthy writing will have to suffice." (Norwegian)
[185] Now I must finally say "Good night." Greet all. (Norwegian)
[186] Yours, (Norwegian)

LILLEGARDS' FRIEND AND NEIGHBOR IS MURDERED.
"The junk men attacked him because he wanted to load wood-oil on the foreign steamers. He was knocked into the river, and though he was rescued right away by his sampan men and brought to the British Gunboat, where the ship's surgeon took care of him, he died 2 A.M. yesterday (June 18th, 1924)…he was our neighbor in Ichang too, when we lived there."[187]

June 25th, 1924

The China Press
Shanghai, China

It is a week since Mr. E.C. Hawley, an American citizen, representing the British Firm of Arnhold Bros., was foully murdered by a mob of coolies, instigated by the Junk Guilds of Wanhsien, and the Upper Yangtse. It is also a week since the Commanding Generals of the Government troops in Wanhsien promised to see to that the guilty persons were punished and that adequate steps would be taken to protect foreign life and property hereafter. Although more of these promises have been fulfilled than the Chinese authorities ordinarily would expect to fulfill, there still remains much to be done before the steps taken to avenge Mr. Hawley's murder can be considered adequate to the gravity of the offense. In response to the insistent demands of the Commander of the British Gunboat in port, two men were executed on the day following Mr. Hawley's death. But these men were not those principally involved, the one being the aged father of an officer of the Junk Guild, and the other the "No. 67 man" of the Guild. The "No. 1 man" is still in the city, but the officials profess to know nothing about him or his connection with the affair and are apparently shielding him, perhaps because he formerly was connected with the military. One or two of the other men who are "wanted" are reported to have fled, and this report is no doubt correct. A reward is said to have been offered for their capture.

It would be hard to point to any attack on foreigners in China of a more sinister nature than this on Mr. Hawley. A mob is a mob the world over, and mobs will do reckless things at times. But one cannot but draw the conclusion that the Chinese in general have gotten over their fear of the foreign military forces, when they proceed to attack a foreigner with a foreign gunboat standing alongside and a boatload of marines actually on the way to protect him. The attack was made so suddenly and the fatal end came so quickly – in less time than it takes to tell it – that it seems it would have been impossible to prevent the crime under the circumstances. But the fact remains that the event makes one feel that there is no use in talking about foreign prestige any more; "there ain't no such animal," at least in this part of China.

The American Gunboat, "U.S.S. Monocacy," arrived from Chungking last week, with the American Consul, Mr. C.J. Spiker, on board, and he has been working on the case since. The Admiral of the American Yangtse Patrol is also due to arrive today.

A representative of the Arnhold Bros. has arrived from Hankow to take charge of the work here. This would be the time for the Foreign firms at Wanhsien to begin shipping wood-oil by foreign steamers, if they are ever to do so. The Junk Guilds have such a hold on the pilots of the foreign steamers, however, that it is doubtful whether any

---
[187] This quote is taken from another letter, written June 19th, 1924, to missionary Klein.

of them will risk taking any wood-oil on board, even if adequate protection is offered here at the time of loading. It is only two years ago that a pilot who had brought one of the French flag boats up river, after it had taken a cargo of goods down in spite of warnings issued by the Junk Guild, was stabbed to death and his heart cut out, in broad daylight, on one of the busy streets on Chungking. There seems to be no limit to the extent to which the Junk Guild is willing to go in order to maintain its control of the traffic on the Upper River. An opportunity is given the Foreign interests to break the power of this monopoly now, which it may not have again very soon. It remains to be seen what results can be obtained, and whether the people of this district will submit quietly to the transition from the old to the new order of things, or whether the change here too can come only after further bloodshed and violence, as has too often been the case in other countries.

GEORGE WRITES HIS IN-LAWS FOR BERNICE IN KULING.
"I think we shall try to arrange to go to the mountain together after this."

Hankow, China, July 5th, 1924

Dear Folks:

Bernice writes me that she has not found time to write home for the last week or two, and so asks me to do so. She has not written very often to me either. They have been left with only one servant for a house of nine grown-ups and three babies, and so have been kept busy doing their own housework, washing, etc.

But to begin at the beginning: Bernice left Wanhsien on Wednesday the 18th of June – that is she went on board that evening; the boat left the next morning at daylight. Thursday evening she boarded a boat at Ichang for Hankow, arriving there on Saturday morning. Schwartzkopfs were along with her from Ichang on. We did not know whether they had left or not, so it was just our luck that Bernice found company all the way. Of course, she had our cook with her to help with the baggage, etc. At Hankow the Zieglers from Shihnan joined the procession. They had come a couple days before and had stayed in Hankow. Saturday night they left for Kuling, arriving there Sunday noon. They were more fortunate than most of our missionaries, in that they had good clear weather. The others struck rainy weather and got all soaked going up the hill.

But since that time Bernice has not been so fortunate. First Betty Ann caught a cold, and has had constipation, and a little fever, and diarrhea, etc., so that Bernice has had extra work taking care of her. There is nothing seriously wrong with baby – teething, I guess. It is about time some teeth are coming through. Then Bernice also caught a bad cold. I am afraid she does not take care of herself when it gets cold. I have a hard time anyway, making her dress according to the weather when I am with her. And up on the mountain, it is of course considerably cooler than down on the plains, especially in rainy weather. It was cold even here Wednesday, when it rained very hard. Then as said, they have had to do most of the housework, as they have been without the usual help. And it seems that our ladies get quite helpless out here when the servants leave them – largely, I suppose, because they are not used to doing the work. Then the rest of the people living with Bernice have been no better off, as they too have been sick or have had sick babies. We are in the big house this summer, which has not been entirely finished, and that means extra work and trouble too. Zieglers, Kleins, the three single ladies, and Mr. Fischer, the new single man, are with us. They are all up there now, except myself. I sent my "boy" up, too, last Thursday night, when I arrived from Ichang, so now they have servant help. I am staying here for the Chinese Conference which begins tomorrow and will last three or four days. I have arranged to leave for Kuling next Wednesday night, and so will arrive next Thursday. That means that I will have been separated from my wife for over three weeks again. And it is not easy to be that when Bernice and Betty Ann are not well or have various difficulties to contend with. I think we shall try to arrange to go to the mountain together after this.

The day Bernice left Wanhsien, a very tragic affair took place – the murder of Mr. Hawley, our neighbor, and the only foreigner we had seen much of in Wanhsien. Perhaps you have seen something about that in the papers. He was killed by junk coolies, who wanted to prevent him from loading wood-oil on to the foreign steamers. The news of his death came as very much of a shock to us, as he was a friendly man, which is more than too many of these business men in the East are. He had been a missionary once upon a time, having charge of a Presbyterian School in North China. The details of his death I shall not enter upon here, as you may have read about it all in the papers. The people in Wanhsien do not seem to be very much afraid of foreigners or of foreign power, since they made this attack on Hawley, right under the nose of a British Gunboat. The Government is trying to get the guilty parties punished, and one result of the affair may be that they will make Wanhsien into a "treaty port," like Hankow. That would make it possible for foreigners to own land there, and to have certain rights and protection which they have not had hitherto.

I left Wanhsien last Monday night, got a boat Tues. night for Hankow, and had an uneventful trip all the way to this place, except for a rather dangerous trip in a small boat across the river at Wanhsien to board the Foreign steamer. The water was rising at that time, and at such times there are bad whirlpools in the river, and a very strong current. A steamer had just gone up too, and the waves from its wake, plus the whirlpools and strong current, got our little sampan into a rather bad place for a time. It whirled around and rocked from side to side and shipped some water, but we finally got away and made it safely. That was the worst experience I have ever had in a boat. I shall try to avoid any others like it. The sampan was too small, and I should have waited till the waves from the steamer had subsided, but I did not realize how bad things could be until I was in it. The steamers anchor across the river at Wanhsien, as there is no suitable place in which to anchor on the city side, and the river is very wide, too, in high water. The current is not so very bad as a rule, except when the water is rising. You may be sure we will be careful when we take our little Betty Ann home.

I am staying while here in Hankow at Bentrups. I am not doing much except talk. There are so many things to talk over with the other missionaries, now that we have not seen them for so long. I am also doing some shopping, so that I will not have to bother with that when I come through in August.

It has not been hot these days, for which I am duly thankful. If this weather will hold another two-three days, we can consider ourselves fortunate. I fear it has been unpleasantly cool up on Kuling.

I know that this letter cannot take the place of Bernice's interesting epistles, but she will no doubt be able to write very soon. With love to you all from us three, and greetings to friends and acquaintances,

Yours,
George

**Chapter 14
Second Verse,
Same as the First**

BERNICE DISBELIEVES THAT SHE'S PG.
"…personally, I think I am suffering from suppressed menstruation…"

Letter No. 155　　　　　　　　　　　　　　　　　　　　　#2397, Kuling, China
　　　　　　　　　　　　　　　　　　　　　　　　　　　　August 10th, 1924

Dear Mama,

　　　This dark spot on the paper is that iodine. I took out a whole bunch of sheets, but I will have to use the rest of the tablet, even if it doesn't look very nice.

　　　Friday evening, just as all our guests were arriving, a huge bunch of American mail arrived, at last. We hadn't received any for about three weeks. There was much excitement, but we had to curb our impatience and wait with reading most of it. I read your #170, but left #171 until later. We in this big house entertained the whole mission Friday evening at a cafeteria dinner. We are thirty-one grown-ups when all are assembled, but three did not come and Mrs. Ziegler, who expects to be confined any day now, did not come down, so we were twenty-seven of us to make the noise. Our invitation read as follows: "On Friday Eve, at half after seven, We would like to see you with the Happy Eleven, On the hill in West Valley, At Two Three Nine Seven." At the bottom of the card, in one corner, we had "Cafeteria Dinner" and opposite "Price – Smiles and Good Cheer." As each guest arrived, he or she was given a small bean bag containing 20 beans and told that for each time he used the words "Yes" or "No" he must forfeit a bean to the one who caught him. He should use "Beans" instead of those two words, or some other affirmatives and negatives. It certainly caused a great deal of hilarity. Each guest was also given a piece of paper on which were some words and this had to be matched with the slips of three other people, the four pieces then showing the verse of a song. These four people were to eat at one table. We had seven small tables arranged in the "Conference Room" and the dining room. We served mashed potatoes, chicken (fried and then stewed tender), gravy, corn relish, dressing, stewed shredded carrots, peas, and warm rolls (really delicious). This we took on our plates and carried to our tables. When we had finished this course and while the servants were carrying away our plates, each table (?) had to sing the song found on their slips. Then we had ice cream (real home-made – no glue in it!) two kinds of cake, and coffee. Before we left the tables, prizes were given to the man and lady having most beans, and booby prizes for the two having least. We played games the rest of the evening – and ate candy, which Mietz had made. They all claimed they'd had a good time. After the guests had all gone, we sat down to read our mail. It took George and me quite awhile as there were two letters from you, two from Geo's folks, and one from Alice…

　　　Conference will finally be over in a day or two. They have had "some" session this year. Since they've had only a few afternoon meetings, it would necessarily take longer, but twice things were brought to a deadlock by one or two members and it meant several extra days of vain discussion. It was really unfortunate, and unnecessary if the ones in question had only been clear thinkers and then somewhat reasonable. And then Schwartzkopfs' and Gebhardt's sick leaves, together with the Board's refusal (after two cablegrams) to send Meyers back this fall, certainly made matters complicated. Allocation was discussed, literally, <u>for days</u>. For awhile we weren't a bit certain we would return to Wanhsien, even though we didn't see how they would or could arrange to take care of that station. Finally they arranged it, however, so Bentrups will go to Shihnan and Theisses will move back from Shasi to Ichang. (Theisses got settled in Shasi in April or May! But I guess they don't mind moving back, if only they can remain there.) Last year I helped George with the Minutes and we were up to date most of the time, but this year we haven't either of us done any of that work yet. I don't feel that I'll be able to help much either, so George has a lot of work ahead of him. He has been busy ever since he came up, too. Summer vacation? That's a joke – anyway for some. It must be admitted there are certain individuals who do make it a real vacation, though.

We've had pretty fine weather this summer. Last year we had so much rain, but we have had very little this last month and then the weatherman has often been kind enough to send the rain at night, so we could get our clothes dry and sports were not interfered with. George has gone along with our mission "boys" a couple times and played basketball. They play outside and late in the afternoon when the field is in shade. The first time he sprained his knee rather badly and he was pretty sore and stiff for a week. It doesn't bother him now, except that he isn't quite as limber as usual. I told him he was getting too old for basketball. He enjoys it, though. Used to play at the Chicago "U."…

I am going to have a frank "visit" with you now. You may decide whether or not it is wise to let Elsa and Ragnar read the following. Do they (E & R) ever open and read your letters? I request that they don't, if they take such liberties.

I have finally been to Dr. Venable, a rather nice, old doctor who practices on Kuling the year 'round. He is trying to find out what is ailing me, if anything. The first four months after Betty Ann was born I experienced the discomforts of menstruation periodically, but there was no flow…In March I did menstruate a little for ten days and in April I menstruated hard. But since April I've had no more menses. Of course, one would naturally think I was pregnant, but I continued nursing Betty Ann until I came to Kuling, as you know, and, although I have felt so punk all the time, I have not felt like I did the three times before. My previous experiences have been different, true enough, but I <u>always</u> recognized my condition in a hurry! Moreover, I didn't grow, not like last time. However, my tummy was bigger, but it was sort of flabby. A couple weeks ago Mietz examined me internally and she also said she could not think I was pregnant, at least not three and a half months along. Last Wednesday Dr. Venable examined me both internally and externally and he, too, seems to think I am <u>not</u> in that condition. At least, he said the uterus was small and hard, so that, at most, I could only be a few weeks along, at such an early stage that an examination would not reveal it. Well, it is almost <u>four months</u> now since I menstruated. So, personally, I think I am suffering from suppressed menstruation and that is what has caused my headaches lately. But, Dr. Venable is looking for other causes as yet. He took a sample of blood to test for malaria. And, when he learned I've had such restless nights, he prescribed santonine. Do you know what that's for? In plain English, it is poison to kill <u>worms!</u> More elegantly, one may say "intestinal parasites"! Don't be shocked. The most careful people get them in this country and I doubt many children escape them. Some doctors claim the germs are simply breathed in from the air…

…Dr. Borthwick remarked more than once that it was strange I could conceive at all – but sometimes "where there's a will, there's a way" and we were happy when we knew Betty Ann was coming to us…

My, the summer is soon gone, and I've not done anything. It seems that by the time I have the bed made, Betty Ann bathed and fed, I am all in. Often I lie down for awhile, or else I putter around with some small odd jobs. Uf! I'm so tired of hanging around like this. Really haven't had any pep since Betty Ann was born. But you haven't felt well for years and I always sympathize with you, even tho' I know that I cannot realize how miserable you feel. That's why I scold so when you write about your housecleaning and so on. You did work hard, you know. I'm sorry I made you "mad" and I'll try to refrain from scolding, but keep on writing about your work as usual. Make Elsa do a little more. She can stand it. By the way, is Elsa's back all right now? Did she have any more adjustments?

Betty Ann was ten months old Friday. We couldn't weigh her, but hope to do so very soon. We took a bunch of pictures today. Hope they are good. You should see Betty Ann pull herself up on her feet. She moves all around in her little bed and is usually on her knees or feet. Will be glad when we get back to Wanhsien where she has a new bed and where I have chance to arrange places for her to play. Last night I cast on stitches for a sweater for her – a sweater-coat, I should say. It is to be blue with grey trimming. Will send sample of wool later on. I like the color so much. You don't like her in a cap? All the girls think her nainsook cap is very becoming to her.

Now, I must close. This is the first time in ages that I've finished a letter the day I started it.

Much love to all you four and greetings to friends from George, Betty Ann, and

Bernice

GEORGE'S 5TH YEAR'S LANGUAGE EXAM IS TOMORROW.
"…he does not seem particularly worried."

Letter No. 156 #2397, Kuling, China
August 20th, 1924

Dear Mama,

It is only 6:36 A.M., but I got to bed quite early last night, for a change, and just now I am waiting for the irons to get hot so I can iron a little. Yesterday I washed the silk, which was my blue accordion plaited dress. I wanted to dye it also – black – but I couldn't buy black dye at any of the stores, so the only thing left to do is have the dress made and then dye it.

My "birthday letter" came on the 15th.[188] That made good time!

8:20 P.M. I wrote this much and then I had to get Betty Ann, who was so impatient for her breakfast. She is growing up, Mama! How you would enjoy her! For over a week she has not used the bottle at all, but does her drinking from a cup. And the last several days she hasn't had her breakfast until seven or seven-thirty, instead of six o'clock as formerly. So now she has a bowl of rice and milk one morning, oatmeal and milk the next. You ought to see how much she eats of them – she likes both very much. At eleven o'clock, or later, she has her potatoes – baked then mashed with butter, salt & milk. It took her quite awhile to acquire a taste for potatoes, but now she is so fond of them and the cook has to bake two, as one does not satisfy her. At 3:00 P.M. I have been trying to give her buttered toast soaked in hot milk, or crackers ditto, but she does not like that very well as yet. This evening for supper she had a boiled custard and she certainly enjoyed it. Anything that has a little sugar in! There are other things she could eat, but it is not so convenient here where we are so many and I'm waiting until we get back to Wanhsien. So far she has digested everything so well…Haven't used anything but "Milkmaid" evaporated milk for her now for a couple weeks and she likes it real well. I mix one part of milk with two of water. It is so much easier than fixing up the "Lactogen."

It will be nice to get to Wanhsien where I can arrange things better for Betty Ann. She is getting so lively and there isn't any place except her swing which is really safe for her. I borrowed Edna's steamer rug today and put her on the floor, but she moves around and gets to the bare floor – she likes that much better than the rug, of course! She had her worst fall so far this evening. I had fed and washed her and put her to bed, but she was unusually lively and wouldn't lie down. She stands up in her bed and gets from one end to the other. As I was going out with the wash dish I noticed the bed was close to the outside edge of the trunk and I hurried to move it in. Then I thought she was safe, since I've been watching right along these weeks and I've never seen the bottom of the bed move at all, even tho' the wicker sides gave a good deal. But the first thing we knew, Betty Ann was on the floor, face down, under bed & bedding. We had her up at once, as we were both in the room. Her mouth bled quite freely and I took her down to Mietz, who washed out her mouth. We think she must have had her fingers in her mouth when she fell and hurt herself in that way. She cried pretty hard while Mietz was washing her, but as soon as I took her after that she snuggled in my arms and closed her eyes. Poor

---
[188] Her birthday was July 17th.

Baby! Didn't notice any other bumps and she has been sleeping nicely. Her bed is on the floor, tho', and will have to remain there. Am glad we have one all made in Wanhsien. Betty Ann loves to stand and she does so very nicely. She seems only to need something to balance herself by. Today she even stood entirely alone for a few seconds. Mietz says she does very well for her age and thinks she will walk early. It won't be too early to suit me! She weighed 23 lbs. a week ago and that is a good deal to carry around. The tailor is making a coat and hat for her out of my old blue broadcloth coat. Am having them lined in grey silk and believe they will be becoming to her.

George and Mietz finally got the Minutes all ready today. George did the typing, Mietz the hectographing. There are about 35 pages and there are 28 or 30 copies of each, so it was quite a job. And tomorrow George takes his fifth year's language examination. He hasn't had a very settled year in which to prepare for it, but he does not seem particularly worried. Hope he gets through all right.

Here's more bad news to report – Bentrups may also leave for home, as Mrs. Bentrup is really very sick. She has not been feeling entirely well for almost a year and the last weeks she has lost so much in every way. Now it seems she has a goiter (I'm not positive that the doctors are agreed on that, but I think so) and the doctors are not agreed as to treatment. At any rate, they cannot go to Shihnan, so the "boys" met again the other evening and it was decided to send Kleins out again. Those poor folks are doing about as much moving as we. They both like Shihnan and have no objections to living there, but it is tough to move three years in succession. They will "camp" this year, as they don't want to take more than the most necessary things along. They want to wait until they are permanently allocated! More than once I thought we'd be going to Shihnan, but I guess nobody wants to go to Wanhsien, so George never received very many votes. The nurse, Miss Bāden, who is coming out – perhaps with Meyers – is a very good friend of the Kleins and was to be in Kweifu. Now, however, they decided to send her to Wanhsien, more especially so that Geo. can outline her language study and help her with it. She, Martha Baden, is also a very good friend, as well as classmate, of Mietz and from what she and Edna tell me, I am sure I will like Miss Baden very much. It will be very nice for me to have a companion, won't it?

A crowd of our missionaries are leaving Kuling next Monday. Plans were changed a good deal after Kleins were allocated to Shihnan. Six from this house will be leaving: Kleins, Frieda (Fritz) and Mietz, George, and Gyps. Since George has work to do in Hankow, which will require several days, he asked if I would care to leave here a little earlier in order that I might travel with him from Hankow. It will save me a lot of trouble in every way and at most I would not have stayed here more than a week or so in September, so now I plan on leaving here Friday, the 29th, and then, if possible, we will leave Hankow the 30th. And, isn't this fine? Mr. Fischer will go down with Betty Ann and me. Have I ever told you that Fischer is from Wisconsin? His home is out on the "thumb" – Algona or some place like that, I believe. Anyway, he didn't live far from Green Bay.

We need rain so badly. The weather is very pleasant, but our water is getting so brown. I dislike bathing or washing Betty Ann in it. Need a shampoo, too, but it won't do much good in such water, I fear.

Your letters 173-174 came today. That means it took the latter only 23 days to get here. Elsa must have had the time of her life! I remember my trip "galavantin'" around the country in 1919. It was great fun, all right.

Haven't sent anything to Elsa yet, but hope to get it off (in fact) very soon now. Of course, I have oodles to do now, since I've been so lazy all summer.

Here comes George, asking, "Haven't you gone to bed yet?"

Best regards to all and lots of love to all of you four from us three.

Yours,
Bernice

GEORGE HAS A STRONG OPINION ABOUT VACCINATIONS.
"The Lord did not intend that we should shoot ourselves full of all sorts of poison in order to keep from getting sick."

Wanhsien, Szechwan, October 2nd, 1924

Dear Louise:

Your letter of July 27th was received some time ago. Thank you. We were very glad to hear that Martin was already up and around again, and that it was certain that he would recover health and strength. May you all be spared further such trials for some time anyway.

I was also glad to hear about Guri. I have never heard anything from Harstad with regard to her, and did not know how she was faring. It is good that the people out there are so kind to her. Do you hear anything about how she gets along with people? Does her old "skjaeldegjest natur"[189] show itself very much?

You asked in an earlier letter whether vaccination helped to prevent typhoid. I suppose you referred to typhoid inoculation, which works on the same principle as vaccination. It is given in injections. I took that treatment when I first came to China, in Nanking. But I have not taken it since, and do not believe much in it. It is not claimed that it prevents the disease for more than a few months or at most a year, and to take those doses every year on the possibility that one might get typhoid, I think would be abusing one's body. The Lord did not intend that we should shoot ourselves full of all sorts of poison in order to keep from getting sick. The proper thing to do is to be careful about cleanliness and about one's food and drink. If you are not sure that your water is absolutely safe have it boiled, before drinking. We boil all our water here, let it cool, and keep our drinking water in bottles. Be careful also about anything eaten raw – fresh vegetables, fruits, etc. If there is any kind of an epidemic around, it is best not to eat too many raw things. At least pour boiling water over them before eating them. This can easily be done with apples and other fruits and most vegetables. If we did not take such precautions in this country, we would be sure to have worms, or cholera or dysentery, or typhoid all the time. The best prevention against any kind of sickness, especially contagious diseases, is a healthy body – plenty of fresh air, wholesome food eaten moderately, and good drinking water. It may be that it would be advisable to take the inoculation against typhoid, or vaccination against small-pox, at times when these diseases are at our door. But otherwise, I for my part would not.

We are all well, and happily engaged in our work, which still includes the process of getting settled. Betty Ann is as always the peppiest and liveliest member of the family. She is standing near me now, playing with her toys. She wants to stand most of the time, but generally leans against something. We have a rug on the floor for her, with several chairs around it, so that she can go from one to the other. She has not walked alone yet, but I think she would very soon if we practiced with her enough. We have not been taking time for such things. She is if anything fatter than ever. We are beginning to think she looks like Everett True in the comics – she has such big cheeks and double chin. She is a pretty happy little girl most of the time, but is naughty too, of course, once in awhile and gets her spankings. She generally takes them pretty nice though. She has been very

---

[189] "irritable nature" – it suggests scolding, fussing, storming and raging. This is NOT a complimentary expression. (Norwegian)

slow about getting her teeth. The first appeared Sept. 20th and the second a few days later, and she is almost a year old. But perhaps she will make up for lost time when she gets started.

Bernice is out this afternoon to a Chinese feast, at the home of the people whose house we were living in the first part of the year. Only ladies are invited, of course, so I am staying home alone. I have not been out very much since coming to Wanhsien, as there is so much work to do at this place where we live and so much of my time goes for literary work and correspondence.

We are still bothered with insects in this place. Now it is flies and mosquitoes that are worst. They give us no peace, even though we have the whole house screened and we are swatting them all the time. I cannot imagine how and where they all get in. When the cold weather comes, we will presumably be rid of that pest anyway. Our place has really been fine though these days, as we have so many flowers, including several large flowering trees, with the sweetest-smelling flowers. Our main courtyard is filled with their odor most of the time. We have had a long spell of cloudy rainy weather, so that we have not been outside as much as we ought to have been, but we hope it will clear up soon. Had a hard rain this morning, which ought to clear the air somewhat.

The doctor that came out to our Mission from Germany is not turning out very well. When he and his wife found out what sort of work was expected of them in the inland of China, they apparently got cold feet, and now they have practically resigned from the Mission. They want to stay in Hankow where there are many foreigners and where they can make more money than our Mission salary affords. They have all sorts of excuses, of course – that we have not been treating them right, etc. But that is mainly excuses, I think. Our people did what they could to make the doctor and his wife feel at home. But she was very German, could not understand any English, and was rather peculiar besides. She took offense whenever anybody talked English in her presence, and in a crowd, where two Norwegian ladies, Bernice and Mrs. Ziegler were present, that could hardly be avoided. In short, neither she nor he had the right mission spirit. So we are perhaps as well off without them. It is good anyway that we "got their number" before we had spent too much money on the medical mission work. What with three of our missionaries incapacitated by illness, one, old Mr. Arndt, becoming rather useless, no new missionaries due to arrive this year at all, and our new doctor failing us, the situation is not the most encouraging possible. But we will have to hope that there will be a better time coming.

I enclose a few pictures of Betty Ann taken this summer. We have not taken any lately. Will have to do so on her first birthday next Wednesday.

Let us hear from you again soon. With best greetings to all the Follinglo friends and love to you and yours from us all,

Your brother,
George

GEORGE RECEIVES HIS DIPLOMA FROM NANKING U.
"He is the only one in the Mission who has done the required five years' work, even though there are others who have been here longer."
Letter 163 Wanhsien, Szechuan, China
October 14th, 1924

Dear Mother,

Have a letter to acknowledge this time, too. #179 came Sunday afternoon. Mange tak![190] I do not quite understand why you had to wait so long for mail in August. I did not write as regularly as I might have, but still I should not think you would have had to wait almost three weeks. I think you probably received one very soon after this letter was sent. At least, I hope so. Betty Ann also received the birthday card from Elsa and says, "Thank you!" The package has not come yet, but that is hardly to be expected.

This is Tuesday afternoon – for once I decided to write in the afternoon instead of the evening. I want to knit tonight. Usually I am rather sleepy and that is a better time for knitting than writing. I am still at that sweater coat for Betty Ann. Will I get it ready before we have cold weather, I wonder! Just these days there does not seem to be much hurry as far as weather is concerned. It has been bright for almost a week, rather, it has not rained for almost that time and we have seen quite a bit of Old Sol. I do not know whether or not I said much about it, but it rained almost all the time for over three weeks. You know what I mean – not exactly rain all the time, but more or less practically every day and the rest of the time it was grey and damp. It seems it was damper those weeks than it had been all summer. Things moulded and some places there was mould on the walls. And how hard it was to get the washing dry, even though we hung it on the veranda of the large inner court! You may be sure we have appreciated a change. It came with the new moon, if I am not mistaken. It has been warm lately, also, and yesterday and today I have actually felt sort of uncomfortable. George thinks I am funny, but it is a fact that right this very minute I am much warmer than I care to be. Just looked at the thermometer to see if I really <u>am</u> so funny and it registers over 80 degrees, so it is no wonder I feel warm. It is sultry, too, which makes it worse.

I wanted to write a letter to you on Betty Ann's birthday, but I was so tired that evening and I was fairly tired the day or two following. I told you I might invite a few neighbors, and I did so. I invited eight ladies, six of whom came. Besides, one came who was not invited, so there were seven ladies and two little girls. I served baking powder biscuits, chicken salad, ginger snaps, angel cake, and two kinds of candy – and tea, of course. I thought the salad was delicious, if I do say so, but I believe only one of the ladies ate any of it – worth mentioning, anyway. I believe we foreigners – at least, we "Shihnan girls" – tried much harder to eat everything at Chinese homes than the Chinese do when they come to our homes. They ate the other things. And how they love to wrap up this and that to take home for the others to taste. I thought I had a great plenty of everything and wanted to have the gatekeeper's wife, mother, and my amah in afterwards to taste of things, but the others simply took all the candy and all there was on the table, so I had only a piece of cake, a couple cookies and biscuits for them. They enjoyed even that, however. Of course the ladies learned that it was Betty Ann's birthday, so they had to give presents. I had purposely not mentioned it in the invitations, although the teacher

---
[190] Many thanks! (Norwegian)

who wrote them suggested putting it in, because I did not want the guests to know. In the forenoon one of the neighbor ladies sent over some flour and a chicken and two others sent over flour, also. The Chinese give quite a different type of gift than we do very often. The flour is ground very fine and I have been using it, but I do not have good success with it. They say it is wheat flour. It does not taste bad, but I cannot make things rise. One lady gave some eggs. Mrs. Wang brought a pretty piece of blue silk, which will make a dress, I think, although I have not measured it yet. Two others gave her money – one half a dollar and one a whole dollar. Both George and I feel that they were too extravagant, even though most of them have some means, and we will have to try to repay them in some way. That is the way here – of course it is more or less all over – but we foreigners feel it more here, that when the Chinese give us something, they expect to get as much, or more, back.

Betty Ann weighed 25 ½ pounds on her birthday. That means she has more than trebled her birth weight. We neglected to measure her until yesterday, when we found that she is 28 and ½ or ¾ inches tall. It is hard to tell exactly, because she does not want to stand still long enough for us to tell and she is so interested in whatever we use to measure her with. I do not know as there are any new accomplishments to tell about, since I have been keeping you quite well informed right along. She seems to try to imitate more these days. We gave her only a wooden whistle as present and took out another toy that she received last Christmas, but has been too small to play with – a little music box. We blew on the whistle for her, of course, and she tried to make the same sort of sound with her mouth, with the result that she got a sound out of the whistle, too! My! How we did laugh at her! Olive sent her a pretty bib with a little Dutch boy embroidered on it, together with a little beauty pin. Edna and the Oelschlaeger girls sent her handkerchiefs. Yes, I can tell you a new stunt of Betty's. She can creep, as I have told you, but so far she has been doing that only on the bed. I was thinking just last night that it was a lucky thing she had not tried to creep on the floor yet. This morning I put her beside the settee in the front room to play for a little while before her bath. The first thing I knew, she was gone, and when I looked I found her at the opposite end of the big rug. I picked her up and put her back and went at my work again, but in less time that it takes to write it, she was off and over at the other end. That means greater watchfulness after this. If only she did not suck those fingers! Uf! It is a terrible thing and to think that we, who are so opposed to finger sucking and tried so hard to break it right from the start, should have one of the worst you ever saw. The coming of these two teeth have made no improvement, so I guess I will have to try a mitten…

Last week George received his diploma from the Nanking University for having completed the five years' work in Chinese. I am glad, and I am sure he is, that he has been able to cover that ground. He is the only one in the mission who has done the required five years' work, even though there are others who have been here longer. They have been very lax about taking examinations or doing systematic study. They made new rules at the Conference this summer so now most of them have taken at least one examination. George has done the third, fourth, and fifth years' work since coming out in 1921 and his average for that work was 92.4%...

Have finished the sewing that amah had basted for me. That is, that part of the work is done. I want to do some outlining on my muslin aprons and will have to find some pattern. There is quite a nice flower on a straw mat we have and I have thought of tracing that for one design. Unless I decide to do a number of odd jobs tomorrow forenoon, I will cut out some more things to sew. It will have to be for Betty Ann this time. She is quite badly in need of clothes.

The other evening I took the little book that you and Papa gave me for confirmation out of the shelf and I see the date is May 19th, 1912. Was that the date I gave you before? This is the correct one, at any rate.

My amah is learning to do her work very nicely and I am so glad of it. She is already quite a help. I feel quite encouraged about that part of the work. I noticed she ironed centerpieces and embroidered pillow slips very satisfactorily today. They surely do learn more quickly when they are young. I think she is anxious to please. But, Hsiao deh is the one who tries my patience to the utmost. Sometimes I think I just cannot hold out any longer, but after a few hours I always decide that we will manage. George suggested sending for a regular cook, but I think not. I do not mind the baking I have to do, but what does irritate me is that I do not seem able to <u>rely</u> on him for anything, even to keep a decent fire when I want it. I have to keep track of every little thing. I don't suppose Hsiao deh means to be so careless, but he hasn't much of a memory, if he has any! He is <u>such</u> a kid! Sometimes he runs away from frying meat or some other duty that needs attention, or I will find him reading a little book, when there are a number of jobs he should be doing – oh! he does all the things that an irresponsible youngster would do and then some, I believe. Perhaps he will have a sudden change for the better some fine day, just like he did with the ironing. You remember how I complained about his ironing? It seemed that all of a sudden this summer he began to do real nice work and now he shows the amah how to do my dresses and some of the more difficult pieces. It is a mighty good thing that the kitchen is so handy here and that I can go in at any time of the day, otherwise I am sure I do not know how we would get along. I was in the kitchen very little in both Ichang and Shihnan – I always had to make a special trip to get there, so I used to leave everything to the cook, perhaps more than I should have.

I want to send off a parcel or two to you folks one of these days. "Not to be opened until December 24th!" I do not know whether or not I will get them off before I write again, but should you receive any parcels, please look around for any such notations as the above…

Had to type this last page after supper anyway. Betty Ann had a real fussy spell. She seemed to have just a fit of bad temper, but she so seldom acts up like that and I wonder if she wasn't feeling just right. She didn't want to go to sleep either. When she fusses like that I get so tired out. It is certainly hard to know if one is doing the right thing or not. I want her to be a good girl, but do we always handle children in the way that will help to make them good? It is indeed a responsibility to train children. Enough for this evening. Much love to all of you from us three.

Your daughter,
Bernice

GEORGE MENTIONS THE LILLEGARD ON THE WAY.
"...there is sewing to be done for our growing baby and the expected arrival."

Wanhsien, Nov. 10th, 1924

Dear Father:

This letter should have been written on the 7th, but I did not manage to get "my pen in hand" that day. Bernice wants me to let you know that we were thinking of you that day anyway. Bernice seems to be keeping busier than ever. We have no experienced servants whom we can trust to look after things, so that B. has to supervise everything. And she seems to be one of the type who find it easier to do things than teach others to do them, so that she has been spending a great deal of time in housework. And then there is sewing to be done for our growing baby and the expected arrival. We hope she will get things straightened out soon so that she can be relieved of some of the detail work she has had hitherto this fall. I have been busy with translation work and other mission matters. I should have been writing at a book on China for the Walther League, but have not gotten around to it yet. I hope I can specialize on it soon, however; when I get through with the translation of Schwan's Catechism Explanation, I intend to let translation work slide for awhile, and put most of my time in at the book.

By this time no doubt the smoke is all cleared away after the great political battle of 1924, which I imagine will be an historic one. If the American gunboat were here, I could get news of the outcome even now by radio, but it happens to be up river at present. So it will be another week or so, before I can expect to get reliable news of the results of the American election. I see England indulged in a complete return to Conservatism after its first Labor Government. Wonder if America will be afraid of Labor too? When you are over the strenuous work of the campaign, I hope you will find time to tell us a little about your work and about "the inside of things." I have had good hopes that "Bob" would win out. But perhaps it will be up to Congress to decide who is to be next President. Let us hope in that case, that it will be Wheeler, if the House refuses to elect LaFollette, which it of course would do. State politics look somewhat muddled at this distance. What is the matter with Blaine? Is he simply vindictive towards personal opponents, or is he trying to betray Progressivism, a la Lenroot? Zimmerman's large plurality ought to have been a pretty good rebuke to Blaine from the people.

As for China's politics – the unexpected is still happening. If there was anything that I did not expect, it was that Feng, the "Christian" General, would turn traitor and act the way he has done. I fear his action will give Christianity a black eye in China – perhaps deservedly so, as the Christians have been making so much of this Christian soldier and his work. It does not pay to boast too much of our Christian friends while they are living, that is certain. They may prove to be anything but worthy Christians. I fear that Feng's defection will mean the prolonging of civil wars for an indefinite period, while if he had remained loyal to his chief, there would have been good prospect that Wu Pei-fu could have brought all the opposing factions under his control in a comparatively short time. However, the unexpected and "unexpectable" may happen again, and peace come to this war-racked country sooner than would now seem possible.

In this province, everything is peaceful at present. We are in a practically independent kingdom here, and are really not very much affected by the war in North

China. The main result so far has been to hasten the departure of the Northern soldiers, which is a good thing. There are enough soldiers around here without them.

Betty Ann weighed 26 lbs. Saturday, at 13 months. Some big girl she is now! She walks around by herself and is continually getting into things that she should stay away from, with the result that the whole force of servants and Bernice are kept busy watching her. But she is only cuter and dearer for all that. It is really remarkable what a difference it makes to one that it is one's own child that is naughty. Any other child doing what Betty does would provoke us very much, I am sure. She gets her spankings frequently enough, but not because we lose patience with her. We are generally much more inclined to laugh at her than to scold and spank her. She understands much of what we say to her now, but does not try to talk, except in her own language. A few times she has said words after us, but generally she does not try to imitate. She does imitate me when I clear my throat, though, and will blow her nose, and do other such things which she would not need to be in a hurry to imitate us in. Such is the perversity of human nature. She has plenty of the old Eve in her and dearly loves to do things that she knows real well we do not want her to do. We just received a fine set of pictures of her and our place here. I shall enclose a few. We got only one copy of each now, and shall send you the rest when we receive more prints.

So much for this time. With love to all the family from us three, and with best wishes to you for many years of increasing usefulness to Church and State,

Your Son,
George

Betty Ann

NINE OUT OF TEN CHINESE ADULTS SMOKE OPIUM.
"Within the last week, strict orders have been given out against smoking,..."

January 12th, 1925

The China Press
Shanghai

The Szechwanese, or at least the people in Wanhsien District, having reached the saturation point in their use of opium, the authorities apparently have decided that the time has come when they can make more money by prohibiting the drug than by taxing it – or in other words, that a heavier tax on the smoker could be justified only by making it a crime to smoke and treating smokers accordingly. Within the last week, strict orders have been given out against smoking, whether in the opium dens or in the homes. All smokers are required to report the number of lamps in their homes and to pay a monthly tax of from $1.00 to $3.00 – according to the ability to pay of the victim – besides the other taxes paid before. Those who do not or cannot pay are simply hauled off to jail. Spies and investigators are abroad searching the homes and dens for opium lamps and apparatus, and where false returns have been made, heavy fines are levied. One opium den keeper is reported to have been fined $500.00 because he reported and paid for ten lamps instead of the twelve he really had in use. The poor people are hard put to it under these circumstances to avoid jail sentence, as they cannot afford the opium under these conditions and do not know how to break themselves of the habit either. There will undoubtedly be much suffering in consequence among them. However, it will be good in the end for this country if the heavy taxes put a stop to the almost universal use of opium, by men and women, rich and poor, and even by children. It is said that nine out of ten adults in this country smoke the poison. There have been no restrictions whatever on the use of opium here for several years, except for the taxes which were levied on opium dens and the opium itself. Opium has been cheap and within the reach of all. If the authorities carry out their prohibition campaign somewhat consistently, the time may come when the drug will be used little by the poor people – who are the great majority of the population even here in wealthy Szechwan.

MARJORIE ELISE LILLEGARD IS BORN IN ICHANG.
"I guess we will have to call her an Onstad anyway."

Sunday morning, February 1st, 1925

This is George, the father of Marjorie Elise, writing. Said young lady arrived this morning at 2 A.M., and proceeded to clear her lungs right away and show that she was all there. Bernice wrote this first page last night, then went down and talked with Mrs. Theiss at the fire place. I was working with the Chinese teacher at the time. About half past eight, Bernice told me to dismiss the teacher and get ready to go to the hospital. She did not have any of the regular pains, but the waters were beginning to come. The pains started about 10 or 10:30 P.M. I stayed at the hospital with her, except when the doctor and nurse were fixing her up. About 1 A.M., the pains began to get pretty severe, so the doctor and nurse came up and I waited down stairs. A little before 2 A.M. I heard the little one exercising her lungs. We had figured pretty strongly on a boy this time, but a girl is just as good any time. In about half an hour, they called me up stairs, and I watched Marjorie get her first bath. She did not like it very well, as it was a bitterly cold night and the room was none too warm – only a fireplace, and you know how drafty they are. However, she settled down nicely after she got in her warm bed, and she has been sleeping most of the time since 4 A.M. I went home a little after 3, and got some sleep between that hour and 8 this morning. After breakfast, Betty and I went to see mother and sister; both were feeling fine. Betty Ann was very interested in her new "baby," of course.

Bernice had a comparatively very easy time of it, and the doctor says everything was entirely normal – no tears or anything that should cause trouble. I think Bernice will get good care from Dr. Scott and Miss Wilson, so there should be no recurrence of such trouble as she had last year. She was feeling ready to get up this morning and talks about going back to Wanhsien with me in four or five days. But the doctor says she will have to stay at least ten days, of course. I plan on leaving for Wanhsien soon, taking Betty Ann with me, as I cannot very well spend any more time away from my station. It is soon a month since I left Wanhsien. Mr. Gebhardt will be coming to Wanhsien, on his return from Hankow, so Bernice and baby can arrange to travel with him. It will be a good thing for me to go ahead and get the house all ready too.

The new Miss Lillegard looks quite different from what Betty Ann did, so far as I can remember. She has about as much nose as Betty Ann has even now. I believe she is a little biggerboned all the way through – long fingers and toes, not such a round face, and a longer body. She has nice fat cheeks, however, and is not at all red, but looks like a regular baby already. She was not near so "dirty" as Betty was when she was born. It's pretty hard to say whom this little one looks like. I don't quite recognize anybody in her. It was easy to see her dad in Betty Ann, but Marjorie may be either like her grandfather Lillegard or the Onstads – I am not sure which. I guess we will have to call her an Onstad anyway. How do you like the name Marjorie Elise? We had quite a time deciding on names, as usual, but this was the choice we had sort of decided upon a few days ago, in case it should be a girl. We had talked most about names for boys. Lawrence Onstad it was to be. Betty Ann was taken care of by Mrs. Theiss last night, and today the Amah has given her a bath, dressed her, etc. So we manage pretty well.

Hereafter, I shall have to take care of Betty Ann nights. She was a good girl last night and caused no trouble.

I want to get this off today, so shall close with this. With love to you all from granddaughter No. 2, Betty Ann, Bernice, and myself,

George

George, Betty & Marjorie

BERNICE & GEORGE BOTH WRITE FROM HOSPITAL.
"And I believe Marjorie will have pianist's hands."
"Marjorie is as angelic as ever."

Letter 174

Buchanan Hospital
Ichang, Hupeh, China
February 2nd, 1925

Dear Mama,

Don't you think I am quite smart this time – writing a letter about 36 hrs. after Baby's arrival? I really feel very spry and am getting along so well. George wrote how suddenly I departed for the hospital – it was rather funny. Had been upstairs awhile and as I don't enjoy brushing my teeth these days – they're too sensitive – I did that in order to have it over with. Went down and started to make a cap for Erna. Didn't feel very comfortable, but that was not unusual. And then my warning came all of a sudden – the membranes burst – and in a few minutes I was on my way over here. George was a bit tired and excited yesterday and I noticed his idea of time wasn't entirely accurate. Baby was born at 2:10 A.M. and George came up less than 15 minutes later.

Tues. Baby needed attention when I had written so much and after that I had callers – Erna, Ruth, and my family and amah – so I didn't get at this again.

Wish you could see your new granddaughter! She, too, is a dear little thing and will be a great joy to us, I'm sure. Little as she is, Betty Ann is quite interested in her little sister. She doesn't know just what to make of my lying here in bed, however, and seems to be a regular Daddy-girl now. I am wondering how you will like the name we chose this time. Marjorie Elise is 20 ½ inches long and weighed 7 lbs. 13 oz. (Geo. called it ¾ lb. as he said it was hard to see. It's only an ounce one way or the other anyway.) She hasn't so very much hair, but she's far from being bald, and what she has is medium brown, a little darker in back. Have nursed her a couple times and must say she has a good deal of hair after all, but it is so short it doesn't show much. Can't say for sure what color her eyes are, as she keeps them closed so much, but I think they are blue. Her ears are close to her head, but quite different from Betty Ann's in shape. And I believe Marjorie will have pianist's hands. She has long fingers & such pretty nails. Just now she is crying because she is troubled with "chi" (chee) in the tummy. I've given her some warm water and she gave a good belch, but there must be more. She has such a pitiful cry when she feels bad. But, she surely hasn't cried much since she was born and when she has, she has always been justified in doing so. Really, the greater part of the time I don't hear a sound for hours. She lies in her nest right next to my bed.

Wed. A.M. Feb. 4th Bernice had some fever and headache last night – the result of her milk "coming in" apparently. She is better today and her breasts are "tight as a drum" she says. Marjorie is as angelic as ever.

We have sent another order to M.W. & Co., for about $12.00. Would you object to extending credit for the few dollars that our account will be overdrawn, till we find out whether or no the Chicago people will be sending any more money? If they do not send money, we shall send from here before we send in any more orders for anything.

I am planning on leaving tomorrow or Friday, taking Betty Ann with me. Of course, I am busy packing and getting ready in consequence. Bernice will write again soon, I suppose, and I shall also try to write on the way up to Wanhsien.

With love to you all from us <u>four</u> (by the way your letter closing with a greeting to "the four of us" came on the day pretty Marjorie arrived – which is guessing pretty close),

                        Bernice & George

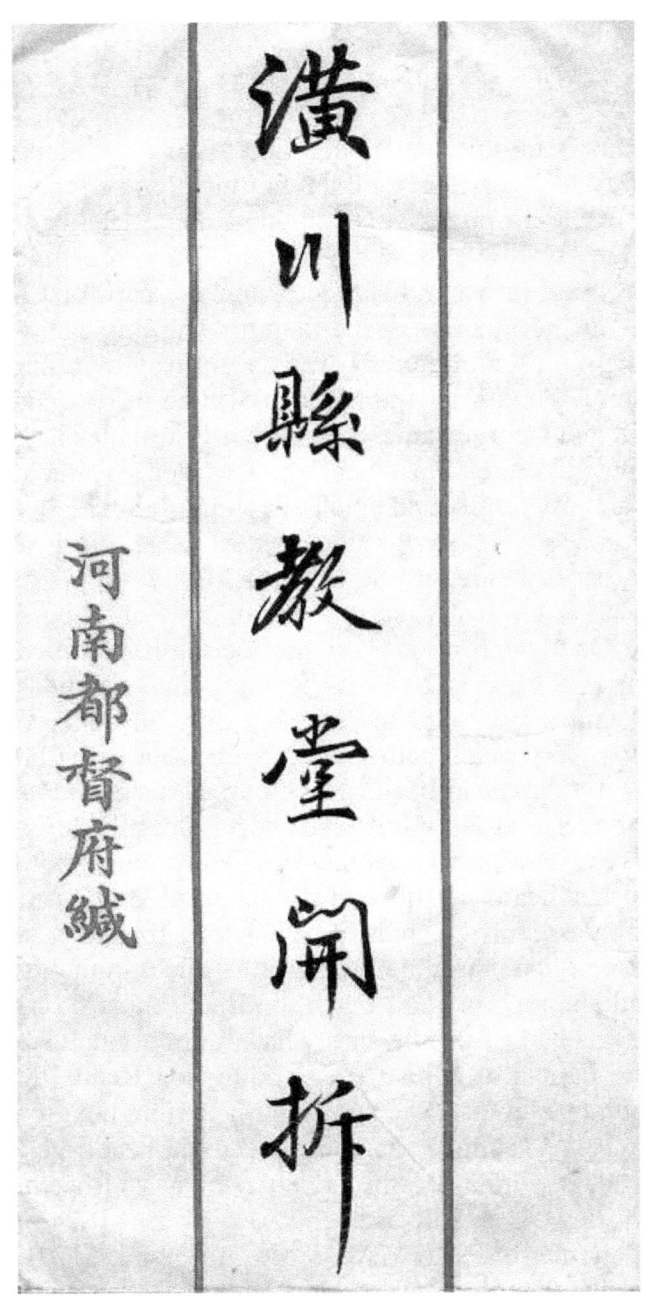

THE FAMILY IS REUNITED AFTER TWO WEEKS.
"It did not take long for her (Betty) to get used to having me around…"

Letter No. 177   Wanhsien, Szechwan, February 25th, 1925

Dear Mother,

Here I am all loaded to write pages and pages and little Marjorie thinks that, since she has been sleeping all day and been such a good girl, she may cry now. If it were earlier in the day, I would feed her, since it is only about half an hour until she is due, but I don't like to take her early in the evening, as she is likely to wake up too early in the night and then she will have a hard time holding out until six in the morning. And I am not hankering to have her howl around four or five in the morning. She really has been doing very well, though, and has not given me any trouble at night. I must say that I think the night "chores" is the hardest in the care of little babies. We have been trying to keep the bathroom somewhat warm and I go in there at night to feed and change on her. Even though we do not keep the fire up, it is considerably warmer than our bedroom. But, I perspire more or less at night, and even under my bathrobe, I feel quite chilly. What a way to start my letter! There is a good deal of news that properly belongs ahead of this sort of rambling.

Have you received No. 176? I wrote it on board the "Chi Ping" in Ichang and gave it to the steward, who promised to get it mailed for me. In case he failed to keep his promise, I will just say that it was written on the 15th and told that I had that day boarded the boat mentioned, was feeling fine, but homesick, and so on. There was nothing very important. Had a nice trip up. The first day there was one other passenger, but after that I was alone. The only other foreigner on the boat was the captain, a very nice young American. The "Chi Ping" has hit the rocks a number of times since Christmas, but this time we had no mishap. I have been unusually blessed during all my travelling in China. We did narrowly escape having a very serious accident, though. At one time when we were in a long gorge, high cliffs on either side and no place where a boat could be beached for miles, a Chinese threw a handful of waste into the steering apparatus so that the wheel couldn't be turned. We were headed straight for the rock wall, but the captain held the steamer in a somewhat straight course by reversing one engine and going ahead with the other until the stuff was picked out again. The captain is very much inclined to believe that it was a deliberate attempt to wreck the boat, but some of the Chinese seemed to think the poor fool who did it, was only fooling around and did it in ignorance. Be that as it may, he was guilty in so far as he was in a place where he had absolutely no business to be, he not being one of the boat's "hands." The fellow was turned over to the authorities here, I think.

As usual, George was right on hand to meet me and he had the house in spick and span order. And he did all the unpacking for me the next day. I stood the trip pretty well, but it did tire me, of course, (rather to my surprise, as I rested most of the time), and I did not feel like doing much of anything for a few days. In fact, I have not done anything outside of a few little jobs like washing the children's wool shirts, etc., besides bathing the kiddies and looking after them.

It was just two weeks from the time George and Betty Ann left Ichang that I arrived here and how many changes I noticed in Betty. When I first saw her she looked ever so much fatter to me. Her face was as round as a full moon! We think she did gain a good deal, but undoubtedly it was not having seen her for awhile that made her seem so very fat. She had not exactly forgotten me, but she was a little bit strange and preferred having her Daddy take care of her that evening. It did not take long for her to get used to having me around and she is almost as much of a mama-girl as she was. She is Daddy's baby now, though, because he does so many things for her when he is in the house, especially when I am taking care of the little baby. He picks her up in the evening and also in the morning and helps with feeding her, besides doing all sorts of little things during the day if he happens to be around. And I am learning to handle her a good deal without lifting her. For instance, I have her bathtub on a fairly low bench and when I am through washing her, she steps out of the tub on to my lap, so I do not have to more than help her keep her balance. She thinks that is great fun! You should see her run! She is all over the house these days, except in the bedroom, and she likes the kitchen best of all, because there are so many more things that she can get into there. She is not tall for her age, but she can reach plenty high enough, it seems, to get into all sorts of mischief. She loves her little sister and when I am bathing or feeding her, Betty Ann comes running every few minutes to love Marjorie up by putting her cheek against her. Of course I have to keep my eyes on her all the time, as she sometimes gets too affectionate and once in a while she is a little rough. It has surprised me a good deal that Betty should take such a great interest in the baby, since Betty is so young. How I am going to keep Betty Ann supplied with proper shoes is a problem. The slippers you sent are still plenty long enough, but they are too tight across the top. If there were any shoemaker here who understood anything about foreign shoes, we would try having a piece of leather put in. She can wear them and they do not seem to bother her when walking as far as we can see, but the straps leave a red mark on her foot. She has been wearing the shoes you sent since coming back. They are much too long yet, but they also, are tight across her foot just where the laces begin. She has such a fat foot and high instep. I am wondering if you have already sent the slippers I ordered. If you have not, will you try to get extra wide (and "fat") ones?

    We looked at the Christmas presents that had come and had Christmas over again the night I came home. George had taken off all the outer wrappings and had looked at some of the other things, but he had left some of mine for me to open. Thank you ever so much for that lovely Boston bag. I know that it will be one of the most useful things I could ever have in that line of article. I have never had anything in which to put those last things that one has to pick up when leaving on a trip and now there are always some little things to carry for the babies. It suffered a little bit through the mail, but it is not enough to make any real difference. The bottom has been bent in a couple places, but I imagine I will always have that bag full enough to keep it from bending any place! Again, Mange tak![191] I suppose Elsa did not know that a pretty bar pin is about the only piece of jewelry that I have wanted for many years. I am delighted with it and know that I will find it as useful as ornamental. Of course Ragnar will read this and know that I am including him in my thanks for the bag. George asks me to thank you all very much for the shirt and collars until he can write and thank you himself. He is pretty busy these days and I am afraid it will be awhile before he gets at writing. The things are certainly very fine – there are always so many new and pretty materials at home and we feel quite

---

[191] Many thanks! (Norwegian)

"nifty" when we have something like that to wear. But, George says that next time you send him a shirt (!!??), please send a 16 or 16 ½!! He wears 17 only in the soft collars, as they usually shrink so much. If this shirt is too large and does not shrink enough, we will fix it. I don't imagine it will be hard to do so…

…I am so sleepy I cannot think – which reminds me that I am now writing on Thursday evening, having succeeded in writing only the first page last night. George had given the little doll to Betty Ann before I came and he said she was as happy as could be over it – she loved and kissed it and "bye-o-bye'd" it. By the time I came she had pulled one arm off and I have not gotten around to sewing it on yet. She likes the dolly very much yet, but, like all kiddies (I suppose), she throws it around with the rest of her toys. She was hugging it to her when she went to bed this evening, though. The big doll is such a nice one that I am not going to let her have it all the time. She has played with it a little, but when she gets to the stage where she likes to throw it down, I take it away. She learned how to make the doll cry in a very short time and it is a joke to watch her turn it over. Have I mentioned everything now? If I haven't, it is only because things were opened before I came and so I have sort of lost track of them in my mind, and then I am sleepy, as said. There is still a package on the way that you sent before Christmas. It is the one with thread in, I believe.

I will not be able to write nearly all I could tonight, so I had better tell a little about Marjorie before I quit. She is a good baby and does not give much trouble, I must say. Of course, she cries some now and then, but I learned quite a few things with Betty Ann and I think Marjorie is benefiting thereby. For one thing, she does not spit up milk after her feeds as a general rule and does not cry so much because of "chi" in the tummy and I believe it is chiefly because I hold her up on my shoulder or against me and pat her back during and after feeds until she belches – and how she does belch! I notice that as soon as I neglect to do that, she will vomit up more or less. How fat she is getting! I can fairly see her grow. She gained ten ounces last week and I expect to see an equally big gain this week. Her face is getting so round. She weighed 8 lb. 12 oz. at three weeks. I have put her in dresses already. I did not put Betty Ann in dresses until she was ten weeks old and I expected to do about the same this time, but I found that the dresses and petticoats fit Baby so nicely, while she was always getting lost in her nighties, so I decided to dress her every day. She is easier to handle and she certainly looks sweeter in a dress and some little jacket. I put a nightie on her in the evening. She has smiled for me a couple times – she has smiled many times ever since she was a few days old, but that was usually when she had a full tummy or was asleep – but now she has smiled when I talked and "clicked" for her. She will be taking more and more interest in the world from now on. She should have been baptized before this, but we have been waiting for Gyps. We thought he would be coming sooner. Expect him next week some time. Have not decided whether we will ask him to perform the baptism or be a sponsor. Have not decided on other sponsors yet, either.

Tomorrow we will have guests for tea. The Jenkins, Captain Cutts and his wife, and Dr. Kaveney are coming. I would have had them next week, but Mrs. Cutts intends to return to Chungking the early part of the week, so I could not postpone it. I am feeling much better these days, however, and do not think I will mind it at all.

There are so many questions in your last letters that I will have to write a special letter to answer them, I think. Have received 197,-8,-9 and Elsa's this week. I will answer only one thing tonight. Where did you get the idea that I had had internal examinations? Didn't I say <u>abdominal</u> exam?[192] You ask Amy if it is not advisable to have examinations to learn if the position of the child is correct or not. Miss Jeffrey told me that if women were more careful about being examined for that beforehand, a great deal of trouble and pain could often be averted. So far as I know or remember, I have not had more than one internal examination during all pregnancies and that was before Betty Ann came – after I had been so sick on the river trip to Ichang. But I have had a good many abdominal examinations. They have been telling me – the Jenkins – that Dr. Kaveney is very anxious to see Marjorie Elise. I am only sorry that he could not have helped her arrive, so that I could have been saved all those weeks away from home.

Tell Grandfather that his nightshirts will have plenty of time to shrink to fit his grandson!

TO BE CONTINUED IN THE NEXT

Goodnight and lots of love to you <u>four</u> from us <u>four</u>

Bernice

Betty & Marjorie, Kuling, August, 1925

---

[192] See Chapter 14, letter No. 155, p. 416.

THE CHINESE SERVANTS' DUTIES ARE DESCRIBED.
"...I find less time for reading and music than I did when I was doing a lot more work than I am now,..."

Wanhsien, Szechuan, China
April 15th, 1925

Letter No. 181

Dear Mother,

    A little after eleven o'clock A.M. I am sitting here at my desk with my wet hair hanging down my back and Marjorie sitting on my lap. And I am wearing that old blue morning dress that you made for me before I was married!! It looks pretty tough now, I must admit, although it is whole, but I wear it part of the mornings, often changing after I have bathed Marjorie. Daddy says I am spoiling Marjorie and sometimes I think he must be right. I do pick her up more often than I did Betty Ann when she was little and one reason for that is that I do it so that Betty Ann will get a decent nap. She will sleep while Marjorie cries, but I find that she does not sleep so long as otherwise – and I certainly like to have Betty Ann take good, long naps. She gets too tired by evening, if she does not have her sleep. She is not regular, exactly. I usually put her to bed between ten and eleven. Sometimes she sleeps only an hour or so, while other times she has slept as much as two hours or more. I do not think that Marjorie is really spoiled, though. She is troubled so much with flatulence, too, and I usually find that when she cries she is either wet or uncomfortable. When she is merely fussy, she does not cry so hard or keep it up very long. She is hollering right now in spite of being held. You suggested that I give water after nursing. I tried it a couple times and couldn't make her take it. Guess I will have to try again, as she would probably be better about taking it now. I do not think my milk is too rich now, though. I have not had such a plentiful supply all the time for this baby. She has been gaining some every week, so she evidently gets enough, but many times I can tell that there is much less. The week before last she gained eleven ounces, while last week she gained only three. That seems so funny, but we always use the same things when weighing her, so it must be correct. And we weighed her twice last time to make sure. No, she gained four ounces last week, not three…

    …Marjorie is such a smiling little thing. In the mornings she often lies and laughs – she actually makes a noise, though it could hardly be called a real laugh – and talks and coos for her own amusement. She has not called for a night feed for almost a week now. Don't you think that is pretty good? She is just over ten weeks. Betty Ann had a night feed until she was five months old and then I had to break her. No two kiddies alike, are there? I certainly enjoy Marjorie – I <u>permit</u> myself to enjoy her more in a way than I did Betty Ann, although my first baby surely gave me as great joy and pleasure as any baby ever could. Betty is a scream at times. It is time for her to get used to the idea of praying before and after meals and at night, etc. She is too small, of course, to learn a whole prayer yet, but we are trying to teach her to say "Amen." She is a great one to say "b" for "m" and so she says "abah" for "amen." When I first held her hands – folded – and said the evening prayer for her, she refused to repeat "amen" after me, but after a few evenings she understood what was wanted. The funniest thing was, however, that she started saying "abah" before I was half through the prayer and kept it up until I was through, and then refused to say it when she was supposed to. Now she starts saying "abah" as soon as her hands are folded and keeps it up during the whole prayer, sometimes going higher – up the scale! She climbs whenever she can. She gets on top of the footstool and from that reaches around for things, climbs into our chairs, etc…

April 16th Did not write any last night as I was rather tired and George did not feel well, so we went to bed quite early. It is four years ago today since I left Madison, but it seems <u>so long ago</u>. I think the next three will pass by more quickly – and then we will be coming home, if all is well. We are having a lovely day, quite different from that day four years ago when we had that terrible blizzard. We have really had such a cold spell lately, tho' that we have been almost uncomfortable, our stoves being put away. We had such nice weather in March that we thought it would be safe to take the stoves down, but we have had quite different weather from last April. Then we had some such hot days that I gave Betty Ann two baths a day at times. Today is very nice for a change and in a little while we are going out to have some tennis. We had our first set last Saturday. Yesterday Mr. Bahnson and Mr. Kahle came over and we played doubles. They have not played tennis before, but Mr. B. is learning very quickly and looks like a promising competitor for George.

(After supper) Bahnson and Kahle did not come up this afternoon, so George and I played alone. Of course I don't get many games, but I have deserved a good few of the points I made and I hope to do better after awhile. I am so glad to have a chance to get some more strenuous exercise. I am sure it will do me lots of good…

Last Friday – Good Friday – was Mr. Chiang's birthday. He had almost made all arrangements for having a lot of guests before he mentioned it to George and it was too late to call it off, so he entertained in spite of our not liking such doings on Good Friday. His idea was to have all those who were interested in the Gospel come and it was really more than he could afford, so George helped out on the expenses, rather he made it a Mission affair in a sense. We served tea and other things to a huge crowd in Shihnan once when we were there as a part of our advertising and George considered it would be a good thing to invite these people for the sake of "advertising." We had services before the feast and the chapel was quite full. I have told you that Mr. Chiang is one of our Christians from Hankow who is helping George, have I not? He came up in November. Until now he has been spending the days down at the Dollar place chapel. He visited with enquirers, showed them our literature and tried to arouse the interest of all he could reach. He also sold books and tracts. But we have no chapel down there now. Saturday evening Mr. Chiang came in and told us that a new manager from Chungking had arrived to take Mr. Wang's place. We had the use of those rooms free through the kindness and courtesy of Mr. Wang, which is one reason why George has continued work down there. It was not a desirable location, however, and this opportunity to withdraw without giving offense was rather welcome. Moreover, we understand that the new manager would not wish to have us there – at least not under the previous arrangements. It is possible he might be willing to rent, if we wanted to pay the price. Attendance down town has been very poor, while up here it has been better right along, so for the present, all the meetings will be held in this chapel. George is trying to find suitable, available place for chapel on one of the busy streets, but so far has not secured any. Everybody (?) in Wanhsien knows that we are in the market for land and property and there are plenty of offers, but because we are foreigners, they are asking "six prices."

There are some questions you asked long ago that I have been intending to answer for the last several weeks, but never seemed to have time for more than just the regular news. You ask about our servants. Surely you know that I have always had three servants ever since coming to China, not including those who carried water. In Ichang and Shihnan we bought water by the load and by the month respectively. Our servants are Hsü sifu, Hsiao deh, Kuang chen, and Amah. Hsü sifu is the coolie. He has many and various duties. His regular duties – or those that I can think of on the spur of the moment – are to wash the floors and beat the rugs, carry water (which is not so little when you think of all the clothes washing, floor washing, etc., etc.) keep the place outside of the kitchen – the back yard, one might call it – swept and orderly, sweep the sidewalks in our small court, fill the lamps, empty the commode twice a day, and so on. Besides that, he has innumerable odd jobs. Today he washed wheat and washed windows. He fixes our water filters, he works in the garden, often gets coal for the kitchen and wash water for us. He goes out and gets wood – that is, finds someone that sells it and then carries it home for us. It costs extra to have someone else carry it way up here. Hsü sifu also is a chair bearer. And when any of us go travelling, he has to help carry the baggage beforehand and then do his duty as chair coolie. He is a slow-going, stupid fellow, and still he is a most handy man. He made our bamboo waste paper basket. He grinds the wheat. Oh, Hsü sifu is called on to do an hundred and one things. Hsiao deh has done practically all the cooking and baking since I returned from Ichang. Besides, he helps wash dishes, of course. He also does the daily dusting, with the exception of two rooms. Every morning about six o'clock he has to make a trip to town to buy eggs, vegetables, meat, or whatever it is we need for that day. The morning is the best time to get things, as that is when the farmers bring their produce in. Moreover, it is the only convenient time for him to go down, as the trip takes at least an hour and a half. Since Hsiao deh is not a regular cook, we call upon him to do many things that we would hardly have asked old Tsen sifu – our cook who died – to do. Hsiao deh has done what pressing and cleaning George's clothes have received lately. He has also helped iron clothes at times. Although he is not any too busy, he has more to do than you would think, as it takes more time to do things because of the nature of the country as well as lack of the most common conveniences at home. Then, too, he is only a sixteen year old kid. Kuang chuen is about the same age, but he is much smaller in size and seems younger, somehow. He sets the table, helps wash dishes, dusts two rooms, washes the kitchen floor once a day (that floor has to be washed twice a day), brings wash water for us and dumps the dirty water. He builds the fire every morning. When we had the heater stove up, he had to tend to that. He has a lot of little things to do. The last months I have had him take Betty Ann out a great deal to play with her and watch her. And Amah has almost more than she seems able to manage, although I think I would get the work she has been doing out of the way a little more quickly. It is not easy for her, though. Half the time when she wants to iron there is either not room on the stove for the irons, or else they are not hot enough. This stove is too small and so dilapidated that it will do well to hold together until summer. She makes the beds and helps with Betty Ann whenever I want her to. She also mends stockings and helps with what sewing I have for her when she has the time. <u>Now</u>, you are wondering what in the world there is left for me to do! It is a fact, it takes about three or more Chinese to do the work one does at home, but you perhaps realize that most things are done in such a primitive way that they simply cannot get as much work done. And I certainly find that I can't get away with what I did in the States. Say or think what you will, we all seem to be busy, many as we are, and I find less time for reading and music than I did when I was doing a lot more work than I am now, as far as accomplishing anything is concerned. I haven't any "get" and, being unused to it, when I do indulge in a splurge of hurrying, I find that I am all worn out after it. A poor stick, am I! I expect to be pepping up a little now when I have more exercise regularly, however – and then watch my dust!! Aa ja![193] After ten o-clock and all in bed save Mother. Will finish tomorrow then. Still have to get ready for bed and feed Marjorie. Wish I could hop right into bed the way I am. I'd be asleep in less than ten minutes. Good Night!

A little more about servants while I am on the subject. You ask why it is necessary to have a gatekeeper. So far we have not really had much need of one, but we will probably be needing one more from now on. You will understand that in a large mission compound – walled – it would be necessary to have a gatekeeper, since there would be Chinese coming and going right along and in China it would hardly do to leave the place open to whoever wished to come in, if they had no business there – inquisitive coolies, for instance, or soldiers. So the gate should be closed ordinarily. Our gate has been open most of the time, but we have ordered the gatekeeper (our present one is the amah's husband, who also writes nicely and has done a good deal of copying for George – catechism, etc.) to keep the gate closed, because it is not pleasant to have kids, dogs, and so on coming in when they have nothing to do here. His duty is also to keep the main courtyard clean, sweep the walks, sweep up the fallen leaves, and the like. Wu sifu is chair bearer. We are entitled to have one chairbearer paid by the Mission. He is a smart fellow and does all kinds of things also. Since over a year ago we have had men working around the place getting it cleaned up and in shape. Some men have been engaged by the day or month and Wu sifu has always been helping with whatever was to be done. There has been an awful lot to do to get this "pig-pen" cleaned up, but we think it is getting to look pretty nice now, although there is still a great deal to be done, if it is to look the way I should like to have it. We plan on planting grass this summer. Wonder if we can afford to buy a lawn mower! If we continue chapel work, have guest rooms and reading rooms up here, I think the Mission should at least pay half. Will have to ask George about that…

Your #205,-6 came day before yesterday. Am glad the news of Marjorie's arrival went through so quickly. We had some acknowledgements from the States almost a week before yours arrived. Must send this off now, even though I could write more. Gave Betty Ann salts this morning, but she has not passed any more of "them things" yet. Hope there are no more, but that would be almost too good to be true.

Lots of love to you all and best regards to friends and relatives from the four of us.

Bernice

---

[193] Oh well! (Norwegian)

THE FIRST CHRISTIANS ARE BAPTIZED AT WANHSIEN.
"...of all the servants on the place, only the wives of Wu and Hsü are not baptized."

Letter No. 186

Wanhsien, Szechuan, China
June 4th, 1925

Dear Mother,

    Betty Ann just came in, having sat down in the mud with her clean rompers and also soiled her clean stockings. Amah was sewing and the two boys, who had nothing to do whatsoever, were too busy (?) to help watch Betty Ann. But, I guess we are all glad that there is a little mud around for a change. It is finally raining and we are all very glad of it. We have had such a long, hot spell and it has been getting hotter day by day until we found it quite uncomfortable. I felt especially sorry for the children. Must say, though, that Marjorie has been just as good as could be, lying on my bed the whole day long and having a fine time all by herself, kicking, talking, and laughing. She is really a good baby, I think. She has had some prickly heat, but she has not been fussy about it. It was several degrees over 90 yesterday and very close. I had to fan Betty Ann last night until she fell asleep. We did not think it could last much longer and how happy everyone was to see some clouds this morning. We almost gave up in the course of the forenoon, but at noon we had a sudden shower and now we have had another hard one. However, we need a lot of rain. Some people have not planted rice yet, since their fields are dry. Right around here they have planted, being so fortunate as to be able to get their water from a large pond in back. And if they cannot put in a big new crop of rice, conditions are likely to be very bad next year. At present there are almost famine conditions here, as well as out in the Shihnan territory. Rice has doubled in price in just a short time, so you can understand that people who were just able to buy enough rice to live on before (and there are so many such in China) are not able to buy nearly enough now. There have been a lot of beggars at our door and other people have come and asked for help also. We have raised the wages of our servants, besides giving them a little extra out of the charity fund. This province has had less famines than any of the others, I believe George said, but now there have been so many soldiers here these years and much opium has been raised, so the Szechuanese are suffering also. In Shihnan our Mission plans on doing fairly extensive relief work, but here there are business firms who are taking a hand and trying to help, so we have not asked for any of the Famine Relief fund. *Hear that a shipload of rice from down river has arrived and is being sold at half price.*

    Betty Ann is evidently struggling with malaria again. She has not been feeling so well since Saturday, but I noticed the change in her at once, so we began feeding her quinine and she did not have a chance to get so bad. Her appetite is poor – she thinks she is awfully hungry and gets so excited when her food appears, but by the time it is ready for her to eat, she often refuses to so much as taste it. She eats fairly well in the morning, though, which helps keep her going. But, what a difference in her disposition when she feels well and when she feels like she has these days! She becomes <u>so</u> irritable! We are going to give her quinine until we get to Kuling – at least two grains per day. The "Palos" is here again and this forenoon Dr. Kaveney called for a few minutes. He thinks it would not hurt to give her another dose of santonine just to be sure she is rid of that trouble. He did not think Betty Ann looked much like an invalid! She doesn't just now, that is sure, but she did for a while.

Friday Eve. Hurrah! Both children have been sleeping since before eight o'clock for a change. I have not even had evenings to myself lately, due to Betty's notion that she was afraid – or something. We have been putting her to bed with music, as we found out that she would lie down, if we promised to play the piano. She falls asleep quite quickly, but it has happened so often that she has awakened an hour or so later. Perhaps it was due to being too warm. It is more comfortable tonight. She has been feeling much better today. At least, she was happier and more content. Her appetite is picking up again, too.

Betty Ann is a regular little Chinese! She cannot pronounce consonants at the end of words. The Chinese have no consonant endings except "n" and "ng." Betty would talk quite well if she used the right endings. She says "bi" for bite, and leaves off the final consonant on cap, hat, hot, wet, and so on. You should hear her say "My, my!" She has been saying that a good deal the last couple days. She says a few Chinese words too, now. The expression she puts into 'aa ja' is certainly good…

Last Sunday George baptized his first class in Wanhsien. There were eight adults, four children in their teens, and five little children. Wu sifu, Kuang chuen (Wu's son), his daughter and other little son; Hsü sifu, Wen tien, a daughter and little son; our amah and her husband, were all baptized. That means that, of all the servants on the place, only the wives of Wu and Hsü are not baptized. They have not been doing much studying, so did not qualify. One of the others is a brick mason who has worked here most of the last year. He could not read a character when he started studying, but he is very bright and they speak so well of him. He has seemed very anxious to learn and has been faithful about attending meetings. Three gentlemen and the children of two – the third has no children – made up the remainder of the class. If only Dr. Liu had lived to be baptized with them!

Mr. Chiang, Hsiao deh, and I were sponsors for the five little children. I was sponsor for the daughters of Mr. Ih (E) and Mrs. Dzou. The wives of these men and of Mr. Dzang – the third gentleman – are very nice and we hope to baptize them in the not too distant future. It is too bad that I have not been able to have meetings with them so that they could have made more progress. Mrs. Dzou and Mrs. Dzang have studied a little at home, but I am sure they would do more, if we had regular meetings. It certainly is a great advantage when the whole family is interested in hearing the Gospel. Mr. Dzou destroyed all his idols shortly after he began attending meetings and I understand his wife was entirely won over by his arguments. She is a dear woman and I want to know her better.

Bed time! Wonder how you all are? How are your feet?
Greetings to all and much love to all you four from the four of us.

Yours, Bernice

GEORGE DEBATES LEAVING THE MISSION FIELD.
"I have done what I could these four years to set things straight. Things will have to either bend or break this summer. It seems to me that four years is about long enough."

Wanhsien, Szechwan, June 17th, 1925

Dear Father-in-law:

It is some time since I wrote you now; but Bernice does so much better than I at the art of letter writing that I have been glad to leave matters to her. I wish to write to you about some more personal matters, which you on occasion might talk over with Ylvisaker, since he is on our Mission Com., and I have already written him about these matters too.

We have not said much about the difficulties we are having in our Mission work this year, as it is rather hard to present the situation without going too much into detail. I shall just state as briefly as possible what we are up against.

Our last Conference took a great deal of time and pains in discussing and deciding a number of important questions, which aimed to get our mission work on a better basis. We had fully expected that the Board would support these moves. Instead of that, it knocks the most important decisions in the head, with the result that things have been in a rather chaotic state ever since. It looks to me as though Meyer, who (to be brief) is a most slippery and unreliable customer, succeeded in pulling the wool completely over the Board's eyes while he was at home, so that the Board took his opinions and his word for things rather than that of the rest of the Conference. This alone would be enough to start a rumpus, of course. But when Meyer came back to Hankow, things began to move there too, and the result has been that I and a number of other missionaries have been kept busy writing protests against the way the Hankow people were running things. I have sent Ylvisaker copies of some of these protests already, and shall ask you to look them over some time. Things finally got so bad that we cabled the Board, asking that somebody be sent out to attend our Summer conference. We have not heard yet whether anybody will be coming or not. At any rate, we are going to have a stormy Conference. A majority of the Conference are with me at heart, but some of them are rather timid, and if things get warm, I imagine I may have to face the music pretty much alone. Others have written very strongly to me, but not all have written to the Conference and the Board as frankly and strongly as I have.

Among the matters that have been causing trouble is the Term Question – what word to use for God. I have sent Y. copies of two papers on that question, which you may be interested in reading. I had fully expected that the Board would come out on the right side, after they had looked into the question a bit, and read some of the materials I had sent them, including my papers. Instead of that, I have just recently received a letter from the Board, taking me to task for some of my statements, which I by no means consider unjustified or unnecessary. I am enclosing a copy of my answer to the Board, which I shall ask you also to show to Y…That the Board writes in this way, means this much, if I am not too bad a guesser, that they are still following Meyer's lead, even on a question in which he is doctrinally wrong. If the Missouri Synod Mission Board takes a stand against what I have written in my papers, I do not hesitate to say that it is deserting orthodoxy and Biblical teaching. On this point, I have any amount of material and would not hesitate to buck the whole faculty in St. Louis, if they should all become so funny as to try to defend the term to which I object. I know it cannot be done, except on the basis of heretical teaching on various lines.

Now what I want to say is this – I have not given up hope yet that the Board will come across on some of the matters to which we have objected, including this Term Question. But at present, things look rather doubtful. Bernice and I have consequently spent considerable time talking over plans and prospects, in case we should feel forced to leave the Missouri Synod Mission. I never was particularly anxious to connect up with the M.S., "having a hunch" that things would not pan out in the best possible way…
Bentrup, who was always on the right side, has resigned – after telling the Board frankly that they did not know anything about Mission work and ought to resign too, I am told! Gebhardt has been forced to stay here in China this year, with the result that I fear he will be too run down to be able to return for a long time, if at all, and more than one of the others in whom I have confidence are getting "cold feet." So if things keep on at this rate, I fear we will find ourselves standing more and more alone. The young kids that the M.S. sends out to the mission field are too often weak in their theology and cannot withstand the unscrupulous methods of Meyer and Co. If things are not corrected this summer, with Gebhardt and others here to help, I do not have any hope that matters will improve any in the future. And so I have to consider the possibility of leaving this Mission, much as I would hate to give up the mission work now.

What I should like to have you do for me, then, if you can, is this: Feel out our pastors and others on the question of supporting my station out here, independent of the Missouri Synod. If there is no prospect that the Synod would be ready to give me whole-hearted support, so that I would be just as independent of the Missouri Synod, while associated with it, as our pastors at home are, although they also stand in fraternal relations with the M.S. – then there is only one thing left – look for work in the home field. How is it – is the Norw. Synod supplied with pastors? Or do they have a hard time supplying the vacant calls? Would there be any desire on the part of our pastors, to have me come home and help with the work there?

One thing that, of course, helps us to contemplate the possibility of returning home for good with more equanimity than we otherwise would, is the circumstance that Betty Ann seems to be having a hard time of it getting rid of her various ills. Bernice has not been so very spry either much of the time of late, and has been rather discouraged. And I have malaria every so often. Perhaps it would be best for us to stay in the States for health reasons if nothing else. You understand, that we have not decided anything yet. Everything depends on how things go at the Conference this summer. If Meyer's strangle hold on this mission can be shaken off, so that we can have some prospect that our work can be run in the future on right, Lutheran lines, instead of the disgraceful way it has been run hitherto in Hankow, I shall want to stay. If not – if something radical is not done to put a stop to the loose way in which things are done there in Hankow, I simply must get out. I have honestly been highly ashamed of my association with this M.S. China Mission at times. When I think of how the M.S. boasts of being the only true Church and then consider how its work in China is built up on the foundations laid by Haugianere, Methodists, Congregationalists, and what not, I get sick in the "tummy." The proselytizing and the unionism which Arndt and Meyer have indulged in down in Hankow has given our Mission a bad name all over the country, and it is a wonder to me that the Anti-Missourian Press has not gotten a hold of it and given them a good raking over for it. Of course, Meyer and Arndt try to lie and bluff out of things, so that the Board does not realize what the true situation is. I have been trying to put the Board wise – and fear very much that they are going to refuse to believe the truth, but will believe the liars instead – something all too common in this world. And that's where I will have a fight on my hands this summer. If a representative of the Board's comes out, I intend to insist on a thorough housecleaning, and if the Board does not back me up in it, but assumes that no housecleaning is necessary, then I want to get into a cleaner house! We can be affiliated with the M.S., without being responsible for all its dirty linen. But we cannot be members of its Mission, without being directly responsible for conditions in that mission. I have done what I could these four years to set things straight. Things will have to either bend or break this summer. It seems to me that four years is about long enough. Anyway I have had enough.

    The papers no doubt keep you informed with regard to the situation in China. Conditions look worse right now than they ever have since the Boxer war, in my judgment. The Lord only knows how things are going to turn out.

    I shall leave other news to Bernice, and shall close with this. With love to you all, and best greetings to friends of mine that you may meet,

George

A bridge over the "little river," Wanhsien, 1926

BERNICE DEFENDS GEORGE'S LETTER.
"...if he did not think that he would be shirking his Christian duty, he would most certainly keep still and let things go."
Letter No. 193   Kuling, China, August 14th, 1925

Dear Father,

Thank you very much for the birthday letter. I think you have never failed to write me on that day, even though your letters have been quite rare treats the last couple years. We realize that you have been very busy.

This letter is for you and Mama and I request that you do not let the "kids" see it. George does not know that I am writing this either. I want it to be just a private little note.

I was very glad that you advised George to be more discreet in his protests and so on. I do think that he takes it better from you than anyone else just at present and I wish that you would try to write to him a little more often and encourage him and give him advice. However, I cannot refrain from telling you that I think he is to be excused to great extent and I want to tell you a few things. First, I must say that I have been urging and urging him to be very careful in his expressions and he always has me read his things before he sends them and he has sometimes rewritten whole pages because I have thought he ought not write this or that. But, I cannot always know what is best and he has often convinced me that what he says should be said. I know that I can say (neither) you nor anyone else not present on the field can appreciate to full extent – perhaps even to small extent – what the situation out here is at this time. Why should one man be privileged? And if Meyer has not been a privileged character, then we don't know who is. Not only that, but it seems he has been shielded by everybody for everything, all the time. If anyone else had done half the things he has done, they would surely have been reported to the Board – if George had done it, for instance. As an example of what I mean, I can take the most recent in that line. I have said that he and Mrs. went to Japan. That was nothing that anyone could really object to, but perhaps you can understand why it was not very much approved of. When he received notice that there would be Conference, he wrote – or at least someone heard through somebody else!! – that they were leaving Japan the 28th of July. But about the day he was expected to arrive here, a telegram came saying he had incipient tuberculosis and a nervous breakdown. The next news was that Mr. Zschiegner should go to Kiukiang last Monday afternoon to meet Mrs. Meyer, who was on her way to Hankow. He brought back the news that she was on her way there to sell their furniture, etc. Meyer had cabled to the Board on his own hook and received permission to come home on sick leave. Last year Gebhardt's case was diagnosed as incipient tuberculosis and he came to the Conference, brought statements from at least two doctors, and then asked the Conference to act. The same in Schwartzkopf's case. In both cases the Conference voted unanimously to recommend to the Board that they be granted sick leave – and the Board came back with such funny answers that Gebhardt did not feel quite justified in going home in spite of being repeatedly advised by the folks out here to do so. Now, Meyer cables to the Board without the advice of the Conference and the Board cables him to come home. I ask you, is that consistent? This is not a matter of principle, but it is of precedent. Moreover, it is all of a piece with things that have been done the last year in regard to principle and policy. George took quotations from a letter from the Board received two years ago and one received this winter and asked them to explain how they could be harmonized and for other information – but, do you think they have answered? He has not received any information on a great many things, but he did get a riffle for writing one of the papers on the Term question. Does anyone think that George simply loves to fight and that he would spend hours and hours of hard work writing papers in order to have a fight <u>with his brethren</u>? In fact, George likes to be on very good terms with all his fellow workers much more than some do and if he did not think that he would be shirking his Christian duty, he would most certainly keep still and let things go.

One thing that makes it a little harder for him than the rest is the fact that he is older and more experienced than any of the others save Arndt. Riedel has been in China longer, but he has not had the experience at home and not <u>nearly the education</u>. But, what do these young college fellows care about education and experience? Some of them even refuse to accept <u>facts</u>. Lately, rather a few weeks ago, those who were here on Kuling had several doctrinal discussions on "The Natural Knowledge of God," chosen because it has bearing on the Term Question and some of them were not quite clear on that doctrine. I think all but one were pretty straight on the question, but that one was – well, either he is stubborn or he is terribly ignorant. All the others came with their commentaries, etc. but the one who should have come with some proofs for his stand, had nothing but his Bible <u>and</u> he even went so far as to practically refuse to accept statements in these commentaries which are used by the best Lutheran pastors! If he has the intelligence to interpret the Bible without commentaries, he ought to have the intelligence to understand them and to accept them. He happens to (be) the youngest save one of all the men – but, you can't tell him a thing! He is perhaps the worst in that way, but a number of the others have pretty much the same spirit about things. I certainly am not writing this in a boasting frame of mind and I think you will know that, but can't you understand that it makes it a little difficult for one who has had a good deal of experience in both mission work and pastoral work, has studied and read incomparably more than almost any one of the others, and has been through such an experience as George had in 1917, to see things being done contrary to Lutheran principle and good Mission policy? And after having tried to inform and instruct some of the younger fellows in a nice way and doing his best to help get things going as they should be in a Lutheran Mission for four years, the doings this last year were raw enough to provoke indiscreet expressions and enthusiastic protests. And, I can tell you, Papa, some unpleasant things have been said about and done to George in personal ways – behind his back – while he has surely tried to be as friendly to one as to the other.

Oh dear! It is so hard to write about such things – perhaps I have written just the wrong things in trying to give you an idea. The unpleasant affairs of the last year are Legion. Anyway, write to George and please ask Rev Ylvisaker to do so also. George will welcome both advice and criticism… I think you and Mother will understand why I felt like writing a little and not misunderstand what I have said – or the spirit in which I have written. We like all our fellow missionaries, but if there is not agreement on principle – well, you know how it goes. We are all having a nice time "playing" together. With much love to you from

Your daughter, Bernice

Chapter 15
Number Three

BERNICE DOESN'T REALIZE THAT SHE'S PG AGAIN.
"All last week I had such a headache...I think I'm crabbier than I was, but George says he thinks I'm the same, only now he tells me what a crab I am!"

Letter No. 206   Wanhsien, Szechuan
                                                                        January 14, 1925[194]

Dear Mom,

    Wanted to write a note last week when I received the enclosed circular letter, but I didn't get at it…

    …I guess "absence makes the heart grow fonder" and so folks in the U.S. like me better – at this distance. They'll all be terribly disappointed then when we get acquainted again. <u>China</u> is not the place to come to to raise a sweet disposition. By the way, will you please tell me what sort of disposition I used to have? I think I'm crabbier than I was, but George says he thinks I'm the same, only now he tells me what a crab I am! So I'm only better informed as to my nature. Now you please tell Geo. whether he's right or not. You ought to know, having lived with me for about 20 yrs!

    All last week I had <u>such</u> a headache. It would let up now and then during the day, otherwise I'm afraid I could hardly have been up and around all the time. And it ached nights, too. Don't know if I was sort of over tired, not keeping regular hours for some weeks, or if it was due to other causes. Have felt better the last days.

    Did I tell you in my last letter that I was making pads for our wicker set – two chairs and settee? Bought some grey Japanese crepe this summer for the purpose. To brighten it a little I made lazy-daisy flowers all over in a half dozen different colors. Since they're small, they don't make it either loud or conspicuous, and still the dull grey is brightened a little. Now I'm going to finish my tea napkins with the crocheted corners – to go with my lunch cloth, you know. 'Bout time! Three have been ready a couple years, yesterday I finished the fourth. Had enough material for ten napkins and think I'll try to make them all now. I seem to have lost a corner or two. Have six in all but thought I had eight. They're easy to make, though, and it is rather fun to crochet for a change.

    The tailor is busy these days making a "prestekjole"[195] for George. It is of silk. George has had Gyps' gown here this fall & winter and the tailor is making it according to that. He seems to be getting along all right. The silk is really too thin, but I guess it will do. It is warm here so much of the time that cashmere is almost too heavy. I dyed this silk myself – about 25 yds. as it's only 20" wide. If only the ordinary Chinese silks were wider! But they don't need them wider for their own clothes…

(The rest of the letter is missing.)

---

[194] This must be 1926, judging by the number of the letter.
[195] "pastor's robe" (Norwegian)

GEORGE DECIDES TO LEAVE THE MISSION IN A YEAR.
"They must think that we know nothing at all about the Chinese language or about 'authorities' on these questions."

Kuling, June 26th, 1926

Dear Father-in-law:

I am sending you herewith copies of letters to the Board and Prof. Graebner, some kodak pictures, a clipping with regard to conditions in Wanhsien, and a copy of some select phrases from Arndt's writings on the Term Question.[196] This week I received a letter from Prof. Graebner which I did not like at all, as my answer indicates. I must say that I am getting rather tired of this Term Question – a question which orthodox Christians should be able to settle without any difficulty at all, it would seem to me, but which these St. Louis people for some mysterious reason insist on looking at in about as "skak-kjoert"[197] a way as possible. Graebner says he is following "authorities." But his authorities are very much in the Minority and it is a mystery to me that even a man who does not know Chinese should not be able to see, at least with the help of the materials that have been sent the Board, that the authorities they follow are all wrong. They must think that we know nothing at all about the Chinese language or about "authorities" on these questions. Or else they have so much confidence in Arndt that they swallow all the wild statements he makes rather than accept the statements quoted from recognized authorities that I have been sending them. I still hope that Graebner does not represent the Board and the Faculty in what he writes on the Term Question. His stand is about the same as the stand of the Board a year ago, and I hope they have learned something about the Term Question since that time. It looks to me as though Graebner is writing just on his own account without reference to what the Board and the Faculty think or know about the question at present. Graebner's letter shows that he is rather ignorant as yet with regard to Chinese religions and the Term Question in particular, and those who have been delegated to study the question should know more than to make some of the statements he does anyway. This letter of Graebner's, however, gave us somewhat of an unpleasant shock, and Bernice and I have been indulging in plans for coming home next year accordingly! I have told the Board plainly that I did not care to work in a Mission that defended the use of the term Shang-Di and shall stick to that.[198] Several other members of the Mission take the same stand. How many of them will stick when it comes to a showdown we cannot tell, of course. I shall try to do what I can to set matters right when I do come home, naturally, by meeting with the Board and discussing this question with them or the Faculty. But I have no doubt that the stand I take is the only right stand and shall expect to show them that it is eventually – if they are not all too prejudiced already. It is strange how hard it is for people to see a point when their prejudices blind them, though, is it not? To identify a god of the heathens with the true God ought to be considered a far more dangerous sin than unionism, synergism, or any of the evils which have caused the Norw. Synod to separate from the other Norwegians. And yet these Missourians, one after the other, have been criticizing me for "separatism" and what not, because I take that stand! Of course they do not admit that the use of Shang-Di involves

---

[196] The Term Question was the debate over which Chinese term to use for God.
[197] "distorted," "perverse;" literally, "pulling to one side" (Norwegian)
[198] Shang-Di or Shang-Ti was an ancient exorcist and wizard worshipped as a god. (See explanation by George in Chap. 13, page 406)

syncretism, but the fact is that it does, and they will never be able to get away from that fact by any amount of quibbling or fallacious reasoning. Arndt and the other Shang-Di men out here really admit that Shang-Di is the name of a heathen god, but say that it is allright to use such a name. That the Board and the Faculty should tolerate such a stand in view of the clear Scripture passages against it is a mystery to me. But hitherto we have not heard a whisper to the effect that they have criticized Arndt and the others for taking such a stand. Graebner even says that it would be allright to use the name of the head-divinity of the pantheon, as if that is not equivalent to recognizing that head-divinity as the true God, which I suppose he would not want to do exactly either. There is where their quibbling and side-stepping come in. It is really too bad that these St. Louis professors were not present to tell Paul and the other apostles that they should use Zeus or Jupiter for the true God, instead of Theos, which was so "contaminated by idolatry," even Venus, Bacchus, and all the other immoral gods being included under that term! But the stand which Arndt and the others so far have taken on this question leads logically just to this conclusion that Paul, etc. were wrong when they used Theos instead of Jupiter or Zeus. Well, there is no use in speculating about this too much. It may be that the Faculty will yet come out on our side. The last letter received from Brand says that the Faculty was still studying the question. Of course they are at somewhat of a disadvantage, not having any knowledge of the Chinese language, and perhaps no ready access to the real authorities either. I suppose the "authorities" to which Graebner refers are such as take their materials at second-hand. There is where Legge has done much harm. He was the first one to write for the English world on these subjects and so has been accepted as an authority, while as a matter of fact, he is on many points entirely wrong, and is admittedly so among missionaries and others who are capable of judging as to the validity of his claims. Well, this will have to do about this matter for today.

We received a letter from Preus not long ago in which he told about the purchase of the Mankato College by the Norwegian Synod. We were quite "thrilled" by the venture that our little Norw. Synod is making, and hope that it pans out allright. It is not easy to work in a Church of which one is not a member, as I find here, although so far as the missionaries are concerned it perhaps makes little difference to them that I am not a member of Mis. Synod. What counts with them is that I have not attended their schools, etc. Even if I should join the Missouri Synod, the situation would remain much the same for me. So I can appreciate that it must have been rather unsatisfactory for our people to work with the Missourians in College and Seminary. May the day be not far distant when we can have our own Seminary too! From what I hear of the St. Louis Sem., I must say that I do not have much confidence in it. It seems that most of the students cheat at examinations, that there is much immorality among the students, and in general anything but the kind of a spirit which one would look for at a Theol. Sem. I think the main trouble is that the boys are too young while at the Sem., and also that there has been little attempt at enforcing discipline. The young boys there are not men enough to be left to themselves the way they are. I believe we have had the best of them here on the mission field, and in some cases, as you know, that is saying none too much!

The doctor says that Bernice can expect to go to the hospital in about two weeks. He also says that it is to be a boy this time. I hope so. If it is, I shall blow myself for a cable to you. "Boyallok" would mean that it is a boy and that everything is allright. If it is "only another girl," (which is quite a Chinese way of saying it), we shall not send a cable.

We have had considerable rain since coming up the mountain. It rained most of last night and is rainy and foggy today too. I have not had much chance for tennis accordingly. However the weather is cool and refreshing, as compared with what we had in Wanhsien.

Kindly pass the enclosed copies of letters to Graebner and Brand on to the members of our Mission Committee. With love from us all,

George

MISS LILLEGARD NO. 3 ARRIVES.
"We have not really decided on a name yet – we were figuring pretty strongly on a boy."

Kuling, China, July 5th, 1926

Dear Folks:

Miss Lillegard No. 3 arrived today at 1:45 P.M. and so far everything is fine. Bernice had a still easier time of it this trip than before. At the dinner table, she noticed that "things were starting," so we sent for a chair. But she decided to walk to the hospital and not wait for the chair. And it is good we did, as everything was just about over by the time the chair reached our place. We got to the hospital about 1:10. Miss Baden, now Mrs. Fischer, got busy getting Bernice ready, and I went back to the house to see about the chair coolies and put the children to bed for their nap. I got back to the hospital by 2:00, to be met by some lusty squawking and the announcement that another girl had come. The doctor did not get there in time either. But there was a lady doctor in residence at the hospital, so she took charge of the case. The doctor came and watched proceedings and got ready in time to help deliver the placenta. By 2:30 I was permitted to see the patients, and everything was over except washing the baby. She weighs 7 lbs. 12 oz., and is a chubby little thing – much the same build as Betty, but more of an Onstad face, I guess. Anyway she has a good-sized nose to start out with. They said she was a very pretty baby, and to be newborn, I must say she was a lot better-looking than many I have seen. I believe she is going to be quite dark, although of course it is hard to tell yet.

We have not really decided on a name yet – we were figuring pretty strongly on a boy. But we shall decide very soon. No doubt we will wait till Brand comes with baptizing her, if everything goes well.

Now I must trot down town with this letter, make a visit at the hospital, and get back to help feed the children and put them to bed. I shall write more tomorrow.

With love to you all from us <u>five</u>,

George

LAURA BERNICE LILLEGARD JOINS THE FAMILY.
"...she has a nice head of hair, more than the other girls had,..."

Letter No. 223

Lot 1228
Kuling, Kiangsi, China
July 20th, 1926

Dear Folks,

Since I am owing you all letters, I shall address this to all, especially as I do not expect to be able to get a great number of letters written for awhile. Kuling is a bad place to try to do much writing and just now I haven't the pep to do much of anything.

First of all, I want to thank for all the presents. The things for the children came while I was in the hospital – on the 10th, if I'm not mistaken. Laura will surely appreciate the comfort of the outfit and the blanket, even if she doesn't understand they are gifts, and so on…

And now a little about my trip to the hospital. I didn't see George's letter, so if I repeat much, please excuse me. Fischers arrived a day later than expected, because it rained so hard on July 2nd that they had to remain in Kiukiang. They came Saturday forenoon (3rd). Sunday morning early I knew my time was limited and how we did wait for F's baggage.

Martha had only a couple dresses here and she naturally wanted her uniforms. Slept at the hospital that night (what little I slept – there was a terrible wind all night) but came back for breakfast Monday. And in the course of the forenoon, I had a good bath and later a dose of c. oil! Martha thought it was a good idea to take oil and I, too, for various reasons. Well, I guess the walks (Sun. eve & Mon. A.M.), bath, oil, and all hurried things along and I couldn't even be polite and wait until everybody had eaten their dinner, but left the table and prepared to leave. We sent for a chair and Geo. went to the nearest phone and got word to Dr. Buswell and then Geo., Martha, and I began walking, as I dared not wait for the chair. And that twenty minute walk certainly brought results in the way of speed. Oh my! Everybody at the hospital were kept on the jump for awhile and it was mighty fortunate that Dr. Thompson (a lady) was right there, because Dr. B. arrived just in time to witness the birth. Excluding him, there were four nurses and a doctor present! Not because the case was difficult, but because there was so little time that it required several to "gadder the things togedder."

Baby was born about a half hour after I walked into the hospital. I lost a great deal of blood the first 12-14 hours after the birth and perhaps that is one reason why I seemed to have less pep and energy than last year. Although I have felt quite well – at least, free from pains – I have had no desire to exert myself. Usually I have wanted to read and write, but I didn't do any writing, except for my diary, and I didn't read much, either. I was more satisfied to rest and take it easy. And how nice it was to have Martha with me! Naturally, she had the time to give me very good care and she did so many things for my comfort. She went home for a few hours every day and then one of the hospital nurses would wait on me, if I needed it.

Dr. Buswell permitted me to come home Friday, which was one day earlier than his regular rules say. I told him I'd like to celebrate my birthday at home. As usual, I found a pile of packages under my plate. The first two, three days I was home, Martha wouldn't let me walk the steps, so George carried me up and down rather than send a tray up to me. Martha gave me a guest towel,…George gave me a pretty luncheon set – a new design. He always asks what to get me and I told him that I'd like to possess more embroideries, if we should leave China – whether we "pull out," are "kicked out," or get a furlough. I have some things, of course, but not very much considering how long we've been here and how plentiful embroideries are.

For some reason or other, Baby was uncomfortable and fussy for a few hours yesterday afternoon and evening, so I didn't get much written. It seems I don't get anything done in the course of the day. Until yesterday, Martha has been bathing Baby and yesterday, too, she helped a little. Today I did it alone – you know it seems quite a task at first, even though I ought to be in good practice. I have to be so careful, because as soon as I become even a little tired, my milk is low. Am drinking more water, eggnogs, and cocoa – liquids in general – than ever before…Certainly hope I'll be O.K. as I gain in strength. I want so much to nurse my baby. It means so much, if they can get a good start.

Baby is, of course, just as dear and sweet as any babe and she has been a good baby, too. We are going to try to get a picture of her real soon and since we are on Kuling, you won't have so long to wait this time. So many weeks are required when we send our films from W. (Wanhsien) for devel. & printing. We can't say yet what color eyes Baby will have. They were so dark at first that I thought surely they'd be brown, but now I am not nearly so sure of it. As Geo. must have told you, she has a nice head of hair, more than the other girls had, but I think it is about the same color. It is not black, but quite dark brown. Laura has not been baptized yet, as we want to ask Rev. Brand to do that. We haven't chosen witnesses yet, either. I think we are going to ask Martin & Louise, Bert and Alice to be sponsors.

Betty Ann certainly does love her baby sister. For a little girl, she is very gentle with her, too. She kisses her hands and holds them and how she enjoys holding the baby! She comes around many times a day and says, "Hold the baby!" And she feels worse if I tell her she may not hold the baby than when she is spanked. Sometimes I've said she was a naughty girl and couldn't hold Baby and then Betty Ann quickly says, "Sorry!" meaning she's sorry she was naughty. Marjorie, also, is fond of Baby, but she is far from gentle. She means to love her, of course, but she grabs so roughly. I think she will learn to be more careful, though.

What wouldn't I give, if my girls could live at a place like Lake Edge? Betty Ann and Marjorie get outside every nice day, but there's no decent place to play – it's just walk here and walk there. They aren't developing any initiative, either, and oh! it seems they cry and scream so much. Betty Ann is fat and heavy, but it certainly isn't because she eats a whole lot. Half the time she says, "Buh iao eat!" and most of the time she just fools around, pretending to eat. Marjorie cut another molar while I was in the hospital and the fourth one is trying to shove an edge through. She seems to be improving again, but hasn't much color. She has been so pale.

I am home alone with the children (& servants) this evening. The rest of the family and several others are out on a moonlight picnic. They didn't ask George at first, knowing I couldn't go, but I said I didn't care to have him miss out on such affairs because of me, if he liked to go. He usually enjoys picnic trips and there's no reason why we should both miss out on them.

Rev. Brand is expected tomorrow afternoon. All the folks will come here in the evening – a little welcome – reception – and ice cream, sandwiches, and cake will be served. I've been saying I am quite excited about his coming, especially since he has seen all of you so recently. Hope very much he is feeling better. We heard he was anything but well at the time he left St. Louis.

There is quite a feeling of suspense amongst most of us and it will be a relief to have Conference under way and begin to find out how things stand.

There is much more I could write, but I know you'd send me to bed, Mama, if you were here, so I shall prepare to obey your unspoken wish. Baby must have a lunch first!

Much, much love to you all – five of you, too, now that Esther[199] joins the family circle – from the five of us. George, Bernice, Betty Ann, Marjorie, and Laura!!!

Marjorie, Betty & Laura, 1926

Marjorie, George & Laura, Betty,

Kuling, August, 1926

---

[199] Bernice's brother Ragnar's new fiancée

LILLEGARDS WILL LEAVE ON FURLOUGH NEXT JULY.
"Arndt came straight out with his opinion that George was to blame for <u>all</u> the troubles…in this mission."

Letter 225

Lot 1228
Kuling, Kiangsi
August 22, 1926

Dear Mama,

 Have been wanting to write all week, but in a way, I guess it's just as well I have not, because they've been discussing the Term Question this week and there have been some committee meetings with Arndt – the result was our moods have been many and various and not the best for letter writing. Conference has been in session for three and a half weeks already and they still have some business to take up. Besides the regular sessions – 8:30 A.M. – 12:00 and 1:30 P.M. – 4:00 P.M. – there have been committee meetings right along. In fact, Conference has adjourned for a half day several times in order to give the committees a chance. Most of the time, until the last couple days, has been taken up with Arndt. He has retracted a number of things in a general way and things are settled "paa en maade."[200] I won't dwell on Arndt now, however. It would take too much time and it would do no good. I'll tell you more about such things when you and I visit together – if you want me to.

 The Term Question isn't settled, as most of the fellows won't accept the Faculty's decision, which says they should use Shang Ti. You may know that. It is very evident that the Faculty members who took this up had the wrong idea as to some things. They came with some "funny stuff" in their report. The first day, the "Shen-ites" were quite cheerful, as their arguments seemed to be shoving the others into a corner. But on Fri. Rev. Brand was well, a bit mean, one might say. George and I were sure this was our last summer on Kuling, because it certainly looked as though we'd <u>have</u> to sever connections. The others were mighty blue, too. Gyps felt pretty badly, because he, also, feels he could not work in this mission if they use Shang Ti.

 We are in a better position than the rest in that respect, as we are not members of the Missouri Synod. And Rev. Brand wasn't any too happy, I guess. Friday evening he as much as said he was prepared to tell them to accept the Faculty's decision or come home. A nice situation! But yesterday morning the tide turned and it seemed as if Rev. Brand finally saw the light. And not only he – some of the others who have been agreed that Shen is the proper translation, but were not convinced it is wrong to use Shang Ti, now seem more and more convinced that it <u>is</u> wrong to use Shang-Ti. The fight isn't over yet and it is possible the ultimate decision may be against us, but the Shen side is 100% more hopeful and confident than on Friday. If the question is settled tomorrow, perhaps I'll get the results written in this letter.

 Have some real news for you this time. The question of furloughs was taken up and a schedule recommended. Rev. Brand thinks the Board will approve of the schedule and we are first on the list. Guess when? We are to leave next July! So many came out in 1921 and '22 that it would be almost impossible for all to go home at the end of seven years. The schedule then arranges for some to go at 6 yrs, some at 6 ½ yrs, and then

---

[200] "in a way," "in a manner" (Norwegian)

others at 7 years. Now, are you going to get excited about our coming home next year? It is quite thrilling, I think. I really had not thought of furlough so soon until we came down this summer and everybody was suggesting that we might be going then. But I have thought we might be coming home earlier because of all the difficulties. Arndt came straight out with his opinion that George was to blame for all the troubles – Term Question & everything else – in this mission. My! I'll have to buckle down and do some work the next nine months. I must confess I don't feel ready to make such a trip, a year at home, etc. etc., but I suppose I never will feel that way. Hope I keep in good health next winter. You know, I plan on doing my own cooking. Am anxious to try to "pull us out of the hole." And I hardly dare tell you what I want to knit before we leave, as you will most likely smile. However, I have wool for sleeveless slip-overs, a winter sweater & cap, and a summer sweater for both Betty Ann and Marjorie…

Fischers are allocated to Kweifu and one of the new missionaries, Simon, is allocated to Wanhsien. We'll have company this year. We don't know whether he will come with a bride or not. Two men who are coming are unmarried.

Betty Ann has been rather restless at night lately, had poor appetite, and been at her fingers so hard, so we had her stool examined. She has worms all right! She is to have a dose of santonine in half an hour, another in two hours, and milk of magnesia tomorrow A.M. early. I rather dread watching for results. Had M's stool examined today and the report was negative. Mighty glad of that. Marjorie has been picking up a lot lately. She has a good appetite, a lot of pep, and she's a fresh little youngster. She not only holds her own with Betty Ann, but she is so naughty to Betty once in awhile that B. cries and I have to punish M. Everybody seems to like Marjorie very much as she always has such a happy smile. Betty Ann talks so much now and she no longer talks Chinese to us. She gets Chinese words and expressions mixed in, but we all do that. Marjorie, too, has acquired quite a few words lately. She says "ahlo" (for "hello") so much and it's fun to hear her chirp "ahlo onkel."[201] She also says "How do!" or How do do!" and "Shame, naughty, Tantan (tante)[202] and other words – oh yes! "Gocking" for stocking, and shoes! Betty Ann is so interested in all pretty things – I try to teach her to notice beauties – and she is learning to enjoy the beautiful sunsets with us…She really walks very well and she takes good, long steps. You should see her run – big strides just like a boy!

Laura is doing very well. She gained over half a pound last week and weighed about 10 lbs. 12 oz. this morning…Rev. Brand baptized Laura on July 25th…She can do a nice little "stunt," also. When I take her by the hands and pull, she will make her body rigid and let me pull her right up on her feet. She is such a strong little one. If she remains well and strong, she ought to be learning to walk about the time we come home next year. I don't look forward to travelling in July. Bet we'll be caked with dirt by the time we reach Wisconsin!...

Must mail this now. Much love to all of you from all of us – big & little.

Bernice

---

[201] Onkel is uncle (German, Norwegian).
[202] Aunt (German)

THE MISSIONARIES ARE SAFE DESPITE A HARROWING EXIT.
"...Hanyang had just fallen into the hands of the Reds[203] yesterday..."

Letter 226

No. 8 Milan Terrace
Hankow, Hupeh
September 7th, 1926

Dear Folks,

  While I sit by Arndts' electric fan, drying my hair, I'll try to get a "bulletin" off. Should have written letters of congratulation Sept 1st, 2nd, & tomorrow, but we are having "hectic" times here and I'm only writing now to let you know we are safe. I imagine you see newspaper reports and so are wondering where & how we are. The situation changes almost daily, so it isn't safe to predict anything. But let me give a brief report of the situation as far as we've been concerned lately.

  Fischers and the Hankowites planned to leave Kuling Sept. 1st but had to give it up. We were booked out of Kiukiang Sept. 3, but ladies & children were advised by Consul not to travel, so finally Geo. & Fischer only left on that day, taking all the baggage we could spare. Sat. P.M. while we were having a children's party at our place for Marie Riedel, a telegram came from George (Hankow) telling us to come. I packed till midnight & was up at 4:30 Sun. A.M. to get bedding, etc. in & things roped. Had a fine trip down the mountain – we were eighteen in the crowd – Scholzes, Theisses, and others – nine adults, nine children. When we came to Kiukiang no definite word as to steamer's arrival could be obtained and we hung around in the "Rest House" – misnomer if there ever was one!! – until 6:00 P.M. Then we went to a hotel, which was "full up," except for 1 double & 1 single bed (for 18 people & children). I can't tell you in a few words of all the difficulties & discomforts of our 14 hr. wait at K. Baby Laura was good as could be, but didn't sleep from about 4:00 – 10 P.M. because she was hungry & I was absolutely flat and no way of giving her a bottle feed. On top of that, I got sick after supper. If it hadn't been for Mrs. Schmidt & Martha, I don't know what I'd have done. Mrs. S. finally nursed Laura and took care of her & M. helped with B.A. & Margie. At 2:30 A.M. after some had had more or less sleep and others none at all, we were routed out to go to the steamer. Hats were slapped on over uncombed hair, sleeping kiddies picked up, & somehow or other, we, the servants, & our lot of baggage got on board the "Suiwo" where we found plenty of cabins, to our relief. The trip then to Hankow was very pleasant, but as we were afraid of being fired on, we travelled for several hours without a bit of light. We heard both rifle & cannon shots in the distance. Arrived in H. we learned that Hanyang had just fallen into the hands of the Reds yesterday P.M. I'd planned to stay aboard until this morning, but Geo. came down and said we must come ashore, so at midnight we pulled out again. I certainly felt sorry for the kiddies. We are at Arndts – only Agnes & Frieda O. are here, as Mrs. A. & Lydia are on Kuling – and we are as comfortable as possible under the circumstances.

---

[203] The "Reds" are the Southerners, led by Chiang Kai-shek, who succeeded Sun Yat-sen upon his death in 1925. Sun's party was originally the KMT, or Kuomintang (Guomindang), a Nationalist party. The Communists from Russia joined him and financed his war to take over China. This offensive was known as the Northern Expedition. It started from the south where the party was headquartered and spread north to Hankow.

Sept. 8 Eve It has been <u>so</u> hot here that all my time has been fiddled away washing & bathing the children and myself, picking things up in our room, etc. etc. We all have more or less prickly heat – Marjorie worst. Sent Geo. out with girls to get haircuts and he came back with two little <u>boys</u>! I was quite disappointed to see almost all their lovely hair gone, but they are certainly more comfortable.

You've most likely seen as lengthy reports as we about the trouble in Wanhsien. We are quite sure the situation is far worse than the published reports. It is evident the British are keeping something quiet. (This is Friday now, Mommy!) George left early this A.M. for Ichang. I hope he has a safe trip. He will proceed to Wanhsien if it is possible and safe (reasonably) to do so. You can imagine I will be anxious for word from him. They say all wires from Hankow are down and there aren't many steamers going now, so I'm rather afraid I may have to wait longer than usual for a message. How long I and the children will be here is very uncertain. It all depends on situation in Wanhsien.

Now I'm going to mail this and then I am really going to make a special effort to get a decent letter off soon. It has been so hot, but is getting a little better. Marjorie's face was swollen with prickly heat. She's better today, but both girls are somewhat crabby. I'm rather "all in," but will feel more rested soon, I'm sure. Baby Laura has been angelic. She's the best baby I've had – so far. Ugh! This is a <u>dirty</u> city. Excuse this terrible scribbling.

Much love to you all from us,

Bernice

(Written in the margins of the front page, top and left side):
Better send mail to No. 7 Milan Terrace for awhile. If I'm not here, they can forward.

Geo. cabled Board "All safe." Wonder if they notified you. You might write Board if at any time the situation seems serious, as there's likely to be word from here.

SHE IS DISCOURAGED; NO GEORGE FOR ALMOST 3 WKS.
"…it certainly isn't easy to take care of three kiddies all under three years and no Daddy around to help."

Letter 228

No. 8 Milan Terrace
Hankow, Hupeh
Sept. 21, 1926

Dear Folks,

Just a note today, as I am a little more busy than usual and haven't much time. I know you will be waiting for news, however, so I will give you what there is. Since writing last week, I've received a number of letters and a couple telegrams from George. Our places in W. are all right. One shell hit the school compound wall, but no other damage was done and none of our people were hurt. George did not go on to Wanhsien, as he was strongly advised not to do so, but he sent one of our Hankow evangelists, who went along with him from here, up to do some business for him and to get some of our boxes. The British planned an expedition up as far as Chungking and they intended to fight it out. They said then it would be unsafe for any foreigner in W. Reinforcements have reached Ichang, but when George last wrote, he did not know if the expedition would materialize or not. One shell shattered Jenkins' kitchen quarters, we have been told – Rev. Brand wired George from Shihnan to await his arrival in Ichang. Whether it has been possible now for Geo. and Brand to go to W., I don't know. Steamers were running again. They wired to Erna & me to come, so we'll be leaving for Ichang Thursday A.M. at daylight – board the boat tomorrow night. When, or if, I get to Wanhsien, is still to be seen. Surely wish I could get back. There is much I'd like to do before furlough…As to furlough, though, don't bank too much on our coming next year. Riedel is sick and Paul Riedel is also, so we'll have to see what this fall's Conference decides. No use making any plans these days.

My! If I don't find George in Ichang, I'm afraid I'll – oh, I don't know what. The girls have been so naughty lately and now Betty Ann is having a cold, so she's been cross besides. And it has been very hot again until today. It was just terrible last evening, hot & sultry, but sometime during the night it rained and cooled off a lot. I am quite discouraged – it certainly isn't easy to take care of three kiddies all under three years and no Daddy around to help. Of course, it wouldn't be so bad in our own home, but it is when living with others. And then I still have a time nursing the baby. She's gaining fine, but she takes it all and lately I've had to give her a bottle once every other day. I'm trying my best to keep away from the bottle, but I just haven't any for her sometimes. Well, I should be as good-natured as my amah. My! She is quiet and she never complains. She puts me to shame.

Laura weighed 11 ¾ lbs. today. That means she's gained 4 lbs. in less than three months. She's so sweet! Just a big sugar lump! Wish you could see her.

Don't know what to say about mail. You can send it either to No. 7 Milan Terrace French Con. Hankow or to Ichang, c/o Theiss. It will reach us in time. Better not send to Wanhsien anyway until we get back there.

Must get busy now writing accounts & doing some odd jobs.

Much love to you all,

Bernice

Mr. Schmidt just told me the "Reds" are going to bombard Wuchang. It's across the river from Hankow. Fact, I hear some big bombs now, but we've heard more or less right along. They've besieged the city for over two weeks. Today they let the women and children out, according to report, so there may be some lively shooting tonight. Guess they're beginning right now.

Haven't time to read my letter over. S's are going out & will mail this.

BERNICE TYPES THE TALE OF DEPARTURE.
"...I finally had my hat on and stood within two steps of the door, all ready to go. And just then came a telegram."

Letter #229

No. 7 Milan Terrace
Hankow, Hupeh
September 23rd, 1926

Dear George,

If I can find my way on a standard keyboard, I will try to type a letter this evening. It seems rather funny to use a typewriter again, especially a Remington. I got so used to that old Corona.

However, there is no time to waste talking about typewriters this evening. There is much other news that I want to write about. I have not written since Monday, since I expected to see you soon. But I guess I will have to plan on writing every day until I am right on a boat, if I want to play safe. Now, for the tale! The first telegram telling Erna[204] and me to come was received Sunday afternoon and I then wired you, asking if we were going to Wanhsien, in order to know whether I should take the groceries along, order a few more things, etc. Your answer to that came Monday around supper time. The "Changsha" was the only boat out this week (the "Shasi" is due to leave Saturday, I just heard today), so Erna and I decided to leave on that. That meant getting aboard Wednesday evening, so I had just two days in which to do the necessary shopping and the packing. That would be oodles of time if I did not have three children to look after, but the kiddies did not appreciate the fact that I would have liked them to be model girls for a couple days and so save me time and trouble! After I had taken care of Baby Tuesday morning, I handed Marjorie over to Frieda, who had offered to take care of her, and then Betty Ann and I went out shopping. Frieda had also kindly given me the use of her rickshaw. Got quite a bit done, but it was a Chinese holiday and the banks were closed, so I could not cash a check. After dinner I wrote a little to Mother and – I forget now what else I did. Since I am living in suitcases and there was washing and ironing to be done, I could not start packing. So much of the stuff was in use that it would hardly pay to start before the last day. Fischer was going to book for us, but as he himself admitted later, "he pulled a big boner." He tried to get the office by phone, but did not succeed, so he just informed us that he could not book. Erna is so very anxious to get home, however, that she was not satisfied and she came over to Agnes Arndt. They went right out to the steamer first, but of course could not book there, so they went over to the office anyway – and they found the doors open and some foreigners there as usual. So they succeeded where Fischer had failed, or been too lazy to make any real effort. Yesterday was some day, though. I wanted to get started with some packing before dinner, but I had to go to the bank and cash a check first and I also had errands to the C. & M.A. and the Associated Drug Co. I did not look for a rickshaw when I started out, so I did not miss them until I came to the drug store and Mr. Vittaly said something about that I would have to walk this morning as the rickshaws were on strike. Then I noticed that the only rickshaws about were private ones. Not a public one in sight. Well, I walked along at a pretty good clip, but you know it is quite a ways. And I stopped in a couple places on the way home so it was almost noon when I returned. Then I tried to straighten up my bills,

---

[204] Erna is missionary Theiss' wife.

etc. so it was after 2:00 P.M. when I got started with the packing. If I could have sent Amah out with Marjorie then and worked entirely in peace for awhile, I think I could have done most of the packing in a couple hours. But, you know how it is. I never like to start out with soiled clothing, so Amah was both washing and ironing and as busy as I. After I had packed for half an hour or more, I picked Margie up and walked the floor for twenty, thirty minutes, finally succeeding in getting her to sleep. She was very cross then and I knew she would not be getting to bed early, so I thought it would be worth the time. I carried her over to Arndts' and put her on one of their beds and there she slept for an hour. Then I had to feed Baby! Well, I felt pretty tired and discouraged and I thought I never would get things packed up. And how to get the baggage down? We found out later that the coolies were not on strike, but all the laborers took a holiday. There was a big celebration out at the Chinese Race Course in honor of the "Reds" and it seems everybody was out there. All afternoon I was wondering if Fischer would come and tend to my baggage. I am sort of helpless, you know, because I have no man servant and so must depend on others to help me with such things. I had not asked Fischer, but with Mrs. Theiss getting hers off, I thought he would be reminded of it and perhaps be so thoughtful as to come over here. I consider that he is in better position to do those odd jobs now, as Max and Schmidt are both very busy, while he is not. But he did not appear, there was no way of getting in touch with him, and it was getting late. Schmidt was still out at the school, so I finally appealed to Max and he was very willing to help. His cook went out about six o'clock to call coolies and came back with the news that he could get none. He went out again, however, and then came back with three. They looked over the stuff and got one or two more coolies. But, as you could guess, they were in position to hold us up on the price, since there were no rickshaws and no coolies. Their first shout for the eight pieces was four dollars! They came down to two dollars, but no less. I was so tired by supper time – and excited, too, I suppose – that after I had eaten a little, I began to feel nauseated and sick, so I drank my coffee and gave the rest of my ice cream to Betty Ann. I was mighty thankful for the coffee, because I was so afraid I would have a spell like I did at the hotel in Kiukiang when we came down. It passed over and I went to pick up all the little things that I had left. Frieda sent her rickshaw over to take Mrs. Theiss and her children down to the boat first and then he came back here to get me. Agnes and the amah walked down with Betty Ann and Marjorie. They took turns carrying the latter. After all the rush and the trouble caused by the unusual circumstances, I finally had my hat on and stood within two steps of the door, all ready to go. And just then came a telegram. Before it was opened – while S. was signing – we joshed about the possibility of telling us not to come, not seriously entertaining that idea. And then we read "Imperative ladies remain Hankow Lillegard Theiss agree Scholz." How would you have felt? I said I wanted to go anyway, but they persuaded me to wait here while they – Schmidt, Fischer, and Max – went to get some more information, if possible. I wanted to go along to the boat and talk it over with Erna, but they thought I had better not, since there was only the one rickshaw. Frieda and Martha came back to see why I did not come and they told me both Betty Ann, Marjorie, and Erna's children were all asleep – on the steamer! The men went, but personally, I do not think they made much of an effort to get information. I know I would have tried to get in touch with someone from the gunboat on the chance that they had received information by radio. All they did, I believe, was to stop on the way hoping to find the "Socony" manager, Mr.

Gregory. Not finding him they proceeded to the boat and they sat there while Erna came up here along to talk things over with me. She was quite determined to go in spite of the wire and so we finally decided we would go. You see, the thing that bothered us was this that it came from Scholz and not from either of you. Had we received a wire direct from either you or Heinie, we would not have discussed the matter at all, but simply obeyed orders. But, coming from Scholz made us discount the seriousness a little and then this "Lillegard Theiss agree" – well, it sort of weakened it, in our opinions. Having just received two wires from you that we should come, it seemed sort of strange that the situation should all of a sudden be so bad, even though we do know that there can be radical changes in the situation in a few hours. That is usually in the war zone, though.

The folks here did not really advise us either way, except Max. Either they were anxious to get rid of us, or they felt, as did we, that it might not be as serious as it sounded. Well, we picked up our things and started off, but got no farther than the gate when we met Max. He thought we ought not to go. He reminded us of the fact that so far all telegrams have been obeyed. We stood there and talked awhile and then I decided that it would be best not to take any chances, but only for the children's sake. Had I been alone, I would surely have gone on. Erna was very loath to give in, but I told her that she would never forgive herself if anything happened to either of the children. And we knew, too, that if we went and anything happened, you boys could say to us that we had that telegram and it was not for us to say that the situation was less serious than the telegram would indicate. Max got an automobile then and got the folks, babies, and the necessary baggage off. And then we had to unpack some things, get nets up, etc. etc.

Friday P.M. This is expensive business. Two dollars to get my baggage down and another $1.20 to get some of it back the following morning. I do not know how much the use of the auto came to. The charges are $5.00 per hour and it was used a little more than an hour, I think. Have not seen Fischer since that evening so I do not know. Yesterday morning I went down to B & S with the tickets and fully expected to be docked half the price – that is the rule – or, is it not 50%? Whatever the percentage – imagine my surprise when they simply cancelled the booking and said the tickets would have to be stamped again the next time we booked! Very decent of them don't you think?

This forenoon I took a trip to Jardines and inquired about steamers. The Kiangwo is due to leave at daylight Tuesday morning. There are steel plates along the decks outside of the cabins, so it should be quite safe from rifle fire at least. I did not book, but they noted our names. They said Monday would be time enough to book. On the way home I stopped in at the Consulate for information. There I was told that the Consulate General was not advising anyone to go up river. If we went, we would go on our own responsibility. They thought Ichang would be safe enough when we got there, although they said Ichang was safe now, but they could not say what it would be in twenty-four hours! Practically, what I was told amounted to advice to remain here. However, you know that attitude is taken so often that people would be sitting around for months if they were always to wait for permission from the Consul.

Sept. 25, 1926

Dear folks,

To save time, I made a copy of my letter to George. Had intended to write more to you, but this morning we received another wire saying we could come – and Erna & I are certainly going. We intended to go Mon. but that steamer doesn't leave now until Thursday, so I asked Max to book us on the first boat out. He came back at noon with the news that he'd booked us for tonight, so now I must hurry and pack things together again. Such a life! I'm rather sore now that we didn't go Wed. eve after all. We'd have been getting in tomorrow, I think. Scholz is easily excited, that's why Erna & I wanted to go anyway, but we could hardly do so in the face of that "<u>imperative</u>." So much for now. If only we can proceed to Wanhsien. That would be fine.

With much love,
Bernice

BERNICE IS ANGRY, MISERABLE, AND FRANTIC.
"...the place here is such that I have to say 'don't this and don't that' from morning to night...there is no place they can really play in the house,..."

Letter No. 230
                                                No. 7 Milan Terrace
Hankow, Hupeh, China
October 11th, 1926

Dear Folks,

    You should have had a letter long ago, but I certainly have not been much in the mood to write letters and it always seemed, at least, that there was so little time. And tonight I really have not much time, but I want to get a note off before we leave Hankow.

    "Before you leave Hankow?" I can hear you think! For in my last letter I hurriedly added a note saying I was pulling out that evening, did I not? Yes, on the morning of Sept. 25th we received a wire saying we ladies could come on any boat, so we booked out for that evening, that is, Erna and I did. Louise did not, as she wanted to go on a Jardine steamer. So, we packed again and thought we would finally get away. When we were all ready and it was about time to eat supper, another wire came saying we <u>must</u> come on the "Kiang Wo," as it had better protection. And letters from Shasi helped to explain why the telegrams had been coming from there. Theiss had gone down there on business and he and Scholz were doing all the wiring. Well, I got really angry when that wire came and at first I said I was going anyway, especially since George's name was not signed to this wire. But, Erna was up in the air, as it was signed by both Theiss and Scholz. After much talking and running about, we finally decided to remain. On Tuesday morning <u>I</u> received a wire from George to come on the first boat and that <u>forenoon</u> <u>tentative</u> bookings were made, which had to be cancelled, as at noon a wire from Scholz, Theiss, George, and Brand (signed by them all) informed us that Conference would be held in Hankow and we ladies should stay. Great life, don't you think? It has been real stale around here the last couple weeks – no telegrams at all! Oh! I forgot. There was one more after that, but it was a cable from the Board saying both "Shen" and "Shang Ti" were admissible! That really made me feel sort of sick for a day.

    It is five weeks tonight since we arrived in Hankow and I believe it is the most miserable month I have spent in a long time. It certainly has been trying. Living in a suitcase is never so very pleasant, but when you have three children to take care of, the inconvenience is rather more than trebled, I think. However, just the inconvenience would not be so much to complain about, especially under the circumstances, but there were other things that were much harder. Both Betty Ann and Marjorie have been so very cross almost all the time. The first two weeks it was so hot that some of it could be blamed to that but I have lately discovered that both of them are teething. Marjorie's two eyeteeth are just coming through – I can feel the sharp edge. And her stomach teeth are coming, also. She has been showing that she does not feel just right in other ways than just being cross lately. Just the other day I also discovered that about half of one of Betty's large molars is through. You can imagine that living away from home like this is in itself hard on the children, too, and teething besides – well, I guess it is not strange that they have been so naughty. Not only that, the place here is such that I have to say "don't this and don't that" from morning to night. You see, they have practically no toys or playthings of their own, there is no place they can really play in the house, and when they get outside, they scrap with the others for their playthings. There is no use trying to tell you all about it now. Suffice to say that I felt absolutely frantic at times and was in no mental condition to handle the children. I had hoped so much that I would be able to nurse this baby for some time, but I think this month has just about spoiled that. I have had to give Baby the bottle more and more lately. I am doing my best to keep on to some extent until we get home in the hopes that active housework and more happy surroundings, etc. will benefit me enough to make me able to keep on for some time anyway.

The men have had a short Conference and closed today at noon. Some business matters were settled, but we are really no further along as regards the Term Question, printing of catechism, and other literature, etc. It is a rather bad situation. Unless something new and unexpected turns up to change our minds, George and I feel that we will be saying goodbye to this Mission when we leave for the States. For a number of pretty good reasons, we will not be sorry to do so, while there are ties that will have to be broken, also, which is not such a happy thought. I am glad that I am so thoroughly in sympathy with George's position on this question. While I do not always agree with his method of procedure and his manner of expression, I do feel that he is justified in his convictions. And I think I can say that I am convinced by the <u>arguments</u>, not by my husband, that "Shang Ti" cannot be used as a translation for "God." However, more of this anon – when we see you, perhaps!...Little Laura, bless her, has been the sweetest, best baby one could wish for. I just wish you could see her big smiles – <u>glorious</u> smiles – and hear her try to talk! And how she can kick! She has been gaining quite well in spite of me and weighed 12 lbs. 4 or 5 oz. this morning.

Scholzes, Theisses, and we had expected to board the "Kiang Wo" this evening, but it has not come in yet, although it was expected yesterday. Hope we can get on board tomorrow. Steamers are not running on schedule now, so there is much uncertainty. Do hope we can go right through to Wanhsien, once we get started from here. We Americans will not likely experience any particular difficulties. There is a good deal of anti-British agitation these days, though.

I wish I had the time to write more, but I shall have to be satisfied with this tonight, as it is already late and there will be plenty to do tomorrow morning, if we are to leave. Do not be alarmed if there is a rather longer period than usual between this and the next letter. Steamers both on this run and the upriver run are running so irregularly these days that mails are likely to be delayed. Moreover, I will be a mighty busy girl the next months. I have to make up for lost time. Have sewing galore to do!

Lots of love from us all to you,

Bernice

GEORGE HOPES THE SOUTHERNERS – REDS – DON'T WIN.

Oct. 3rd, 1926

Dear Sister Louise:

Your letter of August 12th reached me last week at Ichang, having been brought from Wanhsien by a Chinese evangelist whom I had sent to W. to attend to some matters for me. I did not go to W., as I waited at Ichang for Rev. Brand to come back from Shihnan, and then by the time he was ready to sail we could not get boats any more. Large numbers of Szechwan troops are coming down river and are commandeering all the steamers, so the boats have stopped running and are staying at Ichang under the protection of the gunboats. I do not know how long it will be before we can get boats to W. In the meantime we are going to Hankow to have our second Conference with Brand. When that is over with, we hope we can return to Wanhsien without further delay.

Everything is quiet at W. at present, but there is much anti-British agitation going on in the province, and it is hard to tell what may happen next. The opposing armies are preparing for another big battle near Hankow, and also on the upper river below Shasi, or at Yochow. The latest reports are that the Northerners are winning again, so it may be that the Southern "Reds" will yet be driven back. I certainly hope the "Reds" don't win out. It will be hard to carry on mission work in China, I fear, if these Bolshevist "Reds" win out. They came with so much anti-Christian propaganda, wherever they gain the power (they) quarter their soldiers in the mission stations – residences, chapels, and all – and in general have a very hostile attitude over towards foreigners…

The country is becoming more and more chaotic each year and conditions in our Mission are not improving very much.

Bernice and the children have been in Hankow this last month and have not been any too happy living in another's home either. It is hard to take care of three children when there is no place where they can play alone, but must always have somebody watching them. Certainly hope we can get back to W. right away after this Conference.

Our steamer was escorted by a gunboat the first day out of Ichang, as some troops had been firing on steamers at a point near Shasi. After the danger point had been passed the gunboat turned back to escort three steamers that had come up on the way to Ichang. We have not been fired on at all so far. At one place we had to wait for some Chinese soldiers to come aboard and guide the ship through a minefield. So we know we are in the war zone allright. We should be in Hankow tonight, but are not allowed to come in to port at night, so will have to anchor, and pull in tomorrow morning. "It's a great life if you don't weaken!"

Don't worry about us. We are not taking any unnecessary risks. Humanly speaking, we are given good protection by the foreign powers. And after all, our lives are in God's hands and we are as safe here as any other place.

Address us at Wanhsien as usual, unless you get other directions. This month I fear we will not be getting much mail, as it is going to Wanhsien and the interruption in the steamer service means that it will be held up indefinitely.

With love to you all, George

LILLEGARDS ARE DELAYED BECAUSE OF GUNFIRE.
"She (Bernice) does not want to come back at all (to China) under any circumstances!"

On board S.S. "Kiangwo," Oct. 16th, 1926

Dear Folks:

Bernice wants me to write you tonight, as she is busy knitting a sweater for Betty Ann. So I shall give you the last week's news. We finished up our Conference Monday A.M., and had thought to go aboard the same evening. But the boat's sailing was postponed a day. We went on board this ship, the "Kiangwo" Tuesday evening and left Hankow Wed. 10 A.M. We were not fired on at all the first day and night and had gotten five hours beyond Yochow, on Thursday, when we met the British gunboat "Bee" and were ordered back to Yochow, "until further notice." Steamers had been fired on at a place about 18 hrs. above Yochow, and they wanted that matter attended to before permitting steamers to travel. Notice was sent to the commanding generals that if they did not stop this firing on steamers, the gunboats would make an attack on their position, "Temple Hill," and put a stop to it themselves. In the meantime we have been waiting here for 2 ½ days. We are supposed to leave tomorrow at daylight, however. We have two cabins to ourselves and are more comfortable here than we were in Hankow. The main disadvantage is that there is no place where the children can play without fear of their falling into the river or getting into trouble. So somebody has to be watching them all the time. I have spent a good deal of time with Betty and Marjie and have read four novels these four days. Bernice has been busy with the baby and looking after the clothes for the family, knitting, etc. The amah has spent most of her time with the children, and has had some clothes to wash each day. So time has not exactly been hanging heavy on our hands, although we would, of course, like to make some progress toward our destination. We hear that the Ichang – Wanhsien steamers are running, so that we hope we can go direct to W. without having to wait long at Ichang. If we get started tomorrow morning, we should get to Ichang by Tuesday night. Then another two or three days should see us at last in Wanhsien.

We hear that the Southerners[205] are continuing to gain victories also against Sun Chuan-fang's forces. It really looks as though they will yet conquer most of China. That does not promise well for the foreigners in China as the Southerners have been very anti-foreign hitherto. But it is possible they will change their tactics after they once get into power and get settled in their control of the country. Then again much depends on what the foreign powers do about the situation in China. I should not be at all surprised to see foreign intervention in the country – and believe that it would be to the advantage of the country in the long run if they did intervene.

As for mission affairs – most of us are "plum disgusted." Talk about dictators! We certainly have them in this mission. "I am the Board" was a phrase we heard frequently from Brand the last weeks and the wishes and plans of the missionaries on the

---

[205] The Southerners were originally led by Sun Yat-sen, who died in March 1925. Then Chiang Kai-shek took control of the faction, known by many names: Nationalist Party, Kuomintang (Guomindang), or KMT. They were headquartered in Canton, far to the south (by Hong Kong). Sun Yat-sen was the first one to welcome the Communists from Russia as members and financiers. Chiang Kai-shek at first used the Communists in the fighting when he began his "Northern Expedition" to take over the whole country, starting with Hankow. Later he would turn on them and begin to kill them, beginning a bloody civil war.

field were simply overridden and set aside for the plans of the Board in a most arbitrary manner. In short we on the field are considered to be incapable of deciding anything with regard to our work – everything must be decided by the infallible authorities at St. Louis. Most of our missionaries, if not all, feel the same way about these things as I do. The decision of the Board & Faculty on the Term Question is likely to bust this mission up entirely. At any rate, several of the men still stand pat on the question and are not likely to give in. We don't understand how Gebhardt could agree to the Board's action. I rather expect yet to find that there is some catch to the whole thing and that Gyps has been "bluffed out" or tricked in some way. I suppose he had more respect for the Faculty, too, than their utterances hitherto on the Term Question would indicate they deserve. Some of the missionaries out here – two or three – have such implicit confidence in the Faculty that they would believe the earth was shaped like a banana if the Faculty told them so!

At present we are waiting for letters from Gyps and the Faculty before taking any further action. I fully expect to find their letters entirely unsatisfactory to me, and shall then point out to them why they are so. Then it will be their next move. If the Board "gets fresh" and orders me off the mission field because of the position which I hold on the Term Question, they will put themselves in just about the place where I want them. For they "have not got a leg to stand on" if they try on the basis of their interpretation of the Term Question to rule a man out of the mission because he refuses to use the term Shang-Di. I plan to keep up the fight anyway till we get home on furlough next summer, and shall then see what to do next.

If we find this mission an impossible place, do you think there would be any chance of us getting a call at home, or of the Norw. Synod being willing to send us out to China independent of the Missourians? The Term Question may prove the deciding factor. But even apart from that, I must confess that this mission, with half-crazy Arndt still in it and going strong, and with its infallible Board in St. Louis, is getting so on our nerves that I doubt it is worthwhile trying to work in it. "Life is too short" for such continual scraps as this mission is bound to have so long as Arndt is a member and the Board pursues the policy it has indulged in the last couple years. I have done my best to show how impossible Arndt is, and have also tried to show the Board how impractical it is to run a mission in China from an office-chair in St. Louis, but things have gone from bad to worse, and unless a distinct improvement becomes evident in the near future, I shall consider it my duty to "shake the dust of this mission off my feet." Bernice says to tell you that she "is through with China." She does not want to come back at all under any circumstances! I must admit these years have been hard in many ways and it would not be strange if her mission spirit were gone. She is not the only woman in this mission who has had too much!

We would appreciate whatever news of the situation and prospects in the Norw. Syn. you could give us. I am very glad that Dr. Y. agrees with me on the Term Question, and with his help it should not be difficult for me to set our Norw. brethren straight on the question.

The children seem to be happy and peppy enough these days, although both Betty and Marjie are having colds. Betty is getting better now, while Marjie is rather worse. They both have hearty appetites however. This cold weather, the raw winds, and the damp, rainy days are regular colds-producers, so it is not strange they should catch cold,

especially as it is hard to keep them – at the least Marjie – covered nights. Laura is the smiliest baby ever – and has the sweetest smile ever smiled! Bernice and I are well. *No! I have a cold, too. Have been hoarse several days & am coughing plenty.*
    With love to you all from us all,

Yours,
George

P.S. I am sending you a copy of "The Wanhsien Epic" under separate cover…

Refugees from Wuchang after the city was taken by the Southerners, October, 1926

BERNICE PACKS YET AGAIN FOR ANOTHER TRIP.
"It is nearly five months since we left Wanhsien and two since we left Kuling."

Letter No. 231	Ichang, Hupeh, China
October 27th, 1926

Dear Folks,

Now we're here! And we've been here since a week ago yesterday. Had a safe trip up from Hankow and I guess it wouldn't have been necessary to remain in Yochow those two and a half days. But, of course, we had nothing to say and the Captain thought it wisest to await further advice from the naval authorities. I am supposing that you have received George's letter, written aboard the "Kiang Wo" at Yochow. If we had not been delayed those two, three days, we would have arrived here in time to go to Wanhsien on a Jap. boat…One Amer. boat was lying here for over two weeks all ready to leave. In fact, I believe it was ready to sail when it was boarded by soldiers in civilian clothes and carrying concealed weapons. So they didn't go up until this morning. We couldn't go on that, however, as it was booked full.

Thurs. I intended to write a lot this P.M. as I couldn't get more written last night, but this noon George brought the news that a steamer will leave tomorrow and we are to leave with it. So now I must hurry and pack again. And I do hope this is to be the last time I pack until we pack to go home. It is nearly five months since we left Wanhsien and two since we left Kuling. It has been rather trying in many ways, besides has put us behind with our work. I wanted a full year to prepare for furlough and here we've been sitting around so long. Mr. & Mrs. Simon will likely be coming to Wanhsien only a few days later than we, so I won't have much time to get settled. Hope I can get the worst work out of the way, though. Am going to do my own cooking, you know, and that means I'll have a family of seven this winter. And such a lot of sewing!...

We have been much more comfortable and happy here with Theisses than in Hankow, but it surely will be nice to get settled in our own home.

Marjorie has a fever today. She is troubled with teething, I am quite sure. Betty has cut another large molar. Laura is angelic – I couldn't ask for a better, sweeter baby than she has been so far.

There's so much I could write, but let's console ourselves this year with the thought that in less than a twelvemonth, if all goes well, we will be able to talk about all the things that should have been written.

Haven't had mail since yours of Aug. 28th. Hope there'll be some in W. waiting for us. Am anxious to hear about the wedding.[206] Was Elsa bridesmaid?

No more time now. Send mail to W. after this.

Much love to you all from all of us.
Yours, Bernice

---

[206] Her brother Ragnar's marriage to Esther

HAPPINESS DESPITE SICKNESS AND DISREPAIR
"I am not interested in the house, mostly because we are preparing for furlough and also because it is such an old shack."
Letter No. 232

Wanhsien, Szechuan
Nov. 18th, 1926

Dear Folks,

First of all I want to tell you, Papa, that I did not forget your birthday altogether, but I must confess I did not remember it until the evening of the 7th and then I was quite chagrined to think I hadn't written you a letter. Nothing at all has proceeded in a quiet, natural order these last months, so I've been unable to keep track of things. (There it is striking 9:00 P.M. and I'm only starting instead of being half through or so!) We wished you many happy returns of November 7th just the same, Dad, and hope we may celebrate with you next year. Will look forward to an oyster stew, I can assure you.

There is so much to write and so little time to do it in just now that I may only tell of things briefly. We arrived here the evening of Oct. 31st after an uneventful trip from Ichang…Marjorie was not feeling well…Finally, after nine days, George went down and got some medicine from the British gunboat, as there's no Amer. gunboat here. The apothecary (there is no Dr. on this boat) said it wasn't dysentery, but seemed to be a catarrhal diarrhea, perhaps due to her bad cold. The medicine he gave certainly helped and Marjorie is quite well now, save that she is not entirely over her cold…

Marjorie wasn't more than getting back to normal again when George caught a cold. And he grew worse and worse until a week ago, he felt quite miserable…He didn't feel well, but he went to chapel and preached last Sunday. Finally, however, at noon, Monday, he went to bed and he's been there ever since…He has had practically nothing to eat for a week…

11/19…Well, I certainly hope George gets better very soon. He hasn't spent so many consecutive days in bed since we were married.

Betty Ann has been very well and happy. After so many trying weeks between Kuling and here, it was quite a relief to have her rejoicing over all her old playthings. For quite a number of days she wasn't any trouble at all, but played around all day. The novelty has worn off now, but still she and Marjorie play together and are comparatively little trouble. And since I am in a better mental state and have more patience, they are more easily managed and respond to my attempts at training them.

Baby Laura – oh, I could just rave on about her. Please excuse me for doing so, but you should just see her and play with her and I know you'd "love her to death." She finally got a cough, too, poor girlie. It isn't funny, with so many cold germs all about. She hasn't seemed to mind it much and hasn't been a bit cross, but at times she has such hard coughing spells. Her cough seems to be so deep-seated – much like George's. And I've had – well, Margie, too – we've all had colds way down in the chest. Laura has the lustiest cough for a 4-month-old! We feel sorry for her, and at the same time we have to laugh sometimes. She sounds more like a grown-up.

While Margie was sick, we kept her in our bed nights. Now, however, since George became sick, she and Betty Ann are sleeping together as planned. They have great times once in awhile and it seems Betty is the one who is usually most highly amused. And one wants to laugh right with Betty Ann when she gets a'going! She has such a hearty laugh! Betty Ann does a lot of talking these days – she is slower in that respect than some others, tho' Marjorie is talking a lot for her age and will soon be catching up to Betty.

Now a little about Her Highness – The Cook! I surely picked out a great time to do my own cooking – bigger family than ever, two months late with sewing, and trying to prepare for furlough – besides a sick girl for a couple weeks and now a sick husband! But, I've been feeling fine.

Mon. 11/22 Aa ja![207] Now I've skipped two days again. I am some busy woman these days. In spite of all the extras these three weeks, I have felt quite able to manage. Being so behind has of course often made me feel as if I'd like to have several pair of hands – or in fact, be a plural person!!! This fall, getting settled was almost like moving. I think it was seven boxes that had been brought to Ichang, so everything had to be unpacked, and then put in drawers or trunks, etc. as necessary. One thing that I was extremely grateful to T'ang yuen hsin for, was his having cleaned up the whole house, had walls whitewashed, and papered the ceilings and windows. It was very nice not to have to walk about gingerly and find a rag to wipe off some dust before we could put anything down, especially since we arrived at the house after seven o'clock in the evening. Perhaps I told you this spring that our larger pieces of furniture – buffet, bed, chiffoniers, etc. – were to be varnished after we left for Kuling. As the things in the bedroom had been made and varnished at different times, they were not the same color and so we said they were now to make them all the same. Imagine my disappointment and disgust when I walked in that evening and found a pig's-blood red bed glaring at me! And our floors! Expected to find them nicer than ever, since they had two coats of varnish and so many months in which to dry. But, on the contrary, they are worse than ever – I've never had such awful floors in China. The paint is peeling off in every room. They say it is because it was so damp here that the floors were damp too and the varnish wouldn't stick. Perhaps so! Who shall say whether or not it is an alibi for poor work done when the "cat was away"? But I don't care nearly as much this year as I most likely would have another time. I am not interested in the house, mostly because we are preparing for furlough and also because it is such an old shack. There is not much pleasure in fixing it up any more than we already have…

Simons arrived here Nov. 8th – just eight days after we did. They are a young couple – he is 23 yrs., she 19 yrs. It is quite remarkable that of the several who came out, Simons should be the ones to be appointed to Wanhsien, because it is most interesting to discover every now and then what mutual tastes and interests we have…They are very easy to cook for, which is luck for me…

Thanks for that "Times" clipping about the wedding. It gave me some desired information. For instance, nobody told me Elsa was to be maid of honor, but I guessed at it and put this and that together until Elsa's letter came and sort of confirmed my guess…

Well, I could write on, but Mother & Cook must sleep a little, too. I'm enjoying the life, tho! Much love to you all.

Yours,
Bernice

---

[207] Oh well! (Norwegian)

GEORGE REQUESTS NEWS FROM FIELD ON THEIR STATUS.
"We have heard that Shasi and Ichang were looted, but have not heard how the brethren fared during the excitement."

Wanhsien, January 14th, 1927

Dear Missionary Brethren:

This will be a general news letter from Wanhsien, copies being sent to all stations. We wish that similar news letters would be sent out from the other stations, so that we could know something about what has been going on and how our missionaries are faring. We have heard that Shasi and Ichang were looted, but have not heard how the brethren there fared during the excitement. We have received a telegram from Hankow, and have seen reports in the papers about attacks on our chapels at Yin Wu chow and Lao Cwan Miao[208] but have not heard from the brethren as to events.

Everything is quiet here at Wanhsien, and also in other parts of Szechwan, so far as I have heard. The looting of the American boats, Chiping and Chichwan, was a rather bad business, but did not affect us at all – we did not know about the looting till several days afterwards. Yang Sen has punished the soldiers who took part, severely. Several officers were shot, the whole company has been disarmed and disbanded, and in general I believe it will be a long time before his troops try anything like that again. Yang Sen seems to be on friendly terms even with the British gunboat captains. However there may be something brewing under this peaceful surface, since all British have been ordered to evacuate the province, or at least to gather at Chungking and Wanhsien preparatory to evacuation. Nagel was advised by the British Captain here to proceed to Ichang, and so far as I know may have done so by now. I believe that this order was given because of the Hankow disturbances, rather than because of any direct or immediate danger here. If England should get involved in serious difficulties with the Wuchang Government, they would want to have all their nationals in the country inland from Hankow out of the upper Yangtse river region. We have also heard from the British Gunboat that Americans were to be ordered out of this province. To date we have received no direct communication from the Chungking Consulate to that effect. We have heard, however, that Americans are leaving Chungking and that American steamers are being held to take care of refugees, no Chinese being allowed to board. The Monocacy chased a crowd of Military School students off the Iping the other day, according to report, on this ground. So it is possible that we may all have to trek down river ere long, unless conditions improve very much in the Hankow region. I am inclined to believe that we would be entirely safe in this district. But it would not be any fun to be entirely cut off from the outside world, as we would be if things should get still hotter down in that scarlet-red district called Hankow! Even now, our mails came through a month late, if at all, parcels are not being forwarded, and we never know from day to day whether the steamers are going to be running or not. Much depends on whether Yang Sen, who is not a real "Red," will be able to hold his own or not in this district. If he is driven out, or turned out through the machinations of his subordinate generals, we may get the real Bolshevist regime here, as you have it in Hupeh at present.

---

[208] These last two names are illegible.

We are packing some of our goods so that we would be ready to make a quick getaway, if that should prove necessary. We have been advised to do that by the British Captain. Since it would take a month or two to evacuate all the 600 or more Americans and British in this province, we are not planning on leaving here earlier than in February some time, even if we should get the consular order to leave that the British Captain reported was on the way. We want to stick it out as long as possible, and so long as the gunboats are here and the American steamers are running, we might as well stay here too.

We are all quite well at present. The mission work is slowing up a bit, owing to the near approach of Chinese New Year's, but otherwise things are as usual. We have been getting our new chapel quarters fixed up and they now make a real "churchly" impression. The congregation wants to buy a bell, and by adding a little tower to the building, this could be used to good purpose.

We are not worrying about the situation – but we would like to hear something more from the brethren at the various stations as to how they are faring.

With best greetings to you all from us all,

Fraternally yours,
Geo. O. Lillegard

Lillegards at compound, Dec. 15, 1926   **Wanhsien chapel, Dec. 1926**

BERNICE'S FINAL LETTER FROM THEIR MISSION HOME
"...I am a miserable failure in every way -- a poor Christian, a poor daughter, wife, and mother."

China
Wanhsien, Szechuan
January 17, 1927

Letter No. 236

Dear Mother,

    At last we received some mail. We waited so long this time. Your #271, which was so delayed came Jan. 2, but besides that, there was nothing from Madison from Dec. 18 until Jan. 14, almost one month. Last Friday 278 came and yesterday morning I received #277. My, how far ahead of me you are in letters - here I'm only on 236! Oh well! We should worry about <u>numbers</u>, as far as they go. But I am sorry I haven't written more regularly the last two, three years. Sometimes I write whole letters to you <u>days</u> before I get a pen in my hand! It seems so hard to get a chance to sit still long enough to write more than a few lines at a time and I must say I dislike writing at one letter for several days. Won't it be fine to visit with each other over our dishwashing, bed-making, etc. etc. instead of having to sit down to write? So often it seems to me it must be only a sweet dream that I am to see you all again. God grant we <u>may</u> all meet within a few months!

    I think, Mama, that you are disappointed in me. I suppose you wouldn't like to say it or perhaps admit it, but anyway I feel that you may be a little disappointed. It must be mainly because you have wanted to think better of me than I deserve. Where could I have established a reputation for patience? You say you would not say I had expressed myself as being through with China because you would not want to spoil my reputation for patience. If I only were patient! I <u>should</u> have learned patience these years and many other virtues, because, of course, trials and hardships are sent us to train us in Christian virtues. But I am a miserable failure in every way - a poor Christian, a poor daughter, wife, and mother. But I want to improve - and one must have faith in and love for Him in order to be a better person. You say no missionary's life is one of ease. Perhaps that is true to a certain extent, although in the larger cities, many missionaries live a life little different from that at home. But no Christian should expect a life of ease and I have not thought that I should lead any easier life at home as far as <u>work</u> is concerned, than here, nor that it would be a path of roses. But I did expect that the "mission life" would be different. I <u>knew</u> that there are "politics" in the church and that pastors and preachers of the Word are human and so on, but it was somewhat of a jolt to get into such close contact with it as we have here in China. Is there no peace? Seems to me there should be a sort of peace between Christian brethren at least. And as for justice, <u>Ragnar</u> (what <u>am</u> I thinking of)...<u>George</u> got a rotten deal in 1916-1917 and he certainly isn't getting any very nice deal from this Mission Board - and it is the same question really - unionism - syncretism...Let me cease! I almost dread getting to where I can <u>talk</u> to you about these things. If I say anything, I'm afraid I'll say too much.

    Now I must tell you why I didn't write last week. We have been busy packing and doing such things as would make it possible to leave in a short time, if necessary.

The situation down river has been so bad and then Nagel received a wire from the Consul in Chungking which in effect was an order preparatory to evacuating Szechuan - that is the British. Then a wire from Hankow said Americans should go to larger port where there were good transportation facilities, if they felt themselves in any danger. So far, everything has been peaceful and quiet here, and we do not anticipate any trouble in Wanhsien, but if steamers should quit running, we would be sort of cut off from the world. Anyway, we decided to pack as much as we could get along without so that we would not have to leave things around in case we should get orders to leave. And on Tuesday last week the British Captain here sent us word that 400 British and 200 Americans were evacuating Szechuan. The Jenkinses felt quite certain we would receive some word from the Consul, but to date we have had nothing. However, we started packing. George has packed fourteen boxes of books together with some junk to fill in. <u>One</u> box of books is to go home with us. We have also packed all the cut glass, the handpainted china, and the dishes we intend to keep. My cedar chest is almost packed and almost all my linens are in it. Have left out only enough things to put on the dressers. Ruth brought some of her scarfs and doilies over to help out. We are selling all we can of our furniture and quite a number of other things. Simons are buying about $600 worth of our household furnishings: dining room furniture, some kitchen utensils, etc. etc. etc. We are trying to sell the rest of our stuff to Chinese. What large pieces we cannot sell, we will have to leave here, and all that we want to keep - and do not want to take home with us - we will store in Shanghai. We had originally intended to take things only as far as Ichang, but now that the political situation is such, we think it best to take them to Shanghai. It looks pretty much as though we don't intend to return, doesn't it? Well, we won't make any <u>definite</u> statement now. One cannot foretell the future and if it seems that it is our duty to return to the Mission field, I hope we can do so willingly and gladly. But first we want to come home! We will sell the piano, if we can get $1,000 Mexican for it. We think it would be better to do that than to rent or store it...

...Betty & Margie were so funny this evening. They paraded around in their bathrobes and <u>old</u> pith hats, carrying the broom on their shoulder. Margie looks just like Happy Hooligan when she gets that hat on! They never seem to be so well able to amuse themselves as after supper when they should go to bed...

Much love to all of you from the five of us,
Bernice

ALL AMERICANS ARE ADVISED TO EVACUATE.

AMERICAN CONSULAR SERVICE,

Chungking, China, January 14, 1927.

CONFIDENTIAL.

Geo. O. Lillegard, Esquire,
    Evangelical Lutheran Mission,
        Wanhsien, China.

Sir:

    In order that you may be acquainted with the existing state of affairs and guide yourselves accordingly, I beg to give you my understanding of the middle, lower and upper river situation:

    It is my understanding that the Foreign Powers wish to avoid any clash with the Nationalist forces if it is at all possible to do so. However, as you know the Nationalists are in control of the British Concession at Hankow. The assumption of control of this Concession is apparently only one step in the program of Chiang Kai Shek. The Nationalists are closing in on Shanghai. If a repetition of the procedure effected at Hankow is attempted at Shanghai there will undoubtedly be a serious clash. If that occurs it is considered that the interior of Szechwan will no longer be safe for Americans. I wish to warn you that if you wait for a clash to occur before leaving your post for the coast, it may then be too late for you to reach safety.

    For your information I may say that I have urged all Americans west of Chungking to withdraw from Szechwan immediately. I have advised the American women and children in Chungking to proceed immediately to Shanghai.

    I now advise you that in my opinion you should immediately evacuate all American women from your stations and leave only enough men (where men are stationed) to look after property.

    You should telegraph Mr. E.R. Hykes of the Standard Oil Company, Chungking, concerning your passage, cable address SOCONY, giving him the exact number of persons, men, women and children, place of embarkation, asking him to give you the date on which passage will be available.

    You should also notify me of your departure so that your name may be checked off the list of Americans in Szechwan.

Very respectfully yours,

Walter A. Adams,
American Counsul.

300.
WAA/H.

GEORGE IS THE LAST TO LEAVE THE MISSION STATION.
"Bernice and the children left Wanhsien on the 20th, together with the Simons."

En route to Shanghai, Jan. 31st, 1927

Dear Folks:

We are on the way home! The Consuls have ordered all Americans out of Szechwan and Hupeh, so we have had to close down our stations. Since there is no likelihood that we would be able to get back this spring anyway, I have arranged to go on furlough now. Perhaps some of the others will also be going now. Wherever the Southern troops have the power, they have been making it impossible for foreigners to do any work, either business or mission work, and in many places have driven the foreigners out. Foreigners are and have been evacuating Kiangsi, Hunan, Hupeh, and Szechwan accordingly. Most women and children have left Hankow also, but it is possible that the foreign powers will be able to defend that place, although they cannot do much right now, as the water in the river is low and no large war vessels can come up the river. Bernice and the children left Wanhsien on the 20th, together with the Simons. I stayed four days longer to finish the packing and settle up Wanhsien affairs. The others should have reached Shanghai on Saturday. I expect to get in tomorrow. Then we shall arrange to buy tickets home as soon as is possible. I rather expect that we shall be on the ocean within a week or two. Shanghai is so crowded with refugees that we do not wish to stay there longer than absolutely necessary. Besides living is very expensive under these conditions. We shall wire Onstads when we reach Seattle or San Francisco. Perhaps they will let you know when we are expected to reach home. We are not sure yet what route we will be coming, as we want to take whatever steamer will bring us away from Shanghai first. We had planned to go via Seattle, but as it will be rather cold to travel that line now, we shall take the San Francisco route if that will give us the chance to leave Shanghai sooner.

Louise, your letters of Nov. 21st and Dec. 19th were received before I left Wanhsien. Glad to hear that mother is better. And thank you very much for the money sent us for Christmas! We are glad you sent money rather than presents. Some packages are on the way but had not reached us when we left Wanhsien. I suppose they may find us again at Madison some time. Hope they do not get lost. Thanks to you, too, Sarah, and to Aunt Ella, for the money you people sent us. Sarah's letter of Nov. 29th was received just shortly before we left Wanhsien. I suppose there will be a good deal of mail going to Wanhsien that will follow us back to America. The mail service has been very slow of late, because of the disturbed conditions in the country.

I have not heard from Bernice since she left Wanhsien, but presumably she got along allright, as Simons were along to help with the babies, and the naval authorities helped the refugees with transferring from one boat to another, at Ichang and Hankow. They did not stop at either place. Most of our missionaries are now in Shanghai. The Hankow people are still in Hankow, but may leave at any time. The Shihnan people had not left last I heard, but should be leaving. There are no missionaries left at Ichang, Shasi, Kweifu and Wanhsien, of our mission, except Theiss who is staying on at Ichang until the others from Shihnan have gotten through. I shall write again when I learn what date and on what boat we are to leave Shanghai. With love to you all,

George

BERNICE'S LAST LETTER FROM CHINA.
"We intend to leave on the President McKinley, Feb. 20th – two weeks from today."

612 Avenue Joffre
Shanghai, China
February 6, 1927

Dear Folks,

George says he wrote you a short note when enroute to this city, but I guess he didn't give any details of departure, etc. so you probably feel pretty much like question marks. You have undoubtedly read a good deal in the Chicago papers and know about the evacuation of foreigners and what is going on in this country.

The evening of the day I mailed my last letter to you, we received a letter from the Consul urging us to leave at once. We thought we would be leaving in two, three weeks perhaps – and even that almost took my breath. The next morning George & Simon went down to the British gunboat and the Captain was very anxious to have us go immediately. The "I-Ling" was due the following day, but George didn't even consider that. I believe he got the shock of his life when he came home at noon, told me the news, and found me game to try for the "I-Ling." We couldn't have done it if it hadn't been for George's staying on to finish the packing and closing up the house. Well, in a word, Simons, the children, and I left the house twenty-four hours after we'd decided to leave. George left the following Mon. A.M., Jan. 24th. Oh yes! We left on your birthday. Some way to celebrate!

We had quite a trip and I do not want to take time to write all about it, as I hope to tell you about that and many other things very soon. We did not set foot ashore from the time we left W. until we arrived here in Shanghai, eight days later. Of course we did not travel under ideal circumstances and it was very hard on the children. Before we reached Hankow, Marjorie was quite ill with bronchitis, and both Betty Ann and Laura were coughing. Was fortunate enough to find a doctor aboard a steamer at H. and he looked over Marjorie & gave me some advice. Mrs. Bromby, a C.I.M. missionary, was one of our party, and she was a great help to me. Except for a few minutes one day, M. was not out of the cabin from H. to S. and she was getting much better. But day before we arrived, Laura began running a temperature and she was rather unhappy. So a couple hours after I got here – to our room – I called an Amer. doctor. He did not think L. had anything more than a bad cold. She did not get any better, however, so called him again Sun. A.M. That evening I took her to the Country Hospital and she is still there. She has been sick with bronchial pneumonia, but is getting along splendidly now and I hope to have her home again before long. How thankful I am I was where she could get the proper attention. The C.H. is a beautiful, new hospital and there are only foreign nurses attending. Laura's temp. was down to 99° this morning and she has taken interest in toys for a couple days. Am afraid she is forgetting her mommy, though.

We had wired Walter Arndt advising him of our coming, but there was some mistake as to steamer's arrival, etc. so nobody met us. But Scholz & Fischer just happened to come aboard later (details when I see you) and through their help, we secured rooms. I have a large, quite comfortable room – right next to Erna Theiss. My, I was glad to come here and be next door to her. Simons are here, but on third floor. We're on second. George arrived Tuesday night, four days later than we. You can imagine I was glad. It is no fun to be alone with a family of sick children. Betty Ann has had some fever also, so Friday we took both M. & B.A. down and Dr. gave a quite thorough exam. He thinks they're in pretty good condition, but we won't have a full report until Tuesday.

The day before Simons & we arrived, Erna had to take Evelyn to the hospital. She had a fever and at first Dr. feared peri-typhoid. It was not that, but he had not been able to diagnose her trouble by Friday this last week. He said she was not seriously ill, but he would not let her come home until he could locate the trouble, of course. He had her chest x-rayed, but Erna has not heard whether that brought anything to light or not. It is very hard for Erna to be here without her husband. She is the only "grass-widow" and I know how she feels. She worries so much about her children as soon as they're sick. Besides, she didn't have a word from her hubby for over three weeks. Mails are so irregular now.

Besides your Christmas parcel, there are one from Alice and one from Netty in the mails. It would be fine if we could have them before we leave but fear that is expecting too much. George thinks they will reach us eventually – but when that will be, nobody knows.

Erna and her two girls, Fischers, Nagels, Scholzes, Cloeters and we Wanhsien-ites are in Shanghai. We don't know just where the Shihnanites are, but hope they're well on their way to Ichang. Theiss and the two new single men are in Ichang and all the rest are in Hankow.

Well, now for our plans. The Board has not cabled its permission for us to begin our furlough now, but we do not expect them to object. It would be very foolish for them to ask us to remain here under the circumstances. Anyway, we are making definite plans.

We intend to leave on the President McKinley, February 20th – two weeks from today. We are due in Seattle March 7th. We will have to spend a couple days there in order to pass baggage through customs, arrange for freight, etc. etc. Then we will spend a day or so in Tacoma so that we may visit George's aunt Guri, and incidentally, Rev. Harstad. We figure that we should arrive in Mpls. about March 14 or 15. There we will visit with Ella & Eric and a cousin of George a few days. From there to Madison! If you receive this in time and wish to write to us at Seattle, you may address us c/o Thos. Cook & Son and name the "Pres. McKinley," or say, "Passengers aboard the Pres McK." I would like very much to get in touch with Hazel, Marie, & T.T.J. if possible. I don't know their present address, but if I can get word off to Alice in this mail, I'm sure she'd write Hazel or me at Seattle. To make it more sure, would you please send Alice a card about this? Her address is 5309 W. North Ave., Chgo. At Minneapolis mail will reach us if sent in care of Mrs. H. Hartig, 2901 Vincent Ave., No.

Rather late now and I think we'd better get up earlier tomorrow, so will call this enough. My last letter to you from China – in all probability – for who-knows-how-long?

Much love to you all from the five of us.

Bernice

GEORGE WRITES FROM THE PRESIDENT MCKINLEY SHIP.
"The ship rolled so much yesterday that dishes fell off the tables while the children were eating, in spite of the 'fences' they have on the tables,…"

March 2nd, 1927

Dear Folks:

This will presumably be the last letter we will write you – unless it should be necessary to report some change in our plans from Tacoma or Minneapolis.

We received your letters, No's. 285-6 (282-4 are missing) just before we left Shanghai. They had been redirected at the S. Post Office. We left on Feb. 20th. Had rather rough weather the first day, and Bernice was quite sick. Marjie and I also had a touch of it. From the second day until after we had left Yokohama we had nice going – fine weather and beautiful scenery in the Inland Sea of Japan. Our boat stopped ½ day at Kobe and a day at Yokohama. We took an auto ride there and saw something of what the earthquake had done to the city. Since the 26th we have had rough seas, though the weather has often been sunny – no real storms, except perhaps last night for a time. The waves strike the ship on the side so as to send it rolling from side to side, which upsets things in general much more than the pitching up and down would be likely to do. Bernice was quite seasick from Saturday till Monday. Yesterday she began to feel better, and today she seems allright except for the bad head that she always has on board ship. Betty had a spell of some stomach trouble, however, yesterday and this morning. The ship rolled so much yesterday that dishes fell off the tables while the children were eating, in spite of the "fences" they have on the tables, and the commotion frightened Betty so much that she has been crying much of the time since, whenever the boat started rolling a bit extra strong. There is nice sunshine today and I hope the waves will moderate a little too, so that we can feel a bit more safe than we have these days – or at least that the waves will take a direction which will enable our boat to breast them more steadily – or less "drunkenly."

We plan to visit in Seattle and Tacoma from March 7th to 11th, taking the North Coast Limited on the Northern Pacific the morning of the 12th, which should arrive at Mpls. by the evening of the 14th. We shall spend a few days with sister Ella there. Her address is 3933-15th Ave. So., Minneapolis (Mrs. E. Furholmen). Perhaps you will get this in time so that we can hear from you also at Mpls. We shall write or wire you as to what train we will be taking to Madison. Our tickets have already been ordered, reading for the Chicago & North Western, so it will be on one of those trains. Our baggage will be checked through to Madison. As that will arrive some time before we do, I shall perhaps send you the baggage checks from Seattle by mail, so that you can get the baggage out of the depot before storage charges accumulate. We have about eight pieces that will be sent as baggage and a few that will have to go by freight. We shall have to "live in our suitcases" from the time we leave this ship till we get to Madison. If things go as we plan, we will be home by March 20th, at the latest. I do not imagine we will want to stay more than three-four days in Mpls. at this time – if that long. But we want to visit there now, as it might not be convenient for us to go to Mpls. again.

Have you heard that sister Ella got a baby boy on Jan. 21st? Everything O.K., we hear. We got the news just before we left Shanghai.

The boat rocks so much that I have to hang on "with all fours" in order to keep from falling with my chair; so please pardon the irregularity of this writing. I never was much of a penman anyway. (Baby Laura is fine now.)

With best greetings to the friends in Madison and love from us five to you all,

Yours,
George

Seattle, March 8th, 1927

Dear Folks:

    Here we are, all safe and sound. We are at Jacobson's – they met us at the docks, and are having a fine time. Haven't time today to write the news, but wish only to enclose these baggage checks. Kindly get my trunks out as soon as possible, so that they will not be charging storage. They are being sent today, I think. A bill of loading for six boxes sent by freight is also to be mailed to your care. The freight, I suppose, will not arrive before we do, however. We are going to Tacoma tomorrow. (___[209]) will take us down in his Buick Sedan. We plan to leave Tacoma on the 12th, arriving Mpls. the evening of the 14th.

    With love to you all from us all–

                                                                                 George

---
[209] Illegible name

POSTSCRIPT
The Lillegards spent their furlough year at the Onstads' in Madison, WI.
George took a call to Boston Norwegian Lutheran Church in Roxbury (Boston), Massachusetts in 1928 where the family settled in Jamaica Plain (Boston). In 1936 the congregation moved to Cambridge, MA, where the church was renamed Harvard Street Lutheran Church. The family lived briefly in Cambridge, then moved to Newton where they lived until 1952.
Their family was blessed with five more children:
George Onstad, born Dec. 3, 1927, Madison, WI
Lawrence Erik, born May 4, 1929 at Boston, MA
Alice Marie, born Oct. 21, 1930 at Boston, MA
David Theodore, born Sept. 2, 1935 at Boston, MA
Norman Sigurd, born Feb. 24, 1938 at Boston, MA

1935

1941

1944

1960

Left to right: Laura, Marjorie, Norman, Larry, Betty, Alice, George Jr., Bernice, George, David

APPENDIX
TIMELINE

1888	George Oliver Lillegard is born.
1897	Agnes Bernice Onstad is born.
1912-1915	George works on the Chinese mission field for the Norwegian Evangelical Lutheran Church of America.
1918	George and Bernice meet.
	George helps found the Evangelical Lutheran Synod along with 12 other pastors.
May 1920	George and Bernice marry in Madison, WI.
Oct. 1920	George accepts a call from the Missouri Synod to its Chinese mission field.
April-June 1921	George & Bernice Lillegard travel from Chicago to San Francisco, then via steamship to Shanghai, China.
Summer 1921	Lillegards spend the summer in the mountain resort town of Kuling, Kiangsi province, for the annual mission conference.
Oct. 1921-March 1922	They live in Ichang, Hupeh, on the Yangtze.
March 1922-May 1923	They live in mountainous Shihnanfu, Hupeh.
Oct. 1923	Elizabeth Ann Lillegard is born in Ichang.
Jan. 1924-Jan. 1927	The Lillegard family lives in Wanhsien, Szechwan, on the Yangtze River.
Oct. 1924	George receives his diploma from Nanking U.
Feb. 1925	Marjorie Elise Lillegard is born in Ichang.
July 1926	Laura Bernice Lillegard is born in Kuling.
Jan. 1927	Lillegards evacuate from Wanhsien.
March 1927	They arrive in Seattle, WA.

CHINESE NAMES

Old-------------------------------New

Provinces

Honan--------------------------Henan
Hupeh--------------------------Hubei
Kiangsi-------------------------Jiangxi
Kiangsu------------------------Jiangsu
Szechwan-----Sichuan (and Chonqing)

Cities

Chungking------------------Chonqing
Ichang----------------------Yichang
Kwangchow---------------Huangchuan
Kweifu-------------------------Fengjie
Nanking-----------------------Nanjing
Shihnan(fu)----------------Enshih
Wanhsien------------------Wanxian

SOURCES:

Carroll, Vincent. "Is Christianity poised to remake China?" <u>Rocky Mountain News</u> 11 March 2004: A43

Ellis, William. "Shanghai: Where China's Past & Future Meet." <u>National Geographic</u> March 1994: 185.3.

Leppien, Patsy and J.K. Smith. <u>What's Going on Among the Lutherans?</u> Milwaukee: Northwestern Publishing House, 1973.

Lindsell, Harold. <u>The Battle for the Bible</u>. Grand Rapids: Zondervan Publishing House, 1976.

Stanford, Edward. <u>Atlas of the Chinese Empire</u>. London: Morgan & Scott, 1908.

Wehrfritz, George & Lynette Clemetson. "Jesus Is All the World to Me." <u>Newsweek</u> 29 June, 1998: 36-39.

Ylvisaker, S.C., Anderson & G.O. Lillegard. <u>Grace for Grace</u>. Mankato: Lutheran Synod Book Company, 1943.

Zich, Arthur. "China's Three Gorges: Before the Flood." <u>National Geographic</u> March 1994: 185.3.

ACKNOWLEDGEMENTS

I would like to thank the Lillegard family, including my father David, for providing me with the resources for this project. My aunt Laura, who was one of the three daughters born in China, has helped immeasurably by providing and identifying photos and memorabilia, giving pronunciation of Chinese names and answering questions about family history in China and the U.S. My uncle George gave me several wooden file boxes with my grandpa George's writings. My cousin Kirsten (Norman's daughter) sent me Grandma Bernice's letters. My uncle Larry translated a German letter. My aunt Betty & uncle Rudy Honsey provided pictures of her early days in China. Prof. Honsey also translated all of the Norwegian and some Latin, and served as my editor.

My grandpa's sister's daughter Nancy Reid Gallo sent me some pictures of her mother Anna Lillegard and other Lillegards. Thanks to David Furholmen (Ella & Eric's son) for providing pictures and writings of modern-day China from his trip in 1999. Thanks to Rev. Earle Treptow for translating some Latin. Thanks to Mr. and Mrs. David Maeding for translating some German.

I would like to thank my husband, Eric, for listening to my ramblings about this project, giving me some good ideas, making the cover, and publishing the lulu.com edition of the book. Thank you to my brother Matt Lillegard for allowing the use of his painting of people in rickshaws for the cover of the book. Thanks to my son David, because without his birth, I would not realize the importance of heritage or have the opportunity to hand down our family faith. Thanks to Rev. Shawn Kauffeld for formatting and publishing the first edition of this book.

NOTE FROM AUTHOR

I didn't set out to write a book about my grandparents, George and Bernice Lillegard, missionaries in China. It was just a family history project that kept getting bigger and bigger.

In 1995 I started filling out a small book on family history for my family and my husband's family. I also made a family history photo album for both sides of the family. I completed those by 1997, when the Lillegards had a reunion at Bethany Lutheran College in Mankato, Minnesota. At that time, my uncle George gave me a stack of five wooden file boxes containing Grandpa Lillegard's personal files. I started reading through all the material and putting it in chronological order and selecting writings that I thought the family would be interested in reading.

In 1999 my cousin Kirsten Lillegard (Norman Lillegard's daughter) sent me a whole box of Grandma Lillegard's personal letters. They were already organized (by my aunts) chronologically in folders by year, month and date. Some were even taped in order into a binder. She had numbered her letters home from China over a period of six years: they totaled 236!

Between Grandpa's and Grandma's writings, there were thousands of pages. I spent a lot of time reading and trying to select the most interesting and typing them out. That was necessary because of the condition of the original letters. Many were crumbling and fading. Grandpa's were mostly carbon copies, hard to read. Grandma's were handwritten in beautiful cursive, using every inch of both sides of the paper, including the margins.

In 2003 we bought a new computer and scanner. Then I really got busy with all the memorabilia, scanning and inserting photos and documents into the typed material I already had. I wrote material to fill in between the letters so that they would read more smoothly. I wrote footnotes to explain some of the details necessary to understand the letters. I continued to enlist the help of family members to answer questions.

In July of 2006, I completed the typing of this big project. It's exciting to have it done, but I am also saddened because I have enjoyed it so much. It's like getting to the end of a great book and wishing there were more. I wish that all of the Lillegards could have been alive to share in this moment, but George and Bernice have long ago passed on, and two of their children - Marjorie and Larry - have also gone to heaven to be with their Savior, Jesus Christ.

In the summer of 2013, Eric and I went to visit our son David, who lived and taught English in China this past school year. We had the privilege of seeing many places from the Lillegards' past: Hankow (Hankou, part of greater Wuhan), Kuling (Gulingzhen in Mount Lushan National Park, Jiangxi Province), and Kikungshan (Jigongshan in Henan Province). We had the joy of discovering some of the places they lived. Due to this trip, I am publishing the 15th revision of this book, with some pictures re-captioned and re-set.